THE OFFICIAL

History

© Sunderland Association Football Club

1 8 7 9 · 2 0 0 0

© Sunderland Association Football Club

Edited by: John Hudson
                  Paul Callaghan

Written by: Paul Days
                  John Hudson
                  Dave Hudson
                  Bernard Callaghan
                  Paul Callaghan

Design by: (TWO)CAN Design

Sunderland AFC Press
Published in Great Britain by Leighton
in association with Sunderland AFC.

                  The Teleport,
                  Doxford International,
                  Sunderland,
                  SR3 3XD.
                  Tel: +44 (0) 191 525 2400
                  Fax: +44 (0) 191 520 1815
                  www.leighton.com

Publication available as:

Limited Edition   ISBN 0-9536984-2-4
Hardback   ISBN 0-9536984-1-6
Paperback   ISBN 0-9536984-0-8

British Cataloguing-in-Publications Data
A catalogue record for this book is available from the British Library

The publisher has made every effort to obtain permission to reproduce material in this book from the appropriate source. If there are any errors or omissions please contact the publisher who will make suitable acknowledgement in the reprint.

Printed and bound in Great Britain at Butler and Tanner, Somerset.

December 1999

THE EMPIRE STADIUM, WEMBL

The Football Association
Challenge Cup
Competition
FINAL TIE
SAT., MAY 5, 1973
KICK-OFF 3 p.m.
YOU ARE ADVISED TO TAKE UP
YOUR POSITION BY 2.30 p.m.

V.S.Lile CHAIRMAN
WEMBLEY STADIUM LTD

No money refunded or tickets exchanged
NORTH STAND SEAT
£5.00
BE RETAINED

TURNSTILE
F
ENTRANCE
79
ROW
12
SEAT
11

SEE PLAN AND CONDITIONS ON BACK

CONSECTATIO EXCELLENTIAE

SUNDERLAND A.F.C. ®

THE OFFICIAL
History

NIL DESPERANDUM · ASPICIO LUCEM

1 8 7 9 · 2 0 0 0

A Foreword by Bob Murray
Chairman of Sunderland Association Football Club.

As our Club prepares to enter the 21st century, the appearance of The Official History of Sunderland AFC is most timely. The Club has a long and distinguished history dating back to 1879, meaning we are not only one of the oldest football clubs in the country, but in the whole world. In the early days, the Club struggled for survival, moving grounds regularly and working hard to establish itself as a force in North East football. This goal was quickly achieved, and we soon went on to become one of the game's dominant forces, picking up six League Championships by 1936. When we finally added the FA Cup to our list of achievements in 1937, Sunderland could truly claim to be the country's top football club.

Of course, in recent times we have struggled to match the glory days of the pre-War years. In the 1950s, punishments imposed on the Club following an illegal payments scandal hit us hard. With directors and players banned, and the Club shamed, a long period of decline set in. While there have been great highs such as the 1973 Cup win and seven glorious promotions campaigns, there have also been heartbreaking relegations. Painful as such events are, they form an integral part of life as a Sunderland supporter. No other club's supporters have such a rich understanding of the game because none have faced the roller-coaster ride of peaks and troughs like we have. The loyalty of Sunderland supporters is incredible. A constant factor throughout the Club's history has been the huge - and noisy - backing provided by the Sunderland fans, and this is a real source of pride.

Everyone at the Club is working hard to give us something really exciting to shout about. We now have a magnificent new stadium, our finances are on a sound footing, we have a determined manager and a team featuring numerous internationals. The Club is also rich in home grown players, committed to developing youth, and prides itself on having strong community links. All of these are crucial ingredients for our future, but it is the sheer size and passion of the Sunderland support that drives the Club forward. It is the supporters that make this Club great and, with so many exciting developments taking place at the current moment, there is every chance that the 21st Century will mark the start of a glorious new chapter in the history of Sunderland AFC.

As this book makes clear, the problems facing the Club since the 1950s have been huge. Our aim is to restore Sunderland to the position of prominence it held before scandal rocked the Club. Let's hope that future editions of this book recount tales of the Lads winning trophies at home and competing with the best in Europe. No-one is pretending that this will be an easy task. But, we all know that our Club has enormous potential. Harnessing it is our goal for the new millennium. We have reached the very top before, we can do it again.

Best wishes,

Bob Murray.

Introduction

Football - and this is a fact - is the world's most popular game. Almost everyone on Earth holds memories of a match that has gripped themselves, their family, their town or their country. In England, many - probably the majority - have a club they support. Within that majority there is a valiant core of true fans, those for whom a club is for life, a defining feature as thick as blood; those for whom football is a passion. This is a book for those with a passion for football and, more specifically, for those with a passion for Sunderland Association Football Club; it is a book by Sunderland fans for Sunderland fans. This book is for people who believe they have red-and-white DNA.

However, this is also a history book, and few of us have such a passion for history. Yet, there is a need for history. Knowledge of our past enriches our understanding of the present, and this is as true for football as it is for other aspects of history. Most of us stumble through life's trials and tribulations searching for solutions to our problems, blissfully unaware of the fact that previous generations faced up to pretty much the same challenges in their time. Sadly, we all too often commit the same mistakes as they did too. As generations of philosophers have been at pains to point out, the greatest tragedy of human life is that we eternally repeat the farcical errors of our predecessors.

But, history is not just about lessons. It is also about our memories and our heritage. Our Club has a long and proud history dating all the way back to 1879. It goes without saying that no-one alive today can remember the team's first match. Nor can anyone remember what our first ground looked like or recall the faces of the players as they took to the pitch for Sunderland's opening season. This is why official histories are needed: to record those things we should never forget. Indeed, this should be apparent to all Sunderland fans at this particular moment in time, for with every kick of the ball at the Stadium of Light, Roker Park becomes an increasingly distant memory. Soon, young Sunderland supporters will take their seats at our new stadium with no memories - no comprehension - of the fact that people once stood to watch Sunderland, and Roker Park will be nothing more to them than a Victorian public garden where old men play bowls on sunny afternoons.

I hope that you enjoy the book. It is a real team effort, written and designed entirely by Sunderland fans. It began with the vision and determination of Paul Days and Paul Callaghan, but with the mammoth task of producing the book facing them, myself, Dave Hudson and Bernard Callaghan were soon brought in to help see the project through. With the text complete, Paul Briggs of (Two)Can Design then ably turned our words into an amazingly colourful illustrated book. Despite our efforts, we realise that in trying to condense one-hundred-and-twenty years of history there are, inevitably, some great games and great players we have failed to mention. Likewise, in over three hundred pages of text, there will be some errors we have made, particularly for the early years, when records were haphazard and, if present at all, often conflicting. Trying to use historical documents to reconstruct a picture of events is no substitute for actually being there.

Of course, scientists may one day invent time machines that allow us to go back to the early days. If they do, I dare say that all Sunderland supporters would love to be there for that first game, to take in the surroundings of the ground, watch the players' skills and absorb the historical moment of a new beginning. But, without a little history, even the most ardent fan would be thrown: those looking for the famous Sunderland stripes should look towards the team dressed in blue tops and blue-and-white knickerbockers. Perhaps our DNA isn't red-and-white after all!

John Hudson,
Editor.

1879·80	Club formed by a group of local school teachers. First home established at Blue House Field.
1880·81	First competitive matches. Reach semi-finals of Durham and Northumberland Cup.
1881·82	Move to new ground at Groves Field.
1882·83	Reach final of the Durham and Northumberland Cup.
1883·84	Move to Horatio Street. Win Durham Senior Cup.
1884·85	Move to Abbs Fields. Compete in FA Cup for first time.
1885·86	Move to Newcastle Road.
1886·87	Red and white stripes introduced. Beat Darlington to win Durham Senior Cup.
1887·88	Beat Darlington to win Durham Senior Cup but disqualified from FA Cup.
1888·89	James Allan forms breakaway team called Sunderland Albion.
1889·90	'The Team of All Talents' elected to Football League.

The Club started life as the Sunderland and District Teachers' Association Football Club in 1879 and after a shaky start soon made a mark on the region's football scene, establishing itself as one of the best teams in the North East. Our first trophy came in 1884 with victory in the Durham Senior Cup, and by the end of the 1880s the Club had underlined its position as the County's top team by winning the trophy in all but one of the five seasons it competed for it.

Progress in the FA Cup was less spectacular, but impressive performances in friendly matches raised the Club's profile. Dubbed the 'Team of All Talents' in the late 1880s, Sunderland began to push for entry to the Football League.

Off the pitch, the Club was troubled by financial problems in its early years and moved grounds regularly. By the middle of the decade finances were more secure, but new threats to the Club's existence came when disaffected players and officials formed a breakaway team, Sunderland Albion. Regular scrapes with the footballing authorities did not help matters, but the Club's position was secured when we were admitted to the Football League at the end of the 1889-90 season.

THE EARLY

Years

1 8 7 9 · 1 8 9 0

1879-1881
In The Beginning

"The game of football did not immediately grip the town."

Charles W Alcock, FA Secretary 1870.

Our First Home Blue House Field

It is difficult for us today to comprehend the nature of the average 1880s sports ground as stadiums are such a feature of modern life that we take many of their features for granted. While sophisticated examples of sports architecture can be found in ancient times (the Coliseum in Rome, for example), the art of constructing such structures had been lost in the midst of time. In fact no permanent sports stadia were built anywhere in Europe during the middle ages. Sports grounds in the 1880s were little more than fields with appropriate markings on the grass, and Sunderland's first ground at Blue House Field, Hendon, was no exception. Spectators stood behind ropes placed around the perimeter of the pitch and charging for admittance was difficult because the ground was not fully enclosed. Like many other grounds, it was located opposite a public house, in this case the Blue House, which also doubled up as a changing room for the players. Despite the basic nature of the facilities though, the ground was quite expensive, with the owners demanding the considerable sum of £10 a year rent for the field. It was this cost that would lead the Club to quit the site in a couple of years, but it came back into use - and was considerably improved by the addition of stands and a club house - when Sunderland Albion made it their home in 1888.

The nineteenth century was an era of rapid change for many British towns. Economic growth increased their size and moved the workforce from the land into industrial jobs. Sunderland was one of many northern towns that exemplified this change, its population expanding rapidly as the twin pillars of shipbuilding and mining began to provide employment for a growing number of local men. Although association football had for a number of years been an activity associated with the upper class public schools of Southern England, it was to be the working classes of Northern England and Scotland that would take the game of football to their hearts in the late-Victorian era. As the game spread through Lancashire and Scotland it was in no way surprising that a town the size of Sunderland should seek to establish its own football club at a somewhat early stage.

In fact, it was in October 1879 that Sunderland Association Football Club came in to being - some thirteen years before the formation of Liverpool and seven years before Arsenal. Somewhat surprisingly though, the club was formed not by shipbuilders or miners, but by school teachers, local school master James Allan having taken the initiative in organising such a venture. More surprisingly still, the teachers not only formed the club, but made up the entire team too, and the club's original name - Sunderland and District Teachers' Association Football Club - reflected this.

At the time of the club's formation, football was in its infancy and finding suitable opponents was a difficult task. However, the first priority for Allan and his colleagues was to find a home for the team. Over time this was to prove a little more troublesome than might have been expected, but the club initially settled on a site at Blue House Field in Hendon, very close to the Board School where James Allan taught.

The team spent three difficult years there. The game of football did not immediately grip the town. Indeed, at the time, rugby and cricket were Sunderland's main sports, and in particular, Allan's new club had to compete with the popular Sunderland Rovers team that played their rugby in Commercial Road. Further problems for the club lay in the fact that there were only four football clubs in County Durham (which then included Sunderland), meaning they would have to travel further afield for opponents. The lack of teams in the area also meant that Northumberland and Durham were combined into a single region of the Football Association.

At the first official meeting of the club the perennial issue of finance was formally discussed. Running the club would, of course, cost money. The further they had to travel to play matches, the more expensive that would be. Allan had managed to persuade nineteen others to join the club, and was appointed Vice-Captain at this meeting. The members also elected Robert Singleton (Headmaster of Gray School) to the position of Captain and appointed W. Elliott as Club Secretary.

However, they concluded that the size of the club made the position of Treasurer redundant, not least because all of the teachers agreed to pay their own expenses. These arrangements would not prove to be a long-term solution to the financial issue.

Football differed then from now in a number of ways, no more so than in the fact that there was no league competition. Sunderland were eligible to compete in the FA Cup, which had been going since the 1871-72 season, but chose to focus initially on a regional cup competition, the Northumberland and Durham Association Challenge Cup.

Aside from this competition though, football was a matter of 'friendly' fixtures. Although railway travel was widespread at the time, travel was still a lot more difficult than it is today, and as the players were paying their own expenses many of the Club's matches were played against local teams. Early opponents included the likes of Sedgefield, Bishop Middleham, Ferryhill, Ovingham and Newcastle Rangers, and the Club's first 'competitive' match is thought to have been on the 13th November 1880 against Ferryhill Athletic. Robert Singleton captained the blue stripped Wearsiders for that game, and the team lined up in a 2-2-6 formation. With such an attacking outlook, you might have expected the game to be full of goals. In fact the match boasted just one, and unfortunately it was for Athletic: Sunderland lost one-nil - and so it all began.

Hendon Board School, the birth place of football in Sunderland.

The 'Founder' - James Allan

James Allan is commonly identified as the 'founder' of Sunderland and District Teachers' Association Football Club, later to become simply 'Sunderland Association Football Club'. Allan was a Scot, and a graduate of Glasgow University. He taught in one of Sunderland's Board (that is state) Schools at Hendon. The story goes that after a short holiday in his native country Allan was amazed that Sunderland had no football team and so returned with some footballs and a determination to establish a club in the town. What is certain however, is that Allan organised the meeting that led to the establishment of the Club and that he served as our first 'Vice-Captain'. Allan was also a useful player - a left winger with mazy dribbling skills and strong pace, and he holds the Club record for most goals scored in a game: a staggering twelve! However, Allan became disillusioned with the club in the late 1880s, and left to form, manage, and play for rival club Sunderland Albion.

Club founder James Allan.

How the 'People's Game' got started

Soldiers playing an early form of football, 1827.

Drinking Fighting and Football

The North East was not without its variants of the Shrove Tuesday football match. Two annalists witnessed such a game in Sedgefield in 1827, and noted that "an ancient custom prevails at Sedgefield on Shrove-Tuesday, on which day the parish clerk is obliged to find a ball for the use of the townsmen and the country people, who assemble for the purpose of playing a game of football, after which the victorious and the vanquished resort to the public-houses, where they generally 'drink deep e'er they depart'".

A similar game was played in Chester-le-Street between the 'up-streeters' and the 'down-streeters', the aim being to get the ball to the opponents' end of the street. Games typically lasted four hours and such was their violence that shops had to be barricaded for the day and insurance companies refused to provide cover against damage incurred on such occasions. Both games were still being played when Sunderland AFC were formed, but for the most part local games died out when the codified version of the game began to spread.

Since 1879, football has changed enormously in many ways, but the rules have remained extremely durable. Important amendments have taken place since 1879, such as the introduction of goal nets (1890), penalty kicks (1891), the creation of substitutes (1966) and the outlawing of back passes to the goal-keeper (1994). Yet such changes have taken place at the margins. A game played by the 1879 rules would not differ terribly from one played by those of today.

This might seem like a pretty basic observation, but at the time Sunderland were formed, the game of association football was still very much in its infancy. The Football Association, who developed the enduring rules, had only been in existence since 1863 and rival versions of football - most notably Rugby Football - were competing with the association game. As we know, association football, the so called 'dribbling code', went on to become the World's most popular sport, but it is worth bearing in mind that the rules of the game have a history and that it could all have been so different. Sunderland's football club came into being at a time when these rival versions of football were battling to establish themselves as the 'definitive' game, and had rugby, the 'handling code', predominated, this book would have been celebrating some rather different events.

However, the history of football dates back far beyond Victorian times. Football-like games dating back two thousand years have been documented, notably the Chinese game of 'Tsu Chu' and a rather gruesome game played by Roman soldiers where it is rumoured that the head of a defeated enemy often took the place of the ball. Within England, historians believe that rough street games were played in towns and villages as far back as the Twelfth Century, but the inherent violence of these games caused them to be frowned upon by the ruling classes. Serious injuries and deaths were common place and damage to property almost inevitable whenever a game was played. From this period until the Victorian era, football was a game played for the most part without rules. Historian James Walvin sums up the state of the game in Medieval England well:

"It was simply an ill-defined contest between indeterminate crowds of youths, often played in riotous fashion, in tightly restricted city streets, producing uproar and damage to property, and attracting to the fray anyone with an inclination to violence."

Often these games were customary events on public holidays, with Shrove Tuesday in particular being marked in many villages by a game of football. Why this should be is uncertain, but Shrove Tuesday games have been recorded as far back as the 1630s and were widespread throughout the country by the late-1700s/early-1800s. Interestingly, the phrase 'local Derby' originates from such a fixture played between two rival parishes in Derby. Football at this time was both popular and a predominantly working-class affair. However, these traditional games began to die out as the industrial revolution took place, some suggesting the game had become 'unfashionable', but more probably because the mass migration of young men from the countryside to the towns deprived many villages of the players needed to sustain such games.

Curiously it was the upper classes, who had previously frowned upon the game, that kept football alive through the mid-nineteenth century. Violent ball games became extremely popular at the Public Schools, though each had their own specific version of the game. At Rugby School the players were allowed to carry the ball in their hands, but at Harrow the game centred around dribbling with feet and discouraged physical contact.

While the games were exceedingly popular within each school, matches were invariably an internal matter, as opponents from outside did not play by the same rulebook. The same problem arose with local football clubs - the world's first was formed in Sheffield in 1855 - and it was evident that the lack of a common set of rules was hampering the development of the game.

It was to rectify this situation that the leading clubs came together to form the Football Association in 1863. However, agreeing on a common set of rules proved to be difficult. There were three key elements to the various games that had developed through the country: control of the ball with the feet; control of the ball with the hands; and 'hacking'. There was much disagreement over the issue of 'handling' and shortly after the FA's decision to outlaw it, a breakaway Rugby Football Union was set up to govern a 'handling' game. This is well known; what is much less common knowledge is that the association's decision to outlaw 'hacking' caused as much, if not more, controversy and was instrumental in causing the Rugby breakaway. So unpopular was the outlawing of these elements that by 1867 only ten clubs remained as members of the FA.

England v Scotland, 1875. Note the lack of goalnets and rope crossbar.

The Toffs get Tough

Charterhouse was one of the Public Schools that took the lead in developing a set of rules for football. However, the game played there in the mid-1800s shared only the very basic features of modern day football. It was played in the school's Cloisters, a smoothly paved tunnel surrounded by sharp, jagged walls and wooden doors at the north and south exits. Games usually took place between the senior 'Gownboys' and the rest of the school and the aim was to hit the ball against the opposing team's door. In this respect, the game was very much like modern football. Where it differed, however, was in the emphasis on 'scrimmages'. The school 'fags' were charged with the task of defending their team's door, which primarily involved trying to block runs made by the older pupils. Often as many as fifty or sixty boys would be involved in a goal mouth scramble - which could easily last three-quarters-of-an-hour - and clothes would be torn, 'fags' trampled upon and all participants' shins kicked black-and-blue. Extreme violence - hacking - was an integral part of the game, and encouraged by the school because it tested the 'mettle' of the 'fags' and helped 'build character'.

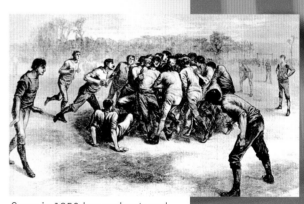

Game in 1850 has goalposts and almost equal numbers on each side!

1881-1884
The Early Years

"Great interest is manifested in the football world as to the issue of the contest."

The Echo, 1883,
commenting on the Sunderland v Tyne Final

Early Sunderland banner.

Agony

"Northumberland and Durham Association Challenge Cup 1883 - Tyne v Sunderland - The final tie was played off in Newcastle on Saturday before a large number of spectators. The weather was delightfully fine. The wind that prevailed, however, rather spoilt the game. The Tyne captain kicked off against the wind, and the game during the first forty-five minutes was very even, no score being made. On changing at half-time, however, the Tyne men showed their superiority, as during the latter half of the game the ball was invariably in Sunderland territory. The first goal was kicked for the Tyne by Redmayne, and was shortly afterwards supplemented by one obtained from a corner kick. When time was called, the Tyne were thus victorious by two goals to nil, which score would have been greatly augmented had it not been for the excellent defence by the Sunderland goalkeeper [Stewart], who was frequently applauded."

Sunderland Echo,
Monday 2nd April 1883.

By 1881 the 'financial question' began to rear its head, and it was evident that the Club faced something of a crisis. Games were not attracting enough paying supporters to make ends meet, and the cost of renting the ground, along with the other overheads involved in running the Club, were becoming a burden for the 'enthusiastic volunteers'. The Club's plight was poignantly illustrated by the fact that it couldn't afford to replace its worn out football. An emergency meeting of the Club's members was convened with two options on the table: disbanding the Club altogether or relaxing its membership qualifications.

Given the enthusiasm for football amongst those who had established the Club in the first place, it is perhaps unsurprising that they decide to go for the latter option. Membership was opened to non-teachers, and the Club's name changed to Sunderland Association Football Club to reflect this; SAFC came into being! However, it was decided that a number of further measures could be taken to guard the Club's position. The first was a raffle, in which one of the committee offered his canary as a prize. The bird was won by another committee member, who raffled it again and the princely sum of a sovereign was raised. Shortly after this, the Club took another decision: to move home. The £10 a year rent for the ground at Blue House Fields was proving to be too costly.

After considering several sites, the decision was made to move to Groves Field in the 1881-82 season. The site was a happier hunting ground for the team, and they began to put in some impressive performances in the Northumberland and Durham Association Challenge Cup. While the Club had managed to reach the semi-finals of the contest in 1880-81, it was evident that the Lads were not up to the task at such an early stage. Their weaknesses were exposed by a Newcastle Rangers team that managed to dispense a 5 - 0 thrashing at their St James' Park ground. The team progressed on the pitch quickly after that and this was underlined by the Club reaching the final of the competition soon afterwards in the 1882-83 season. Importantly, some form of 'cup fever' seemed to be gripping the town, and the Sunderland Echo noted of the final tie that 'great interest is manifested in the football world as to the issue of the contest'. Unfortunately, an evenly balanced game, somewhat spoilt by the wind, did not go Sunderland's way; Tyne ran out 2 - 0 winners.

Before the 1883-84 season, Sunderland were on the move again, this time going north of the river, to Horatio Street, Roker. We were to spend just one year there before moving on, but it was to be a momentous year for Sunderland AFC. Before the season kicked off, major changes were afoot in the organisation of football in the region. The growing popularity of the game meant that there were significantly more teams to provide the opposition than when Allan had formed the Club in 1879 and this was good news for Sunderland.

More than this though, there were now enough teams within County Durham itself to warrant the creation of separate football associations for Durham and Northumberland, and at a meeting in Mrs Brown's Three Tuns Hotel in Durham on 28th May 1883, the Durham FA was formed. There were nine inaugural members including, of course, Sunderland.

With the new association came a new competition. The Northumberland and Durham Association Challenge Cup competition was dissolved, and for the 1883-84 season Sunderland would compete in the inaugural Durham Association Challenge Cup. With the big Northumberland teams such as Tyne and Newcastle Rangers now participating in a separate competition, the main threat to Sunderland came from Darlington, who were developing a useful side that included some talented youngsters. In order to keep travel to a minimum, the Durham competition was split into 'northern' and 'southern' sections, Sunderland competing in the former against the likes of Birtley, Catchgate Red Stars, Hamsterley Rangers, Hobson Wanderers, Jarrow, Milkwell Burn and Whitburn. The winners of each section contested the final. Sunderland topped the northern section in 1883-84 and - unsurprisingly perhaps - Darlington won the southern section. As we shall see the final proved to be extremely controversial.

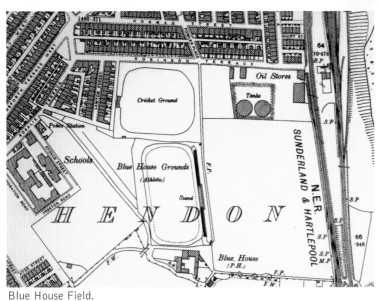

Blue House Field.

On the Move - Groves Field

After a couple of years at Blue House Field, the Club moved to their second home in 1881-82. The Groves Field site was near to where Ashbrooke Sports Club is now located, but Sunderland did not spend long there. The Club were on the move again about a year later, and it has been suggested that the team played as few as four matches on the ground, for most of the team's commitments were away matches at the time. In truth, the move to Groves Field probably had more to do with dissatisfaction with the cost of the Blue House field site than with the qualities of Groves Field. There is some evidence that the Club actually spent a short period between leaving Blue House Field and moving to Groves Field without a fixed home, trying out a number of local fields for size, most notably a pitch near the Cedars, where several games were played. The Ashbrooke site also goes down in history for holding Sunderland Albion's first ever fixture, a hastily arranged game against Shankhouse Black Watch on the 5th May 1888. However, it was Albion's only game there and they lost 3 - 0.

Groves Field.

Sunderland's First Trophy

The first FA challenge cup pictured in 1885.

A Double Anti-Climax

That Sunderland's first trophy victory could have been more auspicious is clear from the match reports. The Darlington officials' politicking and the Durham Association's inability to make a decision and stick to it risked turning the newly created competition into a farce. In the event Sunderland had the last laugh, beating the Darlington team on two separate occasions. However, fans and players alike must have suffered from the anti-climax of thinking they had won the cup, only to be told weeks later that they hadn't. As if this wasn't enough however, the Sunderland captain was still denied the privilege of receiving the trophy after his side's second victory against the Quakers: the newly formed Durham Association did not have enough money to purchase a suitable cup in time for the final! The team would have to make do with silver medals, but even they were presented some time after the match, the Mayor of Sunderland doing the honours on July 6th, some two months after the initial tie.

While the 3rd May 1884, has gone down in history as the date on which Sunderland clinched their first trophy with a 2 - 0 victory over Darlington in the Durham Association Challenge Cup final, the Club's first victory in a cup final had come nearly a month earlier. The opponents in this first match were Darlington, and the competition was the Durham Association Challenge Cup. Observant readers may be thinking that the typesetter has just made an error or the tie was a two-legged affair. In fact, Sunderland's first victory was controversially ruled void by the Durham Association following a series of complaints from the Darlington team.

The cup final was originally scheduled to take place on the 5th April 1884, at the old Cricket Ground, Newcastle Road. The ground, which was later to become Sunderland's home, had been let to the Club for the day and a large crowd of between one and two thousand people made their way there for the game. The Echo judged the 'weather was all that could be desired' and said that the game 'was from beginning to end of a most exciting character'.

Although Sunderland had 'home' advantage, it was Darlington who drew first blood, albeit in disputed circumstances. Not long after kick off, the Darlington players successfully challenged for the ball, but the Sunderland players called for a free kick, claiming handball. They should, however, have continued playing until the referee indicated otherwise, for the Darlington players did not stop their counter-attack and, with only the goalkeeper to beat, soon had the ball between the posts. Sunderland protested that the goal should not be allowed. Darlington claimed there had been no infringement, and the referee sided with the latter: 1 - 0 to Darlington.

The Lads responded in the best way possible, and 'after the leather had been set in motion again, Grayston very cleverly scored the first goal for Sunderland.' The match now began to reach fever pitch, Darlington regaining the lead, and Sunderland hitting the cross bar. Sunderland began to get a grip on the game after this, and from a corner, Murdock put it through the posts "amidst loud applause." All this took place in the first half, and more action was to follow in the second. Darlington again took the lead, but the Lads soon gained the lead for the first time in the game following two quick goals. Time was called, and Sunderland were declared victors 4 - 3, or - as the Echo put it - 'having obtained four goals to two and a disputed one.' Sunderland's top players on the day included club founder J. R. Allan "whose excellent running and dodging were greatly admired and applauded", McDonald, Murdock, Kirtley and Grayston.

This, however, was not the end of the matter. Darlington appealed, claiming that the Sunderland fans had intimidated both the referee and the visiting players. A meeting of the Durham Association was called shortly after the match to consider their claims, but threw them out, firmly awarding the match to Sunderland. Still not satisfied, Darlington continued to complain, and another meeting of the Association was convened on the 19th April, following submission of a petition signed by eleven of the County's clubs.

The charges were the same as in the previous meeting, the pro-Darlington camp moving, "that the amendment which awards the cup to Sunderland be rescinded." Sunderland founder James Allan moved an amendment to the amendment, "that the minutes of the previous meeting be confirmed". Allan lost by four votes to seven and the meeting moved on to consider the Darlington protest afresh. While the Sunderland camp denied there had been any intimidation, evidence from the referee suggesting there had been, helped swing the Chairman towards the view that "the intimidation was quite sufficient to sustain the demand for the match to be played over again". A resolution "that the Darlington protest be allowed, and the match be played over again" was carried by seven to four. Sunderland tried to appeal about the appealed appeal, but to no avail!

The match was replayed on the 3rd May, and switched to a neutral ground at Birtley. A sizeable crowd attended the game, not least because the North East Railway Company had laid on special cheap trains, and this was in all probability the first instance of an organised 'away trip' for the Sunderland fans. Darlington won the toss and decided to play downhill with the wind behind them. This was a smart move, for the strong wind made it "almost an impossibility" for Sunderland to get the ball up toward the Darlington goal. However, the Quakers failed to make the most of their advantage, and as the first half wore on they "made desperate efforts to score, but owing to the wind, which invariably carried the ball over their adversaries' goal post, or to their bad judgement, they were unable to do so." In the second half, Sunderland took control and "displayed some capital play." Joyce scored the first for Sunderland and following a series of corners, McDonald took advantage of the confusion emerging during and scrimmage and charged the ball into the goal. It ended 2 - 0 to Sunderland and this time the Darlington team could have no complaints.

On the Move Again - Horatio Street and Abbs Field

Sunderland's third home, and the first one north of the river, was at a site near Roker Avenue that is now covered by Givens Street and Appleby Terrace. The Horatio Street ground was, however, by no means ideal. Located by a claypit and a brickworks, the pitch was often heavy and apparently dubbed a 'clay-dolly field'. Consequently, the Club spent just one season there - 1883-84 - before moving to Abbs Field, Fulwell. Located near Side Cliff Road, our fourth home was the best so far. A major advantage was that the site was properly enclosed, meaning the Club could at last control admission to their games. Rent for the 1884-85 season was an insubstantial £2 10s for the year, but this had risen to £15 for the 1885-86 season, perhaps because the Club had started to attract large crowds. Sunderland did not spend long there once the rent had reached such a high; we moved home again before the end of our second season at Abbs Field.

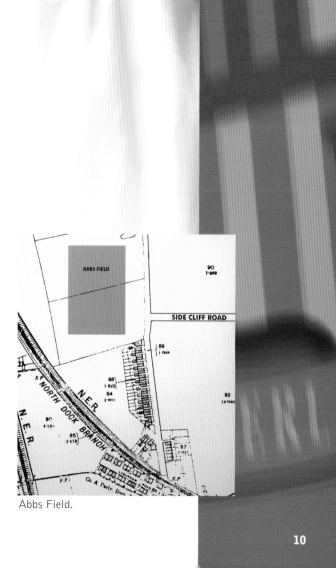

Abbs Field.

1884-1885
Up and Running

"The winter game has made an immense stride in public favour during this season"

The Echo, 1885

The Sunderland team of 1884.

Sunderland's First FA Cup Match

"Sunderland v Redcar (1st round for the English Challenge Cup). This match, played at Redcar on Saturday, resulted in a win for that team by three goals to one. The Redcar kicked off, with the strong wind in their favour, and the first goal was soon scored for them by Bulman, from a pass by Hickeley, a promising young player. The second point was scored by the captain of the Redcar by a magnificent shot over his head, cheer after cheer greeting his feat. Agar, another young player, notched the third point just before time. On change of ends, Sunderland scored their first and only goal in the first five minutes, and it looked as if they would win. Shortly after, the ball was again between the posts, but was disallowed, the player who put it through being offside. Some exciting play followed but the visitors' forwards soon fell all to pieces, and failed to score again. Bulman and Harrison played best for Redcar, and the backs for Sunderland rendered good service."

Sunderland Echo,
Tuesday 11th November 1884.

For 1884-85, Sunderland rented another new home, this time Abbs Field at Fulwell Road. A key landmark in the Club's progress this year was our first ever game in the FA Cup, which took place on the 8th November 1884, at Redcar. At that time Redcar, along with neighbours Middlesbrough, were regarded as the top sides in the North East, and rumour has it that upon hearing of the cup draw Redcar's coach asked "Where's Sunderland?" In the long run we would have the last laugh, but it was not a great start to Sunderland's cup career, Redcar running out 3 -1 winners.

On the 15th November Sunderland put their FA Cup disappointment behind them as they entertained Jesmond and secured a 2 -1 victory. The match was somewhat action packed, with both teams having a goal disallowed for offside, Jesmond having thought they'd secured an equaliser five minutes from time, but Sunderland edged it courtesy of two goals from Club founder James Allan. A week later Rosehill were the opponents, and another victory ensued, Sunderland running out 2 - 0 victors.

Nice as victories in these friendlies were, our early exit from the FA Cup meant our only competitive interest for the season was in the defence of the Durham Association Challenge Cup. The first round of the cup was due to be played five days before Christmas, with Sunderland's opponents being Castletown. As it happened, the fans could not have asked for a better start to the competition: Sunderland destroyed the Castletown team, notching up a Club record victory of 23 - 0, James Allan scoring twelve of them. However, the victory was not as grand as it sounds. Castletown had been unable to field a full team, arriving with just eight players. It was agreed before kick-off that Sunderland should receive a 'bye' to the next round, and the game was played as a 'friendly', with Sunderland lending three players to Castletown for the match. Nevertheless, the scoreline was dramatic and indicative of the strength of the Sunderland team.

Sunderland then played a number of friendlies over a busy Christmas period, including games against Erimus, (a 1 - 0 win on Boxing Day), and Heaton, (2 - 0 the following day). New Year's Day witnessed a home game against St John, who were despatched 2 - 0, prior to the visit of the much fancied Scottish team, Port Glasgow on January 2nd. After a string of good results, the Sunderland team must have been on something of a high. However, they collapsed against the Scots, who annihilated Sunderland 11 - 1. In truth there had been little hope before the game of Sunderland winning and it was all part of the learning curve.

The precise nature of the lessons they took from that defeat will never be known, but three weeks later Sunderland bounced back from their record reverse to dispatch Wearmouth 3 - 1 in the second round of the Durham Association Challenge Cup. This victory put them into a semi-final against Birtley scheduled for the 14th March. A week before this crucial tie, the two teams met in a friendly at Birtley's ground and the latter secured a comfortable 4 - 1 over the Lads. It did not augur well, but once again Sunderland put defeat behind them, coming good when it really counted. This time the match took place on Sunderland's ground and a single goal from McColl secured a place in the final for the home side.

In a repeat of the 1883-84 fixture, Sunderland met Darlington in the final tie, staged this time on Feethams Ground, Darlington. The home team ran out 3 - 0 winners, but the ill feeling from last season's game was evident and the victory was somewhat controversial.

The Echo were in no doubt that the Sunderland team had been badly treated, questioning the referee's performance and pointing out that the grounds for Darlington's complaints the previous season were equally applicable in the case of the 1885 Final. In particular, "the great mass of spectators were in their favour, and constantly "hooting" (or intimidating, if we accept the definition of the word given to the Darlington men twelve months ago) the Sunderland men whenever they claimed their just rights." Certainly the Sunderland players felt this to be so, for they launched a protest immediately after the game. However, their request for a re-match was turned down. In response, Sunderland decided to boycott the competition the following season.

While the cup defeat was a set back, it was clear that the game was beginning to grip the public's imagination and that Sunderland were becoming a force to be reckoned with in the region. Indeed, the Echo noted at the end of the season that "The winter game has made an immense stride in public favour during this season, and has reached a height of popularity never before known in the district even in connection with the popular summer game. Three season ago, all but unknown, and certainly unnoticed, Sunderland AFC played off their matches in a field off Ashbrooke-road. (... Since then) the dribbling code has had a rapid increase in the number of its followers."

The Referee's a Quaker

Sunderland met Darlington in the 1885 final of the Durham Association Challenge Cup. According to the Sunderland Echo, 'The turf was in capital condition,' and, 'the fine weather drew together a large concourse of spectators.' Darlington won the toss and elected to start the match with the wind behind them. Taking advantage of the conditions, the home team wasted no time in mounting a dangerous attack that would lead to a controversial goal. Having forced a corner, the Darlington players lined up to meet a cross that was struck with such force that it ended up between Sunderland's goalposts without an attacking player getting a touch to the ball. The Sunderland players contended, however, that no goal had been scored. The dispute would not have arisen in modern day football, for the issue related to whether or not the ball had actually been put through the goal; nets had not been introduced, and the Sunderland players felt the ball had in fact been kicked over the upright by the keeper. The referee ruled in Darlington's favour.

Following this, the Sunderland players were somewhat riled and raised their game, but the Darlington goalie denied the Lads on a number of occasions, before a quick move by the Quakers led to a second goal for the home side. Again Sunderland disputed the goal, claiming offside. Much confusion followed, and indecision from the referee manifested itself in a farcical incident where the ball was placed for a kick-off, then a free-kick for off-side, before returning again to the centre circle. The referee ruled that it was two - nil to Darlington. In the second half, Sunderland had the wind behind them, and went on the attack from the start. It was to no avail however, and Darlington soon gained the upper hand, adding a third goal. Sunderland refused to give up hope though, and from a corner kick, Hunter headed a goal. To the players' dismay, the referee disallowed it. No further goals were to be scored; the match ended 3 - 0 to Darlington, and Sunderland had lost the Cup.

Fixture card for 1884-85 'session'.

1885-1886
Going Home

"The move to Newcastle Road marked something of a watershed in the Club's history"

1885-86 Sunderland team, in their 'two tone' shirts.

Hearts 2 - 1 Sunderland, 27th February 1886

Sunderland made the five and a half hour trek to Edinburgh, arriving at 11a.m. for a match that many experts thought would result in a thrashing for the Wearsiders. Hearts were generally recognised as a 'crack' side, and having beaten Edinburgh Thistle 8 - 1 and Glasgow Pilgrims 7 - 0, they were unlucky to succumb to local rivals Hibernian 1 - 0 in the Edinburgh Shield.

Sunderland won the toss and elected to play downhill. At 3.40 p.m. the game kicked off, and with Sunderland playing a great defensive game, the Scots were finding it hard to break them down. A beautifully taken Hearts goal was equalised 10 seconds later by Jobes of Sunderland. However, with 10 minutes of the half remaining the 'Jambos' scored what proved to be the winner. Although the game ended 2 - 1 to Hearts, it was generally agreed that Sunderland had done very well to contain the Hearts half back, White, who was 'invincible' on the day. The overall performance was a credit to Sunderland and yet another marker of their progress.

The 1885-86 season would be somewhat uneventful in terms of competitive action. Ruling themselves out of the Durham Association Challenge Cup meant the Lads were left with just the FA Cup, in which they had little experience, and friendly matches.

The season kicked off on 3rd October, with a home match, played over two thirty-five minute periods, against North Eastern. As expected the Wearsiders triumphed, a comfortable 4 - 0 result that got them off to a flier. Mixed fortunes then followed in a series of friendlies before the season's main business kicked off on 24th October with our first match in the FA Cup. Once again the Lads were drawn against Redcar and again the trip south was to prove fruitless. Redcar, who went on to reach the quarter-finals of the competition, beat Sunderland 3 - 0. To come up against a team of their calibre at the start of the campaign was unfortunate, and while Sunderland's share of a bumper £6 gate was welcome, defeat ultimately meant that with just three weeks of the season gone Sunderland had nothing to play for.

Indeed, without the excitement of a cup run, it would prove difficult to sustain interest in the team for the rest of the season. A number of successive victories took place, including 3 - 1 versus Tyne, 4 - 1 against Bishop Auckland Church Institute, a 5 - 2 win over Heaton and a 10 - 3 thrashing administered to South Bank. But, as good as these results were, the gate receipts were poor, so the Club attempted to generate interest by inviting top Scottish side, Port Glasgow, to Abbs Field for New Year's Day 1886. The plan was successful, with around 2,000 fans turning up to see if Sunderland could avenge last season's 11 - 1 defeat. Sunderland were much better prepared for the Scots this time, and as a mark of their progress they lost narrowly by 2 - 1.

Sunderland's run of good results generally continued, with numerous local teams seen off in the New Year. Notable victories included 4 - 0 against Bedlington Rovers and 6 - 0 over Middlesbrough St John. The main test of the team's progress came in games against Scottish opponents however, and the Lads travelled to Edinburgh at the end of February to meet the mighty Hearts. Sunderland put in an excellent performance, and though they lost, the 2 - 1 scoreline was in many ways a great success. Few could have hoped for such a result two or three seasons earlier.

However, if the purpose of Sunderland's trip to Hearts was to raise the Club's profile in the absence of Cup competition, it is likely that the ploy failed. Great as the result - and the occasion - was in retrospect, the chances are that few in Sunderland were aware of it at the time. Although the Echo had begun to show a strong interest in football by this time, the usual Monday match report was missing on this occasion. The entire country had been hit by freak snowstorms of such severity that work in the shipyards was suspended and, crucially, railway travel and telegraphic communication to Scotland were interrupted for most of the week following the game.

Things would soon start to look up again though. While the Club's half yearly meeting concluded that there had been another successful season on the pitch, the main news was the announcement that a field in Newcastle Road, opposite Ellerslie Terrace, had been secured for the purposes of developing a new ground.

The Club moved there before the end of the season, playing their first match at the new ground on the 3rd April 1886 against Darlington. The game was played in fine weather and Darlington kicked off. In those days a kick off was a kick off, and the player simply whacked the ball as far as he could up the field. Sunderland were to dominate though, and raced into a two goal lead before half time. They increased their advantage further through McMillan after the break, but near the end Darlington pulled one back. It was only a consolation goal though, Sunderland winning the first game on their new ground 3 - 1.

The move to Newcastle Road marked something of a watershed in the Club's history, coinciding with the severing of our final links with the Academic community. Prior to this point all committee meetings had been held at Thomas Street School, but it was decided that meetings should now be held in the Workman's Hall in Whitburn Street. Significantly, the hall was owned by the shipyards, whose owners were beginning to exert an increasing degree of influence over the Club's affairs. Indeed, their financial muscle would become of increasing importance as Sunderland tried to establish themselves as a leading club, and the Club's accounts for 1885-86 emphasised the extent to which we were shifting away from being mere amateurs. Expenditure had reached almost £100 - and was to rise to £350 the following season - making it evident that professionalism was upon Sunderland in all but name. Unfortunately the issue would cause the team much heartache in coming seasons.

Almost home - Newcastle Road

Sunderland's fifth proper home was at Newcastle Road, and was clearly to the Club's liking, for they spent over a decade there. The Club secured the ground for an annual rent of £15, the same sum they were paying for Abbs Field, but Newcastle Road was clearly regarded as a better quality site. Indeed, when Sunderland reached the final of the Durham Association Challenge Cup final in 1883-84, they chose to play the tie at Newcastle Road rather than at their home ground Abbs Field. However, this was a one off, and the team's first game at the ground as their home was on April 3rd 1886, a 3 - 1 victory over Darlington. Upon securing the site, the Club erected perimeter fencing, purchased a clubhouse and started to construct wooden stands. Within a couple of seasons it was easily the best ground in the region, and by the early 1890s could hold almost 20,000 supporters; it even had a purpose built press gallery. Throughout Sunderland's tenancy improvements were made to the site, and when the Club published its prospectus for a share issue in 1896 it proudly boasted that "the famous Newcastle Road Ground at Sunderland, where the home matches are played, is one of the best and most comfortable in the Country, and can, with ease, accommodate 18,000 spectators".

Newcastle Road.

1886-1887
Red-and-White

> *"It was the first occasion on which the now famous red-and-white stripes were worn."*

Sunderland's new colours.

Changing Colours

Sunderland's opening game of the 1886-87 season saw the first appearance of the team in their red-and-white stripes. While red-and-white stripes and Sunderland now go together like fish and chips, it was not always the way. The team's original colours were predominantly blue, consisting of blue shirts and blue knickerbockers with a white stripe. By the mid-1880s the team had moved to a strip that consisted of red-and-white halved shirts, which lasted for a couple of seasons before being replaced by the red-and-white stripes. Photographic evidence suggests the team may well have alternated between the halved and the striped shirts for a while, but by 1888 the stripes were the norm and at the turn of the decade the black shorts that complete today's outfit had become a fixture too. Apart from a few brief changes, such as the use of white shorts in the 1960s and the unpopular white with red-pinstripe kit of the early 1980s, our colours have effectively remained the same since. Curiously, Newcastle United once played in red-and-white stripes: things could have been so different! However, it is worth noting that the last time a team wearing stripes won the Championship was way back in the 1935-36 season when, funnily enough, Sunderland won the league!

Before the 1886-87 season kicked off, there was a large attendance for Sunderland's half-yearly meeting on the 13th August 1886. Here it was reported that of 34 matches played the preceding season, 24 had been won with 7 defeats and 3 draws. Goals for stood at 108 and those against at a mere 40. It was noted that the move to Newcastle Road had been a great success, with attendances increasing significantly. On top of that, the Misses Thompson, owners of the field, had been so impressed with their new tenants that over £2 in ground rental was returned to the football club by them. It was generally recognised that Sunderland were one of the finest sides in the North of England, and with all officers re-elected, and entry for the English (FA) and Durham cups approved, the town looked forward to the forthcoming season.

The campaign began on the 18th September 1886, with a 1 - 0 victory over Notts and District (also known as Notts Mellors). This seemingly routine fixture would, in retrospect, be something of a milestone in the Club's history: it was the first occasion on which the now famous red-and-white stripes were worn. It was a great start to the season, the Echo enthusing that "altogether the match was a good exhibition of the association game as it ought to be played." Perhaps the new colours were 'lucky', for it was to be a good year for Sunderland on the pitch.

A couple of exciting matches followed this opener, Elswick Rangers being narrowly defeated 3 - 2 in a game where just about every decision was hotly disputed and South Bank being held to a 3 - 3 draw in the Lads' first away game of the season. The 'real stuff' started on the 16th October though, with Sunderland drawn to play Morpeth Harriers in the first qualifying round of the FA Cup. For once 'Lady Luck' had shone on Sunderland, offering us a tie against a lesser team and home advantage too. This was the first meeting of the two teams and was played in front of a "capital gate". Morpeth, however, took the game to Sunderland, Jopling putting the visitors ahead shortly after kick off. Worse was to follow, R Manners adding a second just before half time.

Whatever was said amongst the Sunderland players at half time, it worked. The Sunderland captain, McMillan, called for more team play from the Lads, and he was not to be disappointed. The Wearsiders turned up the heat and gave an awesome display of pace, especially up front. Davison notched Sunderland's first of the game and then Erskine put through to equalise. Sunderland were now running riot, and the Harriers folded. Lord, Erskine again, a couple from Smith and finally another from Erskine to complete his hat-trick, turned a potentially disastrous situation into a glorious victory. Sunderland had clinched their first win in an FA Cup tie and had done so in a stylish nine goal thriller!

A fortnight later the Cup campaign continued, with Newcastle West End providing the opposition. This would be a trickier match for the Lads, but again we were blessed with home advantage. By all accounts, the match was a close one, finishing 1 - 1 in normal time. In extra-time Sunderland took the lead, and the game finished 2 - 1. However, the West End players complained about bad light during the additional period, and it was ruled that the tie should be replayed at St. James' Park. This time Sunderland's luck was to desert them. West End won the game 1 - 0, and Sunderland's left-back W. 'Dowk' Oliver broke his collar bone during the match. Oliver was one of the Club's better players, later becoming a reserve for the England team. The Club decided to show their gratitude to him, and raised some cash to help Oliver through his injury by organising a benefit match. Two weeks after the fateful Cup match, Sunderland entertained West End for this purpose, running out 1 - 0 winners. It was quite probably the Club's first 'testimonial' match.

In between the Oliver benefit match and the FA Cup defeat, the Lads launched their Durham Association Challenge Cup campaign. Birtley provided the opposition, and were beaten 2 - 0. After a testing Christmas period that included a 5 - 1 defeat at the hands of Darlington and a 5 - 2 reverse against mighty Dumbarton Athletic - interspersed by 1 - 0 win over Glasgow Rangers - attention turned back to the Durham Association Challenge Cup. Here, Gateshead were beaten 2 - 0 in the second round and Whitburn thrashed 5 - 2 in the semi-final, securing the Lads a place in the competition's final for the third time in the three seasons they had entered. Again Darlington provided the opponents, and although they had beaten us 5 - 1 at Christmas, the Echo were a little disparaging of the Quakers before the match. The paper suggested Bishop Auckland would have provided a tougher test for Sunderland and claimed the Wearsiders had had by far the harder run in to the final. They may have been right; the Lads beat Darlington, albeit by the match's only goal, and secured the trophy for a second time.

Sunderland Football Club 1886-87 season.

More Cup Glory

A large crowd of around 6,000 crammed into Newcastle Road to witness Sunderland meet Darlington to contest the Durham Association Challenge Cup on the 26th March 1887. The field was in "splendid condition", having been rolled the previous day, and the sun "radiated heat", though there was, as usual, a strong wind to contend with. Darlington won the toss, and elected to kick down field with the wind behind them. The Lads immediately took the offensive, with good work by McMillan being noted. Darlington had plenty of possession too, and won a corner following a series of attacks. However, Sunderland turned defence to attack. Rooney "executed a splendid run on the right wing" before crossing the ball to the danger area. Davison was lying in wait, and from a scrimmage hit "the sphere between the sticks". Initially the referee disallowed the goal, but on appeal changed his mind. No further score was added in the first period, and Sunderland went in 1 - 0 up at half-time. In the second half, an exciting pace was maintained, with Darlington repeatedly threatening to score an equaliser. However, good defensive play, particularly by Wilkinson, helped to prevent the Quakers from getting back into the contest. The game ended 1 - 0, and the town's Mayoress, Mrs Richardson, at last presented the Cup to the Sunderland team.

R Jackson.

1887-1888
Busted

"Sunderland could now afford to spend 'big money'."

Front cover, 1887-88 fixture card.

'Cock of the North'

On the 7th April 1888, Sunderland took part in their fourth Durham Association Challenge Cup final in five years and aimed to add a third cup win to the honours list. Their opponents, Bishop Auckland Church Institute, were a much better team than their name might imply to the modern reader, and had won the trophy themselves in the 1886, albeit in a competition weakened by Sunderland's decision not to enter that season. The tie was played at Darlington's Feethams Ground, and a good crowd of around 5,000 attended. The Echo expected a Sunderland victory, noting that at the start of the season Sunderland looked a certainty for the competition, but worrying about the after affects of Middlesbrough appeal. In the event, the game was by no means a classic, 'the first half being very uninteresting.' Sunderland played very poorly in the early stages and conceded a weak goal from an Auckland corner. In the second half, however, the Lads improved somewhat, and finished the game 2 - 1 up. That Sunderland were able to clinch the trophy when playing well below their best was a measure of the team's strength. Few would now dispute their claim to be the region's top club.

Flushed with the success of the previous season, the Club's half-yearly meeting on the 25th August 1887 was again crowded. Success on the pitch had also strengthened the Club's financial position, and Sunderland could now afford to spend 'big money'. They did so by bringing Scottish teams down to Wearside (Renton alone were paid £40), and by paying Scotsmen - including four from Dumfries - to play for the team. It was evident that in order to improve, Sunderland would have to dispense with local talent and rely heavily on imports, particularly from north of the border. It was to be a controversial policy that was to be a source of trouble in the coming season.

The Lads started in magnificent style, beating Notts Mellors 8 - 3. Four successive victories followed, Sunderland scoring ten goals and letting in just three, before the arrival of Morpeth Harriers for the first qualifying round of the FA Cup. Having beaten the same opposition at this stage of the competition last season, Sunderland had little to worry about, and scored four goals to Morpeth's two. However, the Morpeth club protested that one of our players - the full back Ford - was not registered in time to play in the tie. The association ordered a replay at Morpeth's ground, but the Lads put in another good performance, beating the Harriers 3 - 2. In the following round, Sunderland were drawn against Newcastle West End, and a bumper crowd at the Newcastle Road ground saw Sunderland win 3 - 1 after extra-time.

This was Sunderland's best season in the FA Cup so far, and the draw for the third qualifying round pitched us against Middlesbrough, away from home. This would be a real test for the Lads, and gave them the chance to prove they were now the top team in the North East. The two clubs had not played each other previously, and a massive 8,000 crowd was attracted to the game. Middlesbrough were fancied to win the tie, but it ended 2 - 2: an excellent result for Sunderland. The replay attracted another 8,000 gate, the biggest at Sunderland's ground to that date, boosted by the news that the winners would receive a bye into the quarter-finals. The visitors had control in the first half and went in two goals up at the break. Sunderland turned it around in the second half, however, and goals from Davison, Halliday, Monaghan and Stewart helped secure a 4 - 2 win.

As so often in the Club's brief history though, the matter did not rest there. Middlesbrough launched an appeal, alleging three of Sunderland's Scots were being illegally paid. At that time, players had to have lived in the area for two years before they were allowed to play as professionals and although all of the players concerned were in employment, an enquiry found that the Club had paid for the players to travel down from Scotland, secured their employment so they could masquerade as amateurs and ensured they were paid above the market rate for these regular jobs. As punishment, Sunderland were ordered to pay the costs of the enquiry, had the three players in question suspended and - worst of all - were disqualified from the competition. In many ways it was a turning point in the Club's history, bringing to a head tensions over its direction and management style. At the end of the season, James Allan would quit the Club and his actions in the close season began to threaten the very existence of SAFC.

However, before this, attention was focused on completing the season's activities on the pitch. As holders of the Durham Association Challenge Cup, Sunderland were given a bye to the second round. The Lads' first tie - against Durham University - took place while the FA Cup enquiry was taking place, but they did not let it affect their performance. An 8 - 0 victory secured Sunderland's passage to the next round, and a series of good victories against Whitburn (1 - 0), Southwick (7 - 1) and Darlington (2 - 1 in a replay, after 1 - 1) put Sunderland into the final of the Durham Association Challenge Cup again. This time they faced new opponents, Bishop Auckland Church Institute, but it made no difference to Sunderland, who retained the trophy by beating their opponents 2 - 1.

At the Club's Annual General Meeting, there was much self-congratulation over the team's success on the pitch. However, this disguised a degree of division within the ranks. Wealthy local industrialists had started to become heavily involved in the Club, and it was their money that had brought the illegally paid Scots to Wearside. The AGM decided that more of the same was needed, and elected shipbuilders James Marr and Robert Thompson to the positions of Chairman and President, and coal owner Samuel Tyzack to the position held by James Allan: Treasurer. Allan and his supporters decided to quit the Club and form a rival team, Sunderland Albion. On the 5th May 1888, just two days after the AGM, Albion played their first match. The town could not support two teams, and a bitter rivalry between the two ensued.

Sunderland Albion team, 1888.

The Scottish Cup comes South of the Border

The icing on the cake of a successful season came when Scottish Cup winners Renton agreed to come to Sunderland for an exhibition match. The Sunderland Echo described the game as "grand" and "important", but pointed out that few fancied Sunderland's chances: "Their warmest friends hesitated to mention them in the same breath with the Scottish champions. On paper the latter had the game in hand, for they beat Cambuslang in a final tie by six goals to one, and Cambuslang in January last played Sunderland on their own field, ran up a total of 11 goals and never allowed their antagonists to score". As an added attraction, Renton brought the Scottish FA Cup trophy with them - the first time it had travelled south of the border - and put it on display in a local shop. Excursion trains were laid on for football fans as far away as Middlesbrough and Stockton; but for higher than normal admission prices and dreadful weather the chances are a record crowd would have witnessed the encounter. As expected, the Scots had the better of the game, leading 2 - 1 at half time and 4 - 2 at the end of the match. Despite this, the game was clearly one of the highlights of the season, and comfort for the Sunderland fans was to come in future years with the signing of a number the Renton players on show that day. Most notably, free scoring forward Johnny Campbell would soon make the move south and establish himself in Sunderland's Hall of Fame.

Inside 1887-88 fixture card.

1888-1889
Albion

"A magnificent spectacle. A dense, black mass met the eye everywhere, rising tier above tier in bewildering continuity our greatest match."

The Echo, commenting on Sunderland v. Sunderland Albion match, December 1888.

Sunderland's Civil War

After the success of the first Sunderland derby, the two teams agreed to meet for a second time, on the 12th January 1889. However, Sunderland refused to go to Hendon for an 'away' game, so the match was again staged at Newcastle Road. A large crowd of around 10,000 packed in to witness a much closer contest this time and twenty policemen were on duty in case of crowd trouble. The game was a tense, but exciting, affair, and Albion raced into a two-goal lead. Sunderland fought back, bringing the score to 2 - 1, and with minutes remaining Sunderland nicked an equaliser. Albion disputed the goal, claiming the ball had gone over the crossbar (there were still no nets), and left the field in a fit of pique. All hell broke loose amongst the fans, and Albion's transport was stoned in North Bridge Street. James Allan sustained a nasty eye injury that required surgery - quite ironic considering that one of the charities receiving the gate receipts was the Eye Infirmary - but it was such a nasty injury that the police interviewed Albion players after the game.

Albion vowed never to play at Newcastle Road again, and an inquiry into the affair put Allan centre stage. The Sunderland Secretary said that Albion could not be free from blame, for the people of Sunderland were incensed by Albion's lack of fair play, evidenced in their tactic of importing players especially for the match. Moreover, Allan was accused of doing everything he could to break up the club he had created. He responded by reminding everyone of the obligation the Sunderland Club had to him for its very existence, and claimed that if he had felt disposed to do so could have blown the lid wide open on the subject of professionalism at Sunderland AFC. It was clear that there was much bad blood between the teams, and although Albion asked for a third match on a neutral ground to determine which of the two Clubs were the better, Sunderland declined, pointing out that they had already had the better of two matches. There would be a long wait for the next Sunderland derby.

The 1888-89 season started in earnest on the 1st September, with a visit from the powerful Blackburn Rovers outfit and a cracker of a match it proved to be. Sunderland won the fixture 4 - 3, a very significant result, Blackburn being one of the strongest teams in the land - a fact demonstrated by their three successive FA Cup wins between 1884 and 1886. The 5,000 hardy souls who braved the monsoon conditions were well rewarded, with entertaining, end to end football against quality opposition. This match was followed by a 1 - 1 draw with Scottish Cup runners up Cambuslang, who had beaten the Lads 11 - 1 the previous January. It was clear that Sunderland were better equipped than ever before to deal with the best teams.

Indeed, a feature of the season was the attempt to pit Sunderland against tougher opposition, in part to boost the Club's profile outside of the region. The Football League had kicked off in 1888, and it was clear that this was the place to be. To make a case for admission, Sunderland would have to prove they could hold their own against the best and other notable visitors in the early months of the season included Grimsby Town (2 - 1), Sheffield Wednesday (2 - 1) and Middlesbrough (2 - 2).

The team's first FA Cup fixture of the season came against Elswick Rangers on the 27th October. The Lads triumphed 5 - 3, with Breckonridge hitting a hat-trick. Three weeks later, Sunderland met Newcastle East End in the next round, knocking them out with a 2 - 0 victory. The Sunderland team had made a great start to the season, due in no small part to the influx of yet another batch of Scottish players. Hopes of building on last season's successful cup campaigns must have been high at this stage of the season, but the Club's management were soon to face a tricky situation. Sunderland Albion had also progressed to the third qualifying round of the FA Cup, and the draw pitted the two teams together. The tie attracted massive interest in the town, but the Club did not want to see a bumper gate swell the bank balance of their new rivals. They decided to withdraw from the competition. Sunderland's FA Cup campaign ended without defeat for the second year running.

Before this decision was made public though, the draw was made for Sunderland's first game in the Durham Association Challenge Cup; astonishingly, the two Sunderland teams were pulled out of the bag together again. There was widespread dismay when Sunderland announced it was withdrawing from both competitions, and the decision was particularly unpopular with the fans. Not only was competitive action over by the middle of November, but the town had been denied the eagerly anticipated battle between the two Sunderlands.

Following immense local pressure, the Club agreed to meet Albion on the 1st December 1888. Sunderland suggested that the gate money should go to charity. Albion declined, but it was an ingenious attempt to prevent Albion benefiting from the bumper gate. Such was the interest that 18,000 turned up at Newcastle Road; the Echo said this was 'a magnificent spectacle. A dense, black mass met the eye everywhere, rising tier above tier in bewildering continuity.' They also described it as 'our greatest match,' running special editions of the paper to bring the people of the town match reports and score updates. In the end, Sunderland proved too strong for their rivals, winning 2 - 0. The victory boosted the Lads, but must have made the decision to withdraw from both of the cup competitions seem a bit foolish. The match was a great success, but a return fixture on the 12th January was to end in unpleasant circumstances, and the teams would not meet again until April 1892.

Having dealt with this 'local difficulty', Sunderland spent the rest of the season trying to prove they could play with the 'big boys'. They did this with some important victories against top opposition, including the likes of Bolton Wanderers (4 - 2), Sheffield Wednesday (2 - 1), Everton (4 - 2), Middlesbrough (4 - 0), Glasgow Rangers (3 - 0), Derby County (3 - 1), Accrington (4 - 0) and Dumbarton (4 - 3). Sunderland saved their best for last though, and towards the end of the campaign met both of the season's FA Cup finalists. First off, the runners up, Wolverhampton Wanderers, paid a visit to Newcastle Road, and were held to a 1 - 1 draw. This was a great result, but better was to come when Cup and League winners Preston North End came to Wearside and were dispatched by four goals to one. The Preston team were clearly the best in England, and beating them by such a margin was a considerable achievement.

It was now evident that Sunderland were more than just a good regional team; they were capable of giving any team in the land a run for their money and were starting to become a force to be reckoned with. Indeed, following their meeting with Sunderland, the Wolverhampton Wanderers team 'frankly confessed that they were harder pressed by Sunderland than in the final tie for the English Cup' and described our team as 'a clever little combination.' Moreover, the emphatic victory over League and Cup winners Preston added much weight to Sunderland's claims that they should be admitted to the recently formed Football League. It would not be long before these claims were accepted.

Double Winners Thrashed

On Monday the 28th April 1889 Preston North End visited Newcastle Road not only as League and FA Cup double winners, but also as quite clearly the best team in England. In topping the League they had finished well ahead of second placed Aston Villa, securing 40 points to Villa's 29, and had finished their campaign undefeated. Their FA Cup record was similarly impressive, the Preston team having lifted the trophy without conceding a single goal. The game kicked off at 6 o'clock in front of a crowd of between 8,000 and 10,000. Sunderland were one up within the first five minutes, much to the joy of the fans. Sunderland's backs were having an excellent game, preventing Preston from playing their famous short passing game by cutting off the supply of balls to the visitor's forwards. This frustrated Preston, but a long ball forward caught out the Sunderland defence and led to an equaliser.

The Lads were not disheartened, and went close on a number of occasions, including a notable effort from "Davison, who sent in a sky scraper, which had it not been a little wide would have been unstoppable." The encounter was a tense and evenly balanced one, but some light relief was brought when Sunderland's Raylson "caused a ripple of laughter by his trickiness with the leather." Kirtley then made a critical save to prevent Preston from gaining the lead and shortly afterwards Sunderland's efforts were justly rewarded when Breconbridge scored just before half-time. In the second half Sunderland took control of the match, a brilliant solo effort from Brand leading to a third and a fourth being added just before time. In the Echo's opinion, "the victory was the most creditable that Sunderland have yet scored, and will give them a lift in the world of football."

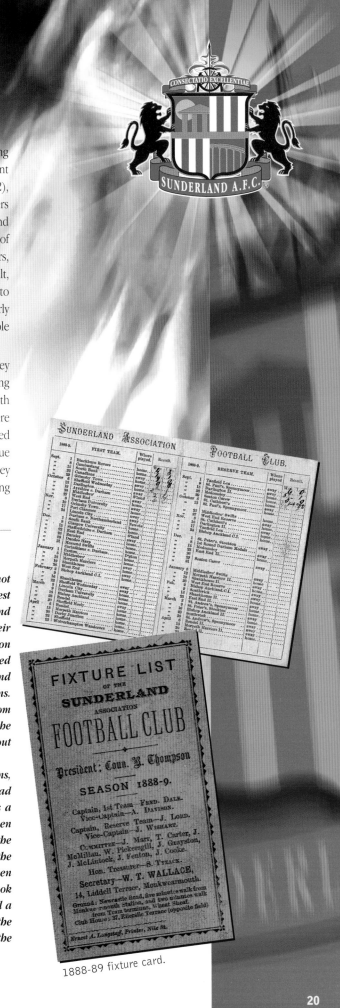

1888-89 fixture card.

1889-1890
Team of All Talents

"A talented man in every position"

William McGregor, Football League Founder, christening Sunderland as the 'Team of All Talents'

Team of All Talents, 1890.

The Safest Hands in Sunderland - William 'Stonewall' Kirtley

The first decade of Sunderland AFC's life was one that saw much change both within the Club and in football more generally. The Club had developed at such a rapid pace that the team, surroundings and opponents of 1879-80 had little in common with those of 1889-90. There were, however, two of the original players left in the side at the end of the 1880s. One was 'Dowk' Oliver, for whom the Club had held their first 'testimonial' match. The other was goalkeeper William 'Stonewall' Kirtley. Both men went on to play for Sunderland in the Football League, but Kirtley made just two such appearances before being displaced by another Sunderland legend 'Ted' Doig. Without doubt one of the early stars of the team, Kirtley regularly put in top performances in big games; indeed, when Wolverhampton Wanderers visited in 1888-89 they were so impressed that they offered him a place in their team. Kirtley declined, preferring to stick with his home town Club. In 1892 he did eventually leave, but did not go far: he joined Sunderland Albion.

Sunderland kicked off their final season of the decade with a home match against Blackburn Rovers. Rovers were still smarting from a previous defeat, but Sunderland beat them again, this time 1 - 0. A good victory against local opposition followed, 3 - 0 against Newcastle West End, and the first eight days of the season were completed when double winners Preston North End paid another visit to Sunderland, and were held 1 - 1 in front of 13,000 fans.

This set the pattern for the season, Sunderland mixing fixtures against local opposition, who were usually played off the park, with high profile games against tough opposition. In the former category, notable results included thrashings given to Darlington (7 - 0), Gateshead (5 - 0), Stockton (5 - 1) and Middlesborough Ironopolis (7 - 0). But even the best teams found Sunderland a tough proposition - we lost just ten out of fifty-five games played in the season - and some major names were defeated. For example, League teams such as Bolton Wanderers (3 - 2), Everton (3 - 2), Notts County (2 - 1) and Accrington Stanley (8 - 2) were beaten, as were major Scottish sides such as Third Lanark (4 - 0), Queen of the South (5 - 0) and Hearts (3 - 0).

Perhaps the most notable result of the season though was a 7 - 2 win against Aston Villa. They had finished second in the League the previous season, and had won the FA Cup in 1886-87. The victory that occurred on the 5th April 1890, was unbelievable. One of the Villa officials, William McGregor, reckoned that Sunderland had a 'talented man in every position': the so-called "Team of All Talents" was born. Significantly, McGregor carried a lot of weight in the Football League, having being instrumental in its formation, and his new found admiration of the Sunderland team increased enormously our chances of election to the League.

Of course, a good campaign in the FA Cup would help the cause too, but Sunderland were unlucky here. Playing in the first round proper for the first time, the Lads were drawn against Blackburn Rovers, away from home. Hannah scored two goals for Sunderland, and at all full time it was 2 - 2. In extra time though, the Rovers team proved too strong, and ran out 4 - 2 victors. It was a little disappointing for the Wearsiders, but the Blackburn team were in excellent form, and went on to win the trophy, hammering Sheffield Wednesday 6 - 1 in the final.

Better was to follow in the Durham Association Challenge Cup though. Here victories against Birtley (4 - 0) and Darlington St Augustines (1 - 0) put Sunderland in their fifth final. Once again Darlington provided the opposition, but they were no match for Sunderland who comfortably beat them 2 - 0. It was the fourth time the Club had lifted the trophy in the five seasons they had competed in it; indeed, one might even have suggested that it was a becoming a little unfair for Sunderland to compete as they were so obviously superior to the rest of the County's teams.

With the trophy secured, attention turned at the end of the season towards the 'small' matter of gaining admittance to the League. However, Sunderland were not the only team pushing for entry, and rivals included a team very close to home. On Friday 2nd May 1890, the Echo noted that "Local footballers will naturally be much interested in the annual meeting of the League to be held in Manchester tonight. Sunderland and Sunderland Albion will be represented at the meeting by delegates who will plead for the admission of their respective clubs to the charmed circle. It goes without saying that both cannot get in, and it is doubtful whether either will succeed."

In the event, it was decided that Sunderland should be admitted, but a clinching factor seems to have been our offer to pay towards the travelling costs of opponents in order to compensate for the extra travelling they would have to do. It was a significant concession to have made, but a clever tactic that did the trick. (And one that in the end cost Sunderland nothing, for no club asked for such a contribution). The Echo argued that Albion's achievements may have warranted admission too, "but as the younger club it can well afford to wait for its turn". In fact, it couldn't. Sunderland's election to the League secured their position as the town's top Club, and interest in Albion began to fade. Despite some good performances on the pitch, it soon became clear that Albion would not gain admission to the League for some time, and the club folded at the end of the 1891-92 season.

Admission to the League was the perfect end to an excellent season. There could have been no better way to end the footballing decade and it was a considerable testimony to the Club's officials that they had achieved such a feat just eleven years after the Club's formation as a teacher's team. Moreover, with four trophies in the bag too, the first decade could quite rightly be regarded as a successful one, but better was to come in the 1890s.

Ready for the 'Big Boys'

Sunderland's fifth Durham Association Challenge Cup final took place on the 22nd April 1890, at the Victoria Ground, Stockton. Darlington again provided the opposition and a crowd of between 7,000 and 10,000 made it to the game. Two heavily laden excursion trains left Sunderland including one with a special carriage for Sunderland's team and committee. After the game kicked off, the Lads took an early lead, Campbell getting the first inside ten minutes. However, early hopes of a runaway victory were dashed as Darlington rallied and their backs began to put in a fine performance, dealing comfortably with successive Sunderland attacks.

It was still 1 - 0 when the second half commenced, but Sunderland faced a worrying few minutes when Porteous left the pitch for treatment to an injury. Despite good play from both teams, the match was somewhat deadlocked and another goal looked unlikely. Indeed, although Darlington had much possession in the Sunderland half, the Lads' goalie Kirtley had little to do. Sunderland went close a number of times, most particularly when a scrimmage followed a corner kick. As the game went on, heavy rain made the pitch slippery, and, much to the amusement of the crowd, a number of players lost their footing. Accurate shooting was becoming a near impossibility, but fifteen minutes from time Smith pulled a brilliant shot out of the bag, perfectly chipping the ball into the Darlington goal.

The Echo's correspondent concluded that "the game was now effectively over," and reported that "many of the spectators began to leave." As time ran out for the Darlington players they began to show their frustration, increasingly resorting to foul play. It did not help them, and no further goals were scored. Sunderland clinched the Cup for a fourth time, with a two-nil victory.

Durham Challenge Cup final winners medal v Bishop Auckland Church Institute. Sunderland won 2-1.

The Sporting Life in Sunderland

Sunderland v Newcastle
at St James' Park, 1889-90.

The 'Code War'

Aside from the Sunderland Albion threat, other sports such as cricket and rugby competed with football for the attention of the townsfolk. In particular, big rugby matches were often staged to coincide with big football matches - a reflection of the war between the two 'codes' perhaps - and many of the town's sports fans would have faced some difficult choices at times. For example, on the day Sunderland played Darlington in the final of the 1888 Durham Association Challenge Cup, the town's rugby club met Durham City in the semi-final of the 'handling' code's Durham Challenge Cup. Similarly, when Albion made it to the final of the Durham Association Challenge Cup the following year, the Sunderland rugby team again met Durham City in the semi-final of the Durham Challenge Cup. That the rugby team lost both ties while the 'soccer' teams won theirs may have played a part in helping the association football bandwagon to roll.

The increasingly affluent late-Victorian Sunderland was a place where organised sports began to flourish and while Sunderland AFC would ultimately emerge as the town's main sports club, a number of competitors for this mantle existed in the 1880s. In particular, James Allan's breakaway Sunderland Albion threatened to destroy the Sunderland club he had helped to found. Though Albion had a brief existence, it was in many ways a very successful one.

Albion's first full season of football commenced on the 1st September 1888, with a 3 - 0 win against Rotherham Town, which was quickly followed up by a 13 - 2 thrashing of St Augustine and 8 - 1 victory over Stockton. The Albion side was a free-scoring one, hitting a staggering seventy goals in their first ten games. As we have seen, the opportunity to contest FA and Durham Cup ties against Sunderland was denied them in this first season, and the Albion suffered a set back when they failed to beat their rivals in two friendly games staged that season. However, while Sunderland withdrew from the Cup competitions in an attempt to prevent the flow of cash into the Albion coffers, the plan partially back-fired, for it gave Albion a free run in the Durham Association Challenge Cup. Emphatic victories over Southwick (6 - 0), Spennymoor St Paul's (13 - 0), Whitburn (5 - 1) and a semi-final victory over Bishop Auckland (2 - 1), put them into the final of the competition. Albion then lifted the trophy - in their first full season remember - by beating Birtley 3 - 0 at Feethams, where over 6,000 witnessed the game. Goals from Miller, Hogarth and McLellan did the damage. It was quite an achievement. However, it was not without drama, for the game was a replay, the original tie having been abandoned following crowd trouble.

The following season, Albion picked up on a Sunderland tradition: going out of both the FA and Durham cups without losing a game. Like their neighbouring rivals, Albion depended heavily on imported players, and made the mistake of using an unregistered player in an FA Cup victory over Bootle. Complaints from the latter led to Albion being disqualified from the competition and suspended from all football for fourteen days. Unfortunately for Albion, they were due to start the defence of their Durham Association Challenge Cup title during this fortnight with a tie against Bishop Auckland. Much to the latter's delight, Albion had no choice but to concede the tie and they went out of the cup without kicking a ball. Undoubtedly this put a bit of a damper on a crucial season, for it meant that the club had little experience of competitive football upon applying for admission to the League at the end of the season. However, Albion had been competing in the Football Alliance - which effectively acted as a 'second division' - and secured a creditable joint-second finish. Nevertheless, it was their Sunderland neighbours who gained admittance to the League for the 1890-91 season.

It was downhill after this. The following season Albion continued to compete in the Alliance - again finishing second - and joined the Northern League, where they finished third. While there were a number of notable victories still - such as an 11 - 1 against Walsall Swifts and 7 - 0 against Crewe Alexandria - the proportion of victories started to fall a little and quality opponents more often than not got the better of Albion. By the 1891-92 season - Albion's fourth - it was evident that they had given up the battle to become the town's top club. They withdrew from the Alliance and focused on the Northern League, but could only manage a mid-table finish.

Moreover, the defeats began to out number the victories and the goal scoring rate had dropped to roughly half that achieved in Albion's first season.

At the end of the 1891-92 campaign, Albion decided to call it a day. The two Sunderland clubs ended their feud shortly before this, and two of Albion's last four games were Sunderland derbies. The gulf that had opened between the two sides was demonstrated in these games, Sunderland winning the tie at Newcastle Road 6 - 1 and the Blue House Field encounter ended 8 - 0 to Sunderland. At least Albion went out on a high note though; their final game - played on the 30th April 1892 - saw them beat Darwen by five goals to one.

Ironically, a second division of the Football League was formed for the 1892-93 season, and Darwen were amongst its founder members, finishing in third place. Other teams competing in its inaugural season included Walsall Swifts and Crewe Alexandria, both played off the park by Albion just two seasons previously. Had Albion maintained their form a little longer, the chances are they would have gained admission to the second division. Had they done so, how many of today's die hard Sunderland fans would instead be committed Albion followers?

Albion Lift the Cup

Albion met Birtley at Bishop Auckland to decide the final tie of the Durham Association Challenge Cup. The initial game took place on the 30th March 1889, in front of 6,000 fans. Albion played well, a Stewart goal putting them one-up by half time, and a second being scored "amid much cheering and hooting" after the re-start. After this, Birtley had little choice but to push forward, and thought they had pulled one back only to be told by the referee that the goal did not stand. An argument broke out amongst the players, and suddenly the crowd behind the goal, mainly Birtley fans, spilled on to the pitch and surrounded the players. Violence broke out, with the Albion captain receiving a nasty wound after being struck on the head. So serious was the injury that the police later offered a £5 reward for information about the perpetrator of the attack.

Unsurprisingly, the players decided to leave the pitch at that point, but the referee would not abandon the match. Forty-five minutes later, the teams reappeared, but Albion were a man down without their captain - there were no substitutes in those days - and Millar was carrying an injury sustained earlier in the game. Despite this, the Albion team appeared to have held out for victory. Three minutes from the end though, fans invaded the pitch again and this time the game had to be abandoned.

Clearly the organising committee had something of a dilemma on their hands, for the game had not been completed, yet to order a replay would somewhat unfairly reward the bad behaviour of the Birtley fans. In the end, they decided that the game should be replayed at the Feethams Ground, Darlington, which "was considered hard lines for Albion, who held that they were in no way responsible for the unruly proceedings at Auckland."

A Sunderland Albion banner.

1890·91   Seventh in League.
Reach the **FA Cup** semi-finals.

1891·92   League Champions.
Reach semi-finals of the **FA Cup** again.

1892·93   Retain the Championship.

1893·94   Finish second in League.

1894·95   Champions again!
Win 'Championship of the World'.

1895·96   Fifth in League.

1896·97   Finish second bottom but avoid relegation
after a series of 'Test Matches'.

1897·98   Runners-up in League.

1898·99   Roker Park opens.
Seventh in League.

1899·1900   Third place in League.

The 1890s saw the most successful decade of football in Sunderland's history. Elected to the recently formed Football League for the start of the 1890-91 season, the Lads wasted little time in putting the town on the footballing map. A respectable first season was followed by a Championship win in our second season of League football. As if this wasn't enough, the Club retained the trophy the following season and added a further success in the 1894-95 season. All told, Sunderland's first ten seasons of League football saw us finish in the top three six times.

However, despite establishing themselves as one of the top two or three teams in the country, the Lads were unable to match their League form in the FA Cup. Sunderland managed to reach three semi-finals between 1890 and 1895 but early round exits soon became the norm. It would be a long time before Sunderland would reach a Cup final.

Off the pitch the Club continued to progress. The Newcastle Road ground was gradually improved but in 1898 Sunderland moved to a magnificent new home at Roker Park. Success on the pitch helped to make the previous decade's financial problems a thing of the past and the Club became a Limited Company in 1896.

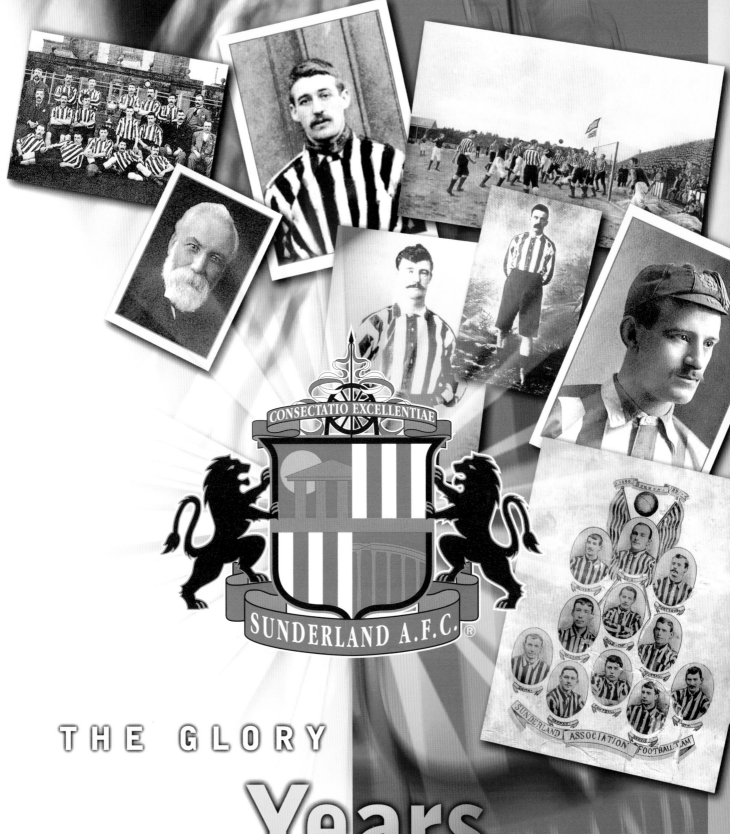

THE GLORY

Years

1 8 9 0 · 1 9 0 0

1890-1891
Welcome to the Big Time

"If Sunderland were not up to the task there were plenty of clubs ready to take our place."

William 'Stonewall' Kirtley.

So Near, Yet So Far

Sunderland's first appearance in the semi-finals of the FA Cup came on 25th February 1891, and took place against Notts County at Bramall Lane, Sheffield. The Lads had thrashed their opponents 4 - 0 in the League a month earlier, so many fans must have expected a first Cup Final appearance to quickly follow.

A massive crowd of 25,000 packed into the ground, a record for the stadium then, and extra stands were erected for the game. Sunderland were weakened by injuries before the game, but a bigger problem was the referee, who ruled against us on a number of occasions. Crucially, he disallowed an early goal from the Lads, and though we managed to put the ball in the net a further three times, the game ended a draw. Against this, it should be mentioned that one of our defenders, Porteous, handled the ball on the goal line (there were no penalty kicks then, so the offence went unpunished) and there were claims that one of our goals had gone over the cross-bar.

The replay was fixed to take place on 11th March, a fortnight after the original tie. The Sunderland team did not have a League game during the intervening period, and spent most of the two weeks in the Roker Hotel. The second match also took place at Bramall Lane, but this time heavy snow had made the pitch almost unplayable. Despite this, the game went ahead and 16,000 Sunderland fans made the trip. The Notts County players responded better to the conditions, running out 2 - 0 winners. The cup dream had come to an end.

The 1890-91 season goes down in history as Sunderland's first in League football. We were admitted to the League at Stoke's expense, the other League members deciding that the Lads would provide them with stiffer competition. While this was good news for us, it was also a warning: if Sunderland were not up to the task, there were plenty of clubs ready to take our place. Until the League season kicked off, it would be difficult to know whether or not we would rise to the challenge. While the Lads had previously met all but two of the League's teams, Burnley and the luckless Stoke, it would be wrong to assume that victories in friendlies would automatically be transferred into similar results in hard fought League games.

Coincidentally, the Lads' first League match was against the one 'unknown quantity', Burnley making the trip to Newcastle Road on 13th September 1890. The game took place before an "immense throng of spectators". While the game was a milestone in Sunderland's history, it ended up as something of an inglorious one, for Burnley took the points with a 3 - 2 victory. Sunderland's first League goal came from Spence. It was a good day for him as he scored another before full-time - but he scored just one more League goal before being transferred at the end of the season.

Two days after the Burnley game, Wolves provided the opposition, again at home, but 5,000 fans witnessed another defeat, this time by four goals to three. Sunderland were 3 - 0 up at half-time, but collapsed in the second half. Goalkeeper Kirtley was largely blamed for the defeat, though he was quite ill during the match, and he would not play another game for the Club. It was not a brilliant start to life in the League, and some fans must have worried that Sunderland would prove to be too weak for the competition. Fortunately, on 20th September, a 4 - 0 thrashing of West Bromwich Albion at their place gave the Lads their first ever League points, and a week later the Lads secured another point in the return match against Burnley, where the score ended 3 - 3.

So, our first month of League football ended won 1, drawn 1, lost 2, a record that suggested the Lads weren't quite ready yet to match the best in the land. The pattern continued over the next few months, though form picked up a little in December, and by the end of 1890, we had won 5, drawn 4 and lost 6, securing 14 points out of a possible 30. Unfortunately, the points secured in the win over West Brom were deducted on the grounds that Kirtley's replacement, Ted Doig, was unregistered at the time, and a final League position towards the bottom of the table looked very probable.

In the New Year, however, things began to pick up. January saw the Lads take maximum points, with Aston Villa thrashed 5 - 1 and Notts County beaten 4 - 0. Moreover, the Club's FA Cup campaign got off to a flier, with a 1 - 0 win over Everton, who lifted the Championship later in the season. The game was played in front of a massive 21,000 crowd and only went ahead following extensive efforts to keep the Newcastle Road pitch clear of snow. Everton's goalkeeper, a former Sunderland Albion player, was singled out for praise, but was unable to stop an early effort from Campbell that ultimately sealed victory for Sunderland. Before the end of the month, the Lads completed an excellent start to the year by beating Darwen 2 - 0 to secure a third round place.

February quickly brought the winning run to an end, the month seeing the familiar 1 win, 1 draw and 1 defeat in the League. However, the FA Cup was providing a compelling distraction, where a 4 - 0 defeat of Nottingham Forest secured Sunderland a place in the semi-finals for the first time. Here the Lads were drawn against Nottingham's other team, but the toils of a hard season began to show, Sunderland going out 2 - 0 to Notts County after a replay.

To their credit, the Lads played at the top of their game after this defeat, taking maximum points from their remaining League fixtures with victories over Preston (3 - 0) and Derby (5 - 1). At the end of the campaign, Sunderland were seventh in a league of twelve, and had two points not been deducted over the Doig 'affair', our excellent goal scoring record would have left us in fifth. Sunderland had made a good start, but had by no means set the football world alight.

Sunderland AFC 1890-91 season.

The Football League

The Football League - the world's first such competition - came into being in the 1888-89 season. While leagues are now part and parcel of football around the globe, the creation of such a competition was a novel idea at the time. Much of the credit for establishing the League is given to William McGregor, the man who dubbed Sunderland the 'Team of All Talents'. In an interview with the Echo in 1892, he eloquently outlined the merits of the contest, arguing "the championship of the League does not fall to the team which happens to be in form during a certain portion of the winter, but can only be secured by the eleven which has played consistently for over five months of the season. Erratic brilliance might easily, with a moderate share of luck, win the English Cup, but it would never get to the top of the League tree."

The competition began with twelve members: Accrington Stanley, Aston Villa, Blackburn Rovers, Bolton Wanderers, Burnley, Derby County, Everton, Notts County, Preston North End, Stoke, West Bromwich Albion and Wolverhampton Wanderers. Sunderland were the first team to gain admission after its creation - at Stoke's expense - but others soon followed. In the 1891-92 season the League was expanded to include fourteen teams (Stoke and Darwen being added) and the following season it encompassed sixteen teams plus another twelve in a second division.

William McGregor.

1891-1892 Champions!

"A Wonderfully Fine Team."

The Times

England international, Thomas Porteous.

England Star

There were many stars in Sunderland's first Championship winning side, but there was one man whose performances over the season had been strong enough to attract the attention of the England selectors, our stalwart back, Thomas Porteous. Born in Newcastle, he grew up in Kilmarnock and joined the local team. He moved through the ranks of the Kilmarnock club, becoming captain of their first team by his early twenties. In 1889, he signed for Sunderland, playing 93 League and Cup games for us before moving to Rotherham in 1893. He took two Championship medals in his time at the Club, and was ever present in both the table topping seasons. In March 1891, he was capped for England against Wales (a 4 - 1 win for the Englishmen), the first Sunderland player to receive the honour.

Sunderland ended the 1890-91 season on a high. After completing the League programme, the Lads played thirteen friendly matches, twelve of which they won! A winning start to the 1891-92 League campaign followed, Wolves being well beaten by five goals to two at home. Unfortunately, Sunderland were soon on the ropes, losing successive away matches against Preston (3 - 1), Bolton (4 - 3) and Aston Villa (5 - 3). Worryingly, one win and three defeats left the Lads bottom of the table at the end of September. Doubts about the team's ability to compete at the top surfaced again.

In the event, these three defeats constituted a 'blip' in the team's performance: the Lads lost just two more League games all season. Maximum points were taken in October, and though November started with a 3 - 1 defeat at Blackburn, the Lads followed this disappointment by going on an amazing unbeaten run. We won all of the remaining fixtures in November - including a 7 - 1 victory over Derby - and went on to take maximum points in December, Darwen being the victims of a seven goal drubbing this time. By the end of the year, Sunderland had won 12, drawn 0 and lost 4, taking 24 points out of a possible 32: this was Championship winning form.

In January, we turned our attention to the FA Cup, where the Lads avenged the previous season's semi-final exit by thrashing Notts County 4 - 0. In the second round, Accrington were beaten 3 - 1, though the opposition were unlucky in so far as the original tie was postponed due to the state of their pitch and had won the friendly played instead that day by one goal to nil. In February, Stoke provided the third round opposition, and after a 2 - 2 draw at Newcastle Road, the Lads triumphed 4 - 0 in a replay.

Sunderland had booked their place in the FA Cup semi-final for the second year in succession. The tie was again played at Bramall Lane, but this time Aston Villa provided the opposition. The crowd of 30,000 was even bigger than for the Notts County game and on several occasions the police had to steer fans off the pitch. Sunderland's recent form in competitive matches, having won fourteen and lost just one of sixteen games since the end of September, made them favourites. Few were surprised when Sunderland took an early lead, Scott bagging a goal in the first ten minutes. However, Villa turned up the heat, charging Doig to make it 1 - 1 at half-time, and in the second forty-five Sunderland ran out of steam. Villa took full advantage scoring three more goals to seal a 4 - 1 victory. The cup dream of Sunderland's shocked fans was over again.

As they had done in 1890-91 though, the team responded in a positive manner to Cup defeat. A mixture of a bad weather and Cup commitments had resulted in Sunderland playing no League games during their progression from the first round to the semi-final, and their League challenge resumed after a two month break. We managed maximum points in March, including a 2 - 0 win over Aston Villa, and when a 4 - 1 victory over Stoke was followed by a 1 - 0 defeat against Notts County, it marked the end of an astonishing run of thirteen consecutive League wins.

While it must have been disappointing to see the run come to a close, it had placed Sunderland at the top of the table, and with just three games left, the Championship looked bound for Wearside. Indeed, a 6 - 1 victory over Blackburn the following week, combined with a defeat for Preston, secured the Championship.

The Lads had won the League in just their second season of first class football. Victories over Darwen (7 - 1) and Burnley (2 - 1) completed the campaign, and the Club ended the season having won 21 of their 26 League matches, including all 13 home games. Sunderland could now truly claim to be a 'team of all talents' and there was no question over their ability to compete at the top. The Lads were comfortable victors in the League Championship, finishing five points clear of second placed Preston (with two points for a win). They had adapted remarkably well to the demands of League football, and were now, in the opinion of the Times no less, "a wonderfully fine team." Thankfully, there was more of the same to come.

Sunderland's League Championship winning team.

The Tale of Two Hotels

It was the best of times, it was the worst of times. In honour of Sunderland's feats on the pitch, the League held its annual meeting in Sunderland on Thursday 12th May 1892. At the meeting, held in the Queen's Hotel, Fawcett Street, tributes were paid to the Sunderland team, and the Champion's trophy was presented. The meeting also made the important decision to create a second division of the League for the 1892-93 season. Newcastle United would join the Second Division in 1893-94.

On the same evening, our main local rivals of the day, Sunderland Albion, held a Directors' meeting at the Empress Hotel, Union Street. It was a somewhat gloomy affair. The 'contest' between the two Sunderland clubs was now clearly over, for Sunderland were not only the town's top club, they were England's too! Two recent friendlies between the teams had underlined this, the Lads cruising to a 6 - 1 victory at home and an 8 - 0 win at Blue House Field. To make matters worse, Albion faced financial troubles. They needed £500 to keep the club on professional terms, but the Directors could not come up with the money. The meeting faced no choice but to wind the club up. That Albion folded on the same night Sunderland received football's biggest prize was poignant, and it emphasised the fact that the two clubs' fortunes were inextricably bound.

1892-1893
Encore

"They were beginning to ease through the League competition as if it were the Durham Association Challenge Cup."

Johnny Campbell.

The Goal Machine

Much of the credit for Sunderland hitting 100 goals in the 1892-93 season lay with goalscoring legend, John Campbell. It was the second season in a row that he had ended as the League's top scorer, scoring 32 League goals in 1891-92 and 31 in 1892-93 - an amazing achievement. Indeed, he repeated the feat in 1894-95 (with 20 goals) and was almost certainly the decade's most deadly forward. Born in Renton, Scotland, Campbell was good enough to be drafted into his local side's first team while still a teenager. Renton were one of Scotland's better teams, and it was in a friendly between Renton and Sunderland that Campbell caught the eye of our financiers. He signed for us in 1889 and stayed until 1897, when he moved to Newcastle United while nearing the 'wrong end' of his twenties. Campbell was one of the smaller players in the side, standing at just 5' 7'', but he was strong for his size and more than capable of holding his own. In his time at Sunderland, he hit 133 goals in 190 League games and 17 in 25 FA Cup matches, a record which leaves him, presently, as the Club's fifth top goal scorer of all time. Without doubt a Sunderland legend, he was, as the Echo put it, "one of the finest forwards that ever donned a jersey."

In an earlier review of the Club's history, former Echo sportswriter John Anderson noted that in their defence of the Championship, "wherever Sunderland went they attracted what were, in those days, great crowds". The Lads started this defence in great style, thrashing Accrington 6 - 0 away from home with Campbell getting a hat-trick. Though our next game, against Notts County, ended in a draw, we soon handed out some heavy defeats to Aston Villa (6 - 1), Blackburn (5 - 0) and West Brom (8 - 1) with Campbell again getting a hat-trick in the last of these. Indeed, the first two months of the season produced a remarkable record, Sunderland winning seven of their nine games, and losing just one, scoring a staggering forty goals against eleven conceded.

The next couple of months saw the Lads produce similar results, though with less dramatic scorelines, and by the end of the year we were already clear favourites for the League title. If there were any doubts about Sunderland's position as the country's number one club, these were surely dispelled in the New Year period when Wolves (5 - 2), Everton (4 - 3) and Aston Villa (6 - 0) were amongst the teams we beat in the first two weeks of 1893.

Once again, the fans had high hopes for Sunderland in the Cup, and our strong form in January augured well. Woolwich Royal Arsenal came out of the hat as our first round opponents with the tie to be played at Newcastle Road. At the time, Arsenal were a non-League side, but one good enough to be admitted to the Second Division at the end of the season. Sunderland brushed them aside, winning through to the next round with a 6 - 0 victory, Millar hitting a hat-trick. Sheffield Wednesday were beaten in the League, 4 - 2, before Sunderland made the trip to the Owls' neighbours, Sheffield United, for the second round of the Cup. The Lads had gone out of the competition on United's ground in the last two seasons, but any worries that the ground might be 'jinxed' were overcome when we won 3 - 1. In the quarter-finals Blackburn Rovers, who we had murdered 5 - 0 in September's League match, provided the opposition. 20,000 fans packed Ewood Park for the game, but Sunderland failed to produce the goods. Rovers, who had a very average season, ran out 3 - 0 winners, and another excellent chance of progressing in the Cup had been thrown away.

The Lads did not have a League match until some two weeks after their untimely Cup exit but, just as in previous seasons, they bounced back in style. Newton Heath (later to become Manchester United) were beaten 5 - 0 away from home, and further victories followed against Derby and Stoke. Sunderland's form then 'dipped' in the last five games, though six points out of ten would have been an excellent return for most teams, and we did manage to thrash Newton Heath again, 6 - 0 this time! By now, however, the Championship was in the bag, and Sunderland could afford to relax. We ran out comfortable winners, finishing eleven points ahead of Preston North End. What's more, the Lads also hit 100 League goals in the season and conceded just 36, quite a record given they played just 30 games!

Comparing teams of over one hundred years ago with those of today is difficult and it is undoubtedly the case that football is a much more defensive game now than it was then. However, the achievements of 1892-93 cannot be easily dismissed, for the Lads' goalscoring feats were remarkable in their own time too.

In that season, Sunderland became the first team to score 100 League goals, and the figure stood as a record until West Brom beat it in 1919-20, when they played 42 matches, 12 more than Sunderland did in 1892-93. The Lads' tally represented an average of 3.3 goals per game, which compared well to the 2.86 goals per game scored by Everton in securing the 1890-91 Championship. (Though, funnily enough, it was some way behind the 3.57 average Sunderland had achieved during their first Championship win.)

It might also be worth pointing out that as 1892-93 was the first season in which there was a Second Division of the League, it was also - logically - the first year in which there was a First Division too. Sunderland can, therefore, lay claim to being the first team to win the *First Division* - as opposed to Football League - Championship. One for the pub quizzes rather than the record books perhaps, but the creation of two divisions was indicative of the game's growing popularity, and the ease with which Sunderland dominated the season's play was a testimony to the skill and dedication of the Club's staff. They were beginning to ease through the League competition as if it were the Durham Association Challenge Cup.

Nine Goal Thriller

On 22nd October 1892, the FA Cup holders West Bromwich Albion made the trip to Newcastle Road. During the Throstles' unexpected Cup winning campaign, Sunderland, who were the favourites, had gone out at the semi-final against Aston Villa, so perhaps this was a chance for Sunderland to see what might have been had they been victorious at the penultimate stage. Sunderland had won both League meetings the previous season - in "dashing style" according to the Echo - and were in top form leading into the game. West Brom, meanwhile, had been undergoing "special training for the match," and were "bent upon inflicting the first defeat upon Sunderland in the league."

The Echo billed the match as the "most important in the league series today". The paper reported that the stand began to fill with a "facility that is unusual except upon great occasions", all this in spite of cold weather that meant "topcoats are an indispensable garment for those exposed to the full blast of the keen wind". The first half was keenly contested, and the Midlands team took full advantage of the wind behind them, going 1 - 0 up inside the first minute. They were delighted, but it was to be their only goal of the match.

Sunderland hit two goals before half-time and in the second period scored a further six! Campbell hit a hat-trick and Millar scored two. If only it had been the Cup Final! It was Sunderland's biggest victory of the season - though we hit five and six regularly - and indicative of the team's ability to dominate games against quality opposition. West Brom were by no means the best team in England, but they were good enough to win the Cup, and Sunderland played them off the park.

1892-93 fixture card.

1893-1894
Nearly Three

"Sunderland had been reduced to the status of mere mortals, but a third successive championship was not out of the question."

Souvenir card dating from about 1890.

Villa Pop

Sunderland met Aston Villa three times in the 1893-94 FA Cup. The first game took place at Newcastle Road, on 10th February 1894, and drew a capacity 23,000 crowd. It ended 2 - 2 with goals from Harvey and Wilson forcing a replay at Villa's Perry Barr home. However, the replayed game was something of a disaster, especially for Villa. The pitch was in a terrible state following heavy rain and the referee had suggested the players give it a go for quarter-of-an-hour, but that if the conditions proved to be too bad, then the game would be a friendly instead of a Cup tie. Villa ran out 2 - 0 winners, and celebrated their hard fought passage to the quarter-finals, only to be told by the referee that the game was to be counted as a friendly. If even the players were unaware of this, one wonders what the fans making their way home must have thought on hearing the news later. The replayed replay took place on 21st February, with another 20,000-plus crowd, but this time Villa were even stronger and beat the Lads 3 - 1. It was probably the fairest outcome all round, but disappointing nonetheless.

Sunderland made a relatively poor start to the 1893-94 League campaign. The season began on 2nd September, with a 2 - 2 draw at Sheffield Wednesday, and for the most part the opening month consisted of drawn games. While the Lads managed to pick up a win at Preston this was more than overshadowed when we suffered a 7 - 1 defeat at the hands of Everton on 30th September. Sunderland took just five points from their first five games, not in itself a bad record but well below what had come to be expected of the 'Team of All Talents'.

This frustrating start to the season continued for the rest of the year. At times the Lads were brilliant, walking over teams such as Derby (5 - 0) and Wolves (6 - 0), but the near invincibility of previous seasons had disappeared and we suffered defeats at the hands of teams as average as Burnley. Most significantly, Sunderland's long period of being unbeaten at home came to an end with a defeat at the hands of Blackburn Rovers by three goals to two on 9th December. Since the opening week of Sunderland's first League season, when Burnley and Wolves had inflicted defeats, Newcastle Road had become something of a fortress. Between 15th September 1890, and 9th December 1893, Sunderland were unbeaten at home in the League and Cup, and had won almost nine out of every ten games they played there. It was a marvellous record, but by bringing it to an end, Blackburn sent a message to football clubs through the land: Sunderland were now a 'beatable' team.

While the position at the turn of the year was poor in comparison to recent seasons, it was by no means a disastrous one. Sunderland had been reduced to the status of mere mortals, but a third successive championship was not out of the question. Indeed, the New Year brought some cheer, for while we suffered a defeat at Wolves, we also took maximum points from the other League games in January, smashing six past Preston on New Year's Day.

Besides, there was always the Cup too, which kicked off on 29th January against Accrington. Sunderland passed this test with ease, winning 3 - 0, and following a 1 - 0 League victory against Everton, awaited the visit of Aston Villa for the second round. Villa were having an excellent season, and looked good value for the League or Cup. It was to be a close encounter, requiring three games, albeit one of them a 'void' match, to produce a winner. Unfortunately, Villa proved to be victorious, making it Sunderland's worst performance in the Cup as a League team.

In the end, Villa were to be knocked out before the final too, but the two teams battled it out for the Championship. The Lads finished with a very strong run, beating Newton Heath (4 - 2), Derby County (4 - 1), Notts Forest (2 - 0) and Darwen (4 - 0 and 3 - 0) in five of their last seven matches. Although Sunderland dropped four points in games against Bolton and Stoke, it made little difference in the end: the damage had already been done in the early part of the season. Villa snatched the title from us, finishing six points ahead of the Lads. It was a much closer contest than in previous years, with a number of teams finishing quite close to Villa, and the Birmingham team's performance was in no way comparable to that of the Sunderland team that had won the 1891-92 and 1892-93 seasons. In particular, Villa's goalscoring rate was inferior, 84 goals in 30 games being some way short of the 100 hit by the Lads in the previous season.

Runners-up in the League is by no means a poor performance; indeed it is one that modern day fans would love to see repeated! However, for a Sunderland team that had dominated the competition for two seasons it must have been something of a disappointment. Explaining why the Lads failed to replicate their Championship winning form is difficult. The team line up was a little less settled than in previous years, and Campbell failed to find his 'shooting boots'. That he was crucial to Sunderland's game plan is clear. He had been the League's top scorer for two seasons but he was at times absent from the team in 1893-94. Sunderland managed just 26 away goals in the League, compared with 42 the previous season and their goalscoring rate (2.4 per game) was well below that shown in the Championship seasons. Why this should be is anyone's guess, but one thing is clear: the Lads were determined to rectify the situation in the 1894-95 season.

The River Wear ferry carried supporters from densely populated areas of the East End on match days. It ran from 1792 until July 1957.

The Sidekick Steps Forward

With Campbell's supply of goals drying up a little in the 1894-95 season, another of Sunderland's star forwards, Jimmy Millar, stepped into the breach. Like Campbell, Millar was a Scot, and began as a teenager at his local club, but transferred to Sunderland while still only 19. Not as prolific as Campbell, Millar, playing as inside forward most of the time, still finished as the Club's leading scorer for the 1894-95 season with 20, and regularly hit double figures. He had two spells at the Club, interrupted by four years at Glasgow Rangers, and in all spent ten seasons at Sunderland. He had a particularly good striking rate in FA Cup games, scoring 17 in 22 appearances, but his League record was impressive too, standing at 106 goals in 238 matches. Millar jointly holds the Club record for the most goals scored in a game - he hit five in the 11-1 FA Cup win against Fairfield. His association with Sunderland ended in 1904, when he was transferred to West Bromwich Albion.

Goalscoring legend Jimmy Millar.

1894-1895
Top of the World

"Sunderland were now, without doubt, the best team in England."

A rare picture of Sunderland Ted Doig without his cap on.

The Game of 'Three Halves'

Sunderland's 1894-95 League campaign started with a bizarre victory over Derby County. At the allotted kick off time, some 8,000 fans had packed a windswept Newcastle Road ground, eagerly anticipating the start of the football season. No doubt the teams were looking forward to the new season too, but unfortunately, one man who was not ready was the referee, Mr Kirkham. In fact, he had not even arrived at the ground. The game kicked off with his deputy in charge, and Sunderland, after winning the toss, elected to play with the strong wind behind them. The Lads took full advantage of the conditions, and raced to a 3 - 0 lead before half-time.

During the interval, however, Mr Kirkham arrived, and gave Derby the option of starting the match again. Naturally, they jumped at the chance of wiping out a three goal deficit, and the teams emerged for the second first half! Ironically, the decision backfired on Derby somewhat. Restarting the game meant a new toss-up, which Sunderland won, and the Lads elected to play with the very strong wind behind them once more. The strength of the wind aided Sunderland again, as they once more scored three goals without reply. When the second - or third - 'half' kicked off, the Derby players were exhausted after having spent 90 minutes battling against the elements, and Sunderland strolled to victory in the 'third half', adding a further five goals!

The Lads signalled their intent to take the League by storm in the first game of the season, when we beat Derby 8 - 0 in a 'game of three halves'. Further victories followed against Burnley (3 - 0), Aston Villa (2 - 1) and West Brom (3 - 0), and though we lost the last match of September against Bolton, the Lads took eight out of a possible ten points in the first month of the season, hitting seventeen goals. In doing so this made it, arguably, the best start to a League campaign so far. Moreover, we had given a direct warning to reigning champions Aston Villa that Sunderland were out for revenge. The good form continued into October and November with us taking five out of six points in October and seven out of eight in November. This put Sunderland into a strong position as the Christmas period approached.

December started in great style, with Small Heath walloped 7 - 1, but it ended in two defeats for the Lads. A busy festive programme saw us play five games over eight days and the Sunderland men found it difficult to maintain top form over this period. Boxing Day saw us win at West Brom, 2 - 0, but the following day the Lads had to make the trip to Nottingham, where Forest beat us 2 - 1. Two days later it was over to Preston, where the year ended with a 1 - 0 defeat. After a couple of days rest, Preston made the return trip to Newcastle Road for a New Year's Day fixture, but the break had given the Lads time to recharge, and we beat them 2 - 0 in front of 10,000 fans. The following day Aston Villa visited Sunderland, and the holiday programme was completed with an exciting 4 - 4 draw witnessed by 12,000 spectators. Sunderland had now dropped five points in five games, and lost another when Forest visited three days after the Villa game. Our only consolation was that the other teams had faced a similarly tough schedule.

Sunderland's first FA Cup match of the season did not take place until February, by which time we had returned to winning ways with victories against Wolves (4 - 1) and Stoke (5 - 2), and the Lads were drawn against unknown Lancashire side, Fairfield, in the first round. The fans were not excited by the fixture and just 1,000 turned out but the 'die hards' were given a treat as Sunderland notched up a record FA Cup victory that still stands today: it ended 11 - 1. In the second round Preston provided the opposition, and this time there was a bumper 12,000 gate. The scoreline was less impressive than in the previous round, but two first half goals from Campbell and solid defending from the backs put Sunderland into the third round.

Both Sheffield teams visited Newcastle Road for League matches and both were seen off before the next Cup tie took place. Here the previous season's runners-up, Bolton Wanderers, made the trip to Sunderland, and a massive 16,000 crowd awaited the outcome. Wanderers started well, nicking an early goal and defending superbly. At half-time the Lads were 1 - 0 down, a scoreline that remained with just ten minutes of the second half left. In desperation, Wilson moved forward, a switch that transformed the game. Within minutes he scored an equaliser and before the end grabbed the winner with a glorious overhead kick. Sunderland were now on their best cup run since the 1891-92 Championship season, and as then the double was a strong possibility. The semi-final draw was not kind though, the Lads being pitched against Aston Villa, a team we would have preferred to avoid.

For once the semi-final was not staged at Bramall Lane (where Sunderland had lost two previous semi-finals), but the venue, Ewood Park, made no difference. Sunderland lost 2 - 1 despite taking an early lead. Villa went on to win the Cup, which they put on display in a local shop. Unfortunately it was stolen by local villains and never found; it would have been better all round had Sunderland won the semi-final tie!

The Lads responded to their traditional Cup exit in the usual manner, winning all remaining League games. In doing so they secured the Championship for the third time in four seasons, and a massive 20,000 crowd made it to Newcastle Road to applaud the team on their last game of the season. The match took place against Everton, who were in second place, but the result mattered little as the Lads had managed to secure the trophy before the season's finish. Campbell had returned to the top of his form in the 1894-95 season and once again he finished as the League's top scorer. Our points haul was just one below the total reached in 1892-93. Sunderland were now, without doubt, the best team in England. In a dramatic gesture, Scottish Champions Hearts challenged us to a match to determine the best team in Britain; the Lads did not let us down.

1894-95 Sunderland team with the League Championship trophy.

Sunderland Crowned Champions of the World

After securing the English League Championship at the end of the 1894-95 season, Scottish League Champions Hearts invited Sunderland to Edinburgh to contest a play-off between the two clubs. The game, which took place on 27th April 1895, was advertised in the Scottish capital as the 'Championship of the World'. There was some justification for the use of such a tag, as England and Scotland were undoubtedly, by some margin, the leading football nations of the time.

A massive 15,000 crowd turned out for the game, which was keenly contested. The teams had met nearly a decade earlier when the Scots were the favourites and they had gone on to beat us 2 - 1. This time, Sunderland were in the ascendancy, and had the better of the game. The fans were treated to an eight goal thriller, which the Lads won by five goals to three. Sunderland were Champions of the World!

Tom Watson.

1895-1896
SAFC Ltd

"In retrospect 1894-95 was probably the swan song of a talented, but ageing, team."

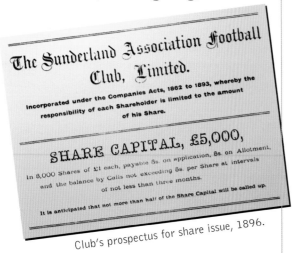

The Sunderland Association Football Club, Limited.

Incorporated under the Companies Acts, 1862 to 1893, whereby the responsibility of each Shareholder is limited to the amount of his Share.

SHARE CAPITAL, £5,000,

In 5,000 Shares of £1 each, payable 5s. on application, 5s. on Allotment, and the balance by Calls not exceeding 5s. per Share at intervals of not less than three months.

It is anticipated that not more than half of the Share Capital will be called up.

Club's prospectus for share issue, 1896.

The Boasting Board

The 1896 share issue was undoubtedly a financial success, and laid the foundations for the Club's future development. The prospectus printed before the issue was a short, two page document, consisting primarily of proud boasts. "The Sunderland Association Football Club is one of the best known and most popular and successful Clubs in the United Kingdom," it argued, and the "famous Newcastle Road Ground at Sunderland, where the home matches are played, is one of the best and most comfortable in the Country". With "reasonable support from their fellow townsmen", the Directors aimed "to maintain the prestige the Club has attained, and make it the best in the Country, and worthy of the traditions of the Sunderland Association Football Club".

Those who think the obsession with the financial aspects of football is a modern day phenomenon should note the document's attempts to stress the economic benefits of football. It argued that the "games played by the Sunderland team away and at home have been the means of bringing the Town and its locale to great prominence, previously to which, in many parts of the Kingdom, it was comparatively unknown. Moreover, the tradesmen of the town have benefited by the many thousands of visitors from all parts which its fame has attracted".

The 1895-96 season was to be a poor one by Sunderland's recent standards. It started well enough, with strongly-attended home victories against Preston (4 - 1) and Blackburn (2 - 1), but the rot soon set in. The Lads only managed to pick up three out of the next ten points and had only won two further games by the end of October. Performances improved a little over the next few months, but by the end of the year the record stood at eight wins, five draws and five defeats. Hardly disastrous form, but not the kind that wins Championships either. Indeed, to put this into perspective, Sunderland had lost just four League games in the whole of the previous season. It was clear that something was missing.

The 1896 fixtures began with the return match against Preston, and the scoreline was the reverse of the season's opener, Sunderland losing 4 - 1. Defeat at the hands of Forest and a home draw against Sheffield United left January looking pretty bleak for the Lads, but they ended the month by thrashing West Brom 7 - 1, Campbell hitting his first hat-trick since the 8 - 1 drubbing of West Brom in 1892. In truth, the score said more about West Brom than Sunderland, the Black Country team going on to finish the season in bottom place.

In February, attention turned to the FA Cup where Preston completed a trio of fixture related 'firsts' as they lined up to face us in the opening round. Amazingly, the score again ended 4 - 1, this time in Sunderland's favour, with Millar and Campbell getting two goals each. It was an excellent result that carried us into a second round tie against Sheffield Wednesday. The game took place in Sheffield, with 22,000 fans paying to see the game. Sunderland were looking to go one better than last year's semi-final finish, but hopes were cruelly dashed in a 2 - 1 defeat. It was Sunderland's shortest Cup campaign as a League club.

Sunderland rallied after the Cup exit in the usual style, winning six of our seven remaining League games, but it was too little too late. The team finished in fifth place, some eight points behind Champions Aston Villa, our worst placing since the 1890-91 season. Of course, it was only a poor performance when judged against Sunderland's excellent record in the competition, and we finished seven points clear of sixth placed Stoke. Moreover, another couple of wins would have seen us joint second, but those extra wins were for some reason beyond the team.

In retrospect 1894-95 was probably the swan song of a talented, but ageing, team and it was evident that funds were required to bring in fresh talent if the team was to continue to challenge for honours. The issue was raised at the Club's Annual General Meeting in 9th July 1896, at which it was emphasised that the Club's finances were on something of a knife-edge. Much expenditure, on players and ground improvements, had been incurred during the close season, meaning the Club were in debt for much of the playing season. Moreover, the Club could never be certain of generating enough income to cover this expenditure, and much depended on success on the pitch: the difference in gate receipts between the Championship season and the 1895-96 campaign was a massive £1,450.

In the past, the generosity of local industrialists had paved the way for signings or the development of Newcastle Road, but it was felt desirable to secure the Club's finances in a more permanent way.

The Board proposed that the Club be turned into a Limited Company, with a share issue being used to raise capital. This would enable the Club to start each season in credit, and plan its expenditure in a more rational way. The proposal was carried, and the Club went into the 1896-97 season with a new title: Sunderland Association Football Club Limited. Sunderland - and football - had come a long way since 1879, when the Club decided it needed no Treasurer for the sums of money involved were small enough to be carried by individual players. Football was becoming a big business and Sunderland's share issue underlined our determination to be at the forefront of this new era in the game.

Thomas Hemy's famous painting of Sunderland v Aston Villa, April 1895. The picture is one of the oldest records of a professional football game and probably one of the biggest. It is now owned by the Club and majestically dominates the reception area of the Stadium of Light.

Hughie Wilson - A Man of Many Firsts

Hughie Wilson, a Scottish international and one time Sunderland captain, was a stalwart of the Club through most of the 1890s. He signed from Newmills in 1889 and left for Bedminster in 1899, after making 258 League and Cup appearances for the Lads. Signed initially as a centre forward, he was soon shifted to right halfback, where he was "considered indispensable". After our first Championship win, the Echo argued he had "proved a priceless 'find' for the Sunderland committee". Even when Sunderland were playing badly he seemed to stand out, and appeared for Scotland against England during our disastrous 1896/97 season.

Wilson was also a man of many 'firsts', being the first Sunderland player to score a penalty in a League match - against Bolton on 19th September 1891 - and the first player to be sent off in a League game, against Stoke, on 14th March 1896. By the end of his time at Sunderland, Wilson had reverted back to the centre-forward position, and ended his career with 45 League and Cup goals for the Club.

Former captain Hughie Wilson.

38

1896-1897

Testing Time

"This was easily Sunderland's worst season so far as a League club, and the fall from grace was all the more dramatic given it came just two seasons after being crowned 'Champions of the World'."

Tom Watson

Tom Watson's decision to leave Sunderland at the end of the 1895-96 season was a bitter blow for the Club. Liverpool, yet to make a big name for themselves in football, were looking for a good manager to steer them through their first season in the top division of the League competition, and offered Watson twice his salary at Sunderland to tempt him away. Watson was by no means a poor man and owned a tobacconist's shop on North Bridge Street, opposite Monkwearmouth Station but the offer proved too good to refuse. Perhaps he also relished the fresh challenge.

Watson was probably Sunderland's most successful manager of all time. He joined in 1889 and assembled the 'Team of All Talents' that not only cruised to Durham Association Challenge Cup glory, but was strong enough to gain admittance to the Football League. After this, he steered Sunderland to those three Championships in four seasons, and though the FA Cup eluded him, it was clear at the time that he possessed special talents. The Echo noted in 1892 that he would go down in history as a key figure in North East football.

Although the manager's job was less 'hands on' than it is today, Sunderland's dip in form after his departure underlined his importance to the Club, and it is worth noting that Liverpool did remarkably well with Watson at the helm, winning two League Championships. Curiously, the Cup jinx 'followed' him to Liverpool and they lost one final and three semi-finals under his charge.

The 1896-97 season was to start badly and get worse. The fans had hoped that the disappointment of the previous season would be soon put behind them but it was not to go as planned. For the first time since the 1890-91 season, Sunderland began their League campaign with a defeat - and a home one to boot - Bury scoring the only goal of the game. The Lads then went on a terrible run, picking up just two points in the opening month, and it was October 17th, the ninth game of the season, before Sunderland managed to win a game. It came against newly promoted Liverpool, in a 4 - 3 thriller, and was followed in the next match by a second win, at Wolves. It was, without doubt, Sunderland's worst start to a League campaign. In the first ten games we had managed to gain just seven points out of a possible twenty, five of which came in the latter three games.

Apart from the share issue, another significant change had taken place in the close season. The Club's Secretary/Manager, Tom Watson, had decided to leave after seven seasons of loyal service. Ironically, it had been Liverpool who had tempted him away by doubling his income so his return to Newcastle Road was not a happy one. His replacement, Robert Campbell, was evidently having trouble living up to the standards set by his predecessor.

Unfortunately for Campbell, his next ten games in charge were, if anything, worse. They began with the return trip to Liverpool, which we lost (3 - 0), and continued on a losing track against Forest (2 - 1) and West Brom (1 - 0), leaving Sunderland without a point from November. December at least began with a draw, the Lads' first point for six weeks, but it ended with 5 - 2 defeat on Boxing Day away at Everton, witnessed by 35,000 fans. Sunderland had played on Christmas Day itself too, and this was a happier occasion, our first win for two months coming against Blackburn at home. The New Year programme brought further misery, a 1 - 1 draw with Preston on New Year's Day was followed by a 2 - 1 defeat by Derby the next day, completing the awful second ten games of Campbell's reign. The results had actually got worse, with a pathetic four point return from a possible twenty.

In the 21st match of the season, Sunderland inexplicably managed to raise their game to beat reigning Champions Aston Villa by four goals to two. It was an excellent result, one of only two games Villa would lose away from home in retaining the League title. However, the Lads couldn't reproduce such performances, and lost the return match seven days later. In the FA Cup, Bury provided the first round opposition, and Sunderland managed to secure a 1 - 0 win thanks to a goal from Morgan. Two weeks later, Nottingham Forest arrived on Wearside for the second round tie, and a massive 17,000 crowd turned out despite Sunderland's poor recent performances. Predictably, Sunderland lost, this time by three goals to one, bringing to an early end Sunderland's hopes of winning some sort of trophy in the 1896-97 season.

The final third of the League campaign saw Sunderland put in some better performances. Eleven of the twenty points were secured, and just two games were lost. However, it was not enough to lift Sunderland out of the 'danger' zone, and we finished second bottom in the League. There was no automatic promotion and relegation at the time, a system of 'Test Matches' being in operation instead.

The Lads and the First Division's bottom team, Burnley, played off against the top two in the Second Division, Notts County and Newton Heath to decide promotion and relegation.

Sunderland luckily scraped through the matches and kept their place in the top flight. But this did not disguise what had been a terrible first season under Campbell's direction. Apart from the final League position and early Cup exit, Sunderland's proud home record was shattered. Newcastle Road had ceased to be a fortress, Sunderland losing five games there after having lost just one in the previous five seasons. The goal scoring record was also poor, the Lads hitting just two more League goals than Johnny Campbell had managed by himself in 1891-92. This was easily Sunderland's worst season so far as a League club, and the fall from grace was all the more dramatic given it came just two seasons after being crowned 'Champions of the World'. Better would be expected the following season.

Everton Box Clever

On Boxing Day, 1896, Sunderland travelled to Everton for a game watched by a massive crowd estimated at 35,000. It was easily the biggest crowd the Lads played in front of during the season, boosted by some excellent encounters between the two sides in recent seasons. The ground was quite heavy, but the weather was summer-like and warm. Sunderland started badly. Doig was caught napping in goal early on and Chadwick put Everton 1 - 0 up after only five minutes. Seven minutes later the Merseysiders had a second, and it "looked somewhat black for the visitors". However, the Lads rallied and Cowan pulled one back. More Sunderland pressure followed before half-time, but they could not turn possession into goals, so the Lads went in at the break 2 - 1 down.

After the restart, Everton were awarded a controversial penalty - "a matter of wonderment" according to the Echo - and though Doig protested particularly fiercely about the decision, the referee stood firm. The penalty was easily converted and Everton went 3 - 1 ahead. Not disheartened, Sunderland pushed forward, but we wasted two or three excellent chances before Everton put the game beyond doubt with a goal from Bell. Though Gillespie scored a second for Sunderland, it was evident that the Lads had given up hope of taking anything away from the match, and Everton added a fifth before the game drew to a close.

The glory days were starting to disappear very quickly and a once magnificent team was beginning to look very ordinary. Everton were not a brilliant team - they finished the season in mid-table - but they cruised to this victory against a side that were invincible two years earlier. It wasn't the only thrashing the Lads received during the season either: it was clear that something was wrong.

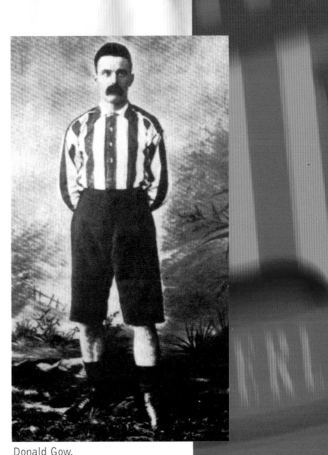

Donald Gow.

Relegation Dogfight Part 1

J Gillespie.

Format of the Test Matches

Although four teams contested the 'mini-league', they did not all play each other. Each of the teams would play just four matches in order to decide promotion and relegation, with the top two in the final test match table gaining - or keeping - their place in the top division. Presumably because they had already played each other in the season, the two first division, and two second division, teams did not play each other. Instead, the fixtures involved teams from the first division playing those in the second division and vice-versa. So, in the Sunderland's case, their first game was against second division Notts County - away from home - and was followed by a return fixture between the two clubs at Newcastle Road. This was then followed with two games against the club that had finished as runners-up in the second division, Newton Heath.

It was a complex format, but it contained some logic. It probably worked in the Lads' favour too, for having to play further fixtures against Burnley may well have produced a different outcome and given either Burnley or Newton Heath the chance to overtake us in the table. As with today's play-off system, the test matches were not without their critics, and were replaced with automatic promotion and relegation - which would have sent us down - in 1898-99.

Sunderland's appalling finish - second from bottom - at the end of the 1896-97 season threatened our status as members of the First Division which we had dominated for much of the previous five or six years. Fortunately for the Lads, automatic promotion between the two divisions had not been introduced, and a series of 'test matches' - similar in principle to today's play-offs - took place instead. However, the format was not of the 'knock out' variety used today, the matches forming a complex 'mini-league'. The bottom two of the First Division and the top two of the Second Division contested the games, and the two teams with the best results in the test matches could claim their place in the First Division the following season. It was possible therefore, that no teams would be relegated or promoted if both First Division teams did well enough in the tests.

Going into the test matches, the Lads had been showing some good form, having been unbeaten for two months. However, Sunderland did not get off to a great start in the tests. Notts County, who had topped the Second Division, were our first opponents. The game was played on 17th April 1897, at their place, and 7,000 fans witnessed a 1 - 0 victory for the Second Division team. This was a disastrous result, and when the return match two days later ended as a goal-less draw, the fans must have expected the worse. Newton Heath and Burnley, the other two teams involved in the tests, had shared the spoils in their two games, each winning the home encounter 2 - 0, and this left Sunderland bottom of the table, being the only team not to have won a game or scored a goal.

Many of the ageing 'Team of All Talents' were still turning out for the Club in the tests, but it had already been made clear that the contracts of the majority of those players would not be renewed in the 1897-98 season, whatever the outcome. To their credit - and Sunderland fans owe the men a lot for their performances over the years anyway - the 'old stagers' lifted their game for the final two matches. A 10,000 crowd saw the match at Newton Heath end 1 - 1 and results elsewhere meant that a win in the return match would keep Sunderland in the top flight. We did manage to win the home match - by two goals to nil - with Gillespie getting both of the crucial goals.

Sunderland owed much to Notts County for the final outcome as they had managed to secure a win and a draw against their first division opponents. We had survived by the skin of our teeth. The final table ended:

	P	W	D	L	F	A	Pts
Notts County	4	2	2	0	3	1	6
Sunderland	4	1	2	1	3	2	4
Burnley	4	1	1	2	3	4	3
Newton Heath	4	1	1	2	3	5	3

It was by no means a convincing performance, just one point separating Sunderland from Burnley and Newton Heath. Had Sunderland drawn the final match against Newton Heath, we would have finished bottom of the table and lost our position in the top division after just seven seasons in the League. Such an outcome would have been a disgrace.

As it was the performance was a blot on the otherwise impeccable record of the team in the decade, but serves as a warning from history: football is a game in which fortunes change rapidly, and even World Champions need to be on their toes.

Scottish international J Hannah.

Moaning Mags

When, in 1990, Swindon's misdemeanours led to Sunderland being promoted as runners-up in the play-offs, many Newcastle fans protested about the injustice of the play off fixtures, arguing their superior League record should have led them to be promoted instead. Curiously, this was not the first time they had made such a complaint. The Magpies were involved in the test matches a year after Sunderland - as runners-up in the second division - but looked to have controversially missed out on promotion and the chance to meet Sunderland in the League for the first time. Before the final test match was played between Stoke and Burnley, it was known that a draw between the two teams contesting it would see both in the top division the following season. An uncompetitive 0 - 0 game followed. Newcastle and Blackburn, the other clubs involved in the tests, complained bitterly about the injustice of this. On this occasion, however, the Mags' moaning did the trick, and the League decided to extend the number of clubs in the top division, meaning all four teams claimed a place in the first division the following season. The controversy also led to the test matches being scrapped. Had the Mags not moaned, we would have waited even longer for the first ever Tyne-Wear League derby.

Matthew Ferguson.

1897-1898
Revived

"Another title win was a distinct possibility."

FA Cup Agony

1897-98 was Sunderland's worst performance in the FA Cup during the 1890s, a first round exit at the hands of Sheffield Wednesday being far from glorious. Arthur Appleton, author of 'Sunderland and the Cup', suggested that a feeling developed during the decade that Sunderland were doomed to failure in the competition. The Lads were favourites for the Cup on a number of occasions, but never managed to live up to expectations, failing to even reach the final. Of course, most teams 'fail' to make the final of the FA Cup each year and many have never appeared in one but what is unusual in Sunderland's case, and acts as evidence to support a 'jinx', is that despite dominating the League we could not produce the goods in the Cup.

The Lads were clearly England's best team for most of the early to mid 1890s, and their regular slips in the Cup become all the more curious when the Lads' performances are compared with those of other teams who have had dominant spells in the League. Preston, for example, won the League in its first two seasons, and also walked away with the FA Cup in one of them. Aston Villa's spell of four League titles in the second half of the 1890s also saw them take the Cup once. Huddersfield's three consecutive League Championships in the 1920s were preceded by an FA Cup win, and the 1930s Arsenal side that won three titles in three years appeared in Cup finals - one of which they won - in the seasons before and after their League success. In more recent times, the Liverpool side that dominated the League in the 1980s eventually succeeded at Wembley and the successful Manchester United team of the 1990s has lifted several FA Cups along with their Premiership titles. So, the question is, 'Why not Sunderland?'

After the disappointment of the previous season, it was crucial that Sunderland got off to a winning start in the 1897-98 campaign. This we did in an away match against Sheffield Wednesday with Morgan getting the only goal of the match. We followed this with a 3 - 2 home win against Wolves in front of 15,000 fans. Our next game was a 2 - 0 away defeat at Preston but the Lads won the return match against Wednesday 1 - 0 and this rounded off September with a very satisfactory three wins from four games, making it our best start since the 1894-95 Championship season.

October was less of a success. We played five games, lost two and won just one. Moreover, one of the defeats was a home game against West Brom, suggesting once again that Newcastle Road was a ground where visitors could come and get results. Fortunately, it was to be the Lads' only home defeat of the season. We played just two games in November and lost both but things began to look up as Christmas approached.

December began with a 4 - 0 victory over Stoke, and we picked up two further points in draws against Derby and Everton. We then began the holiday programme with a defeat against Blackburn on Christmas Day, but two days later the Lads made the trip west to play Tom Watson's Liverpool side, and emerged victorious by two goals to nil. On New Year's Day, Preston visited Newcastle Road and were sent home with nothing, Hughie Wilson sealing the points with the only goal of the game. Two days after this, Sunderland rounded off the festive fixtures with a 2 - 0 win at Notts County.

The Liverpool victory, witnessed by 20,000 spectators, was the start of an excellent period of play by the Sunderland men. After three straight wins in the holiday period, the good form continued throughout January, with wins against Stoke (1 - 0), Bury (2 - 1) and Liverpool again (1 - 0). Sunderland were starting to put together a run reminiscent of their Championship seasons, and another title win was now a distinct possibility.

Confidence must have been high as the Lads started their FA Cup campaign with a home tie against Sheffield Wednesday. However, Wednesday were the Cup holders, and unlikely to give up the trophy without a fight. 18,000 turned out to see the game, but it ended 1 - 0 to the visitors. It was beginning to look as if Sunderland were jinxed in the Cup, with good form in the League regularly deserting them in the Cup.

As usual, the Cup exit was followed by a win in the League, this time by 1 - 0 against Notts County, and more good results were to come our way. February and March saw the Lads win all but one of their games, the other was drawn, and although a number of teams had a chance of winning the title, Sunderland and Sheffield United were the favourites. Significantly, one of the Lads' victories in March was against United, a 3 - 1 home win watched by a 20,000 crowd. There was some confusion before the game though, a mix up resulting in the Sheffield team turning up with just their red-and-white striped outfit, meaning Sunderland had to play in their away kit.

At half-time, heavy rain had soaked the Sheffield players' kits, and in a magnanimous gesture, we lent them our red-and-white kits for the second half.

The two teams played again at the start of April, but a 1 - 0 win for United signalled the end of Sunderland's title hopes. We lost the next three games but rallied on the last day of the season to beat Notts Forest 4 - 0. The result helped us secure the runners-up spot and though Sheffield United finished five points ahead of us, we had given them a good run for their money. It had been a good season for the Lads, the best finish since 1894-95, and it would end up as Campbell's best performance as manager. It was also Sunderland's last season at the Newcastle Road site. A spiralling rent had led the Chairman to seek out a site for a new ground during the close season, and one was found on farmland owned by 'Tushy' Tennant. The 1898-99 season would kick-off at Roker Park.

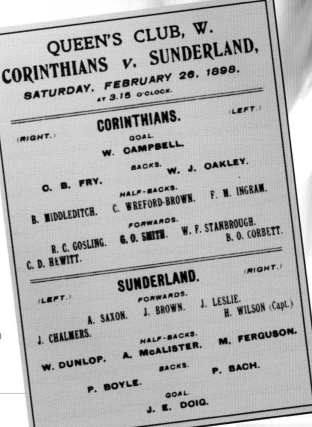

QUEEN'S CLUB, W.
CORINTHIANS v. SUNDERLAND,
SATURDAY, FEBRUARY 26, 1898.
AT 3.15 O'CLOCK.

CORINTHIANS.

(LEFT.)

(RIGHT.)

GOAL.
W. CAMPBELL.

BACKS.
W. J. OAKLEY.
C. B. FRY.

HALF-BACKS.
B. MIDDLEDITCH.   C. WREFORD-BROWN.   F. M. INGRAM.

FORWARDS.
R. C. GOSLING.   G. O. SMITH.   W. F. STANBROUGH.
C. D. HEWITT.   B. O. CORBETT.

SUNDERLAND.

(RIGHT.)

(LEFT.)

FORWARDS.
A. SAXON.   J. BROWN.   J. LESLIE.
J. CHALMERS.   H. WILSON (Capt.)

HALF-BACKS.
A. McALISTER.   M. FERGUSON.
W. DUNLOP.

BACKS.
P. BOYLE.   P. BACH.

GOAL.
J. E. DOIG.

Goodbye Newcastle Road

Newcastle Road had been a good home for the Club, with many glorious victories seen there, but the fact that it was rented, rather than owned outright by the Club, had restricted Sunderland's ambitions since entering the League. Spending large amounts of money developing the facilities was something of a risk when the land belonged to someone else, so it made sense to move to a new home that the Club had the option of owning lock, stock and barrel.

Sunderland's last game there was a brilliant 4 - 0 victory over Nottingham Forest, witnessed by just 10,000 fans, with two goals from Chalmers and one each from Leslie and Brown. Leslie goes down in history as bagging the final League goal on the Newcastle Road ground, and Chalmers doubled his tally for the season in the game! Much had happened in the twelve years spent at the ground, and the Club had made great strides forward while it acted as our base. Success on the pitch was there for all to see and they had been very good times indeed, but it was now time to move on. As ever, the new ground would be bigger, better and more spectacular, but Newcastle Road will always have a special place in the Club's history.

J Brown.

1898-1899
Roker Park

"The Lads pulled some good wins out of the bag, but found it difficult to get into their stride."

Robert Campbell

At the end of the 1898-99 season Robert Campbell left to manage Bristol City. He had, by all accounts, been a very popular man at the Club, and had been important behind the scenes during Tom Watson's time in charge. However, although the papers at the time refrained from mentioning it, the evidence suggests that Campbell was not quite up to the task of 'fronting' the Club himself. Campbell's time in charge had by no means been a disaster - though it certainly could have been had the last game in the test matches not gone our way - but neither was he able to produce the sort of results the Sunderland fans had come to expect. He was unfortunate to have followed the spectacularly successful Watson, for he was always going to be judged against the sensational record of his predecessor. However it should be noted that, excepting William Murray who was in charge for just three games before war broke out, he was the only one of Sunderland's managers before the Second World War that failed to bring the Championship trophy to Wearside.

Robert Campbell's third season in charge at Sunderland began with a 3 - 2 away win against Preston North End, which was followed a week later by our first ever game at Roker Park. A capacity 30,000 crowd, a Club record at the time, crammed into the new stadium, where they saw Sunderland win 1 - 0, Jim Leslie scoring Roker Park's first goal. It was a good opening, but the Club's next five games produced just four points. This set the pattern for a season of mixed results, where the Lads pulled some good wins out of the bag, but found it difficult to get into their stride. While we were winning more games than we were losing, for instance in October and November we had five wins and four defeats, the team were failing to produce the sort of performances that had seen them challenge for the title in the previous season.

December was something of disaster. On the 3rd, Aston Villa defeated us 2 - 0 at Villa Park, in front of 25,000 fans. A week later, Burnley visited Roker Park, and inflicted the Lads' first defeat, by one goal to nil, on our new ground. Sunderland then made the trip to Bramall Lane, where Sheffield United beat us 2 - 0 and on Christmas Eve, Newcastle United made the short journey south to Roker Park. 30,000 fans paid to see the first ever Tyne and Wear League derby, this being the Magpies' first season in the League's top flight, but the result was not a good one for us: Newcastle won by three goals to two.

The rest of the holiday programme brought some cheer for Sunderland fans, with Preston defeated 1 - 0 on New Year's Eve and Derby 1 - 0 on the 2nd January. However, the rest of January proved to be something of a disappointment in the League, two draws being followed by a 6 - 1 thrashing at Bolton. The Cup provided some much needed glee before the month's end with the Lads knocking Bristol City out in the first round with a 4 - 2 win. But, the joy was to be short-lived and we lost our next League game and a week later went out of the Cup in somewhat inglorious fashion. Sunderland's opponents for the second round were non-League Tottenham Hotspur, making their first appearance in the 'proper' rounds of the competition, yet they managed to win through to the third round by beating us 2 - 1. It would be wrong to over-emphasise Spurs' non-League status, they were good enough to win the FA Cup in 1900-01 season, but Sunderland should have won the tie nevertheless.

As if it were a golden rule of life, the Lads yet again responded to Cup disappointment with a succession of good performances in the League. We beat Sheffield Wednesday 1 - 0 away and Wolves were on the wrong end of a 3 - 0 score a fortnight later. Draws against in-form Everton and Notts County were not be sniffed at, and though a defeat against Stoke followed, March was rounded off with a 2 - 1 victory at Bury. Eight points from twelve since the Cup exit was, by the season's standards to that point, a good return.

In the last month of the season, Aston Villa made the trip to Roker Park looking to secure their third Championship in four years, and the tie generated considerable interest: 20,000 turned out for the match. Liverpool were Villa's closest rivals, and the Lads did their old boss Tom Watson a massive favour, sending the visitors home with a 4 - 2 defeat. It was to be the end of Sunderland's mini revival however, and 1 - 0 defeats against Blackburn and Burnley quickly followed.

With just two games left, a mid-table finish was the best we could hope for, but with the placings packed closely together, two victories would make the difference between a top half and a bottom half position.

With pride at stake, there were strong incentives for the Lads to round the season off in style, but the chance to avenge the Christmas Eve defeat against Newcastle added extra spice. Sunderland made their first trip in the League to St James' Park on 22nd April 1899, and took the points with a 1 - 0 win. Revenge was sweet and witnessed by a 25,000 crowd. The Lads' League campaign then ended with a 1 - 0 win over the previous season's Champions Sheffield United.

This left Sunderland in seventh position, well above the Magpies' thirteenth place, but some nine points away from Champions, Aston Villa. Sunderland were in danger of becoming also-rans, Villa laying a strong claim to the mantle of England's top team, and changes were obviously needed at Roker for the following season. Key amongst them would be the appointment of a new manager.

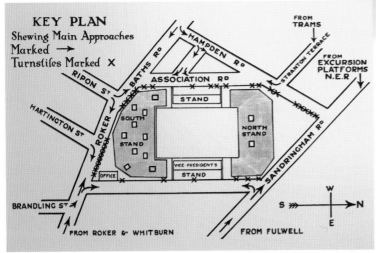

An early map of Roker Park. Note the Roker and Fulwell Ends are named 'North' and 'South' Stands.

If You Hate Newcastle...

Christmas Eve, 1898, saw the first 'non-friendly' match between Sunderland and Newcastle United. The game took place at Roker Park, and saw the new ground's second 30,000 capacity crowd of the season, with demand far exceeding the capacity. Sixteen special trains were laid on from Newcastle station, capable of holding 8,000 Magpies, and it was taken for granted that many more would make the trip by other means. The ground filled quickly and despite the December fixture date, the weather was fair and the lush Roker Park pitch looked good although it was somewhat greasy after earlier rain.

Sunderland started brightly with Leslie scoring after fifteen minutes. The early goal got the match going and Wardrope equalised for Newcastle, dribbling through the defence until he was just three yards out before blasting a shot past Doig. Reddie then hit a second for the Mags before half-time to make it 2 - 1 at the break. In the second period Leslie hit a second for Sunderland, but the Newcastle side also hit another goal and ran out 3 - 2 winners. Much to the dismay of all Sunderland fans, the Mags had won the first ever derby and in the first season at Roker Park to boot. We would get our revenge in the return match later in the season, but most would have preferred to have won the home fixture instead.

Roker Park

Record crowd at Roker Park.

Record Crowd

Sunderland's record gate at Roker Park was a massive 75,118 in an FA Cup sixth round replay against Derby County. The game took place on 8th March 1933, following a 4 - 4 draw at Derby. Those hoping for another great performance from the Lads were disappointed: the Cup jinx struck again, and Sunderland went out of the Cup to an extra-time goal from the opposition, the only of the game.

When Roker Park held its opening game, on 10th September 1898, it was easily one of the best grounds in the country. It would give Sunderland AFC and its fans 99 years of excellent service and become one of the most famous football grounds in the country, staging many glorious - and inglorious - games in the history of the Club.

Amazingly, the ground took just four months to build, and on opening could accommodate 26,000 spectators in its wooden stands and several thousand more on slopes around the ground. The Grandstand contained 3,000 seats, and the Clockstand, which stood opposite, was standing only. Behind the goals were the uncovered North and South ends, their famous Fulwell and Roker End names coming much later. It is difficult to imagine the ground existing without the 'Roker' and 'Fulwell' ends but traditions and 'homely' names emerge over time.

Many additions and improvements were made to the ground over the years. In 1912, as the Club once again sought glory in the League, the Roker End was massively expanded. This was the first major piece of reconstruction, and involved the erection of a complex labyrinth of concrete posts to support a huge bank of terracing. It was a wonderful sight, and an extremely unusual design feature, enabling the stand to hold an enormous 17,000 fans. As result of this, and other incremental changes, the ground could hold a massive 50,000 by the time the First World War broke out.

In the inter-war period further important changes were made to Roker. In 1929, Archibald Leitch, probably the most famous name in football architecture, was commissioned to design a new Grandstand to replace the original wooden one. The resulting structure cost a massive £25,000 and was the most famous piece of the Roker Park stadium, containing Leitch's trademark criss-cross steelwork balcony, painted in glorious red-and-white to match the players' shirts. By now the capacity was a huge 60,000, and as more Championship challenges loomed in the 1930s, Leitch was commissioned to re-design the Clockstand. It was one of his last major works before he died, and was again glorious in its execution. It could hold nearly 16,000 spectators, contained beautiful wooden seating at the top, and ran the full length of the pitch. It opened in September 1936.

Constant re-development of the ground meant that by the start of the Second World War Roker Park was still amongst the best football stadia in the country. Like much of the town, it was hit by German bombs during the war. The lush pitch, again one of the best around, suffered much damage and the car park and clubhouse were quite badly damaged. The main structures remained intact though, and as the country and the people of Sunderland pulled themselves out of the misery of the war, Roker Park was ready to provide another half century of loyal and splendid service.

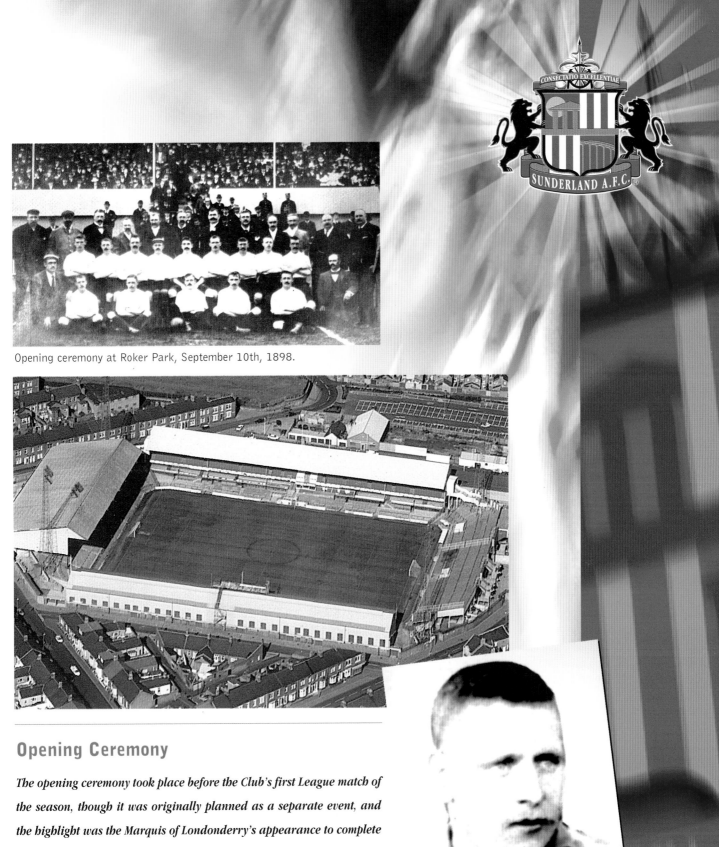

Opening ceremony at Roker Park, September 10th, 1898.

Opening Ceremony

The opening ceremony took place before the Club's first League match of the season, though it was originally planned as a separate event, and the highlight was the Marquis of Londonderry's appearance to complete the 'official opening'. This he did by using a golden key to unlock a gate to the players' dressing room, at which point the teams emerged to an immense roar. The game that followed saw Sunderland win 1 - 0 against Liverpool, led by ex-Sunderland manager Tom Watson. 30,000 witnessed the game and Jim Leslie scored the historic first goal at Roker Park.

Jim Leslie, scorer of the first goal at Roker Park.

1899-1900
Challenging Again

"It was not a question of whether further honours would arrive, but of when."

Alex Mackie

Mackie's first season in charge was a good one, and the start of a successful period at the Club's helm. He probably ranks as Sunderland's second best manager of all time, eventually steering us to another Championship and never finishing below sixth in the First Division. He also goes down in history as the man that brought some much needed glory to Roker Park after the Lads' fairly anonymous first season there. As with Tom Watson, the Club would go through a bad patch after his departure, but Mackie's successor would, unlike Watson's, eventually turn performances around and deliver another Championship. Mackie left Sunderland at the end of the 1904-05 season, after two relatively poor seasons - we finished sixth and fifth in the League! At this time though, again rather like Watson's last season, the team he had put together were past their best, and it was clear that some restructuring was needed.

Alex Mackie took charge of the team for Sunderland's last season of the nineteenth century, looking to improve affairs on the pitch. There were no great changes to the team at the start of the season, though the Hoggs would make an impact as it wore on.

The campaign could not have started with a tougher series of fixtures, Sunderland being pitched against the teams that had finished the previous season in the top three places. Beginning with a trip to Champions, Aston Villa, the Lads put in a good performance but left empty handed, the home side getting the only goal of the match. A week later, we visited runners-up Liverpool, where Sunderland snatched a 2 - 0 victory in front of a 25,000 crowd. The Lads then negotiated the third of their tricky games with the visit of Burnley to Roker Park, and the first home game of Mackie's reign produced a good 2 - 1 win. September was completed with two more victories, against Preston and Notts Forest, to round off an excellent first month for the new manager.

October was to see similarly impressive results with the Lads getting five out of eight points. We won two of November's three games, including a 1 - 0 home win against Everton in front of 20,000 fans. Rather like the 1887-88 season, this good early form put the Lads in with a chance of securing the title, but much would depend on the crucial holiday programme. December started well and we thrashed Notts County 5 - 0 at Roker, but a couple of poor results followed before the Lads made the trip to St James' Park on 23rd December. Again there was a bumper crowd for the derby match, around 20,000, but this time it was the Mackems who would spend Christmas gloating, the Lads securing an excellent 4 - 2 victory, with Hogg hitting a hat-trick.

Unfortunately, the rest of the festive period was something of a let down. A trip to Wolves on Boxing Day ended in a 1 - 0 defeat, and the Lads' last game of the century, at Villa on 30th December, produced a 4 - 2 win for the reigning Champions. Finally, the New Year's Day 1900 fixture saw Wolves complete the double over us with a 2 - 1 win at Roker Park. Three points from a possible twelve after the Notts County win put a severe dent in our Championship hopes.

Liverpool visited Roker Park on 6th January and just 3,000 turned up for the game. Sunderland, however, got back to winning ways with a 1 - 0 victory. Though defeat at Burnley followed, a home win against Preston boosted our confidence for the trip to Derby in the FA Cup. Derby had been beaten finalists in the previous two FA Cup campaigns, and would provide stiff opposition for the Lads. Indeed, a close encounter ended 2 - 2, but an excellent 3 - 0 victory for Sunderland in the replay suggested this might be our year. Anyone thinking this way was soon to be disappointed though, as a fortnight later Notts Forest ended our Cup involvement at the second round, with an easy 3 - 0 victory.

In March the team secured a reasonable set of results, winning three of their five games, but defeats at Everton and Derby underlined what was becoming the main barrier to the Lads' Championship form - a poor record away from home. April began with an away defeat against Notts County, and although three straight wins followed, the flurry had come too late and Aston Villa and Sheffield United had broken away at the top of the table. The season ended with the visit of Newcastle to Roker Park, and the Lads went down 2 - 1. It made no difference to our League placing though, a creditable third.

It was a good start for Mackie, and had it not been for a poor performance in the holiday fixtures and some slack defending away from home, Sunderland may well have ended the season as Champions. That honour went instead to Aston Villa, their fourth title in five years, and their fifth of the decade. It had been an excellent decade of League football for Sunderland, but after dominating the game in the first half of the 1890s, it was Villa who now laid claim to the mantle of England's top team. The Lads were a close second though, and with Mackie in charge, they would be looking to mount a fresh challenge on the Championship and the elusive FA Cup as football entered the twentieth century. It was not a question of whether further honours would arrive, but of when.

Doig in action.

The Safest Hands in Sunderland
'Ted' Doig

John 'Teddy' Doig succeeded the long serving 'Stonewall' Kirtley as Sunderland's goalkeeper in our third ever League game. Kirtley had made a number of blunders in the opening games, and was blamed for a heavy defeat against Wolves. His replacement was brought in rather quickly though, and was unregistered in his first match and Sunderland were deducted two points as a consequence. Indeed, the whole manner of his arrival was surrounded in controversy, for he had signed for Blackburn but then walked out on them after one game - perhaps Sunderland had made him a better offer - and was duly suspended.

Whatever the reasons for him leaving Blackburn, there was no questioning his commitment to Sunderland. Doig was a stalwart of the team for some fourteen seasons, and following his first appearance on 20th September 1890, 'Teddy' played in every one of Sunderland's League and Cup games until September 9th 1895, making him an ever present in all three of the 1890s Championship sides. Indeed, he kept goal for all but eleven of the team's games between his arrival and the end of the 1903-04 season. It was an amazing record, encompassing a total of 456 League and Cup appearances for the Club, a figure surpassed only by another of Sunderland's goalkeeping legends, Jimmy Montgomery.

Ted Doig. He almost always wore a cap to hide his baldness!

1900·01	Second in League, one point behind Liverpool.
1901·02	League Championship returns to Wearside!
1902·03	Secure Sheriff of London's Shield. Third in League, one point behind Champions.
1903·04	Sixth in League. Club rocked by McCombie Scandal.
1904·05	Fifth in League.
1905·06	Robert Kyle becomes manager. Fourteenth in League.
1906·07	Tenth in League.
1907·08	Narrowly escape relegation.
1908·09	Third in League. Thrash Newcastle 9-1 away!
1909·10	Eighth in League.

The 1900's began full of promise after an outstanding first decade in League football. Alex Mackie had taken over from Robert Campbell and in his first season as manager we finished in an improved third place. The squad was full of first class internationals. Doig was still doing the business between the sticks and McCombie was developing into a world class back, with Watson supporting. Players of the calibre of Billy Hogg, Alf Common, and Jimmy Millar were in the attack and it was no real surprise that we were one of the most feared teams in the League going into the new century. Further high quality signings were soon to follow in the shape of Gemmell and Bridgett and the Club seemed set for a decade of success.

The new decade though didn't work out as smoothly as expected, and the Club's whole future was soon in jeopardy following the McCombie scandal, which led to the Club being fully investigated and suspensions being imposed on directors and managers. Our fortunes on the pitch faded with the instability behind the scenes, and a once great Club seemed in real danger of extinction. The arrival, however, of Frederick Taylor as Chairman saved Sunderland, and he appointed Robert Kyle as manager in 1905, an appointment that was to prove one of the best in the Club's history. Initially Kyle's team struggled and we flirted with relegation but he eventually managed to stabilise the Club and made some important signings near the end of the decade. The most notable of these was the arrival of a young nineteen-year-old, George Holley, who was to have a tremendous impact. Thomson and Mordue were also to prove to be inspired signings and we were once more to be back on the football map.

A NEW

Century

1 9 0 0 · 1 9 1 0

1900-1901
Close Finish

"The title race went down to the wire..."

Sunderland and England star Billy Hogg.

Championship Choker

Our home match with Liverpool at Roker was effectively a title decider. Liverpool were closing on the Lads at a frightening rate, and we were losing form at a vital point in the season. Liverpool though, having already suffered defeat at Anfield earlier in the season, were out for revenge, and knew that a similar result would mean curtains for their Championship aspirations.

Sunderland's line-up was not selected until late on as we had five players on the sick list in the early part of the week, and it was doubtful which of them would be able to play. The visitors meanwhile had a strong team, with Robertson being the only absentee.

There was little to choose between the two teams at half time with neither goalkeeper really being forced into a save. Gemmell had gone close just before half time with a header just over the bar. Just after half time, McLatchie sent a right wing cross shot skimming over the bar, but twenty minutes into the second half Liverpool took the lead through Salterwaite. It led to a Sunderland onslaught in the last twenty five minutes, but our shooting was hopelessly off target and the Liverpool defence was exceptionally strong. No further goals were scored, and the 1 - 0 scoreline was to prove crucial.

The 1890s had seen us hit the peaks of English football, and the task for the 1900s was to reassert our claim not only on the Championship, but on the mantle of Britain's greatest football team. The success of our first decade in the League had surpassed everyone's expectations - indeed, it was probably beyond our wildest dreams - but expectations have a nasty habit of rapidly readjusting themselves. With three Championships in the bag already, the pressure was on for more to be delivered. Alex Mackie knew he had taken on one of football's biggest jobs and that the fans were hungry for more of the glory of the sort dished out by Tom Watson's Team of All Talents.

But, Mackie possessed a first class footballing brain. He had already began to knock the team into shape, and the Championship was again a very realistic possibility. Indeed, the 1900-01 season proved to be the first of a number of League title challenges under his charge. Our third place finish in 1899-00 was seen as satisfactory, but the board demonstrated their ambition to do better by financing some important pre-season signings that were needed to improve the side. In particular, James Millar returned for a second spell and the captain of Hearts, George Livingstone, arrived to spice up the attack. The defence was also stiffened up with Watson replacing McNeil in the back line. It worked wonders as the team went on to produce one of the best defensive performances in its history, conceding only 26 goals in the 34 League games for the season.

Roker Park, as was usual in those days, was a fortress. It was a long trail north for most teams and, with transport not what it is today, it often took its toll on away sides in the League. Nevertheless, most visiting teams were not only beaten, but also given a good thrashing! We managed to score 43 goals in only seventeen home games. Yet despite all this impressive goal-scoring and fine defensive play, the Lads were not good travellers themselves. It was not losing games on away days that was the problem, more it was an inability to win them and drawing games seemed a Sunderland speciality. Ultimately, this was to prove costly and an emerging new power would eclipse us in the title race: former Sunderland Manager Tom Watson's Liverpool.

The season kicked off steadily, if not spectacularly, for the Lads. An opening day draw on an away trip to Notts County was followed by an unbeaten sequence of six games. This sequence included a run of possibly Sunderland's hardest games this season. A home fixture versus the mighty Aston Villa in front of 31,000 was drawn 0 - 0, the game being described as very even and 'intensely exciting' with both sides in great form. We then handed out a lesson to the upstarts from Liverpool when we defeated them 2 - 1 on their own patch at Anfield with Hogg and Millar scoring the goals. The following game could not possibly have been harder - Newcastle at home. A 1 - 1 draw, with Livingstone scoring, was in truth not a bad result.

Although the Lads were not getting beaten very often, we were not winning enough games either. However, a run of four wins out of five up to Christmas brought us back into contention. Blackburn were beaten 1 - 0 with a solitary goal from McLatchie, as were Sheffield Wednesday, this time Ferguson getting the goal. In between Everton were beaten 2 - 0, Common and McLatchie again, and Stoke were thrashed 6 - 1.

The game against the Potteries side saw the goals shared. McLatchie, Common, W Hogg, Livingstone, W Hogg again and finally Raisbeck, right on the final whistle, completed the demolition. Our inability to win away from home though was beginning to show and we chalked up five away draws in a row. Fortunately success at home was keeping us in the title race and to emphasise the point we sent Wolverhampton packing after a 7 - 2 thrashing.

Despite League form that made us one of the most feared and respected teams of the day, the usual FA Cup jinx struck when the knock-out ties came around.

This was to be the case all the way throughout the first decade of the twentieth century, with 1900-01 seeing Sunderland lose at home to Sheffield United. Typically, we then played the Blades in the League, once again at Roker, and completely outplayed them, winning 3 - 0.

Coming to the end of the season, Sunderland were in prime position, but Liverpool were about to embark upon an outstanding final run-in, taking 21 points from their last twelve games (at a time when it was still two points for a win). Crucially, this run included the return fixture with Sunderland at Roker. It need not have been a costly result, and we were still placed well in the table for the final run-in after winning three and drawing two of the next five games after the bitter defeat against Liverpool. However, three of the last four games were away from home. The first of these three was at Liverpool's Merseyside rivals, Everton, in front of a bumper crowd of 30,000. The Toffeemen did the Reds a favour, by narrowly beating us 1 - 0.

The title race was going down to the wire! Realistically, with Liverpool in such scintillating form, we had to win our remaining games. Our last home game of the season was against Bolton and we thrashed them 5 - 1 but this was followed by a defeat in the penultimate game away to Sheffield United. The Lads rallied and managed a great 2 - 0 victory over Newcastle at St James' Park in our last game of the season. This win meant that only Liverpool could now catch our points total of 43. To do so they would have to win their two remaining games, away to West Brom and at home to Nottingham Forest. Unfortunately, they did, and the title was lost by one point. The home defeat by Liverpool had been very costly indeed.

Trouble at the Toon

The final game of the season at St James' was, in fact, a replay of the game held on Good Friday between the two sides which had to be abandoned because of crowd trouble. It was estimated that 70,000 people descended on St James' Park, even though the stadium at the time could barely hold 20,000. It was little short of a miracle that there was no loss of life. The ensuing chaos resulted in thousands of people spilling onto the pitch, and the stand's structure was under such severe pressure that it could have collapsed. Most knew that play was impossible, but when it became apparent that the two teams would not take to the field all hell broke loose. The police were charged by the fans and had to use batons to curb the civil disorder. It wasn't until two hours after the scheduled 5 o'clock kick off that the ground was cleared. The game was eventually played a few weeks later with the outcome critical for the League title. Unfortunately, our subsequent 2 - 0 victory was not enough to secure the Championship.

Sheffield Wednesday v Sunderland Programme, 1901.

1901-1902
Back On Top

"The title race would once again go down to the final game of the season."

Sunderland's Championship winning team, 1901-02.

The Ref Runs for his Life!

The frustration of the Sunderland crowd was clear for all to see after the game against Small Heath at Roker. The memories of last season's title being thrown away were still fresh, and after the defeat at Everton a fortnight earlier, tensions were running high. The game itself was a tight affair, Hewitt scoring in the first half, pouncing on a Robertson shot that had been spilled by the goalkeeper. However, on their very first visit to Roker, Small Heath grabbed a point after Doig had rushed out of his goal and lost the ball, which was promptly put in the back of the net. Although having more of the chances from then on, Sunderland's forward play was weak and the final score stayed at 1 - 1. It was not what the fans had expected and the referee, C E Sutcliffe, had given a number of dubious offside decisions against us during the game. A large group of fans waited outside for the referee, wanting to vent their anger. The only way of 'smuggling' him out of the ground was to dress him as a policeman, and although he was subsequently recognised, the local constabulary managed to whisk him away to safety in a horsecab.

During the close season Roker Park had a mini face-lift. The turf was spruced up, the drainage system enhanced, and the stands were given a new lick of white paint. Outside the ground the 'Corporation' had also been busy with a new approach road. It was all to work wonders, as the Lads excelled in their spruced up surroundings. Jimmy Millar was the mainstay in attack, ably supported by Alf Common - who was Sunderland born and bred - while McLatchie was lethal on the left wing. Billy Hogg was still in there to provide vision in the midfield areas, and for this season, he was to be supported mainly by his brother R Hogg. Our main rivals for the season were again from Merseyside, this time in the shape of Everton, and the Toffees were to push us all the way in yet another exciting Championship race.

The first game of the season was at Roker against Sheffield United, yet Sunderland were playing in their change strip of white shirts and dark pants. It made no difference, as Hogg and Common were in fine form and they shared three goals between them in a good 3 - 1 win. After a 1 - 0 victory over Manchester City in the next game, Billy Hogg again scoring, Wolverhampton played host to the Lads in a game that seemed to suggest we might struggle this season. The Wolves were fresh from a drubbing by Everton and were generally expected to be beaten by a Sunderland team that seemed to be shaping up well. Football though has a nasty habit of producing the unexpected and our 4 - 2 defeat was certainly that. An overly fussy referee and some very rough play knocked Sunderland out of their stride and marred the match. A 1 - 1 draw at home to Liverpool a week later didn't provide any real hope either. But, if anyone had doubts about Sunderland's credentials as the top team they were soon to be proved wrong.

A trip to Newcastle the following week was to prove the beginning of a winning run that would push us right up to the top of the table. The crowd of 26,000 was disappointing but the authorities had demanded the gates be closed at 2.30pm to ensure there was no repeat performance of the disgraceful crowd scenes that had marred the Good Friday game the previous season. Sunderland won the toss and attacked the Leazes End. Outplaying Newcastle from the start we had much the better of the early exchanges and it was no real surprise when Gemmell scored to give us a deserved 1 - 0 victory. We also won the next two games 1 - 0 (a score line that was to be quite familiar in this season) before Nottingham Forest were thumped 4 - 0 at Roker, Millar scoring the first of two hat-tricks in the season.

Riding high at the top of the table we now suffered two soul-destroying defeats in a row. The first was a 3 - 0 away to Stoke, the second, and more damaging, was a 4 - 2 home defeat, inflicted by our Championship rivals, Everton. It was a bad blow, but the response to these defeats was mightily impressive and we put together a ten game unbeaten run. It was the away form during this period that was to really improve our chances of the title with some more than impressive results. We beat Manchester City 3 - 0, with Billy Hogg bagging two, while Aston Villa, always a tough game, were beaten 1 - 0 thanks to a McLatchie goal. Although Forest gained revenge for the 4 - 0 beating earlier in the season by bringing our ten match unbeaten run to an end with a 2 - 1 win, we returned to winning ways in the very next game, again away from home, this time Gemmell getting the solitary goal at Blackburn Rovers.

This spell of play made Sunderland title favourites, and the return fixture against Everton on 15th March, 1902, now took on extra significance. Everton were trailing the Lads and needed to win the game to maintain any sort of challenge for the title. After already losing at Roker earlier in the season, we again succumbed to a team from Merseyside in a crucial Championship game and Everton ran out 2 - 0 winners. Despite this poor result, the run-in was kind to us, and with eight games of the season left we had to play only two away from home, and were in a fine position to use 'fortress' Roker to steam roller the title home. The passage however, as always, was never smooth.

Things did not go to plan when Newcastle visited Roker. Gemmell and McLatchie were unable to play, forcing 'A' team players to be drafted into the squad. A 0 - 0 draw in front of 34,819 was perhaps no real surprise in a tense local derby, but we had expected to win. If the die-hards were not yet worried about the team's ability to win the title, three defeats in the next four games would change that! A 1 - 0 defeat at Derby County, where Doig was missing from the side, was followed up by a 2 - 1 home defeat by Sheffield Wednesday. Although Bury were beaten 3 - 0 at Roker, away form seemed to have deserted the Lads by now and we suffered a 2 - 0 defeat in the penultimate game at Notts County. It all meant that the title race would once again go down to the final game of the season.

There was to be no mistake this time however, and we beat Bolton Wanderers 2 - 1 at Roker to win the title by three clear points. The 1901-02 season had brought Sunderland their fourth Championship. Although not achieved in spectacular style, the majority of the nineteen wins being by a single goal, eight of them 1 - 0, it was a solid and deserved Championship after the previous season's failure. Sandy McAllister had also earned an unusual claim to fame for the season: the Wearside faithful had promised him a piano if he assisted the lads to League Championship glory, and in doing so he not only enhanced his musical 'repertoire' but was also given a gold watch!

Goals Dry Up, Victories Keep On Coming

In securing the title the Lads had improved on the previous season's performance by one point and one crucial League place. Somewhat curiously, however, the number of goals scored had decreased quite substantially and the number conceded had increased! Indeed, the season's goal scoring average was the lowest of any of the Championships the Lads had secured, and remains so. Just 32 goals were hit at Roker Park - compared with 43 the previous season - and as a whole, we managed an average of just 1.43 goals a game. Goals were spread between a number of players, Gemmell and W Hogg topping the scoring charts by scraping into double figures with ten each. The veteran Jimmy Millar trailed just behind them with nine League and Cup goals, but six of these came in the home games against Forest and Bury, where he scored the Club's only hat-tricks of the season! In fact, despite finishing one short of being joint top scorer, Millar failed to find the net in 29 of his 34 games. Like his colleagues, though, his focus through the season was on working for the team, and by performing as a unit and, where necessary, grinding out results, the Lads achieved the ultimate reward.

Scottish international Jimmy Millar.

1902-1903
Another Close Finish

"It could, and perhaps should, have been a third League title in a row."

Trouble at the Aston Villa v Preston match, 1888. While the men attending football games were invariably well dressed - with shirt, tie and hat - violence flared at matches still. Gentlemanly dress and gentlemanly behaviour are not, it would appear, inextricably connected!

Those Well Mannered Edwardians...

The 1 - 0 home defeat at the hands of Sheffield Wednesday was taken very badly by the Sunderland fans, who not only stoned the referee, but also the Sheffield players' transport in Roker Baths Road. The result of the game, although the spark for the ensuing violence, was not the most significant outcome of the game. That was the action taken by the FA against Sunderland. For this "indiscretion", Sunderland were banned from playing their next home fixture at Roker, and instead went to St James' Park to entertain Middlesbrough. This meant that our last four games were all effectively to be away from home. Having to play these games away from home undoubtedly affected the Lads psychologically. It was to prove costly.

With the Championship Trophy once again residing in Wearside, the Club could comfortably survey the football world with pride. Missing out in 1900-01 was a real blow, but Mackie had pulled out all the stops to go one better and prove that he was a worthy successor to the great Watson. However, no-one wanted to rest on their laurels. All at the Club wanted to build on the Championship by bringing further success to Sunderland, and another year of hard work lay ahead. Victory in the League meant we would be offered the opportunity of competing for the Sheriff of London Shield later in the season and, as always, there was the elusive FA Cup, but the main contest was undoubtedly the League.

But, our League campaign did not get off to a great start. Nottingham Forest scored the only goal of the game in our opening fixture - at Roker Park - and a second defeat was inflicted a few weeks later at Sheffield United. Though there was the compensation of a 2 - 1 victory against Liverpool, in all, it was a somewhat poor start to our defence of the League title

Worryingly, matters did not improve. A 5 - 1 thrashing of Grimsby at the end of September seemed to suggest that we had merely made a slow start, but instead it only served to highlight our erratic form. The next two months saw the Lads really struggle for form, and by early December we had managed only four victories in the first 14 games. What's more, we had suffered some very bad defeats along the way including a 5 - 2 drubbing against Derby County and 3 - 1 loss against Bury. The fans were undoubtedly mystified by this lack of form. We were, after all, the League Champions, and results like this were simply unacceptable.

The consequence of this poor form was that we were languishing near the bottom half of the table. However, with disaster staring us in the face, we finally got the season going. Out of nowhere, the Lads put together a marvellous winning streak, taking nine victories in eleven games to put the Championship defence right back on track. Unbelievably, we had gone from being threatened with relegation to once again being Championship challengers right at the very top of the table. Included in this run were some fine wins including a 3 - 0 at Everton where Hewitt scored twice, a 4 -2 win at Grimsby, and a 3 - 0 home win against Wolves.

With confidence building, we added the Sheriff of London Shield to the trophy cabinet in February - although quite how it would fit into a cabinet at some six feet tall is anyone's guess! However, we were again knocked out of the F.A. Cup in the first round, losing 3 - 1 to Aston Villa. The possibility of winning two out of three competitions was still there though, and full attention was focused on the League.

Just as the season seemed to be on course for more glory, however, disaster struck. Following the fine win at Everton, the Lads had a home game against Sheffield Wednesday who, along with Aston Villa, were fighting with us for the title. What the Sunderland fans could not have expected after such a fine unbeaten sequence was to lose at home to the Wednesday. Although the 1 - 0 defeat was bad news, it did not seem disastrous, as the advantage was still with the Lads.

But, events off the pitch would come to haunt the team after the game. The next three results were encouraging when a 3 - 0 away win at West Bromwich Albion was followed by a credible 1 - 1 draw at Liverpool and a 2 - 1 home victory over Notts County.

We then played our last proper home game at Roker on April 10th, and could only manage a 0 - 0 draw with Stoke. It was to prove crucial, as the Lads had to play away at Bolton a day later and two days after that at Nottingham Forest. Three games in four days proved too much and a 2 - 0 defeat at Bolton was followed by a humiliating 5 - 2 reverse at Forest. Sunderland could really have done without the hectic away schedule - and the consequent defeats - for the season's final two games were a difficult proposition. Both games were crucial to Sunderland's title challenge, and both were local derbies: Middlesbrough and Newcastle were the opposition. To make matters worse, Sunderland's home tie against Middlesbrough game was to be played at St James' Park as well, a ruling imposed following violence at Roker in the game against Sheffield Wednesday.

Nevertheless, Sunderland defeated the Boro 2 - 1, in what was the very first 'home' Tees/Wear league match, Millar and Hewitt scoring. The game away to Newcastle United would now decide Sunderland's fate, and it was all was set up for a final day three-way title decider between Sheffield Wednesday, Aston Villa and Sunderland. We were confident of victory having won all four of the previous encounters on Tyneside. However, Bob McColl had the last laugh as the black and whites inflicted a crushing 1 - 0 defeat on us. The title was once again lost on the final day. We eventually finished third in the table, only a point behind Sheffield Wednesday, who won it, and Aston Villa. It could, and perhaps should, have been a third League title in a row, a record that would have exceeded that of even the 'team of all talents' from the 1890s.

Left Wing Wizard

The 1902-03 season saw the arrival at Roker Park of one of its greatest ever players, Arthur Bridgett. In time he was to form a lethal left wing partnership with Gemmell, and at international level he was a star, being capped eleven times for England between 1904 and 1909. The most famous characteristic of his play was a lethal shot, something his previous club Stoke City could testify to, as he once broke the net there while playing for Sunderland.

A deeply religious man, he refused to play on 'holy days', and the depth of his beliefs are illustrated by the match day programme for the 1909 game against Sheffield United; it carried the announcement that the international outside left would be leading the Annual Football Sunday Service in the Sheffield Victoria Hall at 3pm.

Arthur Bridgett, 1903-12.

The Sheriff of London Shield Competition

Many Sunderland fans over the years have been intrigued about a famous shield won by the Club at the beginning of the century. The Sheriff of London Shield stands over six feet high and is one of the largest trophies ever competed for in professional football. The Shield was first played for on 19th March, 1898, the intention being that it would be competed for annually in a charity game between the best amateur team of the year and the best professional outfit. Sir Thomas Dewar, who formed a committee and drew up appropriate regulations, offered the Shield as a trophy. Initially the competition was a great success, with money raised from the fixture being distributed to hospitals and other charitable institutions. Although London charities received the greater portion of the money raised, a certain amount was always distributed among the charities of the town that the professional team taking part in the competition came from, meaning Sunderland would have benefited in someway from the Lads' appearance in the contest. Strangely, the Corinthians, who instigated the competition, were actually ineligible to play at first, due to their own regulation number seven which stated that "the club shall not compete for any challenge cup or prizes of any description whatever." Regulations were duly amended and the Corinthians soon began to make their mark on the contest. After winning the League title in 1902-03, it was Sunderland's turn to take part in the Shield competition, and we faced Corinthians.

The game was played on 28th February 1903, at White Hart Lane, Tottenham. The teams selected were:

CORINTHIANS

G. E. Wilkinson (goal); Rev. W. Blackburn, W. U. Timmis (backs); P. P. Braithwaite, M. Morgan - Owen, H. Vickers (halves); M. H. Stanbrough, R. Corbett, R. G. Wright, C. F. Ryder, B. O. Corbett (forwards).

SUNDERLAND

Doig (goal); McCombie, Watson (backs); Farquhar, McAllister, Jackson (halves); Hogg, Robinson, Millar, Hewitt, Bridgett (forwards).

The game itself did not seem much of a contest with Sunderland the far superior side, and the official Corinthians handbook from 1905 tells the story giving the following match report:

"With little or no grass to be seen, and the surface in a greasy condition, accurate passing and kicking became very difficult. Still, these conditions appeared to affect the professionals but little, and they gave a display of collective excellence from start to finish, and won by 3 - 0."

"The Corinthian back division played with Vickers, Blackburn, and Braithwaite continually breaking up the combination of the Sunderland forwards, who were very ably led by Millar in the centre. But the amateur forwards were an untried combination; they had not played together before, and they proved totally ineffective as a whole. Occasional individual breaks caused some anxiety to the Sunderland defence, but before the game was many minutes old it was plain that the amateurs were not likely to fall in with one another's play or show any cohesion in attack.

The Sheriff of London Shield.

Amateurs Fade Away

In the early days of organised football, the game was an entirely amateur affair, with clubs such as Corinthians, Old Etonians and Oxford University dominating the FA Cup. Not only were these teams unpaid, but they were typically made up of upper class players. When the working classes began to take an active interest in the game, northern based teams soon turned professional in order to allow star players to make a living from football. And, when the Football League was formed, it was the professional teams of the working class northern towns that participated in it. The same teams also took a stranglehold on the FA Cup, and pretty soon, the amateurs faded away. The Sheriff of London Shield, therefore, was something of a throwback as soon as it began, and the professional teams tended to dominate. It was, perhaps, a little unsurprising that the competition should be a short lived one.

"The professional backs were complete masters of the situation from start to finish, and it really reflected great credit upon the Corinthian defence that they only allowed three goals to be scored against them".

Afterwards, Lord Kinnaird, President of the Football Association, presented the medals and shield - a huge object that dwarfed most of the players - to the victorious Sunderland. It was, however, to be the only occasion on which we 'lifted' the shield; only a few years later the contest was to go out of existence. A rift within the Football Association (FA) relating to the status of amateurs and professionals led to the FA splitting into two bodies, the FA and the Amateur Football Association. This resulted in the FA forming their own Charity competition, the FA Charity Shield, and the amateur version was, after a bright start, condemned to take a back seat.

The whereabouts of the shield today are unknown as in the early 1980's there was a decision taken to auction it, very much against the FA's wishes. A mystery American buyer apparently bought the Shield for £26,000 and took it out of the country, and the trophy hasn't seen the light of day since.

The 1903 team proudly display the Sheriff of London Shield.

Shielded from Glory

In many ways, the Sheriff of London Shield provided the inspiration for the Charity Shield, and the decision instigate a competition where the FA Cup holders replaced the amateurs was an inspired one. While the contest has always been something of an exhibition match rather than a serious competition, it has provided some great games over the years, and some keenly contested ones. However, the Lads have had few opportunities to participate. Our early League titles came too soon, and victory in the FA Cup in 1973 was not followed by a Charity Shield appearance due to the unsavoury political antics of the Champions, Liverpool. Our only appearances came in consecutive seasons, the Lads winning the shield in 1937 against Arsenal, but losing it the following year against Manchester City.

Scottish international R McNeil.

1903-1904
Crisis

"In truth it had been a poor season and the Club was now in turmoil both on and off the pitch."

James Gemmell.

Left Wing Wizard II

Arriving in 1900, James Gemmell played only a handful of games in that season before establishing himself in the side the next year, scoring ten goals in his first full season. He stayed until 1907, forming a lethal left wing partnership with the English International Arthur Bridgett, and was a tower of strength during a very difficult period for Sunderland, scoring vital goals that kept us in the top division. Gemmell returned to the club in 1910, after spells at Stoke City and Leeds, staying for a further two years, but his best days were in his first spell at the Club. In total he made 227 appearances for the Lads, scoring 46 goals.

Sunderland started off the season once again determined to make amends for a lost title, and set off at a tremendous pace, winning the first four games of the season. Notts County were easily brushed aside 4 - 1, with Craggs, Robinson, Hogg and Bridgett all scoring. Four days later we had an even more emphatic victory against Aston Villa, who had just pipped us to second place the season before on goal difference, the Villains being hammered 6 - 1. Craggs, Robinson, Bridgett and Gemmell each scored one and Hogg netted two. The first away game of the season was at Middlesbrough's magnificent new ground, Ayresome Park. The Lads came away with a hard fought 3 - 2 success, Robinson, Hogg and Gemmell the scorers, with no fewer than 25,000 filling the impressive new arena. This was followed by a 2 - 1 home win over Liverpool. One notable absentee was goalkeeper Doig who had sprained his wrist in training during the week. It didn't matter on this occasion, Lindsay took his place, Gemmell scored both goals, and Sunderland were off to a flying start.

The 1903-04 season, however, was to have far reaching implications for the Club. Events on and off the pitch would affect us for a number of seasons, and the latter would nearly cause the Club to fold. On the playing side Sunderland were to lose the goalkeeper who had been between the sticks for us since our very first season of Football League status. This was to be 'Teddy' Doig's last season, and Sunderland found it hard to replace him, sifting through various keepers over the years before an adequate replacement was found. As a consequence, Sunderland's once proud defence crumbled and goals were leaked in the following seasons at an astonishing rate. Off the pitch, the Club was involved in an illegal payments scandal, with Andrew McCombie, a Sunderland back since 1898, and a £100 payment made to him, being the bone of contention.

The fine start on the pitch did not last, and the team had already started to fade in the League by the time McCombie rocked the Club. We lost four of our next five games after our winning start and thereafter the number of wins was roughly matched by the number of defeats, with only a few draws. Three consecutive victories during November had brought us right back into the leading pack before we travelled to the Baseball Ground, where we suffered a sound 7 - 2 hammering. In fact, we had been 7 - 0 down until the final few minutes when Craggs and Barrie gave us some face. The Lads responded well to this defeat with a couple of good 3 - 1 wins over Newcastle and Middlesbrough over the Christmas and New Year period. We also thrashed Bury 6 - 0 at Roker Park with Craggs and Hogg each getting a couple.

But, three defeats in four League games during March and April put paid to any slim Championship hopes and although we won our final two games of the season against Nottingham Forest and Sheffield United it was all too little too late. With such a mixture of results, we never really put together a title challenge and once again the trophy went to Sheffield Wednesday. We eventually finished in sixth place, due mainly to the fact that we managed to maintain a strong home record, with the Lads winning twelve of their seventeen home games, drawing three and losing only two. In truth it had been a poor season and the Club was now in turmoil both on and off the pitch. It goes without saying that we left the F.A Cup at the earliest possible stage once again, this time going down 3 - 2 at Maine Road to Manchester City.

The opening game at Ayresome Park, Middlesbrough's new ground. 'Boro followed hot on the heels of Sunderland in moving to a new home, and both of the grounds opened in this period gave over 90 years of good service. The game, which took place on 12th September, 1903, saw Sunderland run out 3 - 2 winners.

1903-04 team with the Durham Cup.

Buried

The game against Bury at Roker Park kicked off at 3.30pm, and was a quiet affair at first, with the Echo of the time stating that "there was little in it to interest the spectators." When a dog came onto the pitch it seemed to stir more interest among the fans than the game. By half time there was still no score in what had been a dull match, but the Lads would come out for the second forty-five in sharp contrast to their easy going pace of the first half. Three minutes into the half and a beautiful goal by Craggs got the crowd roaring. Sunderland now seemed inspired and pushed forward. Their reward soon came as Hogg bundled himself and the ball in the back of the net after a dazzling run was finished with the Bury centre-half Thorpe thumping them both in the back of the net. A minute later and there was another goal after Gemmell converted a centre by Bridgett. Only ten minutes into the second half and the game was over. There was no let up though, with Craggs striking an upright soon after, and Bridgett unleashing one of his famous pile drivers which nearly took the Bury goalkeeper, Montgomerie, into the back of the net with the ball! All the play was in the Bury end of the pitch with Doig not yet having touched the ball in the second half, which was by now 20 minutes old. Craggs then got away on the wing and put in a hard shot that Montgomerie could not hold and it was four! The fifth came when Hogg took the Bury defence by surprise, sprinted off from the half way line, and put in a 'lightning like shot' which easily beat the keeper. Three minutes from time, the sixth arrived as Hogg passed the ball across for Millar to put into the empty net.

Sinclair Todd, Sunderland AFC Chairman 1903-04.

Sunderland Rocked by McCombie Scandal

Scottish international Andrew McCombie.

Sunderland Enemy No 1?

Andrew McCombie goes down in history as one of the most significant players ever to appear for the Club. He was certainly a fine footballer, winning a League Championship at Sunderland, picking up caps for Scotland while at the Club, and earning further honours when he left us for Newcastle.

Yet, it is for events off the pitch that McCombie is remembered. Why, after more than half-a-decade at Sunderland, and having played over 150 games for us, did he turn on the Club and plunge us into crisis?

It is clear that he must have been deeply angry at something - or someone - to act as he did. The central issue appears to have been money, and most would agree that the players received less than they were due in those days. However, they were by no means badly paid, and Sunderland had a reputation for looking after their players.

How galling then, that McCombie should plunge us into crisis and then head off to our biggest rivals, Newcastle, and help steer them to glory.

In the early years of the century the outlook for Sunderland was bright. The team was one of the greatest in the land with a nice blend of youth and experience and looked set for a long reign at the top of English football. However, problems that were to very nearly destroy our Club were just around the corner.

In the close season of 1903-04 the Board of Directors of Sunderland AFC gave Andrew McCombie £100 to enable him to start up in business. They did so on the understanding that on receiving a benefit game he would repay the money. McCombie, however, did not see it like this and in time he refused to pay back the money saying it had been a gift from the Club.

Once everything came into the public arena in January 1904, McCombie's future at the Club was obviously over. Other clubs now clamoured for his signature. At the time he had developed into one of the country's finest right backs and had just broken into the Scottish squad, having been with Sunderland for six years. He could have gone anywhere, but his desire to stay in the North East swayed his decision and he eventually signed for Newcastle United.

The Magpies paid a world record £700 for his signature. This beat the £520 we had paid earlier in the season for Alf Common. To put McCombie's playing prowess into perspective, in his first season for the Magpies they would win the League. McCombie was only 25 years of age and had the footballing world at his feet.

This was not the end of the matter however, as the Football Association launched an inquiry into the £100 'gift', Sunderland took legal action against McCombie and a court of law judged that the money constituted a loan. The FA took exception to this ruling and agreed with McCombie that it had been in fact a 're-signing/win/draw bonus', violating the game's rules, and Sunderland's books were deemed as not showing a true record of the Club's financial affairs. The upshot was that Sunderland AFC were fined £250, and six directors were suspended for two and a half years, Alex Watson for eighteen months and Alex Mackie for three months.

This came as a huge blow to the Club, performances plummeted and the side was near to relegation three seasons in a row during the early 1900's. It was also mooted that they may even have to be wound up. The outlook was certainly bleak until the arrival of Fred Taylor. J P Henderson vacated the chair to Sinclair Todd, who stayed less than a year, before Frederick William Taylor, who had been a director in 1897-1899, returned to the Club to become Chairman. It was his efforts that helped save the Club from extinction. He brought Robert Kyle in as manager and his influence helped bring goalkeeper L.R. Roose to the Club, a move that steadied the Club on the pitch. It was also Taylor who supplied money for further signings that season that enabled us, much to the annoyance of other clubs, to 'buy our way out of trouble.' Most of all, he returned some stability to the Club, and with the help of Bob Kyle and Billy Williams, produced one of the most exciting teams ever seen in a Sunderland strip.

Andrew McCombie.

Billy Williams

There is no doubting that the McCombie scandal provided a real hammer blow to Sunderland AFC. The scandal rocked the Club's carefully laid foundations, not least because it separated us from so many of the people who had been instrumental in leading us to success.

However, amidst all the upheaval, one important figure remained at the Club and provided a real calming influence: our trainer Billy Williams. Having arrived in February 1897 - midway through Robert Campbell's first season in charge - Williams stayed in the job when Alex Mackie took over from Campbell and, when Mackie left shortly after the scandal, remained as trainer following Bob Kyle's appointment. Indeed, Williams did not leave the Club until the end of the 1928-29 season, Johnny Cochrane's first in charge. In the list of the Club's loyal servants, few can rival Williams' 32 years at Sunderland.

His importance to our success should not be underestimated, for the trainer's job was hugely important in those days. Williams oversaw many of the tasks that would now belong to the manager, and was largely responsible for getting players fit, honing their skills and disciplining those who stepped out of line. He was also something of a father figure to many players, nurturing the talent - and confidence - of many of our stars. While his was often an unsung hero's role, there should be no doubting the fact that his stabilising influence was crucial in helping us ride out the uncertain period following the scandal.

Billy Williams

1904-1905
Coping

Alf Common, the first £1,000 transfer.

Successful Stewardship

Alex Mackie took over the managerial reigns from Robert Campbell in 1899. Without doubt, his managerial reign at Sunderland was a successful one, as in his six seasons we were only out of the top five once, and that was a sixth place finish. Mackie, along with Billy Williams, was responsible for our three title challenges in the first three seasons of the 1900s. Had it not been for the departure of Doig and the untimely outburst from McCombie, his team could have been set for a long tenure at the top of the Football League. It was the McCombie payments scandal that led to his initial departure, as he was suspended for three months for his part in the deal. After only one more season at the Club though, he left to be Secretary of Middlesbrough, by which time the side was not what it had been in previous years.

In the opening seasons of the twentieth century, Alex Mackie had proved himself to be a man of great talent, and he had built a team that was really going places. The prospect of his team surpassing the achievements of the Team of All Talents seemed at one point to be a realistic one, with the Lads regularly challenging for the League title. However, McCombie had blown a huge whole in Mackie's plan - and even implicated him in the scandal - and his carefully laid foundations were smashed apart. We had struggled as the scandal became public and no-one could be sure what sort of an impact it would have on the Club.

In the event, the full impacts of the affair were not seen on the pitch in the 1904-05 season, but they would come to be more evident in subsequent years. What affected the team on the field of play more in this season was the loss of 'Teddy' Doig as goalkeeper. Lewis, who had taken over in the Sunderland goal from Doig, conceded five goals in three of the first four League games, was then replaced by Rowlandson, who in turn gave way to Whitbourne, and finally Webb was given a chance. It was a tough job replacing 'Teddy' and the position would prove to be a major problem in the coming years. The season, however, did see the arrival of one of Sunderland's greatest ever players in the then 19 year old George Holley. Although not a regular early on, he would go on to be a magical player for the Club. The big arrival at the start of the season was Alf Common, who returned for a second spell for a fee of £520, only to be sold to Middlesbrough before the season was out for almost double the price and a place in the history books as the first £1000 player. The season's results though were merely papering over the cracks that were beginning to appear off the field.

With all the pre-season comings and goings, and the lack of a real backroom board, it was no real surprise that Sunderland opened their season with a defeat, the trip to Deepdale to play Preston producing a 3 - 1 reverse. Yet, we quickly bounced back to crush a hapless Notts County 5 - 0, Bridgett and Common playing exceptionally well and both getting two goals each. Sunderland followed this up with a nine match unbeaten run, winning seven and drawing two. For the time being, at least, the goalkeeping problem seemed not to bother the side. The most impressive result was a 1 - 0 win at Everton, who were to eventually to finish in second place, a game which produced the Merseysiders' only home defeat of the campaign. This impressive start was not maintained, however, and we went down three times in the next four games, including our first home defeat of the season, 4 - 1 to Small Heath, followed by a 5 - 2 whopping at Manchester City.

The strain, instability and the consequences of a number of changes within the team began to show and although we put together a four game winning streak through January we could not keep up the pace. We lost form throughout the end of January and March (during February we had a 100% record as due to bad weather we only played one game and won 3 - 1 at Stoke). These winter months cost us dearly and we were well off the pace for the title. Although Newcastle United took the Championship this season it is worth noting that Sunderland beat them 3 - 1 at both Roker and St James'. In the return game at Newcastle, Holley scored twice after arriving mid-season and managed to get four goals in three games to announce his arrival. The man who brought him to Wearside though, was about to leave Sunderland.

In a real blow to the Club, Alex Mackie left to be secretary manager of Middlesbrough, his position undermined by the McCombie scandal and his carefully developed plans wrecked by one of the players he had nurtured. Fred Dale, who was appointed caretaker until a permanent appointment could be made, was the hot tip to take over. Surprisingly though, Bob Kyle filled the vacancy in August. He had been the secretary of the Distillery club in Belfast and little was know about him.

Overall the season showed a slight improvement on the previous campaign in so far as we finished in fifth position. It was merely covering over the cracks however, and was the calm before the storm. The truth was we were deep in crisis.

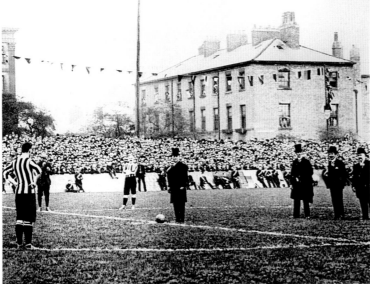

Sunderland v Newcastle United at St James' Park, 1904-05 season. Low stands meant free views were to be had from the surrounding buildings, but there was still room for 30,000 fans inside the ground! Note the formal dress of the match officials. The game itself was a fine one for Sunderland. It ended 3 - 1 to the Lads, Holley scoring two and Buckle hitting the other.

Bill Hogg

Billy Hogg was signed from Willington Athletic and his skills were recognised in November 1900 when he played for the Football League. He played in all three of England's Internationals in 1902, against Scotland, Wales and Northern Ireland. In time he would be transferred to Glasgow Rangers, but would later return as a publican in the Town. Billy would also have a spell coaching at Roker Park. In all he stayed for ten seasons at Roker, making 302 appearances, scoring 85 goals. He was a vital part of the Championship winning side of 1902, and had the honour of scoring a hat trick in the 9 - 1 record away victory over Newcastle United. Without doubt, he was one of the players of the decade.

Billy Hogg.

1905-1906
Worrying

"Your directors have to report a very unsatisfactory season."

(SAFC Annual Report)

Walkover Against Wolves

The weather on the day was fine and the pitch looked in good order as Wolves visited Roker Park. Farquhar was the Sunderland captain and won the toss with the game kicking off at around 3.15pm. There was some early amusement amongst the crowd when a ferocious shot at goal struck the referee and outbursts of laughter were heard all around the ground. We did most of the early attacking and it was no real surprise when Bridgett put a looping cross in and O'Donnell headed in from only a few yards out after 25 minutes. Wolves responded well, and after going close once already, Hopkins tapped in a Pedley cross after Rhodes had been beaten all ends up. Soon after we were awarded a penalty following a handball by Jones in the area. Bridgett struck from the spot at the second attempt after Baddeley had saved the first. Seven minutes before half time Bridgett got another goal after Shaw had taken the ball to the by-line and crossed for him to head in. The fourth quickly followed when Gemmell rifled in a shot, and Hogg brilliantly flicked it into the net. By half-time it was 4 - 1, and the game was over. Wolves did have a goal disallowed for off side after the interval, before Willis fired in an amazing 30-yard drive that flew into the top corner, leading to rapturous applause. The result was not in doubt but Sunderland wanted more. Hogg and Gemmell completed the scoring for Sunderland and although Wolves did manage to get another back, it was a walk over.

Sheffield Wednesday v Sunderland programme, 1906.

After holding together well during the 1904-05 campaign, the aftermath of the McCombie affair at last began to take hold, with results on the pitch being terrible, especially in comparison to what the Sunderland fans were used to. Tommy Tait was recruited from Bristol Rovers and Harry Low from Aberdeen, but our defensive record let us down badly. In some ways it was a transitional season, Robert Kyle taking over the manager's job from Alex Mackie, but if it was a transitional period, it was a long and dangerous one!

The season started off brightly enough with a 3 - 2 home win over Newcastle United, Bridgett scoring twice and Gemmell getting the other. Thereafter, the tone was set for what was to be one of our poorest seasons to date: we lost five successive games in the League, and it was clear that the Club were in big trouble.

By now Naisby, signed from Reading, had replaced Webb in goal. Although not the best of starts to his Sunderland career, he was actually praised for his efforts, and without him, the defeats would have been even heavier than they were. As it was, they were bad enough. 2 - 1 defeats against Aston Villa and Liverpool were followed by a 4 - 1 beating at Sheffield United and a 3 - 1 home defeat by Notts County. To only lose 1 - 0 away to Stoke in the next game was something of a result!

Matters did not get much better throughout the remainder of October and November with a number of bad defeats, including a 2 - 0 at Woolwich Arsenal, a 5 - 2 at Wolverhampton, and a 3 - 0 at Small Heath's ground Coventry Road. Yet our home form was starting to pick up and wins over Blackburn and Everton preceded a mini-revival through December, where we won three games on the trot. Gemmell was the main man behind the run, scoring in each of the games. A couple of Christmas defeats though, 3 - 1 at Bury on the 23rd and 4 - 1 at Notts County on the 27th, let everyone know that it was going to be a long hard New Year. Signs of hope were emerging, however, and the 1 - 1 draw at St James' Park in front of 56,000 in the last game of 1905 added a tad of optimism.

Those who had doubted the Lads and had them already relegated were made to eat their words in what was to be a quite astonishing turnaround. The New Year brought with it new fortunes and we amazingly won seven of the first nine games of 1906. We still managed a few bad defeats, notably a 6 - 2 whipping from Bolton in the middle of February, but it did not dishearten the team and they went on to win four in a row after this defeat, inflicting a few whippings of their own. Aston Villa were brushed aside 2 - 0 at Roker and Blackburn Rovers were taken by surprise as we put three past them without reply at their place. Getting almost confident now, Wolves were swept away with ease at Roker, 7 - 2, and Small Heath quickly followed 3 - 1. Everything seemed back on course and mid-table respectability likely, until the usual end of season loss of form hit. Defeats in the last eight games at Everton 3 - 1, Middlesbrough 2 - 1, Manchester City 5 - 1, and a 1 - 0 home defeat by Nottingham Forest, had us on tenterhooks. Thankfully 2 - 0 wins over Derby County and Preston North End and the fine mid-season run saw us through to a fourteenth place finish. Nevertheless, it was a close run thing: we were only four points from relegation.

Typically, just when League form was deserting us we managed to progress past the first round of the FA Cup. Notts County were beaten in round one, Gainsborough Trinity after a replay in round two and by the time we travelled to Plumstead, the home of Woolwich Arsenal, on 24th February, the Club was quietly confident that this was to be our year. However, the Gunners hammered us 5 - 0 to put us in our place. It had, though, been a nice break from the terrible League form.

In all, it was not really a season to remember, and the directors of the Club were particularly unhappy with matters, the Annual Report dated 3rd July stating: *"your directors have to report a very unsatisfactory season."* Injuries and lack of top class replacements was acknowledged. Robert Kyle's reign as manager had not exactly got off to a flying start. People hoped that this was a mere blip in the Club's fortunes but the next few years were to prove otherwise.

Sunderland v Woolwich Arsenal 1905.

Kyle Takes the Hot Seat

Robert Kyle took over in 1905 after Alex Mackie's departure, inheriting a team in deep trouble. He had previously been secretary of the Distillery club in Belfast and was a relative unknown. He applied for the job with over 70 other candidates. In time he would win a League Championship for Sunderland and lead them to their first FA Cup final, but initially his teams struggled in the League and in today's managerial market he would no doubt have failed to make it past the first couple of seasons. It would have proved a great mistake, however, if he had been shown the door. Bob Kyle went on to become Sunderland's longest ever serving manager, completing nineteen full seasons, and would have been in charge for more but for the outbreak of the war. Kyle's teams were always adventurous and goals were in great supply at both ends. Although only managing to bring the Championship to Sunderland once, in 1912-13, it was a great season, which saw us not only challenging for the League title but for the FA Cup as well. Some of the Club's finest players also played under Kyle, including the legendary Charlie Buchan, the fantastic George Holley and the great Jackie Mordue. Kyle finally left the Club in 1928, after twenty-three years of service, and was replaced by another great manager, Johnny Cochrane.

Robert Kyle.

1906-1907
Mediocrity

"Once again a poor season when judged by the high standards that had been set at the Club in its early years"

Ten Goal Thriller

Twenty thousand fans turned up on the 19th January 1907 to see one of the craziest games ever likely to have taken place at Roker Park. Liverpool arrived on Wearside as League Champions, but were in poor form, having failed to score in their previous five League games. The Lads were quickly put under pressure as Liverpool stormed into the lead, Parkinson placing a weak shot past Ward to open the scoring. The second arrived after Robinson rounded several players, before crossing to Parkinson who from eight yards easily beat Ward. Bridgett pulled one back with a fine shot after steadying himself despite the close attentions of Robinson. It lifted the crowd, who until then had had little to shout about, but they were soon disappointed again as, after some neat passing in front of goal, Raybould scored for Liverpool. Matters got worse too, as Parkinson rifled the ball into the back of the net after a goalmouth scramble to make the score 4 - 1 at half time, and apparently the game was over. For the second half we changed our attacking line up with Gemmell, Hurdman, Holley and Bridgett now all playing up front as by this point there was nothing to lose! The Lads then got the lifeline of a penalty kick and Rhodes stepped up to finish the job calmly. This got Sunderland moving and only four minutes later Hurdman got another. Every attack now looked like yielding a goal, but it was Parkinson who scored next, for Liverpool on a breakaway. This didn't seem to dishearten the Lads and they still poured forward and Hurdman soon got another for the red and whites. With only a few minutes left and heading for defeat, Sunderland were awarded another penalty for handball and Rhodes once again did the job, and a 5 - 5 draw had been salvaged.

Kyle had undoubtedly joined the Club at a most difficult moment. Indeed, his was an almost unenviable position, for he had to cope with both the incredible expectations of those fed on the glorious diet of Sunderland's first quarter-of-a-century as a club, while also dealing with the inevitably unsettling effects of the McCombie affair. It was clear he would need time to prove what he was capable of, but football fans and club directors are not always the most understanding groups of people.

After such a poor previous season, this time around it was inevitable that changes would be made. Kyle's task was one of rebuilding the Club in order to regain the position it held only a few years earlier, and there were a number of arrivals during the season. The goalkeeper's jersey once more changed hands, with Ward replacing Naisby, though this did not really do the trick: we still managed to concede 66 goals in 38 league games this season. Indeed, if the fans had expected an improved season, they were to be greatly disappointed. A year of much the same was in store, and the loss of further great players meant that the squad was becoming devoid of true class.

The first game of the season was the local derby against Newcastle, a fixture which attracted a crowd of 56,378. The Magpies got off to a winning start with a 4 - 2 victory over us, despite Sunderland having taken the lead. We then managed a run of four games without defeat - beating both Liverpool and Aston Villa - giving promise to the season. However, two successive defeats at home to Sheffield United and away to Bolton Wanderers soon underlined the fact that the team was still a long way off producing anything worthy of a challenge on the League title; in fact, it was more likely to be struggling against relegation.

It was not that the team was particularly bad, as on their day the Lads were quite capable of beating the best teams in the land. Indeed, there were fine wins throughout the season, with Manchester United, Newcastle, Small Heath and Middlesbrough all being put to the sword at various points during the season. Nor did the team have trouble scoring, as we managed 65 goals over the season. It was that we simply could not defend or stop leaking goals. Games were won and lost at an astounding rate, and a general lack of consistency was the main problem. A game that probably sums up the season best is the 5 - 5 home draw with Liverpool! Lax defending cost us points in crucial games, and even at Roker Park teams were regularly going home with a point or two in the bag. Indeed, by Christmas, we had won just four home games, with the majority ending in draws or defeats.

The FA Cup was once again to bring a welcome distraction with Sunderland playing enough games to reach the semi-finals stage in today's competition; unfortunately, we did not make it past the third round! In the first round Leicester Fosse were demolished 4 - 1. Southern League side, Luton Town, who at the time were known as the 'Straw Hatters' were next up. The outcome was a rather disappointing scoreless draw, but there was to be no mistake in the replay at Roker Park some four days later, a narrow 1 - 0 victory seeing us into the second round. Here we would clash with Sheffield Wednesday, and the game was a tough affair; the Lads were happy with a 0 - 0 draw. Whilst trying not to be complacent, the advantage was surely with the Lads at Roker Park. It was not to be and we lost 1 - 0 and our interest in the cup competition was once again over at an early stage.

After our Cup exit, the indifferent League form continued. March saw some great wins - including a 2 - 0 victory over Newcastle and a 4 - 1 victory over Birmingham - but we also slumped to heavy defeats. In a terrible week at the end of the month, we slumped to defeat in three consecutive games - all of them away from home - Manchester United and Preston North End beating us 2 - 0 and Everton thrashing us 4 - 1.

The final run in was little different. Cavalier defending again cost us points in games with Arsenal (2 - 3) and Bury (3 - 5), but at least there were some more impressive wins to point to. Most notably, Middlesbrough were beaten 4 - 2 at home - Bridgett scoring a brace - and there was a useful 3 - 2 away win in our final game at Manchester City too.

It was clear that there was still a great deal of talent at the Club, particularly going forward. Bridgett had been showing himself as something of a prolific goalscorer, hitting an impressive 26 goals during the season, and Billy Hogg had weighed in with his share of goals too. But, it was also obvious that we needed extra steel in defence, and that as a whole the team needed to be more effectively organised and was lacking a little extra guile. We were still a decent team - we were certainly in no real danger of relegation - but the dropped points meant we were way off being a top team. The season ended with mid-table respectability - the Lads finished in tenth place. While our off-field troubles had undoubtedly contributed heavily to this, ultimately, it had once again been a poor season by the high standards that had been set at the Club in its early years.

Yet, if the fans thought this was a bad season, they were in for a shock! The Club was still struggling to rebuild itself, and key players were still wanting to leave Sunderland. Indeed, in the season's final stages, we were dealt a real hammer blow when one of our most vital players of the last eight years - Jim Watson - left for Middlesbrough. A Scottish international back, he had been a lynch-pin of our defensive play. Having drawn a blank in the search for a successor to Doig in goal, his departure merely compounded our defensive problems. Leaking goals had cost us points during this disappointing season: what hope did we have now without Watson?

Mean Defensive Machine

Jim Watson arrived at the Club in 1899 from Clyde, and after playing only three games in his first season at Roker went on to become a regular in the back line, playing in some of Sunderland's meanest defensive sides. He was part of the 1900-01 side that conceded only 26 goals in 34 games and was a major part of the 1901-02 Championship winning side. Amazingly, in eight seasons and 225 games he didn't score a single goal for the Club. Watson was also a Scottish International while at Sunderland, gaining four caps. He eventually left us in 1907, for Middlesbrough, and his influence on the side can clearly be seen by the fact that Sunderland were nearly relegated the very next season, and leaked a massive 75 goals in only 38 games.

Jim Watson.

1907-1908 Danger

"The situation was obviously desperate."

Leigh Richmond Roose.

Goalkeeping Dilemma Ends

The departure of 'Teddy' Doig back in 1904 had left an enormous gap in goal for Sunderland and it was not really adequately filled until the Welsh amateur Dr. Leigh Richmond Roose arrived in 1908. He was renowned for taking Sunderland free kicks outside the penalty area, and strangely, as the rule restricting the use of the goalkeepers' hands to the penalty area was not introduced until 1912, he was also 'spotted' bouncing the ball to the halfway line on more than one occasion. Roose was an immediate saviour for Sunderland, making his debut on 18th January at Deepdale, and being instrumental in saving the team from relegation. Without his arrival, it is likely that Sunderland would have been playing Second Division football for the first time in their history in 1909. Roose started his career with Aberystwyth, moving to London Welsh, before a transfer to Stoke City. He then travelled to Everton, back to Stoke, and eventually to Sunderland. He was also the Welsh International goalkeeper, being capped on 24 occasions. Sadly, his life was all too short; he was tragically killed, like so many others, in the First World War.

The 1907-08 campaign was one of the worst in Sunderland's short history to that point, yet it was also one of the most interesting, exciting and significant. It started off disastrously, with us winning only six of the first twenty-one games, and being firmly rooted at the bottom of the table. The team and Club were in deep trouble, and significant changes had to made quickly if we were to survive.

The very first game of the season set the tone and highlighted just how severely in trouble the Club was: a 5 - 2 home defeat by Manchester City. That the score line had any vague respectability was due to Hogg and Bridgett getting a couple of late goals. It could not, however, cover over the facts. The team needed strengthening in key areas or a big relegation struggle was ahead. Early results bore this out, with heavy defeats against Sheffield United 5 - 3, Nottingham Forest 4 - 1, Newcastle United 4 - 2, and Woolwich Arsenal 4 - 0. Yet despite the warning signs there was little urgent action taken to improve the squad.

By Christmas the situation was obviously desperate, so the directors dug deep into their pockets to finance some much-needed new signings. Over £2,500 was forked out to ensure that relegation would be avoided. Foster arrived for £800 from Watford, and promptly scored twice on his debut, a 5 - 2 win over Woolwich Arsenal. When the New Year had got off to a fine start we began to believe that relegation could actually be avoided. A 4 - 0 thumping at Notts County only three days later soon brought us down to earth though, and a humiliating 3 - 1 F.A Cup defeat against New Brompton, who would later become Gillingham, sent the alarm bells ringing. Robert Kyle quickly spent some more of the directors' money. Most significantly L.R. Roose arrived to fill the goalkeeping void left by Doig. Although his first game ended in a narrow 3 - 2 defeat at Preston, this told us little about his talent, for he had only signed the day before. A week later, we managed a 6 - 2 thrashing of Bury, in which George Holley scored twice, announcing that he had come of age and was about to inflict misery on defences all over the land.

Although still losing games away from home, 3 - 1 at Middlesbrough, 2 - 1 at Chelsea and 3 - 0 at Manchester United, we were now winning home games with regularity, a vital factor if the Club was to avoid relegation. Liverpool were defeated 1 - 0, Sheffield United 4 - 1, Nottingham Forest 7 - 2, and Blackburn Rovers 4 - 0, Holley scoring hat tricks against both Rovers and Forest, and also bagging two at United.

The team now believed it could avoid relegation. With Roose at the back, Holley banging them in up front and Thompson having arrived to provide some stability in the midfield areas, Sunderland began to force results away from Roker as well. A 3 - 2 win at Bolton, Holley again on the score sheet twice, was followed by an emphatic 3 - 0 win at Everton, and a 3 - 1 win over Newcastle at St James' in the penultimate game of the season. With such an impressive run-in we could even afford a home defeat against Sheffield Wednesday and a last day defeat at Bristol City.

Holley was quite simply in magnificent form, scoring fifteen goals in the last fourteen games. It was a goal scoring record which quite simply kept us in the First Division. Overall, from a playing point of view the season was regarded as being "most unsatisfactory", although the Directors acknowledged the brilliant performances of Roose.

If the season is taken from the halfway point, however, it must be considered a success as from that point on the only aim was to avoid relegation, which was duly achieved. Another, most significant event of the season for the long-term future of the Club was the successful conclusion of the acquisition of Roker Park. The ground was now ours. Perhaps the Club could now start to go forward once again.

Cup Humiliation

On 11th January 1908, we suffered one of our most humiliating defeats to date, in the FA Cup against Southern League side New Brompton. The season was already going disastrously, and defeat in this game was unthinkable. It was a fine day for football too, and there could be no excuses about the pitch. Sunderland were simply dreadful. Despite opening the scoring through Holley, the floodgates did not open. The reverse in fact happened, and from a beautifully flighted corner McGibbon headed New Brompton level. It did not end there though, as two more were added in front of a 10,000 crowd. Sunderland had been humbled. It was a most embarrassing defeat, and perhaps the only good that came out of it was that it highlighted how poor the team was this year, and the Directors forked out for some new signings. Indeed, the famous L.R. Roose arrived for the very next game.

Leigh Richmond Roose.

1908-1909
9 - 1

"The sticky patch was over."

1908-09 Sunderland team.

Attacking Combo

The 1908-09 season saw the formation of one of the most deadly attacking trios in English football: Holley-Mordue-Bridgett. Mordue arrived at the start of the season from Woolwich Arsenal, and teamed up with Holley - who had risen through the ranks to establish himself as a first team regular - and Bridgett, an established England international who was hitting the peak of his career. The partnership lasted for four seasons, during which time they bagged over 150 League goals between them. All three men were capped by England during their time at the Club. Indeed, Holley and Bridgett played together for England in four matches during 1909, all of them victories. The partnership came to an end when Bridgett left for South Shields in 1912, after a successful season that had seen Holley crowned as the League's top scorer.

In an attempt to draw a line under the turmoil of the previous five years, the board boldly financed a spending spree, and during the summer break, crucial signings were made in important areas to ensure that a repeat of our near relegation performance would be avoided in the coming season. Scotland's centre half Charlie Thomson was recruited from Heart of Midlothian, Jackie Mordue came the long route, from Woolwich Arsenal, having been born just outside of Chester le Street, and Arthur Brown, who had been capped for England at the tender age of eighteen, arrived from Bramall Lane.

With the new signings in place, Robert Kyle's sticky patch was over, but it didn't seem that way at the start of the season. Indeed, it was the same story as in previous seasons, a 1 - 0 defeat in the opening game being followed by a 4 - 2 defeat at Bury, and all seemed set for another battle to avoid relegation. However, in the third game a famous English trio was born, Holley, Bridgett and Mordue all scored in a 3 - 0 win at Middlesbrough. The 'trio' were to inflict more serious pain on our other local rivals later in the season, and set the season alight with some of the most exciting attacking play seen at Roker for some time.

In adopting an attacking policy, our defence was often left exposed and we either won or lost. We played only two draws in the League all season, with a couple of good victories more often than not followed by a couple of defeats. To emphasise this fact, at the end of October, Manchester United were emphatically trounced 6 - 1 at Roker, with Brown, Holley and Bridgett all getting two each, yet the following game was a 4 - 0 defeat at Everton. As if to make a mockery of this result, Leicester Fosse were then quickly beaten 3 - 1 and Woolwich Arsenal 4 - 0.

By Christmas, Sunderland were positioned in mid-table with roughly the same number of victories and defeats. Newcastle, on the other hand, were flying high at the top of the table, and setting an astonishing pace for the League title. A Newcastle victory was expected when the two teams met on December 5th, but the outcome could not have been any further from the truth: the Lads pulled off an amazing 9 - 1 victory!

As we know, the FA Cup was becoming a 'mission impossible' but for a time this season it looked like we could prosper. The first round saw us put out Sheffield United 3 - 2 at Bramall Lane, while in the next round, once again on our travels, Preston North End were dumped out of the competition 2 - 1. A third away tie, this time at Valley Parade, witnessed a 1 - 0 victory over Bradford City, before fate conspired against us. The quarter-final draw paired us with Newcastle United. In front of 53,000 at St James' Park, in the bitter cold with driving sleet, one of the greatest ever games to be held at St James' kicked off.

The excitement over the game was immense and the crowd for the match had started gathering at 10am, with everyone determined to see the match from the vantage of the 'sixpenny end'. By mid-day the entire thoroughfare was swamped with good-natured people. Newspaper reports of the day indicate that two Newcastle United players actually collapsed with exhaustion during the game, a match which incidentally is still regarded as perhaps the finest ever seen at the famous St James' Park arena.

Newcastle took an early lead in the game, but Mordue quickly cut short the celebrations. Brown then gave Sunderland a 2 - 1 advantage, but the Magpies levelled things, and it finished 2 - 2.

The date of the replay was set for four days later at Roker Park, and as if to exact revenge for the 9 - 1 drubbing we dished out earlier, the Magpies continued their assault on the League and Cup double by beating us 3 - 0. In fairness the Magpies were brilliant, all over the pitch, and having taken the lead the turning point of the match came when the Newcastle goalkeeper Lawrence saved a penalty from George Holley. Shepherd rubbed salt into red and white wounds with two brilliant goals late on in the game.

The second half of Sunderland's season was to see more victories than defeats. Five of seven were won from January to the middle of March, before we amazingly recorded our first draw of the season on the 15th of March, 2 - 2 away to Manchester United. The game was also one of three in a row that Roose was to miss. It was to prove significant, as we followed our record away victory with another record, our then record away defeat, 8 - 1 at Blackburn Rovers.

Roose made a swift return in the next game as Arsenal were beaten 1 - 0 at Roker, followed by a 5 - 2 defeat of Sheffield Wednesday, suggesting the Blackburn game was just a one off. In fact, apart from that thrashing at Blackburn we had a fine run-in to the season, winning six of the last eight. This included another victory over Newcastle, 3 - 1 at Roker, but it was not enough to stop the Mags taking the title at a canter. Our third place finish was welcome following the previous season's turmoil and flirtations with relegation. The fans could not argue either that they had not been entertained. In all it had been an exciting season, if not a steady one, and we had returned to winning ways.

Lads on Tour

The close season was to see Sunderland embark upon their first tour, with the following squad: Roose, Allan, Milton, Foster, Tait, Low, Thomson, Jarvie, Clark, Brown, Holley and Mordue. The tour took in Hungary, Austria, Germany and Czechoslovakia, and it was not without success either. In Budapest Sunderland played Torna Club, who had only been formed ten years earlier but put up a good fight, only losing 3 - 2 to the Lads. Magyar FC were also defeated at the same venue 2 - 1. The tour then travelled onto Vienna where we thrashed the Austrians 5 - 0, only to lose 2 - 1 a day later to Vienna Athletic Club. This was to prove the only defeat of the tour though, with 4 - 2 and 3 - 0 victories over Deutscller Club in Prague; a 5 - 2 win in Munich over Bayerne Club, and an 8 - 3 thrashing of Nuremberg following. While the results of the tour cannot be argued with, its usefulness is unclear and there was not another tour until 1913.

Arthur Brown.

Heaven is a Place on Earth

Magpies Stunned as Lads Hit Nine at St James' Park!

Albert Milton.

Great Away Victories

In beating the Mags 9 - 1 at St James' Park, the Lads not only secured a brilliant win, they also set a new League record - in the English game as a whole - for an away win in top flight football. A marker of the magnitude of the victory is the fact that it is a record that still stands today. Although Wolves equalled it in 1955 with a 9 - 1 win at Cardiff City, their opponents were a struggling team relegated to Division Two the following season.

For Sunderland fans, it is one record we do not want to break - unless of course it is in a game against Newcastle. Holding a national record is great; but having achieved it by thrashing our rivals is simply sublime!

At St James' Park on the 5th December, 1908, Sunderland produced one of the greatest moments in the Club's history. Newcastle were well on their way to winning the League title, setting a ferocious pace at the head of the table, and were eventually to finish seven points clear of the second placed team. Difficult as it is for Sunderland fans to admit, the Mags were probably the best team in the country during the decade, lifting the Championship in 1904-05, 1906-07 and 1908-09, while also winning the FA Cup in 1909-10.

Sunderland, on the other hand, were undergoing a transitional phase. But, despite having only just avoided relegation the previous season, the manager knew what he was doing, piecing together an exciting new side. To underestimate the Sunderland team would have been foolish in the extreme, for we had an excellent front-line, all five of our forwards eventually playing for England. Still, the Newcastle fans saw victory as a mere formality, particularly with the tie taking place at their ground, and a big win was expected!

By three o'clock, a 56,000 crowd had assembled at St James' in what was to prove an amazing game of football. The line-ups for both teams were as follows:

NEWCASTLE UNITED:

Lawrence, Whitson, Pudan, Liddell, Veitch, Willis, Duncan, Higgins, Shepherd, Wilson, Gosnell.

SUNDERLAND:

Roose, Foster, Milton, Daykin, Thomson, Low, Mordue, Hogg, Brown, Holley, Bridgett.

The game got underway in misty conditions with a light rain. The first half was a normal enough affair, Sunderland taking an early lead on nine minutes through a simple tap in by Hogg. The game erupted on half time though, as Newcastle were awarded a controversial penalty when Thomson was adjudged to have hand balled. The Sunderland players were incensed with the referee but their protests made no difference. Shepherd smacked home the spot kick and made it 1 - 1 at the interval.

The Sunderland players were livid and came out like men possessed after the half time break. Attacking the Leazes End, they set about destroying this Championship side. A further eight goals were smashed in during an amazing half hour period, six of them coming in only ten minutes!

Holley got the ball rolling just three minutes after the restart, the striker taking advantage when a brilliant run and cross from Bridgett caused confusion in the Newcastle defence. Ten minutes later, the Lads' increasing dominance of the game paid further dividends, as Hogg smashed his second of the game to make it 3 - 1.

By now, Sunderland were clearly on top, but a devastating ten minute spell was about to stun the whole football world. In the 63rd minute, Holley cleverly jinked past a couple of defenders to make it 4 - 1, and four minutes later completed his hat-trick with a thunderbolt shot. Two minutes later, Bridgett won a battle for the ball with Whitson before rounding him and making it 6 - 1.

The Sunderland fans were by now in raptures, and for Newcastle matters got worse when Whitson had to leave the pitch injured; they were now down to ten men! Sunderland, though, showed no mercy. Having just had a taste of a goal, Bridgett hit a second two minutes after his first, this time scoring with a long range screamer.

Then, two minutes later, and just 10 minutes after Newcastle were still in with an outside chance at 3 - 1, Mordue added his name to the scoresheet, making it 8 - 1!

Amazingly, there was still over quarter-of-an-hour to go, but the goal every two minutes act could not continue! In the 76th minute, Hogg completed his hat-trick - making it 9 - 1! - and the Lads decided to ease up a little! The game was won, humiliation for our rivals complete and a place in the history books guaranteed. To add to Newcastle's misery, another of their players - Duncan - was forced to leave the field injured just before the game ended.

When news filtered through to Sunderland about the victory, it was greeted joyously on Wearside, with people dancing in the streets! Newcastle United had been humiliated, and they knew it. For Sunderland and their fans it was a day to remember. We had outplayed - and outbattled - a fine Newcastle team, in one of those days where pretty much everything we hit rifled home. Such days are rare indeed, particularly against such quality opposition. What makes the result even more amazing is the fact that despite this drubbing, and a further three we put past them in the return fixture at Roker, Newcastle finished the season with the best defensive record in the division. The Newcastle fans must have been cursing their luck; the Sunderland fans were pinching themselves in case it was all a dream!

T Daykin.

Harry Low.

What the Papers Said

Many journalists at the game could not believe their eyes as the mighty Newcastle were crushed. Some were a little cynical, attributing our victory to muscle power, one scribe's conclusion being that "the United players were much too light for the heavy and aggressive Wearsiders". Others were quick to sing our praises, noting that the unexpected victory was "due absolutely to the remarkable form of Sunderland". The Sunderland Echo, however, were not at all surprised. With their finger firmly on the pulse of North-East football, they knew exactly why the game had ended 9 - 1: "As to the cause of the collapse of the Newcastle team, it was quite evidently due to their being useless".

1909-1910 Rebuilt

"The last ten years had been a round trip, with good times and bad, but the Lads were now back and set to be better than ever!"

Billy Agnew was the first man to play for the 'big three' North East clubs, spending two seasons at Newcastle before joining Middlesbrough. In May 1908 he made his move to Sunderland.

Violence Spoils Big Match

On 18th September 1909 the League encounter with Newcastle United on Wearside was remembered for all the wrong reasons. There was a 40,000 crowd at Roker Park, a record for the time, but the Fulwell End was so cramped that the crowd spilled onto the pitch. As the playing area was being cleared, which took 15 minutes, violence ensued and a police horse was stabbed. The match was repeatedly delayed and at one point it looked like abandonment was on the cards. The match went ahead and Newcastle won 2 - 0. The referee, fearing for everyone's safety, dispensed with the half time break and both teams immediately changed around at the end of the first period of 45 minutes.

The board's decision to gamble with a mini-spending spree had been a good one. After several mediocre campaigns, the 1908-09 season had been altogether much better performance. While third place perhaps flattered the team, our all round play had been much improved, and there were some excellent players in the team. Of course, the highlight had been the 9 - 1 victory over Newcastle, when our forward line had shown their full potential by ripping the eventual Champions apart. But, while confidence in the team had been bolstered, and disaster avoided, it was now time for Kyle's side to prove that our amazing victory over the Magpies was more than a one off. If the Lads were to challenge at the top again, then the deadly attacking play that had overwhelmed our local rivals needed to be repeated every week.

Given our rapid improvement, it was little surprise that the season started off with much the same team as the previous year. The notable exception here was that the long serving English International, Billy Hogg, had left for Glasgow Rangers. Hogg was one of the central players in the team during the decade, and there is little doubt that his presence was missed. Not only was he a first class player, he was also a real character, playing a big role in generating a strong team spirit. Indeed, his was a position that Sunderland found difficult to fill until mid-way through the season, and there was a fair amount of tactical shuffling as a result of his departure.

While much was expected of the team after the excesses of the previous season - and the fans had been sufficiently encouraged to believe that this would be a good campaign - it took us a while to find our feet without Hogg. Our third place finish had heightened expectations, but it had perhaps done so too quickly. While it was by no means unrealistic to expect the team to develop into one of real class, the youngsters needed time to develop, the more recent arrivals needed time to bed in, and a few more signings still had to be made before the team could really challenge for the Championship. Kyle knew that there was much work to be done, for rather than sit back and wait to see what his team could do, he spent much of the season working on the squad and seeking additional players that might provide the extra boost needed to turn a good team into a great one.

The opening fixture was at Roker Park against Tottenham Hotspur and we comfortably won 3 - 1 with Holley notching twice. The winning start continued with another home victory, this time over Preston 2 - 1, Holley and Brown the scorers. The next home game though underlined the fact that the side was not yet quite up to Championship standard as last year's Champions, Newcastle, inflicted a home defeat on us. However, two impressive victories followed, a 4 - 1 at Liverpool, Holley and Mordue getting one each and Thompson two, and a 6 - 2 thrashing of Woolwich Arsenal, Holley notching yet another hat-trick! A 3 - 0 defeat at Bramall Lane in between, however, once again showed a lack of the consistency and class needed to maintain a serious challenge for honours.

One of the signings needed to make the squad strong enough for a title challenge duly arrived in November, to fill the right back position: Bill Troughear from Workington, who was to be known affectionately as 'tough lugs'. In the run up to Christmas, however, the side was still lacking and we endured a bit of a sticky patch, losing three out of four games, the only victory coming over the previous season's FA Cup winners, Manchester United.

Back to back games at the turn of the year with Bristol City, who lost in the Cup final to Manchester United, resulted in two victories, the first a rare away success, 3 - 2, the second a resounding 4 - 0 victory.

Three League defeats in a row, including a bad home defeat 3 - 0 by Notts County, were broken up by a first round win in the FA Cup, 1 - 0 over Leeds City. Interest in the Cup, however, didn't last much longer than usual, after a victory over Bradford Park Avenue, we succumbed to Everton away, losing 2 - 0.

The team responded well to Cup exit, managing to win six of their next eight League games, including impressive away wins at Manor Field, Woolwich Arsenal's new ground (2 - 1), at Chelsea, 4 - 1, and a 3 - 1 at Nottingham Forest. The run pushed the Lads up into a respectable League placing, albeit one that was some way off the leaders.

Once again though, inconsistency reared its ugly head, reminding all at the Club that there was still work to be done and players to be brought in if the trophy cupboard was to be filled with new silverware. The momentum of the 'winning' streak couldn't be maintained, and the season ended flatly, the Lads falling to defeat in four of their last five games, including 1 - 0 defeats at home to Everton and away to Newcastle. While the final placing - eighth - was respectable in itself, and certainly better than the relegation dogfight of two seasons before hand, there was a worry that the previous season's good finish would not be built on. It was clear now that Kyle had the nucleus of a potentially very good side. However, without the addition of one or two high quality international class players, it would remain little more than potential. If Sunderland were to become a force to be reckoned with again, more team strengthening was essential.

So, as a new decade beckoned once again, much hung on the moves Kyle and the directors had planned during the pre-season break. The first ten years of the twentieth century had been seen the Lads consolidate their position as one of the best Clubs by bringing a fourth Championship to Wearside. However, the Club had also been rocked by activities behind the scenes and another relegation scare reminded all at the Club that Champions can quickly become also-rans. The start of the 1910s were, then, a crucial moment in the Club's history: would we fight to re-establish ourselves as football giants or would we fail to rise to the challenge and allow ourselves to slip down the ranks? The answer would be swift and firm...

Unusual Warm Up Strategy

The game at Manchester United on 16th April 1910 had an interesting twist to it. Sunderland players and staff were making the long journey to the fixture by train, but delays to the Manchester train meant that the team arrived forty minutes later than scheduled. Subsequently, the Lads had to run all the way to the ground for the allotted 3pm kick off. It was hardly the best preparation for the match, though undoubtedly it was a good warm up! The game itself went the way of Manchester, despite the red devils hardly getting a touch in the first half as the Lads outplayed them. United eventually won 2 - 0 as the Lads tired late in the game.

Tommy Tait.

1910-11	Third in League.
1911-12	Eighth in League.
1912-13	Fifth League Championship. Lose 1 - 0 in Cup Final.
1913-14	FA Cup Quarter-Finals, Seventh in League.
1914-15	Eighth in League; First World War breaks out.
1915-19	No League football or FA Cup. Win Durham Senior Cup in 1919.
1919-20	Fifth in League.

Football, as with so much of life, was to be blighted by War for much of this decade. Both the League and the FA Cup were suspended from 1915-1919 as the nation concentrated on fighting the First World War.

Before the outbreak of hostilities in 1914, Sunderland had shown signs of regaining the excellent form of earlier seasons. Manager Robert Kyle had spent much time fashioning an exciting young side that played attractive, attacking football. The decade began with the team securing an excellent third place finish in 1910-11, but the real achievement came in the 1912-13 season when, inspired by the goals of Buchan and Holley in particular, Sunderland secured their fifth League Championship. The season also saw the Lads reach the FA Cup final for the first time. Unfortunately, Aston Villa edged the game 1 - 0, denying us a memorable double by the narrowest of margins.

However, the Lads were somewhat inconsistent during the decade, good finishes one season usually being followed by mid-table obscurity the next. Moreover, the start of the First World War broke apart Kyle's promising young side in its prime. Following the cessation of hostilities, football took some time to re-establish itself, and the Lads spent the early part of 1919 playing in local competitions. This gave the Club a chance to re-visit the past and notch up yet another Durham Senior Cup victory! League football returned for the last season of the decade, and the Lads put in a good performance, securing a top three finish.

WAR AND
Peace

1910 · 1920

1910-1911 Promise

"…if you keep playing like that you'll be King of Sunderland"

Inside Left Jimmy Gemmell's comment to Charlie Buchan after Buchan's debut against Middlesbrough.

Charlie Buchan.

Boro' Offer a Bung

By 3rd December 1910 we were flying in the League and clear favourites for the title. Sunderland took a fourteen game unbeaten run to Ayresome Park, and with Boro' struggling at the wrong end of the table, it was obvious to all that a Sunderland victory was on the cards. The Middlesbrough Chairman, Lieutenant Colonel Poole, had different ideas. He was running for parliamentary elections on the Monday and believed that his candidature and votes would be boosted if his side could beat Sunderland. In true political style, the Boro manager Andy Walker offered our captain, Charlie Thomson, thirty pounds to throw the game. Thomson himself would benefit to the tune of ten pounds, with the rest of the team getting two pounds a piece. Thomson though was having none of this, and informed our trainer, Billy Williams, who made the chairman Fred Taylor aware of the situation. We immediately reported Middlesbrough to the F.A, for which the Club was commended for its honesty, and both the manager and chairman of Middlesbrough were removed. It all proved fruitless anyway, Boro' winning the game 1 - 0 and Poole losing the election!

Although the previous season had produced a lower finish than many had hoped after our '9 - 1' season, it was clear that Kyle's rebuilding process was proceeding at some pace. Important new arrivals were starting to settle into the team and there was more confidence on Wearside than there had been for some time. What's more, Kyle also had some promising youngsters to blood too, and he had once again added to the squad over the summer, most notably with the purchase of England international striker Coleman.

The new decade started off with a home derby game against Newcastle and there is no better way to start a season than a 2 - 1 win against the Black and Whites! The game saw the debut of English International, J.G Coleman, who was to have a spectacular season, yet was later to be displaced by a young centre forward named Charlie Buchan. Coleman and Holley were the scorers that day as they were to be for most of the spectacular opening to the decade. The same two were on the mark in the next game, away to Sheffield United, the result again a 2 - 1 win. Amazingly the two were on target a fortnight later to record another 2 - 1 win over Oldham Athletic. In between, Holley had let the double act down as Aston Villa were sent packing 3 - 2 at Roker in front of 30,000 with Coleman, Gemmell and Tait the scorers.

It was to be one of the best starts to a season ever for the Lads as we remained unbeaten for the first fourteen games. We were flying at the top of the table. Notable wins included 4 - 0 against Everton, with Mordue getting two and Coleman and Holley (who else?) scoring the other two, and another 4 - 0, against Tottenham, with Coleman this time notching up a couple. However, results started to go down hill after our goalkeeper, Roose, broke his arm in a 1 - 1 draw at St James' in November following a tackle by Rutherford. It took only one more game without Roose in goal before our unbeaten start to the season came to an end, Middlesbrough beating us by one goal at Ayresome Park.

The loss of Roose and the first defeat of the season seemed to affect the Lads badly and we could not keep up the electric start to the season. Four defeats in the next eight meant that our grip at the top of the table was weakening, especially as two of the defeats were against Championship rivals. The first was a 2 - 1 home defeat by Manchester United, the second a 2 - 1 away defeat at Aston Villa. Both were to prove crucial. The Cup produced another particularly embarrassing disappointment when Norwich City, a Southern League side, beat us in the first round. In fact our only successes in the period from that first defeat at Middlesbrough at the beginning of December to the beginning of February came against Liverpool. We managed to beat them twice over the Christmas period, 2 - 1 at their place, where Coleman got both, and 4 - 0 at Roker, Mordue, Coleman, Cowell and Holley scoring.

The title race seemed apparently back on course with three wins in four games during February. An important change to the team that seemed to do the trick was the replacement of Allan in goal with Worrall. Suddenly, a 4 - 1 home win over Bury, Holley scoring the lot, a 3 - 1 away victory at Nottingham Forest and a 4 - 0 home win against Manchester City suggested that the run of poor form was over.

However, it was something of a false dawn: we won only two of our remaining ten games after this, a 3 - 1 against Middlesbrough and a 2 - 0 win against Preston.

A 2 - 1 home defeat by Sheffield Wednesday and a 3 - 0 defeat at Bradford, topped off with a 5 - 1 thrashing on the final day of the season by the eventual Champions, Manchester United, saw off our title challenge. The third place finish was more than respectable, but perhaps not quite good enough for the fans. Yet, this season augured well for the future; in the last seven games we fielded a man who was to become one of the greatest players England has ever produced: Charlie Buchan. Although he was unable to turn around the end of season slump, the foundations were now well in place for further success in the coming years, and on his home debut against Middlesbrough he was brilliant, team mate Jimmy Gemmell saying to him: *"if you keep playing like that you'll be King of Sunderland"*.

Thomson leads the team out, followed by Butler and Buchan.

Little 'Jackie'

John 'Jackie' Mordue, played at outside right, and was the smallest player in the team at only 5ft 7inches. Born in Edmonsley, he joined us in September 1908 from Woolwich Arsenal. A clever and tricky winger, he scored twice on his debut against Middlesbrough. Jackie actually preferred to play inside or outside left but after playing on the right with such great success he was not moved. A great penalty taker, it was said that his only fault was bringing the ball back too much instead of sending a cross promptly across goal. He gained two caps for England while at Sunderland in a career that spanned eight seasons. He played 299 games and scored 83 goals. After the war he spent only one more season with the Club before moving on to Middlesbrough.

Jackie Mordue.

1911-1912
Set Back

"A middling season: some great results, but some big disappointments too. There was quality in the side, but the finishing touches still needed to be applied."

Walter Scott.

Boxing Day Massacre

Boxing Day 1911 saw us achieve a most unwanted record that remains today: our record defeat. Sheffield Wednesday completely outplayed the Lads and we were lucky to get off the pitch with the score line as low as it was! A Kirkman goal after four minutes started off the rout, while after twenty minutes Thomson was forced to leave the field. By the time he returned to the pitch, still feeling groggy, it was 3 - 0, following goals by Kirkman and McLean. Glennen made it four, McLean five, Glennen six and then two minutes before the interval it was seven, McLean completing his hat trick. 7 - 0 at half time was simply horrendous. An eighth arrived only ten minutes into the second half when McLean scored again. It looked like plenty more would be added when our goalkeeper, Scott, was carried from the field and taken to the Sheffield Royal Hospital after a 'scrimmage' between a ruck of players. Amazingly, though, there was no more scoring. However, eight was bad enough: the Lads had been humiliated. We can only hope that the reason for such a poor game was that a good night was had by all on Christmas Day! It certainly seems a result very much out of context with the team of the day, and despite a couple of injuries, we had a very strong side out that day.

The start of the new season saw George Holley set off at an electric pace, scoring ten times in the first nine games! Unfortunately the rest of the team was not yet up to speed. We did manage a successful opening couple of games with victories over Middlesbrough (1 - 0) and Blackburn (3 - 1). Holley managed to get all the goals bar one that the long serving Bridgett put in. But, our first defeat of the campaign came quicker than we might have hoped, 3 - 1 away to Notts County. It was not to be the greatest of starts to the new season, with home defeats by Liverpool and Newcastle in the space of a fortnight being particularly disappointing. Strangely though, our away form was holding up during this period and a 3 - 1 away success at Aston Villa was followed up by a 2 - 1 win at Sheffield United, Holley scoring twice in both games to keep up his impressive early season form.

However, November dashed any hopes that might have been lingering that this was to be our year. It was simply disastrous, the Lads failing to record a single victory during the month. For good measure we suffered a couple of bad away defeats, going down 3 - 0 at both Bolton and Arsenal. When these results were followed by a 1 - 0 defeat away to Everton at the beginning of December, things were starting to look grim. However, in a dramatic turnaround, results improved and we had our best spell of the season. Holley was back after injury and contributed a goal in a 3 - 2 win over West Brom to get the Lads going again. This was followed up with a 3 - 0 win over Preston, with Holley again scoring. By now, Buchan was beginning to come to life too, scoring in a 2 - 0 win at Bury on Christmas Day. However, the Lads must have over indulged after their festive victory for on Boxing Day they were well and truly trounced by Sheffield Wednesday, losing 8 - 0!

The result must have hurt, but the Lads had a quick chance to get revenge. After a 3 - 3 draw at Ayresome Park, Wednesday came to Roker for the return game on New Year's Day; a 0 - 0 draw did little to soothe the wounds though. The Lads soon dished out a couple of 5 - 0 thrashings to make amends, the first against Notts County, the second against reigning Champions Manchester United, Holley bagging four. We had proved a point, but with Scott injured during a 3 - 1 defeat at St James' Park results went down hill. Anderson replaced Scott in goal and didn't play too badly, but of the seven games during his spell in the team we managed only one win, a 1 - 0 over Arsenal at Roker.

With our season effectively over by April, Kyle decided to do some early summer spending and brought the English International, Harry Martin, to Sunderland to replace the ageing Arthur Bridgett on the left wing. It was to prove an astute signing. Hall was bought to play up front and Francis Cuggy had also by now forced his way into the side on a regular basis and was to flourish into an English International. The signs were good and this new look Sunderland line up won three of the last four games. A 4 - 0 home win against Everton, with George Holley getting a hat trick, was followed by 1 - 0 over Bury, Holley again. This was topped off with a 3 - 0 away win at Preston on the final day of the season, Cuggy, Mordue and Buchan the goal scorers.

In the FA Cup, we started with an easy 3 - 1 victory against Plymouth Argyle. The Southern League side were mesmerised by what was termed Charlie Buchan's 'don't care' style of play, a complete treat to watch. It was said that he 'couldn't give a monkey's' as he strolled around the pitch taking liberties!

The second round was a little tougher, Crystal Palace forcing a replay, but eventually losing 1 - 0 in extra time on a quagmire pitch at Roker Park. The third round produced a Roker record with over 43,000 in the ground and 10,000 locked out. At one stage even our opponents from West Bromwich were refused entry! Mounted police spent time and energy getting the crowd back from the perimeter of the pitch, but there was a stunned silence when the referee blew the final whistle with the Birmingham side running out 2 - 1 winners. Another Cup run had come to an end, standard fare in this middling season. Eighth place in the League, some great results, but some big disappointments too. There was quality in the side, but the finishing touches still needed to be applied. Fortunately, the manager had the matter in hand…

1911-12 Sunderland team.

The Captain

Charlie Thomson was the Captain and centre-half of a great Sunderland team. He arrived from Hearts, where he had been captain, in 1908 for a fee of £70, giving as his reason for coming the need for a fresh challenge. Born in Preston Pans, Edinburgh, he was affectionately known as Charlie by everyone. A strong but clean player, he was about the finest centre-half to be found in Britain at the time. He achieved a remarkable footballing record and played many times for Scotland. He remained with Club until after the war, but by that time was too old to play. In total he had made 265 appearances, scoring 8 goals, helping us to win the League and reach an FA Cup final.

Former captain Charlie Thomson

1912-1913 Glory

"The Sunderland forwards were having a goal feast!"

Joe Butler.

Buchan Takes Five

The date was 7th December, 1912, the score 7 - 0. It was our highest win since the 9 - 1 defeat of Newcastle United at St James' Park in 1908 and for Charlie Buchan it was a personal triumph. Strangely, the man of the match was Liverpool's goalkeeper Campbell, who was outstanding; but for him it would have been double figures for Sunderland. There were clear opportunities early on for both sides, but it was Sunderland who took the lead. From a quick break Hall ran away, laid off the ball to Buchan, who with a swift low shot opened the scoring. Soon afterwards Martin went on an electric run past several players; the last man, Longworth, put in a tackle but Martin was too strong and from close range he blasted the Lads two up after 23 minutes. 13 minutes from half time, Mordue made it 3 - 0 with a cross shot. With the result not now in doubt, we added a fourth for good measure just before the interval, Buchan coolly slotting home a cross from Martin. After the interval the Lads were straight on the attack looking for more goals. Nevertheless, it took until 21 minutes after break for the fifth goal, Buchan once again the man, registering his hat trick after converting a left wing cross. Five minutes later and Buchan was beginning to make it a one-man show. Mordue took a corner, flighting it in beautifully, and after Campbell parried a shot, Buchan lashed the loose ball into the back of the net for the sixth. Having totally outclassed the opposition, we now took it easy, but with only four minutes left Holley strolled down the wing and crossed to Buchan who put in his fifth goal, and Sunderland's seventh.

This was to be arguably Sunderland's most successful season ever. Kyle's young side had built up a lot of experience and he had brought in some older heads in important defensive positions. We recruited yet another new goalkeeper, Joe Butler, who did a fine job. Centre forward James Richardson, a Scot, arrived from Huddersfield Town and was to prove formidable support for Mordue, Buchan, Holley and Martin. Yet, after a credible opening day draw at Newcastle, 1 - 1 in front of 54,000, the season went disastrously wrong. A 4 - 0 hammering at Blackburn was followed by two successive home defeats, against Derby (2 - 0) and Blackburn Rovers (4 - 2). Oldham piled on the misery, beating us 3 - 0 at their place, before we managed a second point of the season by grabbing a 2 - 2 draw at home to Spurs. A 2 - 0 defeat at Chelsea a week later had us rooted to the bottom of the table by mid-October still without a win to our name! Indeed, five defeats in the first seven games made the season appear over before it had even begun.

The turning point came before it was too late though, with a derby game at home to Middlesbrough. Charlie Gladwin made his debut in defence and his presence was to have a wonderful effect. The right back weighed in at a hefty 14 stone and stood 6 ft 1in tall. He took no prisoners and even had the audacity to boss Charlie Thomson about... no mean feat! With the defence now stiffened, the previously stuttering Sunderland forwards went on a scoring spree. The Lads won 4 - 0. In an amazing turn around to the season we won the next four games, and not just by the odd goal. The Lads served up thrashings of the highest order! Woolwich Arsenal were beaten away 3 - 1, Notts County were seen off 4 - 0 at Roker and a trip to Bradford saw the Yorkshire side hammered 5 - 1, Holley notching a hat trick. The arrival of Manchester United at Roker completed a remarkable run of wins, the Lads seeing them off in a 3 - 1 victory.

The run came to an end with a 1 - 0 defeat against Manchester City and though the Lads responded with an important 3 - 1 victory over Villa in the next game, a 3 - 1 reverse at West Brom the following week suggested to some that the winning streak was a one off and that a challenge at the top of the table could not be maintained. How those fears would be allayed in the next game at Roker: Liverpool were swept aside 7 - 0!

After this resounding victory the good results continued, notable victories including a 4 - 0 whipping of Everton, and a 2 - 0 win over Newcastle at Roker Park, Holley getting both the goals. As 1913 approached, the race for the title was well and truly on, but competition within the team was strong too! Holley, Buchan and Mordue were all battling out for the honour of top scorer at the Club, and all had twelve goals a piece before we hit January. The Sunderland forwards were having a goal feast!

The New Year was to bring us even better fortunes, the tone being set on New Year's Day with a 4 - 1 victory over Arsenal. Spurs were then defeated away 2 - 1, Chelsea at home 4 - 0, Middlesbrough 2 - 0 away, and Derby 3 - 0 away before we suffered our only other League defeat for the rest of the campaign, 2 - 1 at Notts County. It had no lasting effect on the Lads as we won the next seven games. Charlie Buchan was now firing on all cylinders with goals in almost every game. Manchester United were beaten 3 - 1, before a couple of 1 - 0 wins over Sheffield United and Manchester City. We then won 3 - 1 three times in a row, beating Sheffield United, West Brom and Everton. Sunderland were a footballing steamroller, and a visit to Liverpool saw Buchan hit top form, notching a hat-trick in the Lads' 5 - 2 win.

Aston Villa, though, were our title rivals, and with only three games left of the season we travelled to Villa for a crunch match. The ball was very much in their court, the Villains needing to get a win to put the pressure on us. A 1 - 1 draw was enough to make sure that winning the title was in our own hands and there was to be no mistake with the remaining two games - both were won, a 3 - 1 away to Bolton and a 1 - 0 at home to Bradford City. The title was ours, the Lads finishing four points ahead of Villa. Amazingly, despite a terrible start to the season, we still managed to achieve a record number of points for the League too! It had been a grand season, and for once the Lads performed well in the Cup too, securing a place in the Final. Dreams of glory were shattered by Villa though, a 1 - 0 defeat at the final hurdle leaving us agonisingly close to a first Cup victory and an historic double. For the record, it was Buchan who finished as the Club's top scorer, hitting an incredible 32 goals in 46 games.

Sunderland's Championship winning team.

Title Challengers Battle it Out

Having just played Villa in the FA Cup final a few days earlier, a second vastly important match was played against Villa that would settle the issue of the League title. Villa, trailing in the League, had to win the match to force the pace on Sunderland, and the ground was packed well before the kick-off. There were also thousands locked out and in all 70,000 managed to cram inside to see the game. It turned out to be a cracker! The game set off at a fierce pace, and Villa were the first to show, Halse driving a hard shot off the cross bar. But it was Sunderland who took the lead, after 20 minutes. Martin, on one of his powerful runs down the left wing, fought off Lyons, and cut the ball back to Tinsley who lashed it home. Buchan then drove one inches wide and Tinsley had a shot well saved by the keeper. After the break, we once again came forward, Richardson testing their keeper and then having a penalty claim turned down after being fouled in the box. On the hour the Lads paid for failing to convert their pressure into goals, when Halse equalised. Villa almost snatched a late winner, but Butler, the Sunderland keeper, made a significant save to keep the scores level. A 1 - 1 draw proved enough, and with only two games left the title was as good as ours.

A Milton.

Almost the Double

Sunderland's First
FA Cup Final

1913 FA Cup final programme.

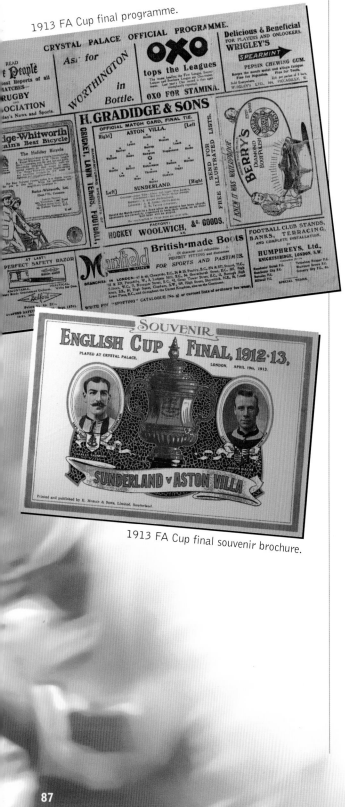

1913 FA Cup final souvenir brochure.

The League title was not the only prize Sunderland were chasing in the 1912-13 season: it was a double assault on League and Cup! A glorious Cup run began on January 11th at home to Clapham Orient, where Richardson, unable to tie down a regular place in the League, emphasised his qualities by hitting four in a six-nil win. The game was played in a blizzard and it was fortunate that the game could be played to a finish. The adverse weather conditions affected the attendance and only 12,895 hardy souls turned out. Clapham were poor, never adapting to the conditions, and their long passing game failed to trouble us.

The second round tie was at Hyde Road against Manchester City and it took place only a week after our right-wing triangle of Cuggy, Buchan and Mordue had played there for the North in a 5 - 0 win against the South. The game was generally regarded as the tie of the round and there was a packed house. The crowd was overflowing onto the pitch, the kick off had to be delayed by half an hour, and the players had to force their way through the crowd just to make it to the pitch. It was amazing the game ever got underway and after fifteen minutes there was a stoppage for twelve minutes as the corner flags were not visible. The score at half time was 0 - 0, but in the second half the Lads stepped up a gear.

Buchan and Richardson scored to give us a 2 - 0 lead after 60 minutes. At this point the City fans could not be held back and the game had to be abandoned. The official attendance had been given as 42,000, but it was clear that many more had forced their way in. Our Chairman at the time, Fred Taylor, put in an official complaint to the FA, criticising City for allowing too many fans into the ground, and suggesting that one City fan even tripped Harry Martin when he was running down the wing. He requested that the return game be played at Roker and this was agreed. City were also fined £500.

After making such criticisms, Sunderland had to be careful: admission prices were raised and the police presence was tripled. Still 28,000 turned out to see justice served. Although Mordue had a penalty saved in the first half, he made amends in the second, putting a free kick over the City wall and into the top corner. It was also from his centre that Holley headed in to make it 2 - 0 and take us through to the next round with relative ease.

In the third round we drew Swindon Town at home and on a fine February day managed to beat the Southern League side with no real problems. The pre-match entertainment for the crowd had centred on the referee who was only four feet ten inches tall, something which caused much laughter amongst the Sunderland fans. Once the game was underway we quickly took control, scoring twice in the first four minutes. Before half time it was three, Gladwin scoring with what was reported as a sixty-yard free kick! The goal, though, was not perhaps as grand as it sounds: the Swindon keeper was watching Richardson when the kick was taken and the ball bounced over him and into the empty net. Richardson added another after half time and we eventually won the game 4 - 2.

The quarter-final draw pulled out a mouth-watering home tie against the old rivals Newcastle United. 30,000 turned out to fill Roker Park and despite being the stronger side, we failed to score past a Newcastle team playing a tight defensive game.

The 0 - 0 result was a fair one and a replay was necessary. It was held only four days later, with a near 57,000 crowd turning out at St James' despite the gates being closed some thirty minutes prior to kick off, locking an estimated 15,000 outside. After sixteen minutes McTavish gave the Magpies the lead, but sixteen minutes later we were level, Holley cracking one into the back of the net. It remained 1 - 1 until three minutes to go when Buchan forced a corner, and headed in the resulting kick from Mordue. It appeared to have given us a dramatic victory, but in injury time Veitch shot desperately for goal and the ball deflected in off Gladwin as he attempted to clear. There was no more score in extra time and so there had to be a second replay! It was rumoured that Gladwin knocked a man off a tramcar that night when he asked him how much he had been paid to keep Newcastle in the Cup.

The third meeting five days later was again held at St James' with just under 50,000 attending. Holley had been due to play in his tenth international that day but was released by England. Harry Low and Charlie Thomson also withdrew from the Scotland squad, which was bad luck on Low as he didn't get another chance of an international cap for his country. It had been snowing in Sunderland on the morning of the game and many thought it would be cancelled, yet it had been clear in Newcastle and so Robert Kyle had sandwich board men walk around the town with 'match on' posters. This time there was no mistake, and after eight minutes we took an early lead through Holley when he cut out a McCracken clearance. Soon after, Martin was tripped in the box by Veitch and Mordue scored from the spot. The weather started deteriorating and there were fears that the game could be abandoned but, despite a heavy pitch, play went on and Mordue rounded matters off with a third. The semi-finals beckoned.

The opposition in the penultimate round were a Burnley side on their way to promotion from the Second Division. It was as good a chance as we had ever had of reaching the FA Cup final! In front of 42,000 at Brammall Lane, Burnley forced the issue in wet conditions and, despite us being given the 'lucky dressing room', we played poorly on the day and were fortunate to escape with a 0 - 0 draw. The replay was at St Andrew's only four days later and was to be a classic. In front of 30,000, we took the lead after just six minutes, Buchan heading in to send the Sunderland fans into delirium. It was to be short lived joy though, as soon after Boyle tucked away a penalty for the underdogs, Low adjudged to have handled. Worse was to come. Not long before half time Burnley took the lead through a fine solo goal from Freeman. A stiff half time talk from Bob Kyle and Billy Williams must have done the trick, as we returned a totally different side. Buchan was brought down after one of his mazy runs through the defence, and as usual Mordue finished off the job, cracking in the penalty to level the scores again. Sunderland finally took control of the game, and with only twelve minutes to go, Holley scored a brilliant goal after running through the defence. There was to be no slip up in the remainder of the tie: after twenty-nine years of underachievement in the competition we were in our first FA Cup final! The bad news, though, was that the opposition was to be provided by our cup bogey side, Aston Villa.

Charlie Gladwin.

Henry Martin.

Preparations for the Final did not go well with Holley picking up a bad injury to his ankle. It was decided that young Walter Tinsley should play instead of Holley but the night before the game he had a nightmare and a subsequent attack of nerves: he refused to play. Holley was ordered to play instead. However, he was clearly not fit and was unhappy about being forced into action.

Any Sunderland players who could not empathise with Tinsley's nerves before the game must have done once they ran out onto the pitch at Crystal Palace: a world record crowd of 120,081 - many of whom could not see anything - were roaring in anticipation! Papers at the time even recorded the attendance as being a few thousand higher. The invasion of London knew no bounds and Mr Daniels, the Traffic Manager at King's Cross Station, indicated that all passenger records had been broken.

The team line-ups were as follows:

SUNDERLAND: Butler (goalkeeper), Gladwin and Ness (full backs), Cuggy, Thomson and Low (half backs), Buchan, Richardson, Holley, Mordue and Martin (forwards)

ASTON VILLA: Hardy (goalkeeper), Lyons and Weston (full backs), Barber, Harrop and Leach (half backs), Wallace, Halse, Hampton, Stephenson and Bache (forwards).

The crowd generated an atmosphere that even made our Captain, Charlie Thomson, 'excitable'. Thomson was the centre of one of the main talking points of the game after a thrilling duel with the Villa forward Hampton. Hampton had scored for England against Thomson's Scotland by charging the keeper over the line. Charlie was determined this was not going to happen during the Cup Final, so early on he laid Hampton out to let him know who was boss! Hampton was later to retaliate by kicking Thomson when he was on the ground, but amazingly neither were sent off, although they were both suspended for the opening month of the next season!

Aston Villa had the sun and wind at their backs and made all the early running with their captain, Bache, instrumental in their meaningful moves. Disaster struck towards the end of the first half when Stephenson was fouled and the referee had no hesitation in awarding a penalty kick. Fortunately for Sunderland, Wallace put his spot kick wide of the upright. Bache then dribbled virtually the full length of the field but none of his team mates kept up with him and his excellent run was smothered.

At the other end Martin dribbled in similar fashion and looked certain to score, but he was denied by the bravery of the Villa keeper, Hardy. It was to prove costly for Hardy though, unable to get up for some five minutes or so due to an injury. Harrop took over between the sticks as Hardy received treatment and for ten minutes Villa were down to ten men. Sunderland piled on the pressure as they tried to make the advantage count but were unable to find a way past the Villa defence.

The teams went in goalless at half-time and as the final whistle approached, the score remained 0 - 0. Twelve minutes from time, however, Wallace forced a corner. The ball was floated into the area and Barber rushed into the box to head past Butler. It was a goal that came as no surprise to Buchan.

The Villa forward Clem Stephenson had told him early in the game that Sunderland would lose: he'd dreamt the night before that Barber would score the only goal of the game and that it would be a header, and so it was to be.

Harry Martin, perhaps the only Sunderland player to really perform well that day, went close at the end, hitting the inside of a post. But, it was not to be. It had in truth been a poor performance by the Lads, Buchan did not play with his usual prowess, and his strike partner Richardson also had a poor game. Holley was obviously injured and should never have been on the pitch, and it is a great shame that on this performance, in perhaps the biggest game of his life, he was described as a 'non entity', because he was a truly great player. Ironically, young Tinsley appeared for the Lads in the League against Villa only a few weeks later where he was man of the match and scored a crucial goal. Had he not felt so nervous before the Cup Final, had Holley been fit, or Buchan fired on all cylinders, then 1912-13 could have been the season Sunderland clinched a glorious double.

Scenes from the 1913 Cup final.

1913-1914
Anti-Climax

"As a whole, the season must go down as something of a disappointment. The free-scoring team that finished just two goals short of a glorious double in 1913, ended 1914 with mediocre performances and a League position to match."

Holley Goals!

George Holley arrived at the Club as a nineteen-year-old in 1904, signing from Seaham White Star. A local lad, he was to gain International honours at Sunderland, winning ten caps before the outbreak of war, and taking part in a tour of South Africa with the national side. His position was inside left and he was probably the most brilliant man in his position in England at the time and a great goal-scorer too, finishing as the League's top scorer in the 1911-12 season. He made a total of 315 appearances for the Lads scoring 154 goals, the fourth highest of all time. After retiring as a player, he later returned to the Club as a coach.

The close season saw the first major reconstruction project at Roker Park with the Roker End being completed. The design was a massive concrete structure holding 17,000 spectators. It wouldn't, however, be filled as often as hoped in its first year as 1913-14 was, on the whole, a disappointing season.

Our defence of the League title got off to a poor start. After a 2 - 2 draw away to Preston on the opening day, we suffered a home defeat by Newcastle 2 - 1. Holley gave us an early lead in the derby match but the game was thrown away with a missed penalty and the Mags came back for victory. This was followed up by a 3 - 1 defeat at Manchester United, and the fans wondered where all that magnificent form of the previous season had gone. It soon returned as we embarked on another fantastic run up until Christmas. Liverpool, a favourite team to play at the time, were brushed aside 3 - 1 away, before a 2 - 0 success over the old enemy Aston Villa, and a classic 4 - 3 win over Middlesbrough. Defeat at home to Sheffield United was only a minor blip, and a couple of emphatic away victories were recorded in November. The first was at Tottenham, where we ran out 4 - 1 victors, Best scoring a penalty, Cringan from a free kick, and Richardson joining in with a couple. In the second, we went one better, running out 5 - 1 winners at Everton. Buchan was on the score sheet this time with two, and Best with a hat trick.

Despite yet another defeat by Sheffield Wednesday, the Lads showed fighting spirit in the next game to get another run going. Bolton, visiting Wearside, were two goals to the good after only 21 minutes and it looked curtains for Sunderland, but a brilliant fight back meant the game ended 3 - 2 to us. Oldham and Burnley were both accounted for over the Christmas period, but the last game of the year was a 2 - 1 defeat away to Newcastle. This was our third game in three days, the first on Christmas Day and was to signal a change in our fortunes for the New Year.

Although a 3 - 1 win on New Year's Day seemed to set things off nicely, a 2 - 1 home defeat only two days later by Liverpool and a 5 - 0 whipping at Aston Villa firmly underlined that this was not to be another Championship season. Defeats began to come with increasing regularity, including eight in the last thirteen games. The result was a relatively poor final League placing of seventh. Amazingly though, only two more wins would have seen us into second place, and but for a weak finish to the campaign, another Championship was a possibility - albeit an outside one.

After getting a taste for the competition in the previous season, the F.A Cup was once again to bring some joy for the Lads. We easily beat Chatham in the first round, running out 9 - 0 winners! Richardson hit four goals in the tie and Best weighed in with two, while Mordue, Buchan and Thomson all got one. The second round proved not so easy. A regulation home victory was expected against Plymouth, but the visitors took an early lead through their English Amateur International, Raymond. It took a penalty kick from Mordue to bring us back on level terms, and a shot from Conner deflected past the despairing Argyle keeper to see us through. Preston were next out of the hat as we were once again awarded a home tie. The 34,000 crowd saw a dull game with Preston defending in numbers. It made no difference to the result though, as Buchan and Connor goals secured a place in the draw for the quarter-finals. On the 7th of March, Burnley arrived on Wearside for the fourth round of the F.A Cup.

In what was described as a footballing classic, the game swung from end to end with some great play. Quite how it ended goalless is a mystery as both sides had numerous opportunities to score. The replay at Turf Moor four days later was to end our Cup hopes once again though, as we succumbed in our first tie away from Roker. An early Freeman goal set Burnley on their way, and despite a late Connor goal, Burnley had the game already won with a second.

Nice as the Cup run was, as a whole the season must go down as something of a disappointment. The free scoring team that finished just two goals short of a glorious double in 1913, ended in 1914 with mediocre performances and a League position to match. What, we might ask, had gone wrong?

Sunderland v Budapest on tour in Budapest in the summer of 1913.

Teesside Tamed

On a scorching day 25,000 fans turned out for the local derby game at Middlesbrough and were supremely entertained. The crowd was in a fine mood cheering every little incident, and there was plenty to cheer, Charlie Gladwin saving the day early on with a couple of fine last ditch tackles. But, just when it looked like we were getting on top with Cuggy cracking one against the bar, Boro took the lead when Elliott fooled Butler with a clever shot. Sunderland tried hard to get back into the game with both Richardson and Buchan coming close before half time.

Buchan though was not to be stopped and early in the second half he toyed with the ball at his feet, beat two men and hit an unstoppable shot into the back of the net. By now, Boro were down to ten men as Jackson had been sent off. Holley soon made it two, after Best had done all the hard work for him and, without further ado, Holley added a third, compensating for a missed sitter that Martin had set up for him. Boro got one back with Elliott scoring from a penalty. Before the end Richardson added a fourth for the Lads. He also claimed a fifth, the ball striking the underneath of the bar and down onto the line but the referee disallowed it. Elliot hit another for Boro in the dying stages of the game, but it was to be no more than a consolation: Sunderland ran out worthy winners in a 4 - 3 thriller.

J Richardson.

1914-1915 War

"There were fewer goals this season than there had been for a long while"

Harry Martin.

Martin on the wing

Harry Martin arrived in 1911 as a young outside left with a big reputation. His job was to fill the legendary Arthur Bridgett's left wing role and this he did with distinct credit. Harry's great forte was speed and strength that took him past defenders and once he had beaten his man his crossing was supreme. Needless to say he was the creator of many of our goals during his stay. Martin helped us to the League title in his first full season, and was one of the only players to come out of the Cup Final with any real credit, almost saving the day when his late shot cracked off the inside of the post and came out. When he was on his best form there can hardly have been a better winger in the country. Martin stayed at Sunderland until 1922, making 231 appearances, scoring 24 goals. He also managed to gain one England Cap while at Sunderland before eventually moving on to Nottingham Forest.

The 1914-15 season was to be marred by the outbreak of the First World War and, as Charlie Buchan stated, there was little interest in the football with the war going on. Indeed, most of the Sunderland players found it difficult to concentrate on their game once their fellow countrymen began to march into conflict. In contrast to the 1945 season when the Second World War broke out, the 1914-15 season was played to a close.

In footballing terms, the campaign got off to a great start as we won our first two League games, the first at home to Sheffield United, 3 - 2, and the second a fine win over Aston Villa (3 - 1 away), with our new signing, Philip, scoring twice. By now Butler had vacated the goalkeeper's position, which was taken over by Scott. In truth Scott was not quite ready for the job, and we started to leak goals again. Seven defeats in ten games, including a 7 - 1 thrashing at Everton, exposed our inadequacies. Five of the goals in the Everton match were scored in the opening half an hour, although we were handicapped for some of that time with Buchan off the field needing treatment. Our consolation goal was actually scored by Buchan when we were again down to 10 men, this time with Philip off the field for treatment.

As if to emphasise that this was not a true reflection of the team, we found some form and won eight of the next eleven matches, including some emphatic victories. Tottenham were thrashed 6 - 0 away, a victory followed up with a 5 - 2 beating of Newcastle at St James' on Christmas Day. However, the Magpies got their revenge on Boxing Day with a 4 - 2 win at Roker. In the other local derby, Middlesbrough were beaten 3 - 2 at Ayresome Park, before we dished out a 4 - 0 drubbing to Aston Villa.

The goals were flying in by now, and a 3 - 3 draw against Bradford Park Avenue was followed by a 5 - 4 victory at Oldham Athletic and a 5 - 1 victory over Blackburn Rovers at Roker. We suffered a couple of defeats at Notts County and Manchester City before normal service was resumed, upon which Sheffield Wednesday were beaten 3 - 1, Middlesbrough 4 - 1, and West Brom 2 - 1.

After this, though, the season started to trail off, the Lads losing 3 - 0 at both Chelsea and Everton. The League campaign was rounded off, however, with another goal feast, and a 5 - 0 drubbing of Tottenham. This result merely underlined the weaknesses of FA Cup campaign: in the two League games against Spurs we had put eleven past them without reply and yet when we drew them in the first round of the Cup we lost 2 - 1 away.

The Lads once more finished the season in a mid-table position - eighth - a creditable enough finish, but a somewhat unexciting one. They had finished someway off the pace, plagued by an inconsistency that saw them struggle to score for weeks and then smash in five or six for a couple of games. Indeed, there were fewer goals this season than there had been for a long while, our goal average being the lowest from a Sunderland team since the relegation near miss of 1907-08.

Football, however, was to take a back seat for the next half-a-decade. The black clouds of war were gathering over Europe with their shadow lying heavy over the latter half of the football season. Many of the young men who had turned out in their droves to watch football in recent years went off to fight in the trenches and football suddenly seemed an altogether flippant and meaningless activity. Rightly, there would be no more League or FA Cup football until after the war.

British soldiers playing football in Salonika on Christmas day 1915.

Sunderland Score Six

Approaching Christmas, 1914, Sunderland went on a goal spree with a 6 - 0 hammering of Spurs. Thanks to a massive thunder storm, the game took place on a sodden pitch, which made defending tricky and our wingers took full advantage. After 17 minutes, Martin and Phillip cleverly interchanged down the wing, before Phillip converted Martin's cross for the first goal. Soon after, Martin left the Spurs keeper helpless, whacking the ball into the back of the net for the second. Spurs were not disheartened and continued to go forward but Scott gave a great performance in goal and the score remained 2 - 0 at half-time. Soon after the restart, Spurs appealed for a penalty, but to no avail. Sunderland were now beginning to dominate the wings, the Tottenham defence unable to cope with our speed and trickery. Mordue dazzled, but it was Best who added the third 25 minutes after half-time from close in. Best did it again after beating both Collins and Clay to put in the fourth, before Buchan hit two, waltzing the fifth past Joyce and hitting the sixth with a clever shot. Spurs had been completely outclassed!

Albert Milton.

94

1915-1919
The War Years

"As life regained some form of normality, the sporting challenges of a Football League campaign beckoned"

Bobby Best scored a hat-trick against Newcastle in the last derby before the First World War.

War Controversy

The decision to continue with football once the War had started was not without its critics. At first, most could see no reason why football should be halted, but as the War became more serious, and casualties began to mount, calls for football to be halted became louder.

To pacify critics, the FA called on unmarried players to volunteer for the armed forces and recruitment drives were staged at matches. This produced some 100,000 recruits in four months, and just 600 unmarried footballers did not volunteer to fight.

However, as the season - and War - continued, interest in football declined, attendances almost halving. At the end of the season, the FA took the inevitable decision to postpone football until after the War in order to allow everyone to focus on a more serious battle than that found on the pitch.

Following the suspension of League football at the end of the 1914-15 season, most of the Sunderland squad entered the Army to serve their country. Notably, Charlie Buchan and Bob Young both went on to win the Military Medal. Sadly there were some casualties amongst the team with up and coming young centre forward Sammy Hartnell tragically killed in action on the 8th of August 1918, and Jimmy Seed being badly gassed. Seed's football registration would eventually be cancelled on medical advice, but thankfully he later made a recovery and went on to have a great career with Spurs and Sheffield Wednesday. In the main, though, the Sunderland squad returned from the War largely intact, and due to the fact that it had been a very young squad of players, most of them continued to play.

Our first game after the War was a friendly match against Newcastle United which we won 4 - 0. We also played four games over the Christmas period, home and away against both the Magpies and Middlesbrough. However, football didn't really begin again until, in recognition of the Armistice of 11th November 1918, the Victory League was formed. This involved friendly fixtures in a league format. The Victory League included us, South Shields, Middlesbrough, Durham City, Newcastle, Darlington, Hartlepool and Scotswood and ran from January 1919 until April 1919. As many players were either still injured, in the processes of being released as war prisoners or being decommissioned, guest players were allowed to play in the league. The first game included only Holley and Best who were regular first teamers before the War. Gradually though Cuggy, Low, Mordue, Buchan, Crossley, Martin, and Hobson returned. The rest of the team had been made up of guest players, our main guests being Baverstock of Wolves, Little from Bradford, Kasher from Crook, Hugall from Crystal Palace and Rodgerson from South Shields.

Our first game was at the University Ground against Durham City on 11th January and ended in defeat. One week later and a home game against Middlesbrough saw one or two old favourites make it back. Players such as Best, Hobson and Mordue featured in a 2 - 0 win. This was followed by an exciting derby game with Newcastle United, the Magpies ending up 4 - 3 winners. We then went to Roker and played out a 3 - 3 draw with South Shields, Cuggy and Buchan included in the team. Thornley opened the scoring for the visitors after 20 minutes, before Travers equalised nine minutes from the interval. It was end to end stuff and Thornley once more netted for Shields, before a mazy solo run from Buchan tied things up once more. With the team now beginning to resemble something of full strength, we began to win games on a regular basis. We beat Darlington away 1 - 0, Hartlepool 5 - 2 at Roker, and Newcastle 2 - 1 at Roker. Buchan, just as before the War, could not stop scoring. Scotswood were accounted for 6 - 1, before the league was wrapped up with a 2 - 0 home win over Durham City. Although players were obviously not fit, it got football going in the region again and the attendances were not bad either with around 20,000 being the average gate.

The Lads also took a trip back in time and entered the Durham Senior Cup. South Shields visited Roker Park first, but left empty handed, drubbed 4 - 1 in front of an 18,000 crowd. The team progressed easily through the stages, demolishing Felling Colliery 8 - 1 in the semi-finals with two a piece for Best, Holley, Travers and Buchan.

The final was no more of a contest, with Crook being thrashed 8 - 0 at Darlington's Feethams ground; the Lads lifted the trophy for the first time since 1890. The Victory League and Durham Senior Cup had been a good warm up, but as life regained some form of normality, the real sporting challenges of a Football League campaign beckoned.

The War had come at a moment when British life was seen as almost idyllic. A steady peace and assured economic growth - the 'golden age' - had been shattered by the horrific War. Lives had been wrecked, families torn apart, careers ruined and people's confidence in the future and in fellow men rocked. Some people would never recover from the shock of the War, but most slowly began to return to their 'normal' routines.

Football had its role to play, and the recommencement of fixtures was a sign that life was being restored to its former state. But, football clubs had been affected too. Sunderland had been in the middle of a footballing peak when the War broke out, but four years on, it was never going to be a case of the players picking up where they had left off.

Joe Kasher

Joe Kasher signed for Sunderland in 1919, just after the War had finished. Like most people in the country, his life was interrupted by the War. Born in 1894, the chances are he would have signed for Sunderland a few years earlier, but at 15 he had joined the Naval Division. It was a decision that took on a whole new perspective when the First World War started, for it meant fighting in the trenches, a dangerous task that brought an early end to hundreds of thousands of young lives. During the War, Kasher almost paid the ultimate price when his officer led them into a German trap. Kasher was taken prisoner, and ended the War alive, but his officer was shot in the head.

After the War, Kasher returned to his native North East and started work in the pit. In the meantime, he also played football for Crook, his home town, where - despite suffering an 8 - 0 hammering at the hands of Sunderland - he caught the eye of the Sunderland selectors. Aged 25, he started his career as a footballer.

The late start did not unnerve Kasher, and soon he was playing alongside men such as Charlie Buchan whom he had regarded as his heroes. His first season at the Club saw the Lads challenge for glory, though ultimately miss out, and he spent three and a bit enjoyable seasons at Sunderland before moving on to Stoke City early in the 1922-23 season.

In all, Kasher made 90 League and Cup appearances for the Lads. His favoured position was centre-half, where he was always good value for the Lads. But, after three seasons good service, Bob Kyle's huge spending spree late in the 1921-22 season effectively marked the end of Joe's career. With competition for places hotting up, and big money internationals lining up to play for Sunderland, Kasher moved on.

A hero on and off the pitch, Kasher's varied career has lessons for us all. Always a hard worker, dependable and down to earth, he was a man prepared to follow his dreams and do his bit. His late start in professional football never held him back, and he more than held his own in football's top flight after all those years as an amateur.

Joe Kasher.

1919-1920
Back in Business

"Fifth place was a credit to the team in what was a difficult year to play football."

Francis Cuggy.

Jack, and Master, of all Trades

Francis Cuggy is probably best described as an early version of a utility player. He was extremely versatile, and while a player at Willingham Athletic once played in six positions in one game! This versatility led to Sunderland signing him in November 1909. Cuggy acquitted himself so well in the reserve side that he was promoted rapidly to the first team. His most common position for Sunderland was at right half and that was where he played in the FA Cup final and helped us win the League in 1912-13. A full international while playing for Sunderland, he gained two England caps, both against Ireland. He stayed until after the War making a total of 190 appearances before moving back to his native Tyneside to join Wallsend in 1921.

As little football had been played in the last few years, the season kicked off on 20th August with a practice match between the stripes and the whites. The 6 - 3 score was immaterial but it gave the manager an opportunity to assess his strongest team. The new season proper kicked off ten days later with the first two Saturdays seeing home and away games against Aston Villa. A somewhat strange change to the fixture list saw us play most opponents in back to back fixtures. Aston Villa were subsequently defeated twice in the first week, 2 - 1 at home and 3 - 0 away, Buchan and Parker scoring in both games. Buchan was to enjoy himself in front of goal in the early stages of the season, starting where he left off: as the most deadly striker in the division. He scored ten times in the first eight games! Results were, however, not always going to plan, and we suffered defeats away to Arsenal and at home to Everton in the opening month.

From November through to Christmas was a fruitful time for the Club. We won seven out of nine matches and people started to talk about a repeat of the 1913 Championship win. The spell included consecutive victories over Newcastle, always a pleasure for the Roker fans! We won the first of the derbies at Roker, 2 - 0, thanks to a couple of Buchan goals in front of an impressive crowd of 47,148 and the return match a week later, in front of an even bigger crowd of 61,761, was a 3 - 2 victory. We then completed a winning sequence of five games with a 2 - 1 win over Manchester City and a double over Sheffield Wednesday with 2 - 1 and 2 - 0 scorelines.

It was difficult, however, to achieve real stability in the side. Predictably, there were many changes after the War and the team line up was in constant flux. In addition, Kyle was once more trying to build up a squad capable of challenging for honours, meaning there was a certain amount of experimentation taking place. Perhaps as a consequence, crucial games were lost, defeats against Liverpool, West Brom, Manchester City and Derby County costing us dear over the festive period.

As 1920 opened, Sunderland kicked off their first post-war FA Cup campaign, and did so in style, whipping Hull City 6 - 2. Buchan bagged four goals in the game and Travers weighed in with the other two. The second round saw the Lads gain a credible 1 - 1 draw away to Burnley, before the boys from Lancashire were seen off with a 2 - 0 victory at Roker Park, where Buchan and Poole got the goals in front of 50,000 fans. Unfortunately, the third round brought a tie against perpetual Cup bogeymen, Aston Villa. As usual they brought our Cup run to an end with a 1 - 0 scoreline.

Back in the League, results continued to be erratic, with three home games in a row all being won, Derby (2 - 1), Oldham Athletic (3 - 0) and Manchester United (3 - 0) being sent home packing. This mini run was followed by defeats in three out four away games - the only success being a 2 - 0 derby win at Middlesbrough. This was to be the story of the season as a whole. We lost only two of our twenty-one home games, yet suffered fourteen defeats on our travels. We finished in fifth place, which was a credit to the team in what was a difficult year to play football after so many years out of the game.

Only five of the players who played in the season's last fixture, a 1 - 0 home defeat against Liverpool, played in the opening game of the season, a fact that tells its own story.

The end of the season saw one of the Club's longest serving players, former England International Jackie Mordue, transferred to Middlesbrough. He had been a brilliant servant to Sunderland AFC and left with everyone's best wishes.

1919-20 Sunderland team.

What a Week!

In November 1919, Sunderland played back-to-back games against Newcastle. Having already defeated them at Roker 2 - 0 in front of 47,000, the teams faced each other again only a week later at St James' Park. There had been heavy frost overnight and there was a thin layer of snow on the pitch. It didn't affect the attendance though, and all ground records were broken. Well before the scheduled kick off the ground was full with over 60,000 packed in. It was decided to make an early start and the game kicked off just after 2pm. Play was treacherous in the opening stages with the players sliding all over the place and playing with no degree of accuracy. They soon adjusted though and it was end-to-end stuff. However, despite doing more of the attacking play, at half time we went in 2 - 0 down! Travers though was to change the game in the second half. Often described as a crude forward, his aim being to get towards goal by the quickest and shortest route, it was undoubtedly his type of game. Yet he levelled the score with two goals that came from clever shots and were due to no mean amount of skill. With the game poised at 2 - 2, Mordue showed coolness and precision and scored to complete a tremendous recovery and a second derby win in a week!

Barney Travers.

A Scholar, a Gentleman, a Goalscorer and a Hero

Charlie Buchan.

Charlie Buchan stands as one of the all time great Sunderland players, and at his peak was arguably the finest forward of his day. Born in Plumstead, London, he started his career with the Northfield Club before moving to Leyton Orient. Manager Bob Kyle signed him for Sunderland on 21st March 1911 for £1,200. It was not always easy for him and he had to be coaxed along by the Sunderland coaching staff. When he joined the Club, Charlie stood 5ft 9in, weighed 10st 5lbs and found it tough. By the end of November he stood just over 6 ft and had also put on some weight and defenders were no longer able to push him around. His physical development though had made him so weak that he could hardly stand up. After each training session he was forced to lie down for hours. His form suffered, the crowd barracked him and he pleaded to be dropped. In mid-November it all got too much and he declared that he would never play for Sunderland again. Bob Kyle though was a wily old fox and refused to accept his position. Both Kyle and trainer Billy Williams took Buchan under their wing and developed his talent. Buchan later said he could never repay Williams for his patience and advice.

An all round sportsman, he was also a fine cricketer and golfer. He played cricket for Kent and East Bolden and in 1919 headed the Durham Senior Cricket league batting table with an average of 68.3. Football was his main game though and his favoured position on the field was inside right. Many said that his playing style reminded them very much of the Corinthian days, praise indeed. He gained representative honours with England and twice played against the Scottish League. Scotland did try to grab him for International honours as both his parents were from Aberdeen, but he declined as having been born in Woolwich he wanted to play for England. His England debut came in Belfast on 15th February 1913 and alongside him were his Sunderland colleagues Jackie Mordue and Frank Cuggy... the Sunderland Triangle. 'Perpetual motion' was its other name. Typically, Buchan scored after 10 minutes. He was just 21 when he played in the 1913 FA Cup final and he often tested the superlatives of the sports writers with comments such as; "he was like a man with four feet", "he dribbled like a Japanese juggler", "he was like the best of the Corinthian dribblers" and "he was full of deft and subtle touches with either foot." The only major surprise was that he did not win more caps for his country but the outbreak of the War had taken his best years away from him.

During the War Buchan served with distinction in the Grenadier Guards and he played football for the Guards Depot before turning out for Chelsea, although this did not last for long. On being given Lance Corporal status he ended up fighting at the Somme based at Marie Court. He also had spells playing for both Birmingham City and Huddersfield Town. When the War ended he of course returned to Sunderland, who had retained his professional registration. Prior to League football starting again he had taken up a teaching position at Cowan Terrace School. He was a clever man, and team mate Joe Kasher said that big Charlie had "more brains in his little finger than the rest of us put together". The rest of the team though became unhappy at his preferential treatment; his teaching duties meant he was allowed to train alone, and he was forced to give them up once the League started again.

By the end of a Sunderland career that had lasted some 15 years (with 4 years lost to the War), he was the only red and white at the time to have scored two hundred League goals, having played some three hundred and eighty-league games before his shock departure to Arsenal.

Charlie was thirty-three at the time, and settled in the Wearside area, having just opened a sports shop in Blandford Street and married a Sunderland girl. He was apparently surprised when the Arsenal manager Herbert Chapman came in for him and was hurt when he was told that he had Sunderland's permission to speak to him. Charlie found it hard to settle in London and, after a 7 - 0 thrashing by Newcastle, asked if he could return to Sunderland. His request was refused and he was asked to develop his tactics of playing a defensive centre half and a roving, scheming inside forward in an attempt to make him stay - such was his value. It was to work too as he went on to score twenty-one goals in his first season for them. He eventually settled well in London and became a leading sports journalist. Many people can still remember the Football Magazine that carried his name, Charlie Buchan's Football Monthly.

Life After Sunderland

When Charlie Buchan left Sunderland, assumed to be past his best, the striker went on to further glory with Arsenal. Indeed, in his first season at the club - 1925-26 - the Gunners' fortunes radically improved, his huge goal haul helping them finish in second place after only managing lowly 19th and 20th place finishes in the previous two seasons. The following year, he helped guide them to the Cup final, though a poor team performance on the day saw the Cup leave England for the only time, Cardiff running out 1 - 0 winners. Charlie then gave it one more year before deciding to call it a day at the end of the 1927-28 season, and his final game came in a classic match against newly crowned Champions Everton, where Dixie Dean needed to score a hat trick to reach the astonishing figure of 60 League goals in the season. This he did indeed do, to great acclaim. However, Dean later claimed that all but one of the players on the field that day ran to congratulate him. Buchan, he suggested, was miffed at being overshadowed, so ignored Dean completely. Establishing the truth of this claim is difficult, for others always point to Buchan as the perfect gent. Perhaps Buchan was merely absorbed in his final moments as a professional footballer. After eleven seasons as a player, and with four of his best years stolen by a savage war, age had finally caught up on him. Who could blame him for feeling a little sad to be leaving?

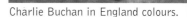
Charlie Buchan in England colours.

1920-21	12th in League.
1921-22	Finish 12th in League; break transfer record.
1922-23	2nd in League.
1923-24	3rd in League.
1924-25	7th in League.
1925-26	3rd in League; break transfer record.
1926-27	3rd in League.
1927-28	15th in League.
1928-29	Johnny Cochrane becomes manager. 4th in League.
1929-30	9th in League.

The 1920s provided another exciting instalment in Sunderland AFC's history. It was a decade in which we would spend big money in trying to bring trophies back to Roker Park, but one that would ultimately add nothing to the trophy cabinet. Sunderland would twice break the world record transfer fee, but the expensive squads assembled by Robert Kyle lacked the stamina necessary for a successful Championship challenge. On several occasions the title would be there for the taking, but the Lads never quite managed to take advantage of good positions, often blowing it in crucial games.

It was also a decade of goals and goalscorers. Even if they didn't win anything, the Sunderland teams of the 1920s managed to entertain. Charlie Buchan and Dave Halliday, in particular, emerged as goalscoring legends, and a future hero - Bobby Gurney - broke into the team as the decade came to a close. In the 1925-26 and 1926-27 seasons, the Lads almost managed one hundred goals in forty-two games.

As the 1930s approached, the decade also saw important changes behind the scenes. After almost a quarter-of-a-century in charge, Kyle left the Club at the end of the 1927-28 season, being replaced as Manager by Johnny Cochrane. The following season, trainer Billy Williams left too, having occupied the job since 1897.

Off the pitch, Roker Park saw a number of developments, including a new grandstand, and season tickets were introduced. In all, despite the failure to bring home the silverware, it must have been a great decade in which to have been a Sunderland fan.

THE

Flappers

1 9 2 0 · 1 9 3 0

1920-1921
All Quiet on the Football Front

"the best word to describe the campaign was quiet."

Billy Moore.

Out Gunned

The Lads began February having just beaten Liverpool and Arsenal - both 2 - 1 victories - and welcomed Arsenal to Roker looking to extend this spell of good form. The weekend proved to be a fairly dull one football wise, with most games around the country being drawn or won by small margins. However, the 30,000 crammed into Roker saw one of the few spectacular results of the day, the Sunderland fans being treated to a real goal feast.

In a close fought match, the Lads were just on top for most of the game, and with quarter-of-an-hour left, the game was evenly balanced, at 2 - 1 to us. In the closing stages though, the Lads exploded into life, scoring three more goals! Buchan was very much at the heart of our play, scoring two goals for the third game in succession. Moore grabbed a brace too and young Marshall also got his name onto the scoresheet.

The first full season of the 1920s kicked on 28th August with a game played at Bramall Lane in tropical conditions; a heatwave had descended on England and some 30,000 basked in the sunshine as the Lads held Sheffield United to a 1 - 1 draw. Johnson had opened the scoring for the Blades on 32 minutes but we came roaring back with a Buchan 'lob'.

September was a pretty good month for us, with only one defeat in six matches. Once more a lot of the fixtures were played on a 'back to back' basis - an arrangement that stuck for the first five seasons after the War - and we soon claimed our first double, Huddersfield being beaten twice. However, October witnessed a footballing disaster as far as Wearside was concerned: two consecutive defeats at the hands of the Magpies. The first, at St James' Park, was an absolute thrashing, ending 1 - 6. In truth the game hinged on a penalty miss by Sunderland after 30 minutes, when Hobson crashed the ball straight at Lawrence. In contrast, Newcastle scored a penalty and from then on never looked back. At half time it was 2 - 0. In the return match at Roker, the Tynesiders once more had too much for Sunderland and we succumbed 0 - 2.

With the Lads' weaknesses having been exposed in such an embarrassing way, the decision was made to bring in some new faces, Jack Mitton and Charlie Parker joining the Club. These were big signings, Parker commanding a new record transfer fee for Sunderland of £3,500. Despite this, November started in much the same fashion, with two consecutive defeats against Middlesbrough! The rest of the month wasn't much better either, the Lads picking up just one point from two games against Everton. We were now perilously close to the bottom of the table.

December, though, finally saw us rack up some points. Though the month started badly, with a 4 - 1 defeat at West Brom, when the Baggies came back to our place the Lads made amends, Buchan hitting a brace in a 3 - 0 victory. A week later, an in-form Manchester City arrived at Roker, looking to extend a nine week unbeaten run. A close encounter ensued, but the Lads edged it 1 - 0, the winner being scored by Fred Cooke after 40 minutes.

The run did not last though. On Christmas Day Sunderland visited Bolton, and though the Lads played well in the first half - being somewhat unlucky to go in 1 - 0 down at the break - in the second half the floodgates opened. A 20-minute hat trick from Smith had us reeling, and the game eventually ended 6 - 2 to the home side. In the return game two days later, the Lads took no chances; a solid defensive performance produced a more satisfying result - albeit a scoreless draw.

In 1921 the festive misery continued on New Year's Day. A trip to Hyde Road for a match with Manchester City produced a 3 - 1 defeat, and the first round of the FA Cup saw another quick exit at the hands of inferior opposition. The home tie against Cardiff City offered a good chance of a passage to the second round, but a lone goal from Dempster gave victory to the visitors. The overwhelming majority of the 41,923 crowd went home disappointed, as did new coach George Holley.

But, the Cardiff game marked the end of a bad run, and after holding Liverpool to a 0 - 0 draw at their place, the Lads started a mini-revival in the return game at Roker, where another brace from Buchan secured a 2 - 1 win. The following week, Buchan hit two again as Arsenal were beaten 2 - 1 and things began to look up.

February commenced with a goal feast, the return game with the Gunners seeing the Lads notch up a spectacular 5 - 1 win. Sunderland were 2 - 0 up inside the first 31 minutes, but most of the goals came in a devastating spell towards the end of the game. A week later, the Lads were at it again! A trip to Villa Park to meet the FA Cup holders looked a difficult proposition, but Villa were put to the sword by a rampant Sunderland. Buchan was outstanding, scoring two gems and there was a notable performance from 17 year old Marshall, who bagged one of the others. Once again, the game ended 5 - 1 to Sunderland!

With fourteen goals in four games, we seemed to have hit top form once more. But, it didn't last. The Lads failed to find the net in their next two games (including the return against Villa), and lost four on the trot. Inconsistency was rearing its ugly head once more, and a merry-go-round of results - draws here, wins there, and a few defeats for good measure - ensued for the remainder of the season. While the Lads managed to prevent Cup Finalists Tottenham Hotspur from scoring at White Hart Lane - the only team to do so that season - and managed to beat League Champions Burnley 1 - 0 at Roker, too many games were being lost or drawn.

A somewhat unspectacular season drew to an end with Sunderland in 12th position. Perhaps the best word to describe the campaign was quiet . The Lads finished in a comfortable mid-table position, well away from either the Championship or relegation.

Buchan Leads the Way

A week after thrashing Arsenal 5 - 1, the Lads travelled to FA Cup holders Aston Villa. Once again it was something of a quiet weekend around the country goal wise, with the exception of Sunderland's game. Buchan notched a brace for the fourth game in a row as the Lads cruised to another 5 - 1 victory. Marshall's impressive development continued, with two goals for him, and the fifth was an unfortunate own goal.

The Times were particularly impressed with the performance commenting that "The chief feature of the Football League competition on Saturday was the victory of Sunderland over Aston Villa by five goals to one. This was the only instance of a side scoring more than three goals, and the Cup-holders were playing at home against a team which until quite recently had done very badly. Sunderland had gained a similar victory over The Arsenal a week earlier, and they have not lost a match since New Year's Day. Their improvement has been largely brought about by the play of Buchan at centre-forward, and for the third time in succession this player scored two goals."

Robert Marshall.

1921-1922
Break the Bank

"as spring approached the team were on the ropes and prompt action was required."

Jim Stephenson.

Another Quick Cup Exit

Sunderland were drawn to play Liverpool in their opening FA Cup match. The Merseysiders were having a good season in the League, but the Lads were hoping to make the most of home advantage. The tie was a close fought encounter, and ended 1 - 1, Stannard getting our goal.

The replay took place four days later, and another tight game was expected. However, the Lads had a nightmare and were thrashed 0 - 5! The result was something of a humiliation, though there were mitigating factors. An influenza bug had struck the squad and eleven players were either out of action or played without being fully fit. Perhaps the Cup jinx was merely manifesting itself in an original form, but whatever the reason, another first round exit was disappointingly predictable.

The 1921-22 campaign opened in fine style, with two victories in front of the Roker faithful: a 3 - 0 triumph over Liverpool, followed by a 3 - 2 success against Burnley. However, in our next two games, the Lads made return trips to play the same teams away from home and, somewhat frustratingly, two defeats followed. Perhaps the manager felt the goalkeeper was to blame, for after conceding six goals in three games, Dempster made way for Scott, the latter returning after almost a year on the sidelines. Following the change, goals-a-plenty were still conceded, but performances improved a little, Sunderland taking a draw and then a win in back to back games against Huddersfield.

Indeed, a new solidity soon became apparent, for the victory against Huddersfield marked the beginning of an excellent run. In a magnificent eight week spell, the Lads took fourteen of a possible sixteen points, notching up seven wins against just one defeat. In addition to inflicting defeat on the formidable Huddersfield, the Lads secured notable double victories against Arsenal and Blackburn, and devastated Oldham at Roker Park. This was more like the Sunderland of old, and the run took the Lads up the table to a strong second position. It was good to see the goals flying in too, Buchan alone having managed to hit eleven in our opening thirteen games.

However, the run did not last and in true Sunderland fashion the fantastic 5 - 1 thrashing of Oldham was followed by a 3 - 0 whipping for the Lads in the return match the following week. As Christmas approached, erratic form set in. The Lads' inconsistency was made more frustrating by the back to back fixtures, weak performances against a team one week often being followed by four or five goal routs that left the same opponents reeling. Clearly this was a cause for concern, but as the season wore on the inconsistency disappeared away from home: the Lads became uniformly poor outside Sunderland! Indeed, the defeat at Oldham that marked the end of our purple patch also marked the start of a black spell, the Lads managing to pick up just four points from the fifteen away games they would play during the rest of the season.

As the calendar turned to 1922, performances became steadily worse, January and February seeing the Lads pick up just three points as they crashed in six of their eight League games. The FA Cup offered a brief respite from the League campaign, albeit something of a miserable one, a close 1 - 1 draw with Liverpool at Roker Park being followed by a disastrous 5 - 0 drubbing in the replay.

As spring approached, the team were on the ropes and prompt action was required. Desperate to help rectify the situation, the Board put their hands in their pockets and forked out for a series of big transfers: England International Warney Cresswell joined for a record £5,500; Scottish International Michael Gilhooley arrived from Hull for a similar fee; and another Scottish International, Jock Paterson, arrived from Leicester. All three made their debuts in the Lads' first game of March - a 1 - 0 home win against Sheffield United - and they were soon joined by another Scottish International, Sandy Donaldson, who arrived from Bolton at the end of the month. Partly as a result of these signings performances picked up a little and the team did enough to see themselves clear of danger. Beyond this, there were even some memorable moments, new man Donaldson hitting a hat-trick in a 6 - 2 victory over his old club Bolton Wanderers.

However, away performances were still poor and by the end of the season the Lads had managed just fourteen goals away from home - our lowest tally since 1900-01 - and, largely as a result, equalled a previous worst in losing fourteen of our League fixtures away from Roker. In unremarkable fashion the 1921-22 season ended, as its predecessor did, with Sunderland finishing in twelfth position. It also ended with a loss of £15,698, the flurry of spending on players hitting the Club's finances.

Buchan and the England Team.

But, the season should be viewed as one of consolidation. In addition to the big money signings brought in towards the end of the season, 1921-22 had seen the arrival of Jimmy Stephenson, a winger signed from Aston Villa for £3,000 and Arthur 'Tricky' Hawes, who always played carrying a handkerchief in his left hand, for £1,750. To make way for this influx, the manager had decided to release a large number of players too - thirteen being set free by the end of the campaign - meaning the squad at the start of the season was very different from that at the end. So, while twelfth place was a little disappointing, it would be wrong to judge the team on the performances of a transitional season; but, with the expensive rebuilding complete, better would be expected in 1922-23.

Sunderland Break the Bank

After a poor showing for most of the season, the Board decided to sanction a massive spending spree in March of the 1921-22 season. When Warney Creswell joined from South Shields for £5,500 the fee was not only a new Club record transfer; it was also a record for a player anywhere in the world. This, though, was only the start, with Patterson and Gilbooley arriving on the same day for similar fees - the latter costing just £250 less than Creswell. With another ace, Donaldson, arriving before the end of the month, the Club's spending on transfers was well over £20,000 in the space of a few weeks.

Making comparisons with current day money is difficult, but it helps to put the figures into perspective. Creswell's fee occupied a similar status to the one Alan Shearer's does today, and with the latter having gone for £15 million it is fair to say that this March spending spree equated to somewhere in the region of £60 million! It is fairly well known that Sunderland were the 'Bank of England' Club in the 1950s, but spending big was also to be the strategy for much of the 1920s. However, big money brought with it demands for success, and in the coming seasons the pressure to produce results would be evident.

Arthur 'Tricky' Hawes.

1922-1923
Almost There

"the Lads seemed unable to go for the kill."

Jock Paterson.

Derbies Hit the Big Time

The back to back derby matches with Newcastle generated huge interest this season. A massive 50,000 crowd packed into Roker Park for the match at our place, and an even bigger 63,000 for the game at St James'. Both games were of more than local significance though, with the two clubs performing well in the League and Sunderland joint top with Liverpool going into the first tie at St James'. To add further spice to the game though, the Monday before the game at Newcastle, Sunderland ace Charlie Buchan was presented with a letter, on which was written "You will be paid £1,000 if you lose the game at Newcastle". This was a huge sum, but the maestro - honest and upright citizen that he was - immediately presented the letter to the Chief Constable of Sunderland's police force and asked him to investigate. There was no suggestion of impropriety on Newcastle's side though and the perpetrator was eventually traced..."an inmate of an asylum at Bristol."

After all this controversy and tension in the build up, the football needed to be good... it was! Unfortunately, the game at their place - a close game - ended 2 -1 to the Mags, a goal from Buchan being too little for even a point. This was deemed a fair result by match reporters, but it took us down to fourth, Boro and Burnley jumping ahead. This made the game at Roker all the more important: we needed to win in order to maintain our title challenge. Fortunately, the Lads did the business this time, goals from Paterson and Hawes helping us to two points and a 2 - 0 win. Crucially, the teams above us had all failed to win their games, Liverpool drawing and both Boro and Burnley being well beaten; we moved up to second, just one point behind the leaders.

Refreshed after the close season break, and largely free from injuries, the remoulded squad took to the pitch ready to do battle in our opening game against Nottingham Forest. But, a close run game ended in a 1 - 0 defeat. Better came a few days later in our first home game of the season when 36,000 crammed in to see us beat Liverpool 1 - 0, Paterson hitting the winner. However, the next three games did little to boost confidence, a 5 - 1 defeat in the return against Liverpool being sandwiched between a couple of draws.

Fortunately, the poor start was merely a 'blip'. Buchan soon began to get into his stride, and hit four goals in a 5 - 1 thrashing of Bolton, the start of a rich vein of form that would see him hit twelve goals in eight games. Propelled by his goal scoring exploits, Sunderland started to notch up important victories and, as importantly, became very difficult to beat.

By the start of November, we were level on points with Liverpool at the top of the League, ready for back to back games against Newcastle. Over 100,000 fans crammed in to the two games, many hoping to see Sunderland consolidate their position. However, in the first tie, at St James', the Magpies snatched the points in a 2 - 1 win, enough to send us down to fourth place, and though the Lads leapt back to second with a 2 - 0 victory at Roker the following week, it was disappointing to drop crucial points against our local rivals. Fortunately, the Lads responded well to defeat, immediately putting together another unbeaten run in the League that would last an impressive four months.

For the first time in a long while, the festive season proved to be a very happy one for Sunderland fans, the Lads securing a series of good wins; Stoke were beaten 2 - 1 at their place on Boxing Day and Birmingham whacked 5 - 3 at Roker on December 30th. This left us in second place at the end of the year, and further victories in the first week of January - a 2 - 0 at home to Stoke and a 2 - 1 at Birmingham - maintained a serious challenge for the title. As usual, the New Year also saw the start of our FA Cup campaign, where a good 3 - 1 victory against Burnley - Paterson scoring all three - raised hopes in this competition too. January ended with an impressive 1 - 0 victory at Huddersfield, the Yorkshire team's first defeat since November.

Sunderland then took this rich form to the Hawthorns to meet West Brom in the second round of the Cup. The game had generated some excitement in the Midlands, and a record crowd of 56,674 turned out for the affair. The home fans were not disappointed, the Baggies running out 2 - 1 winners. Though disappointing, Cup exit allowed the Lads to focus on the League, and further good victories in February - including a 2 - 1 win over Middlesbrough - kept the title challenge on track.

By the end of the month, however, the team were beginning to look a little tired, and there was a noticeable dip in form as spring approached. Sheffield United brought the unbeaten run to an end on March 3rd, and relegation threatened Preston inflicted another defeat before the end of March. In an attempt to revive the players, the directors had taken the players to Buxton for a week's rest and recuperation at the beginning of the month, but it hadn't done much good!

However, the Lads picked up again over Easter, securing 2 - 0 wins against Manchester City and Spurs over the space of two days and closing the ground on Liverpool at the top. The title race was back on now, but the Lads seemed unable to go for the kill, losing a critical game against Manchester City on Easter Monday, and suffering a first home defeat of the season - 5 - 3 against Sheffield United - a couple of weeks later.

Despite poor form in March, the title had still been a possibility, but a weak finish put paid to our Championship hopes; indeed, three of the last five games were lost and the Lads finished as runners-up to Liverpool. After being neck-and-neck with the Merseysiders for most of the season it was a heart breaking finish, our dip in form at the final stages seeing us finish some six points off the pace. Yet, second place was an excellent performance and a justification of Kyle's rebuilding strategy. It was Sunderland's best performance since the 1912-13 Championship season and, but for a superb performance from a very strong Liverpool, could so easily have produced a sixth League title. It was also Charlie Buchan's most prolific season so far, his thirty goal tally landing him the mantle of the League's top goalscorer for 1922-23. In retrospect, it had been a great campaign, but to go so near must have been nothing but agony at the time.

1923 Sunderland team.

Big Signing Returns to Action

One of the big money players signed in our shopping spree at the end of the 1921-22 season had not had much luck since joining the Club. Gilhooley, who cost a massive £5,250, played only four games before being badly hurt in the game against Bradford just three weeks after his arrival. The injury was severe enough to put him out of action for nearly six months, and he only managed brief runs in the team before being sidelined for long periods again. In three seasons, he managed just 20 appearances for the Lads, a story which underlined both the danger of spending large sums on players and the fragile state of even the best footballers' careers.

Michael Gilhooley.

1923-1924 Nerves

"...the pressure now began to show."

1923-24 Sunderland team.

Club v Country

The Club versus Country debate crops up regularly in modern day football, many arguing that players owe their responsibilities to the clubs that pay them and as such should put club commitments above international ones. In the 1920s, though, the clubs were less forceful in putting their case. International matches usually took place alongside club matches, meaning top teams regularly played crucial games without key players.

With the title race really hotting up in April 1924, Sunderland made the trip to London to play Arsenal. The Lads were two points clear at the top, with Huddersfield closing in fast, meaning victory was vital. However, two of our players travelled to London for a different game: the England v Scotland match that was being played to mark the opening of Wembley Stadium. That game ended 1 - 1, with Buchan turning out for England and Clunas for Scotland. The match at Highbury, however, ended 2 - 0 to Arsenal, a defeat which enabled Huddersfield to close the gap to one point. The extent to which this result was down to the absence of two of our star players is difficult to prove, but there is no doubt that their presence was missed. Sunderland had been victims of their own success.

The season kicked off with West Ham United's first visit to Roker Park for a League game, and with the visitors employing "robust" tactics, points were shared in a tight 0 - 0 game. A trip to Ninian Park to play Cardiff City followed, where torrential rain and a 2 - 1 defeat combined to produce a miserable day, and so it was September before the Lads chalked up their first victory, a 1 - 0 win against West Ham at Upton Park.

The next few games produced some mixed form, with a good win at Birmingham being sandwiched between defeats against Cardiff and Manchester City, but the most notable feature of the season's opening stages was our poor home form; though the Lads had notched up two victories in our first five games, both had come away from home, and Cardiff had thrashed us 3 - 0 at Roker. Indeed, our first home win did not come until the last game of September, but the 5 - 2 scorcher against Manchester City was well worth waiting for, Buchan getting a hat-trick as we ripped through the Mancunians.

Following this win our form picked up a little, the Lads losing just one of the six games played during October. The month began with the visit of Bolton to Roker Park, a game watched by Flyweight Champion of the World, Jimmy Wilde. Perhaps the Lads were inspired by his presence, for the fighting spirit seemed to return. The game ended 2 - 2, and our next two home games both produced victories, a 2 - 0 against Chelsea and a 1 - 0 over Spurs.

These good performances continued for the next couple of months, the Lads becoming hard to beat - particularly at home - securing seven wins from the ten games played before the year's end. This was the kind of form upon which a title challenge might be built, and the notching up of points was pleasing. Aside from this, we also had the pleasure of securing back to back wins against Newcastle! The first game was a 3 - 2 victory at Roker, a game that had, at one stage, looked like producing a real beating for the Magpies, with the Lads being 3 - 1 up after just 23 minutes! In the second half, however, we took our foot off the gas and allowed Newcastle the chance to make a game of it, though they managed no more than a consolation goal in the end. The return game took place three days before Christmas, and this time the Lads made no mistake, the 2 - 0 victory being an ideal present for all Sunderland fans!

The New Year provided further cheer, Everton being dispatched 3 - 0 at Roker on New Year's Day, and Notts County being beaten 2 - 1 the following Saturday. However, the first round of the FA Cup saw our cup jinx strike once more, Oldham Athletic beating us 2 - 1 and ending yet another campaign at the first hurdle.

Our reaction to the defeat was good though, and we embarked on a run that would see us remain unbeaten for over two months. Important double victories were achieved during this period too, Aston Villa being satisfyingly defeated home (2 - 0) and away (1 - 0), as were Nottingham Forest. By now, the Lads were in firm contention for the title, and a 3 - 0 victory at Burnley put us at the top of the table with just nine games to go.

As with the previous season though, the pressure now began to show. Two disappointing defeats immediately followed, a 4 - 2 collapse away to reigning Champions Liverpool being followed by a poor 1 - 0 defeat at home to Burnley. The Lads turned their performances around by beating Middlesbrough in their next couple of games - 3 - 1 at their place and 3 - 2 at home - and in doing so kept us a couple of points clear at the top of the table.

However, second placed Huddersfield had three games in hand, making it imperative that we took near maximum points from our remaining five fixtures.

In the event, it was a task beyond the team. Just one of the games - a 2 - 0 at home to West Brom - was won, and three were lost. Consequently, we fell to third in the League at the end of the campaign, Huddersfield winning the title on goal average from Cardiff City. The Lads, though, were just four points adrift, and also finished as top scorers with 71 goals. As with the previous season this was, in many ways, an excellent performance, but one that was bitterly disappointing at the time. Had the team hit its stride earlier or maintained its form that little bit longer, the Championship would have come to Wearside. Once again though, this just wasn't to be.

Buchan (right), Sunderland skipper, shakes hands with Newcastle captain Frank Hudspeth before a Tyne v Wear derby, 1923.

Blunder at Burnley

With the season entering the final straight, the Lads appeared to have the title sown up. In good form and three points clear at the top, they travelled to meet FA Cup semi-finalists Burnley on 22nd March, 1924. The home side, hit by injuries, were playing with a number of reserves in their side, and their minds were likely to be on Cup glory rather than League action. The Lads could not have played them at a better time. Yet, despite having more of the play, we ended up losing 1 - 0. The Burnley side put up a plucky performance, but the Lads played badly on the day, missing a number of great chances. Some pointed the finger at the manager, it being suggested that the defeat was largely a consequence of playing Buchan on the right wing, a position he had not occupied before. But, whatever the reason for the defeat it was unexpected and the race for the title was well and truly thrown open again.

Charlie Parker.

Going Close - The Lads Miss Out Twice On the Trot

Warney Cresswell

One of the big signings brought in by Kyle as he assembled his Championship challenging team was Warney Cresswell. He arrived in May 1922 during our mammoth spending spree, and commanded a huge £5,500 fee, a then world record.

He joined us from South Shields, then plying their trade in the Second Division, and had already been capped by England. A fine defender, Cresswell stayed for five-and-a-half seasons at the Club, making 190 League and Cup appearances for the Lads.

After just missing out on the League title three times with us, he left for Everton in 1927 and picked up a Championship medal in his first full season there!

1922-23 Season Final Placings

LEAGUE DIVISION ONE		Played	Pts
Champions	Liverpool	42	60
Runners-Up	The Lads	42	54

1923-24 Season Final Placings

LEAGUE DIVISION ONE		Played	Pts
Champions	Huddersfield	42	57
Runners-Up	Cardiff City	42	57
Third	The Lads	42	53

Final tables rarely tell the full story. Sometimes teams canter to the Championship, dominating their League and clinching the title well before the season's end. On other occasions there is a close tussle between well balanced competitors, great giants battling it out until the season comes to a dramatic finish. But sometimes, teams blow it at the final hurdle, running out of steam or crumbling under the pressure just as the Championship seems to be in the bag. Like General Elections, Championships are at times lost rather than won.

For two seasons in the 1920s, Sunderland were the team that blew it when the title was all but there for the taking, yet the final tables might indicate we finished some way off the pace in both seasons in question: 1922-23 and 1923-24. Furthermore, while football statisticians often record the runners-up spot as some sort of consolation prize, third place is rarely seen as being significant, yet it was during the 1923-24 campaign - our third place finish - that the Lads looked sure fire certainties for the League Championship right until the final games of the campaign.

In 1922-23, Liverpool were looking for a second consecutive Championship, but after a slow start Sunderland began to mount a serious challenge too, and were the only side in with a chance of denying the Merseysiders. Indeed, as the season entered its penultimate month, March, the Lads were just two points behind Liverpool, with a possible twenty-six points left to play for. Moreover, we were the form team too, unbeaten for four months and closing in on Liverpool at a lightening pace. The title was up for taking.

But, having worked hard to move within one win of top spot, the Lads instantly fell off the pace, losing a vital game against Sheffield United, while Liverpool won elsewhere, pushing the gap between the two teams up to four points. The next two games didn't go well either, with a defeat and a draw leaving us five points behind the leaders before the Easter programme. Our challenge was faltering, and though slim hopes remained - bolstered by the fact we had a game in hand - Championship aspirations were severely dented during the busy Easter weekend. On good Friday, we secured an important victory, only to see Liverpool win too, a scenario which was matched the following day. Liverpool's continued good form was reducing our chances of overtaking them at the top, and *The Times* felt compelled to conclude "The League Championship now looks certain to go to Liverpool for the second season in succession".

On Easter Monday we lent a helping hand, losing at Manchester City, but Liverpool proved themselves to be vulnerable too, going down 4 - 1 on the same day. Disappointing as this was for Sunderland fans, for a chance to close the gap to three points with a game in hand had gone begging, it was important to see the Merseysiders had weaknesses too.

The following weekend, these weaknesses were exposed again, and the Lads narrowed the gap as Liverpool began to falter. A fine 1 - 0 victory for us over Spurs, combined with a draw for Liverpool, led *The Times* to retract its claim that the title was already Liverpool's. "Interest in the League Championship has been increased by the unexpected failure of Liverpool to beat Birmingham and there is again the possibility of Sunderland displacing them at the top of the competition", they argued, for "Liverpool are left with a lead of four from Sunderland, who have played one game less." The race was back on.

A few days later, the Lads entertained Sheffield United at Roker Park, a 5.30pm kick-off. This was Sunderland's game in hand, and a chance to bring the gap back to two points. With Liverpool apparently having run out of steam, the Championship was a real possibility. 36,000 crammed into Roker for the game, yet a Buchan hat-trick was not enough to secure any points. Amazingly, the Lads lost 5 - 3, a scoreline incredible in itself, but one that can only be truly appreciated with knowledge of Sunderland's great home form at the time; before Sheffield United's visit, no team had come to Roker and left with a win. This had been our big chance, and we had blown it.

The following Saturday, Liverpool's poor form continued, and a draw for them, combined with a win for us, cut the gap to three points. With just four games left, though, the odds favoured Liverpool; had we beaten Sheffield United, Liverpool would have only held an extremely vulnerable one point lead. Indeed, Liverpool drew their next two matches, but by now the Lads had lost their momentum; perhaps they felt defeat was inevitable, not least because two of Liverpool's remaining games were against relegation doomed Stoke. The challenge evaporated, crowds dipped and defeats followed. In the end, Liverpool finished six points clear, but in reality it was a much closer race than this and one that was won as much by nerve as by skill.

Billy Clunas

After almost winning the League title in the 1922-23 season, Kyle moved to strengthen his squad during the 1923-24 season by signing Scottish half-back Billy Clunas from St Mirren. He proved to be an astute buy, his performances being assured and attracting the eye of the international selectors. Shortly after arriving at Roker Park, he was capped by Scotland, turning out for his country against England in 1924 in a game that ended 1 - 1. However, despite this, Clunas' contribution was not enough to secure the title, as the Lads missed out once again. While his performances contributed to more title challenges in future seasons, ultimately the Lads remained trophyless in his time at Sunderland.

Clunas was at the Club for eight seasons, making 272 appearances and scoring 44 goals. He left Sunderland in August 1931, as Cochrane focused on his youth policy, returning to Scotland to join Morton.

Billy Clunas

Bobby Gurney

Kyle's teams - particularly in the 1920s - were known for being packed with stars rather than home grown youngsters. However, in between our four title challenges, the manager secured the signature of a promising local youngster known as Bobby Gurney. He joined us in 1925 from Bishop Auckland, and did not feature much in his first season. However, the 1926-27 season saw him break into the first team, and though goals were hard to find, he still showed promise. In the final season of the decade, following Halliday's departure, he really showed what he could do, bagging 17 goals in 25 games.

But, it was in the 1930s that Gurney's star really shone, his goalscoring exploits firing the Lads to glory. While his strike rate was not quite as spectacular as Halliday's, his all round game was superb, and he still managed to hit more than a goal every other game. In thirteen seasons with us he scored 228 goals in 388 League and Cup games, making him our highest scoring player of all time.

Amazingly, with Charlie Buchan our second highest scorer at 224 goals, and Dave Halliday our third, the months of May to July 1925 had all three of our most prolific scorers at the Club at the same time! Unfortunately, there were no competitive games being played during these months, so the trio never appeared together. While, it is fair to say that their careers peaked at different moments too, the Lads fielding Buchan, Halliday and Gurney together is a mouth-watering prospect nonetheless.

Yet, if the 1922-23 run in was a hammer blow, the 1923-24 finish can be described as nothing other than a killer. With just over a month of the season left, the Lads were in top position, and looking comfortable. Once again, we were in a rich vein of form as the season approached its closing stages, but again we crumbled unexpectedly at home when victory was required to consolidate our position; as The Times reported:

"Just as Sunderland seemed to have excellent prospects of winning the Championship of the Football League, they were most unexpectedly beaten at home by Burnley. One of the four Cup semi-finalists, Burnley were compelled to include several reserves in the side, but they played with fine spirit, and 20 minutes after the interval Beel scored the one goal of the match. Sunderland had much the better of the play, but they did not control the lively ball well and missed several favourable chances. The defeat of Sunderland has made the Championship much more open."

Real danger came from Huddersfield Town; though the Terriers were lying in third place, they had games in hand on us, and were proving a difficult side to beat. However, it was a four horse race at this point, with Bolton and Cardiff being very close to us too. It became vital, therefore, that the Lads won as many games as possible, and we responded well to defeat against Burnley, coming from two goals down to beat Middlesbrough, and in doing so, maintaining our position at the top of the table. However, defeat against Arsenal allowed Huddersfield to narrow our lead to one point the following weekend, meaning - once again - the Easter programme would be crucial.

The holiday fixtures began well for us, as a victory on Good Friday - along with a draw for the Terriers - kept us in top spot. The following day, we could only manage a draw, but the same was true of Huddersfield, meaning we remained leaders. By now, though, Cardiff had strung together a useful run of results, and had moved into joint second with Yorkshire club, both teams being just a single point behind us. The pressure was really on now, and the Lads had just two more games left. Maximum points would be needed, not least because the others had games in hand. However, where four points were needed, none were forthcoming; Easter Monday brought a defeat for us, allowing Cardiff to jump into top spot, and to make matters worse, the Lads lost again in their final match. After leading for so long, we had been overtaken on the final bend. It was galling, and the bitter pill was made yet more difficult to swallow by the Magpies' victory in the FA Cup final the same day.

Once more the Lads had come close, and a tight finish saw us blow it at a crucial stage. In the end, Huddersfield took the title from Cardiff on goal average - the Welshmen must have been even more gutted than we were - and the Lads finished four points off the top. Sickeningly, we had the best goalscoring record in the League, and victory in those two final games would have been enough to take the title.

To come so close was a great achievement; for two years running the Lads were so very nearly the Champions. But, if we were to be critical, we might ask why the team lacked the killer instinct necessary to take points in those vital matches that could have delivered the title. This was an *extremely* expensive team, full of international stars. What was it that made them falter in the big games?

Perhaps the expectation was too much; maybe the manager made tactical mistakes; certainly there was some bad luck. But losing out twice in a row, and in such similar fashion, might also suggest that the manager failed to take on board lessons that should have been learnt after the 1922-23 run in. As Oscar Wilde might have put it: losing one title race may be regarded as a misfortune… to lose two seems like carelessness.

Dave Halliday. He is the only footballer to have scored 30 top flight goals in four consecutive seasons.

Dave Halliday

Dave Halliday is one of Sunderland's all time goalscoring legends. He arrived from Dundee at the end of April 1925, his brief being to fire us to glory, and he immediately filled the boots left by Buchan's move to Arsenal.

Halliday certainly kept his part of the bargain, firing a staggering 42 goals in 46 games during his first season. However, it was not enough to secure the title, the Lads coming home in third. The following season, he hit 36 goals in 34 games, but once again we finished third.

In only four and a quarter seasons at the Club, Halliday managed to find the net 162 times in just 175 League and Cup appearances. It was an astonishing strike record, and there were cries of anguish when he followed in Buchan's footsteps by moving to Arsenal in 1929. However, another goalscoring legend - Bobby Gurney - was then ready to take his place.

A player of undoubted class, Halliday is the only man in football to have scored more than 30 top flight League goals for four seasons in succession, a task he completed while at Sunderland. Amazingly, in two of those seasons - 1926-27 and 1928-29 - he scored more than a goal a game. It is unsurprising, therefore, that Halliday ranks as one of our leading scorers of all time, his strike rate making him our third highest goal scorer ever.

Bobby Gurney.

1924-1925 Regeneration

"The Club were determined to continue their fight for the top."

Dave Halliday.

Another Battle With the Mags

The season saw another important encounter with Newcastle played in front of a huge crowd. On 18th October, 1924, a massive 55,632 packed into Roker Park to see us play our neighbours. Once again, the game was of more than local significance, with the Lads in third place and just one point off the top spot. The game did not start well though. Shortly after kick-off, the United winger Seymour made a good run down field and centred the ball for Clark, who headed into the net to make it 1 - 0 Newcastle. However, not long before half-time Marshall equalised from a corner, making it 1 - 1 at the break. With no goals scored in the second period, the points were shared in an even game. Agonisingly, results elsewhere meant victory would have put us in top spot, but dropping a point meant we slid down to fourth. All was not lost though, as the Lads had a game in hand on the two teams above us.

Having disappointingly missed out on the Championship, Sunderland started the 1924-25 season against a side still revelling in the glory of promotion: Leeds United. This was the Yorkshire club's first season in the top flight, and the Lads proved to be a major attraction for the Leeds fans for the game drew a record crowd to the United ground, some 33,722. The home side's promotion was due in no small part to Percy Whipp, who had been allowed to leave Sunderland for £750 in 1922 and scored a hat-trick on his debut for Leeds the next day, and though both teams were looking to get off to a flier, a close game ended 1 - 1.

This was a solid enough opening, but better came in the next game, a 2 - 0 victory against Preston. Buchan scored his 200th goal for the Lads during the game, and our other goal - which came from Clunas - was struck with such force that it broke the net! There was also an amusing incident after the game, with the linesman - a Mr Young from Newcastle - being arrested and ordered to appear before the magistrates for drunk and disorderly behaviour. It transpired that the game had been his first as a match official, and he had stayed in Sunderland to celebrate. He was fined 10 shillings for his misdemeanours!

Following this excitement, Sunderland went on to thrash Birmingham 4 - 0, and it looked like we were all set to make up for the disappointment of the previous two campaigns. This feeling was temporarily dashed by a feeble defeat at West Brom, but three consecutive wins - including a 4 - 1 hammering of Spurs - left us second top at the end of September. However, reigning Champions Huddersfield were above us, and overtaking them would be far from easy.

We then inexplicably crashed to Notts County at Roker Park, a rare home defeat this season. The rest of October saw mixed results - including a 1 - 1 draw at home to the Magpies - and our challenge began to falter a little. However, the Lads recovered well, winning three of their next four matches, and victory over Preston on 20th November put us joint top with Notts County.

In what was becoming a familiar tale though, as soon as the Lads hit top spot their form dipped dramatically; in the next eight games, the Lads could only muster two victories. Moreover, half of the games played were lost, including a 4 - 0 thrashing at the hands of reigning Champions Huddersfield and a 4 - 1 beating at West Ham.

New Year's Day saw us kick off 1925 in fine style, avenging Cardiff's role in our fall from the top the previous season, a goal from Hawes securing the points for the Lads. But in the main, indifferent form continued. A good 3 - 0 victory over West Brom was sandwiched between defeats against Birmingham and Spurs, and although Bury were dispatched 3 - 0 in the first round of the FA Cup, the second round saw Everton outclass us in a replayed tie, the Lads being lucky to escape with the score 1 - 2.

February brought better League form, with three victories from five games. One of the victories, over Everton, resulted in a League double, but was scant consolation for the Cup defeat. Moreover, one of the games we failed to win was against the Mags, where a Sunderland team without Buchan succumbed to defeat, Newcastle running out 2 - 0 winners.

By now, however, the title challenge was all but dead, and with six of the last ten games being drawn, the Lads ended the season in a disappointing seventh place.

After two near misses and a good start to the 1924-25 campaign, fans would have been forgiven for thinking it was Sunderland's year. In the end though, the Lads failed to sustain a challenge because of a poor away record: eleven of our twenty-one away games were lost. By contrast, our home form was good, with just two teams beating us at Roker.

The Club were determined to continue their fight for the top though, and as the season drew to a close, decisions were taken to invest both on and off the field. For the last game of the season against West Ham, the Fulwell End was closed, work having started on re-terracing. Archibald Leitch had been commissioned for both this work and a new grandstand at a combined cost of £35,000, though the latter was deferred for another four seasons. In addition, a new striker was added to the squad, ace marksman Dave Halliday joining from Dundee at the end of April. He would prove to be a great acquisition, but his arrival marked the end of another hero's Sunderland days; Charlie Buchan left for Arsenal shortly afterwards.

The ever present Ernie England in action at Leeds Road, Huddersfield.

Buchan Goes South

Charlie Buchan had, in the latter half of the season, gone through a bad patch, and his scoring ratio dipped: just twelve goals had come from his skilful play during the season, around half the number he had managed in the previous six seasons. Indeed, the Sunderland Echo commented "there is justifiable talk that Buchan is being played on reputation only", and a month later Argus expressed the view that "it is clear that Buchan's days as an effective force are numbered." This bad spell, which every player goes through from time to time, coupled with his age, must have figured in the decision to transfer him to Arsenal at the end of the season. After 15 years at the Club, his transfer was a surprise to many, and Buchan played well for the Gunners. The £2,000 fee seemed something of a bargain at the time, but the terms also specified that Arsenal had to pay us £100 for each goal he scored in his first season at Highbury. He scored 19 and the eventual transfer fee was a much bigger £3,900!

Charlie Buchan.

1925-1926
Big Spenders

"…a familiar tale for the 1920s, the Championship had been there for the taking…"

The Boot is on the Other Foot: Buchan Destroys Sunderland

With Sunderland in top place, the Lads visited Highbury to play second placed Arsenal. Turning out for the Gunners that day was Charlie Buchan, after his controversial move to London. The game generated huge interest, and with 50,000 inside the ground quite early on, the gates had to be locked well before kick-off! To add an extra dimension to the game, cold weather meant the pitch was almost entirely covered in snow, with just the pitch markings being visible!

Before the game kicked off, the funeral march was played to silence in memory of the late Queen Alexandra, but following the start, no punches were pulled. Given the dangerous pitch, match reporters were impressed by the fast and accurate football being played, and Buchan was singled out for praise, one journalist describing him as 'a delight'. Unsurprisingly, he opened the scoring - after just seven minutes - taking advantage of a miskicked clearance by hammering the loose ball home.

After this, though, Sunderland had the better of it. The Lads attacked well, but good goalkeeping by Harper and some excellent defending by the towering Butler prevented us from getting a deserved goal. When the second-half kicked off, Arsenal must have been prepared for the worst, but just four minutes after the restart, a long ball forward caught the wind, allowing Brain the opportunity to nod home a second for the Gunners.

The goal gave Arsenal a huge advantage, and while Cresswell - our man of the match - tried to rally his team-mates with some good runs from the back and a few long range shots, we had few ideas. Prior hit the bar and Halliday had a good chance with a header, but it was mainly Arsenal in the second half. The game ended 2 - 0, and the points were enough to lift Arsenal above us and end our long spell at the top.

The season kicked off at home to Birmingham City, and new signing Dave Halliday had an immediate impact, scoring two goals in a 3 - 1 victory. After this, the Lads went on a real scoring spree, beating Blackburn 6 - 2, West Bromwich Albion 5 -2 and Sheffield United 6 - 1. This was no mean feat - West Brom, for example, had been runners-up in the League the previous season. Indeed, after the Sheffield game *The Times* concluded that "Sunderland's brilliant play has, so far, been the outstanding feature of the new football season". It was difficult to argue with this, the Lads having hit 20 goals in the first four matches! Significantly, half of these were scored by our new front man Halliday, including hat tricks in two of the matches.

Of course, such high praise merely asked for us to be given a beating, which Blackburn duly dished out in our next game, the Lads going down 3 - 0. However, it was nothing more than a hiccup, and the month ended with two further victories, at Cardiff (1 - 0) and at home to Spurs (3 - 0). Crucially, the win against Tottenham lifted us above them and into top spot.

Of course, Sunderland hitting top spot was by now well connected with a run of poor form, and we suffered two consecutive away defeats, at Manchester City and Aston Villa, conceding four goals each time, and dropping down the League as a consequence. Fortunately, the sticky patch didn't last long, and 7 - 3 thrashing of Everton at Roker was enough to put us back in pole position. This meant that, once again, the first derby match of the season saw us needing points to maintain a title challenge; a 0 - 0 draw was enough to keep us at the top.

For the next few weeks, the results largely went our way and until the last weekend of November the Lads headed the table. Arsenal were mounting a strong challenge though, and on 28th November, we visited Highbury for a real crunch match. Agonisingly, we lost 2 - 0, and the Gunners went into top spot.

Though playing well, it was clear that the Lads needed that something extra to mark them apart from the other contenders, and Bob Kelly was bought from Burnley to boost the attack. He had a dream start against Manchester United, the Lads pulling off a good 2 - 1 victory, putting us level on points at the top. The remaining few games of 1925 brought mixed results, but by the end of the year we were in a strong second position, just one point behind Arsenal and having played the same number of games.

Unfortunately, the New Year began with two consecutive defeats, and we slipped to third, Huddersfield leapfrogging above us. The FA Cup, though, brought some cheer; a rule change meant that the top clubs now entered at the third round stage, and non League Boston were drawn as our opposition. We thrashed them 8 - 1! The result must have boosted morale, for the Lads cruised to victories in their next two League games, beating West Brom 4 - 0 and - crucially - Huddersfield 4 - 1. Though our final League game of the month was lost (4 - 1 to Sheffield United), we had done enough to end the month joint top, the Lads, Arsenal and Huddersfield all sharing top place on 33 points!

In February we put in some good League performances, beating Spurs 2 - 0 and Manchester City 5 - 3, and the top three positions, unsurprisingly, switched around from week to week.

The FA Cup, however, was providing something of a distraction for us. Sheffield United were beaten away from home in the fourth round - a 2 - 1 victory in front of a 62,041 crowd - and a home tie with Manchester United beckoned. It was an attractive tie, 50,500 making the trip to Roker, and the Lads should have won it, having enough chances to bury their opponents. Instead, it ended 3 - 3. The replay proved to be a controversial event. With United edging the game at 2 - 1, Halliday scored what appeared to be a perfectly good equalising goal. However, United's Barson complained vociferously and the goal was chalked off. The actual reason for disallowing the "goal" was never accurately determined. Some say that Halliday was offside, and some say that Prior, who was originally adjudged to have forced the ball over the line, did so with his hand. No matter, it wasn't given and we went home out of the FA Cup.

With this defeat, the season began to slip away. Huddersfield, who had games in hand over us following a cold winter, began to pull away at the top, and by the first weekend of March were six points clear of us. When the month closed, the Lads had slipped down to third, and with Huddersfield being eight points clear, the best we could hope for was the runners-up spot.

In the final few weeks, the season fizzled out. Mixed results produced a decent return of points, and though we beat Arsenal 2 - 1 to boost our chances of overtaking them in second, they too had a cushion of games in hand that allowed them to keep the spot safe. We ended a creditable third, but in a familiar tale for the 1920s, the Championship had been there for the taking earlier in the season. The end of the season did see one bright spot though; youngster Bobby Gurney made his debut in one of our last few games, and demonstrated his potential. Indeed, the 18 year old played in our last six matches and scored an impressive four goals. Once again, there was always the promise of next season.

Money Bags Strikes Again

After a good start to the season, having topped the table for much of the early stages of the campaign, the team began to falter a little during November. The Board gave the Manager permission to spend big again, and Bob Kelly joined us on 1st December. The £6,550 fee paid to Burnley was yet another world record transfer fee, and evidence of both the Club's wealth and the Board's desire to do what was necessary to bring trophies to Sunderland.

Kelly was a top quality player who had regularly kept Buchan out of the England team, and his favoured position was outside right. A clever passer of the ball, who also held one or two tricks up his sleeve, his arrival at Sunderland was big news. However, he didn't quite gel into the side as effectively as he might have done, and within two seasons was sold to Huddersfield Town. Though he was often the orchestrater of many of our goals, he scored few himself, hitting just ten goals in fifty League appearances for the Club. In an echo of modern day footballing problems, Kelly continued to live outside the area while on our books, and for some this arrangement was seen as instrumental in his failure to settle at the Club. Following his less than spectacular spell, Sunderland shied away from the big money buys for a while; indeed, a new manager arrived shortly after Kelly's departure, and he favoured a 'grow your own' policy, opting to bring young players up through the ranks rather than spending big.

Sunderland and England international, Robert Kelly.

1926-1927
Just Short

"We had entertained, but fell a little short of what was required of Champions."

Albert McInroy.

Burnley Blitzed

On 6th October, 1926, Burnley arrived on Wearside with happy memories of the North East. The previous month they had hammered Newcastle United 5 - 1, and arrived at Roker in fine form. However, Sunderland were playing well too, and a victory over Sheffield Wednesday had pushed us into top place.

Burnley started better though, and Cresswell and England had to be at their best early on to subdue the visiting forwards. However, Sunderland had Halliday back in their side, the Scotsman returning after a spell out through illness and suspension, and he inspired the side going forward. By half time Sunderland led 3 - 0, and when the final whistle blew, both Halliday and Coglin had netted hat tricks! What's more, record signing Kelly had scored a rare goal, the game ending 7 - 1 to the Lads, Page hitting Burnley's consolation.

A few weeks later though, Burnley got their revenge, beating us 4 - 2 in a game where Sunderland's 'keeper McInroy was the undoubted man of the match, preventing us from receiving a similar hiding.

After yet another near miss and some more big money buys during the previous campaign, there was much cause for optimism as the 1926-27 season kicked off. Yet, it started disastrously, a game played in brilliantly sunny weather at The Hawthorns seeing us go down 3 - 0 to West Brom. Amends were quickly made with a 3 - 0 win at home to Bury, but the crowd of only 18,000 was the smallest for an opening home game since the war. This, however, was not so much a statement about the team, but more a result of the miners' strike, which was in its third month. Indeed, the strike was to have a significant effect on attendances at Roker during this season; the average gate was under 18,000 and the crowd was above 20,000 on only six occasions.

One of those big crowds came when we entertained Huddersfield Town - who had clinched the League Championship for the third time in a row in 1925-26 - and the game ended 1 - 1. Defeat in our fourth game - at Birmingham - meant that we had amassed only three points out of a possible eight, a bad start. September did, however, get better and ended with three straight wins, including a victory over Spurs coming thanks to a goal with the last kick of the game!

Thanks to this little run, a 4 - 1 home success over Sheffield Wednesday at the start of October took us to the top of the table on goal average, a position consolidated with a 7 - 1 thrashing of Burnley! However, once more Sunderland hitting top spot meant a dip in form was around the corner, and we lost three of the next four games, one a revenge mission as Burnley beat us 2 - 4. As a result, we slipped down to sixth in the League and Newcastle leapt above us into second. But, it was tight at the top, and when the Mags visited Roker Park, a 2 - 0 victory for the Lads - courtesy of goals from Halliday and Death - was enough to push us into second and pull Newcastle down to fifth!

Victory over our local rivals put our season back on track, and we lost only two of our remaining nine games in 1926. Notable victories over Liverpool - 2 - 1, with a Halliday winner two minutes from time - and Arsenal - 3 - 2 at their place - helped us back into top spot, and a 3 - 0 win at home to Sheffield United put us two points clear at the end of November.

However, we began December with a defeat at Derby, where circus like blunders helped us crash 2 - 4. Crucially, the result saw us slip into second place, with - worst of all - the Magpies overtaking us. A good result was now imperative in the game against Manchester United at Roker Park, and one came: a 6 - 0 victory! Interestingly, the game was scoreless at half time, but in the second period all hell broke loose. Halliday opened the floodgates, Gurney added a second, and Clunas made it three from a penalty. All this took place in the first fifteen minutes of the second period, and there was plenty of time for Halliday to show what he could do, the player adding three more goals before full time! With Newcastle losing, we were back on top, but Huddersfield - somewhat ominously - were gaining on us, having crept into second spot.

Once more the pole position jinx struck, with points dropped against Bolton (2 - 2) and, on Christmas Day, Everton (4 - 5). Though revenge was gained with a 3 -2 victory at home to the Merseysiders two days later, we ended the year back in third place, and while we were just one point off the top, the teams around us - Burnley, Newcastle and Huddersfield - all had games in hand.

The last thing we needed then was to lose our opening game of 1927. This we did though, crashing 2 - 5 at home to Blackburn. This result was followed by a quick FA Cup exit at the hands of Leeds, a 3 - 2 defeat at Elland Road once again ending our interest in the competition at the earliest possible stage.

The response from the team was a good one though, and we won our next three games, including a 2 - 0 victory at Spurs that was broadcast live on the radio. The results put us in a strong third, just two points behind the leaders Newcastle. However, we blew the chance to close this gap in our next game, when West Ham burst into a two goal lead after just ten minutes. We rallied well, but the game ended 3 - 2 to the Hammers. Results elsewhere did not do us too much damage though, and a 4 - 1 victory over Birmingham City the following week put us within one point of top spot.

This was as close as we would get. A 4 - 1 hammering from Sheffield Wednesday, followed by a very unimpressive 3 - 1 defeat at the hands of Aston Villa put the Magpies four points clear of us with two games in hand. It would take a miracle for us to snatch the title now. Though we finished well, handing out impressive thrashings to Leeds (6 - 2), Arsenal (5 - 1) and Bolton (6 - 2), it was not enough to catch Newcastle. Indeed, a 1- 0 defeat at St James' in the 50th League meeting between Newcastle United and Sunderland - watched by a record crowd of some 67,211 - underlined the sickening fact that our neighbours had the better team!

In the end, we finished third again, seven points behind Champions Newcastle and two points behind runners-up Huddersfield. A lot of goals had been scored - 98 in all - with seven hat tricks being taken in some sensational games. We had entertained, but fell a little short of what was required of Champions. Somewhat worryingly, given the Club's big spender status, the Annual Report indicated that falling gates had contributed to a loss on the year of some £3,120 and a big increase in our overdraft. The funding gap would have to be made good somehow soon.

Highbury Revenge

In November 1925, a Buchan inspired defeat at Highbury knocked the Lads off the top of the table. In November 1926, we visited Arsenal again, but this time victory for Sunderland put us top of the table. The Times described the Gunner's defence as being "baffled", praising the brilliance of Kelly, whose tricky wing play bamboozled the home side's defence.

As with the previous season's game, Buchan hit the first goal, sending the Lads in 1 - 0 down at half-time. In the second half though, Sunderland got their just reward. Clever play by Kelly drew defenders out of position, allowing Ellis to break free and shoot the equaliser. Arsenal, however, regained the lead, Ramsay taking advantage when a fisted clearance from McInroy failed to remove the danger. The Lads kept attacking, and Kelly was at the heart of the second equaliser when Harper found his shot too strong to handle and Halliday smashed home the loose ball. Shortly afterwards, Marshall scored the winner; a long ball forward fooled the defenders with its bounce, and Halliday robbed Parker before setting Marshall free in a one-on-one with the 'keeper.

No further goals were scored, and the game ended 3 - 2 to the Lads. It was an excellent victory that ended Arsenal's proud home record: the Lads were the first team to beat them at Highbury that season.

Albert McInroy.

120

1927-1928
Almost Down

"Sunderland were off the boil."

Billy Ellis.

Bob Kyle Goes

When Bob Kyle announced his resignation on 15th March, 1928, it marked the end of an era at Sunderland. He had been our Manager since the start of the 1905 season, and had put together a number of exciting teams. Highlights included a League Championship in 1913, and an FA Cup final appearance in the same year that almost delivered a famous double. However, huge forays into the transfer market in the 1920s failed to deliver more silverware, and after a number of near misses, some of the Directors must have started to question his position. When performances dipped in the 1927-28 season, the issue came to a head, and when he went, it would appear that he had been pushed rather than having jumped, The Echo reporting that "the directors had taken a stand, and he was left with no other alternative than to offer his resignation".

Though he stayed until the end of the season, performances did not improve, making it a somewhat inglorious end to a fine career. Indeed, when relegation looked likely towards the end of the season, The Echo pointed the finger at the management, arguing that while some players had performed poorly, "the club has been led into its present position by absolutely ignoring weaknesses of the side earlier in the season. That responsibility does not rest with the players"

Sometime after his departure, Argus took a more measured view, suggesting that with Kyle's resignation "a great judge had passed out of the game". Kyle died in 1932, just four years after leaving the Club, at the age of 66. He had been great servant of Sunderland AFC and, as much as any of the players of the time, goes down as one of our legends.

1927-28 was manager Robert Kyle's nineteenth season in charge of the Club, and would mark his twenty-fifth year in the job. The season started off well enough, with the Lads unbeaten in our first five games. The first game, against Portsmouth at Roker Park, produced something of a shock when Sunderland found themselves 1 - 3 down at half time. We rallied and on 50 minutes Halliday reduced the arrears before an own goal by Moffatt gave us a valuable point. Better followed in the next game, when West Ham were beaten away 4 - 2. A 3 - 3 draw at Leicester was followed by a 4 - 2 home defeat of Birmingham City watched by some 27,000 fans. Liverpool then fell 2 - 1 on Wearside to make it an excellent eight points from ten.

But, a massive slump in form soon set in. From 17th September, where the Lads were defeated at Highbury, until 13th November, when they pulled off a convincing 4 - 1 home success over Manchester United, the Lads won just one League game, a run which included six consecutive defeats. The Club was on the verge of turmoil, with one of the directors - Fred Taylor - temporarily resigning because of worries about the direction of the Club and its team selections.

The game against Manchester United, whilst won, was hardly covered in glory. True the scoreline was 4 - 1, but it should be set against a backdrop where the Mancunians played with ten men for three quarters of the game, their left back, Silcock, leaving the field when he "sprained a muscle". It was 1 - 0 at the time.

A revival was signalled with a second successive win, a 1 - 0 at Everton, Hargreaves scoring the goal midway through the first half, and for the rest of the year we played pretty well, losing only one of the next six. However, games were generally being drawn rather than won, and some good victories were needed to boost our points tally. These came in the New Year, West Ham being beaten 3 - 2, and Liverpool thrashed 5 - 2 at Anfield. Unfortunately, the Cup jinx was still much in evidence. After scraping past Northampton in a replayed third round tie, Manchester City knocked us out at home in the following round.

Form was nothing but inconsistent. February saw a great 5 - 3 win at Portsmouth and a tight 1 - 0 win against Bury sandwiched between heavy defeats against Villa and Burnley. Similarly, March began with a 2 - 4 defeat at Huddersfield and a brilliant 5 - 1 thrashing of Arsenal. All this was very frustrating, but it was clear that Sunderland were off the boil. Compared to the performances of the last five seasons, the football was poor. Indeed, feeling perhaps that he had given his best already, the day after our victory against Arsenal, the manager announced he would be leaving his job at the end of the season.

In the month following Kyle's announcement, the Lads managed to win just two of their seven games. By now, the League position was almost perilous, and relegation was a real threat for the first time since the War. The position became steadily worse though. With just five games left, everyone at the Club knew victories were needed to keep us in the top flight. However, a trip to Sheffield United saw us thrashed 5 - 1, and a long journey to Cardiff the following week also saw us leave empty handed, the Lads ending the wrong side of a 3 - 1 scoreline. Four days later, a miserable run of away games was completed with a 2 - 1 defeat at the hands of Manchester United.

We now had two games to save ourselves, but a 3 - 2 home defeat against Sheffield Wednesday made us rank outsiders for survival. The *Football Echo* expressed deep concern:

"The position for Sunderland is now very critical. They were beaten today by a team which, realising the importance of the match, steeled itself against making mistakes and every goal scored by Sheffield against the Sunderland defence was the result of a mistake."

The defeat meant our final game of the season was a real crunch match at Middlesbrough. The Teessiders had only just been promoted and were level with us on 37 points. In a tight table, the eleven teams at the bottom were separated by just two points, but with Boro's goal average being fractionally better than ours, they only needed a draw for safety. We had to win...

In the run up to the game, we were troubled by injuries. Consequently, McInroy played in goal with lots of strapping and there was a debut for George Robinson at outside right. Middlesbrough started furiously and almost overwhelmed us, but we weathered the storm and gradually began to get back into the match. Just before half time, Wright scored for Sunderland, and the pressure was now on Middlesbrough. In the second half, the Lads really turned it on and Halliday and Death made it 3 - 0 before the final whistle. Just like the Team of All Talents had done at the end of 1896-97 season, the Lads had turned in a magnificent last gap performance in order to prevent us from dropping out of the top flight

Whilst there was obvious relief on Wearside there was also concern about the future of the Club. A new manager was needed. Major Frank Buckley of Wolves or George Jobey of Derby County were the front runners, but in the event, Johnny Cochrane arrived from St Mirren, with whom he had won the Scottish Cup. It was to prove an astute appointment.

FA Cup Ignominy

The season's FA Cup campaign began with a 3rd round tie at home to Division Three South side Northampton. It should have been an easy win for Sunderland, but within six minutes the visitors were 1 - 0 up. About ten minutes later, the Lads equalised through Wright, and goals from Hargreaves and Halliday put us 3 - 1 up. It should have been easy after this, but a sloppy goal before half-time made it 3 - 2 and let the visitors back in. For most of the second half the score remained the same, but a goal just seven minutes before the end forced a shock replay. The result was indicative of the team's declining performances, contrasting starkly with the 8 - 1 thrashing handed out to non-League Boston two seasons earlier.

Though the Lads beat Northampton 3 - 0 in the replay, they might as well have not bothered. The 4th round draw again pitted us against opposition from outside of the top flight - albeit this time recently relegated Manchester City. Again the tie was at Roker, and the Lads should have won, but we went down 2 - 1 and were dumped out of the Cup. While it would appear we were extremely unlucky to lose, the City players having the rub of the green, the Lads had once more managed to throw the form book out of the window in the FA Cup. This time, however, the form book did not make for good reading, and critics might fairly suggest that City were the better team, clinching promotion from Division Two just as we almost fell from Division One.

Bill Murray.

1928-1929
New Era

"With both the finances and the team stabilised Cochrane could now concentrate on moulding a new squad for the future."

Manchester United at Roker Park,
November 1929.

Gunners Shot Down

Arsenal's visit to Roker Park on New Year's Day, 1929, attracted a 32,800 crowd. Sunderland had been playing well, and in a repeat of previous season's fixture against the Gunners, the game held the possibility of putting the Lads at the top of the League. First blood went to the visitors, former Newcastle United man Parkin opening the scoring after quarter-of-an-hour. The Lads bounced back immediately, and within a few minutes goals from McKay and Halliday had put us 2 - 1 ahead. Soon the result was in little doubt. Robinson hit his first goal for the Club, and McKay and Halliday also grabbed another goal each. The tie ended 5 - 1 to the Lads, and with results elsewhere going our way, the victory was indeed enough to put us top of the table.

One of the few players to have been in good form the previous season was Dave Halliday, who hit 37 goals in just 41 games; it was part of a marvellous record since his arrival, the Scot having bagged a staggering 115 goals in 121 appearances. Unsurprisingly, perhaps, he scored the side's first goal under Cochrane's charge, but his strike against Burnley was not enough to clinch the points in our opening fixture, the Turf Moor side running out 3 - 1 winners. This was not a great start, but the red-and-whites got off the ground four days later with a 3 - 1 home victory over Cup holders Blackburn Rovers. A 4 - 0 win against Derby County followed, but we then collapsed, losing five out of the next six games, including a 4 - 0 hammering at Portsmouth. Memories of the previous season came flooding back.

However, the last of these defeats - a 5 - 3 against Manchester City - saw a new forward, McKay, make his debut. Signed from Newcastle United, he had scored a hat trick in his debut for them, and he nearly repeated the feat for us, scoring twice in the eight goal thriller. With his arrival performances began to improve. Our next fixture was at home to Huddersfield Town and though the Terriers took the lead after only six minutes, the Lads turned it around, running out 4 - 1 winners. A trip to Wales to play Cardiff produced another victory - with the only goal of the game - before Newcastle visited for the first derby match of the season The game was watched by some 50,519 spectators and a great victory followed, the Lads hammering the Mags 5 - 2. An excellent run of form was then completed with a 3 - 1 win at Bury.

Although a couple of defeats followed, this was nothing more than a temporary setback. The Lads were soon back on the winning trail, hammering Manchester United 5 - 1 at home. Indeed, we remained unbeaten for the rest of the year, and notched up good victories against Leeds (3 - 0 courtesy of two penalty kicks) and Liverpool (2 - 1, McKay hitting a last minute winner). The good form continued into 1929, Arsenal being hammered 5 - 1 at Roker on New Year's Day, a win that took us to the top of the table, and Sheffield Wednesday losing out in a thrilling 4 - 3 game. While in the League this strong play had seen us rise to the top of the table, in the Cup it was the usual story, West Ham knocking us out at the first stage with a 1 - 0 victory.

The Lads started February in good form, avenging an earlier defeat at Portsmouth by thrashing them 5 - 0! However, our first defeat in thirteen League games then came with a 1 - 0 reverse at Birmingham. Though this was our only defeat in the first two months of 1929, a number of games had been drawn, meaning we had slipped off the top of the table. The League leaders, Sheffield Wednesday, began to falter at the end of February though, and victories over Manchester City and Huddersfield helped us close the gap.

But, after a good 1 - 0 win against Cardiff, the Lads' Championship challenge blew up. A 3 - 4 defeat at Newcastle, in front of a 66,275 crowd, was soon followed by a 3 - 1 reverse at Aston Villa, a 2 - 1 defeat at home to Leicester and 5 - 2 defeat at Liverpool. Defeat in the latter was pretty much inevitable when Allan was ordered off eight minutes into the second half. The referee's report claimed Allan had said "that's not a foul, b***** you" to the referee, but Allan claimed he had said "that's not a foul, you b*****" and did not think he was swearing! The FA cautioned him as to his future conduct.

It would be wrong to give the impression the Lads were losing all of their games in this period, for important games were won between these matches, but the scattering of defeats meant too many points were being dropped to mount a serious Championship challenge, and the Lads fell off the pace. While our final home game produced a good victory, West Ham being beaten 4 - 1 largely thanks to a Halliday hat trick, our last game of the season was a bit of disaster, Sheffield United running out 4 - 0 winners. Cochrane's first season in charge saw us finish a respectable fourth, three points behind third placed Aston Villa and five points off Champions Sheffield Wednesday. Halliday had another good season, hitting an all time Club record 43 goals in the season; what's more he did this in 43 games, a perfect goal-per-a-game ratio!

The Club's General Meeting in May reported a net profit for the year of £1,574 with some £1,600 having been spent on Roker Park over the last twelve months. The old grandstand was demolished at the end of the season, and the Directors decided to introduce season-tickets for the centre stand and for the wing stand; each season-ticket holder would have their name printed on their seat. In part this financial turn around was due to the end of the miners' strike and improved performances on the pitch. But, Cochrane's transfer policy was important too; there had been few signings during the season, the Manager merely bringing in some veteran Scottish players - such as Adam McLean and Tommy McInally - to steady the side during his first season charge. With both the finances and the team stabilised, Cochrane could now concentrate on moulding a new squad for the future.

Manchester United at Roker Park, November 1929.

Cochrane Assembles His Backroom Team

When Johnny Cochrane arrived from St Mirren at the end of the 1927-28 season, he brought with him an experienced team of backroom staff. In some ways, the most important member of this team was Scotsman Sammy Blyth, who would be the Club's scout. One of the best in the business, Blyth played a critical role in spotting the young players who would form the core of the team Cochrane built in the 1930s. His role was made all the more important by the Manager's belief in investing in youth rather than spending money on buying stars.

The other key member of his backroom team was Andy Reid, who became the team's trainer. Reid would act as a replacement for Billy Williams, who announced he would be retiring at the same time Kyle made his resignation public. However, Williams stayed on for another season, helping Cochrane to ease his way into the Club. This was significant, for Williams was a constant factor in Sunderland AFC since its early days as League club, having taken up the trainers post in 1897, and serving under Robert Campbell, Alex Mackie and Robert Campbell as well as Cochrane. As Argus later reported, "he was not only a grand trainer but a man who was guide, philosopher and friend to hundreds of players during his career".

Johnny Cochrane.

1929-1930 Flat

*"...the 1920s came to an end
without a trophy."*

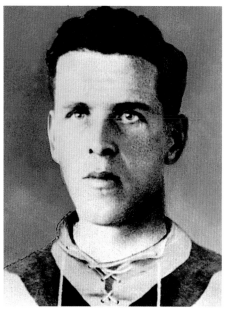

Jock McDougall.

Boro beaten

Middlesbrough visited Roker midway through March. They were looking to put an end to our recovery from the February nightmare and their fans must have been hoping to see us put back in the danger zone given our role in 'Boro's relegation at the end of the 1927-28 season. Having come up as Second Division Champions in 1926-27, we had ensured their stay was the briefest possible, but they had bounced back with another Second Division title in 1928-29. This time, we were the ones on the rocks.

35,000 turned out for the game - much smaller than the crowd drawn by the Newcastle tie - and it was Sunderland who took the lead, albeit with an own goal. Somewhat luckily, a Sunderland corner had struck Ashman on the head, and the ball rebounded into the net! However, Warren soon equalised for 'Boro, and a tight finish was set up. In the 54th minute, Gurney restored our lead, and Eden extended it to 3 - 1 shortly afterwards. With two minutes left, McKay smashed home a header to bring the score to 3 - 2, but by now the Lads had won it, and their recovery was very much on track still.

As part of Cochrane's re-building process a number of players were brought in during the season. Jock Macdougall from Airdrie made the centre half position his own; Tommy Urwin arrived from Newcastle United in early 1930, and so became the first man to have played for all three of the North East's 'big' clubs; Billy Eden came from Darlington; and most notably of all, Harold Shaw came from Wolverhampton, the £7,000 fee leaving gasps in the mouths of English football fans.

On the field, the season opened at Derby, where the Lads crashed to a 0 - 3 defeat, having been two goals down after just 19 minutes. Points were put on the board in our first home game though, Manchester City being hammered 5 - 2, and Halliday - of course - getting our first goal of the campaign. The game also saw the official opening of our new grandstand. However, Archibald Leitch's new structure was not initially graced with fine football from the red-and-whites, with just one point being picked up from the next three games played at Roker. This was a reflection of the generally poor form the Lads were in at the start of the season, with five of the first eight games being lost.

When Newcastle visited on the 19th October though, the massive 58,175 crowd did not leave disappointed - with the notable exception of the Newcastle fans present! Gunson hit the only goal of the match, but it was a controversial win, the referee, Mr Mee, disallowing what appeared to be a perfectly good goal by Hughie Gallacher for Newcastle. The game was tinged by tragedy though; Jack Bartley, a promising left-half from Houghton, had died from pneumonia on the 10th October, and the Sunderland players had worn black armbands in his honour in their game against Sheffield Wednesday.

In spite of victory over Newcastle, the Lads' poor start to the season meant they were near the foot of the table at the end of October. As in previous seasons, the Club v Country debate reared its head, when Jock Mcdougall was chosen to play for his native Scotland against Wales at Ninian Park. The game clashed with a critical Sunderland match against Sheffield United, and with the Lads doing so badly, the Board of Directors controversially refused to release him. Sunderland lost 2 - 4, Scotland won 2 - 0 and Mcdougall never played for his country again!

November saw some mixed results, but the Lads were winning more games than they were losing, and doing enough to keep above the danger zone. The big news of the month though was the transfer of goalscoring hero Dave Halliday. Like Sunderland's previous striking legend, Charlie Buchan, Halliday was sold to Arsenal. This time, though, the fee was more substantial, some £6,500 changing hands. The decision to let him go was an early indication of Cochrane's faith in youth, Bobby Gurney being judged mature enough to act as Halliday's replacement.

The day after his departure, the Lads slumped to a 2 - 4 defeat at Manchester United, a result which put us at the bottom of the table. What's more, we stayed there until the end of December, defeats against Liverpool, Birmingham and Blackburn - the latter a 5 - 3 thrashing on Christmas Day - 'consolidating' our position. After the Blackburn game though, the Lads began to claw their way back. Blackburn were brought back to Roker Park on Boxing Day, where the previous day's defeat was avenged with a good 3 - 1 victory. Two days later, Derby were beaten 3 - 1 at Roker, and with the Lads picking up draws in their first two games of the 1930s, enough had been done to move us off bottom spot.

Our first FA Cup tie of the new decade brought us up against Coventry City from Division Three South. Somewhat embarrassingly, the game - played at Roker - seemed to be heading for a 1 - 1 draw, but six minutes from the end their goalkeeper let the ball slip through his arms and to Gurney's feet; the striker gratefully accepted the chance, smashing it into the net. We were then drawn to play at home to Cardiff City in the fourth round, a much trickier tie, but the Lads secured a good 2 -1 win in front of 40,000 people.

The victory set us up with a winnable fifth round tie against Second Divison Nottingham Forest in the middle of February. Despite a good start to February - a 4 -1 win at home to Aston Villa - the month did not go well. In the run up to the Cup match, we slumped to a 5 - 0 defeat at Leeds, and though we raced into a two goal lead against Forest, the Lads inexplicably lost control of the game, allowing the visitors to get back into the tie with a goal twenty minutes from the end. Sniffing the chance of a replay, Forest went forward and stunned a 42,000 crowd by snatching an equaliser in the 87th minute. Back at their place, Forest ran rings around us triumphing 3 - 1, and once more we 'crept out' of the FA Cup. In the League, the Mags completed our February nightmare, thrashing us 3 - 0 in front of 60,000 at St James' Park.

Fortunately, March was much better! In a complete turnaround the Lads managed to win all of their games, including a pleasing 3 - 2 derby victory at home to Middlesbrough. Indeed, after the horror of February, just three of our last twelve games were lost, and with many of them being won - including a superb 6 - 0 win at Liverpool - the Lads moved well away from the danger zone and ended the season in ninth.

And so, the 1920s came to a rather flat end. The Lads had played a lot of entertaining, attacking football and a team packed with international class stars had thrilled crowds up and down the country. However, despite all of this, the decade ended up as being the first in the Club's history without significant silverware. As the new decade began fans wondered whether it would be a new, glorious era for Sunderland; Cochrane was intent on rebuilding the Club, but would his efforts be in vain?

Patsy Gallacher

One of the young players to emerge during the 1929-30 season was Patsy Gallacher. Nicknamed 'The Mighty Atom', Patsy was born near Glasgow in 1909, and had the distinction of gaining a Scottish cap in 1935, along with team mate Connor. Liverpool once offered £7,000 for his services: it was politely refused...

A loyal servant to Sunderland, he played at the Club for 10 seasons between 1927 and 1938, making over 300 appearances before moving to Stoke City for £5,000. While at the Club, he helped us towards the success that arrived in the 1930s, picking up both an FA Cup and League Championship medal.

Despite his frail frame he was a formidable opponent, and he had a wicked turn of pace that enabled him to set up - and score - many goals from his favoured position at inside left. Indeed, his scoring ratio was a good one, Gallacher hitting 108 goals in 307 games. Most famously, perhaps, he scored the goal that put us through to the 1937 FA Cup final.

Patsy Gallacher.

1930·31	11th in League; FA Cup semi-final.
1931·32	13th in League.
1932·33	12th in League; FA Cup quarter-final.
1933·34	6th in League.
1934·35	2nd in League.
1935·36	Champions!
1936·37	FA Cup Winners; 8th in League.
1937·38	8th in League; FA Cup semi-final
1938·39	16th in League. Johnny Cochrane retires.
1939·40	League declared void after three matches.

The 1930s would prove to be one of the most exciting and successful decades in Sunderland's history. New Manager Johnny Cochrane embarked on an extensive rebuilding process that saw the old guard removed and an emphasis placed on investing in youngsters rather than buying in proven stars. It was a controversial strategy, but one that eventually paid dividends.

From the mid-1930s the Club began challenging for major honours, finishing as runners-up in the League in 1934-35, winning the title in 1935-36 and finally bringing the FA Cup home in 1936-37. Indeed, the decade saw the Lads do much better in the Cup, with the team reaching at least the quarter-final stage on four occasions. At last, the Cup jinx seemed to be beaten!

The decade was a difficult time for the region though and high unemployment contributed towards fluctuating attendances. The 1932-33 season saw the Club record its highest attendance for a competitive match - 75,118 - and its lowest - a mere 4,000.

The decade was also tinged with human tragedy at times. Goalkeeper Jimmy Thorpe died at the tender age of 22 after being badly hurt in one of our matches, and the final season was declared void after just three games when the Second World War broke out. But, in a turbulent era, the Club often provided a focus for the community and brought light and entertainment that lifted the town in times of trouble.

It was also the decade in which Sunderland confirmed their position as one of the nation's top clubs and reinforced their status as the North-East's number one sports team.

YOUNG GUNS

Go for it

1930 · 1940

1930-1931
Up for the Cup

"Elements of a good team were in place… but there was still much to be done."

1930-31 Sunderland team.

Goals a-Plenty

The Lads had just come through a sticky patch, and had dished out a 5 - 0 thrashing to the Mags in their previous home game, when they prepared for the visit of Liverpool in early December. Thick fog and some school boy defending added a couple of extra dimensions to a match that saw a staggering eleven goals! The Merseysiders took a while to get into their stride, and after just 35 minutes we were cruising 4 - 1! It looked all over bar the shouting, but a fight back came. By half time it was 4 - 3 and we had a battle on our hands! 13 minutes after the interval Gurney extended our lead and an own goal from the Liverpool full back, Lucas, made it 6 - 3. Again it seemed all over, but again the Merseysiders came roaring back. Smith scored two late goals to pull the scores to 6 - 5 and set up an anxious finish. However, the Lads managed to hang on - aided by an injury to Hopkin that reduced Liverpool to ten men - and a bizarre victory had been sealed.

The first full season of the new decade kicked off on 30th August with a dramatic match at Roker against Manchester City. With the only new face in the line up coming from the addition of St Mirren's winger Jimmy Connor, the performance mirrored those typical of the previous season. While Connor was a promising winger who would be capped by Scotland while at Sunderland, it was the defence that really needed strengthening. The Lads managed to bag a decent number of goals, Gurney being amongst the scorers as we hit three, but City proved an equal match, the Sunderland defenders being unable to stem the tide. The game finished 3 - 3. In the end, this was a decent result, for the Lads had been two goals down at one point! A similar story emerged in our second game, which saw us travel to Bramall Lane. We hadn't managed to beat Sheffield United on their own ground for some eighteen years, and with defensive weaknesses exposed once again, only Gurney's brilliance and a lucky own goal prevented defeat. Once again, the game ended 3 - 3.

However, Cochrane was a canny manager and wise to the key issue. While his rebuilding process was always going to be fraught with difficulties, he had moved in the summer to snap up a player who would add some steel to the side. Alex Hastings, another Scot, arrived from Stenhousemuir, and he made his debut in our third game of the season - at Portsmouth - where a much tighter performance at the back produced a 1 - 1 scoreline. Hastings, a left-half, would prove an invaluable player, but like many of Cochrane's signings was, perhaps, one whose true worth would only become fully apparent in the future. The rest of the month was still dominated by the defensive problem, Derby (3 -1), Arsenal (4 - 1) and Blackpool (4 -2) thrashing us at home, and Derby (4 -1) and Blackburn (3 - 0) beating us on our travels. By the end of September, twenty-five goals had been hit past the Sunderland defence in just eight games. With the forwards finding it increasingly it difficult to compensate for this at the other end, the League table made less than happy reading.

Indeed, it was October before we managed to notch up our first victory, a 3 - 0 at Leeds United, a result that was followed three weeks later by our second victory, an impressive 4 - 2 at home to Huddersfield Town. However, the team's problems were far from over. Sandwiched between these victories was a close fought match at Middlesbrough, which we lost 1 - 0. Worse still, victory over Huddersfield was followed by the humiliation of a 7 - 2 drubbing at Sheffield Wednesday.

Fortunately, the performances picked up a little after this thrashing as we remained unbeaten for the rest of the month and thrashed the Mags 5 - 0 at Roker Park! The latter was a game our neighbours had much the better of, but Sunderland's short passing game outwitted the visitors and the result was hailed as a tactical victory for the Lads. The following month we went goal crazy, putting six past Liverpool and West Ham, but also conceding five against Chelsea, Leicester and Liverpool. It was clear that going forward, Cochrane's side could be amongst the best around. But, for all our love of attacking football, it was equally clear that the gung-ho approach would never bring silverware to Roker.

Nevertheless, the Lads were determined to have a stab at it and made a good start in the FA Cup. Southampton's 'rough play' in the third round was overcome by our greater guile, a 2 - 0 victory being the outcome. The fourth round brought us a tie at Bolton Wanderers, where a late equaliser kept us in the competition. The game was replayed at Roker Park four days later where the Lads made no mistake, taking control when Leonard converted an early penalty and running out 3 - 1 winners.

As the Cup campaign built up steam, performances in the League showed signs of improvement. February began with an 8 - 2 thrashing of Blackburn Rovers, Eden and Leonard both grabbing hat tricks. Incredibly, we went in at half time with a 7 - 0 lead, though perhaps the result was aided by the weather - it had been snowing heavily - and the fact that Rovers were fielding two reserve backs. Nevertheless, it was a good victory, and was quickly followed by a 4 - 0 win at home to Leeds. The Lads were now on a roll, and a massive gate of 63,016, a new ground record, turned up for the next instalment of the FA Cup, a date with Sheffield United. The game was a close fought classic, and with time running out an absolute peach from Bobby Gurney sealed a 2 - 1 victory for Sunderland.

A fortnight later, Exeter City arrived at Roker Park for the quarter-final tie. An easy victory was expected, and Sunderland laid siege to the City half. Frustratingly, it was one of those days where it proved almost impossible to turn possession into goals. A 51,462 crowd were stunned by a 1 - 1 scoreline. However, Exeter's luck could only last so long, and the replay a few days later saw us ease through to the last four of the Cup with a 4 - 2 victory.

The Cup run underlined the progress Cochrane was making in remoulding the side. Progression to the last four of the competition had been accompanied by a steady improvement in League form, and the Lads followed their sixth round victory with a 5 - 1 hammering of Sheffield Wednesday in the League, Gurney scoring his second hat trick of the season as we ran riot. With good performances having become the norm since the turn of the year, confidence was high as Sunderland travelled to Elland Road for the FA Cup semi-final tie with Birmingham City. However, the game ended in major disappointment for the thousands who made the short journey south. We had plenty of the ball, but Welsh international Curtis scored twice for the Midlanders and our forwards were silenced. The Cup dream was over again.

Defeat was disappointing for fans and players alike, and the Lads took it badly. The result seemed to knock the stuffing out of us: five of the next seven League games were lost. Though we rallied well, winning our last four games, this merely served to underline the fragile confidence of the team. Elements of a good team were in place, but there was still much to be done. While the eleventh placed finish in the League was respectable enough - being bang in the middle of the table - it was a move in the wrong direction for Cochrane's side. The Cup run had been exciting, but mixed form over the season as a whole, and some atrocious defeats, suggested the team was some way short of being capable of competing with the best.

Captain Hastings

A significant addition to the Sunderland squad during the season was Alex Hastings, who arrived from Stenhousemuir in early August 1930. Primarily a left half, who also featured at right half when required, he had few peers in his favoured position, and was capped by his native Scotland twice. In a Sunderland career that stretched over 15 years, he made more than 300 League and Cup appearances - a figure that would have been higher still but for the interruption of the War - and Hastings piloted us to Championship glory when he Captained the team during the all important 1935-36 season.

Alex Hastings.

1931-1932
Disappointment

"the glory days seemed a long way off."

Hastings at Horden.

Disaster

The last weekend of November saw the First Division go goal crazy. 62 goals were scored in the 11 games played, including 11 goals in the game at Everton, where Leicester went down 9 - 2. The fixture at Roker Park saw plenty of goals too. Unfortunately, most of them were for our local rivals Newcastle, as the Lads slumped to a 4 - 1 defeat. The Mags totally outplayed us, their forwards reportedly having 'completely outwitted' our defenders.

It was a poor result, and one that left us fourth from bottom in the League. To make matters worse, we had played a game more than the three teams below us, and both Chelsea and Blackpool were just a single point behind us. The Newcastle fans must, then, have taken particular delight in this derby victory.

Following the previous season's mid-table finish, many fans were hoping that new faces would arrive to bolster the team's fortunes. However, that the days of big money signings were gone was underlined by the fact that there were no major pre-season buys. Cochrane did not depart from his chosen strategy and continued to put faith in youth. 17 year old Charles Thomson was the only arrival, for a measly £50 fee, and he was soon followed by another youngster - local lad Raich Carter - an unknown who joined the Club in November. On top of this, one of the old stars was allowed to leave too, 1920s favourite Billy Clunas moving to Morton for £500 just before the season began. It was clear that the old guard was gradually being dismantled, but it would be some time before the significance of the new arrivals became apparent.

So, it was a familiar line up that travelled to Manchester City for our opening fixture, where a Gallacher goal earned a share of the points in a 1 - 1 draw. A few days later, FA Cup winners West Bromwich Albion, newly promoted from Division Two, visited Roker Park. A 2 - 1 victory completed a pleasing opening week. However, fans had to savour this victory, for there was to be little joy over the next couple of months. Four consecutive defeats followed the West Brom game, including two 3 - 2 defeats at home to Everton and Birmingham. Once again, the new team showed itself to be of fragile quality, and with just three points taken from the first twelve, the signs were not good.

While the Lads managed to bounce back from this spell by putting together a six game unbeaten run - including victories against Blackpool (4 - 0) and Chelsea (2 - 1) - the poor form soon returned, and a nightmare November saw all our League games end in defeat. As if this wasn't bad enough, some of the games were real beatings. Newcastle beat us 4 - 1 in the derby match at Roker Park - in front of our biggest crowd for the season - and Leicester thrashed us 5 - 0. A run of nineteen goals conceded in just six games, combined with a measly return of just four goals in reply, made it clear for all to see that the side had real problems, defensive ones in particular.

Yet, just when it seemed matters could not get any worse, they did. Though December began with good victories against Grimsby and Sheffield Wednesday - both 3 - 1 - and saw us hold our own at West Ham in a 2 - 2 draw just before Christmas, the end of the month saw disaster strike. One of the few players to be turning in creditable performances, and the man at the heart of our purple patch in the run up to Christmas, was Bobby Gurney. Having scored fourteen of our twenty-eight goals so far, and in a rich vein of form that had seen him hit seven in the month's first three games, he was crucial to our fortunes. But, in a Boxing Day encounter at Derby County, Gurney went down injured, and damage to his knee kept him out of action for the next ten weeks. Sunderland's hopes of survival suddenly hung by a thread.

Without our star striker, the Lads found it hard to reply to the increasingly inevitable shower of goals being conceded at the back. January saw us go without a win in the League: Manchester City beat us 5 - 2, with former Sunderland ace Dave Halliday - the man replaced by Gurney - hitting an eight minute hat-trick; Everton beat us 4 - 2 in front of a massive 40,000 crowd; and finally, Blackpool scraped a 3 - 2 win against us to seal the misery in a very disappointing defeat against one of the few teams having a worse season than us. The results left us third bottom, thanks in main to the atrocious form of Blackpool and Grimsby.

However, there was at least one bright note in the Blackpool game. With the League table looking increasingly grim, and Gurney showing no signs of a quick return from injury, the manager at last made a foray into the transfer market, signing Scottish international Benny Yorston from Aberdeen. Yorston made his debut in the game, rounding off a decent performance with a welcome goal.

Ironically, the historical pattern was reversed this season, with the poor showings in the League being accompanied by some good form in the Cup. The Lads played four ties in January and avoided defeat in them all. The third round pitched us against Southampton for the second season in succession, and though the fixture produced a disappointing 0 - 0 home draw, in the replay we hammered the Second Division side 4 - 2, a brace from Poulter - one of the few amateurs to play for the Lads in the 1930s - securing the win. His goals set up a mammoth fourth round encounter with Stoke. We were drawn to play at home, and a close game ended 1 - 1. In the replay, there was again little between the teams, and it also ended 1 - 1 after 90 minutes. No further goals were scored in extra time, and the tie went to a second replay. The game - our first of February - again went to extra time, but on this occasion a winner was found; unfortunately, it wasn't Sunderland, Stoke running out 2 - 1 winners. After playing five Cup matches, we fell out of the competition at only the second hurdle!

The Lads responded positively to the Cup exit though, Yorston doing the business in a 1 - 0 victory against Sheffield United. Though this victory was followed by a 5 - 2 defeat at Blackburn, February was rounded off with an altogether more pleasing scoreline, a 5 - 1 win at home to Portsmouth. What is more, in the second week of March, Gurney returned to the side and results dramatically improved. Although it was Yorston and Gallacher who were hitting the goals rather than Gurney, just two of the last eleven games were lost following the player's return. Indeed, victories now became the norm, and there were some pleasing results. Leicester were beaten 4 - 1, Arsenal beaten 2 - 0 and most pleasingly of all, there was a 2 - 1 win at St James' Park against the Mags!

Spurred on by Gurney and powered by Yorston's goals, the Lads started to rack up points in the closing stages of the season. A final flurry of five wins in the last six matches helped lift us to thirteenth place. After the early season problems, the final position came as a welcome relief. But, while danger had been averted, it was in truth another mediocre finish for Cochrane's side. The season was undoubtedly one of young players, not quite up to the standard, being saved by a late panic buy when things looked truly dim. Following his arrival, Yorston hit thirteen goals in seventeen games; if he had been brought in at the start of the season the Lads may have fared considerably better. As it was, the glory days seemed a long way off, with memories of success fading and prospects for the future seeming dim. To make matters worse, Newcastle finished the season by winning the FA Cup. Our position as the Kings of North East Football was under threat.

Future Star

When Charles Thomson joined Sunderland at the start of the season, for £50 from Glasgow Pollok, no-one knew what the future held for the 17 year old Scot. He would spend most of the first season on the sidelines, appearing just twice for the Lads. The following campaign, however, saw him break into the side at a youthful 18, making 37 League and Cup appearances. It was not long before he became a stalwart of the side, being an ever present in the 1934-35 and 1935-36 seasons. Indeed, he once had a spell where he made 148 consecutive appearances for the Lads, quite a record.

Thomson - who played at right-half - was an excellent dribbler of the ball, and was capped by his native Scotland while at Sunderland. In all, he made 263 League and Cup appearances for the Lads, before retiring from football during the War.

C Thomson.

1932-1933
Hard Times

"In a reflection of the hard times faced by the region the team struggled from the start of the season"

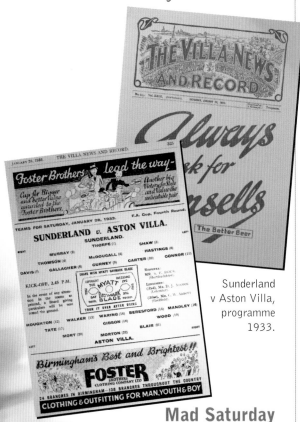

Sunderland v Aston Villa, programme 1933.

Mad Saturday

The last weekend of October saw a series of strange events at football matches as an early blast of winter weather made it difficult to play football. At Blackpool, Chelsea ended their game with just six players, the icy wind causing many to faint! At Blackburn the referee collapsed, causing a temporary interval to the game. Arsenal whacked eight past Leicester in a ten goal thriller. Most importantly though, at Roker Park we hammered Bolton 7 - 4! It was an extraordinary game, with the scoreline 6 - 2 at half-time. Indeed, Bolton did well to rally, and their 'keeper had an outstanding game. The Sunderland front men were just too hot to handle though. Gurney ran riot, hitting four goals, and Carter - described that day as 'the perfect forward' - grabbed one, along with Connor and Temple. Gibson, Dixon and Butler (2) hit goals for Bolton, but in the end it was our day. What a result!

For the North East in general, and for much of the country, the early 1930s were above all else hard times. Mass unemployment plagued many of the area's key industries, and for football fans faced with the harsh realities of life without work, finding enough money to watch the Lads was difficult to say the least. Yet, there were times when passion demanded sacrifices be made, particularly for big Cup games or the annual derby match. The attendance figures for the season tell this story well, for the economic situation was largely responsible for producing Roker Park's lowest crowd for a top class football match, but the season also saw its highest.

Of course, the economic situation impacted on the Club too, and fewer fans meant less money in the kitty; in such circumstances, Cochrane's low budget approach was in many ways a necessity. In a reflection of the hard times faced by the region, the team struggled from the start of the season. The campaign - for the third time in a row - began with a fixture against Manchester City, and while the Lads produced a 3 - 2 victory, it was to be a rare bright spot of a poor opening period. Four of the next six games were lost, including a 6 - 1 thrashing at Arsenal. While in some respects the poor form was due to the absence of key players - Yorston being missing throughout September for example - it was also the case that the team were unable to find their stride.

Fortunately, the sticky patch came to an end in October, the Lads securing good victories against Blackburn (3 - 1) and Middlesbrough (2 - 1) and putting up a superb performance at home to Bolton, where just 9,000 witnessed a classic 7 - 4 win. Although the following month saw us suffer another disappointing home defeat against the Mags - 42,000 seeing the Lads slump 0 - 2 - from October through to the end of the year the Lads were in generally good form, December seeing successive victories against Leicester, Portsmouth and Chelsea. This was more like it! Though the good spell was interrupted by a 5 - 1 thrashing at West Brom on Boxing Day, the year was rounded off with a fine 4 - 2 victory at Manchester City.

The pleasing performances carried on into the New Year, Arsenal - who would eventually be crowned Champions - being beaten 3 - 2 in the League. When the FA Cup came around, the Lads were more than ready for a trip to Hull City. Progression to the fourth round was guaranteed with a 2 - 0 victory, and a tie at Aston Villa beckoned. It was a fact that the famous Team of All Talents had never beaten Villa in a cup tie, but the current crop of young braves excelled and triumphed 3 - 0, Bobby Gurney scoring a memorable hat trick. Victory was in no small part due to a brilliant job by McDougall, the Sunderland back, who subdued dangerman Pongo Waring, Villa's feared striker.

In between the two Cup games, we had been given a 1 - 6 hammering by reigning Champions Everton, and as our Cup run continued, League form noticeably dipped. The fans, though, were excited by the Cup, and the fifth round tie with Blackpool attracted 35,000, our second biggest gate of the season to that point. The game was won by a single goal for Gurney, taking his tally to five goals in three Cup matches. All eyes were now focused on the quarter-final encounter with Derby County. The teams had already met twice in the League - Derby running out winners on both occasions - but the Lads were up for the Cup and battled hard this time.

The game ended 4 - 4, earning us a replay at Roker Park.75,118 - still a Club record attendance - then made their way to see Sunderland challenge for a place in the semi-final. The massive crowd was the largest ever seen in England for a midweek game, and there was trouble keeping the fans on the terraces; at one point the referee had to stop play in order to help the police clear the pitch. The game, though, was not a classic. The Times reported that 'play was considerably affected by the importance of the occasion'. Our forwards fluffed a number of good chances, Davis blasting over the bar from just three yards out. Gurney did manage to put the ball into the net but, after much discussion between the referee and linesman, the goal was disallowed for offside. While most of the pressure came from our side, with Carter and Gallacher being singled out for their contribution, the Derby backs were solid, and coped with everything thrown their way. At the end of the 90 minutes, the game was 0 - 0, and extra time was needed. With stalemate continuing, another replay looked likely, but towards the end of the first period, Rammage hit a crucial goal for the Rams. The visitors then shut up shop and the Lads were unable to reply. We had gone out of the Cup by the smallest of margins.

The effect of this defeat was stunning. In our remaining twelve League games we scored only six times: the team was shattered. Fortunately, the defence tightened up a little, meaning we still picked up points - including two special ones gained in a 1 - 0 victory at Newcastle - but the crowds dipped considerably. Just six weeks after recording our largest ever crowd we recorded our lowest ever: a tiny 4,000 turned out for the last home League game, on 29th April, against Portsmouth. Neither team had anything to play for, and with goals and money tight, few made it to Roker Park for the fixture. The season ground to an end with the Lads in twelfth place, one better than the previous season but still remarkably average. In a story that would become depressingly familiar for future generations of Sunderland fans, there was little sign of the Club achieving success, but it was difficult to think of a realistic alternative way forward either. However, the Club's shirts bore the Sunderland Corporation's famous crest; the next few seasons would show that 'nil desperandum' was a most appropriate motto.

Cup Fever Reaches Boiling Point

The most dramatic moments of the season came in the FA Cup, particularly the two quarter-final ties with Derby. The original tie - at the Baseball Ground - was a classic, ending 4 - 4. The Times concluded afterwards that 'there could hardly have been a more exciting game'. The Lads had much the better of the play, but somehow found themselves two down inside fifteen minutes. It was a thoroughly undeserved lead, but we fought back, and two goals in the space of a minute brought the game level midway through the first half. Just after the half-hour mark, Gurney made it 3 - 2 to Sunderland, but four minutes later the scores were level again.

It was pulsating stuff, but the tie calmed down a little in the second period. Shortly after the restart, Gurney gave us a 4 - 3 lead, and the Lads took control. Derby found it difficult to get the ball out of their own half, but a desperate rally in the last five minutes produced a breakthrough, Duncan hitting a last minute equaliser that fooled Thorpe in the Sunderland goal. The Lads had been desperately unlucky, and the replay brought further pain. The Cup jinx was continuing...

Blizard at Blackpool cup tie 1933.

1933-1934 Promise

"There were real signs of progress now...perhaps Cochrane's faith in youth hadn't been misplaced after all"

Harold Shaw

Spain Conquered

As something of a 'post-script' to the season, the Lads were taken on a three match tour of Spain. The 13th May saw us play Athletic Bilbao - a team who wore red and white at the suggestion of former Wearside shipyard worker Arthur Pentland - and the Lads gave a fine exhibition as an exciting game ended 3 - 3, Shaw hitting our equaliser right at the death. The Lads then travelled to Madrid, where 40,000 watched us play a representative XI, a game that ended 2 - 2. The final match of the tour took place against a Spanish XI, again in Madrid, but this time we triumphed, Gallacher, Shaw and Connor doing the damage in a 3 - 1 victory. It was an unusual end to the season, but a useful learning process for Cochrane's young side.

The Lads began their fourth season of the 1930s inauspiciously. Having failed to secure a top ten finish so far during the decade, defeats against Huddersfield and Portsmouth in our opening two games did not augur well. Once again there were no new signings on display and the fans must have feared the worst. However, the next few weeks brought some remarkable scorelines, with Stoke beaten 4 - 1, Wolves thrashed 6 - 1 and Sheffield United hammered 5 - 0. The Wolves result was particularly pleasing for it was an away game against a side at the top of the table. However, the Wolves result was something of an exception, and over the next couple of months a general pattern emerged that saw us play brilliantly at home but falter on our travels. Home victories against teams such as Liverpool (4 - 1), Leeds (4 - 2), Sheffield Wednesday (4 - 0) and even reigning Champions Arsenal (3 - 0), were interspersed with away defeats at Newcastle (2 - 1), Spurs (3 - 1), Manchester City (4 - 1) and Chelsea (4 - 0) for example.

A pleasing exception to this rule came with a trip to Middlesbrough at the start of December, when a Patsy Gallacher hat trick helped us to a 4 - 0 victory. Hopes of victory must have been high then, when we were drawn to play our neighbours in the third round of the FA Cup. The tie, played at Roker Park, attracted 43,600 fans, and ended in a 1 - 1 draw. The result was tinged with controversy, many feeling the 'Boro goal was well offside. The replay, though, proved more satisfying, Yorston and Gurney getting the goals in a 2 - 1 victory. Our reward was a fourth round tie with Cup bogey side Aston Villa. Having knocked them out at the same stage of the Cup the previous season the Lads had no fear; Villa, however, took no prisoners on the day. A massive 57,213 crowd packed into Villa Park and witnessed a humiliating 7 - 2 defeat for the Lads.

Perhaps it would have been a different result if the game had taken place at Roker Park; indeed, when Villa made the trip to Wearside a week later for a League match we hammered them 5 - 1. The great home form continued, the Villa match being followed at home by a 6 - 0 win against Spurs - no mean feat versus a team that would finish third in the League. Further pleasing victories came with visits from Blackburn (3 - 0), Birmingham (4 - 1) and Newcastle, our rivals being sunk 2 - 0.

Away from home, though, form continued to stink! Draws were the best we could manage, but many games were lost. The trip to West Brom produced a particularly bizarre outcome. In a match regarded as one of the finest played at their stadium, the lead seesawed between two well matched sides. The Baggies struck first after just eight seconds, Richardson giving them an early advantage. Gurney then brought the scores level on seven minutes, but seven minutes later Boyes regained the lead for the home side. Amazingly, after another seven minutes Carter equalised for Sunderland, and sixty seconds later Gurney made it 3 - 2 and - at last - gave Sunderland the lead! Unfortunately, we held out for just five minutes, as Glidden brought the scores level once again. Worse still, West Brom snatched a lead just before half-time, making it 4 - 3 at the interval. When the game restarted, the crowd were given time to catch their breath before the scoring started all over again. On 75 minutes, Shaw made it 4 - 4, but Sandford and then Glidden put the Baggies two goals clear. Still it was not over, and the Lads rallied, Gurney pulling it back to 5 - 6 with just minutes left.

Sunderland pressed for the equaliser, but at the final whistle we had lost. The crowd rose to their feet: they knew they had seen a classic. It is unlikely that Cochrane was quite so pleased with a game that saw Gurney score a hat-trick but left Sunderland without any points to take home.

As the season entered its final month, it was clear that if Sunderland could play away from home as they did at Roker Park then the Championship would be in the bag. Five points were taken from the last three home games, making it 34 points from a possible 42 at home and 15 wins in 21 games. However, this compared to a measly 14 points secured away from home, 10 of those coming from drawn matches; just two League games were won on our travels. As a result, the Lads finished in sixth position - their best performance since 1926-27 - but just four more wins would have been enough to push us into second position.

Overall, the season had been a pleasing one. The emergence of the youthful back line of Thomson, Johnston and Hastings had done much to overcome the defensive weaknesses that had plagued the side in recent years. Indeed, Bobby Gurney later suggested that this trio provided the "springboard" for the success that was to come in the next few seasons. Similarly, the quiet progress of the previous two seasons began to become apparent as other young players, such as Thorpe in goal and Carter in the forward line, began to blossom. While there was still room for improvement, there were real signs of progress now. Perhaps Cochrane's faith in youth hadn't been misplaced after all...

Free Scoring Spell

After a poor start to the season, Sunderland began banging the goals in during September; when a 6 - 1 victory at Wolves was followed by a 5 - 0 win at home to Sheffield United, The Times were suitably impressed, noting "another highscoring day" and pointing out that we were now, by some way, the top scoring side in the First Division. The 5 - 0 victory lifted us to third in the League, just one point behind joint leaders Spurs and Huddersfield.

The Championship challenge did not continue, but it was an early sign that we were about to reclaim our position at the top of football's elite. What's more, it suggested that our free scoring play could be the key to both entertaining footballing and Championship success. Rather like the exciting Team of All Talents that had done so well in the 1890s, we were building a deadly reputation through our attacking play. Bobby Gurney, of course, had done the most damage, scoring 21 League goals. But, others were hitting their fair share too. Raich Carter had weighed in with 17 strikes, as had Patsy Gallacher. Bert Davis just managed double figures with 10 and Yorston had scored 6 in 14 games before moving to Middlesbrough.

With so many of the players still in the early stages of their careers, there was a genuine excitement about the future. Sure enough, there was better to come from our talented front line, but what they eventually delivered exceeded the wildest expectations.

Bobby Gurney in action.

1934-1935

Contenders

Raich Carter.

Cup Classic

Sunderland's FA Cup fourth round replay away to Everton produced ten goals. A massive crowd presented problems for the police and ambulance services, but on the pitch defenders would be equally busy. After just thirteen minutes, Coulter had given Everton the lead with a headed goal, and by half-time the game was already 2 - 1, the home side having the advantage. In the second half, Everton extended their lead through Stevenson, but with just ten minutes left, the Lads rallied. Connor pulled the scores back to 3 - 2, before Gurney hit a spectacular overhead kick on 87 minutes to make it 3 - 3. In extra-time, however, the home side over ran us. Coulter quickly gave Everton the lead again, and though Connor levelled the scores five minutes later, the Merseysiders hit two more goals to make it 6 - 4 at the final whistle. We had been very unlucky, having a goal disallowed in extra time, but couldn't really complain. There had been plenty of chances to score, and we hadn't been as clinical as Everton.

After the success of the previous campaign, the new season began with some hope. With the different pieces of the team coming together, the Lads kicked off in style, showing what they were capable of in a 4 - 1 home win against Huddersfield Town. It was merely the first instalment of a great start to the season all round. Four of the first five fixtures were won, full points being taken in the games against Wolves (2 - 1), Grimsby (3 - 0) and Chelsea (4 - 0). Although by the end of September we had picked up our first defeat - a 4 - 1 hammering at home to Derby - we had also picked up our second away victory by beating Leicester 2 - 0, quickly matching the previous season's number of wins on the road.

This was good news, but in a bizarre reversal of the previous season's scenario, the defeats were coming at Roker and away from home we were unbeatable! Indeed, there were some great performances on the road. November saw Stoke beaten 3 - 0 and Leeds beaten 4 - 2, while in December, we beat the previous season's FA Cup runners up, Portsmouth, 4 - 2. In fact, the Lads did not lose away from home until Christmas Day, when Everton beat us 6 - 2. By this point, however, we had already lost at home four times after having lost just once in Sunderland the previous season! Why this should be is unclear, but it has been suggested that the players were becoming a little over-confident at home, thinking they just had to turn up to win. Unfortunately, it required more effort than this...

However, despite these small problems at home, we were still riding high in the League table. It would be wrong to give the impression that it was all going wrong at home, for our form at Roker was still excellent and the Championship was a real possibility. Perhaps the most notable result of the opening months came when the Champions, Arsenal, visited Roker Park and were sent home pointless, a brace from Carter sealing a 2 - 1 victory. Arsenal were leading the table at the time and the result edged us closer to the top. A 3 - 0 win against Stoke the following week put us top of the table.

Pleasingly, the side now showed signs of real character when necessary. Victory against Arsenal came after being a goal down; similarly, when Manchester City visited a week after the Stoke match, they raced into a 2 - 0 lead, but the Lads fought back to win 3 - 2, City being overwhelmed by the power of our football. Scoring first against Sunderland was once enough to ensure victory, but now it often resulted in annihilation, as Birmingham found out when they had the audacity to go 1 - 0 up against us; the Lads reacted by hammering five past them! Moreover, on the odd occasion we did lose, the reaction afterwards was usually spot on. Defeat at Everton on Christmas Day, for example, was followed by a 7 - 0 thrashing of the same side the following day.

So, when the FA Cup began the Lads were riding high. The third round had paired us with Fulham at Roker, and we triumphed 3 - 2. In the following round, Everton provided the opposition, but a 1 - 1 draw at Roker, after Carter had given Sunderland the lead, was disappointing. The replay, however, proved to be a fantastic game. In a game littered with goals the scores were level at 3 - 3 when the final whistle went. In extra time, the game exploded, with a further four goals being added; however, most of them were for Everton, and the Merseysiders went through to the next round with a 6 - 4 victory.

Once more eliminated at an early stage in the FA Cup, we succumbed to Derby County in the very next League game, losing 3 - 1, before we pulled up our socks and put the Championship challenge back on track with a long unbeaten run. Villa visited Roker Park a few days later and were held 3 - 3. Points were then racked up with a 2 - 0 win over Leicester and a potentially tricky derby match at Middlesbrough ended in a goalless draw. As March began, the Lads prepared for a trip to the League leaders by beating Blackburn 3 - 0.

The game against Arsenal was a massive one. The Lads were just two points behind the Champions, and victory would take us joint top. However, the match was a dull affair, ending 0 - 0. Though we followed the game with good victories against Stoke and Leeds, the Gunners were matching us all the way, and in early April we hit a sticky patch, dropping crucial points in draws against West Brom and Sheffield Wednesday, before seeing our unbeaten run come to an end at Manchester City. As the season drew to an end, we ran out of steam, and three of the final four fixtures ended in draws. As a result, we finished in second place, four points behind Arsenal. In an echo of the previous decade we had fallen just short of being Championship material. In contrast to those days, however, this team was a young one, learning all the time; there was a genuine promise of better to come in the future.

At last the fans were being provided with what they deserved: a team that could challenge for honours. In a fine season, the Lads had put in an excellent performance. Finishing as runners up to Arsenal was nothing to be sniffed at; the mighty Gunners had just clinched their third title in a row. What is more, the improvement away from home had been extremely pleasing and bode well for the future. However, the one sour note was that after doing so well at home the previous season, four of our seven defeats had come at Roker. Had we avoided defeat in these four games, and secured a victory in one of them, the Championship would have been ours. The lesson was clear: if the Lads could turn Roker back into a fortress next season, the Championship would - at last - make its way back to Sunderland.

Heavyweights Battle It Out

With the season drawing to an end, the Lads visited leaders Arsenal on 9th March, knowing that victory would put us level on points at the top. 73,295 - still a record attendance for Arsenal at Highbury - paid to see the game, but it was, by all accounts, a poor match. Both sides were a little edgy, wary of making a mistake that might allow their opponents to gain an advantage in both the game and the title race, and the match became quite negative. Indeed, there was much rough play, and The Times noted that the "tactics, as the match went on, clearly defined themselves. The ball or, if that was not possible the man had to be stopped". At one point our forwards appeared to have wrestled the Arsenal goalie to the ground and it was surprising that no-one received a red card. The Lads had the better of the first half - Carter hitting the post from 25 yards out after the 'keeper was well beaten - but the Gunners were on top after the break. The game ended 0 - 0, a fair result, but not one most of the massive crowd were looking for. It was one of those games that was a classic occasion, but anything but a classic match.

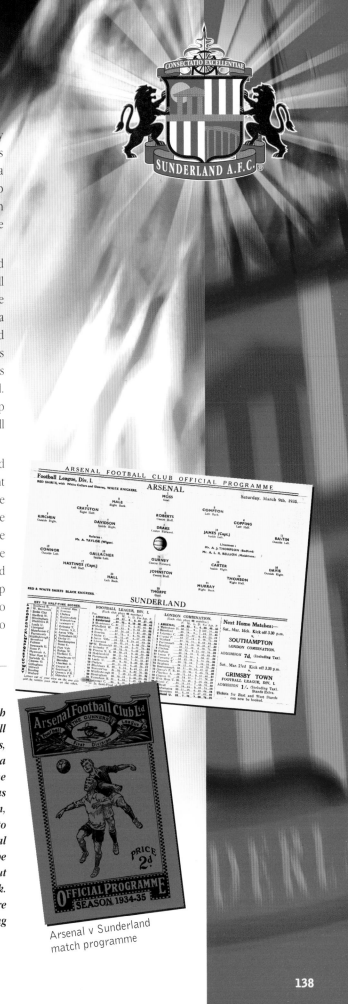

Arsenal v Sunderland
match programme

1935-1936
Kings

"The undisputed Kings of English football"

Bert Johnstone.

Gunners Out-gunned

On 28th December, 1935, the Champions, Arsenal, visited Roker Park. In a game billed by the Sunderland Echo as "The Best Game Yet At Roker" the attendance record for a League game on Wearside was beaten. Arsenal were trying for their fourth Championship in a row, but it was Sunderland who took first blood. After just seven minutes, Davis smashed the ball home to make it 1 - 0 to the Lads. Shortly afterwards, Davis turned provider, his hanging cross being headed home by Gallacher. The Gunners, though, were not prepared to lie down and let the game pass them by, goalscoring legend Cliff Bastin giving the score a more balanced feel with a glorious strike past Thorpe. It was a fast, action packed game, but there was more to come before half-time, and the Lads hit two more goals in the first half, Carter getting a brace to make it 4 - 1 at the interval.

It looked like the game was all over, but a rude awakening awaited. Drake narrowed the gap with a cool finish shortly after the restart, and Bowden headed another to make the scores 4 - 3. All of a sudden the result was in doubt, but as Arsenal pressed for an equaliser, Sunderland upped their game again. Neat play between Connor and Carter created an opening for the latter, and he smacked a beauty past Moss to make it 5 - 3. Though Bowden popped up near the end to steer a shot into the net, it was too late for Arsenal; as the final whistle went, the Lads were 5 - 4 up, and they took away all the points. Both teams left the pitch to thunderous applause. What a game!

While the previous season had undoubtedly been an excellent performance, in football there are no real prizes for coming second. After pushing Arsenal close, the Lads were determined to go one better in 1935-36 and lift the Championship trophy at the end of the campaign. For the second season in a row there were no new signings brought in, Cochrane deciding to stick with his home grown heroes, and a clear first choice XI had emerged: Thorpe in goal; Murray and Hall at the back; Thomson, Clarke and Hastings across the middle; and Davis, Carter, Gurney, Gallacher and Connor up front. Could this team, moulded in the manager's own image, go one better this time and end Arsenal's stranglehold on the League Championship?

In true 'Roy of the Rovers' style, the first fixture of the new season saw us pitted against the Champions, providing us with an early chance to assert our claim on the trophy. The Lads had a good record against Arsenal during the decade, and 50,000 turned out to see the game at Highbury. However, although Gurney managed to open his account with a goal, the Gunners ran out winners, beating us 3 - 1; it was not the dream start we had been hoping for.

Unperturbed, the Lads pressed on, and in the next two weeks they pulled out the stops, sweeping away all the opposition put before them. West Brom were beaten 3 - 1, Gallacher getting a brace; Manchester City were defeated 2 - 1 in our first home fixture; the return against West Brom saw us run out 6 - 1 winners, Gurney grabbing four; and Stoke were despatched 2 - 0. It was great stuff, but better was still to come! When Blackburn visited Roker Park on the 21st September, the opening month of the season was capped with a superb display that sent the Lancashire team home shell shocked. The Lads ran riot in front of a 30,000 crowd, Gallacher scoring a hat trick and Gurney hitting a brace as we ran out 7 - 2 winners.

Though this stunning victory was followed by a disappointing 3 - 1 defeat at Chelsea, this was a minor blemish in an almost perfect spell. The Lads were in a rich vein of form and in the last three months of 1935 they won all but three of their fourteen League fixtures. It was a phenomenal run - reminiscent of the Team of All Talents' glory days - and some brilliant wins were notched up. Notably: Wolves were beaten 4 - 3 at Molineux; FA Cup holders Sheffield Wednesday were hammered 5 - 1; Brentford suffered the same scoreline on their own turf; a 60,000 crowd saw Middlesbrough beaten 2 - 1 at Roker Park; Everton were easily dispatched 3 - 0 at Goodison; and Bolton were hammered 7 - 2 at Roker, Gurney grabbing a staggering five goals! At last, it didn't matter whether we played teams at home or away, for our form was consistently brilliant! But, the most significant result of all during this spell came in our last game of the year, when the Champions visited Roker Park three days after Christmas. A huge 60,000 crowd turned out for the occasion, and they were treated to a classic. In a game that could have gone either way, nine goals were scored, but Sunderland won out in the end, finishing 5 - 4 victors.

After such a glorious end to 1935, it was perhaps inevitable that we would suffer some sort of dip in form during 1936. However, few would have expected it to begin on the first day of the New Year; Villa dampened celebrations by beating us 3 - 1 at Roker Park. This was by no means a disaster, but the FA Cup provided the real ignominy. In a tie we should have won easily, Port Vale - bottom of the Second Division - held us 2 - 2 at home. This was bad enough, but the replay at their place did not produce the expected victory for Sunderland. Instead, the underdogs ran out 2 - 0 winners. The Cup jinx had struck again! All but invincible in the League, we collapsed like school boys in the Cup.

At least the quick exit allowed us to concentrate on the League. Already we were clear favourites for the title, and though our form was some way below that produced before Christmas, games were generally being won throughout January and February. Victories tended to be more modest than the five and six goal hammerings that had been handed out previously, but decent victories were secured against Liverpool (3 - 0), Grimsby (3 - 1) and Wolves (3 - 1). Moreover, we were proving difficult to beat too, and aside from Villa, only Preston managed to overcome us in the League during the first two months of 1936.

With the title seemingly secured, however, we began to falter a little. In March, the Lads failed to win a single game, and lost heavily at home to Brentford (3 - 1) and at Ayresome Park against Middlesbrough (a massive 6 - 0). Both teams had been easily beaten earlier in the season and explaining the slump is difficult. This was not a 1920s scenario, where the team lost their nerve as close rivals started to catch up. Partly it was a case of taking the foot off the accelerator; unlike the 1923-24 season we were well clear of our nearest rivals for the title. But, the team must also have been affected by the tragic death of stalwart goalkeeper Jimmy Thorpe. Thorpe had been an ever present in the team until his untimely death, when a series of rough challenges in the game against Chelsea, combined with his diabetes, had led to his death in early February. For a while, the Lads played superbly, the greatest honour for his memory, but the loss of a friend and team mate must have began to weigh heavy on their minds as the sadness of his untimely departure sank in.

Jimmy Thorpe at Villa Park.

Hero in a Green Jersey

Following our 3 - 3 draw with Chelsea on 1st February, one of the dailies reported that "Atrocious goalkeeping cost Sunderland a point". The goalkeeping referred to was that of James Thorpe; four days later, he died, having sustained injuries to both his ribs and his face, the latter resulting in a very swollen eye. In a rough game that saw Chelsea's right half Mitchell being given his marching orders, Thorpe had sustained serious injuries that brought his life to an untimely end. At the subsequent inquest it was revealed that Jimmy suffered from diabetes and took insulin regularly. He had fallen into a diabetic coma and the official cause of death was given as both diabetes mellitus and heart failure. Thorpe, born in Jarrow on 16th September, 1913, had risen through the ranks at Sunderland, and had made 139 League and Cup appearances for the Lads before he died. He was buried at the tragically young age of 22 years, leaving a wife and a son.

Jimmy Thorpe.

Johnny Mapson in action.

Championship Clincher

Perhaps the best performance of the season came against Birmingham at St Andrew's. That Sunderland won 7 - 2 away from home is impressive itself, that the Birmingham goalkeeper played a blinder tells its own story. Looking for a victory to clinch the Championship, Sunderland toyed with the opposition. It was, quite simply, a brilliant display of football. Gurney put in a marvellous display, hitting four goals, but the game belonged to Raich Carter. In what was described by some as his greatest ever performance in a Sunderland shirt, Carter controlled play and scored one of the Lads' goals. The result confirmed Sunderland's position as the free scoring Champions of England, and brought the League title to Wearside for the first time since 1913. It is a sign of the Club's brilliance in the pre-War era that despite having failed to add another Championship since, only five clubs can boast more League titles than us.

In April, Cochrane drafted in a replacement for Thorpe, Johnny Mapson arriving from Reading. At the same time, the Lads picked up where they had left off before Thorpe's death, finishing off the job of securing the Championship. Mapson's debut saw Portsmouth hammered 5 - 0, putting Sunderland just a couple of victories away from the title as the busy Easter holiday programme came around. On Good Friday we beat Birmingham 2 - 1 in front of 41,000 fans, putting us eight points clear with five games left. The following day we travelled to second placed Derby knowing that a victory would secure the title, but Derby ensured the champagne stayed on ice. They beat us 2 - 1, reducing the lead to six points with eight to play for. On Easter Monday though, it was all over; a trip to St Andrew's saw the Lads really turn it on as they secured their third 7 - 2 victory of the season. Derby had drawn, meaning it was impossible for them to catch us; with just six points to play for, we were seven points clear!

It had been a long wait, but at last the Championship trophy had returned to Sunderland. The silverware was presented at the end of our next home match, a 4 - 3 victory over Huddersfield Town. The game was another stunner, with the winner coming in the last minute. In fact, with just six minutes to go the Terriers had been leading 3 - 2 but, determined to show our Championship credentials, we worked hard to overcome them and thoroughly deserved the two points when the final whistle came. Amazingly, all of the Sunderland players in action that day - with the exception of Thorpe's replacement, Mapson - had come through the reserve ranks, and all but Gurney had been signed by Johnny Cochrane. It was a poignant illustration of the merit in his management strategy, and the Championship was a vindication of his faith in youth. In an attempt to bring back the glory days of the pre-War era, Cochrane's predecessor had lavished money on expensive star signings in the 1920s, but the home grown youngsters had managed something those international star players had found impossible: they had brought silverware to Sunderland.

It had been a season of goals as well as one of glory. We scored a staggering 109, 20 more than our nearest rivals, though we also conceded 74, more than any other Championship winning side. Here there was another vindication of Cochrane's approach. He had always favoured an attacking style. In the early days of his tenure, the Lads often suffered heavy defeats as we were caught short at the back after charging forward in heavy numbers. But, as the League title returned to Wearside, The Times noted that "it is attack which has brought them their success", and commented that, "attack, if there is any reliance in those deceptive things, figures, is always more reliable than defence". Gallacher, Carter and Gurney scored 81 goals between them. In a recent interview, 1930's 'keeper the late Johnny Mapson summed up the Manager's outlook: "Johnny Cochrane had a simple philosophy - he said he didn't mind at all if we conceded three goals a game, just so long as we scored four at the other end".

In securing the Championship for a sixth time, Sunderland joined Aston Villa as the most successful League club of all time to that point. Funnily enough Villa, along with Blackburn Rovers, were relegated at the end of the season; both had been in the First Division since its creation.

This added an extra touch of glory to the season: in addition to being Champions, and jointly holding the record for the most Championships, we were now the only team to have played their League football exclusively in the top division. Sunderland, quite simply, were the undisputed Kings of English football in 1936.

With the title secured, the Lads evidently spent more time partying than was prudent for the final few weeks of the season! No goals were scored in our last two games, and seven conceded. They could afford to take it easy, and deserved the rest. However, the Club had still inexplicably failed to secure English football's other glittering prize: the FA Cup. Could Cochrane's young warriors overcome the Cup jinx?

Sunderland's 1935-36 Championship winning team.

Johnny Mapson

Johnny Mapson was born in Birkenhead in 1917, but moved to Swindon at a very early age. On leaving school he became a baker's boy and played local football in Wiltshire before leaving to take up a football career with Reading.

Following the tragic death of Jimmy Thorpe, a 19 year old Mapson was signed for £2,000. His Sunderland career got off to a great start - with a 5 - 0 win at Portsmouth - and after seven games at Sunderland he finished the season as part of a Championship winning team.

Mapson went on to become a Sunderland legend, and in a career that spanned the Second World War, he played 385 times for Sunderland over thirteen seasons. His final appearance for the Club, a 3 - 3 home draw against Manchester City on 21st March, 1953, came nearly twenty years after his debut. Still a fine player at this time, there is no doubt he would have carried on for longer were it not for a knee injury that required constant attention and, eventually, forced him into retirement.

Johnny Mapson.

1936-1937

Cup Heroes

"The Kings of English Football were ready to claim a long overdue prize"

Members of the 1937 FA Cup Team.

Early Glory

In the early days of the Charity Shield, the game was not, as now, played pre-season at Wembley. Instead, the game took place early in the season, and usually at the home of the League Champions. On the 28th October, 1936, Arsenal - who had made up for us bringing their run of consecutive League titles to an end by lifting the FA Cup - visited Roker Park to contest the season's first piece of silverware.

The match - a midweek encounter - kicked off at 2.15, and the early start had an impact, with only 11,500 turning up for the match. The start time had been dictated by Arsenal who wanted to catch the train home after the match so that they could make it back to London in one day. Before 2.30, Sunderland had taken the lead, a goal after just eight minutes coming when Gallacher crashed the ball home. After this, Sunderland were on top for most of the game, but thirteen minutes from time, Arsenal equalised. After fine work from Denis Compton, Kirchen finished off a sweet move by beating Mapson.

The Lads, however, were not finished, and right on the final whistle, Carter crashed in a shot that bounced off the underside of the bar and was subsequently kicked off the line. The linesman, a Mr H Whitfield of Middlesbrough, flagged and after a discussion between the match officials, the referee pointed to the centre circle. Sunderland had won the FA Charity Shield.

In assembling a team that had brought the League title back to Wearside, Cochrane's place in Sunderland's Hall of Fame had been secured. The same also went for the players in his side, whose assured performances had brought glory to Wearside after eighteen barren seasons. Yet, for all the success the Club had seen over the years, there was still one trophy that had not been secured: the FA Cup. Could Cochrane's lads build on their Championship glory with another title or maybe even a victory at Wembley in an FA Cup final?

Only time would tell, but more immediately, the defence of the Championship began in unspectacular style. The first six games of the new campaign saw the Lads notch up three defeats, in games against Sheffield Wednesday (0 - 2), Derby County (0 - 3) and Arsenal (1 - 4). Our other three matches were well won though, Derby being beaten 3 - 2, Preston 3 - 0 and Brentford 4 - 1. Erratic form is worrying in its own right, but the major concern here was that all the defeats were away from home and all the victories came at Roker Park; it seemed like the bad habits of previous seasons were returning.

Throughout the early stages of the campaign, the Lads struggled away from home, and it was the end of October before we managed to pick up our first away victory of the season, a 4 - 2 win at Manchester City. Amazingly, the previous away match had been a 5 - 5 draw - against Middlesbrough. Moreover, our home record was a perfect one, victories against Everton (3 - 1) and West Brom (1 - 0) making it five victories out of five at Roker. Overall, this wasn't a bad record, and if the away form continued to pick up, we would be in with a shot of another title. In between League games, we had already managed to add to the trophy cabinet, defeating Arsenal - the FA Cup winners - by two goals to one in the Charity Shield. This was the first time the Club had held the shield and it was a welcome addition!

In November, a similar pattern continued to pan out, a 100% home record being maintained with victories against Portsmouth and Stoke, and a reasonable away record seeing the Lads rack up an away victory by beating Chelsea 3 - 1 in front of 40,000 fans. In the middle of the month, we also travelled to France to play Nord FC for an exhibition match. The game was watched by 15,000, spectators including the French Minister for Sport, but the Lads did not give their best display, ending on the wrong side of a 5 - 1 hammering.

As the final month of the year began, the outlook was good. The Lads hammered Grimsby 5 - 1 - at Roker of course - goals from Carter (2), Gurney, Connor and Duns doing the business, and in doing so, we not only maintained our perfect home record, but also climbed back to the top of the League. Strong visions of Sunderland succeeding Arsenal in hauling consecutive titles began to emerge but, somewhat inevitably, the Championship challenge soon faltered as the dodgy away form quickly reappeared. All of our away matches were lost during December, including a 4 - 0 thrashing at the hands of Liverpool. This was frustrating to say the least. Not only had we shown we could win away from home in the previous two seasons, but brilliant displays at home continued to dazzle the fans and raise questions as to why the Lads failed to perform outside of Roker. At least those who turned up at home games were never disappointed. Victories at Roker against Sheffield Wednesday on Boxing Day, a 2 -1 win, and two days later against Birmingham, 4 - 0 with Carter getting a brace, sent Sunderland fans home happy. Amazingly, by the end of 1936, we had won every League game played at Roker during the season.

It was, realistically, only a matter of time before this run came to an end. After a record eleven consecutive home victories, a massive 60,000 saw Arsenal hold us to a 1 - 1 draw on 9th January. All in all, it had not been a good start to the New Year, with defeats at Manchester United and Preston on the 1st and 2nd January seeing us lose more ground in the Championship race. However, there was better news in the FA Cup, where a 3 - 2 victory at Southampton saw us through to the fourth round. 300 Sunderland fans made the trip south, and saw goals from Gurney, Gallacher and Hornby seal the victory. Yet, it was a close escape for the Lads, the defence going to pot in the game's latter stages, conceding two goals in the last twenty minutes.

Our reward was a tie at Luton Town, and after a 3 - 3 draw at Brentford in the League, we made the trip to Bedfordshire for the next instalment of our FA Cup campaign. Sunderland were expected to beat the Second Division outfit, but a frost bound pitch had an adverse affect on our performance. The Hatters raced into a two goal lead, and it looked like the Cup jinx had struck again. However, the Lads rallied, and Dunn and Connor pulled the tie back for Sunderland, earning a replay at Roker Park. No mistake was made the following Wednesday, when 53,000 saw a scintillating 3 - 1 victory, goals from Duns, Carter and Connor putting us through to the fifth round. But, victory carried a price, with Connor picking up an injury that would effectively bring his Sunderland career to an end.

Swansea awaited us in the fifth round, but before the tie took place, the League form continued in a quite predictable manner, the Lads winning their home fixtures - Bolton being beaten 3 - 0 and Huddersfield 3 - 2 - but losing away from home, going down 3 - 0 to Everton. Fortunately, we had been drawn to play Swansea in the Cup, and were a little lucky to be facing another Second Division side and to have them travelling up to fortress Roker. An easy passage to the quarter-finals was expected. The Welsh side won the toss, but they won little else during the day. They elected to play with the wind in the first half, an immense advantage that day, but they could not make it count. The tie remained goalless at half-time, but after the restart, it was a different story. Sunderland rained attack after attack on the Swansea goal and just when it looked as though Swansea might resist the battering, Gurney and Duns effectively sealed our passage into next round with crucial strikes. At 2 - 0, and with the wind behind us, it was game over. Near the end Caldwell extended the lead by turning the ball into his own net and a crowd of some 48,500 went home happy with the 3 - 0 victory.

Ever Presents

During the glory years, Cochrane liked to keep a settled side. The Cup run - which encompassed nine matches - saw six players appearing in every one of these games, namely: Mapson in goal; Hall at the back; Thomson in the middle; and up front, Duns, Gurney and Gallacher. In addition, Gorman, Johnston, McNab and Carter each missed just one game, and these ten players all strode out at Wembley extremely familiar with each others' game. The only 'new' face in the final line up was Burbanks, who came in for Connor after he was injured, and Burbanks still played in every Cup game from the fifth round onwards.

Sunderland's 1936-37 FA Cup winning team.

Carter in Heaven

For 'Captain' Carter, the last few weeks of the 1936-37 season were truly momentous. Not only did he lead his home town club to Cup glory, scoring at Wembley in the final to boot, he also appeared for England against Scotland and celebrated love of a non-footballing kind by getting married just days before the crucial Wembley fixture.

All told, it was probably the best season of the Hendon born forward's career. A true Sunderland legend, he made 279 League and Cup appearances for the Lads, scoring some 130 goals. Widely recognised as one of the finest inside-forwards England ever produced, Raich Carter was a superb tactician, with a wicked shot. His pace and stamina were a trademark, although he used this deceptively, often catching opposition defences unawares. The art of 'creating space' was a speciality of his.

Unsurprisingly, Carter became a key member of the England squad too, being capped thirteen times between his 1934 debut against Scotland (won 3 - 0) and his international farewell against Switzerland at Highbury in 1947 (won 6 - 0). It is fair to say that had the War not intervened that tally would have been considerably more, and during the War he made fourteen unofficial international appearances. After the hostilities ceased, he turned out for Derby County, with whom he won another FA Cup, and he also turned his hand to cricket, appearing for Derbyshire.

In Football Daft, Michael Parkinson argued 'Great inside-forwards' are made in heaven. They are fashioned out of gold and sent on earth to win football matches and weave the stuff that memories are made of. They are the architects who design a game, the artists who adorn it 'a connoisseur's delight'. It was a view shaped by his first clear memory of a football match: a dashing, skilful, slightly aloof inside forward weaving his magic against Parkinson's side Barnsley. That man was one Horatio Carter.

'Hero' is the only appropriate tag for this fine sportsman, who must rank amongst one of Sunderland's all time greats. If we were to try the impossible task of putting together an all time Sunderland XI, Carter's name would surely have to be in the line up. He had the skill, the pace, the flair, the style and can proudly claim to have captained the Lads to glory. On top of this, he was also one of us: a Sunderland fan as well as a Sunderland hero; what a man!

The Cup run was generating great excitement, while the League continued its predestined course, home games being won and away ones being lost. In one of those quirks of the fixture list, details of the competition were almost lost sight of for most of March, as the Lads engaged in a series of battles with Wolverhampton Wanderers. After meeting lower division opposition in the earlier rounds of the Cup, it was inevitable that the Lads would come up against a top flight side sooner or later. The quarter-final saw us drawn to play Wolves, but ominously the tie would take place at Molineux. Fortunately, the Lads managed to avoid defeat on this occasion, and Wolves' then record crowd of 57,751 saw a Duns goal force a replay at Roker. In preparation for the replay, the Lads stayed at the Roker Hotel. This added to the big game feel, and nearly 62,000 fans turned out for the game. The match was a close fought encounter, and remained goalless until four minutes from time. Then, disaster struck, when Wolves sneaked a late goal. The crowd fell so silent that the sound of pin dropping would have reverberated around Roker Park. But, we were not beaten yet! A Thomson throw in, quickly taken, was centred for Bobby Gurney, who somehow managed to creep a shot through a ruck of players for a late, late saving goal. The game then went into extra time, and whilst Duns gave Sunderland the lead, a deserved equaliser saw Wolves take the Red and Whites into a third game at Sheffield. It was pulsating stuff.

At Hillsborough there would be no mistake and a comprehensive 4 - 0 rout saw off the Midlanders' challenge. The turning point came in the final ten minutes of the first half, with Sunderland piling on the pressure. Goals in the 43rd and 44th minutes broke Wolves' resistance. It was a marvellous victory, and the Lads had earned another semi-final tie. As if to underline our superiority over Wolves, we played them in the League just eleven days after the game at Hillsborough, and hammered them 6 - 2, Gallacher scoring a hat-trick as the Lads cruised to victory.

There was nearly a month between the quarter- and semi-final ties, and in the meantime - as if the story needs telling - the home League games were won and the away ones lost; the only exception here came in our fifth game against Wolves, where the Lads really stuck the knife in by holding on for a 1 - 1 draw at their place! All this was really just a backdrop to the big game though, and for the FA Cup semi-final the Lads had struck the jackpot, being drawn against Millwall. The south London side had provided the season's FA Cup sensation, the Third Division South side having put together a marvellous run to reach the penultimate stage of the Cup. Sunderland, however, would - surely - be too strong for them. 62,813 waited in anticipation of the result at Leeds Road, Huddersfield, and when Millwall went 1 - 0 up it looked like the Cup jinx was about to strike in the cruellest and most humiliating of ways. However, the Lads remained cool, and goals from Gurney and Gallacher sealed a place in the final.

With our first ever trip to Wembley secured, the League was now firmly relegated to something of a side-show. The semi-final victory was followed by a 6 - 0 drubbing at Grimsby, and two days later we also suffered our first - and only - home defeat of the season, Manchester City beating us 3 - 1. The latter were on their way to the Championship, while our poor away form meant we had fallen well out of the running. When the campaign drew to a close, the Lads were in eighth place, not the most spectacular defence of the title.

Here the figures reinforce the by now obvious story: just eight points were gained away from home, but 17 of our 21 home games were won. However, with a rare Cup final appearance awaiting, no-one was complaining.

Since Sunderland had joined the Football League in 1890 there had been League Championships a plenty, but the FA Cup had proved elusive. The Team of All Talents, a dominant force in English football, had never made it past the semi-final stage, losing in 1891 to Notts County after a replay, and being seen off in 1895 by bogey team Aston Villa. Robert Kyle's marvellous Championship side had made it to the final in 1913, but a meek performance saw us lose 1 - 0 to Villa and miss out on the double. In the 1930s, Cochrane's side had performed reasonably well in the Cup, making the semi-final stage in 1931, only to be seen off by Birmingham City, but now they had the chance to rectify an anomaly by bringing the Cup to mighty Sunderland. The Kings of English Football were ready to claim a long overdue prize.

So, on May 1st, 1937, the Lads walked onto the Wembley turf before 93,495 spectators - including two Kings - looking to clinch the Cup by beating Preston North End. The teams lined up as follows:

SUNDERLAND: Mapson; Gorman and Hall; Thomson, Johnson and McNab; Duns, Carter, Gurney, Gallacher and Burbanks.

PRESTON NORTH END: Burns; Gallimore and Beattie; Shankly, Tremelling and Milne; Dougal, Beresford, F. O'Donnell, Fagan and H. O'Donnell.

Prior to the game the Mirfield Military Band played musical selections including Blaydon Races. It was Coronation Year and the final was watched not only by the reigning monarchs, George VI and Queen Elizabeth, but also by King Farouk Of Egypt. The stage was all set for an epic encounter.

In the first half, the match did not go our way. First off, Gurney had a goal controversially disallowed for off-side. Then, midway through the first forty-five, Frank O'Donnell scored the opener for Preston. The Lads were unable to find their way through to force an equaliser, and we went in at the interval 1 - 0 down. In the second half, however, Sunderland turned up the heat. From a corner, Gurney backheaded the ball into the Lancashire side's net to make it 1 - 1. Raich Carter then added a second, and Eddie Burbanks, who had come into the side following that nasty injury to Connor in the fourth round, completed what was by now a rout.

At the final whistle it was 3 - 1 to Sunderland. At last, we had won the FA Cup! Cochrane's home grown team had done what 'the Talents' couldn't do. It was a glorious end to the season - perhaps the perfect end - making it three trophies in two brilliant seasons. Cochrane's place in Sunderland's history was now assured and 1937 became a date etched into the minds of all Sunderland fans. The Cup jinx had been smashed!

Lucky Shirts

Successful Cup runs often have a bit of 'magic' surrounding them, and during our successful 1937 campaign, Sunderland's trainer, Andy Reid, thought he had struck upon a winning formula. The Lads wore the same shirts in each of the rounds, Reid refusing to change what he considered to be the Club's lucky shirts. He went to great lengths to ensure that this was the case, and when the Club were presented with a new set - carrying a special Cup Final badge - for the Wembley showpiece, Reid had the commemorative coat of arms transferred from the new jerseys to the old lucky ones! Who can argue? It certainly seemed to do the trick!

FA Cup Final match ticket and programme

1937-1938

Near Repeat

"was this the end of an era?"

FA Cup quarter-final at Tottenham.

Quarter Final Joy

Sunderland's FA Cup quarter-final tie at Tottenham goes down in history as the biggest crowd ever attracted to White Hart Lane. With Spurs plying their trade in the Second Division, their fans relished the visit of a top club like Sunderland, desperate for a taste of their former glory days. Spurs started well, and had more of the ball than us, but our defenders proved too clever for the home side's forwards. Moreover, on the odd occasion they beat one of our backs, Mapson was invincible. The Times described him that day as "a goalkeeper with a perfect pair of hands", as he made a number of difficult saves look "supremely easy". All told, the Lads were just too skilful for Spurs to pose any real threat, and a left foot rocket from Raich Carter was enough to earn us a place in the semi-finals.

Quarter final programme,
Sunderland v Spurs, 1938.

In winning the League and Cup, Cochrane and his side had, in many senses, completed their search for the 'holy grail'. While the fans - as always - were hungry for more, the players and manager might be forgiven if they decided to take things a little easier after three tough seasons at the top. However, with the Cup jinx smashed and the trophy cupboard overflowing, morale was high, and the new season got off to a flier, Gurney hitting two goals as 'Boro were beaten 3 - 1 at Roker in front of 55,000. Although never quite up to the Sunderland-Newcastle game, the 'Boro fixture had become our big derby match during the 1930s glory years, for Newcastle were unfortunately relegated at the end of the 1933-34 season and were finding it difficult to gain promotion from the Second Division. With Middlesbrough to this day having found it impossible to win a single piece of major silverware, the Lads were the North East's top club by a long way during the decade as whole, so victory was to be expected.

However, two days later, we slumped to a 4 - 0 defeat at Leicester, and the first ten fixtures of the season followed the now extremely familiar pattern: all of the home games were won, and all the away games - with the exception of a draw at Derby - were lost. Amongst the results was a 4 - 1 defeat at Arsenal in front of a 60,000 crowd, the Gunners avenging our Charity Shield victory the previous season. In October though, following home victories against Bolton and Birmingham, the form book was reversed. On the 23rd October, we travelled to West Brom and thrashed them 6 - 1, Carter scoring a hat-trick, only to follow this up with a 3 - 2 defeat at home to Liverpool!

November began with our chance to defend the Charity Shield. Playing now as FA Cup winners rather than League Champions, we travelled to Manchester City on 3rd November, for a 2.45pm midweek kick-off. But, the League Champions were too strong for us, and ran out 2 - 0 winners. While it has been suggested the board were pleased with this result - insuring the shield cost a fortune - it would have been nice to have won it; the Club has not competed for it since. Indeed, the month as a whole would be acutely disappointing. While none of our games were won, aside from the Charity Shield, none were lost either, all our matches ending in draws. When December began with consecutive defeats against Leeds (4 - 3) and Portsmouth (2 - 0) it became clear that a Championship challenge was unlikely to be on the cards. A Christmas Day victory at home to Huddersfield - nice as this present was - could not disguise this fact. The sustained effort and consistently high form required to win the League were simply not there.

There was still the Cup though - which for the moment was ours - and the New Year saw us progress through the third round with a 1 - 0 victory over Watford. Even with the team not quite firing on all cylinders, Cup victory was a possibility, for on our day we were still a match for any side in the land. What's more, with the Cup campaign underway, form improved in the League a little too, and another unbeaten run began. Perhaps the commencement of the competition reminded the Lads that they were true Champions. Certainly the competition excited the fans, and a trip to Everton for the fourth round drew a massive 68,158 crowd; memories of the 6 - 4 game at the same stage of the 1934-35 season were still fresh, but this time the Lads controlled the game more effectively, a Bobby Gurney goal being enough to earn us a 1 - 0 victory.

The win set us up for a fifth round tie at home to Bradford Park Avenue. Cup fever was hitting the town again; now the Cup jinx was smashed, perhaps we could do it twice in a row! A massive 59,326 turned out for the game, and again the Lads won through by a single goal. A place in the quarter-finals had been secured. Spurs would provide the opposition here, and going into the game - on 5th March - the Lads were still unbeaten in the League following the start of their FA Cup campaign on 8th January. The Cup, it seems, does not always distract from the League.

The quarter-final tie drew an enormous 75,038 crowd to White Hart Lane - still a record for the famous ground - and for the fourth time in a row the Lads won their Cup match 1 - 0, a goal from Carter sealing a place in the semi-final. We followed the victory up with a good 3 - 0 win at home to West Brom in the League, but a few days later Liverpool brought our unbeaten run to an end, the 4 - 0 reverse being our first defeat in twelve League and Cup games.

With a second successive Cup final now a real possibility, it is fair to say that - at last - the Cup was distracting attention from the League. The semi-final took place a fortnight after defeat at Liverpool, Huddersfield providing the opposition in a game staged at Blackburn's Ewood Park. On the day though, we performed below our best, while Huddersfield raised their game. The match ended 3 - 1 to the Terriers and the Cup dream was over.

Although our run in the Cup had been remarkable - the Lads going for thirteen consecutive ties without defeat - it was very disappointing to miss out on a second final, and with little to play for other than pride, the season petered to a close. We finished - as we had done the previous season - a respectable eighth. This time though, there was no Wembley trip to compensate. The team had again finished a considerable distance off the pace in the League and with some of our stars past their peak, the team that had stormed to the Championship in 1935-36 was starting to break up: was this the end of an era?

Semi-Final Agony

Sunderland were drawn to face Huddersfield in the semi-final of the Cup and while the Terriers had been the dominant force in English football during the 1920s, they were by now a shadow of their former selves, lying fifth bottom in the League, some nine places below the Lads. However, on the day the form book was ripped up, and we were completely outplayed by Huddersfield. Our previously unflappable defence - who hadn't conceded a goal in the previous four rounds - were dragged all over the place. Following a few close shaves in the early stages, we succumbed to the inevitable after 20 minutes, and went a goal down. We held on until half-time, and tried to force the pace after the interval. But, Huddersfield caught us on the break, and with too many of our men forward Wienand had no difficulty in making it 2 - 0. Shortly afterwards, Macfadyen made it 3 - 0, and though we rallied - Carter scoring to make it 3 - 1 - it was too little, too late. We were out of the Cup. As The Times noted, "For nearly two years now Sunderland have had an unbroken run of success in the FA Cup, but... Huddersfield beat them convincingly".

Middleton makes a great save v Arsenal, 1937.

1938-1939
Departure

Johnny Cochrane (left) our most successful manager of the twentieth century.

Johnny Cochrane

When Johnny Cochrane announced his retirement on 3rd March, 1939, it was the end of an era for Sunderland AFC. He had spent 11 seasons at the helm, completely rebuilding the side and delivering success in both the League and the Cup. He was a strong willed man who knew how he wanted to play football. The attacking side he constructed was a joy to watch, gaining plaudits all round for its style, flair and technique. Most notable of all perhaps, was the way his approach contrasted with that of his predecessor, Robert Kyle. By investing his faith in youth rather than proven stars, he set the 1930s against the 1920s as conflicting ways of running a Club. Comparing the two is difficult, for while Cochrane's youngsters delivered the success that the 1920's stars couldn't, their era of glory was brief, and it might be suggested that a lack of new blood in the team contributed to a decline in performances after the League and Cup success. Sometimes new faces are needed to gee the rest of the team up and ensure competition for places; equally, big signings can upset the balance of the team and the dressing room, or - like Gilhooley - suffer nasty injuries shortly after being signed. Whatever the respective merits of the approaches, one fact is clear: Cochrane is a Sunderland legend, and he goes down in history - as far as silverware is concerned - as our most successful manager in the twentieth century.

The 1938-39 season appeared - at the time - to be something of a crucial moment for Sunderland. With Johnny Cochrane's rebuilding process having borne some rich fruits, expectations were high. However, the previous season's Cup adventure could not disguise the fact that the team needed that little bit extra in order to challenge for the top prize again. The question was, would Sunderland be able to respond positively to this situation? Change, as ever under Cochrane, would have to come from within; there were no big money signings, though there was a little more flux in the starting line up than had been the case in previous years. Perhaps competition for places would keep everyone on their toes and spur us on to glory.

Within this context, the season didn't start too badly, a 2 - 1 win at Birmingham being respectable enough. But, two drawn home matches in the next couple of games - against decidedly average opposition - did not bode well. What had happened to fortress Roker? Though useful victories were picked up against Brentford (3 -2) and Leicester (2 - 0), the first ten games produced just four wins, which was nothing more than mid-table form. In a return to the bad old days of Cochrane's early years in charge, performances became somewhat erratic, with good victories - such as a 3 - 0 against Stoke - often being followed by a poor defeat; in this case a 4 - 0 at Chelsea. While in the previous season the Lads had found it difficult to hit top gear, this season they were showing signs of stalling altogether. By the end of the year, the real problem was becoming apparent: Sunderland, once the free scoring entertainers, were finding it difficult to hit the net. Consequently, just eight victories flowed from the 23 games played in 1938, and there were a few heavy defeats, including a 5 - 1 at home to Aston Villa on Boxing Day, a result that would have been unthinkable just two seasons earlier.

In the Cup though, the Lads continued to progress well. A third round tie against Plymouth was easily won by three goals to nil, though this included an own-goal from the Second Division side. In the fourth round there was an excellent victory at Middlesbrough, a 51,000 crowd seeing goals from Carter and Smeaton ease us through to the fifth round, where Blackburn were drawn to play us at Roker. The fans could smell another Cup run, but the game ended a 1 - 1 draw, Hastings scoring a last minute equaliser to earn a replay. Over 47,000 turned out to see the teams play again a few days later, but once again they cancelled each other out. The game went to extra-time, yet still the two sides couldn't score. What's more, matters up front were dealt a huge blow during the game when Gurney broke his leg, a tragedy for both the player and the Club. A second replay would have to take place without our talismanic striker. Although the Lads warmed up for it by putting two past Leicester - to no reply - in the League, they should have saved their shooting boots for the Cup match. The third meeting with Rovers - in front of 50,000 at Hillsborough - was again goalless after 90 minutes, but in extra-time, Blackburn snatched a goal, and the Lads were unable to match them. Our season was over.

A week after the Cup match, we met 'Boro in the League, and were well beaten by three goals to nil. It was to be Johnny Cochrane's last game in charge; a few days later - on 3rd March, 1939 - he tendered his resignation. His assistant, George Crowe, was put in temporary charge, and the season drew to a close with mixed results that left the Lads in a poor 16th place. The team was a shadow of the one that had blasted its way to the Championship some four seasons earlier, scoring less than half as many goals, and losing more than twice as many games.

At the end of the season, William Murray was brought in to replace Cochrane. With a new manager at the helm, the task of rebuilding the side was about to begin once more. However, Murray's first season in charge came to an abortive end after just three games. On 3rd September, 1939, Britain declared war on Germany. There would be no more official football until 1946. Instead, the country turned its attention towards fighting fascism. After the War, football for Sunderland - like life in general - would be a very different proposition. The 1930s had been a great decade for Sunderland AFC, and the pre-War era one of great success. When football recommenced in the 1940s, Murray would have a lot to live up to under difficult circumstances.

Action from one of the best games of the decade: the 1937 Cup Final.

The Season That Never Was

When the 1939-40 season kicked off, war with Germany was looking like a strong possibility. Just three games were played before the Prime Minister, Neville Chamberlain, delivered the shocking news that war had been declared. In a complete contrast to the situation when the First World War broke out, professional football was brought to an immediate halt. On top of this, the results were wiped from the record books - as if the games had never taken place - and the season declared void. Murray's first period in charge was, therefore, a brief one, and strictly speaking his first game in charge did not come until the 1940s. While the results counted for nothing in the end, and were certainly irrelevant in the face of the oncoming war, there will be those who were at the games and can remember them clearly.

Murray's first game was watched by 20,000 and saw Carter hit two goals in a 3 - 0 win over Derby. It was a decent start, but the next two games were less successful. A midweek visit from Huddersfield Town ended in a 2 -1 defeat, despite another goal from a Carter, and just one day before war was declared, Murray's opening trio was rounded off with a 5 - 2 thrashing at Arsenal. The fixtures were replayed in much happier circumstances after the war, and with rather better results.

Billy Murray.

1940·45	League and Cup suspended; reach final of War League Cup in 1941-2.
1945·46	FA Cup resumes. Reach semi-finals of Durham and Northumberland Cup.
1946·47	League resumes; 9th in League.
1947·48	20th in League; one place from relegation.
1948·49	Non-League Yeovil Town knock Lads out of Cup; 8th in League.
1949·50	3rd in League.

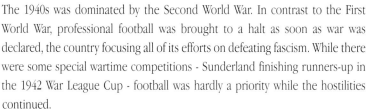

The 1940s was dominated by the Second World War. In contrast to the First World War, professional football was brought to a halt as soon as war was declared, the country focusing all of its efforts on defeating fascism. While there were some special wartime competitions - Sunderland finishing runners-up in the 1942 War League Cup - football was hardly a priority while the hostilities continued.

When the War came to an end in 1945, football - like much of British life - took a while to get into its stride. But, when it recommenced, the Lads put in reasonable initial performances in both the Cup and the League. However, we soon hit a rocky period, coming close to relegation and being famously defeated in the FA Cup by non-League minnows Yeovil Town.

Yet, this was not a period when the Club lacked ambition. As huge attendances filled the Roker Park coffers, the board were keen to sanction transfer activity, and a number of star players arrived for huge transfer fees. Most notably, Len Shackleton joined us from Newcastle in late 1948, the £20,500 fee we paid for him being a world record sum. As the decade drew to a close, the policy appeared to be paying off too, the Lads' all star line up challenging for the League title. However, the real test of the approach would come in the 1950s, as the expensive team reached its make-or-break period.

THE AUSTERITY

Years?

1940 · 1950

1939-1945
The War Years

"British life had been devastated by the horrors and tragedy of war …football was no exception"

League War Cup Final v Wolves, 1942.

Players at War

Footballers, like all others in the country, were called on to do their bit during the War. Many enlisted straightaway in the forces, but this took time, and most had to find jobs to fill in with in the meantime. Raich Carter immediately joined the Auxiliary Fire Service rather than wait for a position in the armed forces, a decision he was to regret as he was taunted for allegedly 'dodging' the call-up. He did, of course, join the RAF two years later. Another of our star forwards, Len Duns, joined the Royal Artillery, whilst other players went down the mines or worked in the shipyards.

During the course of the conflict, many players from many clubs were among those who tragically gave their lives in the service of their country. Of former Sunderland players, Jimmy Temple was killed on active service, whilst Percy Saunders was lost at sea during the invasion of Singapore in 1942. Outside-right John Lynas, who at the onset of war was working as trainer with Blackpool, was captured in Singapore and worked in a POW hospital in Thailand. Future Sunderland stars also played their part, including Ken Chisholm, who was an RAF pilot, and Billy Elliott, who spent his time in the Royal Navy hunting U-boats.

The whole of the 1938-39 season was played out against the backdrop of the infamous 'peace in our time', with many players joining the Territorial Army, and both the Football Association and Football League discussing what to do in the event of a declaration of war. This was a particularly difficult time for football. There had been severe criticism when the full programme had been completed during the 1914-15 season, despite the onset of the 'Great War'. Whilst mindful of the need to be seen 'doing one's bit' for the war effort, the authorities were also trying to balance this with the positive morale effects of 'business as usual'. Ultimately, however, the escapism which has always been associated with football jarred with the images of death and destruction that were becoming part of everyday life.

Five days before the start of the 1939-40 season, the FA waived the rule which prevented members of the armed forces being registered as professional footballers, and the season began with a growing sense of unease. When Sunderland travelled to Arsenal for their third game of the season on 2nd September, 1939, the whole day was overshadowed by Hitler's decision to invade Poland. Although the FA gave permission for games to take place, our kick-off was delayed until 5pm because of evacuations, meaning Sunderland and Arsenal played out a surreal game in front of an unsurprisingly small crowd. Ted Drake scored four as the Gunners triumphed 5 - 2, but football was really the last thing on anyone's mind. Raich Carter said later that he had little recollection of the game itself.

The following day, War on Germany was formally declared, and the Sunderland players and management heard the news in their London hotel. They endured their first air-raid warning of the War, and then travelled back to the North East to receive the news that the Football League had instructed clubs to cancel all League fixtures and to suspend players' contracts. To all intents and purposes, football was over for the time being, and Sunderland effectively went into limbo for the next six months, deciding to take no immediate part in the regional competitions which were already being discussed.

In early 1940, Sunderland re-opened for business, and entered the League War Cup. Victories over Darlington and Leeds were followed by defeat to eventual finalists Blackburn Rovers, but the Club's heart was not really in competitive matches, and they decided to revert to a 'friendlies only' policy for the following season. Gate receipts were handed over to the War Fund.

This decision was in part influenced by the geographical location of Roker Park. Sunderland at the time was suffering heavy air raids, and with the close proximity of the shipyards - one of the main targets for the bombers - it was felt unwise to play regular games. Despite this, Roker Park escaped relatively unscathed from the bombing throughout the War. During one raid in 1943, the clubhouse in the corner of the Roker End was destroyed, whilst a cluster of dropped bombs killed a special constable patrolling outside of the ground and left a crater in the pitch. However, compared to others, Sunderland AFC got off lightly.

Initially, the authorities severely limited crowds, due to concern about how to shelter them during an air raid. Restrictions were eased when the danger of daytime attacks passed, but the limit for Roker Park was set at 35,000 - half of its total capacity - for the majority of the War.

In reality, grounds were never going to be full with the War providing such a dreadful backcloth, although those who did attend matches were frequently treated to numerous 'guest players' turning out for their clubs as scratch sides were put together. This system allowed Stan Mortensen, from South Shields, to fulfil his dream of turning out for Sunderland, who had rejected him as a schoolboy for being 'too small'. Albert Stubbins, who was officially on Newcastle's books, worked as a draughtsman in Sunderland during the War, and turned out a few times for his red and white rivals.

Performances throughout the period of the conflict were at best erratic, despite the plethora of star guests. Sunderland's best 'season' was 1941-42, when we reached the final of the League War Cup, only to lose out heavily to Wolves. Indeed, during that season, the football tended to be very open and entertaining, with the Lads banging in 103 goals, and keeping very few clean sheets!

When the War ended, time was too short to recommence the Football League programme. Many footballers were still in the armed forces, particularly in the Far East, and life would take time to return to what would pass for normality. Indeed, although Germany surrendered unconditionally to Allied Forces on 7th May 1945, with Victory in Europe declared the next day, it would be four more months before VJ day marked the end of the War in the Far East. By September, one of the bloodiest wars in the history of mankind was over. Millions had lost their lives throughout the world, including nine million Jews - more than two out of three - in Hitler's 'Final Solution'. It would take the world many years to recover from the conflict, and the shock waves would continue to reverberate throughout the world for a long time.

Football was to serve its role in the return to normality - although for many, 'normality' could never be recovered. Almost 100 professional footballers had lost their lives, and as teams started to regroup, they did so in the knowledge that some of their former team mates would not be joining them. British life had been devastated by the horrors and tragedy of war, and football was no exception.

Uncertain Future

With the immediate suspension of players' contracts at the outbreak of the War, all professional footballers were effectively made unemployed. For some, there was a little bitterness at this decision. Manchester City's Peter Doherty outlined the tricky position they had been placed in. None of the players were against the War effort, nor did they expect special treatment. However, the plans put in place by the footballing authorities called on the players to appear in morale stiffening war time matches, but ruled they should be denied the appearance money they had received in peace time. This 30 shillings, as Doherty pointed out, was the money they used to look after their families. Yet, finding new work was far from easy. Doherty himself applied for work in Manchester based industries such as Leyland Motors and Vickers Armstrong, but to no avail. Consequently, he widened his search, and seemed to have solved the problem after fixing himself up with work in Greenock. However, he was told in no uncertain terms by the Manchester City Chairman that he would not be allowed to play football anywhere but Manchester; Doherty had to stick to his contract, even if there was no longer any money attached to it. "We seemed to be getting all the kicks and none of the ha'pence" he concluded. In the end, Doherty decided to sign up for the RAF and, contrary to the City Chairman's wishes, turned out for a number of clubs while on service, including Brentford, Lincoln and Grimsby.

Bomb damage at Roker Park caused by air raid on 15/16th may 1943.

1945-1946
The Slow Return

"The Football League programme would begin in earnest the following season and then the real test of the team would begin"

Raich Carter meets the King, whilst playing for Derby, at the FA Cup Final at Wembley in 1946.

Raich Leads the Way - Without us

The War had brought many changes to British life, and when the teams re-assembled in 1945, much had moved on. For Sunderland AFC, one of the biggest losses was inspirational home boy Raich Carter. After a few appearances for the Lads in the 'League of the North', Raich left for Derby County before the 'real' football began, and our loss was very much their gain. Carter helped power Derby to FA Cup victory at Wembley during the season, enabling his new Club secure the first major post-War trophy. The game, against Charlton, was a real marker of the peace and freedom that had been gained with the end of the War. Though life was still far from easy, tuning into the FA Cup final was one of the many basic pleasures in life that had been lost for more than half-a-decade. The match was a real thriller too, going to extra time. In the end though, Derby were too strong, running out 4 - 1 winners. If only Raich had stuck with the Lads...

With the War in Europe only just over, and the War in the Far East still ongoing, the Football League did not officially recognise the 1945-46 season. However, there was an officially sanctioned 'Football League of the North', which provided competition of sorts.

Sunderland's first game in this 'league' took place on 25th August, 1945, at Hillsborough against Sheffield Wednesday. The result was a 6 - 3 hammering for the Lads, but that was immaterial. What was important was that, after the dark days of the war, football was back. Interestingly, guest players were still being utilised, and Dundee's half-back Lurle made an appearance for the Lads that day.

For this season, all games were 'back to back' home and away ties against the same opposition, so when Wednesday arrived at Roker Park, Sunderland were able to gain swift revenge, winning 1 - 0 in front of some 22,300 fans. Sadly, this was to be something of a novelty in the early part of the season, as five straight defeats followed. Two of those defeats were inflicted by high-flying Chesterfield, who surprised Sunderland with 3 - 0 and 5 - 0 wins as they raced away to the top of the table.

The Roker faithful had to wait until 17th October before they again enjoyed that winning feeling, when the Lads beat Stoke City 4 - 0. Manager Bill Murray had really taken to inviting 'guest' players to turn out for Sunderland, a tactic that did not go down overly well with Chairman Colonel Prior, who likened the team to an 'All England XI'. To be honest, the tactic was not actually too successful either, as after 12 games Sunderland's record was 3 wins and 9 defeats, with a paltry tally of 12 goals scored and a frightening 38 conceded.

November saw the return of Johnny Mapson, and he saved a twice-taken penalty in his return game at Bolton. It proved to be a crucial intervention: the Lads ran out 2 - 1 winners. The month also saw an interesting encounter against Manchester United; bomb damage to Old Trafford meant the game was played at Manchester City's home, Maine Road.

The real competition began at the turn of the year though, when the first post-War FA Cup kicked off. This season, the ties were all played over two legs, and Grimsby were easily despatched both home and away in the Third Round. Next up were Bury, who were sent back to Lancashire with a 3 - 1 defeat. The return leg at Gigg Lane was a much closer affair, but an extra-time goal from Burbanks secured Sunderland's progression, despite a 5 - 4 defeat on the day.

In the following round we faced Birmingham City, and some 45,000 fans - the biggest attendance since the end of the War - packed Roker Park for their visit. A single goal from Duns was enough to see the Lads home. However, in the return leg, a 3 - 1 defeat ended our interest in the competition.

With the FA Cup over, there was little to play for in the remaining 16 league games. A number of younger players were given their debuts, but the season petered out with a mixture of wins and defeats. Squad rebuilding also got underway, and we opened negotiations with Huddersfield for the services of their international forward Willie Watson. As Watson himself was still in the army, based in Reading, the deal took some time to conclude. Although negotiations began in February, he did not become a Sunderland player until May!

Crowds at all grounds dwindled, and Roker witnessed attendances just above the 10,000 mark for some of the games. However, the traditional 'derby' games still caught the punters' imagination. The game with Newcastle on 20th April drew some 37,000 fans, and they saw a single goal from Burbanks settle a tense affair in Sunderland's favour. In the return at St James', United exacted swift revenge, with a 4 - 1 rout, including goals from Milburn and Stubbins. The 4th May game with Middlesbrough at Roker Park saw Willie Watson make his long awaited debut. However, his influence was not immediate, and we went down 1 - 0 to a Fenton goal after 20 minutes.

When the season drew to an end, we had escaped the bottom three in the table, but only just. In reality, no one really cared too much. The War was over and football was back. The Football League programme would begin in earnest the following season and then the real test of the team would begin.

Willie Watson scores.

Willie Watson

Sunderland needed a big star to fill the boots left by Raich Carter, and in February 1946, the Club moved in on Huddersfield Town's Willie Watson. Watson, who had appeared for England against Wales in a 'Victory' international held in 1946, was earmarked for the role and snapped up in time for the recommencement of League football in 1946-47.

He gave eight seasons of service to the Club, appearing over 200 times and his fine form meant he received further caps from England while at the Club. While not a prolific goalscorer, he made an excellent contribution to all round play, and his presence was always felt on the field. Indeed, Watson was a great all round sportsman, and holds the distinction of being one of the few men to have appeared for England at both football and cricket.

Willie Watson.

1946-1947
Back in Business

Arthur Housam, 1947-57.

Whitelum Hat-Trick

After suffering our first home defeat of the season, the Lads travelled to Manchester United on 26th October. United were unbeaten all season at their adopted home of Maine Road, making us very much the underdogs. However, an outstanding performance by the Lads led to a surprise win, and a display that left United stunned. In defence, Fred Hall was a giant, and United could find no way around him. Going forward, Duns and Watson were outstanding, and Whitelum - who hit a hat-trick - was deadly in front of goal. His second goal in particular was a beauty, with a flowing move involving Housam and Burbanks leading to a classic finish as the striker buried with ease. All in all, it was a more than satisfying day out, the Lads running out 3 - 0 winners.

With much anticipation around the country, the Football League 'proper' recommenced after seven dark years. In a symbolical display of the nation's ability to overcome adversity, the fixtures for the season were identical to those that would have been played in the 1939-40 season, meaning the War had merely caused football to be 'postponed' rather than 'abandoned'. For Sunderland, this meant the season began with 'replays' of the three games that had taken place before the War broke out, Derby, Huddersfield and Arsenal providing the opponents.

However, while the fixtures remained the same, the teams that took to the field across the country were very different. Older players had retired, younger ones had joined the game, some had switched clubs and many had been injured, or killed, in service. Of the Sunderland team that played against Derby in the opening fixture of the 1939-40 season, just three players turned out for the 'replay': Mapson in goal, and Duns and Burbanks up front. A fourth familiar face came in the form of Raich Carter, returning to Roker Park as a Derby County player. Happily for Sunderland, the Lads put in a decent performance, 50,000 fans - more than double the number turning out for the original game - seeing us sneak a 3 - 2 victory. It was a great start to post-War League football.

Four days later, Huddersfield visited Roker Park. In a game that had ended in a 2 - 1 defeat before the War, the Lads played the visitors off the pitch, running out 3 - 0 winners. The 'replays' were then completed with a trip to Highbury, where 1939's 5 - 2 defeat was replaced with a battling point from a tough 2 - 2 draw. Our big signing, Willie Watson, was settling in well, as was Fred Hall, the half-back bought from Blackburn at the start of the season. However, the headlines were being grabbed by Cliff Whitelum, who had banged in four goals in the first three games. Whitelum, who had made just two appearances before the War broke out, was one of the legacies left by Johnny Cochrane. Signed from Doncaster Juniors in late 1938, the boy that was Whitelum had grown into a man during the War, and he would terrorise defences during his first full season.

After this solid start, however, the Lads collapsed in a 5 - 0 thrashing against Charlton at the Valley, a somewhat disappointing result to say the least. But, the bright note was that Watson and Hall had been absent from the line up; they returned for our next game, and a 3 - 2 victory against League leaders Blackpool followed. After five games, we had a very respectable seven points from a possible ten, putting us third in Division One. The Charlton result appeared to be something of a one off, and winning ways continued with another visit to London, as the Lads notched their first away victory of the season with a 3 - 0 win against Brentford. Sunderland put on some exhibition football during the game, and the Bees' manager Harry Curtis paid tribute to the Lads, saying 'You made us look a poor lot today. You have the best side I have seen for many a day.'

Indeed, the Lads were looking good for a Championship challenge, with our home form being particularly strong. By the end of October, we had won five of our six home games, and also managed to win two of our away games, including a memorable 3 - 0 win against Manchester United. Keen to maintain the momentum, the board sanctioned the signing of another England international forward, Jackie Robinson, joining us from Sheffield Wednesday in the middle of October. This was great news for the fans, who had been flocking to the games in huge numbers. Days after the Robinson deal was clinched, attendances at Roker Park had already topped a quarter-of-a-million for the season, with the average gate well over 40,000. However, his debut was not a happy occasion; despite a goal from the new signing, the Lads succumbed to their first home defeat of the season, Grimsby beating us 2 - 1.

In fact, Robinson's arrival, somewhat unfortunately, coincided with a downturn in form for the team as a whole. All but one of our games during November were lost, including defeats at home to Stoke, Chelsea and Preston, and during the festive period the Lads picked up a 5 - 1 thrashing at Derby in our last game of 1946 and a 4 - 1 beating home to Arsenal in the first of 1947. The table now had us lying in a lowly fourteenth place and - what's more - the defeat against Arsenal was our seventh home defeat in a row, setting an unwelcome Club record.

When defeat against Arsenal was followed by an embarrassing FA Cup defeat at second division Chesterfield, pride appeared to have been stung. In our next game, the Lads trounced Blackpool 5 - 0 at Bloomfield Road - Robinson hitting four - and home form improved considerably, the Lads remaining unbeaten at Roker for the rest of the season. In fact, they even secured victories in six of their ten remaining home games, including a 1 - 0 at home to 'Boro that put a real dent in our rivals' Championship hopes.

As the season drew to an end, we were in a comfortable mid-table position. With little to play for, however, crowds began to tumble, and a very disappointing 12,000 turned out for the last home game, a 2 - 1 win over Brentford. The victory secured a ninth place finish: respectable enough but hardly what was needed to fire imaginations after the long spell without League football.

Dunns, Mapson and Whitelum.

Murray Takes Charge - At Last

When Murray was awarded the Sunderland manager's job in April 1939, he must have thought his career was about to take off. However, by the time he took up his post for the start of the 1939-40 season, war was looking increasingly likely. Just as for others around the world, his life was suddenly put on hold as hostilities flared around the globe. The impact of this on his career can be illustrated by a simple statistic: the excellent 3 - 0 win at Brentford that came in Murray's sixth official League game in charge would have marked his 300th League game in charge had the War not intervened.

The War, however, also created historical opportunities and oddities. For Murray this was the chance to scrap his first three games in charge - which had seen two defeats - and start all over again. Second time around he did much better, winning two games and drawing the other!

Eddie Burbanks 1934-48

1947-1948
On the Brink

"a huge disappointment for a club with major ambitions"

Raich Carter playing in an England v Scotland international.

Destroyed by an Old Flame

Valentine's Day saw the Lads visit the Baseball ground knowing that they had to start performing - or face the dreaded drop into the Second Division. Sadly, the game was an unmitigated disaster. Derby were simply outstanding, and it says a lot that the man of the match for Sunderland in a 5 - 1 rout was the goalkeeper Johnny Mapson. The game was controlled from start to finish by former Roker idol Horatio Carter. Sunderland may have had the big money signing in showman Len Shackleton, but it was the 34 year old Carter who ran the show. Conserving his energy by playing football with his brain, Carter hit a hat-trick and totally embarrassed the Sunderland side. As with Buchan before him, the decision to let Carter go was looking somewhat foolish.

Looking to improve on their previous season's display, the Lads travelled in hope to Highbury, where a 60,000 sell out crowd crammed in to watch us take on Arsenal. In a tight first half, brilliant defensive displays by Hudgell and Stelling meant it was still goalless at the interval. However, in the second half the home side were too strong, their attacking play proving too much for our backs. Three goals by the home side could not be matched, Lloyd's strike being nothing more than a consolation for the Lads. We left the capital with our tail between our legs.

A week later though, a draw with Aston Villa, followed by a 4 - 2 victory at home to Grimsby, meant that the fans were feeling a lot better. However, they were soon in a state of panic once more, as the defeats started rolling in. The first four weeks of the season saw a further four defeats for the Lads. We were leaking goals at the back, and finding it hard to score up front. Already it was clear that the Club were in trouble and crisis talks between the manager and the board saw Murray given the green light to search for new talent. October began with a 2 - 2 draw at Huddersfield, with Murray conspicuous by his absence on a scouting mission. By now, the need for new talent had become glaringly obvious. The Lads were lacking in confidence and looking fragile on the pitch. The game against Huddersfield had seen us throw away a two goal lead, and a week later we were beaten 3 - 2 at Sheffield United as the Lads once again frittered away a two goal advantage.

Uncovering the answer to our problems was from easy though. Chelsea were offered a record breaking £20,000 for the services of Tommy Lawton, but the forward chose Notts County ahead of us. After turning our attentions to Ronnie Turnbull, signed from Dundee, an answer appeared to be have found. He smashed four goals on his debut as the Lads romped to a 4 - 1 victory over Portsmouth. However, in an on-off season, he struggled for form and fitness after this great start, hitting just four more goals over the rest of the campaign.

While the Lads were still managing to put in some good performances - including a 5 - 1 thrashing of Liverpool - defeats were increasingly becoming the norm. Indeed, the Club's plight was illustrated by a disastrous start to 1948. After a reasonable 2 - 1 win at home to Grimsby - Turnbull getting on the scoresheet - we immediately crashed out of the FA Cup at the hands of another Second Division side, Southampton beating us 1 - 0. This result was followed by consecutive home defeats against Manchester City and Bolton Wanderers. An already grim picture was then darkened completely with two awful results away from home, Blackburn beating us 4 - 3 and Derby thrashing us 5 - 1, Raich Carter hitting a hat-trick for his new club.

The Lads were now in real trouble, and everyone knew it. Fortunately, the board were more than prepared to help the manager out, and while the 5 - 1 defeat at Derby marked the peak of our bad spell, it also marked the start of a revival, for it saw the debut of one of our biggest signings yet: Len Shackleton. 'Shack', had been lured away from Newcastle - much to the dismay of their fans - and the huge £20,050 transfer fee broke the national transfer record that had been set earlier in the season when Lawton had signed for Notts County. While Shackleton's debut for Sunderland was hardly the best of starts, he had joined a team low on confidence and in poor form. However, he soon helped turn performances around, and his home debut was rather more satisfying, Shack contributing a goal in a 2 - 0 win over Huddersfield.

As the season entered its closing stages, our form slowly but surely picked up. While defeats were still commonplace - particularly away from home - at least the Lads were starting to win games again. Indeed, following Shack's arrival, five of the remaining seven games at Roker Park were won. Significantly, the points helped us to move away from the relegation places. The Lads had been in danger of the drop for much of the season, but victory in our penultimate game of the season - a 3 - 0 victory at home to 'Boro - finally secured our First Division status.

Yet, while escaping the drop was an important achievement, the final position of 20th - one place off relegation - was a huge disappointment for a club with major ambitions and represented our worst finish ever. Yet, gates held up well, averaging over 42,000, and receipts were a record £77,006, including season ticket sales of over £7,000. The fact that a profit of just over £2,000 was returned was testimony to the size of Sunderland's transfer budget. Over £32,000 had been spent on bringing in new players: relegation following this would have been a disaster. However, much of the investment had come in the latter part of the campaign, and the real worth of the new signings would not be known until the following season. The board would be expecting a decent return on their investment next time around…

Dickie Davis scores.

Dickie Davis

One of the players who began to establish himself in the team during the season was Dickie Davis, who hit 12 League goals in just 26 games.

Signed as a youth just prior to the outbreak of the War, hostilities led to a temporary suspension of his football ambitions. However, he eventually made the breakthrough into the first team towards the end of 1946, hitting four goals in 12 games. His big success came in the 1949-50 season, when he finished as the League's top scorer, powering Sunderland to a Championship challenge.

In total, he played over 150 games for Sunderland, on average hitting a goal every other game. This record stands comparison with the best, but following a dispute with the manager - Davis refused to be transferred - appearances became few and far between. After finishing top scorer in the League, he averaged just thirteen games a season for us, before moving to Darlington at the end of the 1953-54 season.

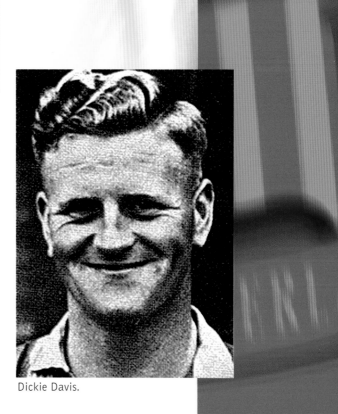

Dickie Davis.

1948-1949 Humbled

"Cup Fiasco"

Col. Joseph Prior

Many modern day managers would love to receive the support Murray was shown by his board during the first few seasons of the post-War era. Despite leading the team to some very poor performances on the pitch, the board stood by their manager in amazing style, giving him huge sums of money to spend on players, even allowing him to break transfer records.

The man who presided over the board at the time was Col. Joseph Prior, who had become Chairman in 1940. His generous approach to spending was to set the tone for the next ten years, as the Club became know for its spending sprees. Indeed, when he was succeeded as Chairman in 1949, his successor - Edward Ditchburn - allowed the transfer fees to get bigger still!

This was a time when the board were determined to return Sunderland to the top of the footballing hierarchy; sadly, their aspirations were destined to remain unfulfilled.

After the relegation struggle of the previous season, it was, perhaps, something of a surprise that almost 48,000 turned up at Roker Park for the opening match against Bolton Wanderers. The huge crowd was a sign of the hope amongst the fans that the new signings would steer the Lads to better times. They were treated to a fine display, as emerging star Dickie Davis hit both goals in an impressive 2 - 0 win. The result was followed by a useful 1- 0 victory at Wolves, spurring the optimists on further.

However, a 4 - 0 defeat at Liverpool soon put the opening performance into perspective. We were half way to being a decent side, but there were still weaknesses. These shortcomings were well illustrated in out next two games: despite scoring three goals against Wolves and two against Blackpool, both matches ended in draws. Moreover, they were home games too.

But at least we were scoring goals again, and a 5 - 2 win at Sheffield United demonstrated our new found prowess. The manager was almost spoilt for choice up front, Turnbull and Watson struggling to get in the team at times. Indeed, having a strong front line was paying dividends, for we were becoming difficult to beat, as the Lads were always likely to score goals. While there were some disappointing draws, only one of our first nine games was actually lost. All in all, it wasn't a bad start to the season.

When FA Cup holders Manchester United arrived in town at the beginning of October, the stage was set for Shackleton to show his true class. With Sunderland taking an early lead, Shack proceeded to tease and taunt the United defence, which contained his England colleague Cockburn. The only surprise was that the final winning margin was only 2 - 1. Almost 55,000 fans went home drooling, having witnessed the full range of magic tricks from one of football's true entertainers. The following week, Shack was at it again, as his old club Newcastle visited for the first 'proper' Tyne-Wear derby since the Mags' relegation in 1934. After a good opening goal from Hair put visitors ahead, a 20 yard screamer from Shack levelled the scores. The game ended 1 - 1.

But, after a solid start, the Lads began to flounder again. In the twelve games left until the New Year, the Lads managed to win just three. When Stoke visited Roker in early November, much was made of the differing costs of the two sides. Our team had been assembled at a huge cost of £50,000, while City, in comparison, had a team consisting entirely of local born talent, none of whom had cost more than a £10 signing on fee. The game ended 1 - 1, showing yet again that money does not necessarily buy success. One of the few victories was, however, a real bright spot, the Lads beating 'Boro 1 - 0 on Christmas Day.

The turn of the year saw matters go from bad to worse. New Year's Day saw us lose 2 - 0 at home to Liverpool, the Lads missing a penalty with the game balanced at 1 - 0. After this, it appeared that the corner had been turned. After losing to second division opposition two years running in the Cup, the Lads eased past Third Division Crewe Alexandra with 2 - 0 away win. Blackpool were then held 3 - 3 in the League, and Derby beaten 2 - 1 at Roker, before the Lads travelled to meet non-League Yeovil in the fourth round of the Cup. The widely expected victory did not materialise, however, as the Lads slumped to one of their most famous and humiliating defeats ever. Our expensive team of all stars were dumped out of the Cup by the unknown amateurs from Yeovil, the 2 - 1 defeat being not only the talk of the day, but for much of the season.

On the Monday following the unmitigated disaster that was Yeovil, the board acted quickly to support their manager, and Sunderland signed Ivor Broadis from Carlisle for a huge £18,000. Designed to boost confidence, the move did not immediately have the desired effect, as Sunderland crashed 5 - 0 away to Arsenal. When three further straight defeats followed - to Huddersfield and Portsmouth at home and away to Newcastle - we were well and truly on the ropes. For all the money spent, it seemed we were doomed to failure.

However, the Lads managed to turn it around just in time. Defeat against Portsmouth marked the turning point, as the players rallied to lift their spirits. We remained unbeaten for the rest of the season, and while many of the games ended in low scoring draws, the points were enough to steer us into a respectable 8th place finish. However, the Cup fiasco meant the fans still had little to shout about, and the board were still waiting for a decent return on their investment.

Stand-in goalkeeper Dickie Dyke makes another save for Yeovil Town, 1949.

Football Hell

The FA Cup always catches the imagination of football fans, and this season's fourth round tie was no exception. Non-League Yeovil, with the usual collection of aircraft workers, glove makers and bar owners, had surprised many by defeating Bury in the previous round. Despite that result, however, the football world sat back and waited to see the cricket score that Sunderland were expected to run up. Yeovil's fans were pleased just to be hosting such a game, and had been queuing since early morning. A crowd of some 16,000, including almost 3,000 who had made the monumental journey from the North East, waited expectantly.

Rumours circulated before the game that Sunderland were about to make another big money signing in Ivor Broadis from Carlisle, and this contrasted starkly with the Yeovil choice in goal - a 22 year old solicitor's clerk called Dyke who had previously played only one game. Everything was set up for the Lads to romp it.

Of course, the non-League club had not read the script. On their famous sloping pitch, the Somerset team's long ball game terrorised their professional opponents. A goal from player-manager Alec Stock after 28 minutes sent the fans wild, but when Robinson equalised on the hour things looked likely to swing the way of the First Division club. Extra time came, and to the amazement of everyone - and the embarrassment of Sunderland - a goal by Bryant saw Yeovil win 2 - 1, securing a place not only in the fifth round, but in football's history books too.

The whole Sunderland team were criticised for an utterly abysmal performance. In truth, they were out played and out fought by a team who were far better on the day. The defeat was nothing short of humiliating.

Sunderland meet Yeovil Town in the FA Cup fourth round, 1949.

1949-1950 Resurgence?

"It all augured well for the 1950s..."

Bill Murray and Ivor Broadis.

Ivor Broadis

Ivor Broadis was born in 1922 in London, and signed as an amateur for Spurs before the War. With the onset of peace, his career resumed, and he made his way to the far northern reaches of English football, signing for Carlisle United. This alone may not seem too surprising for an aspiring 23 year old. However, without a single Football League appearance to his name, Ivor was appointed player-manager for the Cumbrian outfit!

It proved to be a very astute decision, and Broadis quickly established himself not only as a smart manager, but also a talented goalscorer. This alerted a number of bigger clubs, and in January 1949, immediately following our disastrous FA Cup exit at the hands of Yeovil Town, Sunderland stepped in and signed him for a fee of £18,000. Broadis himself handled all of the negotiations, making sure that his employers were getting a decent deal as well as himself.

In the next two years, Ivor made over 80 appearances in red and white stripes, and his strike record of almost one in every three games led to his transfer to Manchester City in late 1951 for a then record fee received by the Club of £20,500. His career continued to blossom, and England recognition soon came, Broadis winning 14 caps, scoring 8 goals, and representing his country in the 1954 World Cup Finals in Switzerland. He returned to the region when signed by Newcastle and eventually moved back to Carlisle as player-coach.

After the near relegation of 1947-48 and the humiliation at Yeovil in 1948-49, expectations surrounding the Club should have been muted. Yet, despite a 4 - 2 opening day defeat at Liverpool, some 56,504 turned out to see our first home game of the season, against Arsenal. The fans were served a real feast, a goal from Shack after four minutes setting the tone as we romped to a 4 - 2 win.

However, the season did not start well. After eight games, we had only six points, having conceded 18 goals. At Bolton, Shackleton had a chance to grab a point with the last kick of the match, but was mortified when he missed from six yards. This pretty much summed up the opening section of the campaign for Sunderland.

Fortunately, there was better to come. When West Brom paid their first visit to Roker Park in 11 years, the Lads marked the start of a revival by beating them 2 - 1. A visit to Old Trafford the following week - Manchester United having eventually returned home following their temporary exile across the city - produced a convincing 3 - 1 victory. The fans, desperate for glory, flocked to Roker following this win, with almost 65,000 cramming in to see us draw 1 - 1 with Blackpool. However, the day was tinged with sadness for all at the Club when the news arrived that Colonel Joe Prior had sadly passed away at his home in Tunstall Lodge during the game.

On the pitch, the revival was short lived. A period of erratic form had the fans biting their nails. Good wins against teams like Charlton, Wolves and Everton were interspersed with defeats and draws. However, we were doing enough to be in with a shout of the title, providing a good winning run could be put together. As the festive period arrived, it was make or break time as the Lads visited Highbury. Sadly, Arsenal were not in the mood for giving gifts, thrashing us 5 - 0. In thirteen visits to Arsenal since the 1931-32 season, Sunderland had a record of two draws and eleven defeats. We had managed to score ten goals, but had conceded a massive forty three - a bogey ground if ever there was one!

While understandable, the defeat meant our season still needed kick starting. The spark was to arrive in the FA Cup. After three disastrous seasons in the competition, the Lads were due a break. Over 55,000 crowded into Roker Park to see us play Huddersfield, and were delighted to see us race into a 4 - 0 lead after only 25 minutes. By full-time it was 6 - 0!

The victory sparked off an improvement in League form too. The next three games were well won, including a 6 - 1 victory over Derby. However, the Cup dream didn't last long: Spurs hammered us 5 - 1 in the fourth round!

But, it was the League that really mattered, and the Lads were putting together a strong unbeaten run. Indeed, our first League defeat of the new year did not come until April 10th, and the improvement had lifted us towards the top of the table. By the middle of March, we were third, and just two points off top spot.

Catching the leaders would be a difficult task, but the Lads were determined to give it a go. After two battling draws, a run of consecutive wins - at home to Aston Villa and Birmingham and away at Fulham - had the fans dreaming of the ultimate glory. When Manchester City arrived at Roker Park, they were almost certain to be relegated and without an away win all season. Everything was set for the Lads to continue their charge for glory - until we lost. Trautmann, the German ex-prisoner of war, saved a twice taken Stelling penalty, and City walked away with a 2 - 1 win. Tears flowed yet again on Wearside, as once more it looked a case of so near and yet so far.

Three games remained, and there was still an outside hope as Sunderland made their way to Leeds Road to take on a Huddersfield team who had been so comprehensively beaten in the FA Cup. Huddersfield themselves were desperate for points to ensure their safety in the First Division, and their desire to win was greater as they triumphed 3 - 1 to put the final nail in the coffin of our Championship hopes. While the season ended well, with a Tommy Wright hat trick helping us defeat Everton 4 - 2, and the last game of the season seeing a convincing 4 - 1 win at home to Chelsea, it was too little, too late, and we disappointingly missed out on the glory of a League title.

Nevertheless, third place was an excellent finish, and we were just a point behind eventual Champions Portsmouth. We had scored more goals - 83 - than anyone else in the division and Dickie Davis had ended as the leading scorer in the First Division, with an outstanding 25. Moreover, attendances during the season had topped the million mark for the first time in the Club's history, with an average gate of 47,832. It all augured well for the 1950s…

1949-50 Sunderland team.

Agony

As the season drew to an end, Sunderland, unbeaten at home all season, met Manchester City, marooned at the bottom of the First Division and without an away win all season. Holding joint top position, this was Sunderland's big chance to make their final push for the Championship, but the match went badly wrong. The game itself was a rather dull affair, with little in the way of goalmouth action, especially in the first half. Four minutes into the second half, Mapson came out for a cross, but the ball dropped from his grasp, bounced off the back of Oakes, and it was 1 - 0 to City. The crowd could scarcely believe it, but things got worse on 60 minutes when a Clarke header put the visitors two up. Stelling pulled one back with a penalty after 65 minutes, and ten minutes later the Lads were gifted a lifeline as the referee again pointed to the spot. Stelling stepped up, only to see his shot saved by the German keeper Bert Trautmann. However, the linesman spotted that the keeper had moved early, and the referee ordered the kick to be retaken. Trautmann, not best pleased, kicked the ball into the crowd, and then broke the hearts of most of them when he again pulled off a magnificent save. The defeat effectively ended Sunderland's hopes of winning the Championship, and did so in the cruellest fashion.

Jack Stelling.

Len Shackleton

When Len Shackleton signed for Sunderland in February 1948, his transfer was the talk of football. Not only was the £20,050 fee a new record for the game of football, but he was the hero of our arch rivals Newcastle. The huge fee had been enough to persuade the Magpies to part with their prized possession, and his arrival was greeted with cheers by the Sunderland faithful. Not only did we have a new hero - but Newcastle had just lost one!

Born in Bradford, Shackleton was one of the game's most dazzling lights. As with many talented players, Len seemed to court controversy, but oh how the fans loved him! Whilst he did his level best to become the 'fans' favourite', the same cannot be said about his relationship with those who ran the game. Most famously, his autobiography, The Clown Prince of Soccer, had a chapter entitled 'What the average director knows about football'. The chapter consisted of nothing more than blank page!

His perceived anti-establishment stance probably goes some way to explaining why one of the most gifted and exciting footballers of his generation managed to accumulate a paltry five England caps. He was not averse to voicing his opinions, publicly criticising referees, the FA, the League and the England selectors - as well as directors. The brevity of his international career was as much England's loss as it was Shackleton's, as the thousands of fans who turned up the length and breadth of the country to witness his outrageous skills would testify!

Len began his career as an amateur with Arsenal during the War, but was regarded as surplus to requirements by the manager George Allison, being told he would never make the grade. In the same way as Decca Records rued the day when they turned down the Beatles, Arsenal lived to regret this hasty judgement, as Shackleton returned to his native Bradford.

He vowed that he would return South to prove himself, but in 1946 a £13,000 fee lured him to the North East - and our deadly rivals at Newcastle. Legends are often made on debuts, and none more so than Shack's - his six goals in a record 13 - 0 victory over Newport seemingly endeared him to the hearts of the Newcastle fans forever. That was, however, until that huge transfer fee brought him to Wearside in February 1946!

Shackleton attracted massive crowds wherever he played. He was loved by many, but hated by many too. An integral part of his play - and attraction - was an impish streak which brought displays that some felt bordered on ungentlemanly behaviour. Primarily this was a case of his superior skills being used to show up average players for what they were; and the Sunderland fans loved it. Shack could make opponents look like fools, and if being a talented footballer of the highest order is an offence, then Shack was as guilty as hell!

Shack's England caps came intermittently, and despite his undoubted talent as a crowd pleaser, he never really had the opportunity to shine brightly on the international stage. His solitary goal at the highest level came against the then World Champions West Germany in 1954, when he contributed to a 3 - 1 England win. Yet, despite having secured only a handful of caps, he remains a huge name in football, and was recently elected as one of only one hundred players in a 'Football League Legends' table compiled to commemorate the centenary of the Football League.

Sunderland and England star, Len Shackleton.

A Football Master

In Masters of Soccer, Edelston and Deleney highlighted the sort of tricks Shack would employ, infuriating half the fans, while delighting the others: a high ball is dropping towards Shackleton, he raises one foot and traps it dead, before pretending to look at his watch and asking the bench "How long to go?". He takes the ball up the pitch, jinking and swerving past opponents until only the keeper is left to beat. He then fools the goalie into diving the wrong way, and dribbles the ball into the empty net. However, he then stops the ball on the line, looks to the keeper and shouts "It's not over the line yet!".

When he did something like this, they suggest, "either you laughed with delighted astonishment at his cheek, or you pressed your lips together and muttered 'Disgusting!' It depended on the sort of person you were, and your motives for watching football."

Just as amazing as the lack of caps in his career, was the fact that he didn't win a single trophy during his career. He was a member of the 1949-50 team which came so agonisingly close to winning the First Division and played in consecutive FA Cup Semi Finals in 1955 and 1956, but ultimately he retired without any medals to his name. Nevertheless, he remains a legend, amongst football fans in general, and Sunderland fans in particular. In total, he made almost 350 appearances for the Lads, and scored 101 goals, just failing to reach the magic century in the League. Injury blighted him towards the end of his career, and with the onset of Alan Brown's rigorous training methods, it was no surprise when he gracefully retired after the first game of the 1957-58 campaign.

Len Shackleton.

The Final Word

Len Shackleton was never a man short of words, and his wisecracks played a huge role in endearing him to fans - and upsetting those he was poking fun at. One comment in particular is worth recording here, and should forever endear him to the Sunderland faithful:

"Even though I was born in Bradford and now live in Cumbria, I still consider the North East to be home. I love the place and the people are smashing. Newcastle people always tell me that I'm biased towards Sunderland, but really I've nothing against Newcastle... I don't care who beats them!"

A class comment, a class act, forever a legend.

Len Shackleton.

1950·51	**12th in League; FA Cup quarter-final.**
1951·52	**12th in League.**
1952·53	**9th in League.**
1953·54	**20th in League, one place from relegation; smash world transfer record.**
1954·55	**4th in League; FA Cup semi-final.**
1955·56	**9th in League; FA Cup semi-final.**
1956·57	**20th in League, one place off relegation; FA and League investigation.**
1957·58	**21st in League - relegated for the first time ever.**
1958·59	**15th in Second Division.**
1959·60	**16th in Second Division.**

The 1950s was, perhaps, the most dramatic decade of the Club's history. It was a time when we became known as the 'Bank of England Club', big money signings flowing in and out of the Club on a regular basis, no expense being spared as we aimed for glory in the League and Cup. We fielded glamorous all star teams full of internationals, played entertaining football and attracted large crowds to our matches. Ultimately, however, we also failed to win trophies.

For football clubs, and most other organisations, the 1950s was a crucial period governing future success. With life returning to normal after the devastation of the War, it was make or break time. For those who had been unsuccessful before the War, it was a chance for a fresh start. For those - like Sunderland AFC - that had been success stories, it was a time when pre-eminent positions had to be quickly re-established or potentially lost for ever.

In a cruel historical blow, just as we seemed to be on track for more glory, the Club was rocked as never before by a behind the scenes scandal. Investigations into illegal payments to players saw the footballing authorities dole out the most severe punishment in the game's history, the Football League and the Football Association making a high profile example of Sunderland in order to warn off other offenders. The effects of this action on the Club were huge. A year later we were relegated to the Second Division for the first time in our history and our position as one of the country's elite clubs was placed in severe jeopardy.

CONSECTATIO EXCELLENTIAE

SUNDERLAND A.F.C.®

NEWCASTLE UN
FOOTBALL CLU
ST. JAMES' PARK · NEWCASTLE · ON

OFFICIAL · 1955 · PROGRAMME · 1956

PRICE 3D

SATURDAY, 3rd MARCH

Photo by Bob Edwards

Kick-off 3.0 p.m.

NEWCASTLE UTD   V.   SUNDERLAND

F.A. CUP 6th ROUND

Programme No. 37

BANK OF ENGLAND

Club

1 9 5 0 · 1 9 6 0

1950-1951
Promise Unfulfilled

"The £30,000 fee smashed the transfer record and sealed Sunderland's position as one of the game's big spenders"

Tommy Wright scoring against Sheffield Wednesday, November 1950 at Roker Park Sunderland 5 - 1 Sheffield Wednesday.

Owls Slaughtered

On November 4th, Sheffield Wednesday, rapidly gathering a reputation for attractive football, made their first visit to Roker Park since 1937. One of the England selectors was at the game, but Ivor Broadis, who fancied his chances of selection, was out through injury. The star attraction that day was a Welshman, Trevor Ford making his home debut.

Strong rain had made the pitch heavy, but the fans did not mind in the slightest as the scoring started as early as the 5th minute, Shackleton heading home. Tommy Wright then forced the ball in from a Cunning free kick(!), but Wednesday reduced the arrears before half time.

At 2 - 1, the game was still anyone's, but the second half belonged to Ford. He volleyed home his opener in the 65th minute, rifled in a second after 85, and with a minute left on the clock, completed his hat-trick - and a total rout - by racing in and forcing the ball - and himself - into the back of the net.

Two years later Gene Kelly would delight movie fans with 'Singing in the Rain' - and perhaps inspiration for the number came from the Roker faithful on this wet, but happy, November day!

As ever, the new season started full of optimism. Having finished a strong third the previous season, and with a forward line containing Len Shackleton and Ivor Broadis, fans were naturally hopeful that this could be a big year for Sunderland. 52,000 turned up expectantly for the opening fixture, a 1 - 0 home win over Derby County. Two days later, however, we were brought down to earth with a bump, losing 3 - 1 at Aston Villa. The result was in some ways a consequence of us losing Stelling through injury in the very first minute, meaning we played most of the game with just ten men and without one of our defenders. However, the result was more than a one-off, being followed by a 4 - 0 thrashing at Liverpool and - after a 3 - 3 draw with Villa - further defeats against Fulham and Wolves.

It was a poor start to the season, and although matters soon improved a little - with draws becoming the most common result - Murray made yet another expensive foray into the transfer market in an attempt to improve our form. Having already been allowed to smash the transfer record with the purchase of Shackleton in 1948, the board gave him the backing to do so again. This time the manager moved in for Aston Villa's Welsh international striker, Trevor Ford. The £30,000 fee smashed the transfer record, and sealed Sunderland's position as one of the game's big spenders.

Like Shackleton before him, Ford's debut was in an away defeat - 3 - 0 at Chelsea - but his home debut was a dramatic win. 48,900 turned out to see him in the game against Sheffield Wednesday, and the new signing put on an exhibition display. As the Lads cruised to a 5 - 1 victory, Ford scored a hat-trick, broke a goal post in the Fulwell End, and did the same to the jaw of the Sheffield Wednesday centre half! The comprehensive win should have signalled a change in fortune, but injury problems for Shackleton proved troublesome. 'Shack' was still the inspiration behind the team, and a run of poor performances in his absence confirmed that we relied very heavily on his unique skills.

Indeed, the victory over Sheffield Wednesday was followed by a 5 - 1 thumping at Arsenal - a game Shackleton missed - and the team started to struggle, going down to defeats against Everton, West Brom and Derby. The latter game, played at the Baseball Ground, was particularly exciting. It took place with two inches of snow on the pitch, and Sunderland were two goals behind on three separate occasions but fought on to the end. At the final whistle though, the score was 6 - 5 in the home team's favour. After this, however, performances began to improve. There were some impressive displays during the festive period, most notably a successful 'double-header' with Manchester United. We beat them 2 - 1 at Old Trafford on Christmas Day, and on Boxing Day - inspired by a Broadis hat-trick - thrashed them 5 - 3 at Roker.

It was in the Cup where the real excitement came though and before the end of January, the Lads had secured a fifth round place. Second Division Coventry were beaten 2 - 0 at Roker in the third round and, with Shackleton back in the team after almost two months on the sidelines, another Second Division side - Southampton - were beaten 2 - 0 in the fourth round, again at Roker Park. With a bad start to the season having ruled out glory in the League, the Cup was providing a real focus for attentions - particularly with the revamped forward line in full flow; the game with Southampton was watched by a huge 61,314 crowd.

Just two weeks after the Southampton game, the Lads limbered up for the fifth round. The draw - which had already been favourable in the earlier rounds - not only gave us another home tie, but pitted us against Third Division South minnows Norwich City. An easy win was expected, 65,125 turning up to see Sunderland make an expected passage to the quarter-finals.

The home fans were not disappointed, a 3 - 1 victory seeing us through to the last eight. However, the draw was now much tougher, and although we were awarded home advantage, our opposition came in the form of a formidable Wolves team that had come even closer than us to the League title the previous season, missing out only on goal average. In a tight match, a Dickie Davis goal was only enough to earn a replay, and four days later we travelled to Molineux. Here, our luck ran out, and Wolves ended comfortable 3 - 1 winners. Not only had they denied us a place in the last four, but also a tantalising semi-final clash with local rivals Newcastle.

Following our Cup exit, the rest of the season drifted away. The Lads put in some decent performances, but draws were the most common result, and with little left to play for, crowds dipped to around the 25,000 mark. The exceptions here were the local derbies, over 55,000 turning out see us beat both Middlesbrough and Newcastle by two goals to one.

When the season ended, we lay in a somewhat disappointing 12th place. Given the poor run at the beginning of the season, this was not too bad, but after a good finish the previous season, and with the huge spending on players continuing, better had been expected. While the Cup run had been exciting, all of our victories came against lower division teams and we had failed in our only tie against top flight opposition. There was no doubting the fact that we had a talented team; but so far, their promise had remained largely unfulfilled.

FA Cup 5th Round, Feb 1951 at Roker Park, Sunderland 3 - 1 Norwich City, Tommy Wright goes into a tackle.

European Clashes

The Bank of England Club were a great attraction across the footballing world, and there were a number of money spinning exhibition matches played against foreign clubs during the season. For example, in April, we travelled to Rotterdam to play a Netherlands XI in front of 50,000 people. We also took on Aberdeen at Pittodrie, while Galatasaray of Turkey had been earlier visitors to Roker Park, and the Yugoslav side Red Star Belgrade took part in a Festival of Britain match at Roker Park, losing 2 - 1.

At the end of the season, we also undertook an overseas tour to Austria, where there were defeats at the hands of Rapid Vienna, FC Austria and a Graz XI. Of the three defeats, the Rapid game was probably the most notable as Sunderland witnessed at first hand the 'Rapid Quarter Hour'. The 'Rapidviertelstunde' was started on 75 minutes as the whole Rapid support started to applaud frenziedly, signalling to their players that they could rise above themselves. Apparently this was a tradition dating back some thirty years, and it certainly seemed to work against Sunderland as we lost 5 - 1!

Johnny Mapson v Galatasaray, 1950.

1951-1952
More of the Same

"Erratic performances had come to typify Murray's side"

Trevor Ford

When he was signed from Aston Villa in October 1950, Trevor Ford was to become part of the 'dream team' combination, adding to the existing flair and talent of Messrs Shackleton and Broadis. The transfer fee of almost £30,000 was a British record at the time, but the three stars never really hit it off, and Broadis and Ford were soon plying their trade elsewhere.

However, whilst he was at Sunderland, Ford managed to make nearly 120 appearances, and scored an impressive 70 goals. He had already won international recognition whilst with Swansea and Aston Villa, and added a further 13 Welsh caps to his tally while turning out for the red and whites. In total, he represented his country on 38 occasions, and ran in a very healthy 23 goals.

The call of his native country lured him back to Cardiff City in November 1953 for another £30,000 fee, and he went on to win 10 more Welsh caps. He ended his career at Newport, and was recently honoured as one of 100 'football legends' by the Football League.

After the mildly disappointing finish to the 1950-51 season, a decent start to the new campaign was needed to boost the fans' spirits and convince them that the all star team might be able to deliver the goods. In the event, the Lads got off to a flyer, with two successive victories and seven goals firing the collective imagination. At Derby on the opening day, we trailed 2 - 0 after thirty minutes, but hit back to win 4 - 3. A week later, our first home game saw Shackleton score a hat-trick as we cruised to a 3 - 0 win over Manchester City in front of a 45,396 crowd. At last, it seemed like our forward line was working together.

Of course, hopes were quickly dashed. The next four games were all lost, including home fixtures with Villa and Blackpool. Already the Lads were reeling, the team being on the ropes with the season barely underway. It was not the start that all concerned with the Club had been looking for, and with the Lads managing just one victory in September, it was clear that - despite all of the spending - the team still needed strengthening. When Stoke City beat us 1 - 0 at home on 13th October - our sixth defeat in the first eleven games - manager Murray and directors Collings and Evans were conspicuous by their absence. There was speculation - and amongst the fans, hope - that there were to be a couple of new signings. However, the only activity to emerge was the sale of Ivor Broadis to Manchester City, the £20,000 transfer having been confirmed earlier in the week.

His departure did not help matters, and by the time Sunderland were beaten by Charlton at the Valley in mid-November, we had amassed only eleven points from our opening sixteen games, losing nine of them. It was all very worrying indeed. However, the board were still keen to spend money, and before our next game had sealed the £20,000 transfer of George Aitken from Third Lanark. Aitken had already won five Scottish Caps, and his form for Sunderland would later see him recalled to the Scotland team.

His arrival helped steady things a little, but his presence could not stop a 4 - 1 drubbing at Roker Park in a Christmas Day derby match with Newcastle. Ironically, he was missing from the line up in a 2 - 0 victory over our other local rivals, 'Boro, earlier in the month. He was, however, at the heart of play during a superb 4 - 1 victory over Arsenal in our last game of 1951.

While the New Year started badly - with a quick Cup exit at the hands of Stoke, and a League defeat at Blackpool - the second half of the season saw a marked improvement in form, as Sunderland buckled down to secure their continued First Division existence. A run of three consecutive victories against Liverpool (3 - 0), Portsmouth (2 - 0) and Chelsea (4 - 1) improved our standing. Somewhat embarrassingly given the money we'd spent, this was our most successful run of the season.

While this winning run was certainly short lived - a 2 - 0 defeat at home to Bolton bringing it to an end - the Lads did not lose too many games following the turn of the year. Defeat at the hands of Bolton - whose side included England hero Nat Lofthouse - was one of only four League defeats inflicted from January onwards. This was more like it, and the Lads ended the season on a bit of a high, being unbeaten for the last eight games of the season. We also managed to pull off some good victories during this spell, most notably a 7 - 1 victory over Huddersfield in April. However, form was good rather than brilliant. A lot of our games were being drawn too, but it was still a radical improvement on the early season run.

Interestingly, the Lads' performances were pretty much the same at home and away. Over the season as a whole, we picked up 22 points from a possible 42 at Roker, almost identical to the 20 points we secured on our travels. Similarly, following the up turn in form in the New Year, the Lads won four, drew three and lost two both home and away. While it was pleasing to be doing well away from home, Roker was far from being the fortress it was in more successful times. But, if the Lads could produce the form shown in the latter part of the season and turn some draws into victories at home, then there would be a strong chance of success. This, however, was asking a lot. Erratic performances had come to typify Murray's side, and this time we paid for some poor spells with another 12th position finish. Again this was comfortable enough, but it did little to satisfy the supporters or justify the manager's huge spending sprees.

Hedley clears v Blackpool 1951

Mags in Cup Glory

With the all-star Bank of England team turning in some frustrating performances, Sunderland fans were already tearing their hair out. Hopes had been raised numerous times when star players arrived at the Club, only to be quickly dashed when they failed to make the glorious impact that had been hoped for. To make matters worse though, Newcastle were doing very well during the period. Not only did they lift the FA Cup in the 1950-51 season, when local lad Jackie Milburn's two goals saw off a Blackpool team containing Matthews and Mortensen. Worse than that, they went on to repeat the feat for a second season in a row in 1951-52, a 1 - 0 win over Arsenal making them the first team to successfully defend the trophy since Blackburn Rovers in the 1890s. 12th place might have been alright under normal circumstances, but with the Mags filling the trophy cupboard at an alarming rate, action was needed.

Len Duns.

1952-1953 Frustration

"at long last we looked like seriously challenging for the Championship again"

Another Shackleton effort, this time blocked by Trautman.

New Year Glee

When Arsenal visited Roker Park in January, Sunderland were lying in a very healthy second spot and the Gunners were just two points behind. The stage was set for a clash of two of the game's big clubs and some 55,000 turned out to watch. Heavy snow had fallen before the game, and whilst it had melted by kick-off, the pitch was waterlogged and very heavy. Despite the conditions, Len Shackleton opened brightly, and danced his way through the Arsenal defence. He was brought down and Ford calmly put away the resulting penalty. A mistake by Sunderland keeper, Threadgold ,allowed Lishman to equalise for the Gunners, but just before half time, Bingham crossed for Shack, who out-jumped the defence and headed home powerfully.

As the players tired in the second half, having slogged through the quagmire, Bingham rounded off an outstanding performance. Shackleton returned his earlier compliment with a cross that the Irishman met with a brave and forceful diving header. 3 - 1 was a more than satisfying result, and was a bright start to the New Year. We were looking good for a Championship challenge.

Having been overshadowed by the Mags' Cup glory, and with a number of rather average seasons behind them, Murray's side were in real danger of becoming an expensive team of misfits. In contrast to the pre-War days, where Cochrane's home grown youngsters slowly developed into a settled side capable of challenging for trophies, Murray's period at the helm so far had seen big money signings coming and going, but with just one decent season in return. He had experimented with numerous combinations of players and made bold forays into the transfer market, but so far, Murray had been unable to find a magic formula desperately needed to bring some semblance of glory back to Roker Park.

With the legendary Johnny Mapson on the verge of retirement - and a knee injury increasingly dogging his fitness - Murray brought in a new goalkeeper for the season, Harry Threadgold joining from Chester. He was the only major signing during the pre-season, suggesting the manager and the board felt the current squad was capable of improving on its previous season's performance. For the third year in a row, the Lads got off to a winning start, beating Charlton Athletic 2 - 1 at home, in front of a 50,000 crowd. A week later, they consolidated the victory with our first win at Highbury in 22 years, Arsenal being beaten 2 - 1. However, we soon slumped again, losing three of the next five fixtures, a run which included a 2 - 0 home defeat against the Mags.

Fortunately, this was merely a hiccup. The Lads soon got back into gear, remaining unbeaten for the next eight weeks. Indeed, we managed to pick up a lot of good victories during this period, wins against Manchester United, West Brom, 'Boro and Liverpool lifting us to second place by the end of October. November then began in glorious fashion, four goal Trevor Ford hitting a hat-trick in the first half-an-hour of our fixture at Maine Road, the Lads hammering Manchester City 5 - 2 on their own turf. A week later, Ford was on the scoresheet again, his goal in the 1 - 1 draw with Stoke being his fiftieth League goal for the Lads.

But, all good things must come to an end, and midway through November, a very strong Preston team inflicted our first defeat since the 17th September, the Lads losing 3 - 2. Following this, we found it a little difficult to hit our stride once again, and although we managed a reasonable six points from six games, this was some way below the winning form we had shown earlier. Moreover, heavy defeats at the hands of Cardiff and Charlton were somewhat worrying, as a return to the bad old ways appeared to be on the cards. However, the return of Mapson in goal for the festive fixtures saw a revival, most notably a 5 - 2 thrashing of Wolves on the 27th December, Bingham and Davis - the latter in just his second appearance of the season - grabbing a couple of goals each.

So, the New Year arrived with Sunderland looking in reasonably good shape, and after a 2 - 2 draw with Villa and a good 3 - 1 win over Arsenal, we prepared for the visit of Scunthorpe in the FA Cup. Our opponents had only been admitted to the League in 1950, and were languishing in Division Three North. In a game played out on a fog-bound Roker Park, the Lads should have cruised to victory. Instead, a hard fought 1 - 1 draw followed. In the replay, though, we secured our passage to the next round, with a 2 - 1 win. However, catastrophe struck in the game when Trevor Ford broke his ankle, an injury which would put him out of action for two months. Amazingly, the injury did not seem to concern him unduly at the time, and he stayed on the pitch for a further 28 minutes - long enough for him to score the winner!

By the time we visited Derby in the middle of January, Sunderland sat proudly at the top of the First Division, and at long last looked like seriously challenging for the Championship again. What actually followed was three months of almost sheer madness. A 3 - 1 defeat at the Baseball Ground marked the start of a run of twelve League games without victory. Needless to say, this put an end to our title aspirations. What's more, we were also dumped out of the FA Cup - in the fourth round - by Burnley as things went horribly wrong. Up front the goals dried up, and at the back we started to leak them. From January to the end of the season, we suffered five goal hammerings at the hands of Portsmouth, Bolton and Burnley.

Oddly enough, throughout this period we remained undefeated at Roker Park. Indeed, our only home defeat during the season came in the game against Newcastle. But, drawn games do not win Championships, and the Lads ended the season in 9th, a somewhat disappointing finish following the early season form. Indeed, the fans were pretty sick of it all; our final match - a 4 - 2 win over Cardiff City - saw the lowest post-War League crowd at Roker Park, just 7,469 bothering to turn up. While this was primarily because the game was a Monday fixture, crowds had been declining anyway, and our final Saturday fixture - a 1 - 1 draw with Spurs - still failed to attract 25,000 spectators. Their mood was summed up in a single word that described the season well: frustration.

The first floodlit game, against Dundee, 1952.

Stadia of Light!

The 1952-53 season saw the Club - and others around the country - experiment with floodlights. On December 1st, we played under floodlights for the first time in England, travelling to Southampton for a friendly match. It ended 3 - 2 to the Lads. Only nine days later, Dundee visited Wearside as, for the first time, Roker Park became the 'stadium of light'. The novelty of the Sunderland floodlights attracted a crowd of 34,352, and they witnessed a 5 - 3 victory for Sunderland.

Indeed, the floodlights at Roker brought with them a whole host of friendly matches. In March, East Fife beat us 3 - 1 in front of over 37,500 fans, whilst Clyde were beaten 2 - 1 later that month. The most attractive fixture, however, was undoubtedly the tie with Racing Club de Paris at the end of the month. Nearly 30,000 turned out to see SAFC win 2 - 0, but the name on everyone's lips afterwards was that of Amalfi, the Brazilian ball player who starred for the French club and thrilled the home fans.

At the end of the season, the Annual Report showed that the Club had turned a healthy profit of £20,342 in the period, and that the floodlit games had brought in gate receipts of £15,800. The temporary floodlighting would be replaced by permanent fittings during the close season, for the experiment had proved to be a huge success.

Fred Hall leads the team out for their first floodlit game at Roker Park v Dundee in December 1952.

1953-1954
Not Good Enough

"throughout the country people smirked at the fact that money cannot always guarantee success"

Billy Elliott.

Topsy-turvy

Arsenal visited Roker Park in September, bottom of Division One, with Sunderland one paltry place above them. It was a stark contrast to the last time these two had met at Roker Park, when they were challenging each other at the head of the table. However, it was still early in the season, and the two were expected to regain their form sooner rather than later; almost 60,000 packed into the ground full of anticipation.

Lishman repeated his feat of the previous season and scored the opening goal for the visitors, but it was very much a false dawn for Arsenal. On 38 minutes, Ford equalised, and just before half time Elliott curled a left foot shot into the net to put Sunderland ahead. The second half was all one way traffic, with the Gunners tiring rapidly under an almost constant onslaught. The Arsenal defence proved just why they were bottom of the League by conceding a further five goals! Ford completed his hat-trick, Wright helped himself to a couple, and Shackleton also found the scoresheet for good measure. Sunderland 7, Arsenal 1. Oh happy days!

Frustration was soon replaced with excitement in the hearts and minds of the Sunderland faithful. Before the 1953-54 season had even begun, fans were flocking to see their team, a crowd of over 15,000 being present for a pre-season exhibition match at Roker Park between the 'the whites' and 'the stripes'. The first team attack and reserve team defence ('the whites') were pitted against the reserve forward line and the first team defenders ('the stripes'). The result was a final score of 8 - 6 to the whites, with Ford and Shackleton having a field day in the second half, the former hitting five goals. It was an amazing turn out of fans, almost double the number who had seen our last home game of the previous season.

The main reason for the huge interest in a practice match was the flurry of pre-season transfer activity Murray had engaged in as he restructured the side following another poor season. Such was the size of the outlay - on top of what had already been spent - that Sunderland were dubbed 'the Bank of England Club'. Nine players were bought for a total of some £70,000. Most notably, goalkeeper Jimmy Cowan arrived from Morton, for £8,000; centre-half Ray Daniel came from Arsenal, for £27,000; and Billy Elliott came from Burnley for £26,000. These three players - Scottish, Welsh and English internationals respectively - were signed to end the 'slump' on Wearside. They were joined by others such as Joe McDonald from Falkirk and Ken Chisholm from Cardiff. An audacious bid was even made to sign Jackie Milburn from arch rivals Newcastle United. Milburn, who it was alleged had 'suffered at the hands of the Newcastle Directors', was interested in the move to team up with his old friend Shackleton, but in the end the Newcastle board turned down Sunderland's approach.

As in any era, a club which is seen as wealthy and powerful is the target for much envy and abuse. Many in the game said that such financial clout was excessive and harmful to the game, and Sunderland became everyone's favourite to beat. It was therefore somewhat predictable, perhaps, that the season would start in a dreadful fashion. The Lads were beaten four times in the first five games, and in two of those matches - against Charlton and Manchester City - we managed to contrive to concede five goals. Although we were hitting quite a few goals ourselves - scoring twelve in five games - at the end of the period we had only two points to show for all of the investment.

However, it finally looked like the team had clicked on 12th September, when Arsenal were routed 7 - 1 at Roker Park. But, this fine performance was followed by two more away defeats, and a home game against Blackpool produced a victory only when goals from Daniel and Ford in the last four minutes saw us turn what was looking like a 2 - 1 defeat into a 3 - 2 victory.

After ten games, we were in dire straits, with just seven points from a possible twenty, but three defeats in the next five games - including a 6 - 2 thrashing at Preston - meant we began November in bottom place of the First Division.

Action was clearly needed, but signing new players would seem a little ridiculous - we already had barrel loads of them! Instead, the manager decided to sell goal hero Trevor Ford, who left for Cardiff for £30,000. It was all very worrying indeed.

Matters hardly improved following his departure. A 5 - 1 thrashing at Burnley was embarrassing enough, but the Bank of England all stars were really humbled in early January when Second Division Doncaster Rovers visited Roker Park in the FA Cup. The Yorkshire club walked away with a 2 - 0 victory that left egg over our faces.

At last, the Lads seemed stunned into some kind of action. Three good victories followed in quick succession, Cardiff being beaten 5 - 0, Arsenal 4 - 1 and Portsmouth 3 - 1. New signing Ted Purdon, a £15,000 capture from Birmingham City, made his debut in the Cardiff game, and his appearance seemed to spur the Lads on. He hit six goals in these three games, including a hat-trick in the win at Arsenal, which - sadly - was Sunderland's first away victory in over fifteen months.

However, Purdon's talismanic effect was short-lived. He scored just five more goals over the rest of the season, and the Lads quickly rediscovered their losing habit. By the time April came around, we were in real danger of losing our First Division status for the first time ever. There were seven games left to stave off relegation, but we started badly. A trip to Anfield saw Liverpool registering their first home win for some four months, as the Lads went down 4 - 3. A draw at home to Preston was followed by the visit to Roker of the two Sheffield clubs. Wednesday went away with a win, and United pinched a point, so it was all down to the last three matches.

A trip to 'Boro ended 0 - 0, which was better than losing, but wins were needed. Fortunately, our last two games produced two points each. Sheffield United were beaten 3 - 1 away and Burnley beaten 2 - 1 at home. This, combined with the failings of others, was enough to secure our Division One status for another year. We were safe, but in truth it was a very close escape. It had been a long, hard season, and throughout the country people smirked at the fact that money cannot always guarantee success.

1953-54 Sunderland team.

Billy Bingham

Born in 1931 in Belfast, Billy Bingham was signed from Irish club Glentoran in October 1950 for a fee of £5,000. One of the most popular players ever to don the famous red and white stripes, Bingham used the upper body strength developed in his early days as a weight lifter to become a devastating right winger.

Whilst with Sunderland, Billy became a mainstay of the Northern Ireland team, and won a total of 56 caps throughout his career. He helped his country to reach the 1958 World Cup Finals in Sweden, where they surprised everyone by making it through to the last eight.

In 227 appearances for Sunderland he scored 47 goals, before joining Luton Town after the 1958 World Cup Finals. He later turned out for Everton and Port Vale, before cutting his managerial teeth with Southport in 1965. From there he went on to spells as manager of Plymouth Argyle, Everton and Mansfield Town, as well as a term as manager of Greece. He then had the honour of managing his country in both the Spain 1982 and Mexico 1986 World Cup Finals, before retiring from the game in 1993.

Billy Bingham.

1954-1955
Back on Track

"This was more like it: a Championship challenge and some brilliant Cup games against quality opposition"

Willie Fraser makes a successful save during a match v Spurs at White Heart Lane.

Goalkeeping Dilemma

During the close season, Johnny Mapson had decided to hang up his boots, and filling the gap left by the legend would prove difficult. Plagued by injury, he had made only a few appearances during his final season, but his replacement - Scottish international Jimmy Cowan - had found it hard to fill Mapson's gloves. Indeed, Cowan himself was replaced during the season by another Scottish international - Willie Fraser - who was brought in from Airdrie towards the end of the 1953-54 season.

Fraser quickly established himself as first choice, and Cowan was soon on his way. However, when the 1954-55 season kicked off, Fraser was unable to get leave from his national service in the army. With Mapson no longer on stand-by, the manager turned to 17 year old local lad Leslie Dodds. It must have been daunting for the teenager, making his debut in front of 57,000 fans, but he performed well in a 4 - 2 win over Cup holders West Brom. However, Fraser was back in time for the second fixture, and Dodds made way for the first teamer. Dodds made only a handful of appearances before moving on a couple of seasons later.

After yet another disastrous - and expensive - campaign, this season must surely have represented Murray's last throw of the dice. The board had backed their manager incredibly well, but in eight seasons under his charge, a third place finish and an FA Cup quarter-final were all they had to show for the massive investment. Of course, it was always going to take time for the new signings to gel together, and everyone involved with the Club was aware of this, but the 20th place finish the Bank of England team secured was the lowest a Sunderland side had ever achieved and was the closest we had come to relegation since participating in the 1897 test matches. Would the board's seemingly undying loyalty to the manager continue if another poor season was returned?

Perhaps the directors were aware of the great potential in Murray's team. With so much change in the personnel during the previous campaign, it was difficult to establish the merits of the manager's preferred line-up, but at the start of the new season they demonstrated their strengths in style. Our opening fixture was a home game against the team that had won the FA Cup and finished as runners-up in the League: West Brom. They were sent away packing as the Lads ran out 4 - 2 winners before a 57,000 crowd.

In a pleasant change from recent seasons, we did not throw away this good start. Further victories soon followed against Spurs (1 - 0), Sheffield Wednesday (2 - 0), Blackpool (2 - 0) and Charlton (3 - 1). By the end of September, we had played ten League games and only suffered one defeat. Amazingly, the victory over Charlton was our first ever triumph at the Valley, while the defeat of Blackpool was notable for the fact we scored twice in only 80 seconds.

The good form continued with a draw at home to Bolton, followed by a superb 4 - 2 victory over Newcastle at Roker Park. 66,654 saw McDonald and Bingham pulling the strings, the latter scoring two goals. The win was enough to put Sunderland top of the League.

Of course, we'd hit the heights two seasons beforehand, only to trail off badly. This time though, the Lads kept on pressing. While draws were, perhaps, becoming a little too regular, we were proving very hard to beat. By the turn of the year, we had suffered only three defeats during the season. Moreover, the impressive performances were being maintained. Arsenal were well beaten 3 - 1, and there was a good 3 - 2 home win over Manchester City, a game which marked Len Shackleton's 250th league game for Sunderland. Fittingly, he put in a sparkling performance.

The FA Cup draw gave us a difficult third round tie against Burnley. We did have home advantage though, and in the end, a Billy Elliott goal shaded the match in our favour. Victory, however, merely presented us with an even tougher tie against the previous season's runners-up, Preston North End. In a marvellous game at Deepdale, dubbed by many as being worthy of the final itself, the two teams cancelled each other out with a 3 - 3 draw. In the replay though, the Lads asserted their superiority, a Chisolm brace securing a 2 - 0 win. The match was watched by an official crowd of over 57,000, but many who were there put the actual gate at nearer 70,000. In addition, an estimated 10,000 were locked outside.

In the fifth round, we were rewarded with a slightly easier draw. Second Division Swansea provided the opposition, but the trip to Wales was still a tricky proposition. A tough battle ensued, the Lads coming away with a 2 - 2 draw. At Roker four days later, however, we moved into the quarter finals with a 1 - 0 win.

There was a downside to the Cup action though. With hard fought ties going to replays, the Lads were finding it difficult to maintain momentum in the League campaign. Our air of invincibility began to disappear as a number of games were lost during the Cup run. Fortunately, the Lads still produced the goods in the big North East derby, 61,550 seeing us beat the Mags 2 - 1 at St James' Park. But, with the team looking strong in the Cup, few fans would have been complaining when Wolves visited Roker Park for the sixth round. This was yet another tough, but mouthwatering tie. Wolves were the reigning League Champions, and the game would be a real test of the progress being made by Murray's side. 54,851 packed into the ground for the game, and the home fans were not disappointed. Two goals from Purdon, and a clean sheet at the back, saw the Champions off. Sunderland were through to the FA Cup semi-final for the first time in seventeen years!

All attentions were now focused on the Cup. All our League games were lost in the run up to the semi-final, where we would meet a promising Manchester City team at Villa Park. However, the game proved to be a massive anti-climax. The pitch was totally waterlogged, and in truth the match should never have been played. But, as was almost customary in those days, the fans were allowed in early, and with almost 60,000 crowded into Villa Park, the game went ahead. A lone goal from Clarke was enough to see City through to the final, where they would meet Newcastle United. Sunderland were deemed to be very unlucky, as they had dominated much of the game, but in the end it was not to be and the tantalising prospect of the first ever all North East FA Cup final had been snatched from our grasp.

Cup exit effectively signalled the end of our hopes of silverware. While we were still in a strong League position, the Championship was, realistically, no longer a possibility, particularly when Championship favourites Chelsea beat us just three days after the semi-final game. Nevertheless, the Lads battled on, and a 3 - 0 home win over Everton in the last game of the season secured a very good fourth place, behind Wolves and Portsmouth on goal average and just four points adrift of the Champions Chelsea. At last the Bank of England team had delivered the goods, an exciting season ending just short of glory. This was more like it: a Championship challenge and some brilliant Cup games against quality opposition. The fans were lapping it up and asking for more of the same.

Rain Stops Glory

When the Lads met Manchester City in the FA Cup semi-final, we were within sniffing distance of Wembley for the first time since the War. However, the heavens had opened for a solid 24 hours before the game, and with only an hour to go, the game was still very much in doubt. But, much to the relief of those fans who had travelled to Villa Park, the game was given the go ahead and Sunderland and City locked horns in a right royal battle.

In truth, the weather spoiled the game, and when Clarke gave City the lead after 57 minutes, things looked ominous. For the last half an hour, Sunderland threw everything at their Mancunian rivals, but in reality they never really threatened Trautmann in the City goal. When the final whistle went, the Wembley dream was over for another year.

As if to rub salt into our wounds, Newcastle were appearing in the other semi-final and had been handed a much easier looking tie against Third Division North side York City. Amazingly, this game ended in a draw, but in the replay - at Roker Park - the Mags went through. Worse still, not only did we miss out on meeting our rivals at Wembley - after beating them twice in the League - but they also lifted the Cup, their third Cup victory during the decade. This took a little of the shine off our own season.

Len Shackleton, FA Cup semi-final v Manchester City.

1955-1956
Another Close Call

"it was clear that Murray's masterplan was finally coming together"

Bill Holden.

Stunned

To lose any game is disappointing. To lose a home game is upsetting. To lose a home game 6 - 1 is distressing. To lose a home game 6 - 1 to your biggest local rivals, the word has not yet been invented to describe that feeling! When Newcastle visited Roker Park on Boxing Day, 1955, the result was a nightmare match that almost belies description. Sunderland were lucky to keep the score down to six, so utterly abysmal was our performance. What's more, the return fixture was played the very next day, with similarly unpleasant results!

So stunned were the Sunderland board by this hammering, that they immediately drove down to Burnley and signed up striker Bill Holden. He made his debut at St James' Park on 27th December, and scored a goal, but Newcastle scored three to make it one of the most miserable festive seasons in Sunderland history. Just imagine going to face your Magpie workmates after that particular double-header!

After the near misses of the previous campaign, Murray invested his faith in the Bank of England team, deciding to stick with his regular line up. A core team had now emerged, focusing around twelve key players: Fraser, Hedley, McDonald, Anderson, Daniel, Aitken, Bingham, Fleming, Purdon, Chisolm, Elliott and Shackleton. Competition for places was toughest amongst the forwards, and early in the season another striker - Bill Holden - was added to the regular squad, further intensifying the competition up front.

Perhaps the need to impress the manager was one of the reasons the team went goal crazy during the opening games of the season. In the first eight matches we scored a staggering 27 goals, hammering Villa 5 - 1, Huddersfield and Villa (again) 4 - 1 and beating Chelsea 4 - 3. Unfortunately, we were also a little lax at the back, conceding 17 goals in the same period. However, almost half of these goals came in a 7 - 3 thrashing at the hands of Blackpool, where an injury to our left back, McDonald, meant we effectively played with ten men, an impossible task against the trickery of Mortensen and Matthews.

It was an excellent start to the season, and once again the Lads pressed on, securing further good wins during October. The Lads were flying and the Championship looked a definite possibility. Certainly our team was one of football's star attractions, and a number of exhibition games were played against top overseas Clubs. In late October, in an ill-tempered match that saw the crowd being calmed down by the French police, we beat Racing Club de Paris 4 - 3 away from home, and in early November, we hosted games against Rapid Vienna (a 4 - 4 draw) and the mighty Moscow Dynamo (a 1 - 0 defeat). The latter game was strongly looked forward to, but was a somewhat disappointing affair. What's more, it marked the turning point in our fortunes, as League performances declined rapidly after the match.

Five days after the Moscow Dynamo game, we crashed to a terrible 8 - 2 defeat at Luton Town. We had begun the game as League leaders, and fielded our first choice team, but left Bedfordshire with our tails firmly between our legs. In the next eight games until the turn of the year, we managed to win just two, and slumped to further heavy defeats. The festive period in particular was a nightmare, with a 6 - 1 hammering from Newcastle on Boxing Day - at home - being followed the day after by a 3 - 1 defeat at St James'. The collapse in form had been staggering.

Fortunately, the FA Cup provided us with a relatively easy draw that might help boost confidence. While a home tie against Third Division South team Norwich was a potential banana skin, in truth the Lads were too strong for their visitors, who were lucky to escape with a 4 - 2 beating. The win certainly seemed to lift spirits. A 3 - 2 victory at Champions Chelsea preceded the fourth round tie, where the Lads made a trip to Third Division North York City. York had been real giant killers the previous season, and a tricky game ended 0 - 0. In the replay, however, we eased them aside with a 2 - 1 victory.

Once again, attentions began to shift towards the Cup. The fifth round pitted us against Sheffield United, who were struggling in Division One. Following a 0 - 0 draw at Bramall Lane, a rare goal from Ray Daniel in the replay secured a place in the quarter-finals. Our reward was a juicy derby clash with Cup holders Newcastle United. The buzz could be heard all round the North East!

The Mags had easily beaten us in both the League games during the season, and were looking to repeat their earlier feat of successive Cup victories.

Their fans must have felt confident, particularly with the game being played at St James', but a superb performance from the Lads - and by Billy Elliott in particular - saw us run out 2 - 0 winners in the first Tyne-Wear Cup game for 43 years. What a victory!

The semi-final game came a fortnight later, against Birmingham City at Hillsborough. Birmingham had only just gained promotion from the Second Division the previous season, and we had beaten them 2 - 1 in the League already. We had been handed a great chance of making it to Wembley for just the second time. But, a ninth minute goal by City made it an uphill battle all the way, and they eventually ran out easy 3 - 0 winners. It was Sunderland's ninth semi-final appearance, but only twice had we made it to the final itself. After the match, Len Shackleton quipped that 'if we get past the Sixth Round next year, I think they will give us a bye straight into the final'. Unfortunately, it would be some time before the Lads made it to the semi-final stage again.

As with the previous season, the FA Cup proved in the end to be a distraction from the League. Six wins from our final sixteen games meant a mid-table finish in ninth place, slightly disappointing after the bright start we had made. Nevertheless, it was clear that Murray's masterplan was finally coming together; with the foundations having been carefully laid over the past few seasons, surely it was only a matter of time before trophies began to make their way to Roker Park?

1955-56 Sunderland team.

Ray Daniel

When Ray Daniel signed for Sunderland in the summer of 1953, he became the most expensive centre half in British football history. The fee of around £30,000 sent shock waves throughout the game as Sunderland became the 'Bank of England Club'.

A Welsh International, Daniel gained his first representative honours whilst still a reserve in North London, making his debut for Wales in 1951. Originally an amateur with Swansea Town, he signed for Arsenal in 1946, and appeared for them in the 1952 FA Cup Final. He gained 12 caps whilst playing for the Gunners. After joining Sunderland, Daniel made a further 9 appearances for his country. He played over 150 times for the Lads before a transfer to Cardiff City in 1957.

On his day Daniel was a centre forward's nightmare, although his desire to play the ball out from the back caused more than a few raised eyebrows among supporters who had not been brought up on ball-playing defenders! His brother Bobby Daniel was also a brilliant player, but his career was tragically cut short when he was killed whilst flying for the RAF.

FA Cup semi-final programme, 1955.

Ray Daniel

1956-1957
Busted

"a joint FA and Football League investigation into illegal payments reported its findings, its implications would shatter the Club"

Ray Daniel takes a long range shot against Manchester United at Roker Park, 1956.

Easy

The 1st September saw Charlton, bottom of the First Division and without a single point to show for their endeavours, visit Roker Park. The conditions were perfect, and within three minutes of the game starting, Shackleton had given the Lads a 1 - 0 lead. After 20 minutes, he thought he had added his second, only for the referee to disallow it, but on 31 minutes Hannigan made it 2 - 0. Two minutes later, Fleming had the ball in the Charlton net, but again the referee spotted an indiscretion and the effort was chalked off. A minute later, and Fleming was through on goal once more, only to be brought down with a bizarre rugby style tackle! Daniel put away the penalty and a half-time score of 3 - 0 was generous indeed to the visitors.

After the break, Hannigan soon increased our lead, before Shack made the scores more realistic with our fifth. Charlton's heads dropped, and goals from Anderson, Fleming and a third for Hannigan gave us the scoreline we all dream about. Two minutes from time Hewie fired in a goal for Charlton, but consolation does not even get near the meaning of this late effort. A great performance and a memorable victory.

After another reasonably good campaign, Murray kept faith in his first team squad once again, the season kicking off without any headline grabbing transfers. Indeed, the opening game saw a celebration of old stars rather than new ones, Len Shackleton captaining Sunderland for the first time. The fixture saw us travel to Luton, who had beaten us 8 - 2 the previous season, and once again they turned us over completely, winning 6 - 2.

The defeat was part of a curious start to the season. It was followed by three home fixtures, which saw a good 3 - 0 win over Bolton, a disappointing 2 - 1 defeat against the Mags, and an astonishing 8 - 1 victory over Charlton! Defeat in the derby match was hard to take, particularly as Newcastle had scored the winner just three minutes from the end. Shack - who had a marvellous game - brushed aside the defeat by enquiring as he left the pitch 'How's the Test Match going?'

But, the huge victory against Charlton - our best League win of the post-War era - was inexplicably followed by a terrible run that saw the Lads win just one of their next fourteen games and slump to defeat in eleven of them. One of those defeats was at Manchester City, where Shackleton was subjected to some horrific tackling, and was eventually booked himself for an uncharacteristically bad challenge. Another was a 6 - 0 thrashing at Preston.

During this run, on October 13th, Manchester United's 'Busby Babes' arrived at Roker Park with an unbeaten record stretching back twenty six matches. Despite a spirited performance by the home side, United ran out 3 - 1 winners. Sadly, it was to be the last that Wearside saw of this fine team, the Munich Air Disaster on 6th February, 1958 robbing football of some of its finest talents. During this game, Denis Violet stunned the 50,000 crowd on 18 minutes, and despite an immediate equaliser from Purdon, further goals from Whelan and Taylor saw the Manchester team comfortably home. Unknowingly, Wearside said goodbye to some great footballers, including, of course, the majestic Duncan Edwards.

As the Lads entered December, the team was in deep trouble, and the Club had already taken action by swooping in mid-November for Manchester City star Don Revie. Signed for £24,000, Revie was an England international, and it was hoped his tactical acumen and intelligent ball play would help steer us to safety. Revie had played a blinder in the previous season's FA Cup final, securing the trophy for Manchester City, and his appearance in red-and-white stripes was hotly anticipated. Typically, he picked up an injury after just two games - both defeats - and was sidelined until February!

Fortunately, performances began to improve a little anyway and - with the exception of a 6 - 2 thrashing at Newcastle just before Christmas - December wasn't too bad at all. Indeed, we even managed to win a couple of games, beating Burnley 2 - 1 and Villa 1 - 0. The latter came on Christmas Day and it proved to be the last time League fixtures would be played on that day.

With the League campaign now a question of survival rather than glory, there was still hope that the Lads might win the Cup. Maybe it would be a third time lucky! The Lads were presented with an easy looking third round tie at home to Queen's Park Rangers, then plying their trade in the Third Division South. A good 4 - 0 win followed. However, dreams of another Cup run were soon dashed; we crashed 4 - 2 at West Brom in the next round.

But, the Cup was the least of our worries. On the pitch, more poor performances soon threatened our place in the top division. A 5 - 2 defeat at Spurs was astonishing given that Sunderland were leading 1 - 0 with only 24 minutes left to play.

For some reason, we completely capitulated and threw the game away. A 4 - 1 defeat at West Brom was equally disappointing.

Meanwhile, off the pitch, the League and FA had launched an investigation into the Club's finances. Allegations of 'illegal payments' were being viewed with the utmost seriousness; if the Club were found guilty of breaking the rules, severe penalties would follow. We were fighting for our lives on two fronts.

Despite putting together a decent seven game unbeaten run towards the end of the season, relegation was still a possibility as we went into the last three games of the season. Having beaten Leeds on Good Friday, we travelled to Manchester United, who brought our run to an end with a 4 - 0 thrashing, a victory that handed the Red Devils their second successive League Championship. We then travelled to Leeds on Easter Monday, our earlier victory being avenged with a 3 - 1 defeat. Fortunately, results elsewhere went our way, and on the last day of the season, Sunderland were already safe - although only just. It was just as well, as Portsmouth beat us 3 - 2 in a game where we fielded one of the oldest fullback combinations in our history, Hudgell (36) and Hedley (33), who had a combined age of 69 years and 267 days! Coupled with the fact that the marvellous Shackleton was himself only two days away from his 35th birthday, it was clear that some new blood was needed in the side.

We had done enough to finish in 20th place - one spot off relegation. It looked like the Club's position had been saved. However, the joint FA and Football League investigation into illegal payments reported its findings on 10th April; its implications would shatter the Club.

Ray Daniel v Manchester City at Maine Road, 1956.

Willie Fraser

Willie Fraser, an imposing six foot tall Scotsman, joined Sunderland in March 1954 from Airdrie. Despite still being on National Service, we agreed to pay £5,000 for the keeper. It proved to be an astute deal, as he went on to become a regular between the posts, making 143 appearances for Sunderland.

An Australian by birth, but of Scots descent, Fraser soon made the goalkeeper's jersey his own, and by the time the FA Cup run of 1955 came round he was justifiably classed as one of the finest keepers in Europe. His agility and total lack of fear were rewarded by Scottish international caps that season against Wales and Northern Ireland.

Although he lost his place for some of the 1956-57 season he reclaimed the goalkeeper's position for the majority of the following campaign, before leaving to join Nottingham Forest in December 1958 for £5,000.

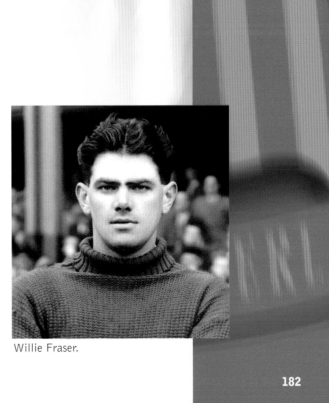

Willie Fraser.

The Curious Affair of 'Mr Smith'

(Left to Right) Bill Murray, Don Revie and Edward Ditchburn.

Hit in the Pocket

The £5,000 fine the Club received following the inquiry was the biggest the League had ever imposed, and remained a record for more than a decade, until a £7,000 fine was meted out to Manchester United in 1969. Even then, if inflation is taken into account, the sum was lower than the fine we received. However, the £10,000 Derby were fined in 1970 can fairly be said to have matched the penalty inflicted on us.

The real impact, however, came with the suspension of key members of the board. The 1950s had seen them spending money like it was going out of fashion, but the Smith affair ended the involvement of many of our most high profile backers. The Club was plunged into turmoil and the board rendered ineffectual. Consequently, when the maximum wage was scrapped in 1961, and players could be legally tempted with huge pay packets, Sunderland were no longer in a position to offer the top salaries.

It is fair to say that in the near 120 years of Sunderland AFC's existence, the last 40 have without doubt been the most frustrating and heartbreaking for its loyal fans. In that time, millions of dreams have been raised and shattered. There was a time though, when Sunderland, along with Arsenal and Aston Villa, were indisputably one of the greatest clubs in the land. Yet, while the other two have continued to prosper, Sunderland has failed to match its trophy winning exploits of the pre-War years. Why this should be is often puzzling, but much can be explained by the effect of events that took place in 1957. The curious affair of Mr Smith requires close analysis in order to help explain some of the problems that have occurred. In telling the tale of the invisible 'Smith', it has to be accepted that many of Sunderland's troubles since 1957 have been self inflicted. However, the events of that year, which shook English professional football to its very foundations, can reasonably be pinpointed to as the catalyst for many subsequent years of mediocrity.

It all started in January 1957, when a letter written by 'Smith' landed on the desk of the Football League. In it, were allegations that Sunderland had made illegal payments to players, and so began a joint inquiry by the Football League and the Football Association. The allegations would be upheld by the six man commission and unprecedented sanctions imposed upon the Club as a result.

The 'illegal payments' in question make little sense to those only familiar with modern day football. In the 1950's, footballers were subjected to a 'maximum wage' that limited the amount they could earn from their talents. What's more, it was a relatively small sum too, the limit being set at £15 per week, plus an initial signing on fee of a further £10. The policy was a bone of contention within the game, many players feeling their wages were far too low. Ironically, the early post-War era was a time when football was buzzing with excitement. Huge crowds were flocking to see games, meaning the clubs had more money than ever. However, no matter how well the players did, or how many people wanted to see them, the clubs were not allowed to pass on their profits to their star players once they had reached the £15 weekly limit.

The six man commission charged with investigating Smith's allegations descended on the Club and searched through our accounts with a fine tooth-comb. Upon doing so, one of the team found a receipt for purchasing straw - amounting to some £3,000 - with a note next to it saying 'where do I put this?' Alan Hardaker, then Secretary of the Football League, rang his brother Ernest, who was Chairman of Hull Rugby League Club. He asked him:

'If I gave you £3,000, would you be able to manage [covering the pitch] for a season?'

'Blow me', replied his brother. 'For that, we'd manage for twenty five seasons.'

It was enough to spark off further investigations, and the commission eventually revealed a system whereby secret additional payments to players were being financed through orders placed with contractors. By charging Sunderland in excess of the amount due, the contractors were able to give the Club credit notes, which were cashed later and paid to players, often as signing on fees. In all, they managed to find money 'appropriated' in this way amounting to nearly £5,450 over a five year period, enough money to buy an international class goalkeeper like Willie Fraser.

Having been caught breaking the rules, punishment was inevitable, but no-one was sure what the penalty would be. The footballing authorities had not dealt with such a case before and decided to pass judgement without remorse. The Chairman, Edward Ditchburn, was suspended permanently from the game, along with his fellow director WS Martin. Another two directors, Stanley Ritson and LW Evans, were removed from the game 'sine die' or indefinitely. In addition, the Club was fined a massive £5,000 - easily the biggest fine in the game's history - and manager Bill Murray was hit by a fine of £200. Other Directors were severely censured as to their future actions. What's more, players were not exempted from the ruling either, with a number of registrations temporarily suspended, including that of Trevor Ford.

It was a devastating blow to the Club, throwing us into disarray. With the affair hanging over us for most of the 1956-57 season, morale at the Club was already low. After the commission delivered its judgement, however, we were not only robbed of the board who had backed the Club so magnificently, but also of the manager - who resigned at the end of the season - and certain key players. The world of football shook at the severity of the punishments handed down and many felt Sunderland had been unlucky; it was assumed that many other clubs were up to similar tricks, but there was no systematic investigation of other top clubs. We had been made an example of.

In 1958, the players successfully sued, claiming damages, on the grounds that the footballing authorities had exceeded their powers. Other punishments were subsequently set aside, and some fines repaid, but the damage to Sunderland Association Football Club had already been done. The 1956-57 season had already proved to be the worst of manager Murray's eighteen year reign, and the following year - with another manager at the helm - we succumbed to relegation for the first time in our history. For the next few seasons, we struggled to re-establish ourselves and, in truth, we have found it impossible to return to the elite position we occupied before the inquiry.

Perhaps the worst thing about this whole affair was that the maximum wage the League and FA were trying to enforce was on its way out anyway. The heavy punishment the Club were subjected to was a desperate last ditch attempt to save a dying system of wage regulation. The 1956-57 season saw Leeds United star John Charles move to Juventus, the first of a number of players to move to Italy where there were no such wage restrictions. In addition, the Professional Footballers' Association - led by Jimmy Hill - were beginning to organise effective opposition to the policy. In 1961, with Sunderland lying battered and broken in the Second Division, the outdated maximum wage was abolished. Almost immediately, star players like Johnny Haynes saw their wages increase to as much as £100 a week.

The knowledge 'Smith' imparted to Alan Hardaker was such that many felt it had to have come from an insider, some suggesting it was the result of a boardroom feud that backfired badly. The former Secretary to the Football League claimed he knew who 'Smith' was, but he took that secret with him to his grave. In truth, the motives behind 'Smith's' letter can only be guessed at, but it is fair to say that from 1957 onwards this famous club has struggled to achieve the success their fans deserve. It is astonishing to think that this situation may have resulted from one of our own pressing the self-destruct button.

Bill Murray

The Smith affair brought an end to the long serving Bill Murray's tenure as Sunderland manager. In eighteen years at the Club, Murray had never really managed to hit the heights of his predecessors, despite receiving generous backing from the board. However, it would be too easy to dismiss his time at the Club as being one of underachievement. Murray took up the post at a difficult time, for the interruption of the War meant he started his career with a scratch side that starred few of the players that had guided us to glory in the 1930s. In effect, he was faced with the task of starting afresh, and after some difficult seasons, Murray finally seemed to be delivering the goods just as the Smith affair intervened. The FA/League investigation cast a heavy shadow over his final season and a better performance would undoubtedly have occurred without it. In the final analysis, however, Murray became the first manager since Campbell to leave the job without having won a trophy. Moreover, in contrast to Campbell, Murray was given much more time, and money, to prove himself. He did, though, feature as a player in the team that won the League under Cochrane and must have been disappointed not to have quite emulated the days of his mentor.

Bill Murray.

1957-1958 Calamity

1957-1958

"an unbelievable and humiliating blow"

Don Revie

In March 1955, Don Revie had been the mastermind behind the 'Revie Plan', Manchester City's tactics which contributed to Sunderland's defeat in the FA Cup semi final. Capped six times by England - with four goals to his credit - Revie was big news when he arrived on Wearside in November 1956 for £24,000. Like City, Sunderland planned to build their team around him, but sadly injury wrecked his first season, as Sunderland struggled to cope with the inquiry into the `Mr Smith' affair.

The following season Revie played a much more prominent role in proceedings, but despite his 12 goals in 39 games, he could do little to prevent the dreaded end of season drop into Division Two. With the Club's first ever season outside the top flight looming, Revie rocked Sunderland by demanding a transfer. He played in nine of the opening Second Division games, but was granted his wish to leave in November of 1958, when he began his long and illustrious association with Leeds United.

He was of course to return to play a part in Sunderland's history in 1973 when, as manager of the mighty Leeds, he had to suffer the ignominy of defeat at the hands of Bob Stokoe's heroes. A year later he was tempted away from Elland Road by the lure of the England manager's job, but controversially walked away from the job in 1977.

The new season began in turmoil, the Club reeling from the traumas and fallout of the official inquiry. With key players suspended and a well respected, long serving manager having abruptly resigned mid-way through a team rebuilding process, it was an inevitably difficult introduction to the Club for Murray's replacement. Alan Brown, who had left his position as Burnley's manager to join us, was a North East man with an obsession for fitness, and he made sweeping changes to both the training regime and the playing staff. His notorious pre-season session was a completely different approach from that of Murray and it came as no surprise when the ageing Len Shackleton retired after the first game of the season. It was indicative of Brown's desire to replace the old guard with new blood, and a number of young players who would go on to have notable Sunderland careers were brought in during the season. However, with the Club already undergoing rapid change, his new broom policy only seemed to add to the shock, and the initial effect of the new regime was a disaster for the Club. The opening eight games of the new manager's reign brought just one victory and a paltry return of four points.

Almost straight away Sunderland were on the rack. In the first eight days of the new season, the inexperience of Brown's side showed as they crashed to defeats against Arsenal (1 - 0), Leicester (4 - 1) and Wolves (5 - 0). The team's problems were perfectly illustrated in a 3 - 1 defeat at Everton three weeks into the season. Bad errors by the goalkeeper, Bollands, gifted the home side two goals in the opening six minutes and though the Lads became more confident as the game went on - Bollands making a great penalty save - it was too little too late.

However, a few weeks after the defeat at Goodison, it seemed like the Lads had turned the corner. A good 2 - 0 win at home to Newcastle, Revie and Grainger doing the damage, was followed a week later by a 3 - 0 win at home to Luton. But, a visit to Blackpool in our next game, which marked the debut of the commanding Charlie Hurley, saw Sunderland limp away disgraced following a 7 - 0 thumping. A week later, we again travelled to Lancashire, to take on Burnley, and were beaten 6 - 0!

The return to Turf Moor was particularly embarrassing for Brown, his Sunderland team slumping as Burnley flourished. There was worse to follow though. A third consecutive game without a Sunderland goal - 0 - 0 at home to Preston - rubbed salt into the wounds, before the Lads travelled to Hillsborough. Here, it looked like we would secure a long awaited win, Sheffield Wednesday trailing with just seconds left. It was not to be; Wednesday equalised with the last kick of the match!

In an attempt to deal with the slump, the Lads had adopted what became known as the 'deep Revie plan'. Playing in the centre forward position, Revie would drop deep, with O'Neill operating at inside left and Fogarty at inside right. While the plan had worked well at City, at Sunderland the plan was less effective, not least because Fogarty had just been plucked from Irish league football and simply did not have enough experience for this sort of tactical approach. But, as the players became used to the system, results improved during the month. Revie must have been pleased with a 2 - 1 win against his old Club, particularly given the fact that he managed to find the net himself, and there was a useful 3 - 2 win at Birmingham City too.

In December, however, form dipped once again. A 2-0 away defeat at Nottingham Forest was described in the press as 'pathetic', and either side of Christmas there were defeats against Arsenal (3-0) and Wolves (2-0). The only bright note came on Boxing Day, when Raich Carter, now with silver hair, made an emotional return to Roker Park on Boxing Day as manager of Leeds United. His side provided some welcome Christmas cheer, the Lads running out 2-1 winners.

In the New Year, the FA Cup did not distract the team for very long. Drawn to play Everton, we held them 2-2 at Roker, but were easily beaten 3-1 in the replay. A few days later, Villa thrashed us 5-2, and after securing draws against Everton and the Mags, we travelled to Luton. With the Hatters having beaten us 8-2 and 6-2 in the previous two seasons, the Lads were undoubtedly dreading the trip. Some say that bad events come in threes, and the Lads provided evidence for this theory, crashing to a terrible 7-1 defeat.

As if this wasn't bad enough, the Lads slumped to defeat against Blackpool (4-1), Burnley (3-2) and Preston (3-0) in their next three games. By now it was as clear as day that the Lads were in real danger of going down to the Second Division. Some fighting spirit was needed. A five match unbeaten run raised hopes of saving the day until a 6-1 home defeat against Birmingham City brought us crashing back to reality. Successive defeats against the two Manchester clubs then left us looking down the barrel of a gun. However, a 3-0 win at home to Nottingham Forest in our penultimate game still gave us a chance of survival: everything would be settled on the last day of the season.

We had to win away at Portsmouth to have any chance of survival. Our rivals for the second relegation spot were Leicester. They had the worst defensive record in the first division by a mile, having conceded 112 goals and lost seventeen of their away fixtures. What's more, their last game was away to Birmingham City. It seemed we were in with a chance.

The Lads pulled it out of the bag at Portsmouth, a clean sheet and two Kitchenbrand goals securing the points. However, Leicester edged a 1-0 win at Birmingham too. It was all over. After sixty-eight years in the top flight we had been condemned to Second Division football for the first time in our history. It was an unbelievable and humiliating blow.

Last Game, Last Hope

Going into the final game of the season, at Portsmouth, Sunderland boasted the longest unbroken run in the top flight of English football. But, we had fallen from grace rapidly since the FA/League inquiry had begun, and our destiny no longer lay in our own hands. We had to win to have any chance of staying up, and then had to hope that Leicester slipped up at Birmingham City.

Torrential rain before the game had left the pitch in a bad way, but Sunderland battled well, and took the lead through Don Kitchenbrand just before half time. The second half witnessed a few defensive wobbles as Sunderland chased a second goal, but we held on and Kitchenbrand made the game safe with his second in the last minute. However, it all proved to be a case of 'too little too late', as news filtered through from St Andrew's that Leicester had also won - and Sunderland were down for the first time in our history.

Heads down following our first ever relegation.

Relegation

When Sunderland AFC were first elected to the First Division of the Football League in 1890, few people would have predicted the length of the unbroken run the team would enjoy in the top flight. From the initial years of success, through the Great War, the depression of the thirties, World War Two and the beyond, Sunderland would establish themselves as a seemingly permanent fixture among football's elite. As such, when the dreaded drop happened for the first time ever in 1958, it was a shock from which everyone expected the Club to quickly recover. But, the next forty years would see Sunderland's efforts to re-establish themselves as a footballing force prove to be woefully inadequate. Before the turn of the century, Sunderland would suffer the indignity of relegation to Division Two on a further five occasions, and would even suffer the unthinkable embarrassment of demotion to the wilderness of the Third Division. Relegation was, unfortunately, something that generations of Sunderland supporters would come to accept as a feature of life as a fan.

The relegation in 1958 came shortly after the devastating investigation into financial irregularities within the Club. Many blame the infamous 'Mr Smith' incident for the start of the downfall, and there is more than an element of truth within that statement. The Club was reeling in 1958, and the final game relegation was like kicking a man when he was down. It would take Sunderland another six seasons before we would regain First Division status, but we were far from the feared force that we had once been. The joy of the 1964 promotion campaign led to a six season run in Division One, but the Club never finished higher than 15th - hardly awe inspiring stuff.

The final game of the 1969-70 campaign saw Sunderland once again in trouble. A victory at home to Liverpool would save our First Division skins for another season, defeat would send us down. The match was played in an almost surreal atmosphere. Liverpool looked as if they were not interested in winning, virtually offering the points to Sunderland on a plate. However, to mix metaphors, you can take a horse to water... After turning past Ritchie Pitt, the Liverpool full-back, Lawler, beat Monty with a strong shot. For the second time in our history, we were condemned to the dreaded drop.

A malaise set in to the Club during the next few seasons following this relegation until, of course, the appointment of the messiah - one Robert Stokoe. The tale of the FA Cup victory in 1973 is told elsewhere, but it was to be 1976 before Stokoe managed to get us back into the First Division. Sadly, the 1976-77 season was another disaster. We looked dead and buried long before the season ended, and the great man himself resigned to be replaced by Jimmy Adamson before the end of the season. An astonishing run of results towards the end of the campaign meant that we went to Goodison Park for the last game knowing that we could actually stay up. A 2 - 0 defeat did not help, but with Coventry and Bristol City playing each other, a win for either would see us safe. History tells us that their game kicked off 15 minutes late due crowd congestion. Reality tells us that our defeat was announced over the PA system at Highfield Road, when that game was balanced at 2 - 2. A draw meant both Coventry and Bristol City were safe, and we were down. Thousands of Sunderland fans at Everton searched for radios to listen to the drama unfolding. No one would leave the ground. In an attempt to get people out, the Everton announcer told us that we were still up - but no one believed him.

Sunderland v Tottenham programme from 1960-61, identical design to the Sunderland v Arsenal programme of 1957 with one notable exception - the line 'Only Club which has never played in any other than the First Division.'

The two teams at Highfield Road played pass the ball, and after only one season, we were down again.

Three seasons later, and we were back in the big time once again, this time for a run of five years. Again, we struggled nearly every year, usually leaving things to the last minute before saving ourselves from the drop. In 1985, we had clearly used up all of our luck in reaching Wembley for the Milk Cup Final. We lost that game, and also our First Division status as our form slumped and we dropped out of sight - coincidentally with the same Norwich team who had stolen our silverware in March!

As if that wasn't bad enough, worse was to follow. The McMenemy era dawned, and with it the total and utter disaster of relegation to the Third Division. We managed to avoid dropping straight through the divisions with a last game victory in 1985-86, but the following season saw us condemned to the terror of the play-offs, and our ultimate demise at the hands of 'mighty' Gillingham. Sunderland, a few short decades after being a permanent fixture in the top flight, were now plying their trade in Division Three.

Denis Smith took us straight out of that division, and following an amazing backdoor promotion in 1990, we had another chance to re-establish ourselves among football's elite. Sadly, this was to be another extremely short stay. Smith had little to play with in terms of funds, and the team were never really good enough to survive. Still, we once again held the slenderest of hopes as we all trooped off to Maine Road for the last game of the season. Over 15,000 Sunderland faithful flocked to Manchester that day, but Niall Quinn inspired City to a 3 - 2 victory. Other results meant that even a Sunderland win would not have been good enough, and we all cried in our beer on the long, long journey home.

And so to the 'second messiah'. After flirting with further relegation for several years, Peter Reid arrived to turn things around completely. We romped to the Division One Championship in 1996, and took our place for the first time in the illustrious and glamorous Premiership. Once again, we hardly had time to learn the way to Highbury and Old Trafford as we slipped down the ladder. After holding a comfortable mid-table position around Christmas, our finger tips slipped off the rungs as our last ever season at Roker Park turned into another disaster.

Wimbledon was the venue for the last game battle this time, and once again fate was to conspire against us. A win would have seen us safe, and 15,000 red and white fans screamed and shouted and chanted and yelled… and then cried. We lost 1 - 0, but hope was still there in the form of our old friends Coventry. Astonishingly, their match at White Hart Lane had kicked off 15 minutes late due to… crowd congestion! As the final whistle was blown at Selhurst Park, once more we all crowded around radios awaiting our fate. A draw would see us safe, but in our heart of hearts we all knew that there could only ever be one outcome - a Coventry win and our relegation. After all, we ARE Sunderland!

The end of the Millennium sees Sunderland back where we belong - in the Premier League. The last forty years have seen heartache, mistakes, disasters, and very little success. The Club is now better placed than ever before in its recent history to make itself a force to be reckoned with. Hopefully, future history books will tell of unbridled success both at home and in Europe, and the dreaded 'R' word will be condemned to the distant memory. Time, as they say, will tell.

Manchester City v Sunderland,
1990-91 season

1958-1959
Long Haul Begins

Don Kitchenbrand and Don Revie.

Don Kitchenbrand

Signed from Glasgow Rangers in March 1958, the £15,000 capture did not prove to be the lucky talisman that manager Alan Brown had hoped for. Despite scoring six goals in only ten outings, Kitchenbrand was part of the Sunderland team which was relegated from the First Division for the first time in the Club's history. He did, however, score four goals in the last three games, including both of the goals in the ultimately fruitless last match win at Portsmouth.

In his first season in the lower league, Don was installed as centre forward, charged with leading the promotion push. He was a near ever-present, and averaged over a goal every other game, but Brown's youthful team lacked the all-round solidity needed for a promotion challenge.

The following season, Kitchenbrand played in only the first three games, his place being taken by Lawther, and he left Sunderland in May 1960 to return to his native South Africa with Durban FC.

Having dined only in the country's top restaurants, the greasy cafe menu now on offer was not to the Sunderland fans' linking. Almost 20,000 fewer fans turned out for our opening home game of the season than had done the previous year. Yet, despite all their experience at the highest level, the team found it difficult to serve up even the most basic of delights. A rather tasteless 3 - 1 defeat at Sincil Bank served as the appetiser in our opening fixture against Lincoln City, and an unappealing 2 - 1 defeat against Fulham followed in Roker Park's first ever Second Division game.

A 2 - 1 home win over Liverpool three days later should have signalled the start of an inevitable charge to promotion. Instead, September 1958 proved to be one of our worst months ever in League football. Six games saw four defeats, and in three successive away games we managed to concede an horrendous total of seventeen goals. Amongst the defeats were thrashings at the hands of Fulham (6 - 2), Swansea (5 - 0) and Sheffield Wednesday (6 - 0). By October, a miserly eight points had been gleaned from fourteen games, and astonishingly it looked like we could drop straight through the Second Division into the total wilderness of the Third.

Having stuck with his relegation team in the opening fixtures, this appalling run persuaded Brown to accelerate his youth policy. The end of the month saw three teenagers pitched in for their debuts against Ipswich - Len Ashurst, Cec Irwin and Jimmy McNab. All would go on to have distinguished careers in red and white stripes. The introduction of the youngsters brought a boost to team spirit. In one memorable incident at Huddersfield, McNab was forced to leave the field injured. Manager Brown, standing on the touchline, realised that the wing half had dislocated his shoulder. He promptly put it back into place, and McNab rejoined the fray!

However, the team were also very inexperienced, a situation that was exacerbated when Don Revie dropped a transfer bombshell. Any hopes Brown may have had of building his young team around Revie were shattered when he demanded a transfer; he was granted his wish and left for Leeds United in November. As a consequence, the average age of the team at this time was a very youthful 21. Yet, the youngsters were soon making a name for themselves. The South African Don Kitchenbrand hit a hat-trick at Rotherham in November and a week later, 19 year old inside right John Goodchild showed that he could match Kitchenbrand, and notched a treble against Sheffield United.

Our form at the turn of the year, while patchy, was a big improvement on the start of the season. The first game of 1959 was a 4 - 0 home win over Leyton Orient, and although Liverpool beat us 3 - 1 at Anfield a few days later - and Everton put us out of the Cup - a run of five wins in seven games eased our relegation worries and pushed us into mid-table obscurity. Some mixed results, including a 6 - 1 thrashing at Orient and a 4 - 1 win against Brighton, did not affect this, and we ended in 15th position. It was hardly a finish to write home about, but something of a relief after the early season form.

If affairs on the pitch were something of a mess, off it they were even worse. At the start of the season, Stanley Ritson had replaced Col. John Turnball as Chairman, becoming the third man to occupy the job in three years. He later told the Echo's 'Argus' that on taking the position he found 'There was a tremendous overdraft and I realised for the first time that the financial position of the Club was pretty disastrous.'

He felt that 'Unless economies are effected, the livelihood of everyone connected with the Club is in jeopardy.'

By the end of the season, matters had not improved, costs increasing and income declining as the Club struggled to readjust to life outside of the glamorous - money spinning - First Division. Expenses, travelling and day-to-day costs were are all up, but with much lower gates at the smaller clubs, one-fifth of away gates were not meeting away expenses. As Ritson put it: 'We are a Second Division side, playing Second Division Clubs, and doing badly.'

Yet, at a time when the Club needed the board to pull together, they were bitterly divided. Ritson, who had returned as a director in 1958 when his suspension was lifted, had been the beneficiary of a ploy to remove Turnbull as Chairman. Turnbull, who had been unwell during his time as Chair, had not, in the opinion of some directors, been able to provide the necessary drive to carry the Club forward. However, many of those who had strove to replace Turnbull with Ritson soon wanted to replace Ritson with Collings, which did indeed happen in 1960. These divisions over control also spilled into arguments over strategy. Some directors wanted to spend big and try to buy success again, while others argued the Club needed to trim down in order to survive.

But, it was not entirely a season of doom and gloom. Some of the youngsters Brown had brought in were showing signs of promise and the Club had invested in its training facilities with the purchase of a training centre in Cleadon. The grow your own policy that had proved so successful in the 1930s was about to get under way again. Ultimately, however, we had just finished 15th in a division that just three years earlier few had thought Sunderland would be competing in. We were in the Second Division, and in danger of becoming second rate.

Billy Elliott

Billy Elliott was already an England international when he made the journey to Sunderland from Burnley in June 1953. The £26,000 fee reflected his international standing, and he joined a string of fellow internationals at the 'Bank of England' Club. The signing of Elliott, Jimmy Cowan and Ray Daniel did not go down too well in other footballing circles, but for those on Wearside, big money signings brought the promise of great things to come.

Elliott was an instant success, but sadly the team as a whole underperformed badly, proving money cannot always buy success. During his career at Sunderland, Billy was dubbed 'the best midfield player I've ever seen' by none other than the legendary Len Shackleton - praise indeed. He went on to make over 200 appearances in six years, before joining Wisbech on a free transfer in 1959.

Billy rejoined Sunderland later in his career as a coach, and had a short spell in charge as caretaker manager just prior to the arrival of Bob Stokoe. He was again invited to manage the Club for half of the 1978-79 season, but with the team just missing out on promotion, his long term managerial ambitions were thwarted. He has remained a regular and most welcome visitor to Sunderland first team games.

Billy Elliott.

1959-1960

Wrangling Continues

"after almost half-a-decade of turbulence the Club was in need of some stability and leadership."

Hurley and Peter Wakeham v Orient

Boardroom Politics

The last few years of the 1950s had seen some intense jockeying for position in the boardroom. Much of the debate had been about the best way forward for the Club, though there were undoubtedly personality issues too. As the Club struggled to find its way during our first season in the Second Division, there was talk of buying Scottish international striker George Herd. Ritson felt it was a bad move - the fee would be high and wouldn't guarantee survival - while Collings supported a £25,000 bid, but Clyde wanted £30,000. The issue divided two sides of the camp in the board, but the ultimate result was something of a stalemate. In the end, Herd did sign for us, but not until the end of the 1960-61 season, and he was an instant success. By then, however, we had endured three seasons of poor football. What's more, his fee had gone up - to £42,500 - and some of his best playing days had been lost to Sunderland AFC.

With the team's performances having declined rapidly over the course of four or five seasons, attendances had dipped noticeably too. Having regularly played in front of crowds of over 40,000 and 50,000 during the 1954-55 season, crowds had dipped to the 25,000 to 35,000 level during the relegation season. Poor Second Division football had - unsurprisingly - failed to halt this decline, and the 1958-59 season had seen crowds steady around 25,000, though the last two home games failed to attract even 20,000 paying customers. If the Club were to challenge at the top level again, a quick return to the top flight - or at least an exciting promotion campaign - was essential.

With the Club still in financial trouble, and boardroom squabbling hampering investment from interested parties, it is a moot point whether the manager's decision to stick with youth was a choice made through belief or necessity. Whatever the case, the season kicked off with the same faces that had ended the previous one. Much would depend, therefore, on the rate at which Brown's boys were maturing into footballing 'men'.

Once again, the season did not start in a promising fashion. Our opening game, at Stoke, was lost 3 - 1, and though we beat Aston Villa 1 - 0 in our first home game, the Villains added our second defeat of the season in the return game a few days later. However, it was not to be a repeat of the previous season's weak collapse. Good wins at Swansea and Sheffield United, and a superb 5 - 1 at home to Sheffield United, left us with a very respectable ten points from the first eight games.

But, there were still moments of panic. A 6 - 1 hammering at Ipswich had the fans worrying, but for the most part we were hard to beat. Indeed, there were just three defeats in our first fifteen games. Brown's youngsters were doing reasonably well and a promotion challenge was a realistic proposition.

However, Sunderland soon pressed the self-destruct button, the Lads going on a disastrous run which saw eight defeats in eleven games. From the 14th November - when we beat Bristol City 3 - 2 - until the 16th January - when Swansea were hammered 4 - 0 - the Lads failed to win a single game. Once again the spectre of relegation was rearing its ugly head. To make matters worse, crowds were heading in the same direction as the team - rapidly downwards. In December, just over 12,000 hardy souls turned up to witness Stoke City's win at Roker Park. The game marked our fifth consecutive defeat, a run extended on Boxing Day at Lincoln City.

With the team in such poor form, it was no surprise that we went out of the FA Cup at the first hurdle. After holding Blackburn Rovers to a 1 - 1 draw at Roker, we were well beaten by four goals to one in the replay at Ewood Park.

Yet, even after beating Swansea to bring our winless to an end, matters did not improve. Defeats against Bristol Rovers, Ipswich Town and Orient in three of our next four games just added to the misery. Relegation was once more on the cards. At last the Lads began to show some urgency. Consecutive wins against Derby and Plymouth - local lad Alan O'Neil helping himself to a hat-trick in the latter match - brought some much needed points and provided our first back-to-back wins since early September. Unfortunately, the Lads' good spell was exceedingly brief: consecutive defeats at the hands of Rotherham, Charlton and Bristol City followed.

With six games left we were rocking. Relegation was a worrying threat, but we were lucky in so far as there was a cushion of teams below us. In the event, victories over Scunthorpe, and Portsmouth home and away, steered us to safety, and we ended up one place lower than the previous season, in sixteenth position. An average gate of just over 23,000 was worrying for a club of our stature, but in truth, the football played did not really merit such levels of devotion. Brown's policy of relying on young home-grown talent or bringing in players on very low fees was hard to swallow for the supporters of a team which earlier in the decade had been dubbed the 'Bank of England Club'.

Behind the scenes, the board room wrangling was continuing. Syd Collings edged out Stanley Ritson as Chairman at the end of the season. He had been on the Board since 1947 and became our fourth Chairman in four years. After almost half-a-decade of turbulence, the Club was in need of some stability and leadership. As the sixties began, would the Collings-Brown partnership prove to be the team that would guide us back to the promised land?

George Curtis and the 1959-60 Sunderland team.

Stan Anderson

Signed from East Durham Schoolboys in 1951, Stan went on to become one of very few players to make over 400 appearances for the Club, notching up a massive 447 games in a career spanning some 12 years. Stan also had the honour of captaining the side in many of those matches, and his contribution as a solid and dependable right half was recognised at international level in 1962, when he was capped by England against both Austria and Scotland.

Stan was sold to rivals Newcastle in November 1963 for £19,000, and later completed the "North East hat-trick" by turning out for Middlesbrough, who he later managed. He was a member of the team that was tragically relegated in 1958, and thought he had fulfilled his dream of regaining First Division football in 1963, when a last match defeat at home to Chelsea saw promotion snatched from his hands. He later blamed the pre-recording of a TV film - which was to be shown after "promotion" - for unsettling the team psychologically. No wonder that today's managers refuse to mention the 'R' word or the 'P' word.

Stan Anderson, 1964.

1960·61	6th in Division Two; FA Cup quarter finals.
1961·62	3rd in Division Two; one point off promotion.
1962·63	3rd in Division Two; miss promotion on last day of season.
1963·64	2nd in Division Two: promoted!
1964·65	Hardwick becomes manager; 15th in Division One.
1965·66	McColl becomes manager; 19th in Division One. World Cup at Roker Park.
1966·67	17th in Division One.
1967·68	15th in Division One.
1968·69	Alan Brown returns as manager. 17th in Division One.
1969·70	21st in Division One: relegated again.

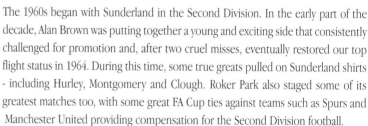

The 1960s began with Sunderland in the Second Division. In the early part of the decade, Alan Brown was putting together a young and exciting side that consistently challenged for promotion and, after two cruel misses, eventually restored our top flight status in 1964. During this time, some true greats pulled on Sunderland shirts - including Hurley, Montgomery and Clough. Roker Park also staged some of its greatest matches too, with some great FA Cup ties against teams such as Spurs and Manchester United providing compensation for the Second Division football.

On returning to Division One, however, the Club immediately lost its way. With the manager, Alan Brown, resigning, we struggled to find a suitable successor. Under George Hardwick and then Ian McColl, we did little more than stave off relegation, and much of the style and confidence of our play began to disappear. Inevitably, top flight football was proving harder than Second Division football, and the Club found it hard to adjust.

After four seasons away from Sunderland, Alan Brown returned to the Club as manager in 1968. It was not, however, a completely successful remarriage. Within two years, Sunderland had hit rock bottom once again, securing relegation to the Second Division in the last game of the 1969-70 season. As the decade closed, relegation underlined a growing feeling that the Club were slipping further away from the top of the game. Promotion to the top flight had not been built upon, and glory seemed a long way off.

THE SWINGING
Sixties

1 9 6 0 · 1 9 7 0

1960-1961
Mixed Fortunes

"a season that seemed to promise so much...ended up some way short of the mark"

Dominic Sharkey & Alan Brown.

Alan Brown

Alan Brown has the rare distinction of being manager of Sunderland on two separate occasions. Joining the Club immediately after the illegal payments scandal, he was brought to Roker not only for his managerial skills but because he had a clean image that might help put the payments scandal behind us. A deeply religious man, he was regarded as a strict disciplinarian both on and off the field. The new style was not enough to halt the decline on field though: relegation immediately followed.

Brown was a fervent believer in the need to develop young talent and this policy brought a rich crop of players through the Sunderland youth system including Jimmy Montgomery, Martin Harvey, Cec Irwin, Colin Suggett and Ritchie Pitt. He also had a great eye for talent from other clubs, bringing in Charlie Hurley, Dave Watson, Brian Clough and George Herd.

After guiding us to promotion in 1964, he left to manage Sheffield Wednesday, a decision which baffled many people. But, Brown was nothing if not his own man and he obviously reckoned that his job at Sunderland was done. It was a surprise, therefore, that he was brought back to the Club in 1968 after the sacking of Ian McColl. His second spell was to last until 1972, during which time he took us back into Division Two in 1970. He was finally sacked in the autumn of 1972, leaving Bob Stokoe the nucleus of a great team. His place in Sunderland history will be one of respect rather than of great affection.

The 'Swinging Sixties' began with Sunderland still languishing in the Second Division, but with Alan Brown attempting to blend home grown talent with some shrewd buys in order to end our exile from the top flight. The Club was undergoing another of its 'transitional phases' as Brown pieced together his ideal team. Anderson, Hurley and McNab were starting to emerge as one of the country's most reliable half back lines and, with young lads like Montgomery, Irwin and Sharkey waiting for their chance, Brown had good reason to feel his hard work would soon pay off.

The season began at Roker, with a 2 - 1 victory over Swansea. While not the greatest of games, it was a decent victory nonetheless, and it suggested we might get off to a good start. Hopes were boosted further in our next home game - a 4 - 0 win against Stoke - but the optimism was short lived. Defeats soon began to follow and, by the end of October, these were our only victories from the first fifteen games.

Brown had already realised that some fresh blood was needed in the team and at the end of September he signed Harry Hooper, a skilful right winger, from Birmingham City for £18,000. Brown's other major change was the introduction of Willie McPheat, a young Scot with a gangling style and an eye for goal. The tide began to turn with home wins against Bristol Rovers and Leyton Orient during November and the crowds that had dwindled to below 20,000 during the early part of the season were drawn back. On Boxing Day, over 46,000 piled into Roker to see the Lads held to a 1 - 1 draw with Sheffield United. The return match the following day saw Sunderland run out 1 - 0 winners, with McPheat collecting his seventh goal in eleven outings for the first team. The team finished the week in real style and gave the fans the best New Year's Eve for many a year when Luton Town came to Roker on the last day of 1960 and were convincingly thrashed 7 - 1.

The Club and the supporters saw the New Year in with heady optimism and no doubt a good few pints. Indeed, it was great to be a Sunderland fan during the first few weeks of 1961! We drew Arsenal at home in the Third Round of the Cup. While they were not having their greatest season in the First Division, they were still seen as formidable opposition. The Lads produced a scintillating performance in front of over 58,000 and two goals from Stan Anderson helped us to a brilliant 2 - 1 victory. Our reward was an away tie at Anfield. At the time, Liverpool were still in Division Two and were not yet the footballing powerhouse that Bill Shankly was to transform them into. Nevertheless, it was a great Sunderland performance in front of a 46,000 crowd that saw us through to the fifth round.

The first two months of 1961 also produced a great patch in the League, with five wins in six games. Particularly enjoyable was a 2 - 0 victory over Boro at Roker. Another 50,000 crowd saw the Lads turn in a great performance against a team that itself had an eye on promotion. The fifth round of the Cup then saw us make a trip to Carrow Road to meet Norwich. A strong travelling support meant the ground was packed with a 42,000 crowd, and they were not let down. The Lads triumphed 1 - 0, a Charlie Hurley goal settling a tense affair.

As all of the Roker faithful huddled round the radio to hear the sixth round draw, the talk was of a promotion and Cup double; heady thoughts indeed! The draw produced a home tie, which was what we all wanted, but when Tottenham Hotspur were pulled out of the bag to meet us, the fans' mouths watered at the prospect. High flying Spurs had a double of their own in mind but for them it was the Holy Grail of the First Division Title and the FA Cup. In the event, the clash provided a highlight of the season. A huge crowd packed into Roker for the game hoping to see us clinch a place in the semi-final.

A close fought match ended 1 - 1. Hopes were still high before the replay, but at White Hart Lane we were played off the pitch, losing 5 - 0.

While losing to Spurs was no great shame, the team seemed to lose confidence in the League and won only four out of its remaining eleven games. The result was a final League placing of sixth, a genuine disappointment to the Club and the fans. We were 11 points off a promotion place and a season that seemed to promise so much in the early spring had ended up some way short of the mark.

Alan Brown, as always, looked to the future and two days before the last game of the season he signed a player who was to become a firm favourite and a loyal servant to the Club, George Herd. Brown's buying spree for the summer was still not over and in July he pulled off a major deal, signing a centre forward of undoubted class. For £40,000 he bought Brian Clough from Middlesbrough. Clough had been the Second Division's leading scorer with Boro for the previous three seasons. He was a genuine goal machine and for many fans this was the perfect signing.

Willie McPheat scores and elated fans invade the pitch.

The Roker Roar scares the Mighty Spurs

The quarter-finals of the FA Cup saw the favourites, Spurs, visit Roker Park. The tie was more than enough to send a tingle through the veins of every Sunderland fan. For the first time since relegation, a really top class side was making its way to Wearside, and both the team and the town wanted to show them we were still capable of matching the best.

The Lads were knocked onto the back foot early on when Tottenham took the lead through Cliff Jones. But the crowd then got behind the team and the famous Roker Roar urged Sunderland on. The noise was so loud that ships on the Wear could hear the sound as every Sunderland move was met by shouts of encouragement. Sunderland went in at half time still a goal down. Brown's talk was enough to do the trick and five minutes after the restart, Willie McPheat grabbed the equaliser. The crowd went crazy and, in the days before barriers and fences, the ecstatic supporters spilled onto the pitch, forcing the referee to halt the game for the playing area to be cleared. The delay gave Spurs the chance to draw breath and play out the draw.

Afterwards, Danny Blanchflower, the great Tottenham captain, described it as the 'most awesome sound' he had ever heard in football. With over 61,000 in the ground it was frightening. The replay at White Hart Lane drew 64,797 and, sadly, saw Sunderland mauled 5 - 0. We were beaten fair and square by the best team in the country and, perhaps, the best team of the sixties. Tottenham went on to win the League and Cup double that season, becoming the first English club to do so in the 20th century.

ENGLISH CUP - Sixth Round
Sunderland v. TOTTENHAM
AT ROKER PARK GROUND, SUNDERLAND,
ON SATURDAY, MARCH 4th - 1961
At 3-0 p.m.
GROUND   Fulwell End
This Ticket is issued subject to the Rules and Regulations of the F. A. and the F.L. Price of Tickets will not be returnable in any circumstances if the match has to be abandoned or postponed.
No 3052
PRICE 3/6

1961-1962
Close Finish

1961-62 Sunderland team.

Mags' Unhappy Return

With four games left to the end of the season, Newcastle visited Roker Park for a tense derby. A draw at St James' earlier in the season had provided us with a useful point but we needed to win the home game to keep alive our chances of promotion.

Before the match, a terrific downpour made the pitch extremely heavy. With over 57,000 fans packed into the ground, the Lads set their stall out early on, George Herd hitting a quick goal to delight the Sunderland fans. In the second half, Willie McPheat scored a simple goal after Harry Hooper's shot had stuck in the goal mouth mud. George Herd then capped a scintillating performance with his second goal of the game to send the Mags back over the Tyne with their tails between their legs. It was a great 3 - 0 win and promotion was there for the taking.

The run up to start of the season was filled with anticipation. With the team starting to look good on paper, a promotion push was expected. But, a picture in the paper put a cat amongst the pigeons. The pre-season photo-shoot showed the Sunderland team line-up wearing white shorts. The traditional black shorts, worn by the team for the previous seventy years, had gone and many people were less than happy. Traditions - then as now - die hard in football and the black shorts would eventually return.

Despite the optimism created by the new signings, the season started badly. Liverpool beat us twice in August by three goals each time. 3 - 0 away at Anfield was not encouraging, but when Liverpool came to Roker a fortnight later and beat us 4 - 1 it looked like the writing was on the wall. However, we had merely come up against a great team; Shankly's side went on to walk the Second Division that year and it was our bad luck to catch them early in the season before our new players had bedded in.

A run of nine games without defeat from the end of September pulled around the bad start and set us up for a good season. By the time December came around we were on the up. Clough scored both our goals in a 2 - 2 draw at St James' Park, before a 54,000 crowd. Newcastle, who had been relegated from the First Division at the end of the previous season, were finding life a little tough in the Second. The following week, Swansea were put to the sword 7 - 2 at Roker, with Clough and Ambrose Fogarty notching hat tricks. Clough was now starting to fire on all cylinders. Never a great goal maker, he recognised that his job was to put the ball into the back of the net - something he was doing with a regularity that delighted the fans.

The League Cup, which had been introduced the previous season, brought some cup triumphs in the run up to Christmas. Victories over Bolton, Walsall, Hull and a bye took us to the quarter final, before a lacklustre performance at Roker Park saw the Lads crash out of the competition 4 - 1 to Norwich City. In the FA Cup, a third round replay against Southampton saw 58,527 cheer Sunderland on to a 3 - 0 victory. However, the fourth round saw us dumped out in a replay by Third Division Port Vale, after a 0 - 0 draw at Roker.

Back in the League, 1962 began with a 6 - 1 victory over Bristol Rovers, and a strong run followed. Ten of the next sixteen games were won, and just three were lost. This excellent spell put us in with a real chance of promotion. However, as was to become very much the norm for Sunderland, everything came down to the last game of the season. With Liverpool already confirmed as champions, the second promotion place would go to either Leyton Orient or us.

The Lads made the long journey to South Wales for a game against Swansea, knowing we had to win to go up. The huge travelling support were preparing for a promotion party when Brian Clough put Sunderland ahead. However, the Welshmen equalised and, despite frantic efforts from the Lads, the score remained 1 - 1 at the final whistle. Orient were promoted instead of Sunderland.

We had come so close to glory, but ended the season in despair. How often we were to feel this way over coming decades! At Roker Park, Sunderland were almost invincible, gaining 37 out of a maximum 42 points.

If only Liverpool had come to Roker later in the season we might not have suffered our only home League defeat of the season. Victory in that game or a couple more wins away from home would probably have been enough to see us back in Division One.

Despite the disappointment, there was much to be positive about. In particular, Alan Brown's youth policy was starting to pay dividends. One player to make his mark during the season was goalkeeper Jimmy Montgomery. Having worked his way through the junior teams, he was given his first run out in the League Cup in October 1961. By the spring of 1962 he had forced his way into the starting line-up and from late February until the end of the season he played in every game, except the derby at Boro, when 'Monty' was allowed to join up with the England Youth Squad. In front of him, Ashurst and Irwin - or 'Cec and Len' as they were affectionately known - also established themselves as the preferred full back pairing. With these youngsters blending well with some of the more established players, the future looked bright...

Brian Clough

"One of the reasons I never became England manager was because the FA thought I would take over and run the show," Clough once said. "They were dead right." One of the most controversial men in English football during his playing and managerial career, Brian Clough was quite simply a 'one off'. Born in Middlesbrough in March 1935, at the age of 18 he signed for his hometown side. He made his League debut in 1955, scoring the first of his multitude of goals a month later. By the time he was transferred to Sunderland in 1961 he had already scored 198 goals in 214 League appearances. When he finally retired in 1965 he had scored a total of 251 goals in only 274 games. Awesome, no other word for it. If Clough had been showing off his talents in the First Division rather than the Second, then he would surely have been selected more often for England. Len Shackleton said 'he was the greatest centre-forward I ever saw. Clough scored goals more consistently than anybody else did and that's a centre-forward's job. He would have shattered the record of Dixie Dean had he played against similar style defences.'

He became the youngest manager in the Football League when he took over the reins at Hartlepool United in October 1965, and led them to promotion before taking over at Derby County in 1967. His managerial exploits were as extraordinary as his playing career. He was, after all, only the second manager in the history of British football to take two different teams to English Championships. That he did so with the relatively 'unfashionable' outfits of Derby County and Nottingham Forest is an even greater tribute. He also went on to win two European Cups with Forest.

His spell on Wearside was all too brief, but at the time very, very exciting. To many it is a great shame that he never came back to manage Sunderland. Clough himself once said that he would have crawled up the M1 on hands and knees over broken glass to be manager at Roker Park. For most of the late 60's and 70's his name was often linked to the job, but it was never to be. Who knows what might have happened with him at the helm?

Goalscoring legend Brian Clough.

1962-1963
Thrown Away

"Could there be a crueller ending?"

A Touch of the Blues

Our final game of the campaign saw us at the top of the table, one point ahead of Stoke on 51, and four ahead of Chelsea. The Blues, however, had a game in hand on us, a match against Portsmouth postponed from earlier in the season and rescheduled after the rest of the division's games had ended. Sunderland needed only one point to clinch promotion. Chelsea had to beat both the Lads and Pompey to go up.

The run-up to the match was tense, with the failure at Swansea the previous season clear in the mind. 48,000 turned out for the game, which proved to be a frustrating affair. The Lads threw everything at the Chelsea goal, but were unable to break down their stubborn defence. Terry Venables was playing for Chelsea that day and he and the team played a hard game. Defender Frank Upton was later fined £25 for persistent misconduct. The game's solitary goal came after 25 minutes and was a complete fluke. Bobby Tambling's corner at the Roker End rebounded off Tommy Harmer's rear end and into the Sunderland net. We piled on the pressure after this, but Chelsea's goalie, Peter Bonnetti, pulled off a string of great stops and the Blues hung on to steal two points - and our promotion spot.

Despite the agony of narrowly missing promotion, there was every reason to believe that the Lads had the wherewithal to finish in the top two by the end of the 1962-63 season. After a slightly shaky start during the previous campaign, Brown's team had shown their qualities with some sparkling displays, including a great winning run towards the end of the season. A solid defensive line up made us hard to beat and this, along with Brian Clough's goalscoring antics, meant we were always likely to finish games with both points.

The new season started well, with home victories against Middlesbrough and Charlton Athletic. Together, the two games brought over 85,000 fans through the gates of Roker Park, underlining the fans' optimistic mood. However, our first away trip was to promotion rivals Leeds. Not only did we lose 1 - 0, but Willie McPheat, who had scored the winner against Charlton three days earlier, was badly injured. Tragically, this marked the end of what had promised to be a great Sunderland career for McPheat and robbed the Lads of a key attacking player.

Alan Brown did not waste time strengthening his team up front after this, moving for George Mulhall from Aberdeen and, somewhat controversially, bringing Johnny Crossan from Standard Liege of Belgium after his lengthy ban from British football. Now, with Brian Clough up front too, Sunderland had as good an attack as anyone in the country and by Christmas we had fired ourselves to second in the League. Hopes that promotion was on its way were understandably high.

On Boxing Day, however, the 42,000 crowd that packed Roker Park for our game with Bury saw disaster strike. With the match evenly balanced, Sunderland were awarded a penalty. Hurley stepped up to take the kick, but the ice bound pitch made precision football difficult, and his strike failed to find the target. Ever the predator, Clough - with 28 goals in 28 games up to that point in the season - challenged the Bury keeper for the ball. As he did so, there was a sickening crunch. Clough did not get up. Having sustained cruciate ligament damage of the utmost gravity, he was grounded in total agony. Not only did the injury keep him out of action for nearly two years but, on his return, Clough managed just three more appearances before having to call a tragically premature end to his playing career.

Without our star striker, we lost the Boxing Day match 1 - 0 and in the return at Bury three days later we were well beaten 3 - 0. The shock of Clough's injury was immense. He was every school kid's idol and the Club's best goal scorer in the post-War period to that point. The town was plunged into despair.

A bitterly cold winter did not help to lift spirits, and we managed just two games during January 1963. The first was a third round FA Cup tie against Preston, which we won 4 - 1, and the other was the home match of a two-legged League Cup semi final against our cup bogey side, Aston Villa. In the autumn we had put together a really good run in the new competition. Having thrashed Oldham Athletic 7 - 1 in the opening round, Clough and Fogarty amongst the scorers, Scunthorpe, Portsmouth and Blackburn were also seen off. This meant we were within spitting distance of a Cup final for the first time since the Bank of England days. The Villa centre forward Derek Dougan turned up at a snowy Roker Park with a mohican haircut and began to pelt the kids in the Roker End with snowballs.

Then, just to rub it in, Villa beat us 3 - 1, a result that all but spelt the end for us. The second leg did not take place until the end of April, but the delay did not improve our chances of victory; the game ended 0 - 0.

With the winter weather completely scuppering our League programme, it was the second week of February before our third game of the year arrived, a fourth round FA Cup tie at non-League Gravesend. A shaky display brought memories of the Yeovil embarrassment flooding back, but a George Mulhall goal gave us a 1 - 1 draw and the chance for a comfortable 5 - 2 win at home in the replay. Following this, we played our first League game for two months, a 2 - 2 draw at Derby.

The long break had given Brown much time to think about how to replace Clough up front. But, rather than signing a replacement, he decided to give young Nick Sharkey a run in the first team. The lad quickly repaid Brown's confidence in him. In only his fifth match he equalled the Club's goal scoring record in an individual match, when he notched five goals in a 7 - 1 rout of Norwich City on 20th March, 1963.

Although our FA Cup hopes came to a feeble end at Third Division Coventry, we still looked a good bet for promotion at the end of March. However, a disappointing 1 - 1 home draw against Plymouth saw the Lads start a run of eight matches in which we only managed one win. What's more, we also succumbed to some poor defeats, including a 5 - 2 thrashing at Cardiff.

This left us with a lot to do in the final run in, but the Lads rose to the challenge. Consecutive victories against Southampton, Swansea and Luton meant we only had to draw our last game - at home with promotion rivals Chelsea - to be certain of promotion. It looked like the long wait for top flight football was finally over.

But, we lost the game 1 - 0, a result which left us waiting on the final match between Chelsea and Portsmouth. The Blues went on to beat Pompey 7 - 0 and were promoted on goal average at our expense. For the second season in a row we fell at the last fence. Could there be a crueller ending?

George Herd

One of the most stylish inside forwards of his day, George Herd was already an established Scottish International and holder of two Scottish Cup Winners' medals when he joined Sunderland. A number of top clubs were interested in signing him when Chairman Syd Collings travelled to Glasgow and met with the Board of Herd's club, Clyde. They agreed on a fee of £42,500, which was regarded as very big money indeed in the early sixties. What made the signing so much sweeter was that we managed to snatch George from right under Newcastle's noses, the Mags believing he was about to join them. He was an excellent signing and Alan Brown had shown once again that he had a good eye for talent.

Herd was just reaching his peak when he came to Roker and was able to inject a touch of Scottish class and guile to blend with the passion and commitment of the rest of the team. He played over 300 games for Sunderland before retiring in 1969. He has continued to work with the Club over the years in a coaching capacity.

George Herd.

1963-1964 Glory

"At last!"

1963-64 Sunderland team.

'We're back'

The expectation before the final home game of the season was incredible. Victory over Charlton would guarantee promotion but, despite our great home record, not a chicken was counted in Sunderland. We had missed out in similar circumstances twice in a row, and Charlton were quite a good side, standing fourth in the table.

As the team took to the pitch, a roar of 50,000 voices greeted them. The stage was set and everyone was hoping for glory. However, the Addicks had the audacity to take the lead early in the first half through their centre forward, Eddie Firmani. There was no question of it being an easy game, and we had to fight to get back into it. Fortunately, George Herd scored just before the break to bring us level.

In the second half, there was only one team in it. Sunderland produced attack after attack, but former Sunderland player Peter Wakeham was having a blinder in the Charlton goal. He produced a stunning performance that rightly won him the man of the match award, but he could not stop Crossan scoring a last minute winner. The goal brought a huge sigh of relief. The fans demanded a lap of honour but were not satisfied with one and called the Lads back in their socks to chair Charlie Hurley around the pitch on Jimmy McNab's shoulders. Celebrations were still going on in and around the ground two hours after the final whistle - we had done it!

Despite a second successive promotion near-miss, Brown made no new signings during the close season. With Brian Usher, a product of the youth system, being the only addition to the first team, some people were asking if Sunderland were up to the task of promotion. The fans, meanwhile, were hoping it would be third time lucky.

The season started brightly with victories over Huddersfield (2 - 0) and Portsmouth (3 - 0). Although the Lads slumped to a 2 - 0 home defeat against Northampton in the third game of the season, this proved to be nothing more than a blip. From then until the end of the year, the Lads lost just four of their 23 League games, showing the kind of consistency needed for promotion. During this spell there were some pleasing wins. The Mags were beaten 2 - 1, promotion rivals Manchester City and Leeds were beaten 2 - 0, Orient were beaten 4 - 1 and Derby beaten 3 - 0. However, aside from the generally good form, there were also some disappointing results too, including a 2 - 0 reverse at Boro and a 5 - 1 thrashing at Northampton.

Having played well before Christmas, in the New Year, the Lads really turned on the style. In the League, January and February saw us win all but one of our games, with Bury (4 - 1) and Swindon (6 - 0) given real hammerings. In the FA Cup, meanwhile, we quickly progressed to the quarter finals. In three games at Roker Park, Northampton were beaten 2 - 0 in the third round, Bristol City were totally thrashed 6 - 1 in the fourth, and First Division Everton were easily beaten 3 - 1 before a 63,000 crowd in the fifth round. The final day of February then saw us hold Manchester United 3 - 3 at Old Trafford in the quarter finals.

With the Lads putting in great performances week-in, week-out, Cup and promotion fever were gripping Wearside. The sixth round replay at Roker saw Manchester United held again, this time 2 - 2, the Lads proving the first game was no fluke. Yet, while these two mammoth encounters against a superb United team were great to watch, they were also tiring for the players. Three days after the replay, we drew 0 - 0 with Boro in the League, before moving on to Huddersfield two days later for a second replay. Alas, the semi-finals were not to be; we lost 5 - 1. Five days after this, an exhausted team travelled to St James', where Newcastle beat us 1 - 0, our first League defeat of 1964. Three Cup games and two derby matches in fifteen days was simply too much.

The Lads were determined not slip up this time though. Consecutive home victories against Preston (4 - 0) and Rotherham (2 - 0), the latter in front of a 57,000 crowd, put us back on track. Further good wins, including a 5 - 2 at Orient, put us neck and neck with the leaders, Leeds, and left us needing just three points from the last three games to go up.

Of course we had been there before and no-one was taking anything for granted. Even when a draw at Southampton reduced the target to two points from two games only the foolhardy were already celebrating. This time, however, we made no mistake. A 2 - 1 win over Charlton in our final home game clinched promotion with a game to spare.

At last! After being at the helm when we first tasted the bitterness of relegation, Brown had returned us to the top flight. Without relegation, of course, there would have been no promotion, and the Sunderland fans experienced the joy of 'going up' for the first time ever.

We had not won a trophy - finishing a close second to Leeds - but the moment was one for nothing other than celebration. The only moment like it in our history had come with election to the Football League in 1890, and few could remember that particular event!

In the final analysis, it was a settled side that drove us to promotion. Brown used just 17 players during the campaign, with Len Ashurst, Johnny Crossan, Jim Montgomery and George Mulhall being ever presents. Despite the relative youth of the side, they had shown much composure, particularly away from home, where we gained 26 of our 61 points, a new Club record. The overall points total was also a Club record, beating the 56 gained when lifting the First Division Championship in 1935-36.

It had been a long and frustrating time in the Second Division, but the Club and the fans were happy to be back where we belonged. Even the Football Echo, which had turned green in despair and shame at relegation, returned to a healthy pink, flushed with the joy of success.

Joyous celebrations at Roker Park following promotion.

Johnny Crossan

Signed in October 1962, Johnny Crossan became an important part of the promotion winning team. In the early sixties it was rare to dabble in the transfer market outside the British Isles. Brown, however, had been keeping an eye on Crossan for some time. Born in Londonderry, Crossan had an eventful career. At the age of 19, having attracted interest from lots of top English clubs, the Irish FA banned him for life after an incident with a referee. This meant he could not play in any of the British Leagues and he was forced to ply his trade on the continent. His banishment was probably the best thing that happened to him, as a four year career with Sparta Rotterdam and then Standard Liege gave Crossan the opportunity to play in almost every major European country against players such as Pele, Puskas and Di Stefano. He even appeared in a European Cup semi final for his Belgian side. Within days of his ban being lifted, he was signed by Sunderland for a big £27,000 fee, and made his debut at Roker on 3rd November 1962, in a 6 - 2 rout of Grimsby Town. He was an ever present in the promotion winning side of 1964 and was our leading goalscorer with 22 goals, the most important of which was most probably the winner he scored at Roker against Charlton to win the game - and promotion.

John Crossan, 1962.

A Season to Remember

"Charlie, Charlie, Charlie"

The Roker faithful calling for their hero.

Match of the Season

The sixth round FA Cup pairing with United was a tie to relish, Busby's side going through a real purple patch that saw them regularly challenging for honours. On 29th February, the Lads travelled to Old Trafford and, in front of 61,700, a quite superb game unfolded. A brilliant performance resulted in us holding a 3 - 1 lead going into the last four minutes, but a 17 year old George Best and the magnificent Bobby Charlton put their genius to full effect to bring the tie level. For the Lads, Johnny Crossan had probably his best ever game in a Sunderland shirt, scoring two memorable goals.

F.A. CUP 5th ROUND BARNSLEY v. UNITED 19th FEBRUARY
Here Foulkes and Crossan go up in a heading duel with Leighton, the Barnsley centre-forward, during an attack on the United goalmouth. United, playing in all white strip, run out easy winners to the tune of four goals to nil.
Photo by courtesy of the Evening News

All this whetted the appetite so much that whilst the official attendance for the replay at Roker Park was given as 46,727, it is legend that that frenzied night probably saw the ground record broken. It is estimated that over 100,000 people descended in or around the ground, and with the gates being crashed open, at one point it was pure chaos inside the ground. Supporters poured in from the collapsed Roker End door and at the end of the night, tragically, two people were left dead.

Oblivious to this, the players put in another great performance. Sharkey volleyed Sunderland into the lead, but Law capitalised on a mistake from Monty to equalise. This forced the game into extra time, where Maurice Setters inexplicably deflected the ball into his own net, before Bobby Charlton saved Manchester United in the last minute with a rare header.

The second replay at Leeds Road, Huddersfield, finally saw United get the better of us. With Denis Law in fine form, the Lads were crushed 5 - 1, Sharkey scoring Sunderland's sole goal. Sunderland had the same line-up for all three games: Montgomery, Irwin, Ashurst, Harvey, Hurley, Elliott (Dave), Usher, Herd, Sharkey, Crossan and Mulhall.

The 1963-64 season provided many great moments for all those involved with Sunderland. A great run in the FA Cup, some scintillating football and - of course - promotion back to the First Division brought joy to the hearts of Sunderland fans everywhere. It would have been nice to have finished the season as Champions, Leeds depriving us of the honour by finishing two points ahead of us. However, this should not detract from the achievements of Sunderland. Not only had they been narrowly pipped by a great Leeds team that would soon been winning trophies, but they had performed better than any Sunderland side for many a year.

While the goalscorers normally grab the headlines, Sunderland's backline were doing their best to catch the limelight during the season. Consistently strong performances meant we conceded just 37 League goals, our best defensive record since 1902-03, the latter coming over 34, rather than 42, games. This was a testament to the superb defence that Brown had built around Charlie Hurley.

Voted Sunderland's 'Player of the Century', Charlie Hurley is regarded as the greatest centre half ever to have played for Sunderland. Born in the Republic of Ireland, he was brought to London as a child. Alan Brown signed him from Millwall in 1957 when he was far from the finished article. A key part of Brown's rebuilding plans, he came into a team that was leaking goals and his first season ended with Sunderland being relegated to the Second Division.

Despite this, Hurley was soon being picked out as a top class player by fans and pundits alike. In 1958, a report in the Daily Express noted: 'Liverpool folk know a footballer when they see one, but I never thought I should see the day when the Kop gave out more polite applause than whacking great roars. It was evident that they enjoyed centre-half back play as Charlie Hurley of Sunderland plays it. This is a man, who strokes the ball as if he loves rather than hates it, who never needs to hurry.'

As a bonus accompanying his great defending, Charlie was also a threat to any opposition team's goal. Whenever Sunderland won a corner or a free kick in a dangerous position, the cry would go up 'Charlie, Charlie, Charlie' and he would stride up field and take his favourite spot at the far corner of the penalty box. As the cross came he would power forward and rise above the opposition to meet the ball.

Whenever he ran onto Roker Park leading the team out to the strain of 'Z Cars' he set the pulse racing. During the season, Everton visited Roker in the fourth round of the Cup. The Club felt that it could not play 'Z Cars' - it was also our opponents' theme tune - so, for one match only, the team ran out to the sound of 'Charlie is M'Darling' instead! Hurley repaid the compliment with a goal in a great 3 - 1 victory. A passionate leader of the Sunderland team, those who were lucky enough to be at the promotion winning game against Charlton will never forget the delight and exhilaration that Charlie showed as he led the lap of honour around Roker Park.

Alongside Hurley was Northern Ireland born Martin Harvey, who signed for Sunderland in September 1957. He made his first team debut at Home Park, Plymouth on 24th October, 1959, and from then on his career rocketed. After only 23 senior appearances he displaced former skipper Stan Anderson at Roker and, 10 days later, he replaced Danny Blanchflower in the Northern Ireland team… aged just 18! He played over 300 games for Sunderland before joining Carlisle as Assistant Manager in 1972.

Completing the half back line was Jimmy McNab, a tough left half. He was born in Scotland and signed for Sunderland in 1956. He made his Sunderland debut at Roker Park, on 20th September, 1958, against Ipswich Town. Ten games later he broke his leg and missed the rest of the League campaign. From 1959 until the mid-sixties he was Sunderland's first choice left half. He made over 300 appearances for the Club and, while not a prolific goal scorer, he did get the odd vital goal including one against Everton in the fifth round of the Cup in 1964. This helped us into the next round for the three game thriller against Manchester United, which he unfortunately missed through injury.

The 1960's also saw the establishment of one of Sunderland's soundest and most consistent full back partnerships, Cec Irwin and Len Ashurst, affectionately known as 'Cec and Len'. Together they brought a combination of tenacity and skill to the team and were a major part of the 1964 promotion side.

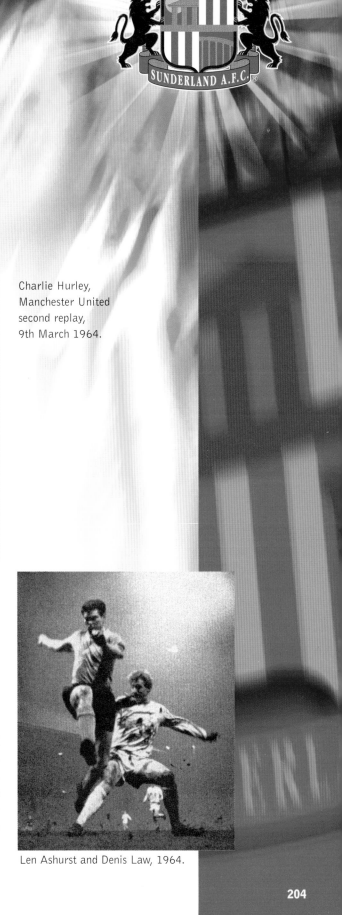

Charlie Hurley, Manchester United second replay, 9th March 1964.

Cec was the younger and the bigger of the two, standing 6ft 1in and weighing in at nearly 14 stone. Born in Ellington, Northumberland, he played for the county team as a lad where he was spotted by Burnley, who, at that time, were always on the lookout for North East talent. However, it did not work out in Lancashire for him and Burnley's loss was Roker's gain. He made his Sunderland debut at the age of 16 years and 165 days, at the time a Club record. Funnily enough, in that first game in September 1958 he was to partner Len Ashurst, who had just forced his way into the team too. While Ashurst, however, was to become a first team regular almost from then on, Cec had to wait until 1961 before becoming a 'regular'.

Len was three years older than Cec and smaller and lighter but, nonetheless, a strong defensive player. He was from Aintree and had always supported Liverpool. On leaving school he joined the Anfield ground staff, where he played as an amateur until the age of 19, gaining 7 England youth international caps. Rejected by his heroes, he signed for Wolves, but when he was again released, Alan Brown picked him up for Sunderland. With Cec playing 350 times for us and Len managing over 450 appearances, they brought consistency and stability to the Roker team of the sixties.

Len Ashurst and Denis Law, 1964.

1964-1965
Expectations

"Hardwick found that life as Sunderland manager was nothing other than tough"

George Hardwick

A Hat Trick against the Hammers

West Ham United were hot property during the 1964-65 season. They had won the FA Cup in the previous season and in May 1965 they beat TSV Munich, in a magnificent game at Wembley, to win the European Cup Winners' Cup. At the heart of their team were three great players of the sixties - Martin Peters, Bobby Moore and Geoff Hurst - all of whom were to star for England in the 1966 World Cup.

But, this season we became their bogey team. We first played them in the League Cup, at the end of September, and sent them back to London with their tails between their legs following a 4 -1 thrashing. Then we played them twice in a month in the League. Both games were a lot tighter than the League Cup win, but we managed to beat them 3 - 2 at home, with two goals from Nick Sharkey, before repeating the scoreline in London, Herd hitting a brace this time.

Having spent half-a-decade working hard to return Sunderland to the First Division, Alan Brown surprised everybody by leaving the Club before we had even kicked a ball in the top flight. Just weeks before the season was due to start, he was tempted away by the managerial vacancy at Sheffield Wednesday and, as a consequence, Sunderland started the campaign without a manager. To make matters worse, we also started the season without a goalie. Jim Montgomery, a star of the promotion season, injured a hand in training and was ruled out of our opening fixtures. It was hardly the ideal preparation for our return to the big time!

In dealing with the goalkeeping problem, the Club made a decision that broke a Football League record. They turned to youth team goalie Derek Forster, aged 15 years and 185 days, who replaced Monty between the sticks. In doing so, he became the youngest goalkeeper to play in the Football League. Forster played in the first three games of the season, but unfortunately conceded ten goals. He did his best, but let in three at home against Leicester, four at West Brom and another three at Chelsea. It seemed that the lad was struggling, so the Club went to Kilmarnock and signed Sandy McLaughlan as cover for Monty. The new signing promptly conceded a goal in the first minute of his debut! However, this was really a case of bad luck, and the defence showed a little more solidity following his arrival.

The managerial situation was not dealt with so swiftly however. Here the matter was allowed to drift until mid-November, when George Hardwick was confirmed as manager. Up until this point, we had managed just one League win - a 1 - 0 home victory over Blackburn - and the Lads were clearly on the rocks. Following Hardwick's appointment, we promptly beat Burnley 3 - 2 at Roker Park and, a fortnight later, thrashed Everton 4 - 0 at Roker.

However, Hardwick found that life as Sunderland manager was nothing other than tough. Early in the season, our great hope - a fit Brian Clough back in action - was quickly dashed. The fourth game of the season saw Clough return to first team action. He dearly wished to be a star in the top division, but his injury was too much to overcome. He played three games, scoring in one, before hanging up his boots after our home game with Aston Villa on 9th September, 1964. Hardwick did not have the money at his disposal to buy another Clough - few managers did - and there is no doubt his talents were missed.

But, life went on without the goalscoring legend. Hardwick's men managed to pick up another two League wins in December, including our first away victory of the season, 1 - 0 at Leicester. In the New Year, however, we failed to win a single League point and, after a good 3 - 0 win at Luton in the FA Cup, soon went out of the competition, losing 3 - 1 at home to Notts Forest in the fourth round.

Fortunately, the Lads started to put a good run together after this, winning six of their next eight games. Not only did this run rack up the points - and see us move away from danger a little - there were some impressive wins too. Manchester United were beaten 1 - 0, West Ham defeated 3 - 2 at Upton Park, Notts Forest were thrashed 4 - 0 and Spurs beaten 2 - 1. These wins came against top quality opposition and suggested the Lads were capable of matching the best teams around.

But, this great form could not last. The final month of the season saw a more realistic mixture of wins, draws and defeats. Three of our last nine games were won and four lost. Nevertheless, the Lads had done enough to steer clear of danger, ending the season 15th in a division of 22 teams.

In all, this was a reasonable performance - albeit one heavily dependent on home form - and in many ways a relief after the poor start we had made. Our purple patch midway through the season augured well, and the players had done much better after adjusting to the pace of First Division football. As always, however, the high expectations on Wearside had proved difficult to match. George Hardwick made way at the end of the season - Ian McColl filling his boots - as the manager's seat at Roker started to hot up.

Roker Park, Fulwell End under re-construction, 1964.

Nicky Sharkey

Nicky Sharkey, a skilful Scot, joined Sunderland straight from school and made a real name for himself in his first season at the Club by scoring an incredible 140 goals in the junior team. He soon progressed through the ranks, and made his full Sunderland debut on 9th April, 1960, against Scunthorpe United, aged just 16 years and 341 days.

Nicky was given the difficult task of filling Brian Clough's boots after the legend's unfortunate injury, but the youngster rose to the challenge. He quickly equalled the Club's goalscoring record for an individual match, when he notched five in a 7 - 1 win against Norwich City. In doing so, he matched the feats of Charlie Buchan in 1912 and Bobby Gurney in 1935.

Nicky was an important part of the promotion winning side, scoring 20 League and Cup goals in that season and going one better in the following season in the First Division. He left the Club in 1966, having made 120 appearances and scored 62 goals.

Nicky Sharkey, 1964.

1965-1966
Close Shave

"This is wonderful I couldn't wish to be going to a better club."

Jim Baxter on his arrival at Sunderland.

Ian McColl and Jim Baxter.

Slim Jim Turns On The Class

In a game that many believe to be his best for the Club, 'Slim' Jim Baxter guided us to a 2 - 0 win over Newcastle in his first Tyne-Wear derby match. Shortly after New Year, the Mags visited Roker Park for the first top flight meeting between the teams since February 1958. A huge 54,668 crowd crammed into the ground for the game, and Baxter dazzled them with his silky skills. Always one for the big occasion, Slim Jim knew exactly how to play derby games, having experienced Rangers-Celtic and Scotland-England ties already. He controlled the game superbly and, as the Lads bossed the game, goals from Herd and O'Hare ensured that possession was translated into points. The win provided us with a great New Year boost, and Baxter went on to prove his worth in the derby games: he finished on the winning side three out of four times against Newcastle.

With Hardwick vacating the manager's chair, Scottish manager Ian McColl became our third boss in three years. He immediately returned to Rangers, a team he had played for, to sign Jim Baxter, a regular in the Scotland side since 1961, and a real class act. Before the season started, however, both McColl and Baxter received a baptism of fire from one of their footballing foes. Celtic were invited to Roker for a friendly and proceeded to give us a 5 - 0 beating...

Once the 'real' action began, McColl got off to a pretty good start. His first game in charge - at Leeds - ended in a 1 - 0 defeat, but a week later, we beat Sheffield United 4 - 1 in his first home game. His second home game, some four days later, saw yet another victory against West Ham, the Lads running out 2 - 1 winners at Roker.

However, this strong start was followed by heavy defeats against Leicester (4 - 1) and Aston Villa (3 - 1). During the latter game - on 6th September, 1965 - a Sunderland 'first' took place when Alan Gauden replaced Mike Hellawell, becoming the very first Sunderland substitute. In some ways it is hard to believe that substitutions, now such an integral part of the game, were only introduced at the beginning of the 1965-66 season.

The Lads soon recovered from these defeats, winning three on the trot, and by the end of September we had a respectable 10 points from a possible 20. On the evidence of his first ten games, McColl's appointment appeared an astute one. In his next ten games, however, performances dipped badly, the Lads notching up six defeats and only two victories. This left us with a very worrying total of just 16 points by Christmas.

Many of our problems were stemming from a lack of fire power up front. This was somewhat ironic, for after our good start McColl had spent £50,000 on bringing Scottish international striker Neil Martin to the Club. Moreover, McColl already had some good strikers at the Club but, there was a lot of flux in the forward line as the manager experimented, struggling to find a line up that satisfied him. Meanwhile, two of the previous season's top scorers - Nicky Sharkey and Harry Hood - struggled for appearances.

After Christmas, we began 1966 by slumping 5 - 1 at home to West Brom and making a quick exit from the Cup, losing 3 - 0 at Everton. A good 2 - 0 win over newly promoted Newcastle provided great joy, but soon the team were on the rocks again. A trip to Liverpool saw the Lads hammered 4 - 0, a result followed by defeats against Leicester, Chelsea, Blackburn and the Mags.

Five defeats on the trot did our League position no favours, and the new manager was in real danger of leading us straight back into Division Two. An improvement was needed if we were to survive. Fortunately, the Lads managed to turn around their home form; five victories were taken from our last seven home games, including good 2 - 0 wins over Spurs and Everton. Away from home, however, our performances continued to be poor, all but one of our away games being lost during the final run in. Indeed, outside Roker, our form was abysmal throughout the season, the Lads winning just one game, and scoring just fifteen goals, on their travels.

Luckily, 13 wins from 21 games at Roker was enough to keep us up - but only just. We finished the season in 19th position, just three points off a relegation spot. All in all, it was pretty miserable stuff. If anything, performances were slightly worse than during the previous season, questioning the validity of the decision to replace Hardwick with McColl.

The end of the season for Sunderland was not the end of the season for Roker Park though. Our ground was chosen as one of the venues for the 1966 World Cup, giving us a chance to settle back, forget our troubles and watch some of the world's best players turn out at Wearside.

Jim Baxter sends the ball between Chelsea Players Housman, Venables and Osgood, to the unmarked Mulhall.

George Mulhall

George Mulhall was another great Sunderland player of the sixties who hailed from north of the border. His professional career began with Aberdeen, where he played for nine seasons. His performances there merited a call up to the Scotland team and caught the eye of Alan Brown, who snapped him up for £25,000 in September 1962.

George was a fast and tricky winger, and he provided Brown with the ideal answer to his problems on the left wing. Indeed, Mulhall made the position his own for the rest of the sixties. As something of a bonus, Mulhall was the sort of winger who scored goals as well as making them; on leaving the Club in 1969, he had managed to bag 66 goals in just under 300 League and Cup games for the Lads.

George Mulhall.

Roker Park and the 1966 World Cup Finals

Temporary seats in the Fulwell End.

Roker Spruced Up

In preparation for the World Cup, the Club received grants to fund a number of improvements to Roker Park. Perhaps the most radical change - and one many Sunderland fans would be grateful for - was the placing of a roof over the Fulwell End. With temporary seating also being added to the stand, it was almost unrecognisable! The Clock Stand also underwent a major sprucing up, with a mixture of temporary and permanent seating added. On top of this, the pitch was extended and, away from the action, new ticket and administration offices and a hospitality suite were built too. As a result, Roker Park was well prepared for the event when the teams arrived in the middle of July.

The announcement that Roker Park had been chosen as one of the venues for the 1966 World Cup brought a buzz of excitement to Wearside. As a hotbed of soccer, the North East was an obvious choice for one of the four groups, but it was still a great privilege to be chosen when such famous grounds as Elland Road and Highbury missed out. Originally, St James' Park had been on the shortlist as a North East venue but, much to the delight of folk from the Wear and the Tees, Sunderland and Middlesbrough received the nod. When the draw was made, Chile, Italy, USSR and North Korea were the sides selected to make the trip to the North East.

The first of the games played at Roker was between Italy and Chile. It was ironic that these two should been draw to meet each other; the previous World Cup had seen the infamous 'Battle of Santiago', where disgraceful scenes of fighting between the two teams' players had marred the entire series. During that game, Chile - the host nation - had two men sent off and Maschio of Italy was knocked senseless after being punched in the face. The Italians were by no means an innocent party however; disparaging comments made before the game had wound the host nation up completely.

At Roker Park, however, there was no repeat of these unseemly incidents. The game was played in drizzly conditions and the Italians went 1 - 0 up after Mazzola latched on to a shot that had been palmed out by the Chilean goalkeeper, Olivares. With two minutes left, Barison scored a beauty, beating full back Eyzaguirre and thrashing it in from a narrow angle. The game ended 2 - 0.

The Roker Park crowd witnessed some of the greatest names in Italian football that day. Albertosi, Burgnich and Facchetti were marvellous players, who later starred in the 1970 World Cup final. And, in Mazzola and Rivera, they had true world class stars.

However, the Italians did not build on their good start. The second match at Roker saw them meet much tougher opposition: the USSR. In a game built up as the best of Group Four, the Italians found Soviet keeper Lev Yashin in inspired form as the USSR triumphed 1 - 0. Chislenko scored the Soviets' goal 10 minutes into the second half, when the usually dependable Facchetti was beaten all ends up by the Russian, who crashed the ball home with his left foot. The goalkeeper's failure to stop the long shot led to a shout from the Roker End of 'I was Monty's double', a reference to both a recent movie about the British General and the Sunderland keeper's tendency to miss the odd long shot.

In the end, this result proved fatal for the Italians. North Korea beat them at Ayresome Park, ending the Italians' interest in the competition at the first stage. On returning to Italy they faced a roasting from both press and public...

The final group game staged at Roker saw the USSR take on Chile. Having all but qualified for the quarter finals already, the Soviets appeared slightly complacent. Eight of their players were rested for a game they were expected to win easily. The USSR did indeed triumph, although the Chileans, who were battling to qualify for the next stage as runners up, gave them a tough time. The game ended 2 - 1, with Porkujan, making his first appearance in the tournament, scoring both goals for the USSR.

Having comfortably qualified as group winners, the USSR then stayed at Roker Park for the quarter finals, where they came up against Hungary. The latter side were slight favourites, having disposed of the Brazilians - Pele and all - on Merseyside. In Florian Albert and Ferenc Bene they had two world class players at the very peak of their games. The Hungarian stars were, however, quite simply marked out of the game.

The Soviets kicked everything that moved, but the Magyars were their own worst enemy. When goalkeeper Gelei failed to hold a Porkujan shot from a corner, Chislenko smashed it into the net from close range. The USSR then made it 2 - 0 after 48 minutes, when Porkujan, unmarked at the far post, simply knocked a Khusainov free kick into an empty net. Later in the game, Meszoly set up a goal for Bene, giving Hungary a chance, but it was too little too late. The game ended 2 - 1, securing a semi-final place for the Soviets.

England, of course, famously went on to capture the trophy with a 4 - 2 victory over West Germany. On a memorable Wembley day, Geoff Hurst became the first - and to date only - man to score a hat trick in the Final game itself. Though there were no Sunderland players involved that day, Roker Park's involvement meant Sunderland had done their bit for England in 1966. Indeed, Roker did very well. Nearly 100,000 people watched the four games played at our home and many millions more saw the games on TV. The welcome that Wearside extended to the visiting teams, media and fans was outstanding and many lasting friendships were made.

Lev Yashin - Hungary v Russia.

Communist Roker?

The socialist anthem 'The Red Flag' was often sung at Roker Park - though as an identification with our Club colours rather than with a political movement - but the Soviets could have been forgiven for thinking the ground was a socialist oasis during the 1966 World Cup. When at Roker, the Soviets seemed to play with added vigour and the results might even suggest they felt it was a home from home! In all, the USSR played in six games during the competition - the same number as England - four of which took place at Roker. Amazingly, all of their games on Wearside were won, but their other two games were lost. Their semi final against West Germany took place at Goodison Park, where the Soviets slumped to their first defeat of the competition, and they were also beaten in the third place play off match, Portugal coming out on top in a game played at Wembley.

G.Crow (Secretary) & Italian Press, 1966 World Cup.

1966-1967

Inconsistent

"we were struggling to establish ourselves as a First Division side"

To Hull and Back

When the fifth round of the FA Cup paired us with Leeds United, the tie was guaranteed to be laced with extra spice. There had been no love lost between the teams since Willie McPheat had broken his leg at Elland Road four seasons earlier.

In the event, it took more than 90 minutes to settle the tie. The first game, at Roker Park, ended in a 1 - 1 draw and was played out in front of 55,763 fans. Critically, the game saw another of our players sustain a broken leg - Bobby Kerr being the victim this time. It goes without saying that this merely increased the bad blood between the teams.

The replay at Elland Road drew a record attendance for the Yorkshire club, 57,892 packing into the stadium, including around 20,000 from Wearside. With some sections of the ground over-crowded, all hell broke loose when some of the spectators spilled onto the pitch. In the game itself, Sunderland took the lead, through John O'Hare, but Leeds equalised to take the game to a second replay.

Boothferry Park, home of Hull City, hosted the third match. This time United took the lead, with Sunderland drawing level in the last quarter of an hour through Alan Gauden. With seconds to go, Cecil Irwin was penalised in the box and Johnny Giles scored from the resultant penalty.

Not content with this piece of bad luck both Herd and Mulhall were sent off for persistent complaining. The penalty decision looked harsh, especially as Jimmy Greenhoff had been standing a mile offside before being 'fouled'. Even the Leeds United President, Lord Harwood, acknowledged his team's luck.

England's victory in the World Cup provided a real boost to football fans throughout the country. Interest in the game was heightened and everywhere fans' hunger for glory was increased. Yet, most fans are also realists, and for Sunderland supporters the hope was merely for something better than the relegation near miss that McColl's side had served up the previous season.

Unfortunately, the Lads did not get off to the best of starts. Our first game of the season was at home to Arsenal, where a 38,304 crowd saw us slump to a 3 - 1 defeat. Although the Lads evened this out with a 2 - 0 win against Southampton four days later, defeats at Manchester City and Southampton left us with a poor two points from four games at the end of August.

A great 4 - 0 win over Blackpool, where Martin hit a hat-trick, was then followed by another poor run. In the League, Leeds, Leicester and West Ham inflicted further defeats, and in the League Cup we suffered a quick exit after being beaten by Sheffield United. With the best the Lads could do being a couple of draws, we finished our first ten League games with a miserable six points.

Luckily, form improved after this, with a brief purple patch seeing us beat Stoke (2 - 1), Sheffield United (4 - 1) and Burnley (4 - 3) at home, and thrash the Mags 3 - 0 at St James' Park! The revival was short lived though; a 5 - 0 hammering at Manchester United quickly brought us back to earth, a result immediately followed by defeats against Spurs and Arsenal.

This inconsistency, combined with a general weakness away from home, was frustrating. The Lads needed a tonic to boost their spirits and, on New Year's Eve, one arrived. After a couple of appearances on the bench, a young Scottish lad made his full Sunderland debut in the home game with Manchester City. His name was Bobby Kerr, and he scored the only goal of the game. In the few fleeting appearances he made during the rest of the season, Kerr seemed like a lucky mascot. His enthusiasm and energy seemed to spread to the rest of the team, and seven goals in his first eleven appearances were enough to suggest that we had found a real gem.

Partly as a consequence, the New Year saw some much better performances. For the first two months of 1967 we were unbeaten in all competitions. In the League, there were good wins against Chelsea and Leicester, but the real magic came in the Cup. January saw us get off to a great start, with a 5 - 2 home thrashing of Brentford in the third round. This was followed by an even better performance in the following tie, when Peterborough were hammered 7 - 1, Martin scoring a hat trick and Kerr hitting two.

The win set us up with a home tie against Leeds. With confidence already high, the Lads sent it rocketing a week before this game by beating the Mags 3 - 0 before a 50,000 Roker crowd, Kerr scoring two of our goals. The Leeds game, however, proved to be something of a disaster. In a bitterly fought match, Kerr's leg was broken. Though the game ended 1 - 1, we eventually went out in a second replay. What's more, without our lucky talisman, form dipped once again.

Five of our first six League games without Kerr were lost, including heavy beatings at Stoke (3 - 0) and Sheffield Wednesday (5 - 0). Despite our good spell, this sort of form made relegation a worry. Fortunately, there were plenty of teams in a worse position than us, and despite losing three of our last six matches, we eventually finished 17th, well clear of the relegation places.

Although there had been some real highlights - including a double over Newcastle - it had been another relatively poor season. In truth we were struggling to establish ourselves as a First Division side.

There was, however, a notable success at the Club during the season. The youth structure that Alan Brown had set up was starting to pay dividends, Sunderland defeating Birmingham City in the final of the FA Youth Cup. The manager of the Youth Team was a certain Brian Clough, showing early signs of managerial promise. The highlights for the Youths were the performances of Chester-le-Street's Colin Todd and Colin Suggett, both of whom were magnificent. There was hope that the future would be brighter than the present...

Baxter penalty v Brentford.

"Slim" Jim Baxter

Baxter, nicknamed 'Slim Jim' was, perhaps, past his best when he signed for Sunderland in 1965, but he was still one of the classiest players to don a red-and-white shirt in the post-War period. For many a Roker fan, the signing of Baxter was a sign that the Club had ambition.

His skill and arrogance had been brought to the attention of English football fans when he had scored two goals for Scotland against England in 1963 and then famously left the Wembley pitch with the ball tucked up his blue jersey. As a Sunderland player, he also gave England a lesson in football in 1967, when Scotland beat the World Champions, England's first defeat since the 1966 World Cup final victory.

At Sunderland, he played for just over two seasons, displaying some of the most creative touches to grace Roker. He scored two on his home debut, a mauling of Sheffield United, and had a magnificent match in a 2 - 0 home win against Newcastle later in the season. By the time we sold him to Nottingham Forest, in December 1967, many people felt that he was becoming too inconsistent and that the £100,000 offered by Forest was too good to turn down. They were probably right. His career never really flourished in the Midlands and he finally retired to become a Glasgow publican in 1970.

Injured Leeds goalkeeper Sprake with Bremner and Mulhall.

1967-1968
A Kind of Homecoming

"the table began to look ominous"

Neil Martin v Newcastle, March 1967

The Scottish Centurian

Neil Martin was one of the many Scotsmen appearing for Sunderland during the mid-1960s. When he joined us from Hibernian, in October 1965, he already had a reputation as good marksman with a tally of over 100 goals. Once he settled into the Sunderland side he confirmed this reputation, hitting goals on a regular basis. Indeed, the records show an impressive goals per game ratio for Martin, the Scot notching up 46 goals in 99 League and Cup appearances for the Lads. He was transferred to Coventry City in February 1968, where he continued to add to his strike tally. On retiring, Martin could proudly came to be a member of the select band of players that have netted over 100 goals in both the English and Scottish Leagues.

McColl's career as Sunderland manager had not exactly got off to a great start. Not only had his two seasons in charge produced two fairly mediocre finishes, but he had also failed to match the supposedly unsatisfactory 15th place finish Hardwick had managed to achieve during our first season back in the top flight. The manager had been given money to bring in his own men and given time to build his team and test ideas. it was now time to deliver... 1967-68 was make or break time for McColl.

The season could hardly have provided a grittier opener: a trip to Elland Road to play Leeds. The Lads secured a creditable 1 - 1 draw. After this, we secured two home victories - against Fulham (3 - 0) and Everton (1 - 0) - and, after a defeat at Fulham, notched up a further victory at Leicester (2 - 0) and managed to hold Champions Manchester United to a 1 - 1 draw at Roker.

In all, this was a solid start to the season. Eight points from a possible twelve was very respectable, suggesting McColl had at last found the formula to make his team 'tick'. However, our fourth home game of the season saw the team's growing confidence shattered by a 5 - 1 thrashing at the hands of West Ham. It was a bad result, but matters soon got worse. Four of the next five games were lost, with the Lads scoring just two goals and letting in ten. Following this, McColl was clearly under pressure to turn things around, but defeats continued, and form was especially poor away from home. Indeed, as a measure of the slump, it need only be recorded that from November 4th to mid-January we did not win a single match, the Lads going out of the League Cup - at the hands of Leeds - and sliding down the First Division as a result.

Something had to give - and it did. McColl was sacked. The final straw for the Board was an FA Cup exit at the hands of Second Division Norwich City. After being held to a 1 - 1 draw at Carrow Road, we capitulated 1 - 0 at Roker, going out of the competition at the first stage. McColl was given his marching orders after just two-and-a-half seasons in charge.

His replacement in the Roker Park hot seat was something of a surprise: former boss Alan Brown took over the reins again. Ironically, his first game back in charge was at Hillsborough against his former club Sheffield Wednesday. Rising to the occasion, his new charges pulled off a 1 - 0 win. But, this winning start did not last. The Lads lost their next four games, failing to find the net in three of them. Once again, the table began to look ominous.

Fortunately, Brown had the measure of the Club, and he firmed the team up during the final run in. The last twelve games of the season produced just one defeat, in a trip to Liverpool, and the team pulled off some good wins too, including a 2 - 1 victory at Manchester United, and home wins against Wolves and Arsenal. In the end, it was enough to steer us clear from danger. Indeed, we finished 17th, and while this was hardly a great performance, it was - once again - a welcome relief after the mid-season scare.

At least the fans could hope that this was all part of another transitional phase. Alongside the appointment of a new manager, the season had also seen a number of changes in the playing staff. Most notably, Jim Baxter left for Nottingham Forest, and he was joined on the departures list by John O'Hare and Neil Martin.

On the incoming side, new faces included Gordon Harris, Brian Chambers, Dennis Tueart and Ian Porterfield. As before, Brown was looking to the future, seeking to bring in promising youngsters that he could mould into his own style.

For now, Brown had steadied the ship. Moreover, he had started to build for the future too. However, his previous Roker experiment had produced a quick fall into the Second Division. The question was, would his 'second coming' lead to the success Wearside yearned for or, would it merely provide another stop off as the Club slowly lost its grip on life in the First Division?

Jim Baxter just clears the far post as Forest defenders look on.

Sunderland See Red

The last match of the season was yet again to be a crucial decider but, thankfully, not for the Lads this time. We were already safe in mid-table when we visited Old Trafford for their final game. United were sitting second in the League, on equal points with their great rivals, City. As the Gods of the Fixture List would have it, both Manchester clubs were scheduled to play against North East teams that day. We were at Old Trafford, while City travelled to St James' Park. The City side of the day had all the fluid skills of Bell and Summerbee, but United were regarded as one of the best teams in Europe. In an unexpected turn, however, we went on the rampage, goals from Suggett and Mulball securing a 2 - 1 win over United. City, meanwhile, picked up a win at Newcastle, and the two points were enough for them to snatch the title. United, however, had the 'consolation' of becoming the first English team to win the European Cup, beating Benfica 4 - 1 at the end of the season.

Colin Suggett, 1966-69.

1968-1969
Don't Leave Home

"Sunderland, it seemed, were hitting new depths"

Hammered!

19th October, 1968, goes down in history as a dark day for Sunderland. We travelled to the Boleyn Ground, home of West Ham United, and crashed 8 - 0, a score that equalled our worst ever defeat. We were well and truly slaughtered.

At the time West Ham were a good, but not a great, team. At the end of the season they finished a modest eighth in the League, only ten points above us. Yet, on that day everything went their way - and everything went in. The West Ham United team included a very young Trevor Brooking and the future Hammers boss Harry Redknapp, but the man who did most of the damage that day was Geoff Hurst, who netted six times - although he did put the first in with his hand! Jimmy Monty did not know what had hit him and, despite pulling off some good saves, was left to spend most of the afternoon picking the ball out of the back of the net.

To make matters worse, Hurst was invited onto Match of the Day that night to gloat and rub a little more salt in the wound.

Having steered us back into the First Division in 1964, Brown left the Club when he appeared to be on the verge of something special. Starting from scratch, he had built up his own side, largely by developing talented youngsters into class players. His promotion winning team was exciting to watch, skilful and full of confidence. Yet, without Brown at the helm, the Lads struggled during their first season back in the top flight and, if anything, had found life even tougher in subsequent seasons. The unusual decision to reappoint Brown gave him a chance to carry on where he left off and, hopefully, re-establish Sunderland as a top flight club after the disaster of the 1950s.

However, in the four years Brown had spent away from the Club, much had changed at Sunderland. Many of the players at the heart of his promotion winning squad had moved on, and of those who were left, age was starting to show in all but a few cases. Some - such as 'Monty' - still had a lot of years at the Club ahead of them, but for most - like King Charlie - their days at Sunderland were drawing to an end. In short, it was less a case of Brown taking up where he had left off than it was starting afresh once more.

With little in the way of transfer activity during the season, Brown was forced to rely on his coaching, tactical and motivational skills to improve results. However, even with his considerable acumen in these areas, turning the mediocre performances of the preceding seasons into something more spectacular would be a far from easy task.

August 1968 provided a packed League programme, with seven games being played during the month. We began with a trip to Stoke, a game which ended in a 2 - 1 defeat, but successive home wins against Ipswich (3 - 0) and Southampton (1 - 0) followed. The month also included a 4 - 1 defeat at Liverpool and a 1 - 1 home draw with Newcastle. In all, we secured seven points from seven games, a reasonable return, but one that relied heavily on home form.

September began with a very quick exit from the League Cup - Arsenal knocking us out straight away - and also saw us suffer a heavy 4 - 0 defeat at home to the League Champions, Manchester City. With just one win during the month - a 2 - 0 victory over Leicester - the outlook was a little less positive.

In October, however, we hit a real low. Although there were good home wins over Forest and Coventry, away from home we continued to be poor. Most notably, we suffered a humiliating 8 - 0 beating at West Ham, equalling our worst ever defeat. In November, the same pattern continued, with the away thrashing being administered by Spurs, who beat us 5 - 1.

After a reasonable Christmas period, which saw us 'avenge' West Ham with a 2 - 1 victory, the New Year brought no real improvement in form. In the FA Cup, a 4 - 1 home defeat against Fulham was somewhat embarrassing, but the next four League games brought more poor results, Everton beating us 3 - 1, Manchester United hammering us 4 - 1 and Chelsea thrashing us 5 - 1.

The latter game was our sixth in London during the season. Fortunately, it was also our last in the capital, for we'd had rotten luck there. Of the six games, we had lost four and won none, conceding 24 goals and scoring just five! While the Chelsea game was followed by a good 4 - 1 win over Stoke on 1st March - our first win of 1969 - we were soon on the losing track again, with five of the next six games being lost. We managed to avoid defeat at St James' - drawing 1 - 1 with the Mags - but this was a small reward. With a month left to play, we were again in real danger of relegation.

Amazingly, by this point we had yet to win a game away from home. A goalless Easter programme failed to rectify this, and defeat at Manchester City left us desperate for points. With just three matches left, the Lads really needed to win some games in order to survive.

In our final home game of the season, Wolves were beaten 2 - 0, securing two valuable points. Then, finally, the Lads at last managed to pull off an away win, beating Burnley 2 - 1. Thankfully, we had done enough to save our skins. Despite a final day defeat at Leicester, we finished in 17th place, four points above the relegation zone.

Once again though, this was little to shout about. As well as equalling the sorry record of our heaviest defeat, we also matched our record for the fewest away wins during a season. The solitary victory notched up in our penultimate game was a performance challenged only by the 1965-66 season.

On top of this, the average attendance of 25,438 was the second lowest post-War figure, with only our first ever season in Division Two being lower. Sunderland, it seemed, were hitting new depths. There was, though, another boost from the Youth set up, with the FA Youth Cup again coming to Roker following an exciting 6 - 3 aggregate victory over West Brom. However, it was unclear if the strength of the youth set up would help us to ride out the storm at first team level. While there was no doubting the fact we held some of the stars of the future, improvements were needed now if another relegation was to be avoided.

Ollie Burton blocks this shot from Denis Tueart in the Tyne-Wear derby.

Colin Todd

One of the finest half backs ever to come through the North East school's system, Colin Todd, a native of Chester-le-Street, signed for Sunderland in 1965. He played his first game for Sunderland at the age of 17 and soon established himself as a first team regular. 'Toddy' had skill in abundance, but his greatest asset was probably his ability to read the game, getting himself into the right spot to intercept dangerous attacking play.

An old head on young shoulders, he captained a First Division Sunderland side at the tender age of 21. After 188 League and Cup appearances for the Lads, we sold him at the young age of 22 to Derby County for £170,000 where he went on to win two Championship medals and 25 England Caps.

Colin Todd.

216

1969-1970 Misery

"Hi Ho, Hi Ho we're off to Mexico, with Baker and Todd in the England Squad. Hi Ho, Hi Ho"

an over optimistic chant from the Roker faithful

The Newcastle Centenary Game

Good Friday 1970 saw the one hundredth game between Sunderland and Newcastle. Both clubs had 36 wins to their credit. But if the record books showed the teams to be about equal the League table did not. Sunderland were languishing at the bottom of the table while Newcastle were riding high in the upper reaches of the division.

Nevertheless we always fancy our chances in a derby, particularly at Roker, and over 50,000 filled the ground anticipating a closely contested game. Sunderland had their backs against the wall from the start. With Colin Todd marshalling the defence and Monty in sparkling form, the Rokermen kept the score sheet level for the first half. This was a hard task, particularly when the Magpies began turning the heat up. Newcastle centre forward 'Big Wynn' Davies had shoulder-charged Monty into the back of the net early in the game but, fortunately, the referee disallowed the goal. Then, just after the restart Jimmy Smith, a skilful Scottish midfielder, smashed an unstoppable shot in the Sunderland net.

The Lads rose to the challenge and pushed forward with the young trio of Kerr, Hughes and Tueart playing their part. With 15 minutes remaining Tueart fed Bobby Park whose shot crossed the line but came back into play. Tueart followed up with a header just to make sure. That was the end of the scoring, leaving the two sides equal at the end of the 90 minutes and in the number of contests won overall. Unfortunately, it was also to be the last Tyne-Wear derby for six years as the Lads were once more plunged into the wilderness of the Second Division.

Having avoided relegation the previous season, we kicked-off the 1969-70 campaign with half-a-decade of continuous top flight football behind us. While this was nothing compared to the 56 seasons we had spent there until 1958, there had been times when it seemed we would never escape from the Second Division, except in a downward direction. Yet, the five years we had spent in Division One were times of struggle. Relegation always seemed to loom large on the horizon. While no-one was expecting us to set the world alight, it didn't seem to be too much to ask for something more than continual involvement in the relegation dog-fight. The failure of two managers to achieve more than this was quickly punished and, for Brown, the brief was clear: keep Sunderland away from the danger zone.

From the start, however, the Lads seemed a racing certainty to be a key player in the end of season relegation scrap. In August alone, we were beaten by Crystal Palace (2 - 0), Burnley (3 - 0), Sheffield Wednesday (2 - 1), Manchester City (4 - 0) and Manchester United (3 - 1). It was an awful start to the season, compounded by further defeats at Liverpool and Stoke in early September. It took us five games before we managed to score a goal, and there were no wins in the first ten League games. What's more, we also fell at the first hurdle in the League Cup, Third Division Bradford knocking us out of the competition.

The fans had to wait until 20th September for our first win of the season - a 2 - 1 victory over Forest - a result followed a week later by a good 1- 0 win at Spurs. However, the poor form quickly returned. The Lads went on an eleven game winless run, failing to score in seven of the games, before notching up their third win of the season on December 6th, a 2 - 1 win at home to Ipswich. With further defeats following during the month, by the end of 1969, relegation was the watch word. The Lads had played 27 League games, but managed to secure just 15 points and had scored only 17 goals.

On the first day of the 1970s, we managed to complete a double over Spurs, beating them 2 - 1 at home, but the misery soon continued. Second Division Leicester knocked us out of the FA Cup - making our involvement in both Cups as brief as possible - before the Lads began a perfect losing streak in the League, taking no more points from the rest of their games in January or from any of the matches played in February. With relegation looking increasingly inevitable, a good winning run was needed. While the Lads managed to beat Wolves at home, they found putting together a run too much. The best they could manage was a 'drawing streak', three 1 - 1 draws in late March - followed by a 1 - 0 win at Manchester City - being the 'best' spell of the season for us.

Amazingly, this appalling form was not enough to condemn us to an early relegation. With two games remaining at the end of the season, we still had a chance of survival. Everton and Liverpool provided our opponents in these games, and the Lads needed three points to survive. This was a hard task, for both teams were strong and Everton were the newly crowned League Champions, having run away with the title.

The Champions were first up and, much to everyone's surprise, we seemed to have done the hard part by securing a point. A scoreless draw at Roker Park gave us hope: victory against Liverpool would do the trick.

Fortunately, the final game was also a home match. A 33,000 crowd turned out to encourage the Lads in their last ditch attempt to avoid the drop. Understandably, it was a tight and tense game. With time ticking away, the game had yet to produce a goal. In need of both points, the Lads began to press forward, searching for a late goal. They could find no way through and, almost apologetically, Liverpool scored with only four minutes remaining. The game ended 1 - 0, and there was stunned silence amongst the crowd. Sunderland had been relegated for a second time.

Instead of turning performances around and securing our top flight status, Brown had done the opposite. Indeed, the 1969-70 season was the worst in our 80-year League history. Out of 42 games we had won just six and lost an incredible twenty-two. Having worked so hard to achieve promotion in the first half of the decade, in the second half we had thrown top flight status away. The harsh reality was that we had flirted with disaster for each of the six seasons since promotion and the eventual outcome - relegation - had an air of inevitability about it. The fans were getting sick of it; the crowd average of 21,789 was a post-War low.

Brown had - again - led us into the Second Division. As a new decade began, the future was uncertain. Would the manager have the heart for another lower division battle? Did he have the desire, or the resources, to put together another promotion winning side? Would the Board want to continue with a manager who had guided their club to relegation? It was clear that the Club was on a downward slide. In failing to respond to the challenge of First Division football, the Club had all but accepted it was no longer a member of the game's elite. What's more, failure to establish ourselves in the First Division meant we were running the very real risk of becoming a permanent fixture in the Second Division. Since the War, a generation of Sunderland fans had been denied the chance of seeing their team win the Cup or the League. But, as the Club continued its downward journey, the chances of the Lads lifting a cup seemed to be nothing more than an impossible dream.

Denis Tueart

'Denis, Denis Tueart, Denis Tueart on the wing', was a cry heard throughout the land during the mid-seventies. But, when Tueart joined Sunderland from Newcastle Juniors in 1967, he took a while to settle in to the team. While he was always fast and tricky on the ball, Denis did not really shine until the 1971-72 season. With experience and maturity came a more balanced game and by the time Sunderland reached Wembley in 1973, he was a lethal finisher as well as great goal maker. Consequently, he became a Sunderland legend, playing over 200 times for the Lads and scoring over 50 goals, before moving on to Manchester City and, later, the New York Cosmos. A great player, who was capped by England, Denis is now a successful businessman.

Denis Tueart.

1970·71	13th in Division Two.
1971·72	5th in Division Two.
1972·73	FA Cup Winners! 6th in Division Two.
1973·74	6th in Division Two.
1974·75	4th in Division Two.
1975·76	Division Two Champions.
1976·77	20th in Division One. Relegated.
1977·78	6th in Division Two.
1978·79	4th in Division Two.
1979·80	Promoted - Second in Division Two.

The 1970s was, above all else, a decade of drama. It was a decade that saw us not once, not twice, but three times finish just one win away from promotion. It was also a decade that saw us stage a dramatic late fight against relegation from the First Division, only to fall on the last day and finish just one point away from safety. But, most famously, the seventies was also a decade of glory, the Lads lifting the FA Cup in 1973 and clinching the Second Division championship in 1975-76.

Ultimately, however, the decade was also one of Second Division football. Just one season was spent in the top flight as we struggled to keep pace with the top clubs. While the glorious Cup run of 1973 saw us beat some of the top clubs in England, and our brief soiree in the European Cup Winners' Cup saw us play well against some of Europe's best, for the most part we were little more than a good Second Division side.

Indeed, while we were unlucky not to achieve promotion to Division One in the season following the 1973 Cup final, our failure to do so meant the Cup winning side began to break up, and the chance to build on our Wembley glory was soon lost. But, the 1970s was rarely a time when the Club took a long term view. In a turbulent era, team building was hampered by a managerial merry-go-round that saw five men installed as Sunderland manager and a further two act as caretaker.

True to its style, the decade closed in dramatic fashion. With the Club celebrating its one hundredth year in existence, we clinched promotion back to the First Division in our final game of the season, beating the newly crowned FA Cup winners in a sell out fixture, ensuring the 1980s would begin with the Club reinstated to its rightful home.

THE IMPOSSIBLE
Dream

1 9 7 0 · 1 9 8 0

1970-1971
Unhappy Return

"the fans could not tolerate much more of this"

St. Hilda's Team, 1957.

Monty...

The holder of Sunderland's all time appearance record - a staggering 623 League and Cup games - Jimmy Montgomery will be forever associated with the 1973 FA Cup Final against Leeds. The wonder save he pulled off in that game is remembered as one of the saves of the century, and Bob Stokoe's emotional dash across the turf to hug Monty at the final whistle is one of the great images of Cup Final history. While Porterfield's goal won the Cup for the Lads it was Monty who had saved the Cup.

Yet, we shouldn't let that one great save obscure the fact that Monty enjoyed a marvellous career in the green jersey for Sunderland, one that began long before that famous save and ended some years after it. Born in Southwick, on 9th October 1943, his first team was St Hilda's RC School, where he was spotted and chosen to play for Sunderland Boys. Here he attracted the scouts and we nearly lost out on him to Burnley, with whom he spent a month on trial.

But, to our eternal relief he was rejected by the Lancashire club and returned home to sign for his boyhood heroes. He started in Sunderland's sixth team before progressing through the ranks to star for the Youths. While playing there he was spotted by the England selectors, and Monty's performances were rewarded with four England Youth International caps.

It wasn't long before Jimmy was knocking on the door of the first team, and he made his full debut in a League Cup game against Walsall on 4th October 1961, just a few days before his 18th birthday. His League debut soon followed, at home to Derby on 24th February 1962. Following this, he quickly ousted Peter Wakeham in goal, becoming the Club's first choice keeper for the rest of the season.

Despite having been on the cards for much of our time in the First Division, relegation at the end of the 1960s was still a blow. It must also have been personally crushing for the manager, Alan Brown, to have led Sunderland to the Second Division for a second time. Yet, as was the case following our relegation in the 1950s, Brown was putting together a team based around some promising young players, and he was perhaps unfortunate to have again suffered relegation in the midst of a rebuilding process. The team had been struggling before he was re-appointed as manager, and dealing with this situation was always going to be a difficult task that was fraught with danger.

However, after six seasons of seeing the Lads struggle against the country's best teams, the supporters expected life to be much easier in the Second Division. Surely, against weaker defences the Lads would score more goals, and having played against the likes of Greaves and Hurst our back line would have no trouble dealing with the tuppence ha'penny strikers found in the second flight. While no-one was pretending the season would be an easy ride, most fans expected to see a good season, with the Lads challenging for - and, with a bit of luck, clinching - promotion.

Unfortunately, the campaign got off to a poor start as the weak away form of previous seasons continued to linger. The first game of the season saw us visit Ashton Gate to play Bristol City, but a battling performance ended in a 4 - 3 defeat for the Lads. Our next two away games also ended in defeat - 2 - 0 at Charlton and 1 - 0 at Orient - setting the tone for the rest of the season. At home, however, we started reasonably well, a 3 - 3 draw with Watford being followed by wins against Charlton (3 - 0), Norwich (2 - 1), Sheffield Wednesday (3 - 1) and Bolton (4 - 1). While these were good, strong wins, the simple fact was that the poor away form cancelled them out. As the Lads had found out in the 1960s, gaining promotion is a tough task, for consistently good home and away form is required to finish at the top of the table.

With performances drifting towards the end of the year, Brown moved to inject some new blood into the side. Having signed Dick Malone from Ayr United - for £30,000 - in mid-October, he splashed out a more substantial fee of £100,000, for Rotherham's centre forward Dave Watson, during December. Results did not immediately improve, however. Indeed, the New Year began disastrously, with Hull beating us 4 - 0 in the League and Orient beating us 3 - 0 at home in the third round of the FA Cup. Though the Lads compensated for this with a couple of good wins at the end of January, in February, they failed to win a single game. What's more, the defence was showing real signs of vulnerability. The month began with a 2 - 0 defeat at QPR and a 4 - 0 defeat at home to Cardiff. Having conceded fifteen goals in the first six games of the year, it seemed clear that our back line needed strengthening. However, Brown instead chose to sell Colin Todd, rated as one of the best half-backs in the game, to Brian Clough's Championship chasing Derby County for £175,000.

It was not the response the fans were looking far, and morale began to sink as the Lads continued to under perform. March proved to be as fruitless as February, the Lads again failing to win a single game. What's more, by the end of the month we had managed to score just one goal in eight games. By Easter we looked more like relegation candidates than a team that had aspirations of return to the top flight.

Fortunately, in the final run in we pulled our socks up. A great 5 - 2 win against Swindon brought our barren winless run to an end and the five games following this saw another three wins, against Orient, Bolton and Sheffield Wednesday, the latter two being away from home. The fans, though, had already had enough.

Crowds had dwindled to well below the 15,000 level, the mediocre 13th place finish being more than many could stomach. It was our worst finish since the dog days of the late 1950's.

Yet, as always with Brown, he had his sights fixed on the future. Once again he was determined to make his youth policy the key to Sunderland's success. By the end of the season the entire squad had cost less than £250,000, with the entirety of that sum having been spent on only four players: Porterfield, Harris, Malone and Watson. The rest of our registered playing staff had either come up through the ranks or been signed on free transfers. But, the fans needed to start seeing quick improvements across the board: they could not tolerate much more of this.

Monty makes a flying save v Northampton Town in 1963.

...Monty

However, after being an ever present in our promotion season, injury kept him out of much of our first season back in the top flight. After recovering, he regained the goalkeeper's jersey, and further impressive performances followed. His reward was yet more international recognition, this time at England Under-23 level, and by the time the 1970 World Cup arrived, many felt Monty deserved a place in the squad ahead of Chelsea keeper Peter Bonnetti. Unfortunately, he didn't receive the England cap he deserved, denied for much of the time by the brilliant Gordon Banks.

While not the tallest keeper, standing 'only' 5ft 11in, what he lacked in height he more than made up for in lightening reflexes. He was renowned as a 'shot stopper', and while the odd-long shot occasionally caught him out, he dominated his penalty box and struck up marvellous relationships with first Charlie Hurley and then Dave Watson at centre-half.

He was at Roker for 16 great years and later came back to pass on his knowledge and experience to Sunderland's youngsters. The Lads have had some great keepers over the years, but it is difficult to make a case for any of them being better than Monty. He is Sunderland's all-time number one.

Jimmy Montgomery.

1971-1972
Improving

"a much better season"

Dave Watson

'King Dave' Watson goes down as one of Sunderland's most accomplished defenders in the post-war era. Yet, when Alan Brown signed him from Rotherham in December 1970, it was as a centre forward, the plan being to use him as a replacement for the ageing Joe Baker.

Dave scored on his debut, a 1-1 draw at Watford, and while he did not shine in that first season, he was the Club's leading scorer with 15 goals the following year. No doubt Dave would have continued in that mode had it not been for the inspired decision to move him into defence. At first, the change might not have seemed such a good idea, as we lost 4-3 away to Carlisle in Dave's first game at the back. But, once he had established a partnership with Ritchie Pitt in the spring of 1973, Dave developed into a centre half of international class. Voted man of the match at Wembley in 1973, he was joint top scorer with Billy Hughes in the Cup run with four goals.

A natural footballer who always looked the part, he was magnificent both in the air and on the ground. He was sold to Manchester City in the 1975 close season for £275,000 after over 200 games for Sunderland.

Expectations had been radically lowered by our mediocre 13th place finish, and when Brown failed to strengthen his squad before the 1971-72 campaign, the fans were generally lacking in optimism. This feeling translated itself into apathy, meaning the attendances for the early part of the season were very poor, averaging out at below the 15,000 mark. The mood was not improved by a miserable opening game, where a 1-1 draw against Birmingham City was marred by a nasty injury to Bobby Park; a broken leg he sustained during the game put an end to what was shaping up to be a very promising career. Our next home match was an altogether happier affair, goals from Kerr and Tueart sealing a 2-0 win over Orient, but this result was followed by a poor 3-0 home defeat at the hands of Carlisle a few days later.

We managed to get a mini-run going in September, with three home wins on the trot - including a 4-1 victory over Boro in the Wear/Tees derby - and even managed a 1-0 away win at Burnley. But, any false promotion hopes starting to flicker were soon snubbed out when we went the next seven games without a win. The defence still had a tendency to be fragile and we were badly shown up in a visit to Oxford where we tumbled to a 2-0 defeat among the dreaming spires.

While form picked up over the next couple of months, wins were still a rarity. But, as the year came to an end, it looked like we had turned the corner. Victories against Fulham and Hull in December were followed by a New Year's Day win at home to Sheffield Wednesday. However, a 5-0 defeat at Orient the following week emphasised the fragility of the team.

At least there was some better news in the FA Cup. Sheffield Wednesday visited Roker in the third round, and we went one better than in the League, beating them 3-0 in front of 25,000. Amazingly, it was our first win in an FA Cup tie since February 1967. The fourth round paired us with Cardiff which, while not exactly glamorous, was certainly winnable. A 1-1 draw brought the Welshmen back to the North East for a replay, and the 39,348 that turned up illustrated the magical aura surrounding the FA Cup. Unfortunately, the team didn't have the magic itself, and another 1-1 draw meant a second replay two days later at Maine Road. This time, the Lads' luck ran out, as we slumped to a 3-1 defeat.

Perhaps inspired by the Cup, Brown's side began to improve dramatically in the League. Four consecutive wins boosted our standing in the table, and though renewed hopes of a promotion challenge were dashed by another winless run following this, the Lads again found their form in the final run in. Most notably, there were exciting wins against Burnley (4-3) and Preston (3-1) over the Easter period. What's more, the youth policy began to show some results too. One of the youngsters to come through the ranks, Joe Bolton, made his first team debut in a cracking 5-0 home win over Watford in April.

Yet, at the end of the season, we had still fallen short of what was required for promotion, being some six points behind second placed Birmingham. A fifth place finish was quite respectable considering the poor early season form, and while it was disappointing to miss out, at least the improvement in form following the turn of the year gave Brown something to build on the following season.

Indeed, 1971-72 had been a much better season than its predecessor. The team were starting to show some shape, and one of the most encouraging aspects of the campaign was that players like Dave Watson, Bobby Kerr and Dennis Tueart were almost ever-presents in the side and, consequently, managed to find the net with regularity, all of them getting more than 10 goals each.

Rather like the early 1960s, it felt that Brown's remoulding of the team was almost complete and that a promotion challenge would follow in the 1972-73 season. Yet, there was also a feeling that we lacked the extra spark needed to turn a good side into a successful one. Nobody knew where it might come from, or how, but if the Lads were to make an impact next season, then we needed someone with a touch of genius to lift the side to new heights.

Pitt scores v Bristol City.

Hooligans

As the season entered its final stages, promotion was little more than a mathematical possibility for the Lads, but loyal supporters still turned out to see their heroes play, hoping for a little fun and entertainment. A 5 - 0 thrashing of Watford at Roker Park certainly provided much cheer, but when the Lads visited Queen's Park Rangers a few days later, a potentially great day out in London turned into a nightmare for many Sunderland fans. The game ended 1 - 0 to the home side, but this was by-the-by. It was events off the field, rather than on it, that marred proceedings. A minority of so called QPR 'fans' ran rampage after the game. Armed with weapons that included knives and meat cleavers, hooligans set about attacking innocent Sunderland fans on the tube. Trapped underground, these fans were truly terrorised in some of the worst scenes of violence ever witnessed at a Sunderland game. Sadly, hooliganism was a growing feature at English football matches, and deplorable scenes dogged the game for over a decade.

Joe Bolton.

1972-1973
Ultimate Glory

"Many felt Stokoe was a jobbing manager, and worst of all, he was a Mag"

Kerr and Tueart, Sunderland v Bristol City, March 1973.

Bobby Kerr

While Bobby was perhaps the smallest winning captain in FA Cup history, what he lacked in height he more than made up for in tenacity and fighting spirit. Born in Alexandria, Scotland, Bobby joined Sunderland straight from school, working his way through the ranks. He got his chance in the first team in December 1966, against Manchester City, and he capped a dream debut with a goal. He had an immediate impact on the team, acting like a talisman as the Lads went on an unbeaten run that lasted until we met Leeds in the fifth round of the Cup in early March. Unluckily, Bobby broke his leg in that game and suffered a further break before he regained his first team place.

Indeed, it was not until 1968 that he re-established himself in the side, but he wasted no time in getting back to business, his performances marking him out as one of the Club's top players. He played over 400 times for Sunderland before leaving to join Blackpool in 1979.

As well as being an extremely skilful player Bobby was a great captain, encouraging and motivating his colleagues and leading by example. His finest hour was obviously at Wembley when he sat on the shoulders of his team-mates holding the FA Cup aloft.

Alan Brown must have started the season with some degree of optimism following the team's form at the end of the previous season. Yet even the most optimistic fan could not have anticipated what was going to happen to the Club in the coming months. The Lads started reasonably well, losing only once in their first eight matches. We then suddenly seemed to hit the buffers. A humiliating 5-1 defeat away at Oxford started the decline and we managed to lose the next two games in similar fashion. The fans began to vote with their feet. The home game against Fulham attracted just over 11,000 and those that were there voiced their displeasure with the performance of the team. Alan Brown, who had left the Club in 1964 in a somewhat hurried fashion, decided to call it a day again. It was not clear whether he jumped or was pushed, but yet again Sunderland were managerless. Billy Elliot stepped in as caretaker and although he was at the helm for less than a month, he did produce the tactical masterstroke of moving Dave Watson from centre forward to centre half. Sunderland should be eternally grateful for that one team change.

When Bob Stokoe was appointed at the end of the month it would be fair to say that the reaction in the press and in the town was not exactly ecstatic. Many felt Stokoe was a jobbing manager who had done the rounds of the lower divisions with spells at Charlton Athletic, Rochdale, Bury and Carlisle United and whose major success had been to win the Anglo-Italian Trophy with Blackpool. What's more - and worst of all - he was a Mag, through and through. At least that was how it seemed. Yet, Bob Stokoe swept into Roker Park as a man with a mission.

Nevertheless, his reign did not start well as we lost 1-0 to Burnley in his first game. However, Sunderland then embarked on a run which saw just five defeats in 32 games, a run which culminated in a day that Wearside will never forget. At the time he arrived, we had won only four games out of 18 and were standing fourth bottom of the League. Moreover, the Club hadn't bought a new player for over two years. By the end of the season, a revitalised team had been judiciously added to, and we were the FA Cup holders, having beaten mighty Leeds 1-0 in the Final.

What Stokoe did was all a case of man-management. He gave the team faith in themselves and told them to go out, play football and enjoy themselves. Players like Tueart, Hughes and Kerr responded to this with little need for encouragement. The Cup-run came as a surprising bonus. Stokoe's main aim, like that of so many Sunderland managers, was to get us back into the top Division and he nearly did that as well as winning the Cup.

From the week after he took charge results started to pick up. We had already comprehensively beaten Brighton 4-0 at home in the week before the Cup run had even begun, and by the beginning of March, when Oxford came to town, he had transformed home attendances from 11,000, when he took over, to 40,000. The fans just loved it. With a number of postponements over Christmas and so many games to play in the Cup, League matches were piling up. In the twenty days before Wembley, Sunderland played eight League games, giving them a return, following Bob Stokoe's appointment, of 30 points from 22 games, clearly promotion standard.

Even after our Wembley triumph we still had two League games to play. We went to Cardiff City on the Monday night, where a Vic Halom goal got us a point and then played QPR at Roker on the Wednesday. By this time the euphoria - and most probably the drink - had got to the Lads and the Londoners showed no deference or sympathy as they gave us a 3-0 beating in front of 43,000. To be honest, nobody really cared about the result as we were still living on a cloud.

To put the Cup Final win against Leeds into perspective, Don Revie's men subsequently travelled to Salonika, Greece, where they were narrowly defeated by AC Milan in the European Cup Winners' Cup final, a dubious refereeing performance hampering their game. They had also finished third in the League, and the following season were crowned English Champions.

By being a football fan you almost agree to take the ninety-nine bad times, so that you can enjoy the one good time. The game kicks you in the teeth far more than it pats you on the back. But, to be a Sunderland supporter in 1973 was to be on top of the world. Wembley was the one good time for those ninety-nine bad. After the euphoria had settled down, however, we were still a Second Division side. What Stokoe had to do now was build on the success.

Billy Hughes.

Vic Halom

One of the players to arrive during the 1972-73 season was Vic Halom, who joined us from Luton for £35,000 in early February. When Dave Watson was moved to the backline, Stokoe needed a replacement for him up front, and Halom was brought in with the express purpose of scoring goals. In his first season at Sunderland, he scored 7 times in 20 games, including a crucial goal in the Cup semi-final against Arsenal. He finished in double figures the following season, bagging 21 League and Cup goals, but he was somewhat less prolific in subsequent seasons. After 130 games, and 40 goals, he moved to Oldham in March 1976. Vic returned to Sunderland during another famous Wembley run in 1992. However, this time it was as a politician rather than a footballer. He contested one of the city's Parliamentary seats in the General Election, standing for the Liberal Democrats. It was not an altogether successful return however; he finished in third place, some way behind the Labour and Conservative candidates.

Vic Halom

Wembley and the Impossible Dream

"I should pack it all in. There'll never be another moment like it."

Bob Stokoe.

Vic Halom scoring against Manchester City
in the 5th round replay at Roker Park

All of Wearside agreed with the sentiments of Bob Stokoe after Sunderland had taken on the best teams that England had to offer and deservedly beat them all to lift the FA Cup. After 36 long years, the most prestigious domestic club trophy in football travelled to Roker Park again. What's more, in lifting the Cup, we became just the fifth club to win the trophy while in the Second Division, following in the footsteps of Notts County in 1894, Wolves in 1908, Barnsley in 1912 and West Bromwich Albion in 1931.

Yet, the Cup campaign all began somewhat inauspiciously on 13th January 1973, when we played Notts County away in the third round. A crowd of just over 15,000 saw County take the lead with a goal from Bradd after 27 minutes. They held the lead for 50 minutes and would have extended it had it not been for a superb save from Montgomery that many of those who were there compare with the famous one he would later make at Wembley. With 20 minutes to go it looked like the Lads were going to suffer another quick exit from the Cup, but Stokoe gambled on Dave Watson and moved him back up front to centre-forward, the position he had been in until the previous November. Big Dave came up trumps, heading in a cross from Dennis Tueart on 77 minutes to snatch a reprieve. In the replay at Roker Park three days later, a crowd of over 30,000 saw Watson score to put us one up, before Tueart put the game out of reach with a second near the end.

Before the third round tie, Stokoe had been back to his old club, Newcastle, to buy Ron Guthrie and David Young for a combined fee of £35,000. The two of them were brought into the team and took over from youngsters Joe Bolton and John Tones for the fourth round home game against Reading. The Roker crowd were delighted to welcome back Charlie Hurley, who was managing Reading at the time, and Charlie brought with him a young goalkeeper called Steve Death who played an absolute blinder. You can imagine what the newspaper headlines would have been if the youngster had kept the Lads at bay, but Dennis Tueart managed to get one past him to equalise Reading's early goal. This meant another replay and we made our way South with some rethinking to do. Stokoe again played the Watson card and he scored with 80 seconds of the start - you can't do much better than that! After the early goal, Sunderland settled down, Tueart and Kerr finishing off a dispirited Reading inside the first half-hour. The home side managed to score a penalty as a consolation, but the Lads were too strong for them.

Whenever your team gets into the last sixteen of the Cup, the pulse starts to race and to be drawn away to Manchester City was enough to whet anyone's appetite. Manchester City arrived at this stage of the competition having disposed of Liverpool after a replay and the Blues must have fancied their chances of going all the way. At that time, the bookies three favourites were Leeds at 4 - 1, Manchester City at 9 - 2 and Arsenal at 11 - 2. According to the bookies, Sunderland were the outsiders.

The Lads travelled to Maine Road with about 12,000 Sunderland fans, who formed part of a huge 54,478 crowd, and they watched spellbound as the match ebbed and flowed. Montgomery made a crucial early save from Rodney Marsh, whose arms were already aloft signalling a goal, but City didn't have to wait long for the breakthrough. Tony Towers, soon to be a Sunderland player, scored after 16 minutes following good work by Mike Summerbee. Mickey Horswill then nipped in to equalise and from that moment on Sunderland were never behind in the FA Cup campaign again.

1973 FA Cup, fifth round replay.

On 68 minutes Billy Hughes was put clear, kept his head and scored. It was looking good for Sunderland but at the death Monty punched the ball into his own goal... cruel, cruel, cruel.

The draw meant we faced our third replay! As the game kicked off, we were into our sixth FA Cup match and we weren't even in the quarter finals yet! We were certainly going to Wembley the hard way. But, the fans didn't mind. Bob Stokoe remembers that some of the Roker faithful were already queuing for tickets for the replay by the time the team had got back from Manchester on the Saturday night!

Voted by supporters the greatest game ever seen at Roker Park, February 22nd, 1973, was one of those nights where everything was right. The 51,872 crowd played their part in generating a superb atmosphere, but they were entertained all the way by two great teams and, of course, most of them went home delighted by a Sunderland win. The Manchester City captain, Tony Doyle, went on record saying there was a feeling in the City dressing room that it was to be their night. How wrong he was. He should have realised his mistake the moment he ran down the tunnel. Dennis Tueart reckoned that the deafening atmosphere was worth a goal start; he later said: 'Quite honestly, we weren't that good at the time but we beat them, the chances we created were enormous, the quality of the performance was superb, they were under the cosh from the start and we beat them well. From then we really started to believe in ourselves.'

Sunderland were awesome, and the legendary Rodney Marsh famously commented that Vic Halom's Fulwell End screamer that put us 1 - 0 up was one of the best goals he had ever seen. When Billy Hughes made it 2 - 0 the Roker Roar just went crazy. But, you can never control all 90 minutes of any football game, and within 10 minutes of the second half City had pulled one back through Francis Lee. Unperturbed, Sunderland dusted themselves off and set about scoring a third. With only 12 minutes remaining Billy Hughes slid the ball home at the Roker End to make it 3 - 1. A famous victory, a famous night.

The draw for the quarter-finals could not have been better. Not only were we picked to play at home, but also against Second Division opposition, Luton Town. Nevertheless, they arrived on Wearside with a brilliant away record, and had already beaten us twice that season, 2 - 0 at Roker in October and 1 - 0 at Kenilworth Road the week before the Cup tie. For the opening 45 minutes it looked as though we might struggle to break down a resolute defence. But, all out pressure had to pay dividends and our patience was eventually rewarded, first with a magnificent Dave Watson header that sent the crowd wild and then a second eight minutes from time when Ron Guthrie smacked a beauty into the roof of the net.

The win put us into the semi-finals of the FA Cup for the first time since 1956. When Arsenal came out of the hat as our opposition, the atmosphere in the town and the area was electric. Tickets were like hen's teeth and a voucher system was used to allocate them. Arsenal had won the League and Cup double in 1971 and they had also been beaten finalists in 1972, losing to Leeds. They were in line for a record third year in a row at Wembley. Unsurprisingly, therefore, they were a class team filled with internationals and stars such as Charlie George. The bookies rightly reckoned they were favourites for the Cup.

The match was played at Hillsborough, and Sunderland were clearly the more uninhibited team, the more eager side, the one that wanted to win most.

Vic Halom, FA Cup semi-final.

Ron Guthrie scoring against Luton Town in the sixth round.

The managers lead their teams on to the pitch, 1973 Cup Final.

Monty's legendary save.

And, we had magnificent support. The roar that greeted the arrival of the Sunderland team was unbelievable. The authorities had given Sunderland the main terraced end of the ground and it was a sea of red-and-white. The Lads started well, and when Bob Wilson just managed to tip over a drive from Horswill there was a stir in the crowd as if the unexpected could happen. A minute later, a long ball had Blockley in a mess and Wilson came out to help. Halom nipped in, got the ball past both of them and tucked it into the net. We had our noses in front and we kept making the chances. But, George Armstrong was proving dangerous for Arsenal and called Montgomery into action with a dangerous low shot.

In the 64th minute, a throw-in from Bobby Kerr was headed backwards by Dennis Tueart. Wilson came rushing out for the ball, but as he did so, Billy Hughes nodded the ball over him into the net to make it 2 - 0. The crowd were delirious! But, Arsenal didn't lie down and six minutes from the end Charlie George scored a simple goal that meant that the final few moments were an eternity for the Roker faithful, Arsenal piling on the pressure as they searched for an equaliser. However, they could find no way through, and at the final whistle the travelling fans refused to move until their 'Messiah', Bob Stokoe, appeared. Taking the salute, he turned and went back to the dressing room... tears running down his cheeks.

The four weeks between the semis and the final were carnival time in Sunderland. Everywhere you looked the town was literally painted red-and-white and, while it seemed impossible, everyone believed we could do it. For those few weeks the eyes of the footballing world were focussed on Wearside. We became everyone's adopted team with all the neutrals both here and abroad hoping we could topple the mighty Leeds.

Former Sunderland player Don Revie was the Leeds manager and he had created a team that was feared and revered throughout the country. Not only did they have skill and guile in the likes of Giles and Gray, they also had some of the hardest men in football in Bremner and Hunter. 'Norman bites your legs' was the banner that summed up their no-nonsense approach. Sunderland, on the other hand, were by-and-large a bunch of Second Division journeymen - or so Leeds thought. What Stokoe had done was nothing short of miraculous: he had transformed a reasonable set of players into a team that believed in themselves, that could play out of their skins. Jimmy Montgomery got it right when he said "We always thought we had a chance. We were hoping that Leeds might more or less take it for granted that they were there and they've got it.' Bob Stokoe instilled in the players that they were as good as the Gileses, the Lorimers and the Bremners.

As the day of the game approached, tens of thousands of North Easterners made the pilgrimage to London, carrying their banners and colours and hope in their hearts. On the night before the game, the centre of London was awash with Sunderland fans determined to enjoy themselves. The mood seemed to pass to the players. As the TV cameras visited the team hotels, there was a noticeable difference in the atmosphere and the mood of the two sets of players. Leeds looked professional and calculating but somehow cool and aloof. When the cameras turned to the Sunderland hotel, all the Lads looked like they were having the time of their lives. Billy Hughes had a laughing box that seemed to set the tone. This was going to be a great day. By strange coincidence, the two managers had met at Wembley once before.

In 1955 Don Revie had been part of the Manchester City team that had played Bob In Stokoe's Newcastle United in the final. As 'Abide With Me' echoed around the Wembley stands it was clear the atmosphere was special, something was in the air.

The nation had taken Sunderland to their hearts and the Lads did not disappoint. They were in no way overawed either by the occasion or by Leeds. In the first few minutes, Pitt upended Clarke as if to show the Leeds striker that he was in for a game.

There had been a considerable downpour in the morning of the match and the pitch was quite greasy. The ball skidded around but Sunderland were really up for it. They chased and harried, taking control of the game, with Watson dominating at the back and Hughes and Tueart making the running down the wings.

After half an hour, Harvey in the Leeds goal lifted a lob from Kerr over the bar. The players took up positions for the corner. Billy Hughes swung the ball into the box, and a superb leap by Dave Watson took a couple of defenders away with him. Vic Halom, following up behind, got a little touch onto Ian Porterfield, who controlled it with his left foot, his good foot, and hit it with his right, which he rarely used. The ball flew into the net in front of the massed ranks of delighted Sunderland fans. It was 3:32pm and the world seemed to go crazy. Yet there was still plenty of time for Leeds to come back. We were ahead - but could we stay ahead?

Porterfield scores.

In the second half, Leeds came much more into the game. Eddie Gray, who had been touted as a match-winner, was substituted for Terry Yorath. This was perhaps the best compliment that Don Revie could have given to Dick Malone, who had been given the job of keeping the Scottish winger quiet. The Leeds team were not going to give up the Cup easily and they kept pressing. Finally, the moment came that would change the game. Mid-way through the second half, Reaney threw a cross into the box and Cherry met it with a powerful diving header. Monty's reflexes were sharp enough to get to the ball but he couldn't keep hold of it. He had only managed to parry it into the path of Peter Lorimer, who was said to have the hardest shot in football. Almost immediately, Lorimer had the ball at his feet and a goal that was wide open. He hit the ball sweetly and swung away to celebrate the equaliser. Monty, still on the floor from his first save, reacted with amazing agility. He threw himself back across the goalline to push the shot up onto the cross bar. It came back into play and Dick Malone was there to belt it clear. It was one of the most fantastic saves ever seen and Monty had pulled it out of the bag when it really mattered. Leeds couldn't believe it.

The final few minutes seemed to be an eternity. Halom had one last effort tipped over by Harvey as Sunderland summoned up every last drop of energy to keep going. As Denis Tueart later said 'I knew it was close to the end and I looked across at the bench and Arthur Cox (the trainer) held up four fingers. I kept running for another half an hour and looked across again - this time he held up three fingers!'

At the final whistle, the place went crazy. Bob Stokoe, a mac covering his tracksuit and a trilby hat on his head, sprinted from the touchline to embrace Jimmy Montgomery. He knew what that save meant. As Bobby Kerr picked up the FA Cup and held it aloft, the whole nation, or at least everyone outside of Leeds, was delighted that Sunderland, the underdogs, had won.

Back in the town itself, those who had been left behind celebrated with sheer delight. The triumphant return of the team on an open topped coach the following Tuesday was met by an estimated one million people who had lined the roads from Carrville to Roker Park. The team had achieved the impossible dream.

Back in Sunderland with the Cup.

1973-1974
Unlucky

"a harsh bump that brought the messiah back to earth."

Mick Horswill.

Team Breaks Up

It is often difficult to keep a successful team together, especially when star players are wanted by other clubs, and this proved to be the case with our Cup winning heroes. As the season drew to an end, both Dennis Tueart and Mickey Horswill were tempted by the bright lights of Manchester and moved to Man City. Tueart cost the Blues a huge £250,000, while Horswill went as part of a package that resulted in Sunderland getting £100,000 and Tony Towers. This proved a good deal for Wearside as Towers established himself as an impressive performer, gaining England recognition while at the Club.
Another of our Cup heroes - Dave Watson - moved to Manchester City at the end of the following season, after another unsuccessful promotion campaign. Dave had started to establish himself in the England team - winning his first cap during the 1973-74 season - and needed top flight football to maintain the momentum of his career.

Following Stokoe's appointment, the Lads had looked an altogether better side. In Manchester City, Arsenal and Leeds, we had beaten three of the country's top teams during our Cup run and, the fans surmised, if the Lads could beat teams of this calibre, then there was no reason why they could not mount a successful promotion campaign. But, the other teams in the Division didn't seem to know the rule that you had to let the Cup winners beat all before them. While we had won the Cup as universally loved under-dogs, on becoming Cup holders ourselves we also became the team that everyone in the Second Division wanted to beat. While the Wembley run had re-ignited the Roker Roar, the added support giving the Lads a real lift, it soon became apparent that we were in for a tough season.

Curiously, it was away from home that we managed to show our early season form. The opening month of the campaign saw the Lads produce some good performances, including a 4 - 1 win at Notts County and a 1 - 0 win at Oxford, but at home we failed to win a single game, Orient and Cardiff holding us to 1 - 1 draws and Luton beating us 1 - 0. The latter defeat was a double blow, for Ritchie Pitt sustained a knee injury during the game that effectively ended his Sunderland career. It was such a disappointment after the success of the previous May.

However, September also saw the beginning of our first - and to date only - taste of European football. As England's representatives in the European Cup Winners' Cup, we travelled to Hungary to meet Vasas Budapest. The game couldn't have gone any better, goals from Billy Hughes and Dennis Tueart, along with an excellent clean sheet, putting us in the driving seat. Consequently, the second leg was something of a formality, and a penalty from Tueart sealed a fine 3 - 0 aggregate victory.

The win seemed to give a slight boost to the Lads' form, and our first home League victory of the season followed a few days later, a 3 - 1 win against Sheffield Wednesday. In a busy week of football, we then took on the 1971-72 League Champions, Derby County, in the League Cup. A fine performance against Brian Clough's team saw the Lads pull off a 2 - 2 draw, enough to bring the Rams back to Roker for a replay. Although this result was followed by a disappointing defeat at Preston, a 2 - 0 victory at Fulham a week later set us up for another epic round of Cup matches.

The second round of the Cup Winners' Cup saw us paired with Portuguese giants Sporting Lisbon. This would be an altogether tougher match than the one with Vasas Budapest but, after our exploits in the FA Cup, the Lads feared no-one. Another excellent performance saw Sunderland race into a 2 - 0 lead, as goals from Horswill and Kerr seemingly set us up with another comfortable buffer for the second leg. However, the Portuguese side scored a valuable away goal in the closing stages of the game, ensuring the tie was delicately balanced.

A few days later, Derby visited Roker for the League Cup replay. Early in the game, Tueart missed a penalty, but he made up for this by netting a goal after 30 minutes. It looked like this might be enough to see us through, until ten minutes from time, when Gemmill equalised. His goal ensured the game went into extra time, but no goals were scored. A toss of a coin then decided the venue for the third replay: Roker. On this occasion, we made no mistake. Over 38,000 turned up to see Sunderland demolish Clough's side 3 - 0, Vic Halom getting a superb second half hat-trick.

The win provided us with a real boost going into the second leg of the Cup Winners Cup. A week after beating the Rams, we travelled to Lisbon 2 - 1 up and with a real chance of progressing to the third round. Unfortunately, it was not to be. Sporting Lisbon ran out 2 - 0 winners, eliminating us by a narrow 3 - 2 margin.

The Lads responded well to the defeat, thrashing Swindon 4 - 1 and Bolton 3 - 0 in the days following the game, before preparing for the visit of League Champions Liverpool in the third round of the League Cup, a match the fans viewed as the 'unofficial charity shield'. Liverpool had decided against playing Sunderland in the usual curtain raiser to the season, citing 'commitments' elsewhere. The Lads had then decided not to enter either, as the spirit of the fixture had been destroyed. The League Cup tie therefore gave Sunderland a chance to show what they could have done if Liverpool had agreed to meet them at Wembley. However, while we played very well, the mighty reds were in top form, and dumped us out of the competition with a 2 - 0 victory.

With the season less than three months old, the Lads had already played a staggering 25 games, as our Cup exploits crowded the fixture list. It was all very exciting, but with Lads out of both competitions, they could focus on the League and FA Cup. When our defence of the latter came unstuck at the first hurdle - Carlisle beating us 1 - 0 at home in a third round replay - the final half of the season was fully focused on the real prize: gaining a place in the First Division.

After a shaky period when Cup commitments stretched our playing resources, the Lads' performances were strong enough in the New Year to put us in the promotion picture. With three-up, three-down having been introduced at the start of the season, our chances of going up had been improved anyway, and as the season entered its final stages, we seemed to have done enough to bag second place. However, disaster struck around Easter time. Defeats against Bristol City and Carlisle knocked us off track, and despite winning our last three League games, we could still only manage to finish sixth. Middlesbrough, under Jack Charlton, walked away with the League, while we finished an agonising two points off the third placed team, Carlisle. Victory over Stokoe's old club - who had also ended our defence of the Cup - would have been enough to have seen us promoted. It was a harsh bump that brought the messiah back to earth.

Tight at the Top

For over sixty seasons, promotion from Division Two had been a prize awarded only to the teams finishing in the top two places. At the start of the 1973-74 season, however, the Football League altered this system in order to improve the chances of teams going up, deciding the top three should be rewarded.

But, any benefit this might have added to the teams chasing promotion was negated by the incredibly close table at the end of the season. While Middlesbrough were run away leaders, Luton, Carlisle, Orient, Blackpool and the Lads were all in with a shout for the other two places. Consequently, two defeats in our last five games - one of them against promotion rivals Carlisle - was enough to snatch a top three place from us. At the end of the season, just two points separated the teams in third, fourth, fifth and sixth.

		P	W	D	L	F	A	Pts
1.	Boro	42	27	11	4	77	30	65
2.	Luton	42	19	12	11	64	51	50
3.	Carlisle	42	20	9	13	61	48	49
4.	Orient	42	15	18	9	55	42	48
5.	Blackpool	42	17	13	12	57	40	47
6.	The Lads	42	19	9	14	58	44	47

Halom header v Milwall.

1974-1975
More Hard Luck

"another end of season hard luck story"

Ian Porterfield, 1974.

Match of the Day

When the Lads visited Blackpool at the start of February, a brilliant top of the table clash that had just about everything, followed. With 5,000 Roker fans in the crowd, the game started at a cracking pace, and there were off the ball incidents galore before things settled down. When they did it was Blackpool who drew "first blood". A corner taken by Bentley was nodded on by Micky Walsh and Alcock headed home. After 42 minutes, ex-Newcastle man Wyn Davies doubled the lead.

At half time, Sunderland received the proverbial 'roasting' from Bob Stokoe and came out fighting. It was little surprise when a Halom rasper halved the lead soon after the restart. Blackpool came roaring back, and just when it looked as though a third might be in the offing, Bobby Kerr broke clear and equalised.

However, Blackpool then won the game with a corking strike, good enough to be judged to be goal of the season by Match of the Day viewers. Micky Walsh picked the ball up on the half way line, shrugged past his markers and unleashed a beauty from 35 yards. Monty had no chance.

While missing out on promotion was obviously disappointing, there was no need for anyone at the Club to panic. The previous two seasons had shown exactly what the Lads were capable of, and they could be expected to be challenging for promotion again once the new season began. However, competition for the top places was likely to be exceptionally tough. Some very good teams had been relegated from the First Division - most notably Manchester United - and the manager moved to strengthen his squad in the pre-season to help deal with this threat. Bob Moncur, a Fairs Cup winner with Newcastle United, made the short trip from Tyneside to Wearside, and Bryan 'Pop' Robson of West Ham joined for a Club record £145,000. These high profile signings signalled the Club's ambition to return to Division One. Without promotion, the legacy of the Cup would be frittered away; while the European adventure, for example, had been great fun, if the Club was serious about building on our Wembley glory, then it could not afford to waste time in the Second Division.

Keen to get on with the job, the Lads got off to a flying start. We began with an away fixture at Millwall, where the Lads ran out 4 -1 winners. A week later, our first home game of the season saw us beat Southampton 3 - 1, in front of 34,000 fans. A 5 - 1 thrashing of Bristol Rovers in our second home game and a 1 - 0 win at York then completed a pleasing opening month that saw four wins and one defeat. While September saw a quick exit from the League Cup and a series of draws in the League, in October we were back to winning ways, beating Sheffield Wednesday home and away and Oxford at home. The following month, the good form continued and, after a defeat at Cardiff, we beat Blackpool (1 - 0), Fulham (3 - 1) and Notts County (3 - 0) before visiting Old Trafford at the end of November.

With both Sunderland and Manchester United in fine form, a cracking game was expected, and some 60,585 turned up at Old Trafford for the game, the highest Second Division attendance since 1959. They were not let down, 'Match of the Day' rating it the best game of the season. An early goal by Stuart Pearson gave the Red Devils the lead before a Billy Hughes' strike levelled matters. The Stretford End was then stunned to silence as a cracking shot, again by Hughes, gave the Lads the lead. In the second-half, Willie Morgan scored, with McIlroy clearly standing offside. The linesman flagged, but the referee ignored it and the score was 2 - 2. Finally, Sammy McIlroy scored the winner as Manchester United came from behind to steal it. It was hard lines on Sunderland, who had contributed to a great match. Manchester United were simply too good for the Second Division, and the result was no disgrace.

The Lads soon put the defeat behind them, thrashing Portsmouth 4 - 1 a week later. But, tragedy struck shortly after that game, when Cup Final hero Ian Porterfield was badly injured in a car crash. The accident put him out of action for the rest of the season and, sadly, he left Sunderland during the following season's campaign. As well as being a personal tragedy, the loss of a player of his calibre was felt badly by the Club and our promotion challenge was severely damaged by his absence. Having played so well in the opening months of the season, we began to fall apart without him in the New Year. Having lost just five games up until Christmas, we managed to lose three in January alone. What's more, we began to struggle badly away from home, finding it almost impossible to beat teams on their own turf. Indeed, our first away win of 1975 did not come until 31st March, when we beat Bolton 2 - 0.

The dip in form was a serious blow to our promotion campaign, but we remained in with a shout. Indeed, on the final day of the season, we still had a chance of going up, but only if we could beat Aston Villa, were also chasing promotion, at Villa Park. In front of over 57,000 spectators, many of whom were from Wearside, we were beaten 2 - 0, and Norwich joined Villa and Manchester United in the promotion party. It was another end of season hard luck story, the Lads finishing two points, and just one place, away from promotion.

While it was another bitter blow, we had competed to the end in an exceptionally strong Second Division. What's more, there were still many positive aspects to take from the season. There had been some great victories during the season, the Lads pulverising teams like Bristol Rovers and Portsmouth. 'Pop' Robson had been a great success up front, adding flair and good finishing to our front line. Meanwhile, at the back, our defence had been strengthened considerably. In conceding just eight goals at Roker Park, a new Club record had been established. And, altogether we had let in just 35 goals during the season, our best defensive record since the turn of the century. Perhaps we could make it third time lucky in 1975-76.

Towers v West Brom.

Another Close Finish

Once again, the Lads were desperately unlucky not to go up. For the second time in a row, we finished just one win away from promotion. With a much better goal difference than Norwich, two points in our final game would have left us the right side of a close finish. As it was, we were again left to rue missed chances and ponder what might have been. Both our games against Norwich - who had been relegated from the First Division the previous season - ended in goalless draws. Had just one of our shots in either of those game beaten their keeper, we would have gone up in their place. A sickening thought...

		P	W	D	L	F	A	Pts
1.	Man Utd	42	26	9	7	66	30	61
2.	A Villa	42	25	8	9	79	32	58
3.	Norwich C	42	20	13	9	58	37	53
4.	The Lads	42	19	13	10	65	35	51

'Pop' Robson

1975-1976
Champions!

"a glorious end to the season"

Joe Bolton v Portsmouth, April 1976.

Hats Off for the Palace

When the sixth round of the FA Cup gave us a home tie with Third Division Crystal Palace, many fans felt that we were already through to the semi-finals. However, Palace were a decent side, and had the added power of carrying a gypsy's good luck message from the third round onwards. What's more, their manager - Malcolm Allison - was a great motivator and he played all the right moves. Before the game, Allison come onto the pitch to wind the Sunderland fans up, strolling around with a giant cigar and an ostentatious Fedora hat. All the talk of gypsies and good luck was also designed to psyche out the Lads. Yet, as the game wore on, Palace did seem to have immense good fortune. Bob Moncur, for example, saw a shot rebound back off the woodwork as the Lads struggled to find the net. In the end, an Alan Whittle goal settled the match in Palace's favour. The 50,850 crowd witnessed what proved to be Sunderland's only League or Cup defeat at Roker Park during the season. Perhaps the gypsies had played a role after all.

Midway through the close season period, we paid the price for failure to achieve promotion. Our England international centre back, Dave Watson, left the Club for Manchester City, in need of First Division football in order to further his international ambitions. The £275,000 fee provided some compensation, and Stokoe used some of this money to bring Jeff Clarke from Manchester City to fill the gap left by King Dave's departure. While the transfer was seen by many as another example of Sunderland being unable to hold onto our best players, Clarke turned out to be an more than adequate replacement. What's more, the manager also used some of the remaining money to purchase Mel Holden from Preston North End, for £120,000. With Holden going on to score some valuable goals during the season, the sale of Watson eventually appeared to have been good business for all concerned.

The fixture list had presented us with two tough games at the start of the season, at home to relegated Chelsea, and away to Bristol City, who had finished the previous season just one place below us. In our opening game, we rose to the challenge, a 30,000 crowd seeing a good 2 - 1 home win for the Lads. At Bristol City, however, we were outplayed, losing 3 - 0 to our promotion rivals. But, with two further wins during August - at home to Blackpool and Fulham - we finished the month with seven points from five games.

The following month began with another quick exit from the League Cup - Notts County beating us 2 - 1 - and a League defeat at Plymouth. But, the rest of September was pure glory, the Lads winning their remaining four League fixtures, with notable wins against relegated Carlisle (3 - 2) and a thrashing of Notts County. This marked the start of an absolutely superb spell, during which the Lads were almost unstoppable. From 13th September until the end of November, we won ten of the thirteen League games we were involved in, with notable results including a 4 - 1 win at York and 3 - 0 home win against Nottingham Forest. While the run was brought to an abrupt end with a 4 - 0 thrashing at Southampton, the points gained had already done enough to mark us out as promotion favourites. Unfortunately, Billy Hughes - whose attacking play had been an important element of our game - was badly injured towards the end of the run, breaking his leg in a 2 - 1 win at Charlton.

Without Hughes we struggled a little during December, and the man signed to replace him in the New Year - Roy Greenwood - found it hard to settle in to the team. But, the Lads were soon back on track, and began to flex their muscles in the FA Cup. Oldham were beaten 2 - 0 at Roker in the third round, before the Lads eased into the fifth round with a 1 - 0 victory at home to Hull. Having met two Second Division sides at home, we were then faced with an away tie at First Division Stoke City. The game, played on Valentine's Day, was a close fought match, both teams defending well, and the game ended 0 - 0. The much anticipated replay drew a huge 47,583 crowd to Roker Park, but another close game had to go to extra time. On this occasion, however, the Lads did the business; goals from Holden and Robson secured a place in the quarter-finals, and an easy looking tie against Third Division Crystal Palace.

Cup runs always get the blood running, and so soon after 1973 there was real excitement and a genuine feeling that we could make another final. As the Lads prepared for their quarter-final tie, there was even the chance of a North East semi-final, for Newcastle were playing at Derby County. In the event, all the speculation was for nothing. Both North East sides went out of the competition, Palace beating us 1 - 0.

But, it was promotion to the First Division that really mattered. The Cup run had interfered with the League campaign a little, and it was time to knuckle down and grind out some results. Having slipped up at the final hurdle twice in a row, Stokoe was determined to go all the way this time. Yet, frustrating form persisted after the Cup exit. Although we beat Orient 2 - 0 a week after the Palace game, a series of draws and a defeat at Forest meant that we had managed just three wins in the first ten games of 1976. With this sort of form, there was real danger that we might once again just miss out as other teams finished the season on a high.

Fortunately, the Lads turned it around for the final run in. Successive victories at home to Southampton (3 - 0) and York (1 - 0) provided a platform to build on, and in the final month we really turned it on. Further strong victories against Blackburn (3 - 0) and Hull (4 - 1) put us in the driving seat. With three games left, we needed just one more win to secure promotion. On Easter Monday, Bolton Wanderers visited Roker Park knowing the home side would be going at them with all guns blazing in order to secure those two points. The game attracted 51,983 supporters and the weather was beautiful, in fact everything was perfect... almost. Bolton included a very young Peter Reid and, as might be expected for any team including Reidy, they certainly came for a game. Towers gave us the lead with a penalty and 'Pop' Robson made it 2 - 0, but Wanderers pulled one back to set a nail biting finish. When Monty was injured in the second half, a hush fell over the terraces. But, all was well. Monty was okay, we hung on and the Lads were up. The scenes of celebration were, as always with Sunderland, a real treat.

On the last game of the season, we then clinched the Championship trophy with a 2 - 0 home win over Portsmouth. Joe Bolton had his shooting boots on that day and scored an absolute 'rasper'. It was a glorious end to the season and an entirely deserved outcome. The Lads had worked hard to meet their goal and everyone was looking forward to our return to the First Division.

'Pop' Robson scores against Bolton, 1976.

Fortress Roker

One of the most pleasing aspects of the season was that Roker Park had again become a fortress. We managed to win 19 of our 21 home games in the League, the remaining two games being draws against the two Bristol sides. Remaining undefeated at home during the whole of a League campaign was quite an achievement, but to actually win almost all of the home games was absolutely superb. On top of this, the atmosphere at Roker Park was again superb. The average crowd of nearly 33,000 was easily the best in the Second Division, beating our nearest rivals by some 12,000. If anyone deserved promotion then it was us. The famous Roker Roar had been magnificent.

League champions cup presentation.

The Football Echo
Sunderland's own paper

For most Sunderland supporters in the North East and for many scattered throughout the world the Sunderland Echo is their daily insight into what is happening at the Club. On Saturday nights during the season for generations of fans getting a Footy Echo has been a ritual that can be filled either with relish or dread depending on the team's performance and the result of that afternoon's game. One feature that always lets you know how the team has performed is the cartoon football on the front page. When we win he raises his hands with joy. A defeat plunges him into despair while a draw always leaves him with a so-so expression on his footy face.

The paper's letters page has, over the years, provided a platform for fans to air their views, both positive and negative, on the progress of the team and the success of the paper and its volume of sales are intrinsically linked to the team's performance - when the team does well, the paper sells and vice versa.

Chapters of Sunderland AFC's history have been marked by the changing colour of the Football Echo. Originally published in pink the colour was changed towards the end of the 1912-13 season because of shortages of pink paper. The first edition printed on white paper appeared on the night of Sunderland's defeat by Aston Villa in the Cup Final at Crystal Palace and it was commonly said that the Footy Echo had turned white with shock.

After the First World War it was printed on blue paper and there were repeated requests by readers that it should return to its familiar pink. A promise was made that if the team won the Cup then the 'flush of victory' would be enough to turn the paper pink. The day came in 1937 and copies of the paper were specially printed in Portsmouth (the home of the Echo's sister paper), as well as in Sunderland. 20,000 copies were rushed from the south coast to London and the "Pink Un" was a sign to all that Sunderland had at last won the cup.

The paper turned blue with shock when the club was relegated in 1958 but returned to pink with promotion on April 18 1964. Relegation in 1970 made the paper blue again but the Footy Echo was able to go pink with delight when we won the cup in 1973. Many Sunderland fans remember being able to read the Sunderland Echo that night in London as copies were printed in Portsmouth and rushed up to London for the revellers to enjoy on their night out in the capital. Coincidentally 1973 saw the Sunderland Echo celebrating its centenary having been established in 1873. The Echo continues to keep fans informed of what's happening and has since 1996 been able to do it on the Internet.

Argus - the voice of the Echo

For the thirty years from 1950 until 1980 the voice of the Echo was Argus, Bill Butterfield. He joined the Echo as a 14-year-old odd-job boy and took up boxing just to familiarise himself with the sport. He ended up winning the North East Amateur title at 18 and perhaps could have had a future as a boxer but decided to follow his first love, journalism. After reporting for fifteen years on Newcastle and Gateshead games under the nom de plume "Novocastrian" he finally got the job he had always wanted - reporting on Sunderland. He took over both the job and the pen name "Argus" from Captain Jack Anderson in 1950 with his first game being a 1 - 1 home draw with Stoke City. As well as writing the football column he was also the paper's racing tipster, using the name "Spot White" and had one exceptional season when his selections were so successful that some bookmakers appealed to the Echo to discontinue its racing service because it was costing them so much.

He came from the old school of journalism where understatement and considered comment were the stock in trade rather than hype and sensationalism. His love of Sunderland Football Club would always come through in his match reports and he felt the disappointment of the relegation in 1958 as much as any fan.

One of the highlights of his career was the World Cup in 1966 when he went out of his way to make his fellow journalists from all over the world feel at home as they reported from Roker Park.

However his most treasured report was on the 1973 Cup Final. He had promised himself that he would not attend a cup final until Sunderland were there. Finally the day came and he was able to produce his most historic report. His verdict printed at the end of that report summed it up.

"They were going to Wembley to make it a cup final that everyone would remember. They did just that. They played Leeds United right out of it, with a display of attacking football which left United not only helpless but also beaten at the finish.

It was heroes all right through the side. Hughes, Tueart and Halom ran themselves to the point of exhaustion in going at the Leeds defence. But they never stopped, and even in those last few minutes when lungs must have been screaming for rest they were still going on. The midfield outfit from Kerr, Porterfield and Horswill was out of this world too, while the back four operation so well conducted by Watson and Pitt in the middle and Malone and Guthrie on the flank denied United the space for their sharp-shooters to get cracking and last but not least was the brilliant work of Montgomery, who made the game safe for Sunderland by two magnificent saves within split seconds of each other at the crucial stage. So the Cup comes back to Wearside with all the pride which goes with such a remarkable triumph."

His final game came in November 1980 when he was able to report a 3 - 2 home victory over Bristol Rovers and round off a great career. In recognition of his services the Echo also decided to retire the name "Argus" with Bill and so his successors have all reported with their own names as their by-lines.

1976-1977

Nightmare Number Three

"the Lads' brilliant never say die performances in the final run in had put us in the driving seat, avoid defeat in our final game and we were safe"

Bob Stokoe and Barry Siddall.

Bob Stokoe

When Bob Stokoe decided to retire from the manager's job in October, he brought an early end to a marvellous career at the Club. In just four years, he had brought more glory to Sunderland than there had been for the whole of the post-War era, clinching a Second Division championship as well as the FA Cup. Indeed, his Cup win ranks as perhaps the greatest achievement of any Sunderland manager. While his predecessors had delivered greater glory in the form of superb Championship wins, challenges for the double and - of course - an earlier FA Cup victory, none had started with a demoralised Second Division team and the reduced resources that second flight football brings with it. Stokoe returned to the Club for a second period as manager at the end of the 1986-87 season, when we were in need of a miracle to prevent a disastrous end to the McMenemy era. Sadly, on this occasion he was unable to pull off a miracle. But, his wondrous achievements in the 1970s earn him a place amongst the true heroes of Sunderland AFC's history. The 'messiah' tag so often applied to his managerial abilities is fully deserved.

During the close season, rumours began to surface that Bob Stokoe was suffering from health problems and that he was thinking of stepping down as Sunderland manager in order to take a break from the exhausting work schedule that the job demanded. For the fans, the prospect of starting life in the First Division without our messiah was a worrying one. Comparisons with our previous promotion in 1964, when Alan Brown had quit before a ball had been kicked in the First Division, sprung to mind. Everyone hoped that the rumours were not true, and that Bob was both well and planning to stay at the Club in order to guide us to a successful season in the top flight.

When the season kicked off - with a trip to Stoke City - Stokoe was indeed in the manager's seat, but the rumours about his ill health had been true, and the early games suggested that perhaps he did need some time off to convalesce. Our opening game ended in a respectable 0 - 0 draw, a result repeated in our first home match - against Leicester - three days later. A 2 - 2 draw in our third game, against Arsenal, was reasonable enough too, and three points from three games didn't seem too bad. However, the next three games did not go at all well. Defeats against Bristol City (4 - 1), Middlesbrough (2 - 1) and Manchester City (2 - 0) left us reeling at the wrong end of the table.

Unfortunately, performances did not improve. A 1 - 1 draw at West Ham increased our points tally to four from a possible fourteen, before consecutive home defeats followed, Everton and Villa both beating us 1 - 0. The latter game - on 16th October - was our fifth defeat in six games, but it took on an added significance when Bob Stokoe decided it was the end of the road for him as manager. His ill health was clearly taking its toll and, feeling had he had lost the ability to motivate the players, he resigned after the game.

Stokoe's decision brought to a premature to end the reign of one of the Club's greatest managers. It also left us without a manager during a crucial phase of our history. Having finally managed to end our exile in the Second Division, we were already racing certainties for an immediate return there. What's more, we were now faced with the prospect of needing a miracle to escape relegation, but without our messiah.

Ian MacFarlane was appointed caretaker manager, but he was faced with an almost impossible task. While results improved a little - his second game in charge saw us record our first League victory, a 2 - 1 win at Coventry - defeat was still the usual outcome when we played. In seven games under MacFarlane's direction, four were lost. What's more, with the free scoring Pop Robson having returned to West Ham before Stokoe's final game, the Lads were finding it hard to hit the net, and the man Stokoe had brought in to replace Robson - Bob Lee - was struggling to make an impact. With the Lads plummeting towards the Second Division, it was clear that a permanent manager needed to be brought in as quickly as possible. So, at the end of November, with the Lads some six points adrift of second bottom placed Spurs, Jimmy Adamson was appointed as manager. His brief was clear: to try to move heaven and earth during our remaining 26 League games in order to prevent an embarrassingly quick return to the second flight.

Unfortunately, the new manager got off to a nightmare start. An unhappy first month saw the Lads lose every single one of the games they played, including a 2 - 0 defeat at St James' Park a couple of days after Christmas. As if this wasn't bad enough, we didn't manage to score a single goal either, and the run continued into the New Year too, with our first three League games of 1977 seeing us both lose and fail to score. When the losing run finally ended - with a couple of draws against Stoke and Arsenal - the result was inevitably 0 - 0. Indeed, it was not until February 11th that one of Adamson's teams managed to score a goal, in a game that also marked his first win as Sunderland manager, a 1 - 0 home victory against Bristol City. The match was his tenth League fixture in charge and ended the worst period of form in the Club's history: ten straight games without a goal. What's more, this run overlapped a nine game losing streak too. With just 16 games remaining, it looked like the Lads had left it all too late.

Yet, the Bristol City fixture marked a real turning point. Having struggled for so long to score a goal, Mel Holden's winner against Bristol seemed to lift a mammoth weight off the Lads' shoulders. All of a sudden, the goals started flying in! Adamson's first victory was followed a week later by his second, an amazing 4 - 0 win at home to Middlesbrough, Holden, Lee, Arnott and Towers grabbing the goals. But, better was still to come. A few days after the 'Boro victory, West Brom visited Roker Park. The Lads ran riot; Lee hit a hat-trick, his strike partner Holden managed to grab one, and two emerging youngsters - Elliott and Rowell - also scored a goal each. The match ended 6 - 1! Astonishingly, there was still better to come. Our next match - our fourth home game in a row - was against West Ham. In a scintillating performance, we ripped the Hammers apart. Two each from Holden and Rowell, one from Lee and a screamer from Bobby Kerr secured a 6 - 0 victory. After going ten games without a goal, we had now scored seventeen in just four matches.

Shaun Elliott v Everton.

Jimmy Adamson

To say that Jimmy Adamson took over the reigns at Roker Park with the team in a bit of a state is an understatement. They were staring instant relegation in the face. What's more, they weren't even making a fight of it. After a rocky opening spell, Adamson dramatically turned events and performances around. A run of nine consecutive defeats was halted on 22nd January 1977, and Sunderland then went on one of the most brilliant fightbacks seen in modern day football. In the last 19 games of the season, we lost only three times, and dished out some memorable thrashings. However, Adamson was unable to work the miracle required to keep us up and, after failing to produce an instant return to the top flight in his first full season in charge, he left for Leeds United early in the 1978-79 campaign, where he replaced the legendary Jock Stein.

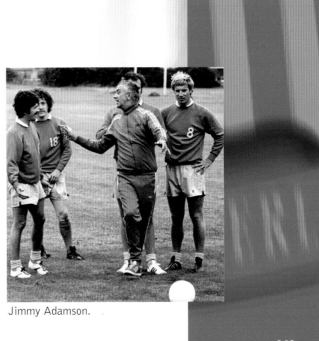

Jimmy Adamson.

Mel Holden v Everton.

Cheated?

After our dramatic last day relegation, there was much sympathy for the turn of events that had led to Coventry and Bristol City's tense relegation dog fight becoming almost a stroll in the park. While there was no way of proving that the two teams had deliberately stopped trying once our result was known, or that the kick off had been deliberately delayed to gain advantage, the national media had much sympathy for us. The circumstances of our relegation were, to say the least, controversial, and attracted much attention. Indeed, one Oxford don even decided to use philosophical analysis to investigate whether or not we had been unfairly treated. The results of his labours suggested we had not deliberately been mistreated. However, few Sunderland fans would have agreed with his conclusions; in this instance, the theory did not seem to match the reality.

Suddenly, we had become the team to watch, and escaping relegation no longer seemed an impossibility. Sure it would be a difficult task, but with the Lads in red hot form, it was no pipe dream. Although the run could never have continued in this vein - Championship challengers Manchester City beat us 1 - 0 four days after the West Ham game - the good form continued. Significantly, the Lads became hard to beat, with a mixture of draws and wins racking up the points needed to give us a chance of escaping the drop. Our new resolve was illustrated over the Easter period, when the Lads faced three tough games, against Newcastle, Leeds and Manchester United. The Good Friday game with Newcastle, who were riding high in the table, ended 2 - 2, a result followed the next day with an impressive 1 - 1 draw at Elland Road. The best result, however, came with the visit of Manchester United on Easter Monday, the Lads beating them 2 - 1, goals from Towers and Arnott bringing delight to the faces of the crowd.

A week after the Manchester United game, we faced a crucial six pointer at relegation rivals Spurs. A battling performance saw the game finish 1 - 1, an important away point for the Lads, which was followed by another 1 - 1 draw, against Derby, and a crucial 3 - 2 win at another of the form teams, West Brom. Having been all but relegated in early February, the amazing turnaround meant that, with three games left, we still had a chance of staying up.

It got better. We defeated Birmingham City 1 - 0 at home, with the Brummies' wonder-kid Trevor Francis missing a sitter at the Roker End. There were now two away games left, and the first saw Sunderland head for East Anglia and Norwich City. At Carrow Road, the 12,000 strong travelling Roker Roar watched on in horror as the Canaries took a two-goal lead. We were dead and buried... relegation had been sealed. But, oh no we weren't! With Sunderland fans streaming out of the ground, we scored... the early leavers came running back. With supporters cramming into any cubby hole they could find in order to snatch a view of the game, the Lads equalised and the place went ballistic! Half the crowd exploded in joy... survival was still on the cards!

By some sort of miracle, the Lads' brilliant never say die performances in the final run in had put us in the driving seat. It was now a simple process, avoid defeat in our final game and we were safe. We could even afford to lose the match if the game between our two relegation rivals - Coventry and Bristol City - produced a winner. The only combination that could send us down was a Sunderland defeat and a draw at Coventry. At the final hurdle, the odds were in our favour.

The date was 19th May, 1977. With Spurs and Stoke already relegated, three teams were competing to avoid finishing in the third relegation place: Bristol City, Coventry and ourselves. With all three teams on 34 points, only goal difference was separating them, but we were above both our rivals on this count and, consequently, had the most realistic chance of survival.

We travelled to Everton full of hope, and around 10,000 of our fans packed a crowd of 36,075 at Goodison Park. The atmosphere was electric. The performance, however, wasn't. After displaying strong form throughout the final stages of the campaign, nerves got the better of the Lads, and we lost 2 - 0.

But, defeat didn't mean we were down. With Coventry and Bristol City playing each other, we just needed one of the teams to emerge from that game victorious in order to guarantee our survival.

Unfortunately, despite a plea for both games to kick off at the same time, the game in Coventry was mysteriously delayed by some fifteen minutes due to 'traffic problems'. This meant that when our game finished, Coventry and Bristol were only half-an-hour into the second half of their game, which was at a delicately balanced 2 - 2. With both teams desperate for survival, a real battle had been taking place, the game played at a tremendous pace. Yet, astonishingly, the result of our game was announced over the tannoy. Both now knew they were safe if the game remained as it was, and an embarrassing quarter-of-an-hour of distinctly uncompetitive football followed. When the final whistle blew Coventry and Bristol City celebrated, while, after an agonising fifteen minute wait, we went home bitterly angry at the injustice of the outcome, and saddened by the brevity of our stay in the First Division.

Hundreds of letters of complaint flooded into the footballing authorities, and Alan Hardaker, who had led the investigation into our illegal payments in 1957, sent a letter from the Football League reprimanding Coventry for their actions. But, there was no stern punishment for their misdemeanours, no investigation into the affair, and no escape route for the Lads. It all seemed so unfair.

To make matters worse, it all came after just one season at the top. In the 1960s, we had managed a six season stay in the First Division, but perpetual relegation battles illustrated the ground we had lost following the 1958 relegation. With our stay in the 1970s being as brief as it possibly could have been, it seemed - Cup win notwithstanding - the gap between ourselves and the best had, sadly, lengthened.

Lost Opportunity

Relegation after just one season in the top flight was a bitter blow. Not only did it suggest we were losing pace with the games' leaders, it also underlined our failure to build on the 1973 Cup win. The team that had beaten Leeds to lift the Cup undoubtedly contained some great players and was led by a great manager. But, after a number of near misses, promotion, perhaps, came too late for the Cup team. By the time our third relegation was sealed - just four years after the Cup win - few of the Wembley heroes remained at the Club. Some, such as Tueart, Horswill and Watson had left for more successful clubs in order to further their careers. Others - such as Pitt and Porterfield - had seen their Sunderland careers brought to an end by injury. Two of the big stars of that day - Monty and Stokoe - had left the Club during our poor run of form early in the 1976-77 season. In fact, the only man on the field in our final game at Everton who had also starred at Wembley was our captain, Bobby Kerr. While there were some great players in the new line up too, it was a tragedy that not even a watered down version of the Cup winning team got the chance to play together in football's top flight.

Shaun Elliott.

1977-1978
Sinking Feeling

Jeff Clarke.

"as the sinking feeling set in, attendances began to slip"

Chaos

On 14th January, 1978, we travelled to Brisbane Road, the home of Leyton Orient. The game ended 2 - 2 - Rowell and Clarke getting our goals - and there were a number of unusual talking points after the game. Firstly, the crowd - a tiny 6,737 - included a number of West Ham United hooligans intent on causing a bit of bother, but fortunately, they were dealt with. Then, the referee ordered Sunderland goalkeeper Barry Siddall to change his goalkeeper's top, because the red kit he wore clashed with the home side's strip. Then, once the game had managed to get in its stride, a dog ran on the pitch and had to be ushered off! But, the most famous incident was linked to events that were well and truly an official part of the match. Sunderland were awarded a penalty, and for the one and only time in his 'competitive' career, Gary Rowell missed.

While the 1976-77 season had produced one of the most dramatic climaxes in the Club's history, its ultimately unsuccessful conclusion gave us what nobody wanted: yet more Second Division football. With the fans now more than used to such fare, early attendances did not suffer too badly, and the real impact came on the playing side. Firstly, in a scenario much like the one that had seen Dave Watson leave two seasons earlier, Tony Towers, who had broken into the England squad while at the Club, left for pastures new during the close season, joining First Division Birmingham City for £140,000. Secondly, after the high jinx of our top flight run in, the players found it hard to lift themselves for early season games against run of the mill teams.

Indeed, just as our two previous spells in the Second Division had done, we began our third visit to the second flight with a defeat, Hull City beating us 3 - 0. At Roker Park three days later we compensated for this. With Wilf Rostron, the man brought in to replace Towers, making his debut, we beat Burnley 3 - 0 before a 31,500 crowd. However, it proved to be an all too brief high point. Over the next eight weeks, the Lads struggled dismally, finding it almost impossible to break down their opponents. In the League, a series of draws gave way to a disappointing mix of draws and poor defeats. Against teams such as Orient we could only manage to scrape a point, while the better teams, such as Brighton, Bolton and Southampton, had no trouble beating us. In the League Cup, meanwhile, we surrendered to Middlesbrough in our first game. Indeed, following our first week victory against Burnley on 23rd August, the Lads did not manage another win - in any competition - until October 15th, when Millwall were beaten 2 - 0. It was not what the fans had been looking for, and as the sinking feeling set in, attendances began to slip.

Yet, in an echo of the previous campaign, once the Lads had ended their winless run, they began to beat all before them. Victory over Millwall was followed by good wins against Mansfield (2 - 1) and Oldham (3 - 1), and after a 3 - 3 draw at Fulham, Bristol Rovers were hammered 5 - 1. It was an amazing turnaround, but it did not last. Soon, the Lads were back to their indifferent form, with a run of draws giving way to a run of defeats. Indeed, December even began with a three game losing streak, Charlton, Spurs and, frustratingly, Bristol Rovers all beating us. The 5 - 1 victory over Rovers had marked the end of a brief purple patch, rather than the rediscovery of our form, and it was six weeks before we managed another victory, a 2 - 1 win at home to Blackpool on Boxing Day.

Incredibly, Bristol Rovers also put us out of the FA Cup - beating us 1 - 0 at Roker Park in early January - underlining our frustrating inconsistency. This was also highlighted by our League form during the early part of the New Year, a good 2 - 0 win at home to Hull being followed by that Cup exit and a weak draw at Orient. Yet, the real indicator of this problem came at the end of the month, when a superb 5 - 1 thrashing of Sheffield United at Roker Park was followed, a week later, by a 5 - 2 defeat at Cardiff City. It seemed that the Lads could turn it on when they really wanted to, but that too often the fighting spirit just wasn't there.

Just as after the 5 - 1 victory over Bristol Rovers, it was some time before the Lads managed another win. Having beaten Sheffield United 5 - 1 on 21st January, the fans had to wait until 18th March for another win, when Mansfield were beaten 1 - 0 at Roker in front of a minuscule 14,033 crowd.

Following this, it was another five games before we managed a further win. However, this time the Lads built on their success. The 1 - 0 win at home to Stoke - in front of just 11,161 - marked the start of a strong finish. It was followed by 3 - 1 victories against Luton and Notts County and, after a defeat against Millwall, further good victories in our final two games, Spurs being beaten 3 - 2 and Charlton beaten 3 - 0.

The winning run was enough to lift us to sixth position. While this seemed reasonable enough, it was a far weaker position than it might sound. We were way off the promotion pace. In a tight finish at the top, the promoted teams - Bolton, Southampton and Spurs - were separated by just two points, but we were a massive twelve points behind the team in third place: Spurs. In truth, our season had failed to get going, and there were few signs of the stunning form that had lit up the end of the relegation season. The widely expected promotion campaign did not materialise - we didn't even push the front runners - and in the Cups we were dismal. The fans were already indicating that they had had enough, and Adamson would have to produce something much better if he was to keep them - and the board - happy.

Barry Siddall stretching for the ball.

Flying Pig

An ever present during the season was goalkeeper Barry Siddall. Signed by Bob Stokoe in his final weeks as manager, Siddall made his debut in Stokoe's final game in charge, replacing Jimmy Montgomery in goal. Siddall remained in the number 1 shirt for the rest of the 1976-77 season, making 36 League and Cup appearances. Amazingly, he also played in all but two of our League and Cup games in the 1978-79 season too and, consequently, strung together an impressive run of 101 consecutive League, League Cup and FA Cup appearances. However, his position as Sunderland's number 1 was threatened following the arrival of Chris Turner at the start of 1979-80 season, and the two men battled for the keeper's shirt over the next three seasons.

A great favourite with the fans, his stocky build and great shot stopping ability led to him being nicknamed 'the flying pig', possibly the most fantastic sobriquet a Sunderland player has ever earned! Barry left the Club in August 1982, joining Port Vale, having made 167 League appearances, and 20 League Cup and FA Cup appearances.

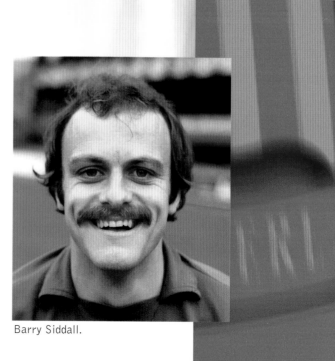

Barry Siddall.

1978-1979
As Close As It Gets

"Another tense, last day drama"

Mick Henderson.

Nine Man Win

When Sunderland travelled to Burnley in late September, we were quickly up against the odds. Joe Bolton and Mick Henderson both received their marching orders in the first half and the travelling Roker Roar wondered how we would cope with just nine men in the second half. They needn't have worried. It is often said that football is as much about attitude as ability, and this was the perfect example of determination overcoming all the odds. The Lads played like their lives depended on the result and an early penalty, converted by Gary Rowell, had the travelling hordes in near hysteria. When Rowell scored again, their cheers lifted the roof off. There were an anxious last few minutes, when Burnley pulled one back, but we held on to secure a superb 2 - 1 win.

With patience wearing thin on Wearside, Adamson knew his team had to start performing. It was, by recent standards, a weak Second Division that faced us, for there were no big clubs such as Manchester United or Tottenham Hotspur to deal with this time, nor were there any of the smaller clubs who had started to hit it big, such as Southampton, who had romped to promotion the previous season after lifting the FA Cup in 1976. Indeed, Sunderland were clearly the biggest club in the division, with Newcastle and West Ham being the only other outfits with big reputations. There could, then, be no excuses for failing to challenge for promotion.

We got off to a reasonable, but shaky, start. At home, there were good wins against Charlton, Preston and West Ham - along with a draw against Fulham - but away from home we were poor, losing at Orient and Brighton and drawing at Palace. We did, however, triumph against the odds at Turf Moor, when we managed to beat Burnley 2 - 1 with just nine men. There were no real questions about our home form, but - while the away form was far from disastrous - we needed to do better on our travels if promotion was to be achieved.

October, however, began with our third away defeat of the season - Sheffield United beating us 3 - 2. We then scraped a 1 - 1 draw at home to Second Division new boys Newcastle, our substitute, Greenwood, scoring the goal, before beating Millwall 3 - 2. The latter game saw local boy Gary Rowell score two goals, bringing his total for the season to seven in eleven games. It also marked the end of Jimmy Adamson's period as Sunderland manager. After a reasonable start to the season, he resigned from the post on 25th October, moving to Leeds United. With our season poised in the balance during a crucial early phase, Dave Merrington took over as caretaker manager.

Unfortunately, his first home game in charge saw us suffer our first League defeat at Roker, promotion rivals Stoke beating us 1 - 0. After this, though, performances improved, the Lads beating Preston (3 - 1) and Luton (3 - 0) away, and thrashing Bristol Rovers 5 - 0 at home. But, after eight games in charge, Merrington made way for Billy Elliott, who was given the task of steering the ship for the remainder of the season.

Like Merrington, Elliott did not get off to a winning start. Indeed, it was some six League games until he produced a win in the Second Division, when Burnley were beaten 3 - 1 in early February. Before that, however, Everton were put to the sword in the FA Cup, the Lads beating them 2 - 1 at home in the third round; if only that result had come on the last day of the 1976-77 season! Although Burnley ended our interest in the next round, the Cup win lifted the Lads, and following Elliott's first League win, we went on a glorious run.

A week after beating Burnley in the League, we travelled to London to play West Ham, and came away with a point following a dramatic 3 - 3 draw. A fortnight later, following our Cup exit, we went to St James', to meet Newcastle, and thrashed them 4 - 1, Rowell scoring a hat-trick! This superb result was followed by further victories, against Millwall, Wrexham and Oldham. Although the winning run was interrupted by a disappointing 2 - 1 reverse at home to promotion chasing Crystal Palace, we were soon back on track, with consecutive victories against Orient, Stoke and Luton.

After struggling for so long to achieve a win, Elliott had now delivered eight in nine games. Moreover, this brilliant run had also catapulted us up the table, our points total being of a sufficient level to make promotion a realistic goal.

Indeed, Elliott continued to build on this run. A 0 - 0 draw at Bristol Rovers was followed by a 3 - 0 win at Notts County and a 2 - 1 win at Leicester. The table was now looking particularly favourable, and everyone expected our position to be further strengthened after the visit of relegation threatened Blackburn. The disappointing 1 - 0 defeat that followed was a real blow, but the Lads picked themselves up, beating Cambridge United 2 - 0 to put us within one win of top place. With another relegation threatened team, Sheffield United, visiting for a midweek game, we could move into pole position if we beat them by four goals. It was asking a lot, but the Lads turned on the magic. A hat-trick from Rostron - and a last minute penalty save from Siddall - powered us to a famous 6 - 2 win.

Now, we were in the driving seat. Surely, it was felt, with just two games left, and with the Lads in such fine form, promotion would be achieved. Sunderland fans should have known better. Disaster struck when our next game - a home match with mid-table Cardiff - ended in a 2 - 1 defeat. With the top of the table incredibly tight, all of a sudden we were no longer masters of our own fate. Even a win in our final game, at Wrexham, would not guarantee promotion. Instead, we needed one of our rivals - Crystal Palace, Brighton or Stoke - to slip up. Another tense, last day drama had been set up. At Wrexham, the Lads did what they needed too, beating the Welshmen 2 - 1. At the final whistle, fans spilled on to the pitch to celebrate promotion, only to hear the tannoy announce that results elsewhere had not gone in our favour.

It was gutting. We finished just one point off second and third place, and just two points behind champions Crystal Palace. Surprisingly, given our early season problems, it was our home form that had let us down, losing five, whilst away from Roker we succumbed only four times. Had we won just one of those games we lost - or even just drawn the games against Brighton or Stoke - promotion would have been ours.

Rowell becomes a Legend

While the season ultimately ended in disappointment, this was partially compensated for by one of the Club's most historic victories. On 24th February we scored a famous victory at St James' Park that is still talked about today. Just six minutes into the game, we took the lead, Gary Rowell converting a Jeff Clarke free-kick. Twenty minutes later, Arnott set Rowell free, and he beat the keeper to make it 2 - 0. Just before half-time, it looked like Bob Lee had made it 3 - 0, but his goal was disallowed.

In the second-half, Newcastle came out fighting, and within five minutes had pulled one back. However, shortly afterwards, Rowell completed his hat-trick, converting a penalty to all but end the Mags' hopes of getting back into the game. Entwhistle then completed the rout, making it 4 - 1 at the final whistle.

Beating the Mags 4 - 1 was glorious enough in itself, but to do it at St James' and, crucially, to see them demolished by a hat-trick from a 21 year old man who was Sunderland born and bred, was just sweet! It was our greatest derby victory since the 9 - 1 demolition in the 1908-09 season.

Gary Rowell, hat-trick hero, Sunderland v Newcastle 1979.

1979-1980
Happy One Hundred

"it was imperative that we didn't slip up again"

Ken Knighton

Ken Knighton played for six clubs during his professional career: Wolverhampton Wanderers, Oldham Athletic, Preston North End, Blackburn Rovers, Hull City and Sheffield Wednesday, making some 350 appearances. During this time, he played under some great managers, including Stan Cullis, Terry Neill and Tommy Docherty. Shortly after his playing career ended, in January 1976, he arrived at Roker Park as a coach, Jimmy Adamson bringing him to the Club in the summer of 1978. Events moved quickly after this, and within a year he was manager himself.

Knighton must have learnt something under his old mentors, for his first season as Sunderland manager brought a glorious promotion - and some great football - to Roker Park. However, during the following season, his managerial career was brought to a somewhat premature end. Life was tougher in the First Division, and with Sunderland struggling a little, Knighton clashed with new Chairman Tom Cowie. There could only be one winner, and four games before then end of his second season, Knighton was sacked.

Many felt it was a harsh act, for Knighton was a promising young manager who had delivered promotion at the first time of asking, a task that had been beyond Brown, Adamson and even Stokoe. What's more, his team had played some good football too. But, Cowie was determined to stamp his authority on the Club, and Knighton was on his way.

Our final season of the 1970s marked a real milestone in the Club's history: it was our one hundredth year as a football club. Much had happened since the early days of James Allan's Sunderland and District Teachers' Association Football Club, and special events were planned to celebrate our centenary. Chief amongst these was a 'testimonial' match for the Club itself, the Lads taking on an 'England XI' in a specially arranged floodlit game on 7th November. While the match - which featured many Newcastle and Middlesbrough players on the opposing team - was great fun, despite ending in a 2 - 0 defeat, everyone connected with the Club was hoping that the real celebrations would come at the end of the season, with the Lads securing promotion to the First Division.

Before the new campaign began, however, there were some important changes at the Club. Ken Knighton replaced Billy Elliott as manager, and Frank Clark had been lured from Nottingham Forest as his assistant. This gave us one of the youngest managerial teams in the country, and they began their first season in charge with all guns blazing. Pop Robson was quickly brought back to the Club to add fire power up front, and goalkeeper Chris Turner was signed too. While Knighton's opening game - at Chelsea - ended in a 0 - 0 draw, the next two games saw two victories, Birmingham and Fulham being beaten at Roker Park. Further victories followed, including a 4 - 0 thrashing of Charlton, where new signing John Hawley smashed a hat-trick on his debut.

However, while we were electric at home, away we were proving easy to beat, slumping to three defeats in our first five matches. This set the pattern for much of the early season, October and November seeing us win all of our home League games and lose all of our away League games. During this period the League Cup also provided a little glory, with Newcastle beaten 7 - 6 on penalties after a 4 - 4 aggregate draw, and Manchester City beaten too, before West Ham ended our interest in the fourth round.

In December, Knighton managed to turn the away form around, picking up a draw at Watford and a win at Fulham, although we did drop a point at home to Wrexham on Boxing Day. The net result was that we entered the New Year well placed for promotion. What's more, Knighton had continued to strengthen his squad during the campaign. Midfield maestro Stan Cummins had joined us in November, a signing followed in December by the capture of Argentine Claudio Marangoni, whose expensive transfer was big news.

But, we did not get off to a great start in 1980. On New Year's Day, the Mags beat us 3 - 1, and four days later, Bolton knocked us out of the FA Cup in a third round tie played at Roker Park. Fortunately, this was little more than a blip. Oldham were thrashed 4 - 2 in our next home game and, after a 3 - 3 draw at Cambridge, Burnley were thrashed 5 - 0, Cummins scoring four. Although this was followed by a poor 1 - 0 defeat at Preston, the Lads dug in for the final run and were not defeated again for the remainder of the season.

With competition at the top tough, a good winning run in was needed and, after an indifferent spell, a 4 - 0 win at Charlton got the Lads going again. Four of our next five matches were won, including a 1 - 0 win at home to Newcastle, where Stan Cummins hit the winner. The run put us in with a real chance of promotion, but once again, nerves began to affect the Lads. With just five games left, a steady hand was needed, but draws against two of the division's weaker sides - Orient and Bristol Rovers - put everyone on tenterhooks again.

A good win was needed to lift the spirits, and the Lads took a hard look at themselves and produced a superb performance at home to Watford, thrashing them 5 - 0, Pop Robson and Shaun Elliott scoring two each.

With just two games left, four teams were contesting the three promotion places: ourselves, Leicester, Chelsea and Birmingham. It was imperative that we didn't slip up again, but in a repeat of the previous season's fiasco, we failed to give our best performance in our penultimate game, which was once again against Cardiff. At least this time we didn't lose, but the 1 - 1 draw meant it all hung on a re-arranged game that would take place after the FA Cup final.

Our opponents for that fixture were West Ham United, and with the rest of the season's fixtures completed, we knew exactly what we had to do. Leicester were already going up as champions, with 55 points, while Birmingham and Chelsea stood in second and third with 53 points. We were fourth with 52 points, but had a better goal difference than either of the two teams above us. All this meant that a draw would be enough to see us promoted. The Hammers, who had just won the FA Cup, were no match for the Lads on the day, and we ripped them apart. A 2 - 0 win put us in second place and guaranteed promotion to the First Division! It was the perfect way to end our centenary season.

1979-80 team celebrate promotion after the game with West Ham.

Cup Comes Back to Roker Park

There is no doubting the game of the season: it was our final match. The game had been postponed twice, firstly because of bad weather, and then because of West Ham's continuing involvement in the FA Cup. This meant that when the game took place, West Ham had already defied the odds to beat Arsenal in the FA Cup final, and Sunderland were in need of just one point to clinch promotion.

Everything was set up for a classic and a full house was guaranteed. Indeed, some 47,129 fans crammed into the ground for the game, and an estimated 7,000 were locked outside. West Ham were given a warm reception as they paraded the Cup before the game, but once it kicked off, everyone was willing a Sunderland victory. Goals from Kevin Arnott and Stan Cummins won the day. The second was a beauty, crashed in from 20 yards at the Roker End.

With our promotion rivals having already completed their fixtures, we knew the result was enough to guarantee promotion, and the partying began straight away! It is hard to imagine a better end to the season…

Kevin Arnott.

1980·81	17th in First Division.
1981·82	Alan Durban becomes Manager. 19th in First Division.
1982·83	16th in First Division.
1983·84	Len Ashurst becomes Manager. 13th in First Division.
1984·85	Runners-Up in League Cup. Relegated to Second Division.
1985·86	Lawrie McMenemy becomes Manager. 18th in Second Division.
1986·87	Relegated to Third Division for the first time in history.
1987·88	Denis Smith becomes Manager. Champions of Third Division.
1988·89	11th in Second Division.
1989·90	6th in Second Division. Promoted via Play-Offs.

The 1980's - from here to obscurity, and back!

Some decades of Sunderland's history tell of heroic achievements. Some tell of FA Cup glory. Others relate tales of Championship success and teams that were the envy of all in football. The 1980s is most definitely not one of those decades.

We began the decade in the top division of English football and ended with promotion to it, but what we suffered in between was a chastening experience for all concerned with Sunderland AFC. This was a decade where, yet again, managers would come and go with almost alarming regularity and where the fortunes of the side would dip from the relatively heady heights of a Milk Cup Final appearance to the embarrassment of our only ever season in the Third Division of the Football League.

The decade tells a story of hope, despair, utter desolation, optimism, and finally extreme good fortune. The decade began with Sunderland newly promoted back into the First Division, and determined to stay there longer than the solitary season of their previous adventure a few years earlier. We would indeed remain in the top flight - for five seasons - but Sunderland supporters would begin to get used to the nerve wracking last game battle to stay up.

Managerial approaches would change throughout the ten years, from Alan Durban's belief in youth, through Lawrie McMenemy's disastrously misplaced faith in experience, right through to the honest and forthright approach of Denis Smith.

If supporting Sunderland is a roller-coaster ride, then this decade sums it all up. The highs are not particularly lofty, but the lows plumb the depths of our emotions.

A ROLLER-COASTER

Ride

1 9 8 0 · 1 9 9 0

1980-1981
Back in the Big Time

"we lived to fight another First Division day"

Stan Cummins, Sunderland v Everton.

Stan Cummins

Born in Ferryhill, Cummins started his career with Middlesbrough before a £300,000 transfer to Roker Park in November 1979. Over the next four seasons he totted up 145 League and Cup appearances for Sunderland, scoring many great goals.

The diminutive striker carried the burden of Jack Charlton's claim that he would be the first £1m footballer, but despite not reaching those heady heights he was always a crowd pleaser with a delightful touch and an eye for goal.

In July 1983, an administrative error over the renewal of his contract allowed him to join Crystal Palace, much to the fans' disappointment. He did return to Sunderland briefly a couple of seasons later, but never really rediscovered his original form.

Stan also enjoyed a few successful seasons in the North American Soccer League, first with Seattle Sounders and then with Minnesota Strikers.

The 1980-81 campaign started full of hope and optimism following the previous season's promotion. On a glorious August afternoon, Everton, who played a major role in the relegation of 1977, were the visitors to Roker Park. A great display saw Sunderland race to a 3 - 1 victory, with goals from John Hawley, Stan Cummins and an Everton own goal.

Amazingly, things got even better four days later. A John Hawley hat-trick at Maine Road helped the Lads to thump Manchester City 4 - 0 and at the end of the night Sunderland sat proudly, albeit briefly, at the top of the First Division. By the time Southampton came to Roker Park on 23rd August, we had gone 22 games on Wearside without defeat, and were unbeaten in 16 league matches. However, an inspired performance by a certain Kevin Keegan saw the record shattered and we went down 2 - 1.

Following this, the first cup campaign of the season was over virtually before it started, when Stockport disappointingly dumped us out of the League Cup, beating us 2 - 1 on Wearside after a 1 - 1 draw at Edgeley Park. However, the Lads then lost only one game in five - albeit a third successive home defeat - in a sequence that saw us hammer Leeds United 4 - 1, with Pop Robson scoring twice. That game also saw the first goal from Gary Rowell in almost 18 months.

At this early stage of the season, we were more than holding our own, and despite a 4 - 0 thrashing at Aston Villa, covered by Match of the Day, things were looking up - or so we thought! Then the inevitable happened: we collapsed. From 21st October until 27th December, we played thirteen games and won only two. Trouble was once again looming on the horizon.

There were a number of key events during this period. The 8th November was something of milestone on Wearside. The match with Stoke City was our 2,500th game in the top flight for Sunderland. Almost typically, the game ended as a 0 - 0 bore draw. Four days later, the Sunderland career of Claudio Marangoni came to an end. His brief appearance in the 2 - 0 defeat of Manchester City was the last that the Roker Roar would see of him. Marangoni returned to Argentina having failed to make the impact that had been hoped for. Ironically, he prospered in his home country, and went on to star for Argentina at International level. Finally, on 20th December 1980, Rob Hindmarch captained Sunderland at the City Ground at the tender age of 19. It was not, though, the best of occasions for him: Nottingham Forest ran out 3 - 1 winners, with a Gary Rowell goal our only consolation.

Early in the New Year, on 31st January 1981, Sunderland AFC was saddened to hear of the death of former fans' favourite Mel Holden. During his time with the Club he had been a loyal servant to Sunderland, and formed an effective partnership with Bob Lee. Mel died from Multiple Sclerosis in Preston General Hospital at the tragically young age of 26. The oft-heard saying amongst the Roker legions was 'Mel rules the Skies' - let's hope it's true.

As winter turned to spring, matters on the pitch showed no real signs of improvement. By 11th April, Sunderland had lost 19 out of 38 games. Something, or rather someone, had to give. Ken Knighton and Frank Clark were sacked, after disputes with Chairman Tom Cowie. Once again, past glories counted for nothing, as the heroes of the previous season's thrilling promotion push were unceremoniously shown the door. The timing of the dismissals was questioned by many, but Mick Docherty was installed as caretaker manager until the end of the season. He had four games to save us from another immediate return to the Second Division - and he did it.

Essentially, Sunderland had to win their two remaining home games to ensure safety, but, as ever, we went about it the hard way. Against Birmingham City at Roker Park, Tom Ritchie netted a hat trick, for a relatively straight forward 3 - 0 victory... then we panicked. Beaten by West Brom at the Hawthorns, it seemed that total disaster had struck in the final home game with Brighton. A last minute goal gave the visitors victory - and left Sunderland facing the daunting task of winning at Anfield to make sure of safety. Liverpool were easily the best team in England, having won the Championship in 1978-79 and 1979-80. They were also one of the best teams in Europe, having progressed to the final of the European Cup, a game they would eventually win later in the month. In short, it looked like we were doomed. Astonishingly, a 1 - 0 win saved us from the drop, and we lived to fight another First Division day.

1980-81 Sunderland team.

Down to the Wire

For Sunderland fans, last game cliffhangers are almost the norm, but few will forget the classic result from this season. Having only been back in the top flight for one season, the Lads were faced with the prospect of needing to win at Anfield to stay in Division One.

At the time, Liverpool were sweeping everything in front of them. Sunderland had sacked their manager a few games earlier and had lost the week before at home to Brighton. Surely, this was to prove just too much for a young Sunderland side?

Rumours and predictions flew around Wearside as the big game drew near. Liverpool manager Bob Paisley was from Hetton, so he would never let us be relegated. Liverpool were a big club like Sunderland, and big clubs always looked after each other. Liverpool liked the money that our fans brought when they visited in their thousands. Liverpool were still embarrassed at having relegated Sunderland in 1970. All, of course, absolute rubbish.

In reality, the match turned out to be a case of 'the great escape'. Sunderland performed way above expectation, Liverpool somewhat below. Stan Cummins scored the only goal and that was that. We had won, we had escaped the drop, and secretly Liverpool probably were quite happy that we would be visiting them again next season!

Tom Ritchie.

1981-1982
Relegation Dog Fight

"Anyone seeking entertainment should go to a circus"

Alan Durban

Alan Durban.

Champion Challenge

Our first home League game of the season was a visit from reigning Champions Aston Villa. The match would be a real test of new manager Alan Durban's approach and a gripping encounter occurred. The Lads began pounding the Villa goal from kick off and only some strong tackling from the visitors kept the score sheet blank in the opening stages. However, after failing to score from their early raids on the Villa goal, the Lads ran out of steam a little. Mid-way through the first half Donovan put the ball past an advancing Turner to make it 1 - 0 to the visitors.

We responded quickly, winning two corners in succession. Both were well taken by Munro, but marvellous goalkeeping from Rimmer prevented what appeared to be two certain goals. It was clear that Durban had been working on set pieces and eight minutes before the break the Lads got their reward, a clever free kick giving Ritchie the space needed to smash an equaliser into the roof of the net.

Just three minutes after the break, the Lads took the lead. Again the goal came from a set piece, Ritchie heading Buckley's free-kick towards goal, and Rowell heading in following a good stop from Rimmer. No more goals were scored, and the match ended 2 - 1 to Sunderland.

It was an excellent display, and The Guardian were particularly impressed, concluding 'on the evidence of this determined, impressively organised performance by Alan Durban's team, the champions will be only one of many sides to leave Roker Park without a point this season.' Sadly, this was not quite to be the case, but a great opening home game had shown what the Lads could do when they played at their best.

Despite our heroic escape from relegation under his charge, temporary manager Mick Docherty did not last long in the Roker Park hot seat. He was replaced during the summer by Stoke City manager Alan Durban, who soon began the task of restructuring the team. One of his first acts was to sign a promising young Scottish striker by the name of Ally McCoist, who joined for £350,000 from St Johnstone, a big fee at the time for an unproven youngster. Another Scot, Ian Munro, was added to the books, but crowd favourites Kevin Arnott and Joe Bolton both departed for pastures new, along with players such as John Hawley, Ian Bowyer and Steve Whitworth. This was also the season that saw the emergence of two of Sunderland's brightest young stars of the decade, Nick Pickering and Barry Venison, while the experienced Jeff Clarke was made Club captain.

In a rule change that was designed to bring about more attacking play at a time when attendances throughout football were starting to fall, the Football League introduced three points for a win. However, the message of entertaining football seemed to pass Sunderland by, as the team struggled from the start and had real problems scoring goals. Maybe a manager who had suggested that those seeking entertainment should go to a circus had something to do with it!

Yet, the season started brightly. The fixture list had produced a real tough test in our first home game, with reigning Champions Aston Villa providing the opposition, but the Lads were equal to the task, running out deserved winners. It was, though, very much a false dawn. Sunderland failed to win any more of their opening fourteen matches, a dreadful sequence that included a 5 - 1 home thrashing at the hands of Manchester United, who included Bryan Robson for the first time following his British record £1.5 million move from West Bromwich Albion.

In a miserable season, the Cups were as depressing as the League. Rotherham provided the early opposition in both the League and FA Cups and were duly despatched. However, that was as far as our progress went, with Crystal Palace and Liverpool both running out winners at Roker Park in the League and FA Cup respectively. Performances did pick up slightly after the FA Cup exit though, when a run of three wins in six games made our position look a little more respectable. Yet, this was followed by another awful run of one victory in twelve and Sunderland were once again plummeting towards the foot of the table. It started to look bleak!

Fortunately, the Lads raised their game to save the day and put in a reasonably good end to the campaign. Just two defeats in the last eleven games helped Sunderland to scrape clear of relegation and finish in 19th place. Yet, despite this, we were still faced with the need to win the last game of the season again in order to stay up, this time at home to Manchester City. A single goal from Mick Buckley was enough to do the trick: Sunderland had preserved their First Division status yet again.

All in all, this was a pretty dire season, with little to commend it. Goals were a problem throughout - despite the presence of Ally McCoist! Sunderland managed only 38 goals all season, equally split home and away. This was our worst tally since the 30 that scored in the relegation season of 1969-70. The football we played was at best average and at times very dull. Crowds held up initially, but after the turn of the year fans started to vote with their feet, and the average attendance ended up below 20,000 for the first time since before the arrival of Bob Stokoe almost a decade earlier.

Given that many of those intervening seasons had been spent in Division Two this was an indicator that things were very bleak indeed; even first class opposition was failing to attract the fans.

Yet, Alan Durban seemed unmoved by it all. He chose to take a positive stance, pointing to the Lads' performances towards the end of the season - six wins, three draws and only two defeats - as evidence of promise for the future. The squad was young and inevitably taking time to develop, but for the fans it was a very frustrating time. The impression was almost that the Club was drifting pretty aimlessly, and this season, like so many since 1958, had little to feel happy about. Unfortunately, things would continue in this vein for a while longer.

Ally McCoist going for goal.

Ally McCoist

Perhaps the most famous Scottish footballer of his generation, Ally McCoist was born on 24th September 1962. He started his professional career with St Johnstone, and in his time with them scored two hat tricks against Glasgow Rangers. After leaving the Saints he joined Sunderland for £350,000 in the summer of 1981. He played less than 50 games for the red and whites before making his switch back home to Ibrox. The rest, as they say, is history.

Arriving at Sunderland as a fresh-faced 19-year-old, Ally was never the prodigious finisher at Roker that he proved to be later in his career. He made 23 League and Cup appearances in his first season, and the same the following year, scoring a total of only 9 goals. During 1982-83, McCoist was paired for a few games with Frank Worthington, then nearing the end of his illustrious career. What would Sunderland fans have given to have seen those two together at their peak!

On his return North of the Border, McCoist simply went from strength to strength. He was Ranger's top scorer for five consecutive seasons, won a record nine Scottish League Cup medals and scored a hat-trick in one of those Finals against old enemies Celtic. With over 300 career goals for the 'Gers, including 13 in Europe and 23 against bitter rivals Glasgow Celtic - all club records - he is quite simply the greatest living Ranger. He is the only Scottish player to win the Adidas Golden Boot, an award he carried away twice. In the late 1990's he was awarded the MBE for his services to football.

Ally McCoist.

1982-1983
Fragile Progress

"a definite improvement with Sunderland ending the campaign in a heady sixteenth position"

Nightmare on Vicarage Road

25th September, 1982 goes into the SAFC record books for reasons that are best forgotten. The Lads paid a trip to Graham Taylor's promising Watford side hoping to regain the form that had seen them beat European Champions Aston Villa at the start of the season. However, a complete nightmare followed as the Lads crashed 8 - 0, a result that equalled the heaviest ever defeat for a Sunderland side.

Watford had a policy of playing attacking football with wingers, and one of the men turning out for the Hornets in that position was a young John Barnes, who turned his fellow England under-21 international Barry Venison inside out. The rout began after 12 minutes, when Callaghan hammered home to finish a well worked move. After this, the Lads pushed forward, but were caught on the break; six Sunderland players were still in attack when Watford made it 2 - 0 through Blissett. Before the break, it was 4 - 0 to Watford, Jenkins and Callaghan grabbing one each.

In the second half Blissett began to grab the limelight, hitting the fifth and, after Jenkins had made it 6 - 0 in the 71st minute, Blissett completed his hat trick to make it 7 - 0 before adding the eighth in injury time. Ironically, it was the first time Watford had ever beaten the Lads. What is more, they also hit the woodwork four times and were denied on numerous occasions by Chris Turner, the goalkeeper actually being one of the few Sunderland players to play well!

All things said it was not a good performance. As the Sunday Times put it: 'Sunderland? They were game for a laugh.'

The opening day of the new season is one that is special to all football fans. For Sunderland supporters, the prospect of a visit to Aston Villa must have filled them with some considerable apprehension. Following the decidedly average performances of the previous campaign, a trip to the newly crowned European Champions - Villa had defeated Bayern Munich only three months earlier - was an interesting proposition. The result was an outstanding performance by Sunderland and a 3 - 1 victory. The turning point of the game was probably the substitution of Peter Withe, the 'Werewolf', who had been terrorising the Sunderland defence in the air. Colin West, Nick Pickering and Ally McCoist helped themselves to the goals as the season started with a major upset.

Perhaps heeding some of the criticism of the previous season, Alan Durban brought some interesting characters to the Club, including Leighton James and Jimmy Nicholl. Ian Atkins was picked up for a song and added much needed steel to the defence. They were joined in November by the marvellous 'Mr Entertainment', Frank Worthington, who many supporters had hoped would join the Club years earlier when Sunderland signed his Leicester strike partner, Bob Lee.

However, rather like the previous season, the Villa victory proved to be a flash in the pan. After a few decent results, including a win against West Ham, a run of four straight defeats soon sent Sunderland heading downwards again. Included in those defeats was the horror story that was Watford away. Sunderland crashed to an horrendous 8 - 0 defeat, one of the three worst beatings that we have taken in our entire history. It was a long journey back to Wearside for the Sunderland fans on 25th September 1982. Many of the supporters had left at half time, and spent the second half sitting in the allotments at the back of the ground chatting to the locals. A truly horrible day!

Fortunately, we managed to recover some face in the next home game, when we demolished our traditional bogey team, Norwich City, 4 - 1 at Roker Park. Almost inevitably it proved to be another false dawn. To add to our worries, the Roker End had been judged unsafe and structural faults had been identified in June 1982. Work began on demolishing part of the massive concrete stand, and the ground would never be the same again. In truth, the demise of the ground in many ways ran parallel to the path of the Club overall in the mid-1980s. Very soon we would hit rock bottom.

The League Cup provided a brief highlight. Following a draw at Molineux, Sunderland trounced Wolverhampton Wanderers 5 - 0 at Roker Park, with Gordon Chisholm in particularly fine form that night, scoring two goals. Our involvement in the competition was, however, short lived again, as Norwich despatched us in the next round. We fared no better in the FA Cup, drawing at home to Manchester City in the Third Round, and then crashing out 2 - 1 in the replay at Maine Road.

Sandwiched between the two Cup exits, form in the League had begun to pick up: a run of ten games without a win was halted on 18th December with a 3 - 0 victory over Arsenal on Wearside. The game is remembered for a number of reasons: the bitterly cold conditions, Arsenal's awful away strip and a brilliant Gary Rowell hat-trick. This was followed by three creditable scoreless draws over the holiday period against Manchester United, Liverpool and Nottingham Forest, and as the Club entered the New Year things were definitely starting to look up.

For teams looking to avoid relegation, January to March is a crucial time, and during the previous two seasons Sunderland fans had been treated to suicidal displays.

This time, though, the Lads bucked the trend. In this period we played eleven games and suffered only a single defeat, away at Southampton. Seven wins had supporters wondering if they were really watching the same team as earlier in the season. As ever, the good run did not last, and any thoughts of a good end to the season were banished by a run of only one win in ten games. Typically, the lone victory came against top drawer oppositon, with a victory over Arsenal at Highbury, a Colin West goal earning the points.

In the end, the League campaign petered out with a very tame 1 - 1 draw with West Bromwich Albion at Roker. Only 16,000 fans bothered to turn out to witness the end of what was in the end another stunningly average season. Yet, as far as our League position was concerned, 1982-83 was a definite improvement, with Sunderland ending the campaign in a heady sixteenth position, having accumulated 50 points. Incredibly, this was our best season since 1967-68, when we finished one place higher - not an illustrious 15 years. However, if the table showed progress being made, it was not to the liking of the fans: the average crowd was just over 17,000.

Frank Worthington.

Nick Pickering

South Shields born Nick joined the Club from school and made his debut on the opening day of the 1981-82 season in the 3 - 3 draw at Ipswich. Originally playing wide on the left wing, Nick was a versatile performer during his time at Sunderland, but it was as a left back that he excelled.

Once in the team, Nick became a regular for the next four and half seasons. He was capped at England under-21 level, and for a time he and Barry Venison, Sunderland's right back, were partners for the young England team. Nick actually won a Full England Cap during the 1983 tour to Australia.

The arrival of Lawrie McMenemy as manager soon led to Nick's departure, and he left for Coventry in January 1986. In all he had played over 200 times for Sunderland, and scored eighteen goals.

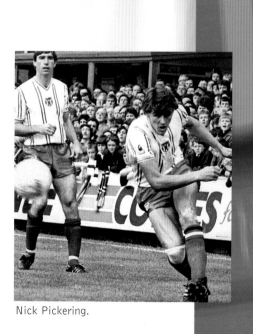

Nick Pickering.

1983-1984
Lowly Peaks

"victory at Leicester City saw the lads fly up to an astonishing thirteenth place..."

Barry Venison

Barry Venison was born on the 16th August 1964, in the Stanley area of County Durham. He signed professional forms from Stanley Boys, and made his debut for Sunderland in October 1981. Sadly for Barry, his debut for the Lads was a 2 - 0 defeat at Notts County.

Venison was to go on to become one of the most accomplished defenders in the country. On as a substitute against Manchester City, Barry scored his first goal in a 3 - 2 win at Maine Road - and it was a beauty too! In 1985, at the tender age of 19, he made history by becoming the youngest-ever captain in a Wembley Cup Final when he led the Lads out for their Milk Cup clash with Norwich City.

After more than 200 appearances in the Red and White stripes, Barry left for Liverpool in July 1986. He later returned to the North East when he signed for arch-rivals Newcastle, but despite the protests of his Sunderland-supporting father, Barry gave good service to the Mags, before joining Southampton. Whilst with Newcastle, he added a couple of full England caps to his Youth and under-21 appearances. His career was cut short by injury, but he has since made a name for himself as a reasoned and snappily dressed TV summariser.

Before the season kicked off, Alan Durban reshuffled his pack a little, selling Ally McCoist to Rangers - for about half the fee we had paid for him - and bringing in Mark Proctor from Nottingham Forest and Paul Bracewell from his old club Stoke. Proctor had spent a short period at Sunderland on loan during the previous season, so the changes were, in truth, little to excite the fans. A little predictably, perhaps, performances continued in the same vein as the previous season had ended. Four defeats in the first six games had Sunderland rocking on their heels before they had really begun.

Fortunately, Durban managed to steady the ship a little after this, even pulling off a 1 - 0 win at Anfield. Indeed, following the poor opening spell, the Lads were beaten just three times before the end of the year, and although one of these matches was a 6 - 1 hammering at the hands of relegation favourites Notts County, it was a commendable achievement. However, our bad start to the season meant that even with this run we were playing 'catch up'. Although the good form had boosted our League position, the outlook could still have been better.

Worryingly, the New Year saw a return to the disappointments that seemed to reign supreme in this decade. A run of four defeats in seven games had the terraces complaining, and once again it was time for another move on the managerial merry-go-round. Alan Durban, who had done a lot of good work in terms of developing young players at the Club, was shown the door following a defeat at Old Trafford. Pop Robson was installed as caretaker manager for one game, a home draw with Arsenal, and then a former Roker stalwart was ushered into Sunderland as the new boss.

Len Ashurst had been a loyal and faithful servant of Sunderland throughout the 1960s. He cut his managerial teeth at Newport County and he was brought back to Roker with many hoping that he could at last provide a period of stability. From the appointment of Tom Watson in the late 19th century to the end of the William Murray era in June 1957 Sunderland had employed just six managers. Ashurst became the fourteenth incumbent, either permanent or temporary, of the Roker hot-seat since then. This is not to suggest that keeping the same manager is always a policy that will lead to success, but it does illustrate that without some element of consistency and stability, a club is often bound to struggle. The 30 years from 1958 onward were not exactly filled with glory.

Ashurst was faced with a potentially 'unlucky thirteen' games to keep Sunderland in the First Division. We lost five, won five and drew three, enough for Sunderland to scrape home yet again. However, for yet another season, our destiny was not safe until the last game of the season, but a victory at Leicester City saw the Lads fly up to an astonishing thirteenth place, the highest finish since the 1955-56 season. Perhaps it was fitting that Pop Robson should score one of the goals to ensure our stay in the top flight, given his extremely brief cameo as manager.

It was also a season in which little solace was to be found in the cup campaigns. Norwich City again proved to be the League Cup bogey team, knocking us out with a 2 -1 win at Roker in the second stage and, despite a 3 - 0 away win at Bolton in the third round, interest in the FA Cup was also short lived as Birmingham walked away from Roker Park with a 2 - 1 win in the fourth round.

While the mid-table League finish might suggest this was one of our better seasons, in reality the position flattered Sunderland somewhat. There was no disguising the fact that the team was still weak in a number of key areas and the average crowd of a little over 16,000 was an indication of what the fans thought of the situation.

With the season at an end, however, Ashurst now had the opportunity to remould the side in an image he saw fit. The fans waited with expectation for the new manager's close season rebuilding, and the optimists had hope that our highest finish for a generation would be built on with the judicious addition of one or two quality players.

Len Ashurst, Manager 1984-85.

Goalkeeping Heroics

October 1st saw Sunderland pay a trip to Anfield to meet the mighty Liverpool. In dire need of points, but having failed to win away from home all season, the Lads needed a miracle against the Champions. Having pulled one out of the bag in order to avoid the drop at the end of the 1980-81 season, it was asking a lot for a repeat performance; lightning rarely strikes twice!

Amazingly, the Sunday Times were able to start their football round-up the following day by reporting 'Plenty of surprises yesterday... and none bigger than Sunderland gaining their first away win of the season at Liverpool'. The Lads had done it again! In a tight game, they did enough to edge a 1 - 0 win. The goal came on 29 minutes. A good Sunderland attack saw a fine header from Gordon Chisholm punched out by Craig Johnston. Good as the save was, Johnston's status as midfield maestro rather than goalkeeping hero meant the referee had no choice but to award a penalty, and Gary Rowell cooly converted it.

After the goal, the Lads did very well to hang on to their lead, with some excellent goalkeeping from Chris Turner doing much to deliver a clean sheet at the end of the ninety minutes. The points moved us up towards mid-table, leaving us 15th out of 22.

Chris Turner.

1984-1985
Roller-Coaster

"we touched the heights by reaching Wembley and plumbed the depths in our dreadful relegation"

Chris Turner

Born in Sheffield, Chris joined his local club, Wednesday, as a youngster, and went on to make over 100 appearances for the Owls. After a period on loan at Lincoln City, he joined Sunderland in 1979 for £75,000. During his early years at Roker, he challenged Roker hero Barry Siddall for the number 1 shirt, but eventually he made the keeper's jersey his own. Loved by the fans, his first season at the Club saw us clinch promotion and he virtually single-handedly carried Sunderland to the final of the Milk Cup in 1985. He will be always be fondly remembered on Wearside for that on its own, although a total of over 220 appearances show him as one of our leading keepers. Whilst not the biggest of goalies, he more than made up for this with his agility and stunning shot-stopping ability. His performances for Sunderland attracted the attention of Manchester United and he signed for the Red Devils in July 1985 for a fee of £250,000.

If there is one season is our recent history that sums up the roller-coaster ride that being a Sunderland supporter is, then it must be 1984-85. The action began before a ball had been kicked, Ashurst determinedly breaking up his predecessor's team with a flurry of transfer activity. Amongst the lengthy list of departures were Paul Bracewell, Lee Chapman, Leighton James, Pop Robson and Ian Atkins. Even folk hero Gary Rowell failed to escape the clear out, as he was despatched to Norwich - although his heart remained firmly at Roker. To compensate for this, Ashurst brought in a whole host of players - some of whom were more successful than others - including Gary Bennett, Clive Walker, Howard Gayle, Steve Berry, Peter Daniel and Roger Wylde. Of these, only Gary Bennett stayed for any real length of time, though Clive Walker undoubtedly had a great impact too. Ashurst's policy was to bring in players for relatively small fees and most failed to make the long-term grade.

In the short term though, the season began well, with a 3 - 1 home win over Southampton. Bennett scored on his debut and his all-action contribution made him an instant crowd favourite. Indeed, we suffered only three defeats in our opening thirteen league games, and there were strong hopes that the last game relegation battles of the previous few seasons would disappear into the past. There were some notable wins during this period too, Luton and QPR both being thrashed 3 - 0. The real excitement, though, was coming in the League (Milk) Cup. November saw us match the country's best in real glamour ties against Nottingham Forest and Spurs; by early December we had beaten both, securing the Lads a place in the fifth round, a welcome change from the early round exits we were used to. Sunderland, it seemed, were really looking up.

But, hindsight is a powerful tool. It tells us in this case that the bright start was merely yet another false dawn. As the Cup heroics against Spurs and Forest grabbed the headlines, our League form dipped worryingly. A 3 - 0 win at home to QPR at the start of November marked the end of the early season promise, and our previously strong defensive play began to crumble as the Lads slumped to defeat after defeat. Of the nine games remaining until the end of the year, seven were lost, including a 4 - 0 drubbing at home to Leicester. Amazingly, one of the games we didn't lose came against a strong Manchester United team, who were beaten 3 - 2 in a keenly contested game, Clive Walker hitting a memorable hat-trick.

The Lads were now in free fall, and form needed to improve quickly. It didn't. The year began with a 3 - 1 defeat at Newcastle, and all but one of the first five League games of 1985 were lost. To add to this, Southampton thrashed us 4 - 0 in the third round of the FA Cup. In the Milk Cup, though, we managed to overcome Watford 1 - 0 earning a place in the semi-finals of the competition, where Chelsea were well beaten. The glory of a Wembley Cup final now beckoned, and attention was distracted from the League campaign: surely if we were good enough to beat the top teams in the Cup we could do it in the League?

After clinching a place in the final, our form picked up . What's more, the week before the Wembley date we beat Norwich - who we would meet there - 3 - 1 at Carrow Road. At last, it seemed that everything might come good. But, it was not to be. Not only did Norwich beat us in the final, but form collapsed immediately afterwards. Of the twelve games left to save ourselves from relegation, eight were lost, and just one was won - a slim 1 - 0 victory at Coventry.

Such poor results, inevitably, sealed relegation for the Lads. We had finished well off the pace, being ten points away from safety, and were joined in relegation by fellow Milk Cup finalists Norwich.

For both teams it was a matter of regret that League form had not matched Cup form. Four of the teams we knocked out of the Milk Cup were First Division teams, and in the eight League games played against them we had picked up just four out of a possible 24 points. Had the Lads raised their game in just half of these fixtures relegation could have been avoided.

So, after touching the heights by reaching Wembley, we plumbed the depths in our dreadful relegation. Ian Atkins, one of the Durban team who left the Club under Len Ashurst, was criticised by his new boss Howard Kendall for saying that Sunderland should be in the top six every week but that they continually thought and acted like a Fourth Division club. It is certain that these views were echoed throughout the pubs and clubs of Wearside in the dark days of the end of the season.

Unsurprisingly, Sunderland once more finished a season by saying farewell to their manager. Despite taking the Club to Wembley, Len Ashurst paid the price for relegation. The task of returning us to the top flight would be placed in another's hands.

Sunderland v Manchester United, 1984.

The Last Rites

Our final game of the season was about as bad as it gets in terms of supporting Sunderland. Not that there were actually many supporters at this match - only 9,398 bothered to turn up. Sunderland had already been relegated from Division One, and this was a case of players and fans bidding 'farewell' to the top league. Matches like this are always strange affairs for supporters. On one hand, they are absolutely meaningless and hold no attraction whatsoever. On the other, there is a sense of morbid fascination to turn up and witness the last rites being issued to your hopes and ambitions for at least two more years. No chance next year of winning the First Division Championship. No chance of trying to sneak into Europe. No attractive opposition. It is an awful feeling.

Ipswich actually had something to play for, and they came to gain the win that would ultimately keep them in the First Division and relegate their East Anglian rivals, Norwich. Sunderland were stretched by injury and Chris Turner was given the opportunity to captain the side in what was to prove his last game for the Lads. Captaincy or not, he was pretty helpless when Wilson gave Ipswich an early lead. Ian Wallace equalised soon afterwards, but somehow everyone knew how it would end, and a second goal from Wilson in the last minute gave Ipswich the victory they deserved.

That was that for another season. As the fans made their way home thinking how dreadful it was being condemned to the Second Division, the news started to come through that a fire at Bradford City had claimed the lives of scores of fellow football fans, all with the same hopes, fears, nightmares and dreams as us. Relegation is bad, but everyone needs a sense of perspective, and the tragic events of that day helped put things into a truer light.

Sunderland v Manchester Utd, 1984.
An exciting game which we won 3 - 2.
Walker scored a hat-trick.
David Hodgson for the Lads and
United's Mark Hughes were sent off.
All the goals came before half time.

The 1984-85 Milk Cup

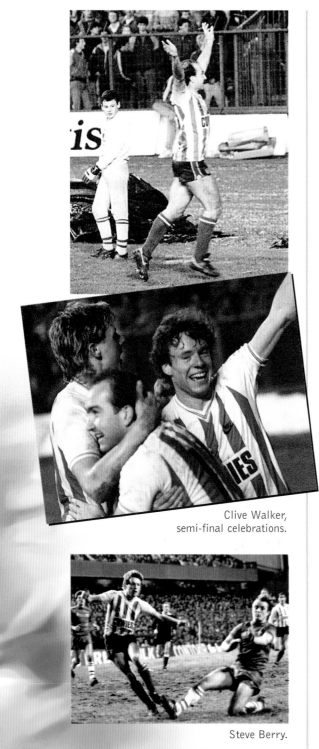

Clive Walker,
semi-final celebrations.

Steve Berry.

Sunderland's history in the League Cup, sponsored in 1984-85 by the Milk Marketing Board and therefore known as the 'Milk Cup', had been nothing short of appalling. In the early years things were not too bad, and we reached the quarter final in 1961-62 and the semi-final a year later. However, in those first few competitions, many of the 'bigger' clubs did not enter, and it was not until 1966, and the guarantee of European football with an Inter Cities Fairs Cup place for the winners, that the football world started to take the League Cup seriously. Sadly, this also signalled the end to any sniff of Sunderland success, so in 1984 the visit of Crystal Palace to Roker Park for the Second Round First Leg tie hardly had the fans dreaming of the Twin Towers.

The visitors actually played very well, but Sunderland scraped a 2 - 1 win in front of 11,600 fans with two goals from Roger Wylde. For Palace, Stan Cummins, who rejoined Sunderland after the second leg of this tie, had enough chances on his own to win the game, but Lady Luck was shining, and the Lads went to South London to defend their lead. A 0 - 0 draw at Selhurst Park was enough to see us through to Round Three, when the opposition would be a bit more fearsome.

An away trip to Nottingham Forest was Sunderland's reward, and a good overall team performance saw the Lads more than a little disappointed to be held to a 1 - 1 draw, with David Hodgson scoring for the Lads. The replay was 'one of those nights' on Wearside. The game started off relatively slowly but got better and better. Scoreless at full time, the match moved into extra-time, and with the atmosphere in the crowd white hot, a blockbuster from Howard Gayle was enough to see Sunderland progress to the dizzy heights of the Fourth Round.

The draw presented Sunderland with home advantage to Spurs, and what turned out to be two classic encounters. Over 27,000 packed into Roker Park on 21st November to see Tottenham adopt a very 'European' approach to the game. They came, basically, for the draw, but in truth had plenty of chances to nick it. If it had not been for the heroics of keeper Chris Turner, our interest would have been over.

As it was, we travelled to North London for the replay, although more in hope than in expectation. What transpired was an even more inspired performance from Turner, who surpassed his earlier heights with a string of world class saves, most importantly stopping a penalty from Graham Roberts. Goals from Clive Walker and Gordon Chisholm combined with Turner's efforts to see Sunderland through 2 - 1 on the night - a result which did not go down too well with the Spurs faithful!

Another trip 'down south' was on the agenda next, Watford being first out of the hat for the Fifth Round tie. At the time, Watford were favourites for the Cup, and had not lost a midweek cup tie at home for years. As a result of injuries and suspensions Sunderland fielded a scratch side but when Clive Walker's shot bounced off Nick Pickering's back and past the stranded keeper, the travelling Red and White Army were beginning to wonder if our name really was written on the Milk Cup.

The semi-final pitched us once again against the team installed as favourites for the Cup, this time Chelsea. In the first leg, another superb all round performance saw Sunderland run up a two-goal lead, with local hero Colin West scoring both. Over 32,000 fans witnessed yet another great cup night on Wearside. The return match was eagerly anticipated. Sunderland now really believed in themselves and had a two goal lead to defend.

An early strike from David Speedie looked worrying, but Turner was again in outstanding form, and two goals from Walker had things looking good.

But, Chelsea's less than wholesome fans invaded the pitch, bringing the threat of an abandonment. Chaos briefly ensued, with the police chasing a supporter on the field as Colin West ran down the pitch and struck his third goal of the tie. The goal effectively sealed it, and though Pat Nevin pulled a goal back late on, it was meaningless. Sunderland had won 3 - 2 on the night, and 5 - 2 on aggregate: we were at Wembley!

Our opponents in the Final would be Norwich City. Before the game both sets of supporters were in good spirits. In stark contrast to the scenes at Chelsea in the semi-final, fans of both Norwich and Sunderland mixed outside of Wembley, exchanging scarves and good wishes before what was to become known as the 'Friendly Final'. It was a sad indictment of Sunderland that in the programme notes at Wembley, Sunderland were now referred to as 'one of the less fashionable clubs'. How far the mighty had fallen.

Milk Cup Final ticket and programme.

Sadly, the game turned out to be a major disappointment to the huge Roker Roar, which could be seen populating almost every section of the ground. After a bright start, with Wallace shooting just over the bar, the game turned flat. In only the second Sunday final in Wembley's history, a bizarre own goal settled a drab affair, a deflection from our captain Chisolm being the only goal of the day. We had our chances - none better than a penalty which Clive Walker missed, the first miss in an English Wembley final.

So it all came to nothing. The hopes of another day were dashed, and the long journey back home was muted. To cap it all, we followed a lacklustre final performance with relegation. Trust Sunderland...

1985-1986
Big Mac

The scenes at Roker Park on the last day of the season "...a mixture of joy, relief, frustration and not a little embarrassment"

Shaun Elliott

Shaun began his distinguished career with Sunderland on 12th January 1977, in an FA Cup match at Wrexham. In his first season with the first team he went on to make 19 League appearances, plus one in the FA Cup. It proved to be something of a baptism of fire for the young defender, as Sunderland eventually lost their First Division status at Everton on the last day of the season.

During the seasons that followed, Elliott made over 350 appearances for the Club, and was captain for many of them. Managers came and went at Roker Park, but Shaun remained popular with all of his bosses and a terrace favourite. His natural leadership abilities shone through, and being a true professional he never gave less than 100% in any game.

Shaun's biggest disappointments undoubtedly came during the 1984-85 season. Instead of leading the Lads down the tunnel at Wembley as captain against Norwich in the Milk Cup Final, he was instead confined to the stands because of suspension. To round off a thoroughly miserable year for Elliott, Sunderland ended up relegated as well.

Shaun played his last competitive game for Sunderland on May 3rd 1986 in a 2 - 0 win over Stoke City, bringing to an end a long and distinguished career with the Club. In August 1986 he signed for Norwich City for £140,000.

Inevitably, the summer was full of speculation about Ashurst's replacement and the rumour factory worked overtime. After lengthy negotiations, the name of Lawrie McMenemy was added to the list of Sunderland managers. His appointment was big news. Having turned an average Second Division Southampton team into a quality First Division outfit - achieving not only promotion to the top flight, but also winning the FA Cup - McMenemy was hot property. A national media figure and a charismatic man able to persuade England stars such as Kevin Keegan to join Southampton, his appointment was greeted with joy by the fans. For Sunderland Chairman Tom Cowie, his capture was a major coup. However, the package offered to McMenemy was a huge one, making his appointment something of a gamble too. In truth, the Club could not afford the deal he had been offered; anything less than an instant return to the top flight would spell disaster.

However, as the euphoria swept across Wearside, few worried about the small print of the new manager's contract. At last, a 'big name' was coming to manage at Roker Park, and the fans had visions of instant success. Promotion was, of course, almost guaranteed, and the more excitable among the Roker faithful expected at least one of the cups to join the silverware in the cabinet. A saviour had been called for and Big Lawrie seemed to fit the bill perfectly. The fans sat back and waited for the long overdue success to return.

The new manager had a tried and tested formula from his days at Southampton, and he decided to apply exactly the same approach at Sunderland. Experienced former internationals were to form the backbone of the team and to that end he brought in a number of new players that fitted the bill: Eric Gates, Frank Gray, Alan Kennedy and George Burley all joined the Club during the early stages of the season.

Sadly, the formula did not appear to be working too well. The season started disastrously, with five consecutive defeats and not a solitary goal to show for all of the optimism. Sunderland were well and truly anchored to the bottom of the Second Division, the lowest point in our history. Crowds were declining at an alarming rate, and no one knew quite what had gone so terribly wrong.

The sixth game of the season saw Grimsby Town held to a 3 - 3 draw at Roker Park, and the first point and goals of the season were greeted like an FA Cup win. That just about summed things up at the time. Two games later we recorded our first win of the campaign, away to Shrewsbury at Gay Meadow, and followed this up with our first home victory, on 28th September, against Huddersfield Town.

But, from then on, it was pretty much a dire affair. The odd single goal victory here, a run of defeats there, and a sprinkling of draws to just about maintain hope of retaining our Second Division status. The Cup competitions brought no relief. Swindon Town, then in the Fourth Division, dumped us out of the League Cup, whilst Manchester United eased us aside in the FA Cup fourth round, easily beating us 3 - 0 at Old Trafford. Even the newly created Full Members Cup - a compensation for England's temporary absence from European football - brought no solace, with Manchester City beating us on penalties at Maine Road at the competition's second stage.

After the high expectations, there were few highlights during a desperate season. One came with the 4 - 2 demolition of Leeds United in January, when a Nick Pickering hat-trick brought temporary relief to the fans, many of whom could still not come to terms with the Club's plight. The same scoreline was also recorded against Fulham, and we also managed to sneak a 1 - 0 victory at home to 'Boro, although they beat us 2 - 0 just after Christmas in the return match.

So, despite having dropped a division, brought in a host of experienced players and appointed one of the country's most famous managers on a huge salary, Sunderland faced a relegation battle for the sixth season in a row. In the end, a turnaround in home form saved the day, the Lads winning their last four games at Roker to pull away from the relegation spots. A 2 - 0 victory against Stoke in our final game ensured safety. Amazingly, the fifth bottom finish sent the fans wild, the Roker faithful demanding a lap of honour from the players and from their manager!

Norwich, who had been relegated along with Sunderland just twelve months previously, returned to the First Division as runaway Champions, whilst SAFC supporters cheered and saluted a team who had escaped relegation by just two places and four points. The scenes at Roker Park that day were extraordinary - a mixture of joy, relief, frustration and not a little embarrassment. But, if fans had felt relived at coming through what seemed a sticky transitional patch, they hadn't seen anything yet: what was to follow made this look like a tea party. Those of you with tender dispositions may be advised to skip the next couple of seasons and rejoin our story at the end of 1987-88. For the rest of you: you have been warned.

1985-86 Sunderland team.

Memories of Better Days

January 11th 1987 saw the Lads pick up what was probably their best win of the season, when Leeds United visited Roker Park. As always, memories of '73 were in the air, and at half-time the scoreline was the same as it had been on 5th May that year: 1 - 0 to the Lads. In the second half, though, the floodgates opened, with five goals being scored. Three of them fell to the Lads, and in what was something of a crazy day, Nick Pickering - not noted for his goalscoring - hit a hat trick! The game ended 4 - 2 to Sunderland, and for once there were some smiles on the fans' faces as they left the ground.

Nick Pickering.

1986-1987

The Unthinkable

"the unthinkable had become reality and we were condemned to football's backwaters"

Gordon Armstrong

Often one of the 'unsung heroes' of Roker Park, Gordon was actually one of our longest serving players. Born in July 1967 in Newcastle, Armstrong joined Sunderland from school, making his debut towards the end of the ill-fated 1984-85 campaign. Within a couple of seasons he was an established first team regular, and held a place in the side for the next seven seasons. Mainly a midfielder, Gordon was often called on to fill in at a variety of other positions, and he never let any manager down. Towards the end of his career he fell from favour slightly, and he eventually joined Bury in 1995.

Gordon will forever remain in the memory for his goal against Chelsea in the 1992 FA Cup Quarter-Final. Having just conceded a late equaliser, Sunderland dug in for that little extra. Brian Atkinson's floated corner from the right was met with a powerful header from Armstrong and the ball bulleted past Beasant to put Sunderland into the semi finals.

He was awarded a testimonial match in 1994, when Bobby Robson brought his FC Porto team from Portugal. Almost 9,500 turned out to support Gordon and see Sunderland beat the European Cup semi-finalists 2 - 0.

With the Club having just endured its worst finish to date, it was essential that attention was focused on putting right the problems that had hampered the previous campaign's performances. However, the season started in turmoil. Chairman Tom Cowie, who had endured something of a love-hate relationship with the fans, resigned. He was replaced by Bob Murray, who had seen a Wembley Cup final and a relegation since joining the board in June 1984. But, his two roller coaster seasons as a director were to be nothing compared to the baptism of fire that awaited him as Chairman.

In buying out Cowie, the new Chairman had inherited a Club in crisis. Against a background of mounting debts and dwindling crowds, the Club was paying huge salaries to a manager and an ageing squad that, to put it bluntly, were not producing the goods. Yet, while radical action was called for, McMenemy saw no reason to depart from his chosen formula. Moreover, while his huge contract might have seemed the right way forward when the Club was looking to secure the services of what all presumed would be a successful manager, it soon became a massive burden when the manager was faring less well. While some felt a mutual severing of ties was prudent, McMenemy wasn't going anywhere: quite simply, the terms at Sunderland were too good to be left behind.

Yet, despite the previous season's disaster, there was always a feeling that McMenemy might come good. A comfortable away win at Huddersfield in the opening game, followed by a home draw with Brighton the following week, suggested that the horrors of the previous season might just be avoided. But, the next game showed us how wrong we were. We travelled to Ewood Park and were thrashed 6 - 1 by Blackburn, the only team still in the division to finish below us in the previous campaign.

It was not all doom and gloom after this though. A mini-revival followed, and victories over Hull, Stoke, Plymouth and Birmingham saw the team move into fifth place. Again the mood swung back towards optimism as faint dreams of promotion were rekindled. Such hopes were soon dashed. From here on in, our form was quite simply appalling. November and December brought just one win in ten games - a 3 - 0 victory over Blackburn - and Sunderland were rapidly slipping back into the mire.

It was clear now that avoiding relegation, rather than securing promotion, was to be the order of the day. The roller coaster started up again in the New Year, with three wins from the first five League matches. However, as the season entered the crucial spring period, our form hit rock bottom. Five out of six games were lost in March. Moreover, the Lads failed to find the net in three of their games, while at the back, goals were being leaked in at an alarming rate, twelve going in during the month. Finally, following a 2 - 1 defeat at home to Sheffield United on 11th April, McMenemy agreed it was time for him to go. If any Sunderland supporter is asked to sum up McMenemy's reign at Sunderland, the word 'disaster' will inevitably be used. Now, with just seven games to go, relegation to the Third Division looked a certainty. We were in big trouble and someone big had to try and get us out of it.

The Chairman made a move for the only man who had been known to perform miracles on Wearside in recent times: Bob Stokoe. He agreed to make an emotional return to Roker Park until the end of the season. His first game back in charge was at Valley Parade, Bradford, on 18th April. The original Messiah was back, 10 years older than when he had walked away from Sunderland, but hopefully wiser as well. It was asking a lot for anyone to save us, but if anyone could, it was Bob.

But, even though we scored twice in his first game, we came away from West Yorkshire on the wrong end of a defeat. Time and games were ticking away, and we desperately needed a win. Against Leeds United at Roker Park we were forced to settle for a draw, but managed to sneak a narrow victory away at Shrewsbury. Bradford then came up to Wearside and inflicted another 3 - 2 defeat, leaving us with only three games in May to save our skins.

A win over Crystal Palace was followed by a well-earned point down in South London at Milwall. This good result set us up for what we all hoped would be our last game of the season - at home to Barnsley. Needing a win to secure safety, Sunderland took the lead, but a penalty miss by Mark Proctor proved very costly as we were beaten 3 - 2.

We were now condemned to the play-offs, facing Gillingham, who had finished fifth in the Third Division. A victory over the Kent side would see us meet either Swindon or Wigan, and surely we would then preserve our status. But, a 3 - 2 away defeat in the first leg was costly, as we crashed out on the away goals rule despite a 4 - 3 win at Roker Park.

Sunderland's demise was now complete. Even the great Messiah himself found this one miracle too far. It was a dark day indeed. When McMenemy had joined the Club in July 1985, he had promised to take us out of the Second Division. Unfortunately, no one had thought to ask him the direction he would take us. Third Division football beckoned for the first time in our history.

The Unthinkable: Sunderland 4 - 3 Gillingham

Without doubt, our final game of the season has to go down as one of the blackest days in the whole illustrious history of Sunderland AFC. Having been condemned to the play-offs by a home defeat against Barnsley on the last game of the season proper, we were to face Gillingham in the first set of play off games to retain our right to stay in Division Two.

The first leg a few days earlier had led to a 3 - 2 defeat, but no one doubted that true class would come through at Roker Park. After all, we were playing Gillingham, and Kent was hardly a hotbed of soccer. This was a Gillingham team who had finished fifth in the Third Division, 19 points behind the champions Bournemouth and 16 behind second placed 'Boro. This was also Sunderland, a big club. We had history and tradition. We had Bob Stokoe who had come back to save us from this fate. Big clubs like Sunderland could not really be relegated to the Third Division - it just was not allowed, was it?

Of course, Gillingham had not read their script properly. Over 25,000 packed into Roker Park, and gave outstanding support to the Lads. If the match had been decided on vocal contributions from the terraces, then someone from the Football League would have apologised to us for all the fuss and immediately told us to go straight to the First Division where we belonged.

The team was decidedly nervous and it was no real surprise when Gillingham took the lead. Two goals from Gatesy restored order, but Tony Cascarino equalised following a missed penalty. Time was running out when Gary Bennett headed us in front on the day, and the game moved to extra time.

Everyone knew we would come through now. We were stronger, and we cost more money than them, and we were at home, and we had great fans, and....Tony Cascarino scored again. A flying header from Keith Bertschin meant little, as the final whistle blew, and the realisation dawned that we would begin next season in Division Three.

For a club with the history, support and potential of Sunderland to end up at this level was a shock for everyone. We would be back, fitter and stronger, but for that moment the unthinkable had become reality, and we were condemned to football's backwaters.

Swindlehurst v Leeds.

The Roker Roar

An Outsider's View

In the build up to the 1996-97 Premiership Season, Paul Wilson of the Observer made the following statement in his Sportsview Section:

'Amid all the hype and hysteria, it might have gone unnoticed that Sunderland are up too, but this will be put to right once Roker's Red-and-White hordes begin their travels through the Premiership. Contrary to popular myth, the Geordies of Newcastle are not the most fanatically exuberant followers in British football; that honour belongs to their Sunderland rivals, the Mackems. Whether disdaining the option of sitting down for the entire duration of matches, standing bare-chested throughout the coldest January afternoon (I'm talking male fans here - Wearsiders are not that exuberant), or collectively ignoring the evidence of their eyes and acclaiming their team as the greatest the world has ever seen, Sunderland followers are in a class of their own.'

Relegation to the Third Division meant one of the most famous clubs and most passionate sets of supporters in football was consigned to the backwaters of football. Whilst Sunderland had many venues before settling at Roker Park in 1898, the ground was made famous by, and became synonymous with, the vocal support displayed by its fans. In time, the supporters of Sunderland AFC became generically known as 'The Roker Roar' - a name that will forever remain.

For years, many fans endured hardship throughout the week, with long hours and physically exhausting jobs in the coalmines and shipyards of the area. The release offered by a visit to Roker Park turned the support into partisanship, and in the early days often led to violent incident. Ground closures in the early part of the century were not uncommon. Like any passion, supporting a football club can sometimes generate white-hot vitriol.

To many, perhaps the overwhelming majority, supporting the Red and Whites takes on an almost religious significance, and the oft heard saying 'keep the faith' is nothing blasé or crass. Unlike Glasgow however, the sectarian divide never played a part. The 'religion' derives not necessarily from a physical community, but more from something intangible, a memory, a story, an emotion, some kind of instinctive family birthright.

Although of a different origin from Rangers or Celtic, it leads to the same intense devotion. It has been said that Sunderland are the 'Bhoys' or 'Gers' of English football. Praise indeed to be compared with such football fanatics. Perhaps it is no co-incidence that the Roker Roar supports with such emotion a club founded by a teacher newly arrived from Glasgow University.

Whilst supporting a football team is a personal thing, to be a member of the Roker Roar is a selfless act. It is a contradiction that cannot easily be explained. If you are not a member willing to help your fellow Sunderland fan, then you betray the forefathers who went before you. Many acts within supporters' branches throughout the world have amply demonstrated a willingness to put group benefit before individual profit. No pain, no gain, as they say.

If something is of importance then the 'downs' are cherished almost as much as the 'ups'. In search of the Holy Grail, it is the historical significance of the Club, and the past glories it has witnessed, that drives many of the fans forever onwards, with tales from their grandfathers and fathers whetting the footballing appetite.

The Roker Roar is demanding, but in truth would the Club have it any other way? At the end of the day it is evident that if something is so worthwhile to so many people then the hard times will be endured so that the good times, when they come, can be enjoyed so very, very much.

Every club thinks that their fans are special and rightly so but some, including the famed Roker Roar, can quite literally change the course of a game. The atmosphere generated by them can, at times, be so intimidating that opposing teams and supporters alike have quite simply capitulated. It should not be regarded as a weakness on the part of our foe, just inevitability.

Throughout the footballing world, there are few areas which can rival the fanaticism and passion of the North East. Glasgow and Liverpool, possibly, parts of South America, Italy and Spain probably. But supporting Sunderland is a love that for many borders on a 'fatal attraction'. Danny Blanchflower once famously said that having travelled the world the Roker Roar was the most awesome display of support he had ever seen. The majestic and brilliant Irishman knew what he was talking about.

The fans are the secret weapon of Sunderland AFC, and it is the reason why one day we will rediscover what past generations have raved about. Wearside is no place for the faint hearted. Shrinking violets need not apply to join the massed ranks.

When success happens you can be sure that the Roker Roar will have been with the Club every step of the way. Whatever success is achieved, it can only be dedicated to the loyal fans. However, the story of the Roker Roar is not of individuals, although many noted fans became legend. It is the story of a travelling band of 'footballing nomads', bound together by a cause that only they can understand.

While statistics alone cannot tell the story of the Roker Roar it should be noted that:

(i) In both 1991 and 1997, Sunderland took over 15,000 supporters to Manchester City and Wimbledon respectively on the final day of the season to witness their team be relegated. The game at Maine Road saw a higher crowd than that of the Manchester derby. Whilst there were expected tears from the rank and file from Wearside, many City fans openly wept with them, the sign of a devotion recognised by fellow 'loyals'.

(ii) In the four decades following the fallout of the 1957 illegal payments debacle, Sunderland have won just one major domestic trophy. They suffered Third Division football, three trips to Wembley in which they failed to score a solitary goal, and did not finish in the top half of the top flight once. The Club had been relegated seven times and a whole generation had grown up on a diet of, at best, mediocrity. In terms of what should be parallel clubs, for example Arsenal, Aston Villa and Liverpool, a lack of 'stars' was painfully evident. Playing Reading on a Tuesday night in February 1998 they attracted 40,579 to what was a Nationwide First Division game.

Enduring the pain of relegation in 1987, the Roker Roar remained loyal and defiant. They know that someday and somewhere a real party will begin. When it does, the People's Game, Pele's Beautiful Game, will smile and say 'it's only the Sunderland fans, taking their deserved bow' and everyone will join in the festivities.

An Insider's View

What does football mean? One day I rang up my grandfather, who wasn't very well, and asked him if he wanted to go over to Roker Park as I had to collect some FA Cup tickets. He said yes, and on we travelled. He hadn't been to the ground in years, but during his supporting days he had walked from his home to the match when he couldn't afford the bus fare. When we got to the stadium he said that he would have a walk about. He had seen some great teams and when I came out of the ticket office he was just staring at the ground as if he was remembering famous players, games, moments. We got into the car and he asked if I could take him to the coast. We stopped off and he got out of the car. He told me all about the football specials and the walk to the ground and talked of how the Club was immersed into the culture of shipbuilding and mining.

He died a couple of weeks later.

And the point of this story? The bloke knew he was dying, but before he went he wanted to go back to the place where he had his memories, his roots, and remember one last time the magic that was his footballing experiences. This is a true football fan; the bloke will always be a special, personal hero.

Paul Days

1987-1988
Back to Basics

"everyone knew we should not be hanging around for too long"

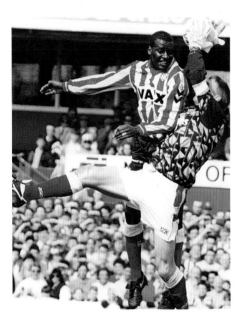

Gary Bennett

Manchester born Gary was always a crowd favourite at Roker Park. Signed for an absolute bargain £65,000 from Cardiff at the beginning of the 1984-85 season, a debut strike against Southampton quickly established 'Benno's' reputation as a rock solid defender who would always contribute goals.

Captain of the side in the dark days of the Third Division, Gary was the only member of the Milk Cup Final side to survive until our next Cup Final appearance at Wembley, versus Liverpool in 1992.

In his career at Sunderland, Bennett made over 400 appearances in all competitions, and knocked in 23 goals. In 1993 he was awarded a testimonial game against Rangers, and Roker Park was packed to the rafters as fans turned out to pay tribute to one of the most popular players seen on Wearside in recent years.

He left the club in 1995 to join Carlisle United, and from there went on to Scarborough and Darlington. He is still a regular, and most welcome, visitor to the Sunderland Stadium of Light.

The Third Division was very much a case of 'uncharted waters' for Sunderland. Relegation had, in truth, been the Club's comeuppance for poor organisation over a number of years, and the Club was on the verge of a real crisis. On the pitch, the Club was about to compete at its lowest level since the 1880s, it had no manager and the team was in tatters following the release of many of McMenemy's ageing signings. Off the pitch, there was uncertainty over the Club's ownership, with a group of 'rebel' directors claiming they should have been offered the chance to buy Tom Cowie's shares, and our debts were increasing by the minute. The season was make or break for Sunderland AFC.

The very real seriousness of the Club's plight at this time should not be underestimated. Relegation to the Third Division had exacerbated our financial troubles; the Club was running at a loss and was already three times over its overdraft limit. Any other business would have had the plug pulled on it, but football clubs had traditionally been given special treatment. However, all this had changed the previous season, when our neighbours Middlesbrough were put into receivership following their relegation to the Third Division. Crucially, both clubs banked with the Midland Bank, who were of the opinion that the same devastating course of action should be applied to Sunderland. In the close season, the Chairman fought off this threat to Sunderland AFC's very existence, lending the Club money from his own pocket and guaranteeing the Club's debts in order to satisfy the bankers.

On the pitch, the decision was taken to appoint Denis Smith as our new manager. The news was not exactly greeted with raptures by the Roker faithful, but he had done a sound job at York City, having guided them to the Fourth Division Championship with a then record 101 points. It proved to be an astute appointment: Smith, a genuine footballing man, had a great knowledge of lower league football, was full of confidence in his own ability and offered an honest and down-to-earth approach that stood in stark contrast to the flamboyant excess of McMenemy's reign.

For a club like Sunderland, the Third Division was something of a sobering experience. Somehow, it just did not feel right and everyone knew we should not be hanging around there for too long. The fans somehow knew that they deserved better. At least the bitter pill was made sweeter by a decent start to the season, the Lads winning their first game in the division 1 - 0 at Brentford. Further victories followed against Doncaster and Mansfield.

However, the Lads then went off the tracks a little. Three draws and two defeats saw Sunderland slip to twelfth place in the Third Division, a new all-time low. Fortunately, help was at hand in the form of Marco Gabbiadini. The young striker joined from York, and along with the more experienced signings of Colin Pascoe, John Kay and John McPhail, was an instant hit.

Six consecutive wins followed and the Lads finally got into their stride. At the beginning of November, we made our claim on the Championship clearly and boldly, bouncing back from a narrow defeat with a superb performance against Southend. In a real treat for the Roker faithful, Eric Gates claimed four goals as we stormed to a 7 - 0 win. The victory - impressive in itself - launched a three-and-half month unbeaten run that stretched for fifteen matches, ten of which were won. When the run came to an end - with consecutive defeats at Bristol Rovers (0 - 4) and Aldershot (2 - 3) - there was no hiding the inevitable fact: Sunderland were going straight back up.

As the season entered its closing stages, the Lads were in fine form still. April began with good wins over Grimsby, Chesterfield and Southend, and it was clear that a couple more victories would clinch promotion. A win over Mansfield in the final game of the month paved the way for a promotion clinching trip to Port Vale. Win and we were up. Would we slip up again at the final hurdle?

Of course not! Eric Gates scored the goal, and we were there. The visit of Northampton on Easter Monday two days later saw the North East's biggest crowd of the season, over 29,000. A 3 - 1 win secured the Championship, and the party was complete, in full fancy dress, with a 4 - 1 win at Rotherham.

Cup hopes were firmly pushed to one side, with defeats by Middlesbrough in the League Cup and Scunthorpe in the FA Cup, but no one was really bothered about that. This season was all about the League. Aside from promotion, the story of the season was the partnership of the young and powerful Gabbiadini with the wise old head of Eric Gates. They had proved unstoppable in the Third Division, scoring a total of forty goals. With winning football back on the menu, crowds were up at Roker, and at almost every ground that we visited.

If the meaning of life is 'to be happy', then in football terms we had gone some way to finding it. Many fans look back with no small degree of fondness on our time in Division Three. We were the best team by a mile. We got the opportunity to go to grounds that we just would not have seen. We were the biggest club, the best supported, and we gave out some spectacular thrashings. All in all, we had a good time.

However, we were pleased to be out at the first attempt. Indeed, it was vitally important that we were. Had the Lads spent any longer there, the consequences may well have been fatal. We bade a fond farewell to the Third Division, and in doing so we hoped to never go back!

Party Time

What goes down must come up - or something like that. While May 1987 had been one of the lows, so April 1988 was to prove to be one of the highs. In reality, Sunderland were quite simply too good for this level of competition, and to finally prove it in terms of the league table was really only rubber-stamping the inevitable.

Having lost the previous Saturday at home to Bristol City, nerves were possibly starting to show a little as the season drew to a close and the Lads prepared to visit Port Vale. However, a 4 - 0 win at Mansfield in midweek had steadied the boat, and Sunderland knew that a win at Port Vale would secure promotion, and in all probability the Division Three Championship as well.

A crowd of 7,569 was swelled by a large contingent of travelling supporters who were keen to see the Club put an end to an enjoyable but rather embarrassing season in the lower leagues. The only goal of the game was in the 79th minute from Eric Gates, his twentieth goal of the season, but in reality Sunderland were never troubled.

And so the worst nightmare was over. If seven days is a long time in politics, twelve months is a lifetime in football. The tears of the McMemeny influenced relegation were washed aside to be replaced by smiles and dancing. It may have only been the Third Division, but we won it by a mile.

Denis Smith.

1988-1989 Consolidation

"the ship had well and truly been steadied."

Marco Gabbiadini

In the last quarter of a century, Marco Gabbiadini is without a doubt one of the most exciting footballers we have seen at Sunderland. He was just what Wearside needed at a crucial time in its history. Newly relegated to the Third Division, and seeking to find their feet, Sunderland fans needed a hero and Marco was ready for the challenge. He arrived on Wearside from York City as a raw 19 year old for a bargain £80,000. Manager Denis Smith had nurtured the young striker at Bootham Crescent, and he was to repay his boss's faith many times over in the years to come. To this day, the money spent still represents one of the best deals ever carried out by a Sunderland manager.

Indeed, by the end of his first season, Marco's partnership with the evergreen Eric Gates had become known as the 'G-Force', and had propelled the red and whites back to the then Second Division, Marco contributing 22 League and Cup goals. From then on, it just got better and better for him, and despite being sent off twice in the following season, he maintained the adoration of the Roker Faithful, whose chants of 'Ole, ole, ole, ole, Marco, Marco' echoed around many grounds.

His performances also gained him representative honours for his country, at under-21 and 'B' international level, and for a time the striker could do no wrong at Sunderland. In 175 League appearances for the Lads, he contributed a very healthy 75 goals, many of them spectacular strikes displaying his key assets of power and speed.

He left Sunderland in October 1991 for £1.8m when he joined Crystal Palace in South London. With hindsight, many think he should not have left Wearside, but the offer at the time was too good to turn down. From then on his career never really hit the same levels, though more recently he has helped revive Darlington's fortunes after rediscovering his old shooting boots. His contribution to the red and white cause during his time with us was immense, and no one will ever forget his goal at Newcastle in the second leg of the 1989-90 play-off semi finals. Class on the grass undoubtedly.

After strolling to the Third Division Championship, Sunderland fans knew that life in the Second Division would be an altogether tougher proposition. While there was optimism that the new strike force of Gates and Gabbiadini would fire us to glory, in truth the priority for all at the Club was to keep a steady presence in the Second Division before rebuilding the squad for a promotion campaign the following season. The Club was still reeling from the McMenemy years and could ill afford either relegation drama or a big spending promotion campaign at this stage.

However, the squad that won promotion found the step up in class a little difficult to cope with at first. Failure to win any of the first six games brought back terrible memories of the relegation season. As the season wore on though, results improved. But, while the team had some good players, we at times lacked that bit of class needed to take us the extra step.

If Marco Gabbiadini had managed to stay on the pitch, perhaps the play-offs might have been a realistic target. He was sent off twice, and the consequent suspensions did little to help the promotion push. The problem was, he was - basically - our only scorer. We knew that, he knew that, and unfortunately the rest of the division seemed to know it too. Marco missed seven games through suspension, and a further four through injury. The scoring rate was halved in his absence, and we were never able to find a successful short term replacement. Billy Whitehurst came and went, and big German striker Thomas Hauser, signed mid-season, failed to provide any real firepower. Peter Barnes, once one of England's most exciting wingers, made a very fleeting cameo appearance, and all in all we simply struggled to score without Gabbers. At the other end of the pitch, Ian Hesford lasted only half the season, and Welsh international Tony Norman joined from Hull in a deal which saw Billy Whitehurst make the opposite journey to Boothferry Park.

Nevertheless, Smith still continued to do a good job. The slow start had supporters once again grabbing their worry beads, but they did not really have too much to fear. A 1 - 1 draw with Crystal Palace in mid-September began a run which saw only one defeat in thirteen games, enough to keep us steady in mid-table, but overall too few of these games were being won to put us in the promotion picture.

Supporters hoped for a little more from the Cup competitions, but had little to cheer here. Smith's old employers, York City, were easily disposed of 4 - 0 on aggregate in the League Cup, but West Ham in the next round were tougher opponents. A 3 - 0 first leg defeat could not be overturned at the Boleyn Ground, and one of our avenues to Wembley was well and truly closed off. In the FA Cup, Oxford held Sunderland to a 1 - 1 draw at Roker Park, and we duly lay down in the replay, finishing on the wrong end of a 2 - 0 scoreline. Even the Simod Cup did not distract fans for too long. An away win at Charlton was followed by defeat at Blackburn Rovers, and that was that as far as the cups were concerned.

Yet, there were some great displays when the team clicked. We managed to beat Swindon, Portsmouth and Ipswich - all decent sides - 4 - 0 at Roker, but with such performances appearing on an irregular basis, we cantered to an eleventh place finish, having won sixteen games, lost fifteen, and drawn fifteen, and scoring as many goals as we conceded. While, ultimately, the performance was nothing more than average, we were back in the Second Division. We had consolidated and were never in any danger of relegation.

For the first time in twenty years, the season had drawn to end without the Lads playing to avoid relegation or hoping for promotion. The ship had well and truly been steadied and we could now look forward to better times ahead.

Thomas Hauser.

Fireworks Fly

Easter Saturday saw Ipswich Town visit Roker Park, and though the Lads had little to play for, the game was filled with action. An excellent display saw Ipswich sent home with their tail well and truly between their legs, a Marco Gabbiadini hat trick - his first for the Club - being instrumental in dishing out a 4 - 0 hammering. However, goals were not the only thing Marco dished out that afternoon, and after completing his hat trick with a penalty, Gabbiadini reacted to some foul play from their keeper and was sent off for violent conduct. It was his second red card of the season, and it brought an automatic four match ban that ended any slim hopes we had of reaching the Play Offs.

Marco was not alone in misbehaving though. His sending off brought the Club as a whole to an extremely high total of disciplinary points; it was our third dismissal of the season, and with almost fifty yellow cards having been dished out too, concern was expressed about the Lads' style of play. Moulded in the no-nonsense style of manager Denis Smith, and with hard men of the calibre of Johnny Kay in the side, there was perhaps a case to be answered! However, the team was hard-but-fair rather than dirty, and Marco's dismissals somewhat out of keeping with his general character. The following season he would score a proper hat trick from open play and avoid the sending off afterwards!

Marco Gabbiadini.

1989-1990
The Play-Offs

"The season that will forever be remembered for the play-offs"

Watford shot down

Early in September, Watford visited Roker Park. The Lads had made a reasonable start to the season, and were looking to press their promotion claims early on. Just 15,042 turned out for the game, but those that had stayed at home missed a real treat. In one of his best games for the Club, Gabbiadini terrorised the Hornets' defence, his pace ripping them apart completely. The match was very one sided, ending 4 - 0 to the Lads, Gabbiadini hitting a hat-trick and Gordon Armstrong scoring too. Glenn Roeder, the Watford manager, made no excuses, conceding the better team had won. Unsurprisingly, he singled out Marco in particular, suggesting the hat-trick was one the best he'd seen.

The win came shortly after an impressive victory over local rivals Middlesbrough, and was enough to lift us into second place in the table. Everyone knew it was early days, but expectations were rising. Perhaps this would be our year?

After comfortably securing our Second Division status, Denis Smith dipped into the transfer market to strengthen his squad during the close season. Having brought in goalkeeper Tony Norman mid-way through the previous season, he added further steel to the defence with Paul Hardyman, a tenacious full back. He was also working hard to bring a quality midfield player to the Club, and in late August Paul Bracewell returned to Sunderland, his brief being to add some creativity to our play. In addition to this, a number of promising youngsters were starting to break into the team, most notably Warren Hawke and Kieron Brady.

The season kicked off with some anticipation then, the Lads making a long journey to Swindon Town, where Warren Hawke scored his first goal for the Club and Sunderland won 2 - 0. A great performance had us looking like promotion candidates already. Ipswich arrived at Roker, however, and soon proved that it would be a long hard slog. Racing into a 3 - 0 lead, they showed Sunderland just what they would be up against this season, and despite goals from Gates and Gabbiadini, the visitors ran out 4 - 2 winners.

Paul Bracewell arrived after this game, however, and he provided a real steadying influence. A 2 - 1 victory at home to 'Boro ensued in our next game, and the Roker faithful were dished up a classic a couple of weeks later when Gabbiadini scored a tremendous hat-trick in the 4 - 0 defeat of Watford. His performance was described by the Hornet's manager Glen Roeder as one of the best he had ever seen. Sunderland crept up to second place, and things were looking good. However, disaster had struck in between these two victories, when goalkeeper Tony Norman suffered a broken arm. He would be replaced for the next three months by Tim Carter. Though Carter acquitted himself well, Norman's presence was missed nonetheless.

In October, though, a couple of awful defeats rocked the boat. A 2 - 0 defeat at promotion rivals Leeds was followed four days later by a 5 - 0 thrashing at hands of another of the favourites, West Ham. It seemed that we weren't quite ready for the big time yet, but the Lads soon dusted themselves off and put the challenge back on track with wins over Bradford, Stoke and Barnsley. Indeed, following these defeats, we lost just one more of the twelve games remaining until the end of the year; in a happy contrast to the days of the McMenemy era, we were becoming hard to beat. Smith's team did not lie down and die.

However, too many of our games were still being draw rather than won, and an improvement was necessary if promotion promise was to be turned into reality. Yet, in the first couple of months of the New Year, our form dipped noticeably. The tone was set with a New Year's Day game against Hull - it ended in a 3 - 2 defeat - and continued for the next nine games, our only victory being a 2 - 1 win at home to Brighton. A small consolation came in the fact that we managed a well-earned 0 - 0 draw in the 110th Wear/Tyne derby game at St James' Park.

Fortuitously, a turnaround in form brought some much needed points. A run of five victories in six games - Bournemouth, West Ham, Bradford, Sheffield United and Stoke being the defeated sides - lifted us into a play-off place by early April.

Three wins in our last seven games was enough to secure the all important sixth position at the end of the season. Our reward was a play-off semi-final against the third placed team: Newcastle United!

In all, it had been our best season for some time, with extra entertainment coming in the League Cup, now know as the 'Littlewoods Cup'. Fulham were well beaten in the second round, and we eased past Bournemouth in a replayed third round. The reward was a long trip to Exeter, where a shock defeat looked on the cards until late goals from Armstrong and Gates levelled the scores, and led to celebrations which, according to at least one newspaper, were very highly spirited indeed. John Kay - the 'red and white tractor' - was targeted, but nothing was proved. John's reputation amongst the fans remained unblemished, and a 5 - 2 win at Roker Park moved us into the fifth round.

Memories of the 1985 run came to the fore, but the main link was the renewal of the Bennett-Speedie grudge match that had peaked in the semi-finals against Chelsea that year. While the first game - at Roker - ended in a draw, the replay saw our dreams crushed in a 5 - 0 hammering.

However, this is the season that will forever be remembered for the play-offs. A scoreless draw at Roker Park in the first leg meant that Sunderland had it all to do at St James' Park. Against all the predictions, Gates and Gabbiadini struck to secure a famous victory and we were off to Wembley to play Swindon, much to the annoyance of Newcastle, who had finished well above us in the division.

The game at Wembley was a bit of an anti-climax however, and a poor 1- 0 defeat followed. It proved irrelevant though, as lady luck shone on Sunderland for once in a decade which had had so few high points. Financial irregularities at Swindon were investigated, and the cloud that hung over the West County Club had an absolutely gleaming silver lining for the men from Roker Park. The Football League ruled that Swindon should be relegated to Division Two as a penalty for the misdemeanours, and Sunderland were promoted to the First Division via the 'back door' in their place. The 1980's ended as they had begun: with Sunderland back in the big time.

John Kay

One of the terrace heroes to emerge during Smith's time in charge was full back John Kay. Signed from Wimbledon for the start of the 1987-88 season, he cost less than £25,000, another of Smith's bargain buys. He was an ever present in the League during our promotion push, but a nasty injury the following season put him out of action for a year. However, he re-established himself in the team during the 1989-90 season, and made over 200 appearances for the Lads.

Affectionately known as the 'Red and White Tractor', he was a no nonsense, tough tackling defender, whose spirit helped drive the team on. Undoubtedly one of football's hard men, he never shirked from a challenge. Perhaps the best word to sum him up was 'dynamite'.

John Kay

Play-Off Glory

A home defeat in the last League game of the season meant that Sunderland were drawn to face arch-rivals Newcastle in the play-off semi finals. Sunderland, having finished in sixth position, hosted the first leg at Roker Park on the 13th May. Unsurprisingly, our biggest crowd of the season packed in to the ground for the occasion, a Sunday lunchtime kick-off. Both the derby games during the season had ended in draws, but Newcastle's superior League position - and the presence of some big money buys in their team - made the Magpies favourites.

The game was typical derby fare, the high stakes adding to the tension. A scrappy, hard fought game saw Sunderland defend brilliantly, denying Newcastle what seemed certain goals on a number of occasions. As the final whistle approached, a scoreless draw seemed to be on the cards, but there was drama right at the end of the match. Sunderland were awarded a very late penalty, and the whole of Roker Park held its breath as Paul Hardyman stepped up for the spot kick. A 1 - 0 victory was about to be snatched and the one goal lead would be a real advantage going into the second leg. We had matched them at St James' in the League, so could do it again in the play-offs. However, the kick was a weak one, and John Burridge saved it well. The Sunderland full back couldn't believe it, and looking for a second chance he followed through for a rebound. None was forthcoming, and the best he could manage was to kick at the ball - and goalkeeper - after Burridge had claimed the loose ball. The inevitable sending off resulted, and attention moved to St James' Park for the second leg on the 16th May.

Despite the 0 - 0 scoreline - and the loss of Hardyman - Sunderland were in good spirits going into the match. Our away form during the season had been excellent, with only seven defeats in 23 games. Moreover, we were still unbeaten against the Mags during the season. But, Newcastle must have thought that all of the hard work had been done. What was to follow will go down as one of the undoubted highlights of this or any other decade.

St James' Park was a cauldron that night, with over 32,000 packed in for a match that was not for the faint hearted. For Sunderland fans, it was glory all the way, and for Newcastle, humiliation. Football is made for nights like this, and the fact that it took place at the home of our greatest rivals made it twice as sweet.

As expected, Newcastle poured forward from the start, although with little pattern to their play. Gary Bennett was colossal at the back, controlling the entire 18-yard area and snuffing out any danger as soon as it arose. After 13 minutes, the travelling red and white fans, housed in the Leazes End, went wild, as Eric Gates slotted home a cross from Gary Owers in front of the crowded Gallowgate End. The Magpies were stunned, and Owers could have doubled the lead shortly afterwards had Burridge not been alert. Newcastle piled forward again, but the Sunderland defence stood firm.

With only five minutes left, Warren Hawke, having probably the best game of his Sunderland career on the left wing, combined with Gates to put Gabbiadini through, and Marco slotted the ball home to make it 2 - 0. Oh what joy, but oh what crowd trouble. Incensed Newcastle fans raced onto the pitch, heading for the Leazes End.

What a goal!

There is no doubting the goal of the season: Marco Gabbiadini's against Newcastle. It came with the game entering its closing stages, Sunderland defending a slender 1 - 0 lead. The game was closely balanced, with both teams playing out of their skins, but we were having the better chances as the game wore on. With ten minutes left, Gabbiadini set up a great chance for Owers, but somehow the Newcastle keeper managed to save his shot. Owers returned the compliment shortly afterwards with a great cross from the right but, with Marco pounding in, the keeper bravely intercepted.

Finally, with five minutes left, Kay headed a long ball forward, which Hawke picked up before feeding Marco some thirty yards from goal. The striker quickly turned and cut inside, charging towards the middle of the penalty area. Surrounded by three defenders, he played a clever one-two with Gates, peeled away from his markers and ran into space before receiving a superbly weighted return pass. With defenders charging after him, Marco pounced on the return and slid the ball past Burridge's left hand.

2 - 0!!! The Lads were through to Wembley and everyone knew it.

The police intervened and the game was held up for twenty minutes. The hooligan elements' hopes of getting the game abandoned were dashed, and when play resumed Sunderland held on comfortably for an historic win.

Our reward was a play-off final against Swindon Town, a one off game for the right to top-flight football. A glorious day saw Wembley packed to the rafters, but the game turned out to be another horrendous anti-climax for Sunderland. If 16th May was one of football's highs, 28th May was surely one of its lows. Sunderland crumbled completely, and offered little in the way of opposition to a vastly superior Swindon side. The 1 - 0 scoreline was a complete travesty - we should have been hammered. Another Wembley own goal, this time by Gary Bennett, was scant reward for the West Country team's total dominance, and everyone headed home with a sinking feeling.

However, the talk on the trains and buses and in the pubs on Wearside was all about the investigation into financial irregularities by Swindon. Maybe, just maybe, we might still go up, despite our poor showing in the capital.

Sure enough, Lady Luck shone through, and during Italia '90 World Cup it was announced that the Wiltshire team should be demoted from the top flight. After leaving Wembley with our heads down, celebrations could start after all. We had done it! Just three years after the play-offs had produced our darkest day with relegation to the Third Division, we were back where we belonged.

Legal Battle

Football is big business and a passionate one to boot. No-one should be fooled into thinking that the stakes have ever been anything other than of the highest order since the very early days of the game. For evidence of this, one only has to look at the way in which Sunderland and Sunderland Albion battled to gain admission to the League in the 1880s, with money being thrown at new players and political lobbying of the highest order being brought to bear on the issue.

At the end of the 1989-90 season, the Football League's decision to replace Swindon with Sunderland in Division One brought a furious response from Sheffield Wednesday, who argued they should stay up as the best placed relegated team, and from Newcastle, who felt they should go up as the third placed Division Two team. Having decided that Swindon should not take their place in Division One, the League knew they had a problem on their hands. There were no rules in place to deal with this one-off situation, so Wednesday, Newcastle and Sunderland all had a legitimate claim on the spare place in English football's top flight.

However, the Football League were keen to protect the integrity of the play-offs system and opted for Sunderland as play-off runners-up. This is well known. However, what is less well known, is that the League had made their decision before the play-off final took place. As the Lads walked out at Wembley, Sunderland Chairman Bob Murray already knew promotion had been secured. Having made their decision, the League were praying for a Sunderland victory to head off the issue, but our poor performance on the pitch meant a legal battle with the losing parties was almost inevitable. In the end, though, we were a match for all such threats, and the strangest promotion in the Club's history was secured.

Play-off final action.

1990·91	Sunderland relegated from First Division on last day of season
1991·92	Malcolm Crosby appointed manager. Narrowly miss relegation. Reach FA Cup Final, but lose 2 - 0 to Liverpool.
1992·93	Premier League starts. Terry Butcher appointed manager. Miss relegation by one point.
1993·94	Mick Buxton appointed manager. Mid-table finish.
1994·95	Peter Reid appointed manager with just seven games to save Sunderland from relegation. Finish fifth bottom.
1995·96	Reid guides team to First Division Championship.
1996·97	Relegated from the Premiership on last day of season. Club becomes a plc. Last ever game at Roker Park.
1997·98	First game at Stadium of Light. Narrowly miss promotion after amazing play-off final.
1998·99	First Division Champions with a record 105 points. Reach Worthington Cup semi-final.
1999·2000	Begin new millennium in Premier League. Stadium of Light hosts England international game.

In the 1990s the rollercoaster ride continued. The decade began in the old First Division, where an exciting young team won plaudits for their attacking football but suffered the agony of relegation on the final day of the season. The following year, a glorious run in the FA Cup took us all the way to the final, but a strong Liverpool team proved too much for the Lads on the day.

A succession of poor performances in the League saw a merry-go-round of managerial changes and relegation to the third flight became a real possibility again. But, the arrival of Peter Reid in 1995 provided some much needed stability and success, his first full season in charge producing a First Division title. Back in the big time again, we were once more the cruel victims of a last day relegation, but the Lads fought back and another First Division title saw the decade end where it began, with Sunderland back in the top flight.

Off the pitch, we moved home for the first time since 1898, Roker Park bowing out after 99 years of fine service. The Club's new state of the art home, the Sunderland Stadium of Light, opened at the beginning of the 1997-98 season and is recognised as one of the finest stadia in Europe. The 1990s also saw the Club become a Public Limited Company, one of the first clubs to make a move into the stock market.

As the new millennium approaches, the Club looks in better shape than it has done for many years, both on and off the pitch. Indeed, there is much to suggest that we are on the verge of a new dawn, with huge crowds at the new ground roaring on a young and spirited side. At last, it seems like the big time is here again!

CONSECTATIO EXCELLENTIAE

SUNDERLAND A.F.C.®

Sunderland A.F.C.
New Stadium Opening
Vs. Ajax
Date 30/07/97   Kick Off 5.30
West Stand
Stiles: 17   TO 20
Access: 5   TO 20
22   Seat 0281
Adult   Price
YOU ARE REQUESTED TO TAKE YOUR SEAT
20 MINUTES BEFORE KICK-OFF   TO BE RETAIN

INTO THE

Light

1 9 9 0 · 2 0 0 0

1990-1991 Drama

"Although the Lads put in good performances, the bottom line was that we were winning too few games."

Tony Norman

One of the most reliable - and likeable - players in Smith's team was Welsh international goalkeeper Tony Norman. Signed by Smith during the 1988-89 season, the keeper cost around £650,000 in a deal that saw Ian Hesford and Billy Whitehurst go to Norman's old club - Hull - as part of the deal. He proved to be an astute buy. The goalkeeper's position had been something of a problem for Sunderland since the departure of Chris Turner in 1985, but Norman ended our troubles between the sticks, his solidity adding confidence to the back line.

Tony put in some memorable performances in his time at the Club, but one that really sticks in the mind came in our 1992 FA Cup quarter-final replay against Chelsea. He was superb that night, pulling off some trademark reflex saves that denied our opponents what appeared to be certain goals.

In all, Norman made some 227 League and Cup appearances for the Lads, before moving on to Huddersfield in 1995. Since retiring from the game, Norman has returned to work in the region, as a policeman in the Durham area. If he can catch criminals as well as he could catch footballs, Durham villains are in for a hard time!

Good fortune had ended the Lads' long exile from the place where they belong - English football's top division - and they began the first season of the 1990s in Division One. The team that had won promotion featured some excellent young players, chief amongst them striker Marco Gabbiadini, but it was evident that the squad would need strengthening if it was to cope with the rigours of First Division football. With this in mind, Denis Smith invested in defender Kevin Ball (a £350,000 purchase from Portsmouth) and striker Peter Davenport (£300,000 from Middlesbrough) before the season kicked-off. The two were welcome additions, but some fans craved further signings. However, with a court case over the Club's ownership looming, there was still much uncertainty behind the scenes and this inevitably limited investments.

On the pitch, the Lads' first game of the campaign was away to Norwich City, a closely fought encounter that included a fantastic goal from Gabbiadini. The scoreline, however, did not end in our favour, with the home side running out 3 - 2 winners. A few days later, Tottenham Hotspur made the trip to Roker Park. Spurs were, arguably, the most glamorous side in the country, including England World Cup heroes Gary Lineker and Paul Gascoigne amongst their number. The stadium was crammed with over 30,000 fans and, although it ended 0 - 0, the match was an exciting one and the Lads notched up a well earned point.

Our next game was another glamorous home match, FA Cup holders Manchester United making the trip to Roker Park. Another big crowd turned out and hopes were high when Gary Owers put the Lads ahead. Manchester United, however, pulled one back in the second-half, and as the game wore on, it looked like Sunderland would have to wait at least another week before recording their first victory. In the 89th minute though, Gary Bennett picked up the ball on the edge of the box and cleverly beat his man before curling a wicked shot into the corner of the goal. It was a glorious strike and it clinched a marvellous victory for the Lads, their first in the top division since April 13th, 1985.

It was a promising opening to the season, but a number of difficult games followed. Although the Lads put in good performances in these matches - winning many plaudits for their attacking play and scoring some spectacular goals - the bottom line was that we were winning too few games. By the end of September, we had gained just five points out of a possible twenty-one. Indeed, Sunderland's second League win of the season, a 2 - 0 victory over Luton Town, did not come until 20th October, and their third, another 2 - 0, this time against Sheffield United, came a month after the Luton game on 24th November. By the end of the year, the team had managed to gain just fifteen points from a potential sixty - relegation was looking a distinct possibility.

Yet, the team were playing good football, and had been genuinely unlucky in many games, often losing points as a result of late goals or coming out on the wrong side of a close game. As a measure of this, it is worth recording that only twice in twenty games had the Lads lost by more than a single goal. This good work began to pay dividends in the New Year with victories over Southampton and Chelsea providing a much needed boost in January and the following month the Lads secured a good win at Notts Forest and were beaten just once, by Everton.

Smith looked to have done enough to maintain the team's place in Division One, but as the season drew to a close, the tolls of a difficult campaign began to show, and the lack of depth in the squad was exposed by injuries, particularly to star striker Gabbiadini, and suspensions. Three consecutive defeats in March - against Sheffield United, Liverpool and Aston Villa - severely weakened our League position and April began with a 5 - 0 thrashing at Leeds. That match was followed by further defeats at QPR and Southampton, leaving the Lads in a relegation place and five points behind their nearest rivals, Luton Town.

With just four games left, relegation looked inevitable. Hopes were raised when the Lads beat Luton 2 - 0, but failure to win our game in hand, against Wimbledon, gave the Bedfordshire team the upper hand. In the end, it wasn't to be, with defeat on the final day of the season sealing Sunderland's fate. The flirtation with top flight football had been cruelly brief.

Gary Owers.

Six Goals at Spurs

One of the season's most exciting games came when the Lads visited White Hart Lane to play Tottenham Hotspur. Spurs were having a good season, but in an electric first half, the Lads tore the home side apart, going 2 - 0 up before half time. In the second half though, Spurs fought back, pulling the game level. More was to come, and the Lads regained the lead. With seconds left, it looked like Sunderland had achieved a famous victory, but right at the death Spurs hit an equaliser. The Lads made giving away late goals something of a habit; they were 2 - 0 up at Wimbledon with ten minutes left, but drew 2 - 2; similarly at Derby they were 3 - 0 up but drew 3 - 3. Had we managed to hold onto leads in these games, the extra points would have been enough to keep us in the top flight. It was a bitter pill to swallow.

Kevin Ball.

Singing the Blues

"How can you be relegated and have people chanting for you like that?"

Denis Smith

Sunderland players celebrate, but eventually loose 3 - 2 to Manchester City on the final day of the season.

Reidy takes note...

As Sunderland fell to a strong Manchester City team on the final day of the 1990-91 season, who could have predicted that two of the men behind City's good form would later become Sunderland heroes? Peter Reid had put together one of the best Manchester City sides of recent decades - but was unbelievably sacked in 1993 after twice leading them to fifth place - and a young Niall Quinn was one of the First Division's leading marksmen, hitting 22 goals in the 1990-91 campaign.

Nearly four years after their Maine Road defeat, Sunderland would be desperately searching for a saviour. We were not in a strong position to attract a good manager, but the board managed persuade Reid to take what had become one of the hottest seats in English football. The passion of the fans that day must have left an impression!

Sunderland's last game of the season was away to Peter Reid's classy Manchester City team. City were riding high in the League and were looking to finish ahead of rivals Manchester United. Their manager had organised an effective team that defended well and scored goals. The Championship was beyond their reach, but victory in their final game would probably secure a place in the top five and see them finish above United.

With just four games remaining the Lads had been five points behind fellow relegation contenders Luton Town, but victory at their place closed the gap to two points, and the Lads had a game in hand. That extra game - a bad tempered affair spoilt by the opposition's gamesmanship - was a 0 - 0 draw against Wimbledon that cut the margin to one point with two games remaining.

Sunderland's penultimate game was against League leaders Arsenal, who needed points to help them secure the Championship, and the Lads did well to produce another 0 - 0 draw. Indeed, they were a little unlucky on the day, Gary Owers having a marvellous shot tipped away by David Seaman in the game's closing minutes. The good news for Sunderland though, was that Luton had lost again, putting the teams level on points going into the final match of the season. Amazingly, the two clubs had an identical goal difference, but Luton remained ahead of Sunderland because they had scored more goals. This meant that Sunderland had to better whatever Luton did on the final day of the season, if they were to stay up. Luton, though, were playing at home to bottom placed - and already relegated - Derby County. It was Sunderland who needed the points most for we stood in a relegation position before the match kicked off.

So, the Lads kicked off their final game hoping to avoid the drop, but knowing the odds were against them. Within ten minutes, Manchester City had lengthened these odds, Niall Quinn scoring a well taken goal. The Lads did not give up though. Marco Gabbiadini equalised with one of the goals of the season, a bullet header from John Kay's cross, and Gary Bennett put us into the lead with a deflected header just before half-time. By now, the fans were going wild, but they were soon brought back to earth by Quinn, who made it 2 - 2 following a mistake by Owers.

In the second-half, the Lads battled on, but were unable to break down the City defence. News began to filter through that Luton were winning by two goals to nil leaving Sunderland with the difficult task of scoring a further two themselves in order to stay up. In the dying seconds another goal was scored but by City rather than the Lads and the dream was over. Sunderland had lost 3 - 2, and finished three points away from Luton. But, they had gone out fighting.

The game - in fact the season as a whole - had been a mammoth encounter. Yet, what marked this match out was not so much what happened on the pitch, as what went on off it. 15,000 Sunderland fans had made the trip to Maine Road, which as The Guardian pointed out, was around 5,000 more than the average Luton crowd. At the end of the game they refused to go home until they had cheered their heroes on one last time; indeed, they stayed for 45 minutes after the final whistle, singing their hearts out for the Lads. Manager Denis Smith found it hard to control his emotions: 'Unbelievable. How can you be relegated and have people chanting for you like that? Grown men out there are crying, kids are crying - they hurt as much as the players. It's difficult to put my feelings into words.'

The Guardian noted that 'Though someone had to go down from the First Division on Saturday, there will be many who wished it had been Luton [for] Sunderland are a club carried so deeply in the hearts of their supporters that their passion warms the hearts of even those who would be neutral.' Both on and off the pitch, the Club had won friends up and down the country, and our relegation was viewed with sadness beyond the confines of Wearside.

1990-91 Sunderland team.

Kevin Ball:
Defensive Rock - Midfield General

The 1990-91 season provided Kevin Ball with his first taste of football Wearside style. Despite the disappointment of relegation at the end of that campaign, it must have been to his liking, for he has remained at the Club throughout the 1990s. Kevin arrived at Sunderland at the start of the season, signed on the basis of the tough, no-nonsense defending that had won the hearts of fans at Portsmouth. On arrival in the North-East these same qualities, along with his fighting spirit and desire to win, soon saw the Roker faithful warm to him. It quickly became apparent that Ball was a great motivator too, regularly seen calling on his team mates to raise their game, and it was only a matter of time until he became Captain of the team. He has gone on to lead the Club to two First Division Championships.

Signed as central defender, he has shifted to central midfield more recently, where he has played a crucial role in linking play between the middle and the back, and where his presence at the heart of the team has been of great importance. Always one to stamp his authority on the game, Bally is widely acknowledged as one of the toughest players in football; indeed, no less an authority the Vinnie Jones branded him the 'hardest man in football'! Always a gentlemen too, Kevin Ball is without doubt a Sunderland legend, and the new millennium marks his testimonial season at the Club.

Kevin Ball.

1991-1992
A Tale of Two Teams

"The FA Cup was becoming the main attraction"

Le Brace is Ace

At the end of the 1991-92 season, one of Roker's heroes, Paul Bracewell, left the Club for a second time. Signed initially by Alan Durban in 1983, 'Le Brace' played just one season for the Lads before moving to Everton, where he was part of a hugely successful team that won most of the game's big trophies.

He re-joined the Lads in 1989-90, and his silky skills and midfield vision graced Roker for three further seasons. His final game in this second spell was an appearance in the 1992 FA Cup final, his fourth Cup final appearance, and sadly it ended like his previous three - in defeat. During the 1991-92 close he controversially moved to Newcastle, where Kevin Keegan saw him as just the man to turn around their team. Keegan's judgement proved sound, and Bracewell not only helped guide the Magpies to the Premier League, but also continued to play a role in the top flight, despite his by now advancing years.

Fortunately, all was not lost for the Lads, and in the summer of 1995, Peter Reid brought Bracewell back to Roker as his player-assistant manager. Reid, who had played with Bracewell in Everton's midfield, knew exactly what Le Brace was capable of, and his trust in the player was not misplaced. However, after another two and a bit seasons at the Club, it was clear that his playing days were numbered with the arrival of a youthful Lee Clark in the summer of 1997, and Bracewell moved on again, rejoining Keegan at Second Division Fulham, eventually becoming manager of the club following Keegan's appointment as England manager.

Whenever a team suffers relegation the manager faces a difficult task in motivating his players in the face of great disappointment, and Sunderland's 1991-92 campaign was to be a difficult one for Denis Smith. The season did not start too badly, with a respectable home draw against fellow relegation suffers Derby being followed by a 3 - 0 midweek win at Barnsley. The second Saturday of the season, however, saw disaster strike as the Lads crashed 4 - 1 to Millwall; it was one of a number of heavy defeats the team would suffer before Christmas.

September proved to be a particularly devastating month for the Sunderland faithful. It began with a 1 - 0 defeat at Portsmouth, ended with a 2 - 1 defeat at Middlesbrough, and included a 3 - 5 reverse against Swindon Town. The month's only bright spot was a 4 - 1 win at Charlton Athletic, where a lightning quick hat-trick from Gabbiadini ripped the Londoners apart. The next couple of months were no better, the Lads managing to win just two League games in ten, and suffering the humiliation of a 6 - 1 aggregate defeat against Huddersfield in the League Cup.

It was clear that radical action was required, and Smith decided to sell his star player, Gabbiadini, to Crystal Palace for a massive £1.8 million. Two new strikers came in to replace him: John Byrne for £250,000 from Brighton and Don Goodman, for a Club record fee of £900,000, from West Brom. Unfortunately for Smith, Goodman's debut was something of a disaster, the Lads ending with just nine men as they crashed 1 - 0 at Wolves. Significantly, one of those sent off was Goodman's new striking partner Byrne, and the latter's subsequent suspension meant the two would have little opportunity to play together before Christmas. Though two narrow victories followed the Wolves game, defeats against Tranmere (1 - 0) and Oxford (3 - 0) over the Christmas holiday proved to be too much for the board and Smith was sacked before the New Year began. The Goodman-Byrne partnership had been the last roll of the dice for Smith, but they managed just two full games together under his management. It was too little, too late.

So, the New Year began with Smith's assistant, South Shields born Malcolm Crosby, in charge of team selection. His first game saw a reasonable 2 - 0 victory against Barnsley, and three days later the Lads beat Port Vale 3 - 0 in the FA Cup third round. The following weekend things really began to look up, Goodman hitting a hat-trick as Millwall were thrashed 6 - 2. A League win at Derby (2 - 1) and a thrilling 3 - 2 FA Cup win at Oxford then capped an excellent first month for Crosby. Under his guidance, Sunderland had picked up maximum points in the League, scored a hat full of goals, and reached the 5th round of the FA Cup for the first time since the 1975-76 season. Unsurprisingly, he walked away with a well earned Manager of the Month award.

Inevitably, such form could not be maintained for long, and over the next few months, the League form began to dip. However, in the FA Cup we were unbeatable, leading some to observe we had two teams: a poor one in the League and an heroic one in the Cup. First Division West Ham were beaten after a replay in the fifth round, and another top flight London team, Chelsea, were seen off in the quarter-finals. Crosby had put the Lads into their first semi-final since 1973.

Inevitably, this Cup run led to a stockpiling of postponed League fixtures, for which the Lads would pay at the end of the season, with six games being played in a gruelling thirteen days between 8th and 20th April.

Furthermore, poor League form at various points of the season meant that the Lads needed to pick up points in these matches in order to avoid relegation. However, this seemed to be of little concern when a moment of pure glory in the Cup semi-final against First Division Norwich saw a header from Byrne seal a place in the Cup Final.

After this high, the battle for survival re-commenced. Relegation was a very real danger, and at one point it looked odds on that we would go in to the Cup Final as a Third Division team. Safety was not guaranteed until a 2 - 2 draw at Blackburn, in our penultimate game, gave us enough points to avoid the drop. The match was Crosby's first as manager, his appointment having been confirmed before the game. That point - along with another secured in our final match - ensured the Lads scraped to an 18th place finish, just three positions away from relegation. It was a disappointing performance from a team that had graced the First Division a season earlier and - without Goodman, its Cup-tied star striker - managed to reach an FA Cup final. What's more, the battle had taken its toll too, and it was a tired team that made the journey to Wembley for the Cup Final, where Liverpool proved too strong for Sunderland and ran out 2 - 0 winners. It was great to have made the Final, but it proved to be yet another bitter end to the season.

John Byrne.

Smith Leaves the Club

The 1991-92 season brought Denis Smith's reign as manager to an end. He was perhaps unfortunate to have lost the job, but after four good seasons there were signs that the strong team spirit he had built was starting to fade. His arrival at the Club was unforgettable. Following in the wake of McMenemy's disastrous period in charge, Smith promised to bring the good times back. He had charisma and self-confidence that rubbed off on the players and a good eye for bargain transfers, qualities which helped him to catapult Sunderland back into the Second Division during his first season in charge. His second season was very much one of consolidation, but in the third - albeit with a little luck - he steered the Lads back into the top flight. It was a great achievement, but his luck ran out the following season, when relegation was sealed at the end of the season. An honest and hard working manager, Smith always gave 100%, and was committed to the Club. His personality and approach were a complete contrast to that of McMenemy, and the fans remember him fondly. He goes down as one of the Club's best managers in recent years.

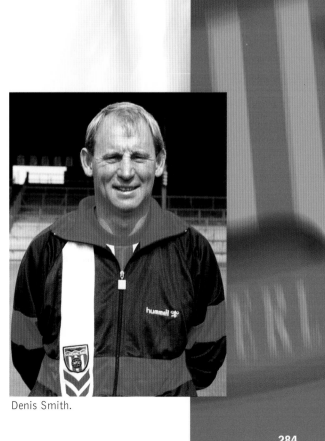

Denis Smith.

The Road to Wembley

Malcolm Crosby.

Crosby the Caretaker

The man who had guided Sunderland to Wembley was caretaker manager Malcolm Crosby. As the Lads started to build up momentum in their Cup run, calls for Crosby to be given the job on a permanent basis - the most vocal, perhaps, from London based pundits such as the BBC's Des Lynam - began to increase. The board, however, were acting cautiously, feeling his best role was a coach rather than manager, concerned that his lack of experience in the position might create problems. However, when the Lads reached the Final, the board had no choice other than to offer him the post. Partly the offer was a reward for the Cup run, but there was also immense pressure from the fans and the media to give him the job. Much had been made of the possibility of having a caretaker manager leading the team out at Wembley, and victory over Norwich made his appointment inevitable.

In the event, the board were probably right to act with caution. Crosby, an excellent coach and very well liked within the Club, had no real experience of management, and found it difficult to reproduce the heroics of the Cup run in the League. Indeed, he departed before the 1992-93 season was completed. Crosby has successfully teamed up as an assistant to old boss Denis Smith on a number of occasions since, notably at Oxford United and West Bromwich Albion, demonstrating his strengths as a number two.

The 1991-92 FA Cup campaign proved to be one of the Lads' best ever. As in 1973, no-one expected it to happen. The team had been playing poorly in the Second Division, and the Cup 'jinx' had been in evidence for much of the previous ten years, the Lads having won just four FA Cup games in the whole of the 1980s (against Rotherham in '82, Bolton in '84, Newport in '86 and Darlington in '87). Again much like 1973, a new manager took charge before the first Cup tie, and somehow turned around the team's performances.

The Cup run began with a home tie against Port Vale. As the team were in such bad form, and with new record signing Don Goodman 'cup tied', no-one would have been surprised had the Lads lost. However, Davenport, Byrne and Atkinson scored the goals as Sunderland recorded a 3 - 0 win. A good result, but it was hardly reason to believe we were about to start a glorious Cup run.

The Fourth Round draw pitted us against Oxford United, at their place, and an excellent performance saw the Lads in full control for most of the match. Indeed, we were cruising at 3 - 0 with goals from Byrne, Hardyman and Davenport before a crazy final five minutes saw the home side hit back, first with what everyone assumed to be a consolation goal, and then with a worrying second that put them in the hunt for an equaliser. Fortunately, we held on for the final few minutes, and clinched a Fifth Round tie at home to West Ham.

Difficult conditions spoilt the tie against the Hammers, and for a long time it looked like the First Division side would put the Lads out of the contest. However, a 64th minute goal from Byrne was enough to keep us in the hunt, the match ending a 1 - 1 draw. The replay at Upton Park was to prove a dramatic encounter. In the 6th minute, Byrne picked up on a dreadful backpass to give the Lads a 1 - 0 lead. Less than twenty minutes later, Byrne struck again, to put us in a commanding position. However, the Londoners hit back just before half-time, and early in the second half grabbed an equaliser to set up a grand finale. Inevitably, a tense encounter followed, but the critical goal came twelve minutes from time, when David Rush knocked home the winner.

In the Quarter-Finals, Sunderland made another trip to the capital, with high flying Chelsea providing the opponents. The First Division team had much the better of the tie, Clive Allen giving them a 1 - 0 advantage after 36 minutes. As the game wore on, it looked like Sunderland's luck had run out, but with just seven minutes left, Byrne headed home a joyful equaliser to bring Chelsea back to Roker Park. In the replay, the Lads played magnificently, and led 1 - 0 for most of the game. In a dramatic last five minutes though, Chelsea equalised, before Sunderland grabbed an astonishing last minute winner.

The Semi-Final against Norwich took place at Hillsborough, the first Semi-Final at Sheffield Wednesday's ground since the tragedy in 1989 that had killed nearly 100 Liverpool fans. Off the pitch, the famously friendly relations between the two sets of fans continued, and on it a headed goal by John Byrne was enough to put Sunderland into the Cup Final! Amazingly, the Irishman had scored in every round of the Cup so far, and if he could grab one in the Final would be able to join a very select group of strikers to score in every round during a single season.

The Final, though, was to be deeply disappointing for Sunderland fans. The players, tired after a gruelling League programme, found it difficult to match the Liverpool team. It was the team's 56th competitive match of the season, and their twelfth in the five weeks that began with the Semi-Final. The game was not helped by the rain that had made the Wembley pitch greasy, but Sunderland had their chances in the first-half. Most notably, Byrne had a great opportunity to put us 1 - 0 up, but the striker was not at his best, having carried an injury in the run up to the match. When the second-half began, Liverpool came out all guns blazing, and a spectacular strike from Michael Thomas gave the Merseyside club the lead. Rush added another soon afterwards, and there was no way back for the Lads after that.

Briefly, the Lads held winners' medals - the FA having given the wrong ones to them - a mistake which heightened the heartache faced by many players. For some, it was perhaps worse than others :Paul Bracewell had just played in his fourth Cup final, and all of them had ended in defeat. The Cup always creates dreams, but this time the impossible dream remained unfulfilled.

Semi-final action

Armstrong Heads for Glory

The Quarter-Final replay against Chelsea was without doubt one of Roker Park's all time classics. A fantastic atmosphere backed the Lads throughout the game, and a first-half goal from Byrne gave Sunderland the lead until late in the match. Tony Norman had performed heroics in the Sunderland goal, but in a reverse of the Stamford Bridge tie, Chelsea, through Dennis Wise, hit an equaliser with just three minutes left. The Roker Roar fell silent, and Norman's face was a picture of anguished dejection. Thirty minutes of nail biting extra-time seemed inevitable, but the Lads refused to lie down after the equaliser and continued to surge forward. A corner was forced in the last minute, and Brian Atkinson swung it towards the edge of the box. Unmarked, Gordon Armstrong ran to meet it and within seconds his head connected with the ball, unleashing an astonishing header that powered its way into the top corner of the net. Roker exploded with noise, joy and disbelief. The Chelsea players were stunned. It was a glorious winner in a glorious match.

1992-1993
Too Close for Comfort

"once again, it all hung on the last day of the season."

Stadium Struggle

While the Club battled for survival on the pitch, off it, there were even bigger problems on the horizon. With the Taylor Report requiring all First and Second Division clubs to upgrade their stadia into all seated facilities, the Board faced a difficult decision as to how to proceed. Converting Roker Park was far from straightforward. The ground had been allowed to decline since the War, there being a continual failure to invest in it. The only structural changes had come following external investment for the 1966 World Cup and in the early 1980s when safety requirements forced changes to the Roker End. In the latter case, Chairman Tom Cowie merely opted to demolish most of the stand rather than rebuilding or redesigning it. In short, Roker Park was an ageing ground that had been left behind by decades of under-funding. Consequently, the Board opted to move to a new purpose built stadium and leisure complex in Washington, a project that would receive substantial financial backing from the European Union. A ballot of the fans had backed this move, but the Club were facing resistance from those fans who could not bare to part with Roker and there were potential pitfalls in receiving planning permission too. Uncertainty surrounding the outcome of the move made life difficult for the Club, not least because a failure to move to the new ground would result in the government forcing us to invest huge sums in rebuilding Roker Park.

Crosby, like Smith the previous season, faced a difficult task in lifting his players after a disappointing end to the preceding campaign. To make matters worse, inspirational midfielder Paul Bracewell had controversially decided to leave the Club for Newcastle United. However, against this, the manager had strengthened his squad, spending £700,000 generated by the Cup run on Grimsby captain Shaun Cunnington, and bringing in a number of new faces in addition, such as Hearts winger John Colquohon, former England captain Terry Butcher and Sunderland born striker Mick Harford.

Despite our lowly position in the previous year's Second Division, Sunderland started the season in the First Division. We had not, however, been promoted: a new Premier League had been formed in place of the old First Division, and the Second now became the First. It was a controversial move, with Sunderland Chairman Bob Murray making strong efforts to promote the welfare of smaller clubs, many of whom would lose out as money started to flow more directly to the top teams.

On the pitch, Sunderland started badly. The opening game saw defeat at Swindon, and though the Lads beat Tranmere in our first home game, by the end of September we had picked up just eight points from twenty-four, defeat being the most common outcome. Furthermore, Second Division Huddersfield had knocked the Lads out of the Coca-Cola Cup at the first stage. Though October started with a win against Millwall, matters soon became somewhat embarrassing; with the exception of a 2 - 2 draw at home to Notts County, the rest of the month's games were all lost, including a humiliating 6 - 0 televised defeat at West Ham. Now we had just twelve points from thirty-nine.

Matters improved a little over the following month, with good victories against Wolves, Derby and Southend, but it was a far from solid recovery, a 5 - 2 defeat at lowly Peterborough illustrating the frailty of the team. Indeed, performances soon dipped again, and as the festive period came and went, a familiar pattern continued, wins being few and far between, and teams that should have been beaten such as Brentford and Watford coming to Roker Park and taking all three points from the Lads.

At the end of January, with Sunderland out of the Cup following a fourth round defeat at Sheffield Wednesday, the board decided that enough was enough. Relegation to the Second Division was looming, so changes needed to be made: Malcolm Crosby made way for Terry Butcher in the managerial hot seat. However, it was not the appointment the board were looking for. They had tried hard to attract a proven manager to the Club, someone with the wherewithal to guide us back to the top flight, but were knocked back by all those offered the job, including the promotion specialist Dave Bassett. Quite simply, the Sunderland manager's job was not an attractive one. While it was clear Crosby had to go, lining up a suitable replacement was a fraught task. The new manager was another inexperienced appointment from within. The Club drifted into the Butcher era, just as it had drifted into the Crosby era.

Unsurprisingly, perhaps, the new appointment made little difference. After promising wins against Oxford and Charlton, the old, indifferent form reappeared very quickly. The next eight games produced just two victories, and the Lads were unable to find a goal in five of those matches. Consequently, we entered the final stages of the season with relegation still very much on the cards. Significantly, we faced a number of 'six-pointer' games against fellow relegation contenders, including ties with Southend, Brentford, Birmingham and Luton.

The outcome of these matches did little to help the nerves. Southend thrashed us 4 - 2 at home, Brentford held us to a 1 - 1 draw, Birmingham, again at home, beat us 2 - 1, and the match with Luton was saved only by a late, late equaliser. A trip to Newcastle, who were running away with the First Division leadership, rubbed salt in the wounds at the end of the month, the Magpies beating us 1 - 0 to put the Club into real trouble.

As if things weren't bad enough, the derby game was followed by a visit from the team favoured by many to join Newcastle in winning promotion - Portsmouth. Amazingly, the Lads pulled out a great performance, beating Pompey 4 - 1. Would it be enough? A few days later, we visited Tranmere, only to lose 1 - 2, meaning, once again, it all hung on the last day of the season.

In our final game, the Lads made a trip to Notts County knowing that a win would keep us up. A draw or defeat might be enough, but that would rely on others losing elsewhere. County themselves were below Sunderland in the table, but a win would catapult them above us. On the day, a 14,417 crowd in the tiny Meadow Lane ground, around half of whom were Sunderland fans, witnessed a terrible performance from the Lads, and though Kevin Ball grabbed a goal for us, the Notts County team ran out easy winners. The match ended 3 - 1 in the home team's favour.

Sunderland were now left hoping results had gone their way elsewhere. For once they did, Bristol City beating Brentford 4 - 1 and West Ham overcoming Cambridge 2 - 0. Sunderland had, luckily, escaped the drop, finishing just one point, and one place, away from relegation. It was a terrible performance from a club that had reached the Cup Final twelve months earlier, and had graced the old First Division a year before that. Indeed, discounting our successful solitary season in the Third Division, it was the second lowest League placing of all time for a Sunderland team.

Butcher Buckles at Brentford

The Lads' crucial run in to the 1992-93 season, and the very real danger that they may finish the campaign in a relegation position, placed a great deal of pressure on the Sunderland management team. During our last nine matches, we would play against five other teams involved in the division's relegation dog-fight. Following a home defeat against Southend, where a young Stan Collymore helped to pull apart our defence, the Lads made a midweek trip to Brentford. The Bees had been promoted from Division Three the previous season, and were finding life in the second flight hard. After failing to pick up three points against Southend, the fans made it clear that they expected amends to be made against the London team. However, the game did not go to plan, and although Sunderland managed a draw, it was evident that the fans were unhappy. Discontent was aired during game, and player-manager Terry Butcher lost his temper with some fans to such an extent that he was reported to the police for using foul and abusive language. It was clear that the tension was getting to him, but the manager apologised immediately after the incident, saying: 'I think with all the frustration and attention to play and be manager of a team, as well as the worries and the pressure - I just snapped. A few supporters did state their feelings in no uncertain terms. I said something back which I obviously regret. It was a heat-of-the-moment reaction.'

It was a telling moment in his brief managerial career. A lion on the pitch as a player, as a manager he often seemed to crack under the pressure. While the old bulldog spirit works well for a team captain, managers need to draw upon a much broader set of skills and characteristics. Sadly, Butcher often seemed helpless to prevent his side from playing badly, and the frustration was evident for all to see that night at Brentford.

Terry Butcher.

1993-1994
Butchered

"The board backed new manager Terry Butcher to the hilt with over £2 million of talent joining the Club."

Phil Gray out-jumps his markers.

Leeds in the Cup

Despite the generally poor League results that ensued during Butcher's reign, there were still moments of great football to savour. Indeed, when firing on all cylinders, the team he started to construct during the 1993-94 season was an excellent one, a fact demonstrated in a two-legged Coca-Cola Cup tie against Premier League Leeds United. Leeds had won the Championship in the 1991-92 season, and were a formidable side; indeed, they had thrashed Sunderland 5 - 0 the last time they had met, in 1991.

Unfazed, Sunderland took the game to Leeds, goals from Don Goodman and Phil Gray securing a 2 - 1 lead at the end of the Roker Park leg. Despite this, Sunderland were not expected to hold onto their lead in the return match at Elland Road, but another sterling performance produced an identical result - with Goodman and Gray again bagging the goals - to put Sunderland through 4 - 2 on aggregate. Aside from the result, it was the quality and passion of the performances that impressed; yet, this was a two-edged sword for Butcher, as it led many to wonder why his team could not produce such football week-in week-out.

With a third manager at the helm in as many seasons it was clear that something had gone astray in the Sunderland master plan. The board, at times criticised for keeping a tight hold of the purse strings, were keen to rectify the situation, and backed new manager Terry Butcher to the hilt in the run up to the start of the campaign, with over £2 million of talent joining the Club. Butcher had publicly stated that a new broom was required to sweep the cupboard clean, and he set about the task of rebuilding his team. Amongst the pre-season signings were goalkeeper Alec Chamberlain, midfielders Derek Ferguson and Ian Rodgerson, Welsh international defender Andy Melville and Northern Ireland striker Phil Gray.

The spending spree generated much excitement amongst the fans, and boosted hopes that the team would launch themselves into the Premiership. However, just days before the season kicked off, fate once more conspired against Sunderland, when a bizarre car crash involving Sunderland's big new signings temporarily robbed us of the services of Gray and Rodgerson.

Following the incident matters somehow got worse, the Lads losing their opening game of the season 5 - 0 to Derby, the biggest opening day defeat in the Club's history. Butcher didn't disguise his disgust at the team's performance, and any optimism that the supporters may have had pre-season was instantly blown away. The Lads bounced back in their first home League match, thrashing Charlton 4 - 0, but three defeats followed, leaving Sunderland with just three points from their first fifteen. Once again, this was relegation form, and Sunderland were already gracing the foot of the table.

Towards the end of September, matters began to improve. Two draws at least stopped the run of defeats in the League, and following the dismissal of Chester in the First Round of the Coca-Cola Cup, Leeds were beaten both home and away in the Second Round. The following month brought further improvements in the League, with four of the month's six games being won, and in the Coca-Cola Cup, an excellent performance against Aston Villa was acknowledged by the national media. Unfortunately, the Lads lost the tie, a 4 - 1 result in no way reflecting the game.

But, October proved to be Butcher's best month in charge, and the losing habit soon returned. Indeed, matters came to a head on 20th November, when Southend inflicted the Club's fifth successive defeat. Butcher admitted defeat and resigned as manager. The Club were now in crisis mode again, and Chairman Bob Murray decided to take a back seat for a while too. Disillusioned by a lack of progress on the pitch after the summer transfer activity, frustrated by Nissan's efforts to block the building of a new stadium and enduring severe criticism in the local media from former Chairman Tom Cowie, he handed over the Chairmanship to John Featherstone, but remained on the board as the Club's major share holder.

The Club's increasing malaise did not help in the search for a new manager. Butcher was replaced by Sunderland Coach - and former Huddersfield Town boss - Mick Buxton. Another internal appointment, at least Buxton was an experienced manager. He was also a Sunderland lad and a firm manager who would knock the squad into shape.

He was not, however, a long term solution to the managerial problem, and his appointment further emphasized the difficulty the Club was having in attracting a new manager to Sunderland. The position was not the most attractive in football: expectations were high, the chances of surviving more than a year low, Butcher had emptied the coffers, the team were playing badly and Roker Park was an increasingly dilapidated stadium, comparing poorly to the revamped grounds that supposedly smaller clubs like Watford were playing in.

Buxton's first game in charge was a 3 - 2 defeat against Notts Forest, a result which completed a pointless November for Sunderland, but in December he steered the team clear of defeat, delivering three wins and a draw. January produced similarly pleasing League results, with ten points being taken from a possible fifteen, and Carlisle were dispensed with in the FA Cup following a replay. A Fourth Round tie away to Wimbledon rounded off the month's fixtures, but the Dons were too strong for us, running out 2 - 1 winners.

This New Year upturn in form led some of the more optimistic fans to dream of a play-off place, but just two points from February's games put paid to such hopes, and soon mid-table respectability seemed the best the fans could hope far. On the bright side, for the first time in the 1990s relegation was not on the cards!

Promisingly, Buxton had started to get the players working as an effective unit, and March saw four out of five games being won. The last month of the season produced some less spectacular displays, but by then there was little to play for. Buxton, it had to be said, had done a good job since coming in as manager. Indeed, many wondered what might have happened had he taken over earlier in the season. The Lads finished the season in twelfth place, hardly an amazing performance, but a welcome position after the previous season's drama, and a position that seemed improbable during the three months that Butcher led the team. The season had started with high hopes and rapidly descended to invoke the fans' worst fans, but in the end most were happy to settle for the tranquillity of a mid-table finish.

Mick Buxton.

Butcher is Chopped

Terry Butcher will not be remembered as one of the Sunderland 'greats'. An excellent defender throughout most of his playing career, Butcher was in the twilight of his playing days when he joined Sunderland, and had already had one unsuccessful spell as a manager at Coventry before Crosby signed him. Somewhat predictably perhaps, he stepped into the breech as manager when results did not go Crosby's way, but the season's performances actually got worse after his appointment. In his defence, it is worth pointing out that it was not 'his' team that he managed for the second half of the 1992-93 season. However, his massive spending before the start of the 1993-94 season did not help matters on the pitch. In all, he managed the Lads for 38 League games, but steered them to victory just ten times and witnessed defeat in over half. It was a dismal record, particularly given the fact that much the same team had achieved promotion and reached the Cup Final not long before his arrival.

Terry Butcher.

1994-1995
The Great Escape

"just seven games left to save the team from a seemingly inevitable relegation."

'Big Bad Don'

The 1994-95 season saw the departure of another of Sunderland's goal scoring heroes: Don Goodman. Signed by Denis Smith for a then Club record £900,000 in December 1991, Goodman was a committed - and skilful - striker who always gave 100%. He did not spend long under Smith's tutelage following his transfer - Smith left the Club after Goodman had played just five games as a Sunderland striker. Indeed, it was a somewhat turbulent period that Goodman spent at the Club, playing under four managers in his three years at Sunderland. Nevertheless, Goodman hit a respectable 40 goals in 112 League starts.

At the start of the 1994-95 season, though, his form dipped a little - perhaps the result of dissatisfaction at the Club's lack of success - and he scored just three goals in nineteen games before being transferred to Wolves for £1.4 million. Ironically, Goodman had the misfortune to be excluded from the Club's main success during his time at Sunderland. He was Cup-tied on his arrival on Wearside - having played a first round game for West Brom - which meant he had to sit it out as his team mates made the trip to Wembley in 1992, a loss for the team as well as for Goodman.

Sunderland started the 1994-95 season with their fourth manager in four seasons, but with Buxton having produced some good performances at the end of the previous season there was some cause for optimism. Indeed, the 1994-95 campaign started well, and for the first time in the post-war era, Sunderland remained unbeaten for their first eight games. In fact, this was our longest unbeaten start in 84 years, which prompted the question 'Was this to be the Lads' season?'

Unfortunately, the answer was to be 'No.' Although the team managed to start the season well in so far as they avoided defeat, they were also finding it difficult to achieve victories; six of those first eight games were draws. This gave the Lads a respectable twelve points from a possible twenty-four, but it was something short of promotion form. If the Club were to end their exile from English football's top division, more of these draws would have to be converted into victories.

But, rather than improving as the season wore on, results in fact became worse. The eight game unbeaten run came to an end with a 1 - 0 defeat at Tranmere Rovers on 24th September, and the Lads endured a miserable period for the rest of 1994. In the seventeen League games that took place from the end of the unbeaten run until the end of the calendar year, just four were won, and more were lost than were drawn. Out of a possible fifty-four points on offer during this time, the Lads managed to secure a paltry eighteen. Once again early hope had rapidly faded and relegation was on the cards.

Matters failed to improve in the New Year. In January the Lads failed to pick up a single point in the League, and after struggling to beat Carlisle in the FA Cup - eventually overcoming the Third Division side in a replay - the team were thrashed 4 - 1 by Spurs in the fourth round. The following month was a little better; after two draws and a defeat, we managed to beat Watford 1 - 0 - our first League win for over two months - and followed this with a 1 - 0 win against Southend, but in March performances took another turn for the worse again. It was a busy month - the Lads had seven League matches - and wins were clearly needed to improve our points tally. Unfortunately, just three points were secured - the result of a 1 - 0 win over Stoke - with six of the seven games being lost. To make matters worse, the team managed to hit just two goals in the month and the home win against Stoke was our first victory at Roker Park - in all competitions - for three months. What's more, our final game of March, at Barnsley, saw the Club field an unregistered player. An administrative cock up meant that the paper work for Dominic Matteo's loan move from Liverpool had not been processed before the transfer deadline; consequently, he was not eligible for selection and should not have played. To top it all, we were now in big trouble with the Football League.

It was the final straw. A points deduction was the normal penalty for such an offence, and with relegation already looking a probability, rather than a possibility, for the fourth time in four seasons urgent action was needed. Bob Murray returned to the Chairman's position, Buxton was relieved of his services as manager and instant lobbying of the football authorities began in order to avoid a points deduction.

But, once again, the board were not in a strong position to attract a new manager to the Club. The job had become one of the most insecure in football, the team were playing badly, and there were just seven games left to prevent a seemingly inevitable relegation. We needed a miracle worker, and turned to former Manchester City manager Peter Reid, an appointment viewed with some scepticism by fans at the time. Reid had been out of work for 18 months, a successful spell as Manchester City manager having come to an acrimonious end after clashes between Reid and City Chairman Peter Swales. To the fans and the Board, he was something of an unknown quantity, and the Club proceeded cautiously, offering Reid an initial short term contract until the end of the season in order to allow both the Club and manager to take a look at each other.

As it happened, however, Reid did know how work miracles. With little time to take stock the new manager instantly added one of his most famous characteristics to a team that was on the floor: fighting spirit. Amazingly, Sunderland came roaring back! Reid's first game in charge was against Sheffield United - at Roker Park - and the Lads put in a stirring performance for their new boss, a last minute winner from Craig Russell giving Reid all three points from his first game. More wins would be needed though, and he managed to secure another two; furthermore, just one of the games under his management were lost, in a game against Champions-to-be Bolton. With the board having worked hard to avoid a points deduction over the Matteo affair - a fine was imposed instead - the Club had pulled together with a real Dunkirk spirit, working hard to stave off relegation.

Astonishingly, Reid had done enough to keep Sunderland in the First Division. It was an amazing performance considering the state of the team when he arrived and testimony to his motivational skills. However, after a series of false dawns, the fans were still to be convinced that a new season, and another new manager, could deliver the sorely missed Premier League football they deserved.

Tottenham on the Telly

Sunderland's biggest crowd of the season came when Tottenham Hotspur visited Roker Park for an FA Cup fourth round tie at the end of January. 21,135 made the trip for the game - not a massive crowd, but as big as the diminishing capacity at Roker would allow - which kicked off on a Sunday in order to allow the game to be televised. Spurs were riding high at the time, with their front line being led by prolific German international Jurgen Klinsmann. Sunderland, however, were not being regarded as a push over, and the Lads' trip to Wembley in 1992 was still fresh in the fans' minds.

Buxton knew that if the Lads were to progress the Spurs forwards would have to be silenced, and in a departure from the norm, we fielded a five man defence. In a tense opening period, the game was evenly balanced, and a great first half performance from the Lads meant it was all level at the break.

In the second period though, the game swung dramatically. Only minutes after the restart a strong Tottenham move came to an abrupt end when Gary Bennett handled on the goal line; he was sent off and Klinsmann buried the resulting penalty. With the Lads' 5-3-2 formation now disrupted, Spurs took advantage. Two more goals quickly followed, and though Phil Gray snatched one back, it was too little too late. Before the end, Klinsmann hit a second, making it 4 - 1 to Spurs at the final whistle.

1995-1996
The Unexpected

"Reid had done an amazing job, turning a team of relegation regulars into Champions overnight."

Martin Smith skips past Neville and Giggs in the third round replay.

Manchester United Held

Some of the most exciting moments of the season came when the Lads took on Manchester United in the FA Cup Third Round. Drawn to play at Old Trafford, few expected Sunderland to make any impact on the Lancashire team, and the game seemed set to follow the form books when Nicky Butt put the home side 1 - 0 up. In the second half though, Sunderland struck back, Steve Agnew equalising for the Lads, and Craig Russell putting us into the lead. A famous victory was on the cards, but in the dying moments Eric Cantona put the scores level.

In the replay, a packed Roker Park urged the Lads on to success, and memories of 1992 started flooding back when Phil Gray put us in front with a brilliant goal. Agnew almost put us 2 - 0 up before the break, but Peter Schmichael made a good save. In the second half though, United took control, Paul Scholes hitting an equaliser and Andy Cole heading a winner towards the end of the match. The FA Cup wasn't to be, but a strong performance against English football's top team demonstrated the progress Reid's team were making.

The disappointment of recent seasons had severely impacted on expectations surrounding Sunderland. No longer were we amongst the bookmakers' favourites to go up, being quoted at 25-1 for promotion and 85-1 for the Championship. Few fans anticipated anything more than a play-off place at best. The team had narrowly escaped relegation for two seasons running, but the manager had added just one player to his squad before the season kicked off, bringing Paul Bracewell back to Sunderland for his third spell at the Club, this time as Assistant Manager. Many viewed this inactivity as signifying a lack of ambition.

Hopes were hardly boosted by a home defeat, 2 - 1 against Leicester, on the opening day of the season, or by a 0 - 0 at Norwich in the Lads' second game. Indeed, in a manner that had come to typify Sunderland in recent years, it was the end of the month before the Lads secured their first League win, 2 - 0 against big spending Wolves.

September began with a defeat at Ipswich, leaving the Lads one point from the relegation places, but they bounced back with wins against Southend, Luton and Millwall, the points helping the Lads to climb the table. Moreover, a good Coca-Cola Cup performance against Premier League Liverpool, albeit one that ended in defeat, helped to boost spirits. The manager also moved to strengthen his squad, buying striker David Kelly for £900,000 and adding Paul Stewart on loan.

The following month, Sunderland's quiet progress began to suggest that better times might be around the corner. Victory over Crystal Palace at the start of October saw the Lads move to third in the table, and by the end of the month Sunderland had gone nine games without defeat. This unbeaten run was extended into November, with a well earned draw and a good win against Sheffield United, but Stoke then brought the run to an end with a 1 - 0 win at their place.

However, the good spell had provided a platform on which to build a push for promotion, and victory in a difficult game against Crystal Palace in early December put us into second place in time for the visit of top of the table Millwall. Suddenly, the Lads' season took off, as four goals from Craig Russell helped us to destroy the League leaders by six goals to nil. Millwall did not recover all season, and Sunderland did not look back. We were now top of the League, but not for long! Second placed Derby beat us 3 - 1 in a tough game just before Christmas, and the three points were enough to give them top spot.

In the New Year, attention turned to the FA Cup, where we were drawn against Premier League giants Manchester United. United were lucky to survive the first tie, at Old Trafford, a late equaliser earning them a replay. Unfortunately, the return at Roker did not go our way, Manchester United running out 2 - 1 winners, and to make matters worse the intervening League game against Norwich was lost, and David Kelly sustained an injury that would keep him out for the rest of the season.

With the FA Cup behind them, the team began to focus on the League. The manager had picked up two new players in January, defender Gareth Hall and young goalkeeper Shay Given. The team had started to lose the winning way a little, and it was hoped the new faces would boost the team. Given, a loan signing from Blackburn, proved to be inspirational. A clean sheet was kept on his debut, and he repeated the task in eleven of the further sixteen games he played for the Club.

However, the slight downturn in form had seen the team begin to fall off the pace at the top of table, and a good run of form would be needed to reverse this.

On 20th February, a 1 - 0 victory against Ipswich marked the start of a brilliant winning streak that would fulfil this very need. A week after the Ipswich game, Luton were beaten 1 - 0, a few days later Southend were overcome 2 - 0, and March began with a 4 - 0 thrashing of Grimsby. League leaders Derby then visited Roker Park, where the Lads gave them a footballing lesson, the game ending 3 - 0.

By now, promotion was looking a strong possibility, and a 2 - 1 win at Oldham made it six wins in six, putting Sunderland just one point behind Derby with a game in hand. A thoroughly professional 2 - 0 victory at Birmingham then made it seven out of seven and put the Lads back at the top of the table. Further wins against Oldham - 1 - 0 - and a 3 - 2 versus Huddersfield gave us the ninth in a row, and a massive 27 points from a possible 27. Unfortunately, as April started, a thrilling 3 - 3 draw at Watford brought the winning run to an end, but as the season entered its closing stages it was clear that Sunderland had an excellent chance of going up and doing so as Champions.

Indeed, by the end of April we had clinched promotion to the Premiership and on the penultimate game of the season the Championship was secured. Reid had done an amazing job, turning a team of relegation regulars into Champions overnight. He had boosted confidence and morale throughout the Club and if ever there was proof that a manager can make a difference, he had provided it. What a difference a year makes!

Craig Russell celebrates.

First Division Champions of 1996.

The Statistics...

Reid's first full season in charge was an amazing one, as the statistics and records testified. The nine game winning run equalled the Club record set by the Team of all the Talents in 1891-92. An 18 game unbeaten run towards the end of the season passed the previous record set in the 1922-23 season. The points total of 83 set a new record for Sunderland at this level. At the back, the Lads had conceded just 23 goals away from home, a record surpassed only in the 1900-01 and 1901-02 seasons, when fewer games were played, and by letting in just 10 at Roker Park they equalled a record set twenty years earlier. On top of this, the 25 clean sheets kept by the goalkeepers smashed the Club record of 21 set in 1974-75. It was quite a season!

Peter Reid, 1996.

294

1996-1997
Yo-yo

"an immediate return to the First Division was…a serious threat"

Lionel Perez.

Chelsea Blues

Ten days before Christmas, Chelsea visited Roker Park. The Londoners were the team of the moment, managed by the flamboyant Ruud Gullitt, and including Italian international stars Gianluca Vialli, Roberto Di Matteo and Gianfranco Zola amongst their number. The game, being broadcast live on Sky Television, was seen as a showcase for the talents of the multi-national Chelsea side, but the Lads showed no fear. Aided by the Roker Roar - and a bitterly cold Roker wind! - they took the game to the visitors, attacking from the off. However, Chelsea were out for all three points too and a long period of stalemate followed. But, shortly before half-time the Lads achieved the crucial breakthrough when a deflected shot put Sunderland 1 - 0 up. This proved to be the turning point, and filled with confidence the Lads really turned the heat up after the break. Kevin Ball added a second goal - with a fantastic diving header - and Craig Russell hit a third; what's more the defence silenced the visitor's international strike force, delivering a clean sheet for the manager. It was a brilliant victory and one completed with some style. For a moment, it looked like the Lads were world beaters, and the national press sang our praises. The team had given their best and were worthy winners against a team that would end the season by lifting the FA Cup at Wembley.

At last, Sunderland were back in the top flight, but after the euphoria of promotion, the question now was 'Will we stay up?' Reid had brought in new faces, including 'keepers, Tony Coton (£600,000 from Manchester United) and Lionel Perez (£200,000 from Bordeaux), Republic of Ireland international striker Niall Quinn (a Club record £1.3 million) and attacking midfielder Alex Rae (£1 million from Millwall). 1996-97 was to be our last season at Roker Park, work having begun on a new stadium at Wearmouth, so there was an added incentive to make it an extra special one and keep us in the top flight for 1997-98.

The opening fixture of the campaign was - again - at home to Leicester City, and it ended goalless, but a few days later the Lads made the trip to Notts Forest, where a superb first half display secured a 4 - 1 win, Quinn scoring two of the goals. The first month's fixtures were then completed with a trip to Anfield, where the Lads silenced the Kop by securing a 0 - 0 draw against Liverpool. It was a good start to the season, putting Sunderland in fifth place.

September, though, did not start well. Newcastle arrived for the last Tyne-Wear derby at Roker, where the Mags ran out 2 - 1 winners. A series of mixed results left us in a solid mid-table position at the end of the month, but a bizarre encounter at Arsenal marred proceedings. Sunderland crashed 2 - 0, and finished with just nine men, but the referee - who had a poor game - later admitted he had made a mistake in sending Paul Stewart off, and the player escaped an automatic suspension. The reprieve, however, came too late to prevent the loss of points.

October kicked off with the last Tees-Wear derby at Roker, and an excellent match ended 2 - 2. However, Sunderland received their third red card in two games, Richard Ord taking the early bath. With suspensions piling up - and serious injuries to star signings Niall Quinn and Tony Coton threatening to put both out of action for the rest of the season - the Lads suffered a slump in form, losing three of their next four League games. Nevertheless, a superb 3 - 1 away victory against Everton meant the Lads went into December in a respectable twelfth position.

The year ended with some mixed performances, being notable for an excellent win over Chelsea and a 5 - 0 humbling from Manchester United. But, as the New Year started, the Lads were in a promising 13th place, and mid-table security looked likely. This position was consolidated in January, a useful victory against Championship challengers Arsenal avenging the nine men game in September.

The following month though, our form hit rock bottom, with all League fixtures being lost. The first week of March then saw defeats against Blackburn (1 - 0) and Tottenham (4 - 0), leaving the Lads dangerously near the relegation positions as Manchester United prepared to visit Roker Park. United were riding in Europe at the time and, having thrashed us 5 - 0 earlier in the season, most pundits expected an easy win for the visitors. Amazingly, the Lads pulled a victory out of the bag, beating United 2 - 1, but it was a false dawn. A 2 - 1 defeat at Sheffield Wednesday was then followed by a devastating 6 - 2 reverse at Chelsea, a Zola inspired side wiping the floor with us. While the Lads had at one point threatened to get into the game, turning a 3 - 0 deficit into a 3 - 2 one, in truth Chelsea were just too good for us. Worse still, a relegation 'six-pointer' against Forest - where Chris Waddle made his debut - ended 1 - 1. Failure to pick up three points against one of the weakest teams in the division - and one of our biggest relegation rivals - was a massive blow. Just four points had been taken from a possible twenty-four, and an immediate return to the First Division was becoming a serious threat.

A trip to Newcastle saw the Lads secure a point, but a 2 - 1 defeat against Liverpool the following week left us in a relegation position for the first time all season. Two crucial games against fellow relegation candidates Middlesbrough and Southampton then followed; victory in these would probably ensure survival. While the Lads managed to overcome our local rivals, they were unable to score against Southampton at Roker Park, and the Saints left with all three points, enough to lift them above us, and put the Lads back in the relegation pack.

Two games were now remaining. Everton travelled to Sunderland on May 3rd for the last ever League game at Roker Park. The Lads put in a fine performance, a 3 - 0 victory giving everyone hope and, once again, it all fell on the last game of the season. As long as we claimed a draw at Wimbledon, relegation would be avoided. But, Wimbledon are tough customers, and in the event, we lost. There was still hope, however, as long as Coventry - playing against Spurs - failed to win. In an echo of the 1976-77 season, their game had kicked off late, and fifteen agonising minutes were spent waiting for the result. Astonishingly, our relegation rivals pulled off a win to match our defeat, the only combination of results that could see us relegated. It was unbelievable. As with the Manchester City game five years earlier, 15,000 had made the trip to the game; they left completely gutted.

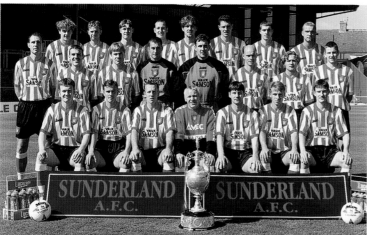

1996-97 Sunderland team.

Sunderland PLC

During the 1996-97 season, the board decided to raise £12 million by floating the Club on the stock market. Valued at £47.7 million, the Club's shares started trading on Christmas Eve, 1996. Much of the money raised was earmarked for transfer spending, and some of it used to help fit out the new ground being built at Wearmouth.

The move to make Sunderland a Public Limited Company (PLC) came almost 100 years after the Club became a Limited Company (Ltd), and - like the move to Limited status in the 1890s - was tied in with the move to a new, bigger stadium.

Sunderland were moving with the times, and it was clear that a new era in Sunderland Football Club was emerging. Since flotation, the Club's shares have held their value well, while those of most other clubs - such as Newcastle, Leicester and Southampton - have dipped badly. This is an indication not only of the high esteem we are held in by the City, but also of the Club's underlying strength.

Hello Goodbye

Last League Game

Sunderland's last ever League game at Roker Park took place against Everton on 3rd May, 1997. It was an emotional affair, for in addition to being a milestone in the Club's history, Sunderland needed to win the match in order to stave off relegation. A full house witnessed an excellent performance from the Lads. Just after the half-hour, Sunderland took the lead, Paul Stewart burying a penalty kick following a hand-ball in the area. Sunderland born Chris Waddle then hit a glorious free-kick to make it 2 - 0, before Allan Johnston made it 3 - 0 - and in doing so scored the last League goal at Roker Park. It was a great way to say goodbye, but the Lads' precarious League position necessarily put a damper on the occasion.

At the end of the 1996-97 season, the final whistle blew on the Club's long serving home, Roker Park. The stadium had provided ninety-nine years of loyal service, hosted thousands of memorable matches and held happy memories for generations of Sunderland supporters. Amongst the best grounds in the World when it opened in 1898, Roker Park was regularly upgraded during its lifetime; in the pre-War era the addition of the famous Archibald Leitch stands in the 1920s and 1930s gave the stadium much of its shape up until its demolition, but significant changes were made after the War too. For example, in 1952, Sunderland became the second club in the country to add floodlights to their ground - the first being Arsenal - and in the 1960s, in advance of the World Cup, a number of improvements, most notably the addition of a roof to the Fulwell End, further enhanced the ground. In the 1970s, executive boxes were added and the floodlights improved. Despite these changes though, the ground which held 50,000+ crowds during the 1973 FA Cup run was not too different from that which hosted the 1937 FA Cup run, a testimony to the quality of the buildings erected during the inter-war years, but also a sad indictment of the Club's failure to invest in facilities during the post-War era.

Despite the fine quality of the original structures, from the early 1980s onwards a combination of ageing buildings and increasingly stringent safety requirements began to erode the capacity of Roker Park. In 1982, a large section of the Roker End - a massive banked terraced held up by a series of concrete pillars - was removed. Not only did this diminish the grandeur of the Roker End, it also reduced the ground's capacity by 10,000. Indeed, the capacity diminished rapidly during the 1980s, from 48,000 at the start of the decade to a much smaller 36,000 by the mid-1980s. Just 9,000 of this total was accounted for by seated accommodation, not unusual at the time, but a fact that would take on great significance in coming years.

The 1980s saw a number of fatal tragedies at football grounds, including an horrific fire at Bradford which saw fans burnt alive and devastating scenes at Hillsbrough, where nearly one hundred fans were crushed to death during an FA Cup semi-final. Following these incidents, the footballing authorities and the government of the day became convinced of the need to upgrade football stadia in order to make them safer and more comfortable. In addition, football had, for a number of years, been making strenuous attempts to eliminate the hooligan element of its fan base, hoping to attract exiled fans, families in particular, to matches. It was felt that improving stadium facilities would help to achieve this objective too.

In many ways, Roker Park was a typical English football ground, for despite numerous improvements over the years, the similarities between the Roker of the 1930s and 1990s were huge. Though significant, changes since the war had been incremental, modifying what was there rather than replacing it altogether. Significantly, many of the improvements were made for the 1966 World Cup and, had it not been for this event, some modifications may not have occurred at all. Perhaps the only major change seen was the demolition of much of the Roker End in the early 1980s, an action taken on safety grounds. For many fans, football at Roker Park was about standing in the open air, facing the elements and toilets and catering of the most basic standard.

Of course, the priority was football, not luxury accommodation. Faced with the choice of spending money on the ground or the team, most Chairmen plumped for the latter. Most fans would have backed this choice too, for there was little point in having a super stadium and a sub-standard team. As ever, competition for players was stiff and transfer fees were rising; forgoing a star striker for new toilets or a roof was rarely the preferred option.

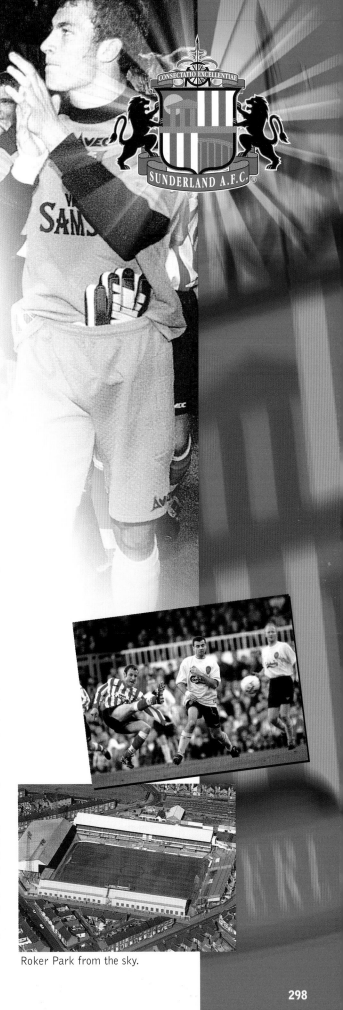

Changing this situation required action from the football authorities; if all clubs were made to improve their grounds then none would lose out unfairly as a result. Following an extensive investigation into the Hillsborough tragedy, the Taylor Report recommended that such action be taken, and all clubs be mandated to upgrade their grounds to make them safer. In particular, they argued that top clubs should possess all seated stadia, and that standing at matches be quickly phased out. The report's suggestions were taken up, though some groups were opposed to the changes; many felt that the removal of terracing would strike a hammer blow to the spirit of football, and that the atmosphere at all seated stadia be somewhat subdued. However, government backing for the report meant there was no going back, and at the start of the decade all top clubs - Sunderland included - had to make plans for implementing the report's recommendations.

For many clubs, there was an obvious route forward, usually the installation of seating in existing stands, or the slight modification of older structures. Some faced difficulties that enforced the rebuilding or replacement of sections of their grounds. For others, the only realistic option was to abandon their home and start afresh with a brand new stadium. Sunderland were torn between the latter two options. Given the age of Roker Park, and its location in a built up area, there was much to support the case for a move to a new home. Upgrading Roker would be difficult and very expensive. There were severe space limitations around the ground - roads and houses hemming it in - and this would inevitably limit the capacity to a level unfitting of a big name club. On the other hand, clubs in similar situations - such as Arsenal - had found a way around such problems, and there was much to be said for remaining at a site that held so many memories for the fans. Consequently, when the Club announced its decision to move home, it was not without its critics. However, when plans for the new ground were published, the majority of fans appeared to be won over, and a ballot on the move lent favour to this view.

Support for the move was undoubtedly increased by the enforced reduction of Roker Park's capacity. Irrespective of the long term future, immediate measures had to be taken to comply with new safety requirements, and the ground's capacity was a mere 29,000 during the 1992 FA Cup run. This seriously restricted the number who could see famous encounters such as the Chelsea replay, and by the time Sunderland had returned to the Premiership for the 1996-97 season, the capacity at Roker was just over 22,000: well short of the demand for big games. What's more, within this total, just over 8,000 were seats. If the Club were to upgrade Roker Park to a 25,000 seater stadium - a modest total for a club with such a huge fan base - then the task was one of putting 17,000 seats into a space that had capacity for just 14,000 standing spectators. At best this would have produced a small and cramped stadium and, for the board, it was clear that the sums just didn't add up: there was no option but to leave Roker.

"There will never be another place like Roker."

On 13th May, 1997, Sunderland made their last appearance at Roker Park, in a ceremonial 'closing' match. A full house of 22,000 were there to say goodbye to the famous ground and, fittingly, the last opponents were Liverpool, the first team to visit Roker Park way back in 1898. Before the game, heroes of yesteryear paraded the pitch, including 'Player of the Century' Charlie Hurley, 1973 Cup heroes Jimmy Montgomery, Billy Hughes, Bobby Kerr, Bob Stokoe and Denis Tueart, and goalscoring legend Gary Rowell. The match itself ended 1 - 0 to Sunderland - John Mullin scoring the historic final goal - the same scoreline that had occurred 99 years earlier in Roker's opening game. After the match, another of Roker's legends - Len Shackleton - summed up the feelings of Sunderland fans everywhere: "There will never be another place like Roker."

Roker Park from the sky.

Stadium That Never Was

In late 1992, it looked like Sunderland were all set to move to a purpose built 48,000 seater stadium in Washington. Based on a huge site near the Nissan factory off the A19, the stadium was to be part of a multi-purpose leisure, entertainment and conference complex. Alongside the stadium, there was to be a 10,000 seat North East Arena (later built in Newcastle), a multi-screen cinema, leisure facilities such as a bowling alley and an international conference and exhibition centre.

Chairman Bob Murray remains convinced that the site would have been ideal for the Club, for it would have put Sunderland on the map - and not just for footballing reasons. Moreover, the project would have provided a much needed economic boost to the region, generating several thousand jobs. Because of this, the European Union were very keen to support the project, and were ready to offer generous financial support.

However, Nissan, who had initially supported the bid, turned hostile, and the project ran into planning difficulties as a consequence. Their change of heart still rankles with Bob Murray, not least because it plunged the Club into crisis. Indeed, it was the latest in a series of knock backs from the motor manufacturer. With Nissan having made a huge financial commitment to the city by opening their plant in Sunderland, Murray quickly explored the possibility of them becoming involved in the football club too, offering them the opportunity of buying a substantial shareholding. Nissan, however, declined the offer, dashing hopes that they might use their substantial wealth to bring star players to the Club.

On top of this, as other clubs began upgrading their grounds, fans travelling to away matches became increasingly aware of the general inadequacies of Roker Park. The facilities at the ground were basic to the say least, and it was obvious that the ground was no longer amongst the best in the country. Be it in terms of toilets, catering, bars, executive hospitality or media facilities, it was becoming obvious that Sunderland had been left behind by the rapid development elsewhere. Roker's ageing stands could not cope with the increased demands being placed on football grounds in this new era. Not only was there an absence of such facilities but, again, limited space meant there was little scope for adding them. The most poignant illustration of this problem came when the TV cameras visited Roker. In order to accommodate their commentary team, temporary structures would have to be constructed in the Roker End and, for the unlucky ones, the most hostile accommodation imaginable - an exposed gantry on the roof of the Clockstand - would be taken advantage of. When the winter winds were blowing - as they regularly are in Sunderland - you had to feel sorry for the poor fellows up there!

While most fans would have loved to have seen the old lady reach her century, the overwhelming majority agreed that at ninety-nine Roker Park was very much past her best. By 1996-97, it was time for her to go. Parting, of course, was still a bitter-sweet moment, for the bonds between Sunderland AFC and Roker Park were of the strongest kind. History is also a strong force, and many worried that the powerful memories of games in the past, and times spent with friends and family, would be lost once Roker was gone. Sunderland fans loved Roker Park, but the relationship had to come to an end. Like all true love affairs, though, it will be remembered with fondness of the good times, not heartbreak at the parting.

The pain was eased by the fact that for the 1997-98 season, Sunderland kicked off in the biggest and most exciting new football ground in England, the Sunderland Stadium of Light. Quite simply, there is nowhere else quite like it for football. However, the move was far from straightforward, for while the board had made the controversial decision to move during 1992, building work on the new stadium did not begin until some four years later.

From the outset, plans for the new ground were dogged by planning issues. On announcing their intention to move to a new site, the Club outlined plans to build on a site off the A19, close to Hylton on the outskirts of Sunderland. Here, the Club would be able to acquire enough land to build a huge stadium and leisure complex, and be able to take advantage of European Union funding to help finance the costs of the new stadium. However, as soon as the local council had granted outline planning permission, the Department of the Environment launched a public inquiry due to opposition from a major objector: Nissan.

The inquiry meant a significant delay in the move was inevitable and, moreover, the outcome of the investigation was unlikely to be in the Club's favour. The motor manufacturer, one of the most powerful multi-national companies in the world, had close links with the Conservative government. Nissan's access to Number 10 was likely to be a significant factor in their favour and it was extremely frustrating for the Club that, after initially backing the move, Nissan decided to oppose it. The change placed the Club in turmoil again. With a long inquiry likely to rule against the application, the Club effectively had no site for the new ground and, as a consequence, no plans to comply with the Taylor Report.

The board decided, therefore, to look for an alternative location. This was a matter of extreme urgency; the footballing authorities had agreed to allow Roker Park to retain standing accommodation, but only on the understanding that a new stadium was in

the pipeline. If a new site was not forthcoming, they could force the closure of the non-seating areas in our ground. The possibility of Sunderland having to play in a converted Roker Park, with a capacity of just over 15,000, was a very real one.

Significantly, as the Club searched for a solution to their problems, a superb new site in the centre of Sunderland became available; the Wearside Colliery had ceased production and the Club moved quickly to secure the location. In many ways, it was an ideal site. Sunderland AFC is as much a community as it is a big club, and through proposing to relocate a mere few hundred yards from Roker Park, the Club stuck to its roots as a community club, remaining in the heart of the city. Moreover, the choice of a former pit site was apt too, for it is a testament to the miners who constituted so many of the team's fans in previous decades. Similarly, the ground's location by the River Wear brings echoes of the city's past as a great shipbuilding town and the Club's historic links with that industry. However, the generous European Union funding was not available this time; nor would the site include the job creating multiplex cinema or conference facilities that would have accompanied the Washington site. With the region's economy suffering badly - not least through the closure of pits like Wearmouth - the loss of those new jobs must be counted as a blow.

Having waited so long to secure a location, it was imperative that work was conducted at double speed as soon as we did, and attention immediately turned to the detail of designing and constructing the Club's new home. At the outset the stadium blueprint was for a 'bowl' containing a continuous lower tier and a second tier over the west side of the ground. The bowl concept represents the optimum in stadium security, spectator comfort and ground circulation and generates a tremendous atmosphere within the ground. It allows all Sunderland fans to freely circulate around the stadium and its facilities, removing restrictions and classes evident in so many in other grounds. With no pillars, posts or square corners, all seats in the ground - be they concession corner or directors' box - offer a perfect view of the pitch. What's more, the continual bowl generates tremendous noise and a strong feeling of togetherness, bringing together the red-and-white army in a way that a revamped Roker Park could not possibly have done. The site of 42,000 Sunderland fans lined up in a continuous circle really is a marvellous one, and it should be emphasised that the Club specifically set out to create the tremendous atmosphere found within the stadium. Because they were starting from scratch, the Club were able to go back to first principles, and the most fundamental one was that the new ground should harness, as well as serve, Sunderland's great support.

New Stadium, New Badge

To accompany the move to a new stadium, the Club decided to commission a new crest. This was a controversial move, for the badge carrying a ship on top of red-and-white stripes was popular with the fans. For many, it felt like past traditions were being quickly jettisoned; first Roker Park, and then the Club's badge. Yet, the Lads had only be wearing the famous badge since the 1970s; it just seemed like it had been around for longer. Indeed, there had been many changes to the badge over the years, and the Club felt it was again time for a new look.

The redesigned crest has an altogether much grander feel. Between two roaring lions - known in heraldic terminology as 'supporters' - a quartered shield carries fragments of two of the city's most famous sights - Penshaw Monument and the Wearmouth Bridge - while the other segments feature the team's famous red-and-white stripes. On top of the crest, the Club's new motto - 'Consectatio Excellentiae' (In Search of Excellence) - and a colliery wheel signify the Club's vision for the future and its links with the past. The crest is rounded off with a banner of the famous name 'Sunderland AFC' being unfurled at the foot of the shield.

Wearmouth Colliery

The Sunderland Stadium of Light.

Kevin Ball meets the Ajax captain at the opening game.

Carnival Time

On 30th July, 1997, the doors of the Sunderland Stadium of Light were opened for the first time, and a full house roared the team on to the pitch for an exhibition match against Dutch giants Ajax Amsterdam. Before the game, fans were entertained by a star studded line up, including live appearances from rock band Status Quo, who were flown especially to the stadium for the celebrations, and top pop bands F.K.A., Upside Down, Clock, Kavana and Code Red. Somewhat less noisily, the Bishop of Durham also made an appearance in order to bless the stadium and the pitch. The game, of course, was the main feature, and full strength sides - Ajax featuring international stars such as Marc Overmars and the De Boer brothers - played out a 0 - 0 draw. Sunderland captain Kevin Ball did manage to hit the back of the net on the night, but the goal was disallowed, denying him an historic first he would have loved to have completed! The whole event was designed to have a carnival atmosphere - which it did - and to top the celebrations off, the fans were sent home with a massive fireworks display.

Beyond this, the Club also aimed to develop a ground that structurally reflects the three major industries that have historically dominated the Sunderland area - glass manufacturing, shipbuilding and coal mining - and the designs drew visual inspiration from these sources. In addition, there was a desire to maintain a link with the Club's past by incorporating bits of Roker Park; the famous Archibald Leitch latticework and the Clockstand's clock, for example, have been accommodated around the new ground.

Perhaps the most important decision to be made though, concerned the planned capacity of the new ground. The initial planning application had indicated the Club wanted a 29,000 capacity, expanding to a maximum of 34,000 if demand and finance allowed this. However, shortly before construction began, the board felt they had been far too conservative. In taking full advantage of their knowledge, contacts and reputation, Bob Murray and his colleagues had managed to secure finance for their dream stadium, and revised proposals were submitted seeking permission to open with a capacity of 42,000. This was a very important decision, although at the time we didn't know how crucial it would be. Persuading bankers to lend the Club money to build a 42,000 seater stadium when we were only getting crowds of 20,000 was not an easy task. The common view was that a big ground would be a white elephant, half-filled and devoid of atmosphere. But, crowds of over 40,000 are common place at our new home, Sunderland's attendances leaving the football world staggered at the level and passion of the Club's support. The Chairman, however, did not have any doubts about the strength of Sunderland's fan base, and he was prepared to stake his reputation on it.

With the plans in place, the construction team moved in. The Club selected Ballast Wiltshire plc, part of the leading international construction group Ballast Nedam NV, as the main contractor for the new ground. Again this was significant. The company have a huge experience in stadium construction, and were in the process of completing work on Ajax's internationally acclaimed Amsterdam Arena at the time. The decision confirmed the Club's ambition to create a stadium of the highest quality.

Construction work began in May 1996. Some fourteen months later, the new ground opened for the 1997-98 season. To celebrate the move, a special match was arranged against the aforementioned Dutch giants, Ajax, and it was a race against time to complete work in time for the match on 30th July, 1997. Although the main structures were in place well beforehand, many of the finishing touches had to be put in place before the council could grant a safety certificate, and in the days leading up to the opening game, round-the-clock work ensured that the ground met all necessary requirements in time.

Upon opening, the magnificence of the new structure became a wonder for all Sunderland fans to behold! Inside, the stadium is decked out mainly in red seats, with white, yellow and black seats being used to display huge versions of the Club's new badge and a few selected phrases such as 'Sunderland AFC' and 'Ha'way the Lads'. The pitch is very similar to Roker Park's, being the same width at 68 metres (75 yds) but a couple of metres longer at 105 metres (115 yds). In a far cry from 'clay dolly field' the Lads played on at Horatio Street, the current pitch is one of the most technologically advanced in the country. Under the grass there are five layers of gravel, sand, soil and polypropylene fibres to anchor the roots firmly; seventeen sprinklers can pop up through the grass, and more than a mile of drainage pipes carry excess water away. In addition, the pitch carries under-soil heating; some 15 miles of 25mm pipes can carry hot water through the soil, and sensors close to the roots automatically trigger a computer that switches on the heating and can telephone the groundsman at home to let him know the temperature has fallen!

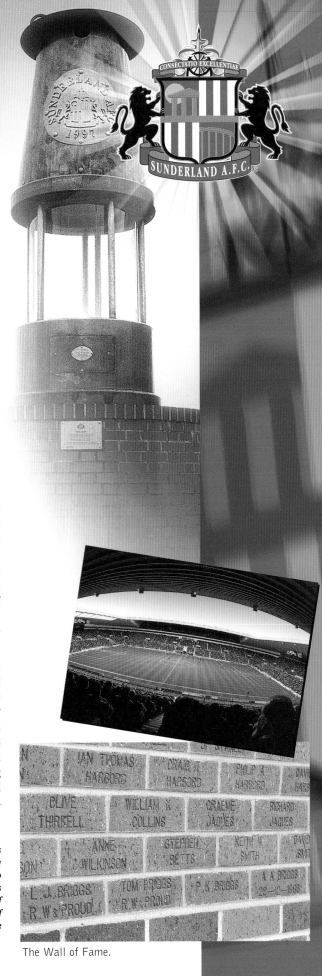

Underneath the West Stand, the players have state of the art dressing rooms. The facilities were designed to meet Premier League and FIFA requirements and set a benchmark for other clubs. The home and away dressing rooms are designed and fitted out to the same specifications, though a sports psychologist was employed to devise unwelcoming colours for the visitors' room and motivating ones for the Lads' room! Our excellent home form at the new stadium suggests this was a smart move. In addition, there is also a warm-up room, a coaches' room and, of course, the manager's office. New and unique facilities for the next millennium also include a medical and drug testing centre, a ball boys' dressing room, and male and female match officials' dressing rooms!

In an interesting move, the Club decided against locating its main offices - including the ticket office - within the stadium itself, and instead opted for a purpose built, state of the art, £1 million office complex just outside the stadium. This, of course, freed up more room within the stadium for other uses, and here there is much on offer for the fan. Aside from copious refreshment booths, there is a large Club shop that stocks a massive range of SAFC merchandise and a themed sports bar and restaurant that contains many parts of the old Roker Park ground. Toilets are palatial - and in stark contrast to the Roker facilities - and those needing to nip out for a wee during the game needn't miss the action, for the entire concourse area is fitted out with television monitors displaying the game as it happens.

Some of these features were announced in the run up to the stadium being opened; others only became known to fans once the ground opened. But the biggest mystery surrounding the new stadium was its name. The board had kept this under wraps until late, only announcing it on midnight of 29th July 1997, the day before the ground's official opening. When the Club made the long awaited announcement, however, many were disappointed with the choice. 'Wearside Stadium' and 'New Roker Park' were thought to be the front runners, but no-one had expected it to be named the 'Sunderland Stadium of Light'.

The expected choices were, perhaps, a little parochial. There is a certain arrogance attached to the new name, but the sheer size of the stadium justifies it. Like the stadium, the name is bold and brash, evoking visions beyond the confines of Sunderland. It has an international flavour, reflecting our desire to reach for the top. A desire, of course, which has already been met, it being England's first choice after Wembley for their fixture with Belgium in October 1999.

At the same time, however, the name is rooted in a vision of what the Club and the stadium mean for the local community. It evokes the history of the area as well as the international fut're of both the Club and the City of Sunderland. The electric light was invented by Joseph Swan, a Sunderland born man. The miners at the former Wearmouth Colliery - like those elsewhere - carried with them a Davey Lamp as part of their everyday working lives. The lamp, invented by Sir Humphery Davey, was tested at the mouth of Morton West pit at Fence Houses. When Sunderland played in the 1913 FA Cup Final, there were 304 pits in the Durham coalfield alone, employing some 165,000 men. In recent decades that number has been whittled down, and

Wall of Fame

One of the more unusual features of the Stadium of Light is its 'Wall of Fame'. Supporters of the Club were given the opportunity to leave a legacy for future generations to see by purchasing a commemorative brick. Designed for those loyal supporters who wished to literally cement their support in stone, for little more than the price of a match ticket fans could have a brick containing a short message of their choice placed on the outer wall of the stadium. A unique feature amongst British clubs, the stadium now has thousands of bricks engraved with supporters' names and messages, giving many fans a permanent link with the Club's new home.

The Wall of Fame.

Artist's impression of the North Stand expansion.

Flexible Capacity

In putting together the blueprint for the Stadium of Light, the directors emphasised the need for planned growth. The board knew that if the Club's vision could be delivered, then the initial 42,000 capacity would be insufficient to meet the demand of the passionate Sunderland following. Consequently, the stadium was built in a way that allows for a relatively straightforward expansion.

While the bowl structure forms the basis of the stadium, each stand can accommodate an additional upper tier. Upon opening, the West Stand already carried an upper-tier, but if the Club needs to expand, similar tiers can be added in stages around the ground.

Significantly, the demand for tickets is such that the Club is already planning to add an additional tier to the North Stand, boosting capacity to 48,000.

If necessary, the Club can add a similar tier to the South Stand - lifting capacity to 54,000 - and, should the 2006 World Cup come to England, then an upper tier will be added to the East Stand, producing a staggering 63,000 capacity.

when the Wearmouth Colliery closed, putting some 2,000 men out of work, the number of had been reduced to zero. In naming the ground which replaced it the 'Stadium of Light' the Club aims to maintain a link with the region's industrial past, a tribute to the generations of miners who played such a crucial role in our history as fans and, sometimes, players. To emphasise this, a sculpture of a Davey lamp stands at the stadium's entrance, with an eternal flame burning to signify the continuous journey of time that links Sunderland fans past, present and future.

Beyond this, the name also signifies the stadium as the way forward and a focus for a club - and a city - that have suffered in recent years. From darkness follows light. As Bob Murray puts it: 'We want to be a successful club at the centre of a booming city in a thriving North East - and when people all over the region see the lights they will know we are here and lighting the way forward, carrying Wearside's hopes confidently into the new century.' The name - like the stadium - radiates like a beacon to the football world. And shine it does. The glorious West Stand is swathed in red and white lights, while on top of each corner stand four of the world's most powerful searchlights, radiating 'one billion candlepower' beams of white light into the sky. Bright enough for a newspaper to be read six miles away, the searchlights are turned on each evening from darkness until midnight, making the stadium a permanent landmark on the Sunderland skyline.

The Stadium of Light tag is undeniably controversial. Rather like a new hair cut, the name of the new stadium was always going to take some getting used to irrespective of its faults or strengths. Yet, the unusual name was a shock for all fans. Since its announcement though, the name has started to sink in, and its brashness is appealing. Reflecting on the name, what it suggests and the vision it tries to evoke, it was an inspired choice. Rather than locating the stadium with a place, it locates it in a vision.

That the Stadium is central to the articulation of the Club's philosophy cannot be denied. Since moving home, the Club has been able to expand on its full range of activities. On the pitch, the pull of the stadium and the additional finance brought through huge gates have enabled us to attract star players to the Club. The Stadium is indicative of our ambition, making it easier for Reid to persuade big name players to join Sunderland, and easier for Murray to persuade Reid that Sunderland is a club he can take all the way to the top. Off the pitch, the size and nature of the ground allow the Club to include all of its fans. Affordable and accessible football are the themes, the new ground carrying bigger and better facilities for all, including families, disabled fans and those on low incomes. With a 42,000 capacity, the Club can accommodate everyone and offer sensibly priced tickets while also generating the huge level of finance needed to sign the top class players needed if Sunderland are to compete in the Premier League. The commitment from Bob Murray is that Sunderland 'is a club for all, a club which promotes family involvement, social inclusion and accessible football.' And, as he points out, 'The Stadium of Light is absolutely central to this philosophy, and is here to be enjoyed by the future generations of this great region.'

In all, the Stadium of Light cost some £23 million to construct. It was money well spent. The ground, of course, is still developing. New features are regularly being added, and fans are still exploring their new home. Home, though, it is. Legendary games have already been played, legendary figures are being created. One of those games came at the end of the stadium's first season, when Sheffield United visited for a Play-Off semi-final. The late Johnny Mapson, Sunderland's heroic 1930s goalkeeper, attended the match, and at its conclusion he was asked 'What do you think of the atmosphere of the Sunderland Stadium Of Light compared to Roker Park?' His answer was simply 'Noisier!'

On an unashamedly personal note, I will abuse the editor's power to recount a tale that illustrates, for me, what a huge boost the new ground is to the Club and those who love it. In 1994, I brought a friend who supported Watford to Roker Park to see our teams clash. He had never been to Sunderland before and I wanted to show off Roker Park. I was proud of our home; I loved it and readily admit to being sceptical about moving elsewhere. But, after his team had the audacity to beat us 3 - 1, he rubbed my nose right in it by saying he was thoroughly unimpressed with our ground. Vicarage Road, he said, was in a totally different class. The sad fact is that he was right. A trip to their ground later in the season confirmed what I didn't want to accept. Theirs was a smart, colourful, comfortable and well appointed stadium. But, Watford! They are smashing club, but undeniably small. We had been surpassed by one of football's minnows… it was embarrassing.

After this, I didn't want friends who supported other clubs to visit us. I didn't want another session in the pub with them telling me how Roker Park was not what they expected or that it was a throwback to the 'old days'. I knew that we were being left behind. Now, all that has changed. Owning the Stadium of Light - which we do, because it belongs to us all - is like having a flash new car or a big new house. You know it's wrong, but you just can't help yourself, you want to show it off, you want to brag, you want to say 'Look at what I've got, it's brilliant and it's much better than what you have!'. It brings out the monster in you. Hell, we can even have England around to play and not have to worry about looking out of place. Best of all, it's big and noisy, a footballing cauldron. When Prokofiev blasts out you can taste the atmosphere. And when the teams run out, you can see the opposition thinking "Bloody hell! This Club are bigger than I thought.' It unnerves them, it plants the seed of doubt in their minds, and it gives the Lads a few crucial minutes to get at them and take control of the game. You just know that we are going to do well at home. We have a fortress, a base from which to build successful campaigns. Yet, even if we don't win there is something to crow about, for friends have to admit that ours is the best stadium they've seen. Before, we might have pretended it was so, but now it is indisputable fact: we have one of the biggest and best grounds in Europe, in which we can properly show off the biggest and best support in England. The Stadium of Light is a badge of pride, a beacon, our standard bearer. It's something to shout about, it's ours… and I love it!

International Honours

With Peter Reid's team full to bursting with international players, Sunderland fans have become used to seeing players temporarily leaving the Club for international duty. In 1999, however, there was an unusual international call up that really underlined the progress being made by Sunderland AFC. When England agreed to play Belgium in a friendly match, they found that Wembley Stadium was unavailable for their preferred date, for the old ground was booked for a pop concert. However, rather than cancel the fixture - or switch it to Belgium - the FA asked if they could stage it at the Stadium of Light, a ground they knew was of sufficient quality to stage a high profile international fixture.

The Club, of course, were delighted and immediately agreed to stage the game. In choosing the Stadium of Light, the FA signalled the high regard in which the arena is held in footballing circles. It also highlighted the fact that there are only a handful of grounds in the country that can match the facilities at the Stadium of Light.

There can be few higher honours for a stadium than hosting the national team's fixtures. Hosting a major Cup final or semi-final would come close, and with Wembley about to undergo rebuilding, that could become a possibility. Ultimately, of course, there is the World Cup, and if England are successful in their bid to host the competition in 2006, then an expanded Stadium of Light is likely to feature heavily, perhaps even hosting a semi-final. Such an event would reveal the stadium in its fullest glory, allowing it to truly shine on the international stage.

1997-1998 Cruel

"...penalties shattered our dreams for another season."

Kevin Phillips.

Kevin Phillips
Goal Machine

The big success story of the campaign - and one of the biggest surprises - was Kevin Phillips' emergence as a goal machine. On his arrival from Watford, for a bargain fee, few Sunderland fans had heard of him and some lamented Reid's failure to buy a big name striker who would score 30 goals a season. In the event, Phillips proved that bargains can be found, as he hit goal after goal, producing a staggering thirty-five goals, enough to beat Brian Clough's post-war Club record of thirty-four goals in a season. Phillips was selected for the England 'B' team during the season and voted Nationwide League Player of the Season.

The following season, better came! Despite a long period on the sidelines through injury, Kev still finished as the Club's top scorer, with a superb total of 25 goals. On top of this, he was also called up to the England squad, making his international debut against Hungary. Since then, he has remained in the England manager's plans and, in the Premiership, has continued to prove his goalscoring credentials, knocking in a hat-trick in just his eighth top flight game and topping the goalscorers' table as a result.

Dubbed 'Super Kev' by the fans, his record breaking feats have already guaranteed him a place in the Sunderland hall of fame.

After the glory of promotion, and a solid start to the Club's first season in the Premier League, fans once again faced a new season with some degree of despondency: relegation had been a huge kick in the teeth. For Reid, as for Smith some six years earlier, the task was the difficult one of rallying his players following the disappointment of dropping a division. Unlike Smith though, Reid took the opportunity to invest heavily in new recruits, most notably new record signing Lee Clark, a £2.3 million fee going to Newcastle United. Other, less well known, faces joining included striker Kevin Phillips from Watford and defender Jody Craddock from Cambridge.

But, it was not only the new signings that boosted hopes in the pre-season; the Club's new home was also generating much interest. However, the season did not get off to the best of starts. The Lads' opening match at Sheffield United ended 2 - 0 to the home team, and though we bounced back shortly afterwards - a 38,821 crowd witnessing a 3 - 1 victory over Manchester City in the new stadium's first competitive match - three of the first four games were lost, leaving us a poor 17th at the end of August.

September was much better, with victories over Bradford and Birmingham helping the League position, but the month ended with a disappointing home defeat at the hands of local rivals Middlesbrough, and October started very badly indeed, a 4 - 0 thrashing at Reading leaving the Lads mid-table and the manager somewhat displeased. It was to be the turning point of the season. Reid began to shuffle the team for the next few League games, and with the introduction of new players the performances began to improve.

For the rest of October, the team remained unbeaten in the League, and a run of good results - notably wins at Portsmouth (4 - 1) and Tranmere (3 - 1) - saw the team start to climb up the table, and as the New Year started, the Lads were sitting in a respectable fifth place. More importantly, we were on a roll, and started the year by thrashing Rotherham 5 - 1 - away from home - in the FA Cup. League victories against Sheffield United and Manchester City then lifted us to fourth, but just as the team began to look invincible, the bubble was burst at the end of January with Cup exit at the hands of Tranmere and a League defeat at Norwich.

The Lads remained confident though, and a good string of victories pushed us into third place at the beginning of March, just one place off an automatic promotion spot. Above us, were the two teams that had dropped out of the Premiership with us - Nottingham Forest and Middlesbrough - and dislodging them did not look an easy task. Both had started the season well, opening up a fifteen point gap between themselves and the Lads. However, when a trip to Forest produced an amazing 3 - 0 win for us, automatic promotion began to look a realistic option; indeed, a 4 - 1 win against Stockport days later put us into second place. A nail-biting end to the season was now guaranteed, with the big three spending the following weeks swapping positions regularly. Things were looking good for Sunderland though, with consecutive victories against Portsmouth, Bury and Tranmere consolidating second place as the Easter programme began.

Crucially, the Lads lost badly needed points over the holiday programme, a 2 - 0 lead being wiped out by a couple of late goals for QPR on Good Friday, and a disappointing 3 - 3 against West Brom on Easter Monday seeing Sunderland end with ten men. Despite this, we were still in second place, and home victories against Crewe and Stoke helped put us back on track.

With just two games left it was all in our own hands, and the Lads visited Ipswich with the chance to put us clear of third placed Middlesbrough. Again though, our form dipped at a key moment, and a disappointing 2 - 0 defeat was a bitter blow. Suddenly the odds swung against us, for promotion would now depend on results elsewhere.

As so often in Sunderland's recent history, those results did not go our way. Despite a final day win at Swindon, the Lads had to settle for third - being an agonising one point away from automatic promotion - and the play-offs beckoned. Here, a semi-final against Sheffield United saw defeat in the first leg at the their place, but a wonderful performance at home put us through to a Wembley final against Charlton. It proved to be a dramatic encounter, but it didn't go the Lads' way, as defeat on penalties shattered our dreams for another season.

Kevin Phillips tearing through the Reading defence.

Reading Avenged

On February 17th, 1998, Reading made the trip to Sunderland for a Tuesday evening game. The Lads, thrashed 4 - 0 by the Berkshire team in October, were looking for revenge, and needed the points to maintain their promotion challenge. A massive 40,579 packed into the Stadium of Light, making it the best attended game in the Nationwide League at that point of the season. The Lads played superbly, demonstrating the art of attacking football. While we scored four goals - two from Phillips and one each for Rae and Quinn - many more could have gone in. The visitors managed a consolation goal, but that was all it was: they were never in the match, Sunderland's marvellous passing and wing play being too much for them.

306

Agony

"a footballing classic, but one Sunderland fans would rather forget."

Niall Quinn

After an injury stricken first season at the Club, Niall Quinn recovered well to become one of the stars of Sunderland's 1997-98 season. As a towering centre forward, he provides the target for many of our wingers' crosses, but Quinn also has a huge amount of skill and close control, meaning there is much more to his game than simply being the 'big man' up front. He hit seventeen goals in the 1997-98 campaign, and set up many chances for others, particularly his striking partner Kevin Phillips. His never say die spirit was particularly evident in the Play-Off Final, where his two well taken goals so nearly gave Sunderland promotion. Niall's good form continued in the 1998-99 season, where he finished as second top scorer with 21 goals.

An experienced Republic of Ireland international, he has won over 60 caps for his country and is only a few goals away from being the Republic's all time top goalscorer. Off the pitch he is one of football's ambassadors, having done much to promote anti-racism campaigns and writing an intelligent weekly column for The Guardian. A true professional, Quinn has been well worth the £1.3 million the Club bought him for.

Missing out on an automatic promotion spot was disappointing, but all was not lost, for the Play-Offs gave Sunderland an excellent chance of making an instant return to the Premiership. The series kicked off with a trip to Sheffield United - who had finished sixth - for the first leg of the semi-final. The Lads made an excellent start to the game, Kevin Ball firing us into a 1 - 0 lead. In the second forty-five though, the home team came back, hitting two goals as they tore the Lads' defences apart. United now had the upper hand: something special would be required in the return match at the Stadium of Light.

A massive 40,092 crowd packed into the Stadium of Light for the ground's first really major occasion, an attendance that would have been bigger still had Sheffield United managed to sell all of their allocation. The atmosphere was electric, all doubts that the new ground would be unable to replicate the Roker Roar being dispelled. On the pitch, it was a tense affair, but Sunderland were at the visitors from the off. The Lads had a great first forty-five minutes, an own goal and a cracker from Phillips putting the Lads 2 - 0 up on the day - and 3 - 2 on aggregate - at the interval.

In the second half, Sheffield came at Sunderland. Making use of all their substitutes the Blades piled forward, with the prolific Dean Saunders always a danger. The game was on a knife edge, for a goal from the visitors would tip the balance of the tie completely. Sunderland's goalkeeper, Lionel Perez, was in fine form though, and made one particularly notable double save that denied what appeared a certain goal. It was enough to win the tie for the Lads, and set up a Final at Wembley, against Charlton.

The decider would prove to be a footballing classic, but one Sunderland fans would rather forget. A massive 77,739 crowd turned out for the game - a record for a Play-Off Final - and the majority of them were Sunderland supporters. Once again, the atmosphere was first-class, but the Lads had a disappointing first-half, Sunderland raised Clive Mendonca getting a 24th minute goal that gave Charlton a 1 - 0 lead at half-time.

In the second-half though, the game changed rapidly. The Lads came out for the restart all guns blazing, and within five minutes had their reward when Quinn powered in a header to level the scores. Suddenly, Charlton looked scared, and eight minutes later, Phillips made it 2 - 1 with a cheeky chip over the Charlton 'keeper. The fans went wild, and it at last looked like it was going to be Sunderland's day.

But, the Addicks were in no mood to surrender, and Mendonca hit once more to make it 2 - 2. The game - indeed, the season - was now reaching boiling point, a dramatic climax being inevitable. It could have gone either way, but Quinn looked to have sealed it for the Lads when his second of the day made it 3 - 2 to Sunderland. With just five minutes left though, Charlton brought the party to an early end with a late equaliser: extra-time would be needed to decide it.

The second-half had been packed with drama: it was difficult to believe that the game was really happening. As a footballing spectacle it had been marvellous, but for partial observers it was gut wrenching agony. When extra-time kicked off, there was no let up, the ball moving from end to end. On the 100th minute, the Lads took the lead for a third time, when Summerbee fired home a rocket shot. Surely, this would be the winner? Again, it looked to be, but again, Charlton fought on, and with the clocks ticking towards the end of the game, they levelled once more, Mendonca completing his hat-trick with a well taken goal just minutes after Summerbee's strike.

Ninety minutes of football could not separate the two teams, nor could thirty minutes of extra-time. The match would be decided on penalties: five each. Charlton went first, Mendonca stepping up to the spot. A well hit penalty beat Perez to make it 1 - 0 to Charlton. Summerbee then appeared for Sunderland. With an entry in the Guinness Book of Records for the hardest shot in football, we expected him to score. He did! 1 - 1. On it went. Brown, Jones, Kinsella and Bowen all took kicks for Charlton, and all scored. Each step of the way though, the Lads matched them, Johnston, Ball, Makin and Rae doing the business for Sunderland.

With all five penalties taken, the scores were still level. Incredibly, it would now be decided on 'sudden death': the first team to miss one would lose. So, Robinson stepped up for Charlton, and another well taken penalty produced a sixth goal for the Addicks. However, Sunderland fans felt confident when Republic of Ireland international striker Niall Quinn moved towards the penalty area to take the Lads' kick. He made no mistake: 6 - 6. Six perfect penalties each, four goals each and over two hours of breathtaking football: it seemed unfair to penalise either time.

However, a winner was needed. Newton struck Charlton's seventh penalty, and sent it clear of Perez. The pressure was really on. Sunderland born Mickey Gray stepped up to take Sunderland's kick. A short run up before he struck the ball did not augur well, and the shot was saved by their 'keeper Sasa Ilic. After ten months of football, and some of the best performances seen from a Sunderland team, fate had intervened to deny us at the death: Sunderland would start the 1998-99 season in the Nationwide League Division 1.

Mickey Gray

Mickey Gray's transition to left-back during the season - and his developing partnership with left-winger Allan Johnston - was one of the real successes of the season. Gray is, without doubt, one of the stars of the Reid era, noted for both his work rate and his skilful play. The Play-Off Final, however, thrust him into the spot light for a missed penalty-kick. One of the most touching - and choking - moments of the game came after his miss, when Sunderland fans immediately put their disappointment to one side after his miss to chant "There's only one Mickey Gray": it was mark of the affection with which they hold him in and their appreciation of his work on the pitch. A true professional, Gray has not let the incident affect his game, and he has gone from strength to strength since, his performances attracting the eye of England manager Kevin Keegan, who has rewarded him with full international caps.

Mickey Gray.

1998-1999
Fantasy Football

"The perfect season"

Thomas Sorensen

Seventh Heaven

Saturday 19th September, 1999, saw one of the highlights of the season as Oxford arrived at the Stadium of Light. Within three minutes, Michael Bridges had put the Lads 1 - 0 up with a clinical finish from close range. Minutes later it was 2- 0, Michael Gray firing in a free kick struck hard and low. Oxford, however, refused to give up, and went close with a couple of great shots, but on 35 minutes, Daniel Dichio put the Lads 3 - 0 up from the penalty spot.

It had been a great first half, but better came in the second! Eight minutes after the restart, devastating wing play from Johnston opened up the defence, and Alex Rae took advantage, hammering home the Lads' fourth. Three minutes later, Bridges fired in a fifth - game over - and ten minutes later it was 6 - 0, Dichio adding his second of the match. It was exhibition stuff, the players pulling all sorts of tricks out of the bag; indeed, it was only a matter of time before the seventh came, and eight minutes before time, Rae scored his second of the game. The match ended 7 - 0, but it could easily have been more; in fact, Bridges and Dichio both had goals disallowed! While Oxford were not the best team in the League, it was still a great result: it was Sunderland's biggest win for over a decade and Oxford's heaviest defeat ever.

Wembley had been crushing, heart breaking for all involved in the Club, but the players, officials and, of course, the fans, made their way back from Wembley vowing to be stronger for the experience. Talk is cheap though, and behind the brave faces were worries that the play off final had left a scarring legacy. In the event, the sleepless nights were all for nothing. From the moment the new season kicked off it was clear that disappointment had given way to a determination to get the job done.

With the intention of adding steel to the defence, Reid made two new additions to the squad. Paul Butler - a tall, imposing central defender - arrived from Bury for £1 million, along with young goalkeeper Thomas Sorensen, a £1 million capture from Odense in Denmark. Yet, this renewed concern with defensive play did not come at the expense of attacking football, and August saw some great displays. Watford were thrashed 4 - 1, Allan Johnston scoring a beautiful curling goal, Tranmere were humiliated 5 - 0, and one of our big promotion rivals, Ipswich, were easily beaten 2 - 0 at Portman Road. Not only were the results great, the football was a joy to watch.

But, this successful start wasn't without its costs. The opening fixture saw record-signing midfielder Lee Clark injured during a 1 - 0 win against QPR. Clark's leg was broken in a freak incident that put him out of action for three months. As if this wasn't bad enough, Niall Quinn and Alex Rae were missing for most of the first couple of months too, and two weeks into September record breaking striker Kevin Phillips injured a toe in a Worthington Cup second round tie against Chester City; this seemingly insignificant ailment proved to be serious enough to put him out of action for the rest of 1998.

Yet, the Lads marched on unfazed. With Danny Dichio and Michael Bridges deputising for Quinn and Phillips, Oxford were hammered 7 - 0 at the Stadium of Light, both of the youngsters hitting a brace, Rae - on as a sub - also hitting two, and Mickey Gray scoring with a free-kick. What a day! September ended with the Lads unbeaten in all competitions, top of their division and through to the third round of the League Cup. Amazingly, the Club were unbeaten at reserve and youth level too, a marvellous illustration of the Club's strength.

October was to be tough month though, with the Lads up against a number of teams pushing us at the top of the table. Draws were secured against Bradford and Huddersfield - the latter game drawing a record crowd to the McAlpine Stadium - but it was a game against West Brom, managed by former Sunderland boss Denis Smith, that stood out. The Lads took a fifteen game unbeaten run into the match and had conceded just eight goals all season. Yet, we were 2 - 0 down before half-time. As the second half wore on with the score still 2- 0, it looked like the unbeaten run was over. However, Reid threw on Bridges and the game turned around. The youngster's pace tore the Baggies apart, and victory was snatched from the jaws of defeat. Three late goals sent the fans wild, three vital points being secured and the unbeaten run maintained. It was a fitting way to secure the Club's 500th away win. The month ended with a victory against Grimsby in the third round of the Worthington Cup and the Lads still at the top of the League table.

As if it wasn't clear already that the Lads were flying, the opening weeks of November confirmed it beyond doubt. Promotion rivals Bolton were dispensed 3 - 0 at the Reebok Stadium, newly capped Scottish international Allan Johnston doing much of the damage. Then, Crewe were thrashed 4 - 1 at Gretsy Road and Grimsby beaten

3 - 1 at home in front of 40,000. The Lads then visited Premier League Everton for the fourth round of the Worthington Cup; a magnificent opening goal from Bridges looked to have secured a victory for Sunderland, but a late equaliser eventually took the game to penalties. This time we made no mistake, a save from Sorensen securing victory - and a quarter-final place - for the Lads.

Ten days later, however, we suffered our first defeat of the season. In a gritty game, ten men Barnsley dug in to beat us 3 - 2 at home, bringing our twenty four game unbeaten run to an end. The Lads' response was magnificent though. A trip to fourth placed Sheffield United saw one of the games of the season; within ten minutes the home side were reeling from two Sunderland goals, and the game ended 4 - 0, a result which flattered the home team.

The final month of 1998 saw four straight home games at the Stadium of Light, all of which the Lads won. Notably, this run included a 3 - 0 victory against Luton Town in the Worthington Cup, securing a League Cup semi-final spot for the first time since 1985. Though Tranmere inflicted our second defeat of the season on Boxing Day, the year ended on a high, with 41,433 witnessing a 2 - 0 win against Crewe.

The New Year, as usual, saw the start of our FA Cup campaign, Lincoln being beaten 1 - 0 at Sencil Park. The following week saw Kevin Phillips return to the team, scoring a spectacular goal in a 2 - 2 draw at QPR. A good win against Ipswich followed, but the month ended with three consecutive defeats. Blackburn beat us 1 - 0 - very much against the run of play - at Ewood Park, knocking us out of the FA Cup. A few days later, Leicester visited the Stadium of Light for the first leg of the Worthington Cup semi-final, and a below par performance from the Lads resulted in the visitors running out 2 - 1 winners. Reeling from these defeats, the Lads failed to get into their stride against Watford in the League, losing 2 - 1 at Vicarage Road. It was a terrible ten days, but the Lads learnt from the experience: there would be no more defeats during the season.

February saw some useful wins in the League, but the main fixture was the return leg of the Worthington Cup semi-final. The Lads knew they could push Leicester harder than they had done at home, and we attacked from kick-off in the second leg. Quinn was in fine form, his ability in the air causing many problems.

Paul Butler

A huge, imposing centre back, Paul Butler arrived at Sunderland for a £1 million fee at the start of the 1998-99 season. His arrival caused much discussion amongst the fans, as Reid replaced the young, attacking centre back pairing of Craddock and Williams with the more rigid, but defensively more solid pair of Butler and Melville. While the new duo were certainly less attack minded, the strategy paid off, for the Lads won more games and conceded fewer goals, although credit here went to new keeper Sorensen too.

Butler's size also caused much discussion. An intimidating figure to say the least, few would want to pick a fight with him! A no-nonsense defender, his successful part in the promotion campaign has brought him to the verge of international honours with the Republic of Ireland, and a new defensive pairing with Steve Bould in the Premiership has caught the eye of pundits.

Paul Butler.

We're On Our Way...

On Tuesday 13th April, the Lads finally sealed promotion to the Premier League. The tiny Gigg Lane, home of Bury, was packed with an 8,669 crowd; most were Mackems, and the fans roared the team on for the full 90 minutes and a good half-hour after the game too! Within ten minutes we had taken the lead - Kevin Phillips coolly slotting home a penalty kick - and the stage was set for an almighty thrashing of lowly Bury. However, the home side equalised 14 minutes later, their fans going wild as a rocket shot flew past Sorensen. Fate was not on their side. Within 60 seconds the Lads were back in the lead, Niall Quinn bundling in Nicky Summerbee's precision cross. Bury were reeling, and six minutes later, Phillips hit his second of the night, taking advantage of goalmouth confusion to make it 3 - 1. It was great stuff, but a couple of minutes later, Phillips secured his hat-trick, nodding home an Allan Johnston cross to make it 4 - 1 ten minutes before half-time!

By now the party was well under way. The win we needed to secure promotion was clearly in the bag! The second half saw Bury pull one back - and at times threaten to get back into the game - but in truth, there was only one team in it. Phillips made it 5 - 2 shortly before the end with a superbly struck shot that curled into the top corner. At the final whistle, the ground was ringing out to the sound of the fans' new anthem: 'We're on our way, we're on our way, to the Premier we're on our way...'

Indeed, it was the big Irishman who broke the deadlock, firing the Lads in front on the day - and pulling the scores level on aggregate. At half-time we were on top, but a tactical change in the Leicester line up swung the balance; a goal from Tony Cottee made it 2 - 3 on aggregate, and the game ended that way. A brave effort, but not quite enough to secure a Wembley appearance. All attention would now be on the League.

We responded well, and March saw a perfect set of results; five games were played, five victories delivered. The win at Bradford was a real headline grabber; not only were the Yorkshire side gunning for promotion too, but Tommy Sorensen was stretchered off during the match. With no reserve keeper on the bench, Quinn - who had just scored for us - stepped into the breach, and made a number of good saves to keep the score at 1 - 0! Another important victory came when Bolton visited the Stadium of Light; Colin Todd's pre-match comments that his side could still catch Sunderland added extra spice to the game, but a stadium record crowd of 41,505 saw Bolton humbled. From the first kick we tore into the Trotters, and Reid's 100th Wearside home game - Sunderland's 50th at the Stadium of Light - produced a 3 - 1 victory that flattered the visitors. During the game, Kevin Phillips scored his fiftieth goal for Sunderland.

As the Easter programme got underway, it was not a case of if, but when Sunderland would secure promotion. Unsurprisingly, there were full houses every week at the Stadium of Light, fans being eager to witness the moment celebrations could start. Home games against West Brom and Huddersfield saw over 41,000 pack into the ground, securing our place as the country's third best supported team, but in the event, promotion was secured at one of the division's smallest grounds: Bury's Gigg Lane. With a capacity of less than 9,000, the moment was savoured by the lucky few, though most of the crowd were Sunderland fans. In a storming match, the Lads were on fire, being 4 - 1 up well before half-time; Phillips notched a first half hat trick, and he added a fourth goal in the dying minutes of the game; with a month of the campaign left, a 5 - 2 victory had secured Premiership football for 1999-2000.

Predictably, the Bury game had something of a carnival atmosphere, and the partying continued three days later when we visited Barnsley. Another win would secure the Championship, and in driving rain, the Lads turned it on again, Summerbee, Clark and Phillips hitting the goals in a 3 - 1 victory. It was nothing less than we deserved. The Lads had topped the table for most of the season, and no-one else had occupied it since 24th October. In short, we were just a class above the rest; with nine points left to play for, no-one could catch us.

The hard work did not stop there though. Reid's team were in record breaking form. The win against West Brom had broken the post-War record for consecutive home League victories, and another against Sheffield United would equal the record of thirteen set by the team of all talents in the 1890s. Sadly, a slightly flat 0 - 0 performance fell just short. However, there was still more to play for. The Lads were in sight of English football's all time record points haul; victory against Stockport gave us a staggering 102 - equalling the total set by Swindon - with a game left to play. What's more, in between the two matches, half the first team were on international duty. As usual, Niall Quinn turned out for the Republic of Ireland, and Allan Johnston put in another great display for Scotland. In addition, Thomas Sorensen made it on the bench for Denmark, underlining his claim as Peter Schmichael's future replacement, and Andy Melville continued to press his claims for a place in the Welsh side. But, the big news was the appearance of two Sunderland players in England's team against Hungary, Kevin Phillips and Michael Gray topping great seasons with their first England caps. It was the first time since October 1926 that England's finest had included two red-and-whites.

Our final match, a 2 - 1 victory against Birmingham, completed a marvellous season and made it a new English football record of 105 points from 46 games. The Lads had finished 18 points clear of second placed Bradford - illustrating the gap between us and the rest - and in beating Birmingham had completed a 'full set' of victories: no team in the division had avoided defeat against Sunderland during the season. A new record crowd at the Stadium of Light, some 41,634, saw the Lads crowned as the 100th Football League Champions. To add to the glory, the reserves had also pipped Manchester United and Liverpool to the Pontins League Premier title, making it a double success, and the 33,517 that had turned out for the reserve match against Liverpool smashed the all time Pontins League attendance record. Indeed, it was a figure that exceeded the season's top crowd for many of the Premier League's first teams!

After the devastation of 1996-97 and 1997-98, this had been the perfect season, and the message was clear: Sunderland are back in the big time and ready to go!

Goodbye Andy

One of the stars of the season was Welsh international central defender Andy Melville. Signed by Terry Butcher in the 1993-94 season, Melville had been a central figure in Reid's first promotion campaign, but after losing his place at the Stadium of Light early in the 1997-98 season, it looked like his Sunderland career was over. 'Mary' - as the other Lads dubbed him - fought back brilliantly though, and after winning his place back early in the 1998-99 campaign, established himself as a regular, making 52 League and Cup appearances. Much of the credit for the defensive record during the year goes to Melville, who established a solid pairing with Paul Butler, and forced his way back into the Welsh national squad. However, the season was also his last at the Club. At the end of the campaign he moved on to join former Sunderland assistant manager Paul Bracewell's Fulham. He had provided six seasons of great service to the Club and a testimony of his talent and application comes from the fact that he was one of the few players to survive the transition from the Butcher & Buxton to Reid eras. A great defensive player who was always comfortable going forward too, he was a great servant to the Club.

Andy Melville.

Into the New Millennium

"Sunderland are a true Premiership force."

Colin Wood, Mail on Sunday.

Stefan Schwarz

The Club signalled its ambition before the season began by pulling out all the stops to sign world class Swedish international Stefan Schwarz. His three previous Clubs - Arsenal, Fiorentina and Valencia - are all appearing in the 1999-2000 UEFA Champions' League, so it was a considerable coup to persuade Stefan that Sunderland had the ambition to match these teams. No doubt the new stadium and the fact that our team features numerous internationals helped to sway his decision, but the Club went to great lengths to make sure Stefan would be happy in the region, something for which the player was very grateful.

His transfer fee of £4 million set a new Club record, but there was an unusual feature in his contract. Stefan had, half jokingly, expressed an interest in being a passenger on the first civilian space flight, but the Club were a bit worried that this might be a dangerous activity. Most appropriately as we enter a space age new millennium, Stefan became the first footballer to have a 'no space travel' clause in his contract!

As Sunderland AFC prepare to enter the new millennium - the third century in which we have played professional football - there is much to be positive about: the Club are back in English football's top flight; for the first time in decades we can truly claim to have one of the best grounds in British football; behind the scenes, the Club at last has a strong, modern business structure; and on the pitch, the team contains more quality international players than it has done since the Bank of England days. While football is full of uncertainties - no-one knows what the year 2000 holds for Sunderland AFC - the signs are that the Club has finally turned the corner and is ready to shake off the problems that have dogged it since the late 1950s.

Before the season's fixtures had even been announced, the Club's rude health - and the fans' excitement at the forthcoming season - was firmly underlined by phenomenal season ticket sales. 36,000 were snapped up, thousands of fans being disappointed at missing out. However, for a large number of fans, season tickets are not a viable proposition, and the Club chose to limit the number available in order to allow fans to buy tickets for individual matches. Nevertheless, the huge capacity of the Stadium of Light means Sunderland can still boast the highest number of season ticket holders in English football. What's more, this number includes a higher proportion of women supporters than any other team and the biggest number of families with season tickets, the latter contributing towards the Club's season ticket holders having the youngest average age of any of the Premiership teams, all healthy signs for the future of Sunderland AFC.

Armed with transfer funds bolstered by these ticket sales, Peter Reid spent much of the summer looking for players that might strengthen his squad for the Premiership challenge. Speculation in the press surrounded some top quality players, including Argentinean international Ariel Ortega, Croatian international Davor Suker and Swedish international Stefan Schwarz. Not only did these stories create great excitement, they also illustrated the huge strides froward the Club has taken in recent years.

However, as the Lads returned for training - and before the expected flood of pre-season signings had taken place - the fans were rocked by the announcement that three of the previous season's stars had been placed on the transfer list: Lee Clark, Michael Bridges and Alan Johnston. Geordie born Clark had made a gaffe of immense proportions when, while at Wembley to watch Newcastle in the FA Cup final, he had temporarily worn a t-shirt insulting Sunderland fans. When pictures of this later appeared in the Sunday papers, Reid had little choice but to sell him, and a £3 million switch to Fulham followed.

As such, Clark's move was expected - and encouraged - by many fans; he had lost their support. But, the listing of Bridges and Johnston was more difficult to stomach. Both players, who had pleased the crowds with their eye-catching performances, had just one year left on their Sunderland contracts. Keen to keep them, the manager offered both improved and extended deals, which they shook hands on. However, both then went back on their word, refusing to sign the deals. Angry at their refusal to commit to the cause, and worried too that the players might leave the Club on a 'Bosman' free transfer when their contracts expired, Reid put both on the transfer list and froze them out of the squad. Bridges soon left in a £5 million transfer to Leeds. For Johnston, though, there were no buyers, and the situation remained unsolved as the season kicked off.

It was a controversial move by Reid, but the manager is 100% committed to Sunderland and he needs players who are prepared to match this commitment out on the pitch. Better news came with the confirmation that in-coming transfer dealings had been planned.

Steve Bould, stalwart of a great Arsenal defence, joined the Club for around £500,000; Thomas Helmer, a veteran German international, joined on a 'Bosman' free transfer from Bayern Munich; and Swedish international Stefan Schwarz became the Club's new record signing when he joined from Valencia in a £4 million deal. The trio joined Carsten Fredgaard, a Danish international whose signature had been confirmed before the end of the previous season, £1.8 million bringing him from Lyndby. Finally, a week into the season, Reid also captured Welsh international John Oster, who joined from Everton for around £750,000. Helmer's stay was short lived. Just a month into the season he returned home. He had been unable to force his way into the team, a testimony to our strength in depth.

The fixture list dealt the Lads a difficult start to the season, with games against three of the previous season's top four in our opening fortnight, along with a crunch derby game at Newcastle. We kicked off with a trip to Chelsea, scene of a 6 - 2 hammering on our previous visit in 1997. This time, it was little better. The Lads were completely outclassed and slumped to a 4 - 0 victory. It was men against boys throughout the pitch, and early season optimism immediately turned into gloom. Perhaps we wouldn't be up to the challenge.

Our second game came at home to fellow promoted team Watford. The Lads ran out 2 - 0 winners, Phillips scoring a superb goal, but the result told us little about our ability to survive at the top. A more significant result came at home to Arsenal, the previous season's runners-up. An excellent defensive performance silenced their attack, and the game ended 0 - 0. Our opening fortnight was then completed with a trip to Leeds United. When Phillips put us 1 - 0 up, we looked good value for at least a point. However, some appalling referee decisions contributed to an undeserved 2 - 1 defeat.

At this point, it was difficult to tell how well the team might fare. Arsenal, Chelsea and Leeds - having finished second, third and fourth in 1998-99 - were all good teams. As such, four points from four games wasn't too bad, particularly given the circumstances surrounding the Leeds defeat. However, there were still doubts that we might struggle, particularly away from home. Some good wins were needed to settle the nerves. Fortunately, they soon began to arrive.

Bosman Ruling

Jean Luc Bosman goes down in history as one of the most important footballers of the 1990s. However, his fame was not achieved on the pitch - where he was a decent, but unspectacular player - but off it. He argued that the transfer system operating in European football placed unfair restrictions on players' freedom of movement, and took his case to the European Courts. At the centre of his dispute was the claim that clubs treated players as if they were their property, because contracts tied players to clubs even if neither the player or the club wanted the working relationship to continue.

Bosman had a point. His club were refusing to play him - he had no part in the manager's plans and his contract had run out- but, at the same time, they were unwilling to sell him to anyone else until they were offered a transfer fee matching their valuation. Yet, without first team football, Bosman had little chance of clinching a move elsewhere, because his club's valuation was simply too high for a reserve player. All Bosman wanted to do was play football but, because his club 'owned' him, he was unable to do so.

The European Courts agreed that this situation was unfair and ruled that across Europe, players would be free to move wherever they wanted once their contracts had finished. Clubs would no longer be able to hold on to a player's registration until someone else bought it off them. However, the ruling has created a whole new set of problems. The balance of power has shifted from clubs to players, and managers are finding it increasingly difficult to plan for the future. If star players refuse to sign extensions to their contracts, then clubs are faced with the difficult choice of cashing in on their asset and losing a key player, or waiting until their contracts have expired and see them move to another club for nothing.

Steve Bould

SUNDERLAND ACADEMY
...aiming for the stars

INSPIRED BY TRADITION · DEDICATED TO THE FUTURE

Youth Academy

In building for the future, the Club is aiming to expand its youth facilities considerably by developing a purpose built Youth Academy. With transfer fees continuing to escalate, competition for the players of the future is hotting up too, clubs being eager to catch potential stars before they cost millions of pounds. By developing state of the art training facilities and accommodation at the academy, the Club hopes to be able to attract some of the best youngsters of the day to Sunderland. More importantly, the hope is that the modern coaching facilities contained within the academy will also help those youngsters develop into star players.

Who knows? When the academy is firmly established, perhaps we will see a repeat of the 1930s, with a team of home grown youngsters leading us to League and Cup glory.

Our fifth game of the season was a real biggie: Newcastle at St James' Park. With the Mags in trouble at the bottom of the table, the Lads knew they were in with a shout of pulling off a win. Yet, the Newcastle team was packed with stars - including England captain Alan Shearer - and we hadn't won at Newcastle since the 1990 play-offs semi-final. When the Mags took an early lead, the fans were braced for the worst. But, the Lads responded superbly, goals from Quinn and Phillips securing a delightful 2 - 1 win. The defeat proved to be the end of the road for Newcastle boss Ruud Gullitt, who left the club shortly after the game. What an outcome!

A televised 1 - 1 draw against Coventry followed - not the best result - but the next two matches were pure class. The visit of Leicester City to the Stadium of Light was expected to be a real benchmark for the Lads. Leicester, promoted with us in 1996, had established themselves as a useful, battling team. Indeed, we had come up against them in the Worthington Cup semi-final the previous season, when the Midlands team proved strong. This time, however, we were wiser. The Lads bossed the game, goals from Butler and McCann securing a 2 - 0 win. Better was to come though. Our next match was a trip to the other team promoted with us in 1996: Derby. Like Leicester, Derby had established themselves as a robust Premiership side following promotion, but the Lads swept them away. A hat-trick from Super Kev and goals from McCann and Quinn produced an unbelievable 5 - 0 away win! It was our our biggest top flight away win since January 1947, when the Lads thrashed Blackpool 5 - 0 in the first post-War League campaign.

The result lifted us to fourth place after eight games, a position few expected us to occupy. What's more, it also placed Kevin Phillips at the top of the Premier League goalscorers' table. Amazingly, the Lads travelled to Walsall for a Worthington Cup tie some three days later and repeated the feat! With the manager making nine changes to the Derby team in order to give some of his other first team squad players a chance to prove themselves, the new line up completely overpowered their First Division opponents. Two goals apiece from Dichio and Fredgaard, and one from new signing Eric Roy, made it a second 5 - 0 away win a row! The result put us through to the next round with an 8 - 2 aggregate score, and the emphatic nature of the win illustrated the increasing gap between the strength and depth of our squad and the standard of that found in the First Division.

The wins were no flukes however. We quickly consolidated our League position with a string of wins, Schwarz scoring the winner in a 1 - 0 victory at home to Sheffield Wednesday, Phillips hitting a brace in a superb 4 - 0 win at Bradford and another couple from Phillips securing the points in a 2 - 1 win against Aston Villa. Agonisingly, a late goal from West Ham - with the Lads reduced to ten men - brought our run to an end, and while the 1 - 1 away draw was still a good result, the three points would have put us on top of the Premier League with a third of the season gone. As it is, the Lads are hitting heights unseen since the 1950s, holding down a place in the top four against all the odds. While no-one can predict how well we will perform over the rest of the season, a great start has been made. The Lads have shown early on that they are ready for the challenge and, already, they have surprised more than a few people and confounded the pundits who predicted another season struggling against relegation. Indeed, following our emphatic victory at Bradford, Colin Wood of the Mail on Sunday was forced to concede that "Sunderland are a true Premiership force."

Once thing that is certain, however, is that Sunderland need to stay in the Premiership this time if the forty year cycle of decline is to be broken. After decades of incremental decline it really is make or break time for the Club. Our highest placed finish since the illegal payments scandal remains the pitiful 13th place secured in 1984.

But on all fronts we seem much better placed now than we were then to mount an assault on the top half of the top division. Indeed, there may never be a better chance to break the cycle of decline. We have the strongest squad of players for some time, with genuine international class players who can grow with the Club. Schwarz, Phillips, Gray and Sorensen, for example, are players recognised as being amongst the best in their position who still have years left in them. While in the past our 'international' players have often been men past their best, their true international days being spent with previous clubs, this is not the case with our current batch of star players. In Reid, we also have our most talented manager in a generation. While there are always those who start to question the manager following a couple of bad results, Reid's contribution to our revival cannot be understated. When he arrived at the Club, we were in crisis, continually flirting with relegation to the third flight. He changed this overnight, and while his first spell in the Premier League didn't quite work out, he showed the determination and commitment to take us back there as quickly as possible. The number of Club records broken under his period in charge is phenomenal and a testimony to his managerial skills. On top of this, of course, we have the new stadium. Its state of the art facilities, and the huge crowds it pulls in, not only boost the Club's finances, but also signal the Club's ambition to grow, the embodiment of a team that is going places. Last time around, a crumbling Roker Park and 22,000 capacity attendances hampered the manager's efforts to attract players to the Club; this time around our ground is a key selling point used to draw players to Sunderland.

But, Sunderland fans are well aware of the thin line that exists between survival and relegation. A good start can easily go wrong; injuries at crucial moments can be devastating; and the quality of the opposition is undeniably high. The new millennium does, therefore, present a real crossroads for Sunderland. A successful season could act as the springboard for future success. A top half of the table finish will keep the momentum of change going. Success breeds success. If opposition players see the crowds continue to increase, the stadium expanding and the team doing well on the pitch, then they too will want to be part of the action. Reid will be in a strong position to attract new talent to the Club and strengthen the team in order to challenge for European places and domestic honours. If, on the other hand, disaster strikes and we drop back into the First Division, then the chances are that some of our key players will feel the time is right to move on to pastures new. It is only fair that international players consider their own personal future and if Sunderland cannot provide them with the platform to build a career at the top of their profession, then they cannot be blamed for moving. In such circumstances, Reid's priorities would inevitably focus around trying to persuade his best players to stay rather than trying to fruitlessly persuade new internationals to join a second flight team.

England at Sunderland

On 10th October, 1999, the Sunderland Stadium of Light received a compliment of the highest order, when it played host to England's international fixture against Belgium. With Wembley being unavailable due to the Net Aid concert being played there, the national team turned to our home, recognising it as one of the best stadiums in the country.

In a great day for Sunderland, a full house witnessed the game, and the organisation behind the scenes was a credit to the Club, for it was a smoothly run operation. But, it was a double reward for Sunderland, because Kevin Phillips was chosen to start up front for England, meaning the game underlined our rapid progress both on and off the pitch in recent years.

The game itself ended 2 - 1 to England, with Alan Shearer and Jamie Redknapp getting England's goals, the latter being a real screamer from outside the box. Phillips played well too, Sky Television viewers voting him man of the match.

Kevin Phillips shoots for goal, England v Belgium, Sunderland Stadium of Light.

SAFCommunity

In order to facilitate its community activities, the Club has a stand alone, non-profit making arm known as 'SAFCommunity'.

Established in 1988, when it was based in a terraced house opposite Roker Park, it has grown rapidly over the years.

Headed by the Community Officer, Bob Oates, it currently operates in three areas - education, coaching and junior supporters - and employs two full time teachers, 37 coaches and a junior supporters' co-ordinator.

There is, for sure, a certain element of luck in football, and Sunderland are due some. As Blackburn Rovers proved in the 1998-99 season, clubs with good players can quite easily find themselves sucked into the relegation places. And, as others such as Coventry continually demonstrate, it isn't always the best teams that stay up. But, the belief that Sunderland can do more than survive this time is not confined merely to ever hopeful fans. Following our 5 - 0 rout of Derby County, The Observer confidently predicted that the Lads had more than enough skill and fighting spirit to hold their own in the Premiership.

Perhaps our resurgence is being timed to perfection. While it may well be true that we have never had such a good chance of re-establishing ourselves as a force in English football, it is certainly the case that English football itself is undergoing dramatic changes that are pushing it towards a new era. The game is changing thick and fast. Hillsborough and Taylor brought a new era in football stadia; the formation of the Premier League has increased the wealth of the top clubs and brought an influx of foreign players; the trend towards the flotation of clubs on the stock exchange has both increased the level of finance in the game and brought a new set of issues in relation to the ownership of clubs; and, the satellite, cable and digital revolution in television and internet based media has, and will continue to, bring changes to the ways in which people watch the game and the times and places at which it is played. Whether these changes are for better of for worse, it is imperative that Sunderland don't get left behind. Football is on the verge of new era, and if we are to be a successful club, competing at the top level, then we must keep a careful eye on such developments and be prepared to make bold moves when necessary. Indeed, if we can take the right turning at the right time, then we can be amongst the small band of clubs in the leading pack, just as we were in the pre-War era.

Already, we have moved to become one of the growing number of clubs listed on the stock exchange, becoming a plc (public limited company) in 1996. Since flotation, our shares have performed well, reflecting a belief within the City that Sunderland are one of the few clubs in the game who still have the potential to grow both on and off the pitch. It is also a vote of confidence in the Club's managerial structures, which have been radically modernised since flotation. Most notably, perhaps, the plc board includes a series of distinguished non-executive directors, led by Chairman Bryan Sanderson, and accompanied by Sir Richard Storey and David Chance. Each of these men have worked at the top of their respective fields, and the advice that they can offer is invaluable and will help ensure the Club's growth continues.

In opening up the boardroom to people such as Sanderson and his colleagues, flotation provided a positive step forward for a club that has often suffered some serious backroom troubles in recent decades. In addition, flotation also opened up the possibility of ordinary Sunderland fans legally owning part of their club. For as little as £5, fans can now purchase Sunderland AFC shares from the stock market, giving them the chance to participate in the Club's decision making processes and pass judgement on our annual performance. While many have expressed concern at football clubs being listed on the stock exchange, these positive moves are important steps forward. The new boardroom is radically different from the closed shop that existed at Roker Park, when only the extremely wealthy could have a say and, even then, only if they were invited onto the board by its existing members.

At the same time, however, it should not be denied that there are some undesirable aspects surrounding recent changes to the game. As money becomes more important, there are certain clubs who have abandoned their traditional fans and decided to focus on making profits instead. Unfortunately, there is inevitably a competitive dynamic in professional sport that means if one club increases its profiteering in order to spend more on players, then others have to follow suit or fall behind. While Sunderland are committed to restoring the team to the prominent position it enjoyed in the past, the fans can be reassured that they will not seek to do this at their expense.

Indeed, at the heart of the Club's philosophy for the new millennium is the belief that Sunderland AFC is a community club that needs to focus on putting as much back into the city and the region as it can. Shameless exploitation is not on the agenda.

As an illustration of this, it should be noted that for well over a decade the Club has been running an ever expanding community programme, using the Club's image, facilities and resources to help improve life in the region. For example, over 10,000 school children visit the Stadium of Light's classrooms each year, where they are given free, national curriculum based lessons, taught by the Club's two full time teachers. The excitement of visiting the stadium enthuses many of the kids involved in the scheme and boosts their desire to learn once back in school. On a similar note, the Club has pioneered an attendance reward scheme to help combat truancy. Here, free match tickets and stadium tours were given to pupils whose attendance at school was excellent, or those whose attendance had dramatically improved. The Club also employs 37 community coaches, who make a combined average of 55 school coaching visits per week throughout the region and beyond, often to some of the poorest areas of the North East. On a slightly different note, the Club has also launched the 'Sunderland AFC Health Accord', a partnership between the Club, council and local health agencies. Its aim it to harness the power of the SAFC brand in promoting health messages to children, such as anti-smoking campaigns. Similarly, the Club has also used its position to promote anti-racism messages, distributing 40,000 'show racism the red card' posters and organising a schools' anti-racism painting competition. These are less well known aspects of the Club's work, and are all non-profit making activities that it funds out of its own pocket. It does this because it is committed to putting something back in to the community, and it is proud to be the most active football club in this field.

The board know that without the fans, Sunderland AFC is nothing. The Club's huge and passionate following is the key to its success; it is what makes the Club what it is. One of the key reasons for moving to the Stadium of Light - and continuing to expand it - was that it would enable the Club to achieve its goal of 'affordable and accessible football'. The huge crowds at the new ground generate tremendous revenues that can be used to fund transfers and players' salaries. But, with our 42,000 capacity, we can do this while offering 17,000 concessionary tickets for each game - more than any other Club in the country. Sunderland are committed to keeping a balance between generating the finance needed to compete in the modern game and keeping football open to all Sunderland fans, irrespective of their income. A measure of our commitment to this goal comes in one simple statistic. For the 1998-99 season, our average home gate exceeded that of our nearest local rival by several thousand. Yet, our rival's average gate receipts were roughly double ours. High ticket prices might help to buy short term success, but in the long term there can be no future in selling the fans short. More importantly, it is also wrong. Football is the people's game, and Sunderland will remain the people's club. Ours is a club for the many not the few, a club with no exclusions, a one class club.

Women and Football

As football enters the 21st Century, one trend we can expect to grow is that of women taking a more active interest in the game. While at one time it was rare to see women at matches, not least because the men dissuaded them from attending, this is no longer the case, and Sunderland can now boast the highest number and proportion of female season ticket holders in England, some 19%. The Club is committed to 'opening football up' to women, and in order to help achieve this objective, it runs the North East's only FA Centre of Excellence for female footballers, one of just twenty around the country. The Stadium of Light has also tried to keep ahead of the times by including male and female changing rooms for the referee and referee's assistants.

Bob Murray

Bob Murray joined the board in 1984, as a director, and was appointed Executive Chairman in 1986, when he acquired a major shareholding in the Club. Except for a brief period between November 1993 and June 1996, he has remained in the post since.

His lasting contribution to the Club is clearly the Stadium of Light, a project that was very much driven by his own vision and determination. Indeed, Murray suffered a great deal of personal abuse when he announced plans to move from Roker, few believing the vision he articulated would be seen through. In the end, however, the critics were proved wrong.

Yet, Murray feels his most important seasons in charge came not when we were moving home, but when he first took over the Chairman's job. 'There are', he says, 'two things that should never have left Southampton, Lawrie McMenemy and the Titanic!' His first task was to try to remove McMenemy from the Club, a job which took the best part of a season. By the time he did go, Sunderland were in deep trouble, and our relegation to the Third Division presented Murray with a real challenge. The Club were in danger of going bankrupt, and with the bank closing in, he had to work hard to prevent this from happening, while also providing Denis Smith with the support he needed to take us back into the Second Division at an important first attempt.

Chairmen rarely get credit for their actions, but they play a crucial role in laying the foundations for success. Few can doubt that Murray has managed to do this at Sunderland. Indeed, the greatest testimony to his efforts is that when Murray decides to leave the Club, he will be the first Chairman for a long while able to truthfully say that he has left Sunderland in a far better position than he found it in.

Murray & Reid - A Winning Partnership

One of the darkest moments in the Club's recent history came on 24th March, 1995. After flirting with relegation for a number of seasons, we were in deep trouble again, and travelled to Barnsley needing a win to boost our chances of survival. With just eight games left, manager Mick Buxton had brought Dominic Matteo on loan to the Club on transfer deadline day, the hope being that the Liverpool youngster would help us to play our way out of trouble. The game was a complete disaster. Not only did we lose 2 - 0, heightening our relegation worries, but the Club had made an error in processing Matteo's registration and, consequently, we had broken the rules by fielding him. A points deduction looked inevitable, making our slim chances of survival worse.

After the match, Bob Murray decided it was time for him to again take an active role in leading the Club, having taken a back seat role for a couple of years, and his first action was to replace Buxton with Peter Reid in the manager's position. It was a masterstroke. In the remaining seven games, Reid guided us to safety, and the following season he transformed a set of relegation regulars into Champions. What's more, he did this not by spending huge amounts on new signings, but by using his managerial skills to motivate the players, organise them and convince them they were winners.

In hindsight, Reid's appointment was a real turning point for the Club. Since his arrival, Sunderland have been an altogether much better team, and the quality of the football being played is the best seen on Wearside in a generation. Two First Division championships tell their own story, with our most recent achieved in an emphatic style that is likely to see the Club in the record books for some time to come.

However, during the dark days of 1995, no-one could foresee the success that Reid would bring to Sunderland. Bob Murray had spent several months scouring the country for a new manager, and much time was spent investigating and pondering Reid's merits as a manager. In his first managerial job, at Manchester City, Reid had done well, twice steering his side to a fifth place finish in the top flight, and as a player, Reid had always been a winner, lifting two League Championships, the FA Cup and the European Cup Winners' Cup with Everton, and reaching the World Cup quarter-finals with England. But after being unceremoniously dumped by City in 1993, he had been out of the managerial game completely, spending nearly two years making occasional playing appearances for Southampton, Notts County and Bury. Moreover, while at City, Reid had something of a confrontational relationship with his Chairman, Peter Swales, with disagreements between the two being largely responsible for his untimely sacking.

Weighing up these plusses and minuses was a difficult task for Murray, who wanted to avoid making a weak appointment. The Club had been drifting since the departure of Denis Smith, and a firm guiding was required. He decided, therefore, to give Reid the job on a trial basis. Both parties would have until the end of the season to see what they thought of each other and see if a good working relationship could be established. With the team soon performing miracles on the pitch, it was evident that Reid was the man for the job. What's more, he seemed to take to the Club too, and the relationship was soon made a permanent one. Indeed, such was the turnaround in the team's performances that people quickly began to see Reid for what he is: one of the most talented English managers in the game today.

But, the problem with having a first class manager is that pretty soon, everyone else wants him too. Yet, Murray was wise to this, and was determined to ensure that the Club matched Reid's ambition to win by doing everything it could to lay the conditions for success. With Roker Park being reduced to a shadow of its former self, a new stadium was essential and, just as Reid arrived at the Club, the closure of Wearmouth Colliery opened up the possibility of building a brand new ground in the heart of the City. After a series of frustrating delays, the new stadium was at last back on track. Crucially, however, Murray took the bold step of deciding to plan for a 42,000 seater stadium, and one that could easily be expanded to a maximum of 63,000, sagaciously foreseeing the need to provide a stage fit for Reid's international packed Premier League team. At the time, people though he was crazy, and many predicted it would be a white elephant. Instead, the original 42,000 seats already needs to be expanded in order to cope with the demand for tickets now that Reid has revived the team.

Just four years on from that dark day at Barnsley, so much has changed. Not only have our fortunes been radically changed on the pitch, but a Club on the brink of disaster has been transformed into a Club with fantastic prospects for the future. That we are in the position to realistically contemplate challenging for honours in a stadium that is good enough to be a centre piece of England's bid for the 2006 World Cup is, sometimes, hard to believe. At the same time though, we have travelled so far recently that is often hard to remember just how desperate the situation was a few short years ago. But we should not forget. The bad times make the good times so much sweeter, and we should pay tribute to the winning combination - Murray and Reid - that has done so much to turn events around. It is clear that there is a special bond between these two men and that both are intent on building on the Club's strengths. The Chairman has a great respect for Peter Reid and believes that Sunderland is the 'club of destiny' for our manager. There are rare moments in footballing history when a club and manager come together at a time when both are ready to hit the game's highest peaks. Shankly at Liverpool, Revie at Leeds and Clough at Nottingham Forest all took teams from the Second Division up to the top of the League. Who would want to bet against Reid doing it at Sunderland?

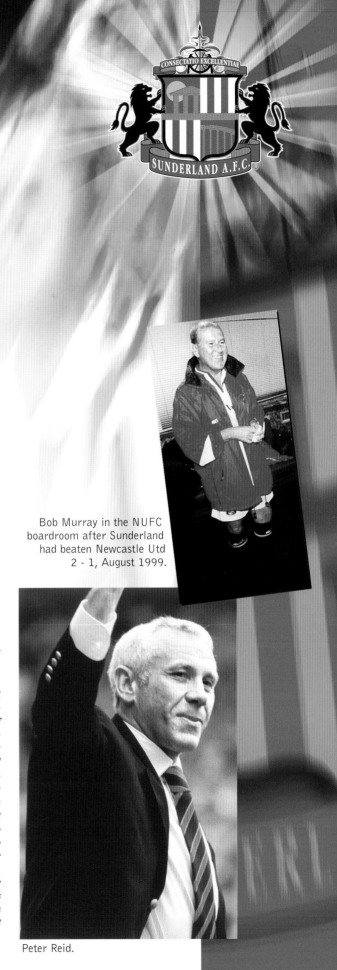

Bob Murray in the NUFC boardroom after Sunderland had beaten Newcastle Utd 2 - 1, August 1999.

Peter Reid

The legendary Bill Shankly once described Reid as 'the yard dog scrapper'. You could see where he was coming from. Reidy always gives 100%, always battles to win, and is not afraid to fight for his side. Yet, the phrase hardly does justice to the intelligence of the man who has masterminded Sunderland's revival. While there is no doubting the fact that Reid is a tough customer - few would want to mess with him - you cannot achieve what he has without also possessing a great footballing brain. Real tactical nous, first rate man management skills and a comprehensive knowledge of the ins-and-outs of what's going on in football are some of Reid's key characteristics, yet they are often overlooked because of his passion and fighting spirit. If battling alone could win trophies and medals then Sunderland would have had few problems over the years. But real winners need more than this, and Reid is a real winner. As a player he won two League Championships, an FA Cup and the European Cup Winners' Cup. He was also capped eight times by England, appearing in the 1986 World Cup quarter-finals, where the team were denied by Maradonna's infamous 'Hand of God' goal. Most notably of all, perhaps, he was also named the Players' Player of the Year in 1985. As a manager, he has already delivered two First Division championships at Sunderland and guided us to the League Cup semi-finals. The best, though, is surely still to come. If anyone can guide Sunderland to glory it is Peter Reid. There is no doubting that Reid is our best manager in a generation, and his considerable skills are already widely recognised.

Peter Reid.

Conclusion:
History Lessons?

Club founder James Allan.

Life can move at a frighteningly quick pace. At the outbreak of the Second World War, Sunderland AFC had been in existence for just sixty years. Our development from an amateur, voluntaristic teachers' football Club, to what was then the most successful team in a recognisably modern game, all came within an ordinary lifetime. It is amazing to think that for someone of Winston Churchill's age at the outbreak of the War, childhood years were a time when football was a game for dedicated enthusiasts. While established rules had been in place for sometime, there were few football clubs in existence then, even in large towns such as Sunderland. Yet, by the time Churchill was a young man, football had rapidly organised itself. No town worth its salt was without a football club and the creation of the Football League meant regular, organised football took place throughout England.

Given the almost omnipotent presence of football in today's media age, it is difficult to imagine a time when football was nothing more than a minority sport. Yet, in the space of just two lifetimes, it has gone from nothing to what it is today. But, no-one should be fooled into thinking that competition was any less tough then than it is today. Indeed, as the early years of our Club's history illustrate, life was often very tough in the late 1800s. When James Allan and his colleagues took the first steps towards establishing a football club in Sunderland, the long term future of their venture was extremely uncertain. Money - as always - was the key issue. A football club, like any other institution in life, cannot survive without cash, and without sufficient funds to cover the costs of maintaining such fundamental facilities as the pitch itself, Sunderland almost folded after two years in existence.

But, the Club struggled through. While a fable suggests it was the successful raffling of a prize canary that saved the day, in truth it was a dedication to the cause, married with a more realistic view of how the Club might cover its costs, that saw us through. Opening up membership of the Club to all of those with an interest in the game was undoubtedly the crucial decision during those early years. James Allan had initially envisaged a team just for school teachers in the Sunderland area, but this plan limited the pool of members on which the Club could draw, and weakened us in both playing and financial strength. But, the significance of turning the Club into one for the whole town was not immediately apparent. Allan and his colleagues had hoped the move would boost the Club's coffers by increasing the number of players who joined, but as the game's popularity rapidly increased, it became clear that football's future was as a spectator sport. With the Club operating as Sunderland's team, rather than being an academically based sporting society, its fan base was now huge.

Pretty soon, watching football had become the activity of choice for thousands of Sunderland's working men. Indeed, the town very quickly came to be one filled with keen followers of the new game. Even in the Club's early days, the fans proved themselves to be passionate and noisy. When Sunderland made it to the first ever Durham Cup final in 1884, our opponents complained that the noise generated by the Sunderland supporters was so great it was nothing less than intimidating. That a travelling army of fans should generate noise to support their team was, it seems, viewed as simply unsporting in some Victorian circles.

But, this huge level of support quickly marked the Club out as one of great potential. Early ground moves were fuelled in part by the need to find a home that could accommodate our fans - and ensure they paid to get into matches - and the revenue generated from games helped to attract some excellent players to the Club.

With working class men becoming increasingly fascinated by football, it was only a matter of time before their employers - notably the shipyard and coal mine owners - began to take an interest in the game too. Men such as Samuel Tyzack could see the importance of the game to their workers, their workers' morale and even their workers' perception of local bosses. These men knew that a successful team in Sunderland would provide a real boost to the town and began to provide financial backing for the Club, funding the signing of talented Scottish players such as Millar and Campbell and bringing the hugely talented Tom Watson to the Club as our secretary/manager.

Team of all Talents 1890.

Amazingly, in just ten years, we travelled from being a voluntarstic teachers team to a wealthy, well organised and successful football club, as Watson's 'Team of All Talents' took the footballing world by storm in the late 1880s, beating great teams in front of large crowds at our excellent Newcastle Road ground. Few Clubs could compare to Sunderland at the time, for we were totally focused on winning, our aim being nothing less than to be the best, and our goal being a simple one: to gain admittance to the newly formed Football League.

Such was our prowess, that the Football League admitted us for the start of their third season, and by the end of their fourth, we were Champions. Two further Championships followed in the space of three seasons, and in 1895 we were crowned 'World Champions' following victory against Scottish League winners Hearts. By this time, the Club had firmly sealed its place in footballing history and life was a story of glorious success rather than a struggle for survival. The Club was a thoroughly professional outfit and played other equally well organised clubs. All of this was a contrast to our first cup win - in the Durham Senior Cup - some ten years earlier, when stiff opponents had included the likes of Bishop Auckland Church Institute. At that time, many clubs had their roots in small local institutions such as churches, illustrating the truly amateur nature of the game. Football - and Sunderland AFC- had travelled a long way in a short time.

Jimmy Millar.

Tom Watson.

That these were changes for the better seems hard to dispute. The competitions that were forged, and the clubs that were formed, in those years have proved enduringly popular. Yet, despite our success, the route the Club had taken in seizing its opportunity was a controversial one. Much of our early success was the result of employing talented Scottish players, but this was denounced by those who felt such 'foreign players' were ruining the character of the game; Sunderland's team, they argued, should be made up of Sunderland born players. Good players were also attracted to the Club by offering them financial rewards in return - such as a good job in Sunderland - but this was a policy that got us into trouble when rules were broken, and was unpopular even when the rules were observed. The prevailing attitude was that sport should be an amateur activity, and that paying someone to play the game was wrong. This was all very well for the upper classes who had the means to live without employment, but if a working class man was to play football for Sunderland, he needed money to survive.

Sunderland Albion 1890-91 season.

These issues have clear modern day echoes; while the nationalities and cash figures involved might be very different, the underlying arguments are pretty much the same. But, the most important event in determining the Club's future came when we were granted admission to the Football League. All the spending on top players and our superb facilities would have been called into question had we failed to gain entrance to the top competition. Indeed, Watson's ability to attract the best players would also have been jeopardised, for all the best men wanted to show off their skills in the Football League. Again, the echoes with the present are very clear; for the contemporary Sunderland AFC, becoming an established part of the Premier League is crucial to our future plans. And, who knows, in the not too distant future, it could even be a case of having to battle for entry to a European League in order to survive as a footballing force. The penalty for failure at that crucial moment in 1889 would have been extremely severe. We know this to be true, for Sunderland Albion narrowly missed gaining admission to the League at the same time, and within five years the club had been wound up. With Sunderland playing against the top teams every week and romping to Championship glory, fans soon lost interest in Sunderland Albion.

Of course, in the early days, the fans' loyalties were less well developed. With both Sunderland and Sunderland Albion being young clubs, many Sunderland folk supported both teams. Today's Sunderland fans are part of a tradition that goes back 120 years and the possibility of them abandoning the team during the hard times simply does not arise. Yet, it is strange that more than a century after the battle to gain admission to the League, we are repeating the events of the 1880s and 1890s, knowing that money has to be invested and facilities developed to gain admission to the game's top division, and that the penalty for failure will be severe. With the gap between the Premier League and First Division widening each year - in financial and footballing terms - the early days of the Club's life, somewhat curiously, provide the nearest historical parallel to our current situation.

The past does, then, have lessons to offer the present. But there are plenty of warnings from history. The good times - those early Championship glories for example - tell us much about what to do in order achieve success. But there have been bad times and frustrating times too, and we should examine these and ask what we might learn here as well. Another big debate that has strong echoes in the present is the youth versus experience or spending versus developing players debate.

Peter Reid has come under fierce criticism from some fans in recent years because of his reluctance to splash the cash and break transfer records. There have, however, been times when Sunderland managers were very keen to spend money in trying to bring success to the Club, most notably during the 'Bank of England' years of the 1950s and under Bob Kyle in the 1920s. Both periods saw exciting international players - real entertainers - arrive on Wearside, with British transfer records smashed and many players brought in for huge fees that fell just short of being records. On both occasions the end result was remarkably similar: great teams entertained the fans and challenged for honours, but that extra element needed for success - be it team spirit, a fighting character, luck - was lacking, and potentially glorious seasons ultimately ended without silverware.

In contrast, these two periods sandwiched the successful 1930s, where Johnny Cochrane preferred to follow a policy of developing young kids into star players, and our sixth League Championship in 1936, and first FA Cup win in 1937, came through a team that had cost next to nothing. A canny eye for spotting young talent, proper coaching at the Club and an investment of faith in the youngsters brought more success to Wearside than spending, in modern day terms, millions of pounds on proven star players. The spirit of his team, and their dedication to the Club and each other, were crucial elements of the winning formula, and Cochrane was able to create the right climate by catching talented players at an early age, and moulding their attitudes as well as their footballing skills. As such, he gave the team a quality that all the record breaking transfers could not buy, for one man, no matter how great, does not make a team.

Yet, all this must be balanced against times when youth has not helped us through, such as our two relegations under Alan Brown. As a manager, Brown twice came to the Club during difficult times, but his faith in youth rather than experience saw us slip out of the top flight. While the eventual pay off was, in both instances, a talented crop of youngsters, it is also true to say that the Club slipped behind the standard of play in the top flight and found it difficult to compete after gaining promotion.

Johnny Cochrane - 1930s

Bob Kyle - 1920s

Alan Brown - 1960s and 70s

Peter Reid - 1990s

1937 and 1973, Sunderland's two FA Cup victories.

Similarly, there have been numerous occasions in recent years when the team have struggled for want of one or two quality players, but managers have been unable to sign these players because finance was lacking. The recent roller coaster ride that has seen us yo-yo between divisions must, in part, be a consequence of the fact that we have lacked the international quality centre forward who can score twenty goals a season or the creative midfield genius who can turn play with a single pass.

Of course, even great teams and great players need motivating and organising. Experience also suggests that the man who pulls the strings behind the scenes plays a crucial, pivotal role. If ever anyone doubted that the manager makes a difference, the appointment of Reid surely dispelled such thoughts. Having taken over a team languishing in the relegation places, he completely turned performances around. With largely the same group of players that had struggled to avoid relegation, he instantly delivered a Championship. The turnaround was similar to that achieved by Bob Stokoe, who took charge of a team low on morale and languishing at the bottom end of Division Two, and instantly turned them into an FA Cup winning side.

In football, as in any walk of life, getting the best out of your workers is a difficult task; it takes an understanding of their strengths and weaknesses, knowledge of their individual characters and an ability to motivate each and every one of them, all of which is easier said than done.

The Club's history also suggests that when you have a good manager it is important to give him time to develop the team, for success is rarely an instant phenomenon, a point perfectly illustrated by Johnny Cochrane's career. The 1930s Sunderland team was undoubtedly one of the best in the Club's history. At a time when English football was immensely competitive at the top levels, the team held their own and delivered silverware, including our first ever FA Cup. But, it took Cochrane many years to develop his winning team. Having committed himself to developing a team around talented youngsters, Cochrane oversaw a difficult transitional period where the Lads struggled for three or four seasons. Many would have questioned Cochrane's strategy as the Club slid to consecutive midtable finishes. However, when the rebuilding came to fruition, Cochrane and his backroom team proved to be masters of the game. Wonderful attacking football propelled the team to glory, the Lads managing to both entertain and win, no mean feat.

Indeed, in the early days, managers were generally given a long run in the job. While it would wrong to suggest that given time all managers deliver the goods - some people are clearly not up to the task - the modern tendency to call for the manager's head after a few bad results makes it difficult for a Cochrane style project to be seen through to its glorious conclusion. It is often said that businesses need stability in order to plan for the future, and to an extent this must also be true for football clubs. The managerial merry-go-round that has existed for much of the past three decades has hardly helped the Club in going forward. More recent periods of stability - such as those under Smith and Reid - have demonstrated the benefits of giving a good manager a proper run at the job.

But, the Club's history also shows that it is not always possible to attract the right manager to the Club. Sometimes seemingly great appointments just don't work out - Lawrie McMenemy being the finest example. Other times, the right managers aren't available or simply don't want the job. Who knows, if Brian Clough and the Sunderland manager's job had both been free at the right time, perhaps he would have guided Sunderland, rather than Nottingham Forest, to League and European glory.

In more recent times, the board have found it very hard indeed to persuade top managers that the Sunderland job was one worth taking. With the team almost constantly battling against relegation and Roker Park slowly but surely declining, Sunderland did not look like a Club going places.

Now, however, that perception has changed. Progress on the pitch has been matched and supported by progress off it. The board have shown the necessary ambition to back the manager in his quest for success. But, this is not a simple matter of throwing money at players. Instead, it is one of laying the foundations for success. In constructing a marvellous new stadium, developing state of the art training facilities and placing the Club's finances on a sound footing, the board have done far more good than throwing ten million pounds on a transfer would have done. The Club now has genuine capacity to grow and has the facilities needed to attract the best players to the Club. Here, there are strong parallels with the Club's successful years before the War. In the 1880s there was a constant search for a suitable home until the Newcastle Road site was secured. Here, a state of the art football ground was constructed - including special gantries for match reporters - and it acted as a base for our campaign for League admission and our early Championship success. Once established in the 1890s, the Club did not rest on its laurels. Instead, it completed a successful share issue to finance further building, and overcame the constraints of the Newcastle Road site by moving to a new home at Roker Park. Once there, the Club did not rest either. The 1900s through to the 1930s saw constant investment in our facilities, most notably the addition of the magnificent Archibald Leitch stands.

In the post-War era, however, the Club seemed to lose sight of the need to be constantly improving the behind the scenes set up. The ground that saw in the 1973 Cup run was little different from that which saw in the 1937 Cup run, and had it not been for the World Cup in 1966, significant investment in the ground would have been almost completely absent. Indeed, the media facilities provided to visiting television crews in the 1990s were particularly primitive, in many ways being less hospitable than those provided to newspaper reporters in the 1890s.

In short, the Club were being left behind, something that would not have been allowed in the pre-War years. Sports are by their very nature competitive activities, and to be the best you have to work hard on all aspects of your game. As our history makes clear, it takes a complex interaction of a whole host of factors to produce a successful football club: money, ambition, facilities, good players, a quality manager, and dedicated fans to name but a few. Whoever it was that said "At the end of the day it's about eleven men against eleven men" was way off the mark, way off.

Niall Quinn, a great partnership with Kevin Phillips.

Kevin Phillips equalises from the penalty spot in the Sunderland v Aston Villa Premier league fixture at the Sunderland Stadium of Light, 18th October 1999.

The Lads went on to get all three points with Phillips also scoring the winner.

Acknowledgements

A great number of people have helped us in the production of this book. Without them it would not have been have the book it is and, for the record, we would like to express our gratitude to some of those people and organisations who have been especially helpful to us.

For identifying, tracking down and supplying illustrations we are particularly indebted to Brian Leng, George Hoare and Alan Brett, all of whom have been a great help and, without whom, pictorial evidence of the Club's history would be very scant indeed. We are also grateful to the Sunderland Echo for allowing us access to their important, and extensive, picture archive.

Rob Mason is owed a huge thank you for providing assistance with the historical narrative. His encyclopedic knowledge of all things Sunderland was a great help to us. Thanks are also due to Suzanne Robertson for allowing us access to the archive built up by her father, Billy Butterworth, which contained vital information about the Club's early days in particular. John Musgrave and Barry Newton provided us with access to their extensive personal collections of programmes, newspapers and match reports. Dave Harrison offered valuable assistance with the Second World War material, and Dave Hillam's footballing brain was a huge help in plugging the gaps too.

Sunderland AFC offered us a huge helping hand during the production of the book. Bob Murray, whose comments and assistance were hugely important, gave freely of his time, and Jim Slater and Lesley Callaghan were a big help too. The Local Studies Centre at Sunderland Library were extremely helpful when we needed to track down old match reports and Jackie Richardson came to the rescue a number of times when we needed help with finding ancient newspaper copy.

Finally, a big, big thank you to all those at Leighton and (TWO)CAN Design who helped bring the book into being, especially Andrea Murphy at Leighton and Paul Briggs, Paul Montgomery and Sally Peirson at (TWO)CAN Design. They put in many, many hours to make sure the book hit the press and their hard work is really appreciated.